Lecture Notes in Computer Science   **13628**

More information about this series at https://link.springer.com/bookseries/558

Weihong Deng · Jianjiang Feng · Di Huang ·
Meina Kan · Zhenan Sun · Fang Zheng ·
Wenfeng Wang · Zhaofeng He (Eds.)

Biometric Recognition

16th Chinese Conference, CCBR 2022
Beijing, China, November 11–13, 2022
Proceedings

 Springer

Editors
Weihong Deng
Beijing University of Posts
and Telecommunications
Beijing, China

Di Huang
Beihang University
Beijing, China

Zhenan Sun
Institute of Automation
Chinese Academy of Sciences
Beijing, China

Wenfeng Wang
China Electronics Standardization Institute
Beijing, China

Jianjiang Feng
Tsinghua University
Beijing, China

Meina Kan
Institute of Computing Technology
Chinese Academy of Sciences
Beijing, China

Fang Zheng
Tsinghua University
Beijing, China

Zhaofeng He
Institute of Automation
Chinese Academy of Sciences
Beijing, China

ISSN 0302-9743   ISSN 1611-3349 (electronic)
Lecture Notes in Computer Science
ISBN 978-3-031-20232-2   ISBN 978-3-031-20233-9 (eBook)
https://doi.org/10.1007/978-3-031-20233-9

This Springer imprint is published by the registered company Springer Nature Switzerland AG
The registered company address is: Gewerbestrasse 11, 6330 Cham, Switzerland

Preface

Biometric technology, which performs automatic person recognition based on physiological or behavioral traits such as face, fingerprint, iris, gait, and signature, has numerous applications in the modern society. In recent years, biometric recognition systems have been extensively deployed worldwide in law enforcement, government, and consumer applications. It is also becoming essential to develop diverse approaches towards trustworthy biometric applications. In China, thanks to the huge population using the Internet and smart phones as well as to the great investment of the government in security and privacy protection, the biometric market is rapidly growing and biometric research has attracted increasing attention. The researchers have been addressing various scientific problems in biometrics, developing diverse biometric techniques, and making significant contributions to the biometrics field. The Chinese Conference on Biometric Recognition (CCBR), an annual conference held in China, provides an excellent platform for biometric researchers to share their progress and thoughts in the development and applications of biometric theory, technology, and systems.

CCBR 2022 was held in Beijing during November 11–13, 2022, and was the 16th in the series, which has been successfully held in Beijing, Hangzhou, Xian, Guangzhou, Jinan, Shenyang, Tianjin, Chengdu, Shenzhen, Urumqi, Zhuzhou, and Shanghai since 2000. CCBR 2022 received 115 submissions, each of which was reviewed by at least three experts from the Program Committee. Based on the rigorous double-blind review process, 70 papers were selected for presentation. These papers comprise this volume of the CCBR 2022 conference proceedings, which covers a wide range of topics: fingerprint recognition; palmprint and vein recognition; face detection, recognition, and tracking; gesture and action recognition; affective computing and human-computer interfaces; speaker and speech recognition; gait, iris, and other biometrics; multi-modal biometric recognition and fusion; quality evaluation and enhancement of biometric signals; animal biometrics; trustworthiness, privacy, and personal data security; and medical and other applications.

We would like to thank all the authors, reviewers, invited speakers, volunteers, and organizing committee members, without whom CCBR 2022 would not have been successful. We also wish to acknowledge the support of the China Society of Image and Graphics, the Chinese Association for Artificial Intelligence, the Institute of Automation of the Chinese Academy of Sciences, Springer, and Beijing University of Posts and Telecommunications for sponsoring this conference.

November 2022

Zhenan Sun
Fang Zheng
Wenfeng Wang
Zhaofeng He
Weihong Deng
Jianjiang Feng
Di Huang
Meina Kan

Organization

Academic Advisory Committee

Tieniu Tan   Institute of Automation, Chinese Academy of
                              Sciences, China
Anil K. Jain   Michigan State University, USA
Yaonan Wang   Hunan University, China
Qiang Yang   WeBank, China
Jun Guo   Beijing University of Posts and
                              Telecommunications, China
Jianjun Yang   China Electronics Standardization Institute, China
Jianhuang Lai   Sun Yat-sen University, China
Yunhong Wang   Beihang University, China

Industry Advisory Committee

Zhifei Wang   Ministry of Human Resources and Social
                              Security, China
Hongchuan Hou   Ministry of Public Security, China
Xiaodong He   JD Group, China
Shiliang Pu   Haikang Research Institute, China
Liang Li   Ant Group, China
Xiaoliang Chen   Beijing SoundAI Technology Co., Ltd., China

General Chairs

Zhenan Sun   Institute of Automation, Chinese Academy of
                              Sciences, China
Fang Zheng   Tsinghua University, China
Wenfeng Wang   China Electronics Standardization Institute, China
Zhaofeng He   Beijing University of Posts and
                              Telecommunications, China

Program Committee Chairs

Weihong Deng   Beijing University of Posts and
                              Telecommunications, China
Jianjiang Feng   Tsinghua University, China

| Di Huang | Beihang University, China |
| Meina Kan | Institute of Computing Technology, Chinese Academy of Sciences, China |

Organizing Committee Chairs

Fei Su	Beijing University of Posts and Telecommunications, China
Man Zhang	Beijing University of Posts and Telecommunications, China
Liang He	Tsinghua University, China
Xiaobin Zhu	University of Science and Technology Beijing, China

Program Committee

Baochang Zhang	Beihang University, China
Bingyu Liu	Beijing University of Posts and Telecommunications, China
Bo Peng	Institute of Automation, Chinese Academy of Sciences, China
Caikou Chen	Yangzhou University, China
Cairong Zhao	Tongji University, China
Changhui Hu	Nanjing University of Posts and Telecommunications, China
Chao Shen	Xi'an Jiaotong University, China
Chaoying Tang	Nanjing University of Aeronautics and Astronautics, China
Cunjian Chen	Michigan State University, USA
Cunjian Chen	Canon Information Technology (Beijing), China
Dewen Hu	National University of Defense Technology, China
Di Huang	Beihang University, China
Dong Liang	Nanjing University of Aeronautics and Astronautics, China
Dongdong Zhao	Wuhan University of Technology, China
En Zhu	National University of Defense Technology, China
Eryun Liu	Zhejiang University, China
Fan Liu	Hohai University, China
Fanglin Chen	National University of Defense Technology, China
Fei Peng	Hunan University, China
Feng Liu	Shenzhen University, China

Lei Zhang	The Hong Kong Polytechnic University, Hong Kong SAR, China
Leyuan Liu	Central China Normal University, China
Li Yan	Taiyuan University of Technology, China
Liang Chang	Beijing Normal University, China
Liang He	Tsinghua University, China
Lifang Wu	Beijing University of Technology, China
Lin Zhang	Tongji University, China
Lingyu Liang	South China University of Technology, China
Linlin Shen	Shenzhen University, China
Linzhi Huang	Beijing University of Posts and Telecommunications, China
Lu Leng	Nanchang Hangkong University, China
Lu Yang	Shandong Jianzhu University, China
Lunke Fei	Guangdong University of Technology, China
Man Zhang	Institute of Automation, Chinese Academy of Sciences, China
Manhua Liu	Shanghai Jiao Tong University, China
Mei Wang	Beijing University of Posts and Telecommunications, China
Min Xu	Capital Normal University, China
Muwei Jian	Ocean University of China, China
Nan Zhou	Beihang University, China
Nannan Wang	Xidian University, China
Nizhuan Wang	ShanghaiTech University, China
Qi Li	Institute of Automation, Chinese Academy of Sciences, China
Qi Zhu	Nanjing University of Aeronautics and Astronautics, China
Qijun Zhao	Sichuan University, China
Qingyang Hong	Xiamen University, China
Quanxue Gao	Xidian University, China
Shan Li	Beijing University of Posts and Telecommunications, China
Shan Zeng	Wuhan Polytechnic University, China
Shasha Mao	Xidian University, China
Shengcai Liao	Abu Dhabi Artificial Intelligence Innovation Institute, UAE
Shenghua Gao	ShanghaiTech University, China
Shiqi Yu	Shenzhen University, China
Shiquan Wang	Amazon, USA
Shunli Zhang	Beijing Jiaotong University, China
Wangmeng Zuo	Harbin Institute of Technology, China

Wanjiang Xu	Yancheng Teachers University, China
Wankou Yang	Southeast University, China
Wei Jia	Hefei University of Technology, China
Wei Wang	Institute of Automation, Chinese Academy of Sciences, China
Weicheng Xie	Shenzhen University, China
Weihong Deng	Beijing University of Posts and Telecommunications, China
Weihua Ou	Guizhou Normal University, China
Weijun Li	Institute of Semiconductors, Chinese Academy of Sciences, China
Weimin Tan	Fudan University, China
Weiqi Yuan	Shenyang University of Technology, China
Weiqiang Zhang	Tsinghua University, China
Weishi Zheng	Sun Yat-sen University, China
Wenxin Li	Peking University, China
Wenxiong Kang	South China University of Technology, China
Xiancheng Zhou	Hunan Technology and Business University, China
Xiang Ma	Chang'an University, China
Xiangbo Shu	Nanjing University of Science and Technology, China
Xiangqian Wu	Harbin Institute of Technology, China
Xiangyang Luo	Information Engineering University, China
Xiao Luan	Chongqing University of Posts and Telecommunications, China
Xiao Yang	Sichuan University, China
Xiaoguang Li	Beijing University of Technology, China
Xiaohua Xie	Sun Yat-sen University, China
Xiaoyuan Jing	Wuhan University, China
Xin Liu	Huaqiao University, China
Xiuzhuang Zhou	Capital Normal University, China
Xiuzhuang Zhou	Beijing University of Posts and Telecommunications, China
Xu Jia	Liaoning University of Technology, China
Xun Gong	Southwest Jiaotong University, China
Yanxiong Li	South China University of Technology, China
Yi Jin	Beijing Jiaotong University, China
Yi Wang	Dongguan University of Technology, China
Yi Wang	Hong Kong Baptist University, Hong Kong SAR, China
Yiding Wang	North China University of Technology, China
Yiguang Liu	Sichuan University, China

Ying Chen	Nanchang Hangkong University, China
Yingchun Yang	Zhejiang University, China
Yinjie Lei	Sichuan University, China
Yongliang Zhang	Zhejiang University of Technology, China
Yongxin Ge	Chongqing University, China
Yuchun Fang	Shanghai University, China
Yuhang Zhang	Beijing University of Posts and Telecommunications, China
Yuli Xue	Beihang University, China
Yunlian Sun	Nanjing University of Science and Technology, China
Yunlong Wang	Institute of Automation, Chinese Academy of Sciences, China
Yunqi Tang	People's Public Security University of China, China
Zengfu Wang	Institute of Intelligent Machines, Chinese Academy of Sciences, China
Zhaofeng He	Beijing University of Posts and Telecommunications, China
Zhaoxiang Zhang	Institute of Automation, Chinese Academy of Sciences, China
Zhe Guo	Northwestern Polytechnical University, China
Zhenan Sun	Institute of Automation, Chinese Academy of Sciences, China
Zhengning Wang	University of Electronic Science and Technology of China, China
Zhenyu He	Harbin Institute of Technology Shenzhen Graduate School, China
Zhi Liu	Shandong University, China
Zhicheng Cao	Xidian University, China
Zhifeng Li	Institute of Advanced Technology, Chinese Academy of Sciences, China
Zhihui Lai	Shenzhen University, China

Publicity Chairs

Wei Jia	Hefei University of Technology, China
Kuerban Wubli	Xinjiang University, China
Wenxiong Kang	South China University of Technology, China
Qingyang Hong	Xiamen University, China

Sponsorship Chairs

Shiqi Yu   Southern University of Science and Technology,
                                      China
Jiwei Song   China Electronics Standardization Institute, China
Zhen Lei   Institute of Automation, Chinese Academy of
                                      Sciences, China

Forum Chairs

Jing Dong   Institute of Automation, Chinese Academy of
                                      Sciences, China
Feng Liu   Shenzhen University, China
Jun Du   University of Science and Technology of China,
                                      China
Yi Wang   Dongguan University of Technology, China

Publication Chairs

Qijun Zhao   Sichuan University, China
Huibin Li   Xi'an Jiaotong University, China
Qi Li   Institute of Automation, Chinese Academy of
                                      Sciences, China

Competition Chairs

Xianye Ben   Shandong University, China
Yi Jin   Beijing Jiaotong University, China
Peipei Li   Beijing University of Posts and
                                      Telecommunications, China

Contents

Fingerprint, Palmprint and Vein Recognition

Multi-modal Biometric Recognition and Fusion

Quality Evaluation and Enhancement of Biometric Signals

Fingerprint, Palmprint and Vein Recognition

A Finger Bimodal Fusion Algorithm Based on Improved Densenet

Wenhao Lv, Hui Ma$^{(\boxtimes)}$, and Yu Li

Electronic Engineering, Heilongjiang University, Harbin 150080, China
2011043@hlju.edu.cn

Abstract. Compared with single-mode biometric recognition, multimodal biometric recognition has been widely used because of its high security and high accuracy. Among them, finger based multimodal biometric recognition is the most common and efficient way. However, biometric recognition has lots of problems such as too high feature dimensions, high computational complexity and insufficient correlation between modal classes. This paper propose an improved DenseNet network, which uses dual channel input and feature layer fusion to obtain richer features. Then, in order to make the network learn the multimodal representation adaptively, we introduce the attention mechanism and optimize the loss function. The network solves the problem of performance degradation caused by insufficient correlation between different modes in the fusion process, and it can effectively improve the recognition accuracy. Finally, we verify it on two public multimodal datasets and achieve good results.

Keywords: Biometrics recognition · Multimodal fusion · Convolutional neural networks · Loss function

1 Introduction

Biometric recognition has gradually replaced the traditional recognition methods and has been widely used in various fields because of its convenience and security. Common biometrics include fingerprint, iris, face, finger vein, etc. [1–4]. Among them, multimodal identification technology integrates a variety of feature information for identity authentication, which has higher anti-counterfeiting and stability than single-mode identification. Fingerprint has been widely used because of its accessibility and convenience. It plays an important role in payment, device login, access control assessment and many other scenes. However, fingerprint identification is easy to be stolen. In addition, people in specific occupations may have fingerprint worn, which has caused some problems for its use. Finger vein recognition uses the vein characteristics of human fingers, which has the advantages of living body recognition, high anti-counterfeiting, non-contact safe collection and so on [5]. Therefore, this paper selects the bimodal features of fingerprint and finger vein for recognition, which can be safe and universal.

The recognition of finger related features usually leads to high intra class differences and low inter class differences due to pose shift, illumination and acquisition spectral

W. Deng et al. (Eds.): CCBR 2022, LNCS 13628, pp. 3–11, 2022.
https://doi.org/10.1007/978-3-031-20233-9_1

wavelength, which makes feature extraction difficult, and increases feature dimensions and computational complexity in the process of multimodal fusion. Prommegger et al. [6] used images from different angles to train finger veins, and used the DenseNet161 model with softmax as the loss function, which achieved good results on the PLUSVein dataset. Kuzu et al. [7] used the improved DenseNet161 to conduct experiments on multiple databases such as SDU, and achieved an EER of about 1.5. Song et al. [8] used deeper DenseNet and combined input of two venous images. The experiments were carried out on SDU and HKPU databases to achieve eer within 0.5. Moreover, some Palmprint related methods are also worth learning [9, 10]. Although the use of finger vein single-mode recognition can achieve high accuracy, there are still some problems. The first is the problem of data volume. The main problem of biometric recognition is the small number of samples within the class and the large number of samples between the classes, which also leads to the problem that the training results may be over fitted to a certain data set. In addition, finger vein recognition is easily affected by temperature, which leads to the problem that recognition may fail. Therefore, this paper proposes a finger multimodal fusion method based on DenseNet, which adopts the method of dual-channel input to extract the depth features of finger vein and fingerprint and fuse them. In addition, we also add attention mechanism and improve the loss function, so that the network structure can deal with multimodal biometrics on large data sets. The main contributions of this paper are as follows:

1. Using the DenseNet161 network with dual channel input, the finger vein and fingerprint images are input into the network at the same time, and the feature level fusion strategy is adopted to fuse the two images, which has wider applicability than single-mode recognition.
2. The attention mechanism module is adopted which greatly reduce the decline in recognition accuracy caused by ignoring the correlation and contribution gap between modes. And the loss function is improved so that the network can learn the similarity between classes to a greater extent and adjust the weight adaptively.

The other chapters of this paper are arranged as follows. The second section mainly introduces the backgrounds of our research. The third section mainly introduces the improved DenseNet network. The fourth section is the relevant experimental results and the discussion of the results. The fifth section is a summary of the full paper.

2   Research Backgrounds

2.1   Multimodal Fusion Strategy

First, we will give a brief introduction to multimodal feature fusion. Multimodal feature fusion is mainly divided into image level fusion, feature level fusion and score level fusion. Image level fusion is to fuse the unprocessed data obtained from different channels to get a new image. Feature level fusion is to fuse the biometric information of different modes to get a feature set containing more information; and score level fusion is to make the matching scores of each mode compatible.

This paper chooses a feature level fusion scheme which has more abundant fusion information. However, the features of different modes are different, so it is necessary to design an effective feature fusion scheme. At present, the multi-modal feature fusion scheme based on CNN mainly includes two network structures, as shown in Fig. 1 below, that is, learning different feature information by fusion in different positions. The right side of the picture shows the fusion of shallow networks which focusing on capturing the underlying element information of images, while the left one incline to the fusion of deep networks abstracts the high-level semantic information of images.

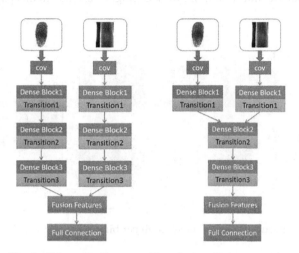

Fig. 1. Schematic diagram of two feature fusion strategies.

Although deep integration may more time-consuming, it can help us extract richer features, so we choose the deep feature level fusion strategy.

2.2 DenseNet161

DenseNet161 is a convolutional neural network trained on Imagenet database. This architecture has 161 layers. The network also realizes the classification of 1000 objects. Compared with ResNet, DenseNet reduces network parameters and enhances feature reuse, making it easier to train. DenseNet also includes models with different parameter quantities, such as DenseNet121, DenseNet161 and DenseNet201 [11].

3 Methodology

3.1 Overview

In the multimodal recognition method based on convolutional neural network, learning efficient feature representation and information complementation between modalities is the key element to realize accurate classification and recognition. Advanced techniques

based on attention feature representation, such as positional attention and channel attention, recalibrate the contribution of features and focus on useful information. We propose
a recognition framework consisting of feature extraction network, fusion network and
classifier. First, DenseNet161 network is used for biometric extraction task. Then, the
attention mechanism module is introduced to dynamically weight the importance of different modal feature maps through cross modal information interaction, so as to further
improve the system performance. Finally, the classifier makes decisions based on the
multi instance feature vectors output from the fusion network. Figure 2 shows the whole
improved bimodal identification framework of finger designed in this paper.

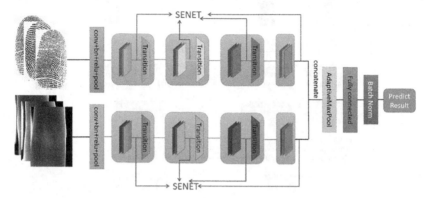

Fig. 2. Schematic diagram of improved finger bimodal recognition framework.

3.2 SENET

SENET [12] adopts a new feature relocation strategy. Specifically, it is to automatically
obtain the importance of each feature channel through learning, and then according to
this importance to enhance useful features and suppress features that are not useful for
the current task.

The use structure of SENET is shown in Fig. 3 below. If we use W and h to represent
the width and height of the feature map and use C represents the number of channels,
and the size of the input characteristic diagram is $W \times X \times C$:

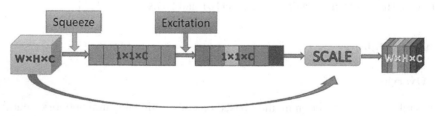

Fig. 3. Schematic diagram of SENET.

First, through a global average pool. After compression, the characteristic graph is compressed to a $1 \times 1 \times C$ vector. Then through two full connection layers, in which SERatio is a scaling parameter, the purpose of this parameter is to reduce the number of channels and thus reduce the amount of calculation. The first fully connected layer has $C \times$ SERatio neurons, and the input is $1 \times 1 \times C$, output is $1 \times 1 \times C \times$ SERatio. The second fully connected layer has C neurons with input of $1 \times 1 \times C \times$ SERatio and output of $1 \times 1 \times C$. Finally is the scale operation. After we get $1 \times 1 \times C$ vector, the original feature map can be scaled, where the channel weights are multiplied. Supposed that the original feature vector is $W \times X \times C$. The weight value of each channel calculated by SE module is multiplied by the two-dimensional matrix of the corresponding channel of the original characteristic diagram, then we get the final output result.

After testing, we choose SERatio $= 16$. We tested to add SENET before each dense block, before each transition block and before the full connection layer. Finally we chose to add SENET before the transition block and before the full connection layer and we got the best results.

3.3 Loss Function

The loss function is an index to measure the performance of the prediction model in predicting the expected results. We have improved the cross entropy loss function in DenseNet161 fusion network by adding circle loss [13].

Circle loss puts forward a unified perspective for data pair learning and classification label learning, that is, maximize the similarity within classes and minimize the similarity between classes. At the same time, it is found that for most loss functions, actually the similarity S_p, Sn is embedded and reduced $S_n - S_p$. While the traditional loss method has equal punishment for each similarity, it should be punished according to the degree of dissimilarity. Therefore, circle loss, which can learn data pairs and samples of classification labels at the same time, is proposed.

Circle loss can be expressed by the following formula (1):

$$L_{circle} = \log[1 + \sum_{i=1}^{K} \sum_{j=1}^{L} \exp(\gamma(\alpha_n^j s_n^j - \alpha_p^i S_p^i))] \tag{1}$$

where α_n^j, α_p^i is nonnegative weight parameter. In training, the gradient of $\alpha_n^j s_n^j - \alpha_p^i S_p^i$ will be multiplied by α_n^j, α_p^i. Proposed that the optimal s_p^i is O_p, the optimal s_n^j is O_n and $(O_n < O_p)$. When there is a large difference between the similarity and the optimal value, it should have a large weight for effective updating. The weight parameter is defined as follows (2):

$$\alpha_p^i = \left[O_p - S_p^i \right]_+, \ \alpha_n^j = \left[S_n^j - O_n \right]_+ \tag{2}$$

where [.]+ Represents the truncation operator from 0 to ensure that the weight parameter is non negative. Usually there is a scaling factor in the loss γ, the weighted term of circle loss actually replaces the role of scaling factor, and the weighted term will be adaptive.

Through the previous design of the fusion network and the improvement of the loss function in the classifier, we have effectively improved the accuracy of bimodal recognition.

4   Experimental Results

4.1   Datasets

This paper will use two databases for experiments. The first database is SDUMLA-HMT [14], which is a multimodal database. We selected the images collected by FT-2BU sensor in the finger vein database and fingerprint database. There are a total of 106 samples, with 6 pictures for each sample. Figure 4 shows an example sample of SDU fingerprint finger vein bimodal state library.

Fig. 4. Sample diagram of SDUMLA-HMT.

The second database is NUPT-FPV [15], which is a bimodal database of fingerprints and finger veins. There are 840 samples, 10 pictures of each sample, a total of 16800 fingerprint images and 16800 vein images. Figure 5 shows an example sample of the fingerprint finger vein bimodal database of NUPT.

Fig. 5. Sample diagram of NUPT-FPV.

4.2   Experimental Results

In this section, we introduce the multimodal biometric data set used, and use the following super parameter to set the training process of the network. The initial learning rate is set to 0.001, and the final attenuation is 0.0001. We use random horizontal flipping to increase the bimodal data to reduce over fitting, and improve the training speed by adjusting the image size. In order to better verify the effectiveness of this method, we randomly divide the training set, and set the proportion of training set, validation set and test set as 5:2:3. Our framework is implemented using pytorch. All experiments are carried out on NVIDIA RTX 2060 GPU with 16 GB memory and 6 GB video memory.

Table 1 shows the comparison of test recognition accuracy after training on different networks.

Table 1. Comparison of test recognition accuracy(%) after training on different networks.

Dataset	DenseNet121	DenseNet161	Proposed method
SDU-MLA-HMT	98.3	98.5	**99.2**
NUPT-FPV	97.9	98.2	**98.7**

Table 2 shows the comparison of test recognition accuracy after adding SENET in different parts of the model and improving the loss function. Here, Plan A represents original network, Plan B represents adding SENET before each dense block, Plan C represents adding SENET before each transition block, Plan D represents adding SENET before the full connection layer, Plan E represents adding SENET before each transition block and the full connection layer, Plan F represents modifying the loss function on the basis of Plan E, Plan G represents fusion methods use ResNet [16].

Table 2. Comparison of test recognition accuracy(%) after adding SENET.

Dataset	Plan A	Plan B	Plan C	Plan D	Plan E	Plan F	Plan G
SDU-MLA-HMT	98.5	98.1	98.6	98.8	98.9	**99.2**	98.3
NUPT-FPV	98.2	98.0	98.4	98.3	98.5	**98.7**	97.6

Figure 6 shows the schematic diagram of accuracy changing with training epochs on two datasets, which also shows the convergence speed of the modified DenseNet network. The training period is about 5 min.

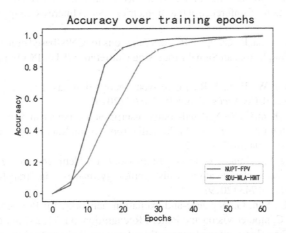

Fig. 6. Schematic diagram of accuracy changing with training epochs.

Through experiments, we prove the progressiveness of the proposed fusion recognition method. It not only has good convergence ability, but also has good accuracy. The recognition rate on two public datasets achieved 99.2% and 98.7%.

5 Conclusion

This paper proposes a bimodal feature level fusion recognition algorithm of finger based on improved DenseNet. The proposed network achieves a good balance between training time and recognition accuracy. In addition, our proposed algorithm solves the loss caused by the different importance of feature maps of different patterns in the fusion process, so as to further improve the accuracy. Finally, feature fusion is carried out in the full connection layer and the improved classifier is used for recognition. Compared with the existing technology, our proposed method considers the correlation between multi-modal features, and reduces the expression effect gap of different modal features through the attention module. In the future, we plan to make more improvements in training speed and learning cost.

References

1. Yin, X., Zhu, Y., Hu, J.: Contactless fingerprint recognition based on global minutia topology and loose genetic algorithm. IEEE Trans. Inf. Foren. Secur. **15**, 28–41 (2019)
2. Al-Waisy, A.S., Qahwaji, R., Ipson, S., Al-Fahdawi, S., Nagem, T.A.M.: A multi-biometric iris recognition system based on a deep learning approach. Pattern Anal. Appl. **21**(3), 783–802 (2017). https://doi.org/10.1007/s10044-017-0656-1
3. Chandrakala, M., Durga Devi, P.: Two-stage classifier for face recognition using HOG features. Materials Today: Proceedings (2021)
4. Banerjee, A., Basu, S., Basu, S., Nasipuri, M.: ARTeM: a new system for human authentication using finger vein images. Multimedia Tools Appl. **77**(5), 5857–5884 (2018)
5. Lu, Y., Yoon, S., Wu, S., Park, D.S.: Pyramid histogram of double competitive pattern for finger vein recognition. IEEE Access **6**, 56445–56456 (2018)
6. Prommegger, B., Wimmer, G., Uhl, A.: Rotation tolerant finger vein recognition using CNNs. In: 2021 International Conference of the Biometrics Special Interest Group (BIOSIG), pp. 1–5. IEEE (2021)
7. Kuzu, R. S., Maiorana, E., Campisi, P.: Loss functions for CNN-based biometric vein recognition. In: 2020 28th European Signal Processing Conference (EUSIPCO), pp. 750–754. IEEE (2021)
8. Song, J.M., Kim, W., Park, K.R.: Finger-vein recognition based on deep DenseNet using composite image. IEEE Access **7**, 66845–66863 (2019)
9. Leng, L., Li, M., Kim, C., Bi, X.: Dual-source discrimination power analysis for multi-instance contactless palmprint recognition. Multimedia Tools Appl. **76**(1), 333–354 (2015). https://doi.org/10.1007/s11042-015-3058-7
10. Leng, L., Zhang, J.: Palmhash code vs. palmphasor code. Neurocomputing **108**, 1–12 (2013)
11. Talo, M.: Automated classification of histopathology images using transfer learning. Artif. Intell. Med. **101**, 101743 (2019)
12. Hu, J., Shen, L., Sun, G.: Squeeze-and-excitation networks. In: Proceedings of the IEEE Conference on Computer Vision and Pattern Recognition, pp. 7132–7141 (2018)
13. Sun, Y., et al.: Circle loss: a unified perspective of pair similarity optimization. In: Proceedings of the IEEE/CVF Conference on Computer Vision and Pattern Recognition, pp. 6398–6407 (2020)
14. Yin, Y., Liu, L., Sun, X.: SDUMLA-HMT: a multimodal biometric database. In: Sun, Z., Lai, J., Chen, X., Tan, T. (eds.) CCBR 2011. LNCS, vol. 7098, pp. 260–268. Springer, Heidelberg (2011). https://doi.org/10.1007/978-3-642-25449-9_33

15. Ren, H., Sun, L., Guo, J., Han, C.: A dataset and benchmark for multimodal biometric recognition based on fingerprint and finger vein. IEEE Trans. Inf. Foren. Secur. **17** (2022)
16. He, K., Zhang, X., Ren, S., Sun, J.: Deep residual learning for image recognition. In: Proceedings of the IEEE Conference on Computer Vision and Pattern Recognition, pp. 770–778 (2016)

A Lightweight Segmentation Network Based on Extraction

Chuanbo Qin, Xihua Lin, Yucong Chen, and Junying Zeng[✉]

Faculty of Intelligent Manufacturing, Wuyi University, Jiangmen 529020, Guangdong, China
zengjunying@126.com

Abstract. Most of the existing finger vein segmentation models require great memory and computational resources, and the global correlation of the models is weak, which may affect the effectiveness of finger vein extraction. In this paper, we propose a global lightweight finger vein segmentation model, TRUnet, and build a lightweight Lightformer module and a plug-and-play module, Global-Lightweight block, in the proposed model respectively. The network not only has global and local correlation to achieve accurate extraction of veins, but also enables the model to maintain its lightweight characteristics. Our approach achieves good results on the public finger vein dataset SDU-FV, MMCBNU_6000.

Keywords: Finger vein segmentation · Lightweight network · Image segmentation

1 Introduction

Among many biometric identification technologies, finger vein recognition technology has many advantages such as contactless and user-friendly experience. Among them, finger vein pattern extraction is the key step of finger vein recognition technology, which has a large impact on the accuracy of finger vein feature extraction, matching and recognition. Therefore many works are dedicated to extracting clear finger vein pattern features efficiently. Recently many researchers have applied deep learning to extract the veins of finger vein images with the aim of improving the drawbacks of traditional methods. Some work has emerged that has done well. Lei et al. [1] proposed an iterative graph cut (IGC) method for automatic and accurate segmentation of finger vein images. Li et al. [2] created a finger vein infrared image segmentation dataset and investigated how to segment finger vein images using pyramid structures and attention mechanisms, and investigated how to segment finger vein images using pyramid structure and attention mechanism. Although better finger vein segmentation can be achieved by previous finger vein segmentation works, these methods require a large amount of storage space and computational resources, and in addition these works are difficult to obtain global feature information of the image, resulting in unsatisfactory finger vein segmentation results. In order to make finger vein recognition a grounded application of algorithms on low-cost terminal devices and to enhance the correlation of global information of images, this paper focuses on how to build an efficient lightweight finger vein segmentation network.

W. Deng et al. (Eds.): CCBR 2022, LNCS 13628, pp. 12–21, 2022.
https://doi.org/10.1007/978-3-031-20233-9_2

Directly addressing the above issues, we make the following contributions:

1. In this paper, we propose a lightweight Lightformer mechanism, using this module not only has a small impact on the model size but also enables the model performance to be improved.
2. In this paper, a plug-and-play lightweight Global-Lightweight module is designed. It effectively combines the global and local information of the image to improve the image segmentation effect.
3. In this paper, a lightweight finger vein segmentation network TRUnet is constructed based on the Unet base network with Global-Lightweight as the foundation block, and SOTA performance is obtained on two-finger vein public datasets, SDU-FV and MMCBNU_6000.

2 Method

2.1 TRUnet Network

In this paper, we propose a lightweight finger vein segmentation network TRUnet that can fully utilize the global and local information of the image, combining Transformer and CNN, the model can not only extract the underlying features of finger vein but also enhance the ability to correlate the global features and obtain better segmentation results. TRUnet is more than the existing lightweight networks. The network structure is shown in Fig. 1.

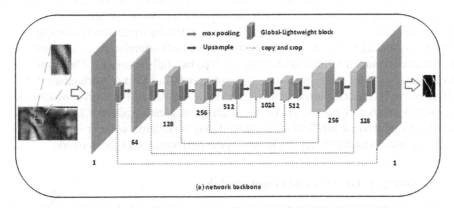

Fig. 1. Light-weight finger vein segmentation network TRUnet

TRUnet consists of 5 encoding layers and 5 decoding layers, and the finger vein features are extracted in an encoding-decoding manner, with a jump connection operation reserved between the encoding and decoding layers, which allows the deep features to be combined with the shallow features to highlight the finger vein pattern information more. In both encoder and decoder parts, the Global-Lightweight module designed in this paper is used as the basis for construction, as shown in Fig. 2. This module encodes the local information by layer-by-layer convolution, and point convolution projects the tensor to the high-dimensional space by learning the linear combination of input channels. Finally, the Lightformer mechanism in Fig. 3 is used to effectively unify these two parts of information, making the overall network more globally and locally relevant.

2.2   Building the Lightformer Mechanism

Since the introduction of the traditional Transformer mechanism will increase the model parameters significantly, in order to solve this challenge, this paper proposes a lightweight Lightformer that not only preserves the global relevance of the Transformer but also makes the introduction of the mechanism have little impact on the model size. The network structure diagram is shown in Fig. 2.

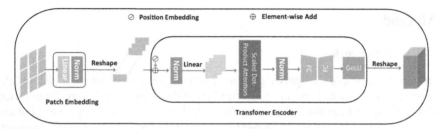

Fig. 2. Lightformer

The Lightformer mechanism is similar to Transformer in its overall structure, by dividing the image into multiple patches, arranging the input image into a set of vectors, finding the corresponding k, q, and v conditional vectors by triple matrix multiplication, multiplying and adding the k, q, and v vectors by the self-attentive layer, and then using the extracted feature information as the input of the two fully connected The Lightformer mechanism has two improvements over the traditional Transformer mechanism: 1. In the self-attentive layer, Lightformer only uses a single-headed self-attentive, which makes the overall number of parameters of the mechanism greatly reduced. 2. Number. The improved Lightformer mechanism ensures global correlation without introducing too many parameters to the model and improves the performance of the network.

2.3   Building the Global-Lightweight Module

In order to improve the segmentation performance of the model, this paper combines the designed Lightformer with group convolution and proposes a plug-and-play lightweight Global-Lightweight module, the structure of which is shown in Fig. 3

Suppose $X_i \in R^{H \times W \times C_i}$ is the size of the input image, first, use 3×3 layer-by-layer convolution to extract features from the input feature map in the depth direction to get C_i scattered feature maps, the feature map size is $X' \in R^{H' \times W' \times C_i}$, the scattered feature maps are randomly assigned to G group convolutions to extract deep features according to the set number of groups G. The first group convolution compresses the feature dimension in proportion r. The output feature map size is $X'' \in R^{H' \times W' \times \frac{C_i}{r}}$, and then

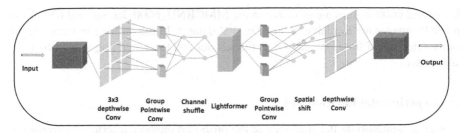

Fig. 3. Global-Lightweight block

$X''' \in R^{H' \times W' \times \left(G, \frac{C_i}{r}\right)}$ is obtained after channel shuffle to reorganize the feature information between groups and break the information imbalance between groups of group convolution. The feature map obtained after layer-by-layer convolution has extracted the local information of the input image, and after the first group convolution on the linear combination of pixel points on different channels, but the global correlation of the feature map obtained at this time is still weak and cannot model the global dependency, so we add the Lightformer mechanism and use the Lightformer mechanism to model the feature map We take the feature dimension obtained by channel shuffle as $X''' \in R^{H' \times W' \times \left(G, \frac{C_i}{r}\right)}$ input, expand it into n blocks with block size $X'''' \in R^{O \times D \times \left(G, \frac{C_i}{r}\right)}$, and encode the output as $X_1 \in R^{O' \times D' \times \left(G, \frac{C_i}{r}\right)}$

$$O = H_i \times W_i \tag{1}$$

$$D = W_i \times H_i \tag{2}$$

$$X_1 \in R^{O' \times D' \times \left(G, \frac{C_i}{r}\right)} = \text{Lightformer}\left(X'''' \in R^{O \times D \times \left(G, \frac{C_i}{r}\right)}\right) \tag{3}$$

The second group convolution restores the number of picture channels to C_o, and after the second group convolution, we get $X_1 \in R^{O' \times D' \times (G, C_i)}$, and then after a layer of spatial shift, the spatial information of the image is reorganized to get the feature map in G group Conv. To compensate for the partial loss of local spatial information when performing point convolution, another layer of 3 × 3 layer-by-layer convolution is added at the end of the module, thereby extracting the global information of the image while preserving the local information of the image. The module not only has the global correlation of spatial induction deviation, but also strengthens the correlation between spatial information and channel information, and at the same time realizes the lightweight operation of the module, which lays the foundation for building a lightweight model.

3 Experiment and Analysis

3.1 Data Pre-processing

The publicly available finger vein databases used in this paper include MMCBNU_6000 of Jeonbuk National University in Korea and SDU-FV of Shandong University. 600

classes and 6000 images are available in the MMCBNU_6000 dataset, and 639 classes and 3816 images are available in the SDU-FV dataset. In the training process, we randomly select one-fifth of the dataset as the test set and the remaining four-fifths as the training set.

3.2 Experimental Environment

In order to demonstrate the efficiency of the proposed method, a series of comparative experiments are conducted on a PC with Ubuntu 18.04, Intel i9-10900k@3.7 GHz CPU, 32 GB RAM, Nvidia GeForce RTX 3090 TURBO, CUDA 11.2, Pytorch 1.8.1, and Python 3.6.5. Gradient descent is performed using an Adam optimizer with a learning rate of 0.001 and a batch size of 512.

3.3 Network Performance Evaluation Index

In the comparison experiments of this paper, we use five segmentation metrics, Accuracy, Specificity, Precision, AUC, and Dice, as the evaluation of good and bad network performance, and the most important evaluation metrics are Dice and AUC and Accuracy.

3.4 Network Experiment Comparison

3.4.1 Comparison with Large Networks

In order to evaluate the representation learning capability of our proposed network and to understand the data requirements of each model, we conducted comparison experiments between the proposed network TRUnet and the conventional segmentation network U-net, the changed network R2U-net, DU-net, and the pure Transformer structure network Swin-UNet on two datasets SDU-FV and MMCBNU_6000 (Tables 1 and 2).

Table 1. Experimental results of TRUnet series network and large-scale network on SDU-FV data set

Network	Params	Mult-Adds	Dice	AUC	Accuracy	Specificity	Precision
CNN							
R2UNet	48.92 M	–	–	90.29%	91.87%	98.21%	62.18%
DUNet	26.73 M	–	–	91.33%	91.99%	97.26%	64.20%
UNet	13.39 M	1.928 G	44.46%	84.34%	91.17%	96.48%	53.79%
Transformer							
Swin-UNet	27.14 M	–	48.96%	88.85%	89.95%	93.24%	46.29%
TransUNet	**102.12 M**	–	49.64%	88.34%	91.82%	96.06%	56.25%
TRUnet	**401.586 k**	**12.550 M**	**50.38%**	**89.36%**	**92.07%**	**96.23%**	**58.69%**

Table 2. Experimental results of TRUnet series network and large-scale network on MMCBNU_6000 data set

Network	Params	Mult-Adds	Dice	AUC	Accuracy	Specificity	Precision
CNN							
R2UNet	48.92 M	–	–	90.58%	92.94%	97.22%	54.68%
DUNet	26.73 M	–	–	91.25%	93.30%	97.89%	58.82%
UNet	13.39 M	1.928G	43.72%	84.74%	91.03%	95.70%	49.49%
Transformer							
Swin-UNet	27.14 M	–	52.34%	91.53%	91.43%	95.65%	55.00%
TransUNet	105.12 M	–	53.22%	91.93%	92.96%	96.08%	57.09%
TRUnet	**401.586 k**	**12.550 M**	**53.56%**	**92.87%**	**93.72%**	**96.18%**	**57.17%**

Under the condition that the dataset is SDU, the number of TRUnet parameters is only 2.9% of that of Unet, and the Dice, AUC, and accuracy are improved by 5.92%, 5.02%, and 0.9%, respectively, compared to Unet. On the MMCBNU_6000 dataset, TRUnet has significantly improved the performance indexes compared with U-net, R2U-net, and DU-net. TRUnet has improved Dice, compared with U-net. The number of TRUnet parameters is only 401 K, which is much smaller than that of large segmentation networks, but its segmentation performance exceeds that of large networks U-net, R2U-net, and DU-net. The segmentation of our network is better than the pure Transformer structure. This proves that our proposed network TRUnet is robust.

3.4.2 Comparison with Lightweight Networks

In addition, we also compare some classical Unet-based lightweight networks with our proposed TRUnet in a comprehensive manner in several aspects such as model size, segmentation performance, and running time (Tables 3 and 4).

Table 3. Experimental data of TRUnet series network and other lightweight networks on SDU-FV dataset

Network	Params	Mult-Adds	Dice	AUC	Accuracy	Specificity	Precision
Unet	13.39 M	1.928 G	0.4446	0.8434	91.17%	96.48%	53.79%
Squeeze_Unet	2.893 M	287.61 M	0.5017	0.8630	91.02%	94.72%	51.90%
Mobile_Unet	3.932 M	481.35 M	0.5025	0.8554	91.31%	95.34%	53.68%
Ghost_Unet	6.783 M	128.97 M	0.4853	0.8864	91.84%	96.75%	58.47%
Shuffle_Unet	516 K	57.97 M	0.5116	0.8859	91.48%	95.28%	54.49%
TRUnet	**401.586 k**	**12.550 M**	**0.5038**	**0.8936**	**92.07%**	**96.23%**	**58.69%**

Table 4. Experimental data of the TRUnet series network and other lightweight networks on the MMCBNU_6000 dataset

Network	Params	Mult-Adds	Dice	AUC	Accuracy	Specificity	Precision
Unet	13.39 M	1.928 G	0.4741	0.8834	92.42%	95.80%	49.24%
Squeeze_Unet	2.893 M	287.61 M	0.5105	0.9216	93.08%	95.34%	52.60%
Mobile_Unet	3.932 M	481.35 M	0.5003	0.9054	92.06%	94.52%	53.37%
Ghost_Unet	6.783 M	128.97 M	0.5110	0.9243	93.01%	96.43%	58.38%
Shuffle_Unet	516 K	57.97 M	0.4792	0.9066	91.80%	94.15%	46.33%
TRUnet	**401.586 k**	**12.550 M**	**0.5356**	**0.9287**	**93.72%**	**96.18%**	**57.17%**

In the SDU-FV dataset, TRUnet not only has a lighter model size but also outperforms other lightweight networks in terms of performance metrics. In the segmentation metric Dice, TRUnet is only lower than Shuffle_Unet, and in the other segmentation metrics, TRUnet achieves better performance than other lightweight networks. On the MMCBNU_6000 dataset, TRUnet outperformed the previous lightweight networks Squeeze_Unet, Mobile_Unet, Ghost_Unet, and Shuffle_Unet in all performance evaluation metrics, and TRUnet outperformed the lightest classic lightweight network, Shuffle_Unet. TRUnet improved 5.64%, 1.92% and 2.21% in Dice. Compared with classical lightweight networks, TRUnet achieves a significant performance improvement while taking into account model compression. Overall, TRUnet achieves better performance with less number of parameters, and the experimental results are already significant without spending a lot of training overhead, which proves that our proposed network does not lose performance but improves performance with lightweight, demonstrating the efficiency of our proposed method.

3.5 Model Visualization

Figure 4 and Fig. 5 show the segmentation results of TRUnet and various lightweight networks, respectively. In order to compare the segmentation performance of different networks, we selected the same image of SDU-FV dataset and MMCBNU_6000 dataset for segmentation. The comparison shows that our proposed network TRUnet not only achieves outstanding results in terms of performance metrics, but also the segmented finger veins are more detailed and smoother, thanks to the global correlation and local correlation of TRUnet, compared with other comparison networks. The details highlighted in the red box show the strong local correlation of our network, and the finger vein features in the overall image are less burly, smoother, and more consistent with the real characteristics of blood vessels, which also verifies the strong global correlation of our network.

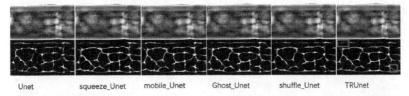

Unet   squeeze_Unet   mobile_Unet   Ghost_Unet   shuffle_Unet   TRUnet

Fig. 4. Actual segmentation effect of TRUnet and other lightweight networks on the SDU-FV dataset (Color figure online)

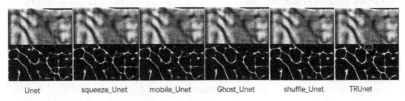

Unet   squeeze_Unet   mobile_Unet   Ghost_Unet   shuffle_Unet   TRUnet

Fig. 5. Actual segmentation effect of TRUnet and other lightweight networks on the MMCBNU_6000 dataset (Color figure online)

As can be seen from Fig. 6, the performance metrics and model size of TRUnet are better than those of previous classical lightweight networks. As can be seen from (a, b) of Fig. 6, TRUnet has significantly improved the Dice segmentation metrics on the MMCBNU_600 dataset based on the relatively substantial number of covariates, and on the SDU-FV dataset. From (c, d) of Fig. 6, it can be seen that TRUnet not only dominates in the number of covariates, but also in AUC and Accuracy on both MMCBNU_600 dataset and SDU-FV dataset, surpassing previous lightweight methods, proving that TRUnet takes into account the improvement of segmentation performance while compressing the model. Therefore, our proposed model TRUnet achieves good results in lightweight and significant improvement in performance metrics, and this result proves the correctness and progress of our proposed method.

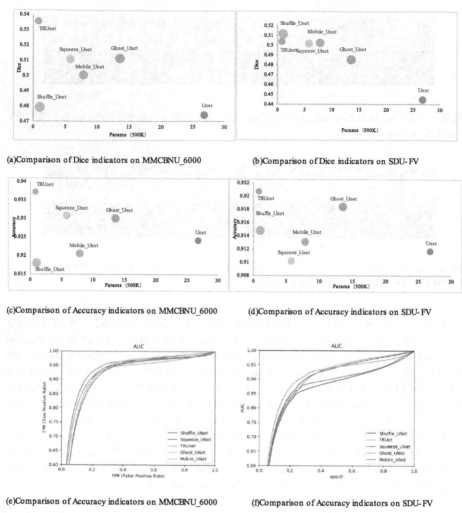

Fig. 6. Comparison of important metrics with classical lightweight networks

4 Conclusion

To address the problems of high memory and high computational cost of existing finger vein segmentation networks, as well as to compensate for the difficulty of convolutional neural networks to obtain global information of finger veins. In this paper, a novel lightweight segmentation network TRUnet is proposed, in which the proposed Global-Lightweight module, not only can establish the global correlation of images and compensate for the shortcomings of convolutional neural networks, but also has the features of translational covariance, localization and insensitivity to data enhancement in CNN. The network achieves the extraction of local and global feature information of finger veins with only 401.586 k parameters and 12.55 M Mult-Adds, and its segmentation performance exceeds that of previous Unet-based large segmentation networks and lightweight segmentation networks.

References

1. Lei, L., Xi, F., Chen, S., et al.: Iterated graph cut method for automatic and accurate segmentation of finger-vein images. Appl. Intell. **51**(2), 673–689 (2021)
2. Li, X., Lin, J., Pang, Y., et al.: Fingertip blood collection point localization research based on infrared finger vein image segmentation. IEEE Trans. Instrum. Meas. **71**, 1–12 (2021)

A Novel Multi-layered Minutiae Extractor Based on OCT Fingerprints

Wenfeng Zeng[1,2,3], Wentian Zhang[1,2,3], Feng Liu[1,2,3]([✉]), Xu Tan[4], and Qin Li[4]

[1] College of Computer Science and Software Engineering, Shenzhen University, Shenzhen, China
cengwenfeng2021@email.szu.edu.cn,feng.liu@szu.edu.cn

[2] SZU Branch, Shenzhen Institute of Artificial Intelligence and Robotics for Society, Senzhen, China

[3] The National Engineering Laboratory for Big Data System Computing Technology, Shenzhen University, Shenzhen, China

[4] School of Software Engineering Shenzhen Institute of Information Technology, Shenzhen, China
{tanx,liqin}@sziit.edu.cn

Abstract. Fingerprints of Optical Coherence Tomography (OCT) imaging provide 3D volume data which have the nature property of multi-layered tissue structure. This paper, for the first time, attempts to extract minutiae for OCT-based fingerprint by making full use of the merits multi-layered structure of OCT imaging and powerful convolution al neural network (CNN). In particular, a novel multi-layered feature fusion minutiae extraction network is proposed, involving a multi-layered feature extractor to integrate the rich information of multiple subsurface fingerprints, and a two-stage object detection framework using reweighted concatenation feature to detect minutiae points. Compared with the results achieved by typical traditional and learning-based methods, our method outperforms the best one by about 2% of F1-score in minutiae extraction, and achieves the improvement of 0.09% than the best one in matching performance, which further demonstrate the effectiveness and robustness of our proposed method.

Keywords: Optical Coherence Tomography (OCT) · Minutiae extraction · Two-stage detection framework · Channel attention mechanism

1 Introduction

Minutiae are very important features for fingerprints and widely used in automatic fingerprint identification systems (AFISs). Most AFISs suffer from poor-quality fingerprint image, like altered or worn-out fingerprints and ultra-wet or dry fingerprints. Many existing fingerprint acquisition systems are all based on the texture of surface fingertip skin, which is not friendly to extract minutiae.

W. Deng et al. (Eds.): CCBR 2022, LNCS 13628, pp. 22–31, 2022.
https://doi.org/10.1007/978-3-031-20233-9_3

Optical Coherence Tomography (OCT) technology [1], as a non-destructive and powerful in vivo tomography imaging technology, provides a possible solution to avoid these negative factors, which expands the imaging dimension and further obtains information in the depth direction. Multi-layered skin tissues, including the stratum corneum, viable epidermis and papillary dermis can be obtained by OCT imaging in the form of B-scans and A-lines. Each A-line, which reflects the imaging capability of the OCT device for the subsurface characteristics of the skin, reaches a certain penetration depth and corresponds to pixels along the depth direction. Each B-scan, also known as a cross-sectional image, is formed by all the A-lines scanning along the horizontal direction [2].

Unlike traditional fingerprint imaging technology, OCT fingerprint imaging results in a set of cross-sectional images of a finger, which can provide an internal representation of the fingertip skin and can be reconstructed to a usual sense fingerprint texture image like the traditional 2D fingerprint image, as shown in Fig. 1. There is some complementary information among them, for example, we can see the clear texture in the same position of stratum corneum and papillary dermis, as outlined in the red rectangle, but it is not better at the corresponding position of viable epidermis. And the green rectangle indicates that ridge lines are very distinct, except for stratum corneum. As well as the quality of stratum corneum and viable epidermis is superior than papillary dermis in the blue rectangle. Ridge lines and minutiae features can also be detected robustly for OCT-based fingerprints when it takes full advantage of the textured and complementary information. However, the lack of dataset limited the development of OCT-based fingerprint recognition techniques including the related minutiae extraction methods. Thus, we analyze the natural advantage of OCT imaging, the distinct properties of reconstructed subsurface fingerprints, the merits of multi-layered feature fusion strategies and previous learning-based algorithms on plain [3–5] or latent fingerprint [6–8], we proposed a new framework for 3D multi-layered minutiae feature extraction for OCT-based fingerprint images by fusing multi-layered subsurface fingerprints' features.

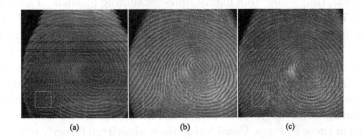

(a)   (b)   (c)

Fig. 1. Reconstructed results. The image from left to right correspond to (a) stratum corneum, (b) viable epidermis and (c) papillary dermis fingerprints.

2   Related Work

The application of OCT technology in fingerprint is an emerging area, that there is no specific method to extract minutiae for OCT-based multi-layered fingerprints at present. And the existing methods of minutiae extraction are aimed to single-layered surface fingerprints. In general, minutiae extraction methods can be divided into two categories: traditional algorithms using handcrafted features designed by domain knowledge, and learning-based algorithms using various neural network structures.

Most of the traditional methods [9,17] operate on skeletonized binary fingerprint images. These algorithms consist of a series of processes: pre-processing, binarization, thinning, minutiae extraction, and post processing. However, these operations are heavily interdependent. If the previous stage is not handled well, it will directly affect the performance of the next procedure. The computational complexity of such kind of binarization technique is also relatively high. Moreover, a significant amount of information may be lost during the skeletonization process, which may introduce a large number of spurious minutiae. Although some algorithms [10] detect minutiae from gray-scale image, it is still greatly affected by image quality and domain knowledge.

Inspired by rapid development and success of convolution al neural networks (CNNs) in a variety of computer vision and pattern recognition tasks, researchers turn to regard minutiae extraction as a learning problem, which have designed many kinds of novel algorithms for minutiae extraction and deploy them to commercial verification systems [18]. Some researches [3] have focused on combining domain knowledge and deep learning representation ability to obtain more accurate minutiae extraction on latent fingerprints. However, the accuracy of the final result seriously depends on the quality of the enhancement and segmentation stage while ignoring the ridge pattern in the raw fingerprint texture. Some methods [5,8,11] divide the whole fingerprint image into many small patches, and feed them to a minutiae descriptor which can identify whether each patch contains minutiae or not. Although these approaches result in accurate minutiae extraction, they suffer from highly time-consuming problem. There are other methods [6,7] regarded minutiae extraction as a point detection problem in pixel level using fully convolution al networks (FCN). Each point at the raw fingerprint got a minutiae-like score, then a detection network was used to classify the regions centering at candidate minutiae-like points and calculate their orientations. To design a fast and accurate neural network-based algorithm. Zhou et al. [4] analyzed the properties of fingerprint images and proposed a two-stage network sharing several layers to extract full-image features and then extracted minutiae from these features. Considering their algorithm directly extracts minutiae from raw fingerprint images without any traditional pre-process, the network only requires datasets with minutiae labels for training.

3   Proposed Method

3.1   The Network Architecture

Inspired by the idea of regarding minutiae extraction as a point detection problem, we also apply a two-stage detection framework and extract minutiae directly from raw fingerprint. The two-stage architecture is shown in Fig. 2. It mainly consists of three parts: feature extraction, feature fusion with a Squeeze-and-Excitation block (SE block) [12], and prediction.

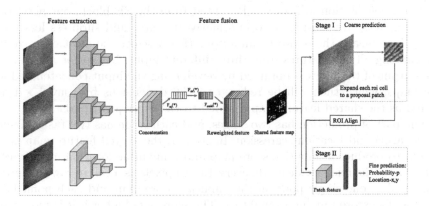

Fig. 2. The architecture of the proposed SECFMENet. The three-tier parallel structure corresponds to the three subsurface fingerprints of stratum corneum, viable epidermis and papillary dermis.

Table 1. Architectures of shared convolution al layers

Input	Output	Residual Block	Block Num
640 × 640 × 1	320 × 320 × 64	conv 7 × 7, 64	1
320 × 320 × 64	160 × 160 × 256	conv 1 × 1, 64 conv 3 × 3, 64 conv 1 × 1, 256	3
160 × 160 × 256	80 × 80 × 512	conv 1 × 1, 128 conv 3 × 3, 128 conv 1 × 1, 512	3
80 × 80 × 512	40 × 40 × 1024	conv 1 × 1, 256 conv 3 × 3, 256 conv 1 × 1, 1024	3
40 × 40 × 1024	40 × 40 × 256	conv 3 × 3, 256	1

The part of feature extraction has three branches. Each branch independently takes a single layer fingerprint image as input and then extracts the features through a series of (Conv, BN, ReLu) down-sampling layers. The pretrained

Resnet model [13] is used to initialize the convolution al layers of each branch. In order to fix the downsample stride at 16, we only use part of these pretrained model and add a smooth layer that consists of 3×3 convolution al kernels to reduce output dimension and calculation parameters, which are indicated in Table 1.

The output of three branches are passed to the feature fusion part to mix these three features together at a high-level layer. In order to boost the representation power of a network, SE block is utilized to explore channel relationship. This mechanism helps the network to recalibrate channel-wise feature responses adaptively by explicitly modelling interdependencies between channels of the network's convolution al features. Benefited from the SE block, our network is able to increase its sensitivity to informative features and suppress less useful ones, which means the network can automatically select the most effective features among all the features from three different input fingerprint images. The final output of the block is obtained by reweighting the input concatenated feature maps, which then will be reduced to 256 dimensions by conv 1×1 and treated as the shared feature map that fed to the subsequent part.

The part of prediction has two stages, and each stage has two tasks, namely classification and location regression. In stage I, the shared feature map is calculated to produce a minutiae score map and a minutiae location map by conv 1×1. Due to the fixed stride as 16, every 16×16 pixels as a cell in raw fingerprint is mapped to one single point in the minutiae score map and each point has a minutiae-like score ranging from 0 to 1. The score gets higher if it is more likely to contain minutiae in the corresponding cell. Each point of minutiae location map means the relative position offset of minutiae to the center of the cell. To generate candidate patches that have sufficient information for precise minutiae extraction, Stage II expands each proposal cell to a 32×32 pixels centering on the predicted minutiae location in the cell and reclassifies these candidate patches to obtain more reliable minutiae scores and precise location. We select the top 100 patches after non-maximum suppression (NMS) as the candidate patches fed to the network in the second stage. For the dataset, this number of candidate patches will be sufficient because it is larger than the number of true minutiae in a single OCT reconstruction fingerprint image. To reduce unnecessary calculations, our method extracts the features from the shared feature map using an operation known as ROIAlign [14], which aligned the extracted features with the raw input image properly and preserved precise spatial location information. Therefore, the network in the second stage uses 2×2×256 features to calculate every result by two fully connected layers.

3.2   Loss Definition

For the loss function, we use binary cross-entropy loss for the classification as Eq. 1, and adopt the smooth L1 loss [15] to regress the location deviation between the minutiae and the cell's center as Eq. 2:

$$L_{cls}(p_{n,i}, y_{n,i}) = -y_{n,i} \cdot log(p_{n,i}) - (1 - y_{n,i}) \cdot log(1 - p_{n,i}). \tag{1}$$

$$L_{loc}(t_{n,i}, t^*_{n,i}) = smooth_{L1}(\|t_{n,i} - t^*_{n,i}\|_2). \tag{2}$$

where n is the index of a training sample (i.e., the index of a cell in Stage I and the index of a candidate patch in Stage II) and i means the number of stage. $p_{n,i}$ and $y_{n,i}$ represent the predicted probability of a minutiae and its corresponding ground truth. $t_{n,i}$ is the location regression predicted by the network, while $t^*_{n,i}$ denotes the difference between the locations of the true minutiae and the cell center. We can use hyper-parameter λ_1 multiply the values of regression loss to balance the weight of different tasks in the first stage, as well as λ_2 to regression loss in the second stage. Meanwhile, we also add a hyper-parameter μ to balance the loss between two stages.

4 Experiments

4.1 Dataset and Training Protocol

To evaluate our proposed method, we select the public OCT fingerprint benchmark dataset [16] and adopt our previously proposed reconstruction method [2] to obtain three layers of subsurface fingerprints, namely stratum corneum, viable epidermis and papillary dermis, which is shown in Fig. 1 We randomly selected 410 fingerprints from the successfully reconstructed texture image and manually marked about ten thousand minutiae coordinates. Hyper-parameters λ_1, λ_2 and μ of loss function are set to be 1, 0.5, 1, respectively. The learning rate is set to be 0.01 at the beginning and reduces by a factor of 0.5 when the loss has stopped decreasing within 10 epochs. We train the networks by means of stochastic gradient descent (SGD) with a momentum of 0.9 and a weight decay of 0.0005. The maximum epoch is 200. Meanwhile, we adopt k-fold cross validation strategy and choose k = 5 in our experiment. The database is randomly divided into five parts without overlap.

An extracted minutiae is assigned to be true if its distance to a ground-truth minutiae is less than a certain pixels, we set the threshold as ε. The performance of minutiae extraction is evaluated in terms of the positive predictive value (precision), true positive rate (recall), and their harmonic mean (F1 score).

4.2 Effectiveness of SECFMENet

To verify the effectiveness of our proposed methods, we will carry out several experiments.

Firstly, we replace the SE block of SECFMENet with 1×1 convolution and call it CFMENet to confirm the role of SE block. Then, we also demonstrate the power of cascades by replacing three cascaded branches with one in the part of feature extraction, and call it as SFMENet. Table 2 shows the comparison. The average precision, recall and F1-score of SECFMENet are about 1% higher than CFMENet, which confirms that embedding SE block in our multi-layered fingerprint fusion framework does further enhance the learning ability of the network. In addition, a improvement of 0.5% for average F1-score to the CFMENet has moderate advantage comparing with SFMENet. And increasing by 1.7% of average F1-score in the comparison between SFMENet and SECFMENet. By combining cascading and SE block, we can draw a conclusion that using a reweighted concatenation feature is effective for detecting minutiae points. Fig. 3 shows several visualized minutiae detection results of the proposed SECFMENet. In order to visualize minutiae point more clearly, we draw the predicted position of minutiae with blue circles in the viable epidermis fingerprints, and mark the target minutiae with red crosses. It is obvious to see that most predicted minutiae and manually marked minutiae are superimposed.

Table 2. k-fold results of different fusion methods(ε=12 pixel).

	SFMENet			CFMENet			SECFMENet		
Fold	Precision (%)	Recall (%)	F1-score	Precision (%)	Recall (%)	F1-score	Precision (%)	Recall (%)	F1-score
1	88.99	79.37	0.839	89.08	79.26	0.839	89.67	80.30	**0.847**
2	88.59	79.37	0.837	87.36	81.14	0.841	89.03	80.65	**0.846**
3	85.52	75.23	0.800	85.84	75.92	0.806	86.62	79.66	**0.830**
4	86.52	77.23	0.816	86.27	78.43	0.822	87.72	79.93	**0.836**
5	87.82	78.65	0.830	88.11	80.08	0.839	88.17	81.72	**0.848**
Avg	87.49	77.97	0.825	87.33	78.97	0.830	88.24	80.45	**0.842**

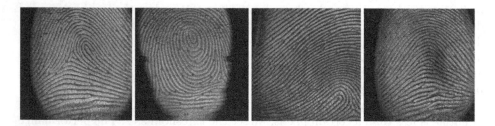

Fig. 3. Some example minutiae extraction results. The blue circles indicate the extracted minutiae and red crosses denote manually marked minutiae.

Then, we carry out experiments that the input is from single-layered fingerprint, fused features from any two fingerprints or fused feature from all the three fingerprints. As shown in Table 3, results of multi-layered fingerprint fusion are always better than that of any single-layered fingerprint among them. Specifically, the result of internal fingerprints has proved to be the best among the three layers, but one can further improve the accuracy if features from other layers of fingerprints are combined. When the information of all the three fingerprints is fully utilized, we can achieve the best performance. In addition, for the stratum corneum and papillary dermis fingerprints, feature fusion of them will be better than just using either fingerprint alone. Experimental results prove the effectiveness of our proposed multi-layered feature fusion strategy.

4.3 Comparisons

To evaluate the performance of our proposed algorithm, we compared ours with several methods. There are MINDTCT [17], VeriFinger [18], JudgeNet [5] and FMENet [4]. And in order to make full use of the information of each subsurface fingerprint in the above mentioned comparison method, we use the fused fingerprint obtained by our previous method [2] as the input of these methods. The first two methods are mature products which can be applied directly, while the codes of the remaining methods are not open source but they provided a detailed description of the network architecture and training preparation. Thus, we reproduce it by ourselves on the public OCT-based fingerprint benchmark dataset.

Table 3. Comparison of different feature fusion results (ε=12 pixel).

Feature			Precision (%)	Recall (%)	F1-score
Layer1	Layer2	Layer3			
$\checkmark$	$\times$	$\times$	39.70	17.09	0.239
$\times$	$\checkmark$	$\times$	87.28	77.29	0.820
$\times$	$\times$	$\checkmark$	83.79	62.48	0.716
$\checkmark$	$\checkmark$	$\times$	**89.81**	76.92	0.829
$\times$	$\checkmark$	$\checkmark$	88.99	76.87	0.825
$\checkmark$	$\times$	$\checkmark$	85.86	68.14	0.760
$\checkmark$	$\checkmark$	$\checkmark$	88.24	**80.45**	**0.842**

In order to demonstrate the robustness of our proposed methods, we set parameter ε to three values: 8, 12 and 16. Table 4 shows that the performance of traditional methods on OCT fingerprint database is unsatisfactory, which may due to the divergence between traditional plain optical fingerprint images and reconstructed OCT-based texture images. The approach of JudgeNet can obtain a very high recall of 90%, which crops each region in the raw image to a small patch and sends it to a trained classification network. However, this method often misdetects some non-minutiae as true minutiae, resulting in low precision. The overall F1-score of JudgeNet is not as good as our proposed SECFMENet. The performance of FMENet is also inferior to our model, whether precision, recall or F1-score. That is, the proposed SECFMENet outperforms other approaches under all settings of thresholds ε, which confirms the effectiveness of our method.

Besides, we also evaluate the fingerprint matching performance using the extracted minutiae. The matching algorithm which we used is [17] and the matching performance comparisons of different minutiae extraction algorithms are shown in Table 5. Our SECFMENet achieves the best result with 2.58% matching EER.

Table 4. Comparison with other methods.

Methods	Setting1 (ε =8 pixel)			Setting2 (ε =12 pixel)			Setting3 (ε =16 pixel)		
	Precision (%)	Recall (%)	F1-score	Precision (%)	Recall (%)	F1-score	Precision (%)	Recall (%)	F1-score
MINDTCT	36.67	60.55	0.457	45.96	75.36	0.571	51.33	83.16	0.635
MINDTCT + quality threshold of 30%	42.03	54.52	0.475	52.60	67.72	0.592	58.51	74.48	0.655
VeriFinger	45.02	64.38	0.530	55.63	77.59	0.648	63.28	82.80	0.717
JudgeNet	51.00	**91.87**	0.656	73.22	**91.57**	0.814	76.35	**91.70**	0.833
FMENet	77.48	71.81	0.745	86.35	79.38	0.827	89.51	82.19	0.857
Proposed SECFMENet	**79.81**	72.29	**0.759**	**88.24**	80.45	**0.842**	**91.24**	83.26	**0.871**

Table 5. Matching results and efficiency comparison with other methods.

Method	Matching EER(%)
MINDTCT	10.69
MINDTCT + quality threshold of 30%	7.31
VeriFinger	5.85
JudgeNet	5.08
FMENet	2.67
Ours-SECFMENet	**2.58**

5   Conclusion and Future Work

A novel multi-layered feature fusion strategy was proposed in the paper. In the strategy, the most effective components are obtained using a SE block, which helps the network to increase its sensitivity to instructional features and suppress less informative ones, so as to robust minutiae extraction. Experimental results show that our method is efficient and reliable, which achieves superior performance in terms of precision, recall and F1 score over published approaches on a benchmark public OCT-based fingerprint database.

This work mainly focuses on obtaining the locations of minutiae on raw fingerprint images without the orientations, future work will expand our framework to detect the direction simultaneously.

Acknowledgements. The work is partially supported by the National Natural Science Foundation of China under grants no. 62076163 and 91959108, the Shenzhen Fundamental Research fund JCYJ20190808163401646, and the Innovation Team Project of Colleges in Guangdong Province under grants no. 2020KCXTD040.

References

1. Podoleanu, A.G.: Optical coherence tomography. J. Microsc. **247**(3), 209–219 (2012)

2. Liu, F., Liu, G., Zhao, Q., Shen, L.: Robust and high-security fingerprint recognition system using optical coherence tomography. Neurocomputing **402**, 14–28 (2020)
3. Tang, Y., Gao, F., Feng, J., Liu, Y.: FingerNet: an unified deep network for fingerprint minutiae extraction. In: 2017 IEEE International Joint Conference on Biometrics (IJCB), pp. 108–116. IEEE, October 2017
4. Zhou, B., Han, C., Liu, Y., Guo, T., Qin, J.: Fast minutiae extractor using neural network. Pattern Recogn. **103**, 107273 (2020)
5. Jiang, L., Zhao, T., Bai, C., Yong, A., Wu, M.: A direct fingerprint minutiae extraction approach based on convolution al neural networks. In: 2016 International Joint Conference on Neural Networks (IJCNN), pp. 571–578. IEEE, July 2016
6. Tang, Y., Gao, F., Feng, J.: Latent fingerprint minutia extraction using fully convolution al network. In: 2017 IEEE International Joint Conference on Biometrics (IJCB), pp. 117–123. IEEE, October 2017
7. Nguyen, D.L., Cao, K., Jain, A.K.: Robust minutiae extractor: integrating deep networks and fingerprint domain knowledge. In: 2018 International Conference on Biometrics (ICB), pp. 9–16. IEEE, February 2018
8. Sankaran, A., Pandey, P., Vatsa, M., Singh, R. (2014, September). On latent fingerprint minutiae extraction using stacked denoising sparse autoencoders. In IEEE International Joint Conference on Biometrics (pp. 1–7). IEEE
9. Zhao, F., Tang, X.: Preprocessing and postprocessing for skeleton-based fingerprint minutiae extraction. Pattern Recogn. **40**(4), 1270–1281 (2007)
10. Fronthaler, H., Kollreider, K., Bigun, J.: Local feature extraction in fingerprints by complex filtering. In: Li, S.Z., Sun, Z., Tan, T., Pankanti, S., Chollet, C., Zhang, D. (eds.) IWBRS 2005. LNCS, vol. 3781, pp. 77–84. Springer, Heidelberg (2005). https://doi.org/10.1007/11569947_10
11. Darlow, L.N., Rosman, B.: Fingerprint minutiae extraction using deep learning. In: 2017 IEEE International Joint Conference on Biometrics (IJCB), pp. 22–30. IEEE, October 2017
12. Hu, J., Shen, L., Sun, G.: Squeeze-and-excitation networks. In: Proceedings of the IEEE Conference on Computer Vision and Pattern Recognition, pp. 7132–7141 (2018)
13. He, K., Zhang, X., Ren, S., Sun, J.: Deep residual learning for image recognition. In: Proceedings of the IEEE Conference on Computer Vision and Pattern Recognition, pp. 770–778 (2016)
14. He, K., Gkioxari, G., Dollár, P., Girshick, R.: Mask R-CNN. In: Proceedings of the IEEE International Conference on Computer Vision, pp. 2961–2969 (2017)
15. Girshick, R.: Fast R-CNN. In: Proceedings of the IEEE International Conference on Computer Vision, pp. 1440–1448 (2015)
16. Liu, F., Shen, C., Liu, H., Liu, G., Liu, Y., Guo, Z., Wang, L.: A flexible touch-based fingerprint acquisition device and a benchmark database using optical coherence tomography. IEEE Trans. Instrum. Meas. **69**(9), 6518–6529 (2020)
17. Ko, K.: User's guide to nist biometric image software (nbis) (2007)
18. Neuro Technology. https://www.neurotechnology.com/verifinger.html

An Overview and Forecast of Biometric Recognition Technology Used in Forensic Science

Zhen Peng[1], Jun He[3], Fan Yang[2], and Xingchun Zhao[1,2(✉)]

[1] Shanxi Medical University, Shanxi 030001, China
zhaoxchun@sina.com
[2] Institute of Forensic Science, Ministry of Public Security, Beijing 100038, China
[3] Institution of Physical Evidence Identification LuoYang Municipal Public Security Bureau, Henan 4741000, China

Abstract. With the development of modern technology, the mainstream biometric recognition technology applied in forensic science in China has experienced an evolution from fingerprints, footprints, DNA STR loci, portraits and voiceprints to current technology, among which gait and long-distance iris recognition are representative methods. In this paper, we summarize the typical applications of these biometric recognition technologies in forensic science in China, their important contributions to solving criminal cases, and some shortcomings, such as the shortage of reference material databases with independent intellectual property rights. Biometric recognition technologies require increasing investment and targeted niche research if they are to play a more significant role in forensic science in the future.

Keywords: Forensic science · Biometric recognition · China

1 Introduction

There has been a long history of using biological characteristics in forensic analysis, providing the most common model for establishing individual identification, which significantly contributes to determining persons of interest (POI) in criminal cases. Biological characteristics that can be used for identification in forensic science will generally meet the following conditions: a. universality, or a biological characteristic common to everyone; b. uniqueness, or a characteristic that is unique and different in each person; c. scalability, meaning this feature can be collected and measured; and d. stability, meaning this feature will not change with differences in time and environment [1, 2].

With the development of modern technology, new methods for individual identification in forensic analysis have become increasingly common, using different types of biological characteristics, which consisted early on of fingerprints, dental images and DNA markers and more recently, of video portraits, voiceprints and irises. At the same time, the criminal suspects have also increasingly enhanced their awareness of counter-reconnaissance techniques to reduce the probability of being identified by wearing gloves and masks and taking other protective measures to avoid leaving physical evidence at the crime scene. As the saying goes, "While the devil climbs a post, the priest climbs ten"; the fierce battle between criminal suspects and police makes it mandatory that more new methods for forensic analysis are continually developed, using new biometric recognition modes such as gait, remote iris and vein recognition and so on.

Here, we will summarize several major types of biometric recognition technology that play important roles in different development stages of forensic science and put forward prospects and suggestions for the improvement of these technologies in the future.

2   Traces for Biometric Recognition that Are Left at a Crime Scene, Such as Fingerprints

According to the chapter "digging holes for theft" in "Feng Zhen Shi", a book of forensic investigation provisions from the Qin Dynasty that was recorded on bamboo slips unearthed at Shuihudi, Yunmeng, Hubei Province, ancient Chinese people gave attention to biological trace evidence left by the suspects at the crime scene. For example, at the scene of a burglary conducted by digging a hole into a house, evidence was recorded on the Qin bamboo slips: "There are, in total, six partial knee marks, handprints and fingerprints on the soil inside and outside the cave" [3]. In the earliest systematic forensic monograph in Chinese history "The Collection of Grievance Relief Stories", written by Song Ci in the Nan Song Dynasty, there are also details on how Nan Song officers collected fingerprints of suspects to solve cases. This means that the identification of biological trace evidence represented by "fingerprints and handprints" played a very important role in helping judicial officers to crack criminal cases during the long history from the Qin Dynasty to the Nan Song Dynasty and then to the present.

In modern times, fingerprint identification technology was introduced to Japan and India and then spread to European countries around the 1860s. In 1892, Sir Francis Galton published his famous book "Fingerprints" in which he systematically elucidated the uniqueness and stability of fingerprints and defined the basic characteristics of whorl, arch and loop, laying a scientific foundation for the large-scale application of fingerprint forensics. Then, in 1901, Scotland Yard, the forensic science department of the British government, established the first systematic fingerprint identification database in the world, which was the start of the wide use of fingerprint identification in forensic analysis [4].

As time went on, modern science and technology were introduced into the field of fingerprint identification, effectively solving problems in obtaining fingerprints with fingerprint ink printing, fingerprint fuming and multiple comparisons. At that time, fingerprint comparison technology was valued greatly, and the fingerprint was defined as "the king of evidence" for the first time. The fingerprint database size in major countries increased as well. In 1971, the number of fingerprint files at the FBI reached 200 million (including repeated entries of fingerprints of the same person). At present, the number of ten-digit fingerprint data entries gathered by Chinese public security departments has also reached 150 million, while the number of two-digit fingerprint data entries has reached 530 million. With the help of this fingerprint database, more than 170 thousand cases of all kinds are solved every year [5]. In the "fingerprint-dominant case solving battle" organized by the Ministry of Public Security from July 2003 to February 2004, more than 12000 cases were solved by relying intensively on the fingerprint automatic identification system and information network; among the most famous of these was an intentional homicide case that occurred in Huangshan City, Anhui Province 19 years ago that was successfully cracked by Jiangsu Police [6].

Similar to fingerprints, footprints (usually containing both bare footprints and shoeprinting) are also widely used for biometric recognition. A footprint is a kind of visual trace left on the surface of mark-bearing material, such as the ground when a human steps on it, which provides information related to age, height, sex and walking habits. Footprints have a long history of forensic application in China. In the 1950s, Ma Yulin and others began to use the information about a person's gait contained in footprints to solve crime cases, opening the door to the modern history of footprints in forensic analysis in China. Then, in the 1960s, footprint comparison was used in public security departments all around China [7].

The development history of footprint comparison technology can be divided into three different periods: the period that relied on individual experience, the period that relied on quantification and the period that relied on automatic testing. The developments in quantification, automation and objectivity of footprint comparison made it more scientifically reliable and transferable to other cases. At present, the forensic technology department mainly uses footprints at the scene of the crime to narrow the scope of investigation and track criminals, as it can reflect the features of criminal activities. In this process, the characteristic information about age and height that footprints can reflect is widely used for criminal identification [8]. For example, in the case that occurred in Yongcheng, Henan Province in 2010, when a large-scale crop of greenhouse vegetables was frozen to death, footprint testing expert Wang Qingju inferred the approximate age, height and walking characteristics of the suspect based on footprints at the scene of the crime. He then screened out a group of people with matching characteristics and finally caught the criminal by comparing their footprints with those on record [9].

Over time, the application of biometric traces represented by fingerprints and footprints for identification in forensic analysis encountered a choke point. On the one hand, as a result of the continuous enrichment and convenience of access to information, the counter-reconnaissance means of criminals were increased, significantly enhancing awareness of how to prevent fingerprints and other traces from being left at the crime scene. At the same time, with the process of urbanization and the hardening of mark-bearing surfaces, the nature of crime scenes changed, making it difficult to obtain enough footprint information [10, 11]. In some complex situations, the scope of application for biometric traces was also restricted because of a low capability for the automatic discovery and collection of fingerprint or footprint evidence and an insufficient ability to deal with incomplete prints [12]. These factors then became obstacles for further expanding the application of traces for biometric recognition in forensic science.

3   DNA Sequence Information of Hereditary Materials, Such as the STR Locus

While fingerprint identification and footprint comparison continue to play important roles in forensic analysis, forensic scientists have also expanded the range of available biological characteristics that can be used for identification. After DNA was confirmed to be the main carrier of genetic material, this double helix polymeric compound, which exists widely and spreads stably in organisms, attracted the attention of forensic scientists. In September 1984, Alec J Jeffreys, a British biologist, prepared the first DNA fingerprints using a set of hybridized probes designed for detecting multiple minisatellite regions in human DNA. This technology of using restriction fragment length polymorphism (RFLP) to prepare personal DNA fingerprints was soon used for kinship identification as well as individual identification [13] and opened up a new era for forensic scientists to use DNA polymorphism in the birth of forensic genetics.

With the discovery and continuous development of PCR technology, forensic geneticists have screened out more suitable individual identification genetic markers: microsatellite DNA or short tandem repeats (STRs). STRs make it possible for technicians to obtain individual identification in a relatively short time (2–4 h) utilizing a very small amount of DNA templates (at the nanogram or even picogram level), which makes it possible to use infinitesimal quantities of biological material left by the suspects at the crime scene. In recent years, with the development of Y chromosome STR locus detection technology, public security departments have obtained the ability to narrow the scope of suspects through paternal relationships, providing a solution for individual identification with unmatched comparison DNA samples.

Chinese public security departments started using DNA biometrics early on after their discovery. In the early 1990s, the Institute of Forensic Science, Ministry of Public Security of China, had mastered the use of RFLP and then kept up with cutting-edge research in the field of STR detection, resulting in the invention of the first domestic DNA STR multiplex amplification reagent system, DNATyper™15, in 2004 [14], which greatly enhanced the application of forensic genetics technology in China. At present, China has established a DNA STR comparison database with tens of millions of data points, which supports the detective work in hundreds of thousands of criminal cases every year [15]. At the same time, the Institute of Forensic Science improved the technology for identifying infinitesimal DNA material and DNA in obsolete biological samples. As a result, a large number of influential homicide cases and cold cases have been solved, such as the murder of three little girls in Jiangxian County, Shanxi Province in 2010 and the "silver case" in Gansu Province, solved in 2016. Similarly, forensic DNA analysis has played an important role in combating child trafficking. In 2021, in the yearlong program "Reunion Action", public security departments used technology integrating DNA comparison and face matching to recover 10,932 children abducted for various lengths of time of which the longest was 74 years [16].

There are also some limitations in the application of forensic DNA analysis. First, DNA amplification may fail if the DNA template is limited or severely degraded; second, biological material left by suspects at the crime scene may be mixed with samples from other sources, resulting in mixed test results that are difficult to identify; in addition, factors such as sample pollution and laboratory environmental pollution can also influence the application of DNA recognition technology.

4 Biological Characteristics Relying on Machine Recognition, Such as Portraits and Voiceprints

Portrait recognition is a kind of biometric recognition technology based on human facial feature information, also called face recognition. Usually, the face is unique, consistent and highly irreproducible, which makes it suitable for identity recognition. Portrait recognition technology has also been used in forensic analysis for a long time but has played only a marginal role in history because the method of comparison was primitive and inefficient. In recent years, the development of modern imaging technology, artificial intelligence, computing technology and some other new "machine recognition" technologies has made portrait comparison and recognition more automatic and intelligent. Moreover, the popularization of security cameras and other monitoring equipment in public areas laid the foundation for the large-scale application of portrait recognition. As a result, the role of portrait recognition in individual identification in forensic science is becoming increasingly important.

Currently, the 2D portrait recognition technology mainly utilized in forensic analysis always uses the following steps: image acquisition, image material acquisition, appearance detection, feature extraction and information comparison [17]. Individual recognition is finally achieved by face feature matching and comparison, which are extracted from the facial appearance. Compared with fingerprints and DNA, the collection of portrait information has many advantages, such as nonmandatory acquisition (namely, portraits can be collected without the cooperation of the ones to be identified) and noncontact acquisition (namely, the ones to be identified do not need to directly contact the equipment). Moreover, the face recognition technology widely embedded in the security video monitoring of the public security system can help collect real-time pictures, greatly improving the efficiency of the detection of suspects in theft, homicide, robbery and other cases [18]. During the "Reunion Action" in 2021, artificial intelligence was used to "age" portraits, and integrated with DNA technology, achieved the effect of "$1 + 1 > 2$" [16]. Additionally, there were many reports of achievements in arresting fugitives through the automatic recognition of the cameras arranged by the public security departments at important gateways, greatly improving the efficiency in solving cases.

The development of modern "machine recognition" technologies brought benefits to another biometric recognition technology, voiceprint recognition. Voiceprint recognition relies on the process of recognizing speakers by deconstructing the characteristics of their speech [19, 20], so characteristic extraction and pattern recognition became the key obstacles to widespread adoption. In the field of characteristic extraction, deep learning algorithms are widely used at present, which can learn to abstract and summarize the features for identification in speech signals through training with massive amounts of speech data. In the field of pattern recognition, the current applications are the template matching method, probability model method, artificial neural network method and other modeling methods developed with artificial intelligence and computer technology [21, 22]. Voiceprint recognition technology is also widely used in forensic analysis, especially in the field of combating telecommunications fraud. Public security departments collect the marked voice of fraudsters, extract and store the voiceprint characteristics of the people involved, establishing a voiceprint database. Then, when a new call is accessed, the voice of fraudsters can be realized automatically through voiceprint extraction and comparison [23].

The advantage of both portraits and voiceprints is that they can be easily collected, but it is also easy for suspects to take corresponding preventive measures, such as obscuring portrait features with the help of shelter or disguise and changing voiceprint features using sound simulators [24]. In addition, judicial acceptance of the reliability of individual identification conclusions drawn from portrait or voiceprint recognition is still an important issue that needs to be solved further.

5 New Biometric Recognition Technology Such as Gait and Long-Distance Iris Recognition

Gait refers to posture and motion characteristics of the human body when walking, and the gait is different between people because of the large differences in individual muscle tendons, muscle strength, bone length, bone density, center of gravity, coordination and so on. Gait is a kind of dynamic feature that requires coordinated actions of multiple parts of the body, so it is difficult to camouflage. At the same time, gait can be easily and effectively obtained through monitoring equipment in public areas even at long distances, and there is no need for the cooperation of the target person [25]. Moreover, it is extremely difficult for the suspect to avoid the acquisition and recognition of gait features by means of camouflage even if he or she has a strong counter-reconnaissance ability [26].

The iris is a ring-shaped muscular diaphragm between the pupil and sclera in the eye and appears as a radial texture from inside to outside. It has the characteristics of uniqueness, stability and anticounterfeiting. Iris recognition technology has many advantages, such as high precision, rapid comparison, strong anticounterfeiting ability and noncontact acquisition [27–29]. Above all, it is not easily affected by facial occlusion, and the probability of suspects changing or blocking their iris features when committing crimes is also low. Both gait and iris biometrics are difficult to camouflage, shadow or change, so the prospect of their wide adoption in forensic science is bright. However, they have been introduced into this field for too short a time, and there are still many key technical problems to be solved and broken through. For example, there is still a significant need for further optimization of the gait recognition algorithm so that technologists can lock on targets quickly amid multiple moving objects through gait recognition under complex monitoring conditions, even ignoring the interference of bad weather or bright light [30]. The prioritization scheme for iris recognition is to further improve recognition at long distances and with high accuracy to meet the need for complex crime-disposal situations.

6 Summary and Prospects for Biometric Recognition Technology in Forensic Analysis

In conclusion, during the 2000-year history of forensic science, an increasing number of biometrics have been utilized for individual identification (Fig. 1). With unique characteristics and advantages, biometric recognition technology has played an important role in case investigation, court litigation and other parts of criminal investigations, constantly contributing to the prosperity and progress of Chinese forensic science (Table 1). At the same time, the shortcomings of biometric recognition technology currently utilized in forensic analysis must be recognized so that optimized solutions can be sought.

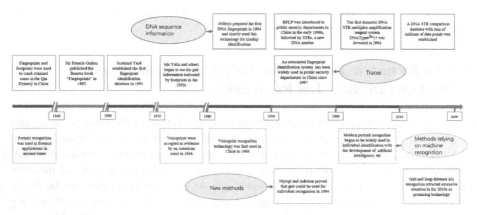

Fig. 1. A brief history of biometrics in forensic science

Table 1. Advantages and shortcomings of biometric recognition technology used in forensic science

Biological characteristics		Technology readiness level*	Advantages	Shortcomings
Traces	Fingerprint	★★★★★	1. Unique and stable 2. Complete application system 3. Large amount of data gathered	1. Many modern ways to prevent them from being left 2. Can be forged
	Footprint	★★★★	1. Must be left when people walk 2. Can narrow the scope of investigation	The changing nature of crime scenes makes it difficult to obtain them
DNA sequence information	STR	★★★★★	1. Unique and stable 2. Can be used for individual recognition as well as genetic relationship identification 3. Large amount of data gathered	1. Many modern ways to prevent them from being left 2. Difficult to analyze when biological materials are mixed

(*continued*)

Table 1. (*continued*)

Biological characteristics		Technology readiness level*	Advantages	Shortcomings
Methods relying on machine recognition	Portrait	★★★★	1. Nonmandatory and noncontact acquisition 2. Real-time pictures can be collected easily	1. Can be easily obscured or forged 2. Judicial acceptance needs to be addressed
	Voiceprint	★★★	Nonmandatory and noncontact acquisition	Judicial acceptance needs to be addressed
New methods	Gait	★★	1. Difficult to camouflage, hide or change 2. Nonmandatory and noncontact acquisition	Much work is needed to solve the key technical problems
	Long-distance iris recognition	★★	Nonmandatory and noncontact acquisition	

* The evaluation is made according to the normal use of these technologies in forensic applications.

First, with the continuous emergence of new technologies, the accuracy and efficiency of forensic identification have been improved. Especially in recent years, the development of big data and artificial intelligence technology have greatly improved the identification and comparison efficiency of DNA, fingerprints and portraits, effectively improving the efficiency of case investigation and resolution. What follows is the problem of reliability of the interpretations made with auxiliary decision-making information provided by the artificial intelligence algorithm. As there are high requirements for the interpretability of evidence in court, finding ways to break the "black box" of the current artificial intelligence algorithm used in individual recognition to promote the interpretability of technology has become the most urgent research problem to be solved [31–34].

Second, in the process of forensic analysis, the limitations of individual recognition with a single biometric have gradually emerged. On the one hand, limited by the size of the database, there is an unignorable possibility that the biometric information cannot be matched; on the other hand, it is difficult to avoid the adverse effects brought by the suspect's counter-reconnaissance measures or background noise pollution when only a single biometric modality is used [35]. In response to this requirement, new individual recognition technology that can combine multiple biometrics should be established. This multibiometric recognition technology works with a data fusion algorithm in which the data comparison results of different biometrics intersect automatically to obtain optimal recognition results. This multimodal way partly compensates for the deficiencies of single biometric recognition to effectively improve the accuracy of the recognition system [36–40].

Finally, we should also pay attention to the standardization and traceability of biometric recognition technology used in forensic science. For example, the datasets ImageNet and MSCOCO that are currently used to evaluate the key indicators of image recognition algorithms, such as accuracy, are maintained by foreign teams; in the field of forensic genetics, the allelic ladder for individual identification of DNA by multiple-PCR amplification detection kits are ultimately traced to the database at the NIST (National Institute of Standards and Technology) in the United States [41, 42]. Currently, facing as the international situation dynamically changes, the risk of being "stuck at a bottleneck" is increasing rapidly. Therefore, the need to build a forensic scientific biometric dataset as a standard for comparison in individual identification, along with a basic database and reference material database with independent intellectual property rights and suitability for the Chinese population is urgent, calling for continually increased investment in forensic scientific research.

References

1. Lu, G.M., Li, H.B., Lang, L.: A survey on biometrics. J. Nanjing Univ. Posts. Telecom. (Natl. Sci.) **1**, 81–88 (2007)
2. Zhao, X.P.: A survey of biometric recognition technology. Forensic Sci. Tech. **6**, 44–48 (2011)
3. Chen, J.L.: Fingerprint identification and investigation of the case in ancient times. People's tribune. **1**, 126–128 (2022)
4. Wang, SH.G.: A survey of fingerprint recognition technology. J. Inform. Security Res. **2**, 343–355 (2016)
5. Li, X.J.: The past and present of fingerprint identification technology. Chin. Govern. General Serv. **4**, 64–66 (2021)
6. The Chinese Police Have Cracked 12,000 Cases in "Case Solving Battle with Fingerprint Identification". http://www.chinanews.com.cn/n/2004-04-22/26/428797.html
7. Yang, L., Tong, D.X.: Review on research progress of footprint identification technology. J. Liaoning Police Acad. **3**, 93–96 (2017)
8. Chen, F., Ling, S.H.: Overview of the discovery and identification of footprints at crime scenes. Legal Sys. Soc. **20**, 275–276 (2016)
9. Wei, B., Wang, Q.: The magical crime solving expert in footprints identification. Democracy Legal Sys. **2** (2013)
10. Zhou, X.P., Quang, H.P.: Thought on the current situation of footprint inspection technology and its development in our country. J. Hum. Public Sec. Coll. **4**, 36–38 (2010)
11. Zhou, F., Chen, Y., Li, Y.B.: A multiple research on examination technology of the footprints. Legal Sys. Soc. **33**, 272–273 (2013)
12. Chu, K.: Public security technology informatization achievement "footprint information identification system" and its role. J. Chifeng Univ. (Natl. Sci. Ed.) **21**, 37–39 (2015)
13. Jeffreys, A.J.: The man behind the DNA fingerprints: an interview with professor sir Alec Jeffrey. Invest. Genetics **4**, 21 (2013)
14. Yin, J., et al.: An approach on the forensic science DNA STR typing reference materials. Forensic Sci. Tech. **6**, 3–6 (2009)
15. Liu, B.: Data mining of the national DNA database. Forensic Sci. Tech. **5**, 345–352 (2015)
16. "Reunion Action" Illuminating the Way of Family Reunion. http://cpc.people.com.cn/n1/2022/0113/c64387-32330286.html
17. Li, ZH.Y.: Review of face recognition technology research status. Elec. Tech. Software Eng. **13**, 106–107 (2020)
18. Hao, T.R.: Application of face recognition technology in smart public security system. Digital Comm. World **12**, 5–7 (2021)
19. Zheng, F., Li, L.T., Zhang, H., Askar, R.: Overview of voiceprint recognition technology and applications. J. Info. Sec. Res. **1**, 44–57 (2016)

20. Li, H.P.: Progress and reflection on voiceprint identification in speech recognition. Tech. Outlook **21**, 280–280 (2016)
21. Zheng, Y.H.: Development and application strategy of voiceprint recognition technology. Tech. Wind. **21**, 9–10 (2017)
22. Xiong, J.: Theory and experiment of sound pattern identification. Audio Eng. **4**, 73–75 (2018)
23. Liu, X.CH., Pan, X.Q., Cao, J.X., Lu, T.L.: Application of voiceprint recognition and speech recognition technology in public security. Network Sec. Tech. Appl. **4**, 153–155 (2021)
24. Tang, L., Wang, K.: Research on application and limitation of face recognition technology. Info. Sec. Comm. Privacy **6**, 82–95 (2021)
25. Zhu, Y.ZH., Li, M.: Current situation and development trend of gait recognition. Telecom. Sci. **8**, 101–110 (2020)
26. Liu, X.F., Zhou, H., Han, Q., Zan, M.E., Han, D.: Survey of vision-based gait recognition. J. Chin. Comput. Sys. **8**, 1685–1692 (2018)
27. Sun, Y., Zhang, M., Sun Z.: Demographic analysis from biometric data: achievements, challenges, and new frontiers. IEEE Trans. Pat. Anal. Mach. Intel. **2**, 332–351 (2017)
28. Li, SH.G., Zhao, SH.W., Tan, L.: Application of Iris recognition technology in public security system. China Sec. Prot. **3**, 94–99 (2018)
29. Chen, Z.L., et al.: Tentative exploration into artificial selection and labeling of iris feature. Forensic Sci. Tech. **3**, 221–227 (2021)
30. Zhang, SH., Zeng, Y.: A review of research on gait recognition techniques. Sci. Tech. Vision **22**, 30–30 (2014)
31. Chen, K.Q., Sun, Y.X.: Exploration and expectation on the "embedded" style of police enforcing the law with the artificial intelligence under the background of big data. J. People's Pub. Sec. Univ. China (Soc. Sci. Ed.) **2**, 101–110 (2019)
32. Wang, M.ZH.: Research on the Application of Artificial Intelligence in Judicial Decision. Nankai University (2020)
33. Zhang, Q.: Risks and legal responses in the age of artificial intelligence. J. Liaoning Admin. Coll. Police Justice **1**, 75–80 (2020)
34. Wu, J.J., Guo, W.E.: The governance of the algorithm black box in the era of artificial intelligence. J. Sci. Tech. Law. **1**, 19–28 (2021)
35. Liu, H.B.: Multi-biometric fusion recognition technology. China Sci. Tech. Info. **13**, 49–50 (2017)
36. Fang, ZH.G., Ye, W.ZH.: A survey on multi-biometrics. Comput. Eng. **9**, 140–142 (2003)
37. Liu, Y.J., Feng, X.L., Ma, Y.D., Du, H.F.: A survey on multi-biometrics identification techniques. Ship Elec. Eng. **1**, 36–39 (2006)
38. Liiu, X., Guang, J.J., Zhong, B.N., Du, J.X.: Survey on multi-feature fusion in biometrics and its developments. J. Chin Computer Sys. **8**, 1792–1799 (2017)
39. Nie, H., Lu, X.L., Guo, W.ZH., Li, Y.J., Han, G.J., Zhao, X.CH.: Research progress and prospects of multi-modal biometrics identification technology. Life Sci. Inst. **5**, 20–28 (2020)
40. Li, X.M., Chen, Y.: Multi-biometric feature fusion recognition based on fractional layer fusion. Changjiang Info. Comm. **10**, 7–11 (2021)
41. Zhao, X.CH., Yin, J., Sun, J., Jiang, CH.T., Ye, J.: An brief introduction of DNA standard reference materials in forensic science of United States. Chin. J. Forensic Med. **4**, 263–266 (2009)
42. Zhao, X.CH., et al.: Certified value study for alleles on STR loci of forensic DNA reference materials. China Meas. Test. **4**, 55–57 (2012)

Combining Band-Limited OTSDF Filter and Directional Representation for Palmprint Recognition

Chaoxiang Hou and Wei Jia[✉]

School of Computer Scinece and Information Engineering, Hefei University of Technology,
Hefei 230009, China
2020171167@mail.hfut.edu.cn, jiawei@hfut.edu.cn

Abstract. Correlation filter is one of important and powerful tools in pattern recognition. Recently, the method of band-limited phase-only correlation (BLPOC) has been successfully used for biometrics. Motivated by the method of BLPOC, we propose the band-limited optimal tradeoff synthetic discriminant function (BLOTSDF) filter in this paper. Compared with BLPOC and original OTSDF filter, BLOTSDF filter has faster matching speed and can achieve better recognition performance. We then propose a method combining BLOTSDF filter and directional representation (DR) for palmprint recognition. Since DR is insensitive to illumination changes and contains rich information and the BLOTSDF filter has good recognition ability, the proposed method can achieve promising recognition performance, which is comparable with that of other state-of-the-art methods. Particularly, the matching speed of the proposed method is about 20 times faster than that of several classical directional coding algorithms, which is very suitable for industrial applications. The experiments results obtained on two palmprint databases validate the effectiveness of the proposed method.

Keywords: Biometrics · Palmprint recognition · Correlation filter · OTSDF filter

1 Introduction

In recent years, as one of promising biometrics technologies, palmprint recognition has drawn wide attention from academia and industry [1, 2]. In the past twenty years, researchers have proposed many effective palmprint recognition methods. These methods can be roughly divided into traditional machine learning methods [3–7] and deep learning methods [8]. Among the traditional algorithms, the directional coding methods such as Competitive Code [3], Ordinal Code [4], and Robust Line Orientation Code (RLOC) [5], local texture descriptors [6], and correlation filter-based methods [7] have achieved good performance.

In biometrics field, correlation filter-based methods such as Phase-Only Correlation (POC) [9], minimum average correlation energy (MACE) filter, optimal tradeoff synthetic discriminant function (OTSDF) filter, have shown their effectiveness [10, 11]. For palmprint recognition, Hennings-Yeomans et al. [12] proposed a method with the use

W. Deng et al. (Eds.): CCBR 2022, LNCS 13628, pp. 42–51, 2022.
https://doi.org/10.1007/978-3-031-20233-9_5

of multiple correlation filters. Ito et al. [13] proposed a palmprint recognition algorithm using Band-limited Phase-Only Correlation (BLPOC) method. It should be noted that these correlation filter-based methods mentioned above were only directly applied to original palmprint images. For convenience, we call original image as original representation (OR) in this paper. In [7], Jia et al. proposed a method combining BLPOC and directional representation (DR) of palmprint, have achieved very promising performance. In biometrics field, BLPOC has become the most mainstream correlation filter, which is applied to different biometrics technologies.

Motivated by the method of BLPOC, in this paper, we propose the band-limited optimal tradeoff synthetic discriminant function (BLOTSDF) filter. Compared with BLPOC and original OTSDF filter, BLOTSDF filter has faster matching speed and can achieve better recognition performance. We then combine BLOTSDF filter and DR for palmprint recognition. Since DR is insensitive to illumination changes and contains rich information and the BLOTSDF filter has good recognition ability, the proposed method can achieve promising recognition performance. For each class, BLOTSDF filter can form multiple training sample images into one feature template, so increasing the number of training samples will not increase the matching time. For BLPOC, each training sample will form a separate feature template, so increasing the number of training samples will linearly increase the matching time. Our work enriches the biometrics technologies based on correlation filter. Because BLOTSDF filter has very fast matching speed and good recognition performance, it is very suitable for industrial applications.

2   Brief Review of BLPOC

In this section, we will introduce the fundamentals of BLPOC [9, 13]. Firstly, the definition of POC is described as follows: Consider two $N_1 \times N_2$ images, $f(n_1, n_2)$, and $g(t_1, t_2)$. Let $F(t_1, t_2)$ and $G(t_1, t_2)$ denote the 2D DFTs of the two images. Here, $F(t_1, t_2)$ is given by:

$$F(t_1, t_2) = \sum_{n_1=0}^{N_1} \sum_{n_2=0}^{N_2} f(n_1, n_2) e^{-j2\pi \left(\frac{n_1 t_1}{N_1} + \frac{n_2 t_2}{N_2} \right)}$$

$$= A_F(t_1, t_2) e^{j\theta_F(t_1, t_2)} \tag{1}$$

where $A_F(t_1, t_2)$ is amplitude and $\theta_F(t_1, t_2)$ is phase. $G(t_1, t_2)$ can be defined in the same way. The cross-phase spectrum $R_{FG}(t_1, t_2)$ is given by:

$$R_{FG}(t_1, t_2) = \frac{F(t_1, t_2)\overline{G(t_1, t_2)}}{|F(t_1, t_2)\overline{G(t_1, t_2)}|} = e^{j\theta(t_1, t_2)} \tag{2}$$

where $\overline{G(t_1, t_2)}$ is the complex conjugate of $G(t_1, t_2)$ and $\theta(t_1, t_2)$ denotes the phase difference $\theta_F(t_1, t_2) - \theta_G(t_1, t_2)$. The POC function $r_{fg}(n_1, n_2)$ is the 2D Inverse DFT (2D IDFT) of $R_{FG}(t_1, t_2)$ and is given by:

$$r_{fg}(n_1, n_2) = \frac{1}{N_1 N_2} \sum_{t_1 t_2} e^{j\theta(t_1, t_2)} e^{j2\pi \left(\frac{n_1 t_1}{N_1} + \frac{n_2 t_2}{N_2} \right)} \tag{3}$$

From formulas (2) and (3), we can see that original POC exploit all components of image's 2D DFT to generate the out plane. Miyazawa et al. [9] found that BLPOC can achieve better recognition performance by removing the high frequency components and only using the inherent frequency band for matching.

Here we denote the center area of $\theta_F(t_1, t_2)$ and $\theta_G(t_1, t_2)$ as $\theta_F(t_1, t_2)_{BL}$ and $\theta_G(t_1, t_2)_{BL}$, whose size is $J_1 \times J_2$. Thus, the BLPOC function is given by:

$$r_{fg}(n_1, n_2)_{BL} = \frac{1}{J_1 J_2} \sum_{t_1 t_2} e^{j(\theta_F(t_1,t_2)_{BL} - \theta_G(t_1,t_2)_{BL})} e^{j2\pi(\frac{n_1 t_1}{J_1} + \frac{n_2 t_2}{J_2})} \quad (4)$$

3   The Proposed BLOTSDF Filter

It is well known that MACE [10] and OTSDF [10] are two important correlation filters. When designing MACE and OTSDF filters, 2DDFT will be applied to training images firstly. As we have introduced above, in BLPOC method, the center part of 2DDFT phase spectrum was selected for filter design. In this Section, we will extend the similar idea to construct band-limited MACE (BLMACE) and BLOTSDF filters by exploiting the center part of 2DDFT magnitude spectrum for filter design. Given an image, $f(n_1, n_2)$, whose size is $N_1 \times N_2$, its 2D DFT i.e., $F(t_1,t_2)$ could be calculated by formula (1). Generally, the size of $F(t_1, t_2)$ is also $N_1 \times N_2$. And it should be noted that we should move the zero frequency component of $F(t_1, t_2)$ to the center of the spectrum for convenient use.

If we have a training set which has C classes and each class has C_j training samples, the total number of training samples is $\sum C_j$. For class j, the MACE filter design is used to synthesize a single filter template using C_j training samples. And the goal of MACE filter design is to produce correlation output plane (COP) that the value at the origin is constrained to a specific peak height (usually chosen to be 1) while minimizing correlation values at other locations. Therefore, when the filter is cross-correlated with a test image that belongs to an authentic, the filter will exhibit sharp correlation peaks. Otherwise, if the test image belongs to an imposter, the filter will output small correlation values with no discernible peak.

However, in any practical application, the factor of noise introduced from varying sources should be taken into consideration. Thus, OTSDF filter was proposed [14], which is obtained by minimizing a weighted sum of Average Correlation Energy (ACE) and Output Noise Variance (ONV).

In [10], we know that all components of training samples' 2D DFT are exploited to generate MACE filter and OTSDF filter. However, the 2D DFT of training samples might include meaningless components in high frequency domain. That is, the original MACE and OTSDF filters emphasize the high frequency components, which may have less reliability. Thus, we propose BLMACE filter and BLOTSDF filter by removing the high frequency components and using the inherent frequency band for filter design. Figure 1 shows the framework of palmprint recognition using BLMACE and BLOTSDF filters.

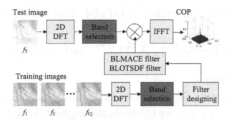

Fig. 1. The framework of palmprint recognition using BLMACE or BLOTSDF filters

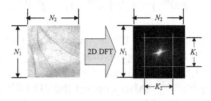

Fig. 2. The $K_1 \times K_2$ area surrounding the center of 2D DFT spectrum is used for filter design

Now, we present how to generate BLMACE and BLOTSDF filters in detail. Suppose that we have C_j training images in class j, which are denoted by $f_1, f_2, \cdots, f_{C_j}$. Given an image, $f_i^{(N_1 \times N_2)}$, whose size is $N_1 \times N_2$, we can obtain its 2D DFT, $F_i^{(N_1 \times N_2)}$. BLMACE only uses the components located in the center area of the magnitude spectrum for filter design as shown in Fig. 2. Here we assume that the size of center area of $F_i^{(N_1 \times N_2)}$ is $K_1 \times K_2$, and define this center area as $F_i^{(K_1 \times K_2)}$. We perform 2D DFTs on all images in class j and then convert the 2D DFT arrays $F_1^{(K_1 \times K_2)}, F_2^{(K_1 \times K_2)}, \cdots,$ $F_{C_j}^{(K_1 \times K_2)}$ into 1-D column vectors by lexicographic ordering, which are denoted by $X_1^{BL}, X_2^{BL}, \cdots, X_{C_j}^{BL}$, respectively. Then, we define the training image data matrix X^{BL} as:

$$X^{BL} = \left[X_1^{BL}, X_1^{BL}, X_1^{BL}, \cdots, X_{C_j}^{BL} \right] \tag{5}$$

Consequently, the BLMACE filter expressions H_{MACE}^{BL} can be calculated by the following formula:

$$H_{MACE}^{BL} = D^{BL^{-1}} X^{BL} \left(X^{BL^{+}} D^{BL^{-1}} X^{BL} \right)^{-1} u \tag{6}$$

where $D^{BL} = (1/C_j) \sum_{i=1}^{C_j} D^{BL}_i$, in which D^{BL}_i is a diagonal matrix of size $(K_1 \times K_2)^2$ whose diagonal elements are the magnitude squared of the associated element of X_i^{BL}; the superscript "+" denotes conjugate transpose, and the column vector u with C_j elements contains the pre-specified correlation peak values of training images, which are often set to 1.

As we have mentioned, the OTSDF filter can be accomplished by minimizing the following tradeoff energy function:

$$E(H_{OTSDF}) = \alpha(ONV) + \beta(ACE) \tag{7}$$

where $\beta = \sqrt{1 - \alpha^2}$. In this paper, the BLOTSDF filter H_{OTSDF}^{BL} is given by:

$$H_{OTSDF}^{BL} = (\alpha I + \beta D^{BL})^{-1} X^{BL} \left(X^{BL+} (\alpha I + \beta D^{BL})^{-1} X^{BL} \right)^{-1} u \tag{8}$$

where I is the identity matrix.

For simplification, we fix the value of α to 1 in this paper i.e., in our experiments, we only adjust the values of β to try to obtain the highest ARR and lowest EER. In this situation, the formula of (9) can be rewritten as:

$$H_{OTSDF}^{BL} = (I + \beta D^{BL})^{-1} X^{BL} \left(X^{BL+} (I + \beta D^{BL})^{-1} X^{BL} \right)^{-1} u \tag{9}$$

After designing H_{MACE}^{BL} and H_{OTSDF}^{BL} filters, we can correlate the filter with test image to produce COP as shown in Fig. 1. Suppose that $f_T^{(N_1 \times N_2)}$ is a test image, whose size is $N_1 \times N_2$, we apply 2D DFT to it to get $F_T^{(N_1 \times N_2)}$. Then select the center area of $F_T^{(N_1 \times N_2)}$ to form $F_T^{(K_1 \times K_2)}$. Also, convert the 2D DFT arrays $F_T^{(K_1 \times K_2)}$ into 1-D column vectors by lexicographic ordering, which is denoted by X_T^{BL}. The cross-correlated vector (CCV) between X_T^{BL} and H_{MACE}^{BL} (or H_{OTSDF}^{BL}) can be calculated by the following formulae:

$$\begin{aligned} CCV &= IFFT \left((X_T^{BL})^+ H_{MACE}^{BL} \right) \\ CCV &= IFFT \left((X_T^{BL})^+ H_{OTSDF}^{BL} \right) \end{aligned} \tag{10}$$

where the *IFFT* means inverse Fourier transform. Finally, the 1D vector, CCV, should be converted to 2D array by lexicographic ordering to generate final COP.

There are some different measures to evaluate the similarity between test image and BLMACE/BLOTSDF filter such as peak-to-correlation energy (PCE), and peak-to-sidelobe ratio (PSR). As the name suggests, peak is the maximum peak value in the COP. PCE and PSR are defined as:

$$PCE = \frac{peak - mean_{COP}}{Std_{COP}} \tag{11}$$

where $mean_{COP}$ is the average of the COP, std_{COP} is the standard deviation of the COP.

$$PSR = \frac{peak - mean_{sidelobe}}{Std_{sidelobe}} \tag{12}$$

where $mean_{sidelobe}$ is the average of the sidelobe region surrounding the peak (21 $\times$ 21 pixels with a 5 $\times$ 5 excluded zone around the peak), and $std_{sidelobe}$ is the standard deviation of the sidelobe region.

4   Combining BLOTSDF and DR for Palmprint Recognition

In [7], Jia et al. used DR of palmprint to improve the recognition performance of BLPOC method. They proposed modified finite Radon transform (MFRAT) to extract DR of palmprint. In this paper, MFRAT is used to extract DR of palmprint due to its simplicity

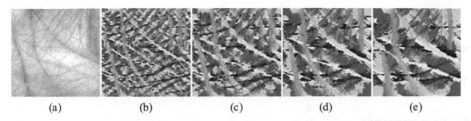

(a)   (b)   (c)   (d)   (e)

Fig. 3. Different DRs extracted from(a) under different p of MFRAT. (b) $p = 11$, (c) $p = 17$, (d) $p = 25$, (e) $p = 33$.

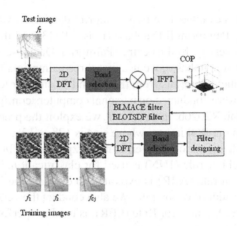

Fig. 4. The framework of combining BLOTSDF filter and DR for palmprint recognition

and effectiveness. The detail of MFRAT can be found in [7]. MFRAT accumulates the pixel values of line segments passing through the center point in 12 directions. Using winner-take-all rule, the MFRAT can be used to calculate the direction value (index value of direction) of each pixel, and the direction value can be used as the new pixel value of the image, so as to obtain the DR of the palmprint image. MFRAT has an important parameter, p, which is used to determine the size of MFRAT. Figure 3 illustrates the DR images extract by MFRATs with different values of p. It can be seen that if the value of p is small, the orientation feature of short and thin palm lines will be very clear; when the value of p becomes larger, the direction feature of long and thick principal lines will be more distinct. In this regard, it can be concluded that, besides structure and direction information, DR also contains scale information, which is valuable for recognition as well.

The framework of combining BLOTSDF filter and DR for palmprint recognition is shown in Fig. 4. The main steps of the proposed method are given as follows:

Step 1. Given training images $f_1, f_2, \cdots f_{Cj}$, which are belong to class C_j, we extract their DR.

Step 2. Perform 2D DFTs on all DR images in class C_j, and select the center part of 2DDFT magnitude spectrum for filter design.

Step 3. Build BLMACE and BLOTSDF filters.

Step 4. Given a test image f_T, we extact its DR.

Step 5. Perform 2D DFTs on DR image of f_T, and select the center part of 2DDFT magnitude spectrum for matching.

Step 6. Correlate the BLMACE and BLOTSDF filters with the center part of 2DDFT magnitude spectrum of DR (test image) to produce COP.

5   Experiments

5.1   Databases and Experimental Environment

The proposed method is evaluated on two palmprint databases, which are Hong Kong Polytechnic University Palmprint II Database (PolyU II) [3] and the blue band of Hong Kong Polytechnic University Multispectral Palmprint Database (PolyU M_B) [15], respectively. In these two databases, we use first three palmprints from the first session for training and leave the palmprints from the second session for test.

Most experiments were conducted on personal computers configured with Microsoft Windows 10 and Matlab R2020b. In our paper, we exploit the preprocessing algorithm proposed in [3] to crop the ROI image, whose size is 128×128.

We conduct both identification and verification experiments. In identification experiment, the nearest neighbor rule (1NN) is used for classification. The statistical value, i.e., accurate recognition rate (ARR) is exploited to evaluate the identification performance, which is rank 1 identification rate. We also conduct the verification experiment. The statistical value i.e., Equal Error Rate (EER), is used for performance evaluation.

5.2   Performance Evaluation on PolyU II Database

In the proposed method, there are three important parameters. The first parameter is p, the size of MFRAT. The second parameter is K_1, the size of center area of $F_i^{(N_1 \times N_2)}$. In our method, the center area of $F_i^{(N_1 \times N_2)}$ is a square, that is $K_1 = K_2$. The third parameter is β, which defines the noise tolerance of filter. We conduct identification and verification experiments on different DRs extracted by MFRAT with different size of p. For each filter, we can know the "best value" of p corresponding to the highest ARR and lowest EER. It is interesting to know the recognition performance of three filters under different 2DDFT bands. For each filter, we fix their best value of p of MFRAT firstly, and then conduct identification and verification experiments under different K_1. In this way, we can obtain the best value of K_1. We then fix the best value of p and K_1, and conduct identification and verification experiments to determine the best value of β. (See Additional Materials to view the experimental results).

The recognition performance comparison of BLPOC, BLMACE and BLOTSDF between on OR and on DR is made in Table 1. The experimental results show that three correlation filters can achieve better recognition performance than OR when combined with DR, which validates the effectiveness of the methods. Among three filters, the proposed BLOTSDF + DR achieves the highest ARR and lowest EER.

Table 1. Recognition performance comparison between on OR and on DR of BLMACE, BLPOC and BLOTSDF filters

	BLMACE + OR	BLMACE + DR	BLPOC + OR	BLPOC + DR	BLOTSDF + OR	BLOTSDF + DR
Highest ARR	99.35	99.79 $(p = 11)$ $(K1 = 36)$	99.02	99.94 $(p = 15)$ $(K1 = 22)$	99.61	**100** $(p = 13,15,...,25)$
Lowest EER	0.28	0.2075 $(p = 11)$ $(K1 = 30)$	0.238	0.1293 $(p = 13)$ $(K1 = 24)$	0.207	**0.0397** $(p = 19)$ $(K1 = 30)$ $(\beta = 0.05)$

Besides ARR and EER, we are also concerned about the matching speed of proposed BLMACE and BLOTSDF filters (See Additional Materials to view the experimental results). While K_1 is 30, the matching speed of BLMACE/BLOTSDF filter is 20 times faster than that of original MACE/OTSDF filter (K_1 is 128). Here, we make a performance comparison between the proposed method and other state-of-the-art methods by using four performance values i.e. ARR, EER, ZeroFAR and matching time. The definition of ZeroFAR is presented as follows:

$$ZeroFAR(t) = \min_t \ t\{FRR(t)|FAR(t) = 0\} \tag{13}$$

Table 2. Performance comparison among different methods on PolyU II database

Method	ARR (%)	EER (%)	ZeroFAR (%)	Matching speed (us)
BLOTSDF + DR	**100**	**0.0397**	1.139	**72**
BLMACE + DR	99.79	0.207	3.1	170
BLPOC + DR	99.94	0.1293	2.53	168
RLOC	100	0.057	2.82	1396
Competitive Code	100	0.048	0.26	1461
Ordinal Code	100	0.025	0.29	1485
BLPOC + OR	99.02	0.238	12.02	187

Table 2 lists performance values of different methods. In this paper, we implement RLOC, Competitive Code, and Ordinal Code on PolyU II Database using the identical experimental protocol. In Table 2, the matching time is the execution time of a test image matching with a template which contains three training images. From Table 2, the performance of the proposed methods is comparable to other state-of-the-art methods. Specially, the method of BLOTSDF + DR has fast matching speed. Especially, the matching speed of BLOTSDF + DR method is about 20 times faster than that of directional coding algorithms such as RLOC, Competitive Code and Ordinal Code.

5.3 Performance Evaluation on PolyU M_B Database

In this subsection, we evaluate the performance of the proposed methods on PolyU M_B database. We conduct similar experiments on PolyU M_B database as we have done in Subsect. 5.2. Here, we only list the final recognition results and related parameters in Table 3. The recognition performance of BLOTSDF + DR is better than that of BLPOC + DR. These results are same to those we have obtained in PolyU II database. In this table, we also make a performance comparison between the proposed methods and other methods such as RLOC, Competitive Code and Ordinal Code. From Table 3, it can be seen that the performance of the proposed methods is comparable to other methods.

Table 3. Performance comparison among different methods on PolyU M_B database

Method	ARR(%)	EER (%)	ZeroFAR (%)	Parameters
BLOTSDF + DR	**100**	0.018	0.2	$p = 17, K_1 = 46, \beta = 0.05$
BLPOC + DR	99.97	0.033	0.7	$p = 11, K_1 = 26$
BLMACE + DR	99.93	0.093	1.56	$p = 11, K_1 = 30$
BLOTSDF + OR	99.63	0.188	9.7	$K_1 = 24, \beta = 100$
BLPOC + OR	99.93	0.099	2.83	$K_1 = 28$
BLMACE + OR	99.4	0.31	9.8	$K_1 = 38$
RLOC	100	0.03	1.98	------
Competitive Code	100	0	------	------
Ordinal Code	100	0.03	0.7	------

6 Conclusions

In this paper, we proposed a method combining BLOTSDF filter and DR for palmprint recognition. The proposed BLOTSDF filter has better recognition performance than BLPOC, thus, it can be widely used for biometrics in the future. On PolyU II database, the proposed method has achieved the ARR of 100%, and the EER of 0.0397%, which is better than that of the method of BLPOC and is comparable with the performance of other state-of-the-art methods. On PolyU M_B database, the proposed method has achieved the ARR of 100%, and the EER of 0.018%, which is again better than that of the method of BLPOC. Particularly, BLOTSDF filter has faster matching speed if there are multiple training samples within a class, because the BLOTSDF filter design is used to synthesize a single filter template using multiple training samples and the inverse Fourier transform can be performed very fast. Particularly, the matching speed of BLOTSDF + DR method is about 20 times faster than that of directional coding methods such as RLOC, Competitive Code and Ordinal Code, while the recognition accuracy of BLOTSDF + DR method is comparable to these directional coding methods. This advantage is important for some real applications.

Acknowledgments. This work is partly supported by the grant of the National Science Foundation of China, No. 62076086.

References

1. Fei, L., Lu, G., Jia, W., Teng, S., Zhang, D.: Feature extraction methods for palmprint recognition: a survey and evaluation. IEEE Trans. Syst. Man Cybern. Syst. **49**, 346–363 (2018)
2. Zhong, D., Du, X., Zhong, K.: Decade progress of palmprint recognition: a brief survey. Neurocomputing **328**, 16–28 (2019)
3. Kong, A., Zhang, D.: Competitive coding scheme for palmprint verification. In: Proceedings of the 17th ICPR, pp. 520–523 (2004)
4. Sun, Z.N., Tan, T.N., Wang, Y.H., Li, S.Z.: Ordinal palmprint representation for personal Identification. In: Proceedings of CVPR, pp. 279–284 (2005)
5. Jia, W., Huang, D.S., Zhang, D.: Palmprint verification based on robust line orientation code. Pattern Recogn. **41**, 1504–1513 (2008)
6. Luo, Y.T., et al.: Local line directional pattern for palmprint recognition. Pattern Recogn. **50**, 26–44 (2016)
7. Jia, W., et al.: Palmprint recognition based on complete direction representation. IEEE Trans. Image Process. **26**, 4483–4498 (2017)
8. Genovese, A., Piuri, V., Plataniotis, K.N., Scotti, F.: PalmNet: Gabor-PCA convolutional networks for touchless palmprint recognition. IEEE Trans. Inf. Forensics Secur. **14**, 3160–3174 (2019)
9. Miyazawa, K., Ito, K., Aoki, T., Kobayashi, K., Nakajima, H.: An effective approach for iris recognition using phase-based image matching. IEEE Trans. Pattern Anal. Mach. Intell. **30**, 1741–1756 (2008)
10. Kumar, B.V.K.V., Mahalanobis, A., Juday, R.: Correlation Pattern Recognition. Cambridge University Press (2005)
11. Rodriguez, A., Boddeti, V.N., Kumar, B.V.K.V., Mahalanobis, A.: Maximum margin correlation filter: a new approach for localization and classification. IEEE Trans. Image Process. **22**, 631–643 (2013)
12. Hennings-Yeomans, P., Kumar, B., Savvides, M.: Palmprint classification using multiple advanced correlation filters and palm-specific segmentation. IEEE Trans. Inf. Forens. Secur. **2**, 613–622 (2007)
13. ITO, K., Aoki, T., Nakajima, H.: A palmprint recognition algorithm using phase-only correlation. IEICE Trans. Fundament. **e91-a**, 1023–1030 (2008)
14. Kumar, B.V.K.V., Carlson, D., Mahalanobis, A.: Optimal tradeoff synthetic discriminant function (OTSDF) filters for arbitrary devices. Opt. Lett. **19**, 1556–1558 (1994)
15. Zhang, D., Guo, Z.H., Lu, G.M., Zhang, L., Zuo, W.M.: An online system of multispectral palmprint verification. IEEE Trans. Instrum. Measure. **59**, 480–490 (2010)

Cross-dataset Image Matching Network for Heterogeneous Palmprint Recognition

Yuchen Zou[1], Dexing Zhong[1,2,3(✉)], and Huikai Shao[1]

[1] School of Automation Science and Engineering, Xi'an Jiaotong University, Xi'an, Shaanxi 710049, China
[2] Pazhou Lab, Guangzhou 510335, China
[3] State Key Laboratory for Novel Software Technology, Nanjing University, Nanjing 210093, China
bell@xjtu.edu.cn

Abstract. Palmprint recognition is one of the promising biometric technologies. Many palmprint recognition methods have excellent performance in recognition within a single dataset. However, heterogeneous palmprint recognition, i.e., mutual recognition between different datasets, has rarely been studied, which is also an important issue. In this paper, a cross-dataset image matching network (CDMNet) is proposed for heterogeneous palmprint recognition. Feature representations specific to a certain domain are learned in the shallow layer of the network, and feature styles are continuously aligned to narrow the gap between domains. Invariant feature representations in different domains are learned in the deeper layers of network. Further, a graph-based global reasoning module is used as a connection between the shallow and deeper networks to capture information between distant regions in palmprint images. Finally, we conduct sufficient experiments on constrained and unconstrained palmprint databases, which demonstrates the effectiveness of our method.

Keywords: Palmprint recognition · Heterogeneous recognition · Style transfer · Global reasoning networks

1 Introduction

Modern society has a close connection with individual authentication, which is needed in payment, travel, security, criminal investigation, and other fields. In recent years, biometric technologies such as such as face recognition [1] and fingerprint recognition [2] have gradually applied to identity verification. During the outbreak of the novel coronavirus 2019 (COVID-19), the previously more widely used face recognition technology is limited for scenarios where the face is obscured by a mask. Contactless palmprint recognition technology, on the other hand, is not subject to this constraint and has a wide range of potential uses in many identity authentication situations [3].

W. Deng et al. (Eds.): CCBR 2022, LNCS 13628, pp. 52–60, 2022.
https://doi.org/10.1007/978-3-031-20233-9_6

In the past decades, a variety of effective palmprint feature extraction methods have been proposed, which are mainly classified as structure-based, statistical, subspace, coding, and deep learning-based methods [4]. However, most of the current palmprint recognition algorithms are mainly suitable for recognizing samples from the same dataset. When the palmprint images come from different datasets, e.g., from different devices and different lighting conditions, it may not match the correct identity in the palmprint gallery. This limits practical applications of palmprint recognition strictly. Therefore, we propose a cross-dataset matching network to accomplish heterogeneous palmprint recognition between different palmprint datasets.

The contributions can be briefly summarized as follows:

(1) A novel and feasible cross-dataset palmprint matching network is proposed to solve the heterogeneous palmprint recognition problem.
(2) Style alignment and graph-based global reasoning are applied to reduce the inter-domain gap of datasets and strengthen the connection between key identity features in global palmprint images.
(3) Extensive experiments on constrained and unconstrained benchmark palmprint databases show that the proposed method achieves satisfactory performance on heterogeneous palmprint recognition.

2   Related Work

Palmprints contain rich features and many explorations have been conducted in palmprint feature extraction methods. Xu et al. [5] proposed a competitive code based palmprint authentication method using more accurate dominant direction representation. Jia et al. [6] proposed a new palmprint frequency domain recognition algorithm that jointly explored directional information at multiple scales, multi-directional levels, and other aspects. Fei et al. [7] proposed a double-layer direction extraction method for palmprint recognition, which extracted directional features from the palmprint surface layer and energy map layer.

In recent years, feature extraction methods based on deep learning have shown powerful capabilities. Genovese et al. [8] proposed PalmNet based on convolutional neural network (CNN) to extract discriminative palmprint features using Gabor filter and PCA. Zhong et al. [9] used deep hash network (DHN) and biometric graph matching (BGM) to multimodal fusion of palmprint and dorsal hand vein features for end-to-end palmprint verification. Liu et al. [10] extracted the features of palmprint images at the structural and pixel level, and achieved few-shot palmprint recognition.

The above approaches mainly revolve around palmprint recognition on a single dataset, but the actual recognition conditions are often not consistent with those at prior acquisition, thus requiring matching across different datasets. Earlier, Jia et al. [11] tested various traditional feature extraction approaches for cross-device palmprint recognition. Shao et al. [12] proposed the joint pixel and feature alignment framework (JPFA), which can match unlabeled target images with source or pseudo images across datasets. In this paper, we propose CDMNet for heterogeneous palmprint recognition, which can obtain excellent performance.

3 Method

As shown in Fig. 1, we propose a two-branch network structure for a cross-dataset palmprint recognition scenario, where the inputs are palmprint images from two different domains. After a shallow feature extractor with non-shared parameters similar to pseudo-Siamese network, the feature representation specific to a domain is obtained. And the styles of features are continuously extracted in multiple layers to complete the alignment of image styles in the shallow network. The network intermediate insertion graph network module captures global information and models global relationships. The deep network is a parameter sharing feature extractor that extracts common features of two domains and finally generates feature codes with cross-dataset discriminability.

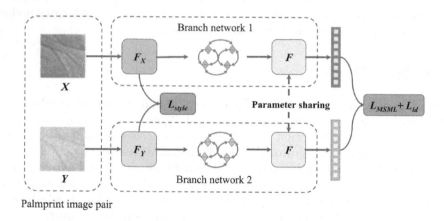

Palmprint image pair

Fig. 1. The architecture of our CDMNet method.

3.1 Style Alignment

We hope that the palmprint features extracted by the shallow network can separate itself from the style of its own original domain as much as possible, which would be more conducive for the deep network to be able to extract palmprint features that are independent of the image style. However, this is in contradiction with the strategy of non-sharing of parameters in the shallow network.

Inspired by image style transfer [13], we use Gram matrix to analyze the feature maps extracted by the shallow network and introduce style alignment. The number of selected layers from shallow network is l. The feature map is

$F^l \in \mathbb{R}^{H_l \times W_l \times C_l}$, which is reshaped as $F^l \in \mathbb{R}^{N_l \times C_l}$, where $N_l = H_l \times W_l$. The Gram matrix is $G^l \in \mathbb{R}^{C_l \times C_l}$, G^l represents the inner product of feature map i and j in layer l, which can represent the modal style of the original image to some extent:

$$G^l = \sum_k F_{ik}^l F_{jk}^l \, , \qquad (1)$$

where F_{ik}^l and F_{jk}^l are the activation of the ith and j^{th} filter at position k in layer l.

The distance between the mean squared error matrices of the two domains in the shallow network extracted from the feature maps is calculated as the difference in style, and this difference is introduced into the loss function to continuously draw closer the style of the feature maps in the shallow network. For different palmprint datasets in X and Y domains, the Gram matrices of the lth layer feature maps are G_X^l and G_Y^l, and the inter-domain style difference loss is:

$$\mathcal{L}_{style} = \sum_l \frac{1}{4C_l^2 N_l^2} \sum_{i,j} \left(G_X^l - G_Y^l\right)^2 \, . \qquad (2)$$

3.2 Global Reasoning

To enhance the global representation of feature maps and strengthen the connection between feature maps containing key palmprint information, a graph-based global reasoning module in [14] is used as the connection between the shallow and deep networks. Graph network relationships are established between the palmprint feature maps extracted from the shallow network.

The palmprint feature maps in X and Y domains are extracted by the shallow network as $F_X, F_Y \in \mathbb{R}^{H \times W \times C}$, and it will be reshaped into $F_X, F_Y \in \mathbb{R}^{L \times C}$. Divide the node set into $V = \{N_X, N_Y\}$, assigning N nodes to each node set:

$$V = B \cdot \phi(F) \, , \qquad (3)$$

where $V \in \mathbb{R}^{N \times C'}$ is N nodes of length C', $B \in \mathbb{R}^{N \times L}$ is projection matrix, $\phi(F) \in \mathbb{R}^{L \times C'}$ is the feature map after dimensionality reduction and reshaping.

After projecting the features from the coordinate space to the interaction space, a graph with different feature nodes is obtained. Edge E is defined between nodes V in graph G. The weights and state update functions of the interaction edges between the nodes are learned using graph convolution and the node feature matrix is obtained as follows:

$$Z = GVW_g = ((I - A_g)V)W_g \, , \qquad (4)$$

where $G, A_g \in \mathbb{R}^{N \times N}$ is the adjacency matrix between nodes for diffusion information across nodes, W_g is the state update function. The projection of the node feature matrix after global reasoning is returned to the original space, and the residual connection is formed with the original feature F to complete the aggregation of contextual palmprint information.

By constructing graph network, the modeling of remote relationships of palm-print images becomes the inference of the relationships between nodes in the graph. In training, the learning process of the adjacency matrix reflects the continuous adjustment of the relationship weights between the underlying features of each node. If the nodes in it include these important texture features such as main lines, wrinkles, valleys, and ridges in the palmprint, continuously learning and reinforcing the weights of these inter-node connections will enhance the interaction of this information in generating the final feature vector.

Combining cross entropy identity loss L_{id} and margin sample mining loss L_{MSML}, the overall objective function is:

$$L_{total} = L_{id} + \alpha L_{MSML} + \beta L_{style} . \tag{5}$$

4   Experiments

4.1   Dataset

XJTU-UP palmprint database is collected under unconstrained conditions. Five common brands of smartphones are used as acquisition devices, namely Samsung Galaxy Note 5 (denoted as S), LG G4 (denoted as L), Xiaomi 8 (denoted as M), Huawei Mate 8 (denoted as H), and iPhone 6S (denoted as I). Indoor natural light (denoted as F) and cell phone flash (denoted as N) are used for lighting. Ten sub-datasets are divided into SN, SF, LN, LF, MN, MF, HN, HF, IN, IF, and each sub-dataset contains 2000 palmprint images of 200 categories. A typical sample is shown in Fig. 2.

PolyU palmprint dat*abase is acquired under four spectra. According to the different light spectra, it is divided into four sub-datasets: Blue, Green, Red and NIR, and each sub-dataset contains 6000 palmprint images in 500 categories. A typical sample is shown in Fig. 3.

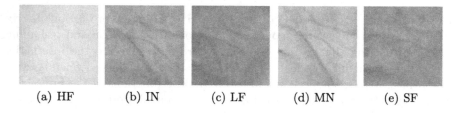

(a) HF   (b) IN   (c) LF   (d) MN   (e) SF

Fig. 2. Samples of five sub-datasets in XJTU-UP database.

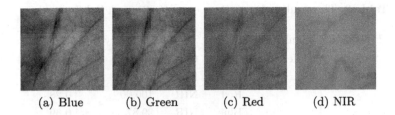

(a) Blue   (b) Green   (c) Red   (d) NIR

Fig. 3. The ROI samples of PolyU database under different illumination.

4.2   Implementation Details

In experiments, different datasets are selected as source datasets and target datasets. The ratio of training set and test set is 1:1 and there is no overlap in categories. Palmprint images with similar features in target dataset are queried in source dataset. The initial learning rate is 0.008 for training with epoch 40, batch size 16, and Adam optimizer. The hyperparameter α and β in Eq 5 are set to 2 and 10, respectively. The experiments are implemented using Pytorch on a NVIDIA GPU GTX3070 and CPU i7-2.7 GHz processors.

4.3   Experiment Results

In XJTU-UP database, the experiments are divided into three classes according to the different acquisition equipment and illumination conditions, and a total of nine sets of experiments are conducted. The recognition accuracy is shown in Table 1. When IF is source dataset and IN is target dataset, the accuracy reaches 98.70% and the EER reaches 1.09%.

In PolyU multispectral palmprint database, two groups are taken from each of the four datasets according to the different shooting spectra, which are divided into four groups of experiments as source and target datasets, and the experimental results are shown in Table 2. Among the four sets of experiments, three sets have recognition accuracy as high as 100.00% and the lowest recognition rate is 99.87%. The EER is kept below 0.7% (Table 2).

Table 1. The results of cross-dataset recognition on XJTU-UP database

Equipment	Illumination	Source	Target	Accuracy (%)	EER (%)
Same	Different	SF	SN	97.80	2.75
		LF	LN	97.70	2.58
		IF	IN	98.70	1.09
Different	Same	SF	HF	97.20	3.29
		LN	IN	94.50	4.01
		MF	HF	97.60	2.73
Different	Different	HF	MN	94.60	3.94
		LF	HN	93.00	3.54
		SF	IN	94.50	4.69

Table 2. The results of cross-dataset recognition on PolyU database

Equipment	Illumination	Source	Target	Accuracy (%)	EER (%)
Same	Different	Red	Green	100.00	0.24
		Green	Blue	100.00	0.14
		Red	NIR	100.00	0.28
		Blue	NIR	99.87	0.69

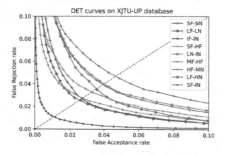 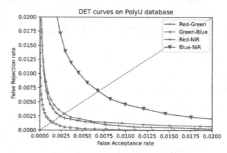

Fig. 4. The DET curves of palmprint recognition. The former of the label is target dataset and the latter is source dataset, e.g. SF-SN, SF represents target dataset and SN represents source dataset.

4.4   Compare with Other Palmprint Recognition Methods

To evaluate the effectiveness of CDMNet for palmprint recognition across datasets, we compared CDMNet with Retnet50 [15], the backbone network of this framework, and other advanced palmprint recognition methods, such as Apparent and Latent Direction Code (ALDC) [7] and Learning Discriminant Direction Binary Palmprint Descriptor (DDBPD) [16]. Tested by the more difficult cross-dataset identification between SF and IN, and Table 3 lists the identification results of our method with the above three methods. It can be seen that our proposed method are capable of achieving higher accuracy and lower EER.

Table 3. The results of cross-dataset recognition on PolyU database

Source	Target	Model	Accuracy (%)	EER (%)
SF	IN	CDMNet	**94.50**	**4.69**
		Resnet50	85.60	10.28
		ALDC	89.00	9.93
		DDBPD	93.40	12.48

5   Conclusion

In this paper, a cross-dataset palmprint matching network is proposed to address the heterogeneous palmprint recognition issue. By adjusting the mechanism of parameter sharing, invariant feature representation among different palmprint datasets is learned. Meanwhile, style alignment is introduced to align the feature styles of different domains in the shallow network. Further, global reasoning is performed in the middle of network to capture and reinforce important feature relationships between distant regions in palmprint images. Adequate experiments in two palmprint databases, XJTU-UP and PolyU, yielded competitive results for accurate heterogeneous palmprint recognition.

Acknowledgments. This work was supported in part by the National Natural Science Foundation of China under Grant 61105021, in part by Natural Science Foundation of Zhejiang Province under Grant LGF19F030002, in part by Natural Science Foundation of Shaanxi Province under Grant 2020JM-073, in part by Young Talent Fund of Association for Science and Technology in Shaanxi, China, under Grant XXJS202231.

References

1. Xu, Y., Zou, H., Huang, Y., Jin, L., Ling, H.: Super-resolving blurry face images with identity preservation. Pattern Recognit. Lett. **146**, 158–164 (2021)
2. Agarwal, S., Rattani, A., Chowdary, C.R.: A comparative study on handcrafted features v/s deep features for open-set fingerprint liveness detection. Pattern Recognit. Lett. **147**, 34–40 (2021)
3. Shao, H., Zhong, D.: Towards open-set touchless palmprint recognition via weight-based meta metric learning. Pattern Recognit. **121**, 108247 (2022)
4. Zhong, D., Du, X., Zhong, K.: Decade progress of palmprint recognition: a brief survey. Neurocomputing **328**, 16–28 (2019)
5. Xu, Y., Fei, L., Wen, J., Zhang, D.: Discriminative and robust competitive code for palmprint recognition. IEEE Trans. Syst. Man Cybern. Syst. **48**(2), 232–241 (2018)
6. Jia, W., Zhang, B., Lu, J., Zhu, Y., Zhao, Y., Zuo, W., Ling, H.: Palmprint recognition based on complete direction representation. IEEE Trans. Image Process. **26**(9), 4483–4498 (2017)
7. Fei, L., Zhang, B., Zhang, W., Teng, S.: Local apparent and latent direction extraction for palmprint recognition. Inf. Sci. **473**, 59–72 (2019)
8. Genovese, A., Piuri, V., Plataniotis, K.N., Scotti, F.: Palmnet: gabor-pca convolutional networks for touchless palmprint recognition. IEEE Trans. Inf. Forensics Secur. **14**(12), 3160–3174 (2019)
9. Zhong, D., Shao, H., Du, X.: A hand-based multi-biometrics via deep hashing network and biometric graph matching. IEEE Trans. Inf. Forensics Secur. **14**(12), 3140–3150 (2019)
10. Liu, C., Zhong, D., Shao, H.: Few-shot palmprint recognition based on similarity metric hashing network. Neurocomputing **456**, 540–549 (2021)
11. Jia, W., Hu, R., Gui, J., Zhao, Y., Ren, X.: Palmprint recognition across different devices. Sensors **12**(6), 7938–7964 (2012)

12. Shao, H., Zhong, D.: Towards cross-dataset palmprint recognition via joint pixel and feature alignment. IEEE Trans. Image Process. **30**, 3764–3777 (2021)
13. Gatys, L.A., Ecker, A.S., Bethge, M.: Image style transfer using convolutional neural networks. In: 2016 IEEE Conference on Computer Vision and Pattern Recognition, CVPR 2016, Las Vegas, NV, USA, pp. 2414–2423 (2016)
14. Chen, Y., Rohrbach, M., Yan, Z., Yan, S., Feng, J., Kalantidis, Y.: Graph-based global reasoning networks. In: 2019 IEEE Conference on Computer Vision and Pattern Recognition, CVPR 2019, Long Beach, CA, USA, pp. 433–442 (2019)
15. He, K., Zhang, X., Ren, S., Sun, J.: Deep residual learning for image recognition. In: 2016 IEEE Conference on Computer Vision and Pattern Recognition, CVPR 2016, Las Vegas, NV, USA, pp. 770–778 (2016)
16. Fei, L., Zhang, B., Xu, Y., Guo, Z., Wen, J., Jia, W.: Learning discriminant direction binary palmprint descriptor. IEEE Trans. Image Process. **28**(8), 3808–3820 (2019)

Dual Mode Near-Infrared Scanner for Imaging Dorsal Hand Veins

Zhibo Zhang[1], Lin Cui[1], Qingyi Liu[1], Guozhong Liu[2], Ran Zhang[1], Meng Tian[1], Yingxia Fu[3], and Peirui Bai[1(✉)]

[1] College of Electronic Information Engineering, Shandong University of Science and Technology, Qingdao 266590, China
bprbjd@163.com
[2] College of Physical Education, Shandong University of Science and Technology, Qingdao 266590, China
[3] College of Energy and Mining Engineering, Shandong University of Science and Technology, Qingdao 266590, China

Abstract. In this work, a novel near-infrared (NIR) scanner called MultiVein is designed. The self-produced device can efficiently collect near-infrared dorsal hand vein (DHV) images in real time. It has two attractive characteristics. First, MultiVein can work in two imaging modes that can switch freely, i.e. the transmission mode and the reflection mode. Second, MultiVein can adjust flexibly illumination intensity of the infrared backlight LED array. Balanced illumination and high adaptability of ambient conditions can be achieved by this operation. The quality of the images acquired by MultiVein was evaluated qualitatively and quantitatively, as well as comparisons with competitive instruments were conducted. The experimental results demonstrated that MultiVein can acquire reflection or transmission NIR dorsal hand vein images with high quality and effective acquisition. It was believed that MultiVein has promising application in DHV biometrics and health care.

Keywords: Dorsal hand vein biometrics · Near-infrared imaging · Dual imaging mode · Reflection mode · Transmission mode

1 Introduction

Personal identification based on the analysis of NIR dorsal hand vein (DHV) images is an emerging biometrics technology [1]. The DHV biometrics has several attractive and distinguishing characteristics, e.g. high recognition performance, liveness detection, high capability of anti-counterfeit, high acceptability, etc. [2, 3]. However, image skeletons extracted from vein images are often unstable because the raw vein images suffer from low contrast [4]. Therefore, collecting high quality DHV images is crucial to enhance the performance of the DHV biometric system [5].

Infrared imaging technology is the most common means to acquire DHV images. The effective infrared window for penetrating the hand skin and passing through the tissues is $0.7\ \mu m$ to $1,000\ \mu m$ [6]. The infrared DHV imaging technology can be divided roughly

W. Deng et al. (Eds.): CCBR 2022, LNCS 13628, pp. 61–71, 2022.
https://doi.org/10.1007/978-3-031-20233-9_7

into NIR-based imaging and FIR-based imaging in terms of the working wavelength. The NIR-based imaging technology usually exploited infrared radiation with wavelength of 0.7–0.9 μm, which can penetrate into human tissue 5–10 mm. In contrast, the common working wavelength of the FIR-based imaging technology is 1.5–400 μm, which can penetrate the tissues less than 2 mm [7]. The advantage of the FIR-based imaging is that it does not need external lighting. However, the capture camera of the FIR images is usually high cost and is sensitive to ambient conditions as well as human body temperature [8]. So, the NIR-based imaging becomes the most popular means in DHV biometrics [9–11].

The NIR imaging of dorsal hand veins can be divided into two modes i.e. the reflection mode and the transmission mode [12]. As shown in Fig. 1(a), the CCD camera and the NIR LED array was placed in the same side of hand back in the reflection mode. The infrared light reflected from hand back was captured. As shown in Fig. 1(b), in the transmission mode, the LED array was placed under the hand palm, whereas the CCD camera was placed above the hand back. The transmission infrared light was captured by the CCD camera. In general, the transmission mode was more robust against skin conditions and ambient illumination [13]. However, it required higher light intensity and consumed more power. In contrast, the reflection mode can employ smaller sensors, but it is more sensitive to illumination intensity and ambient imaging environment.

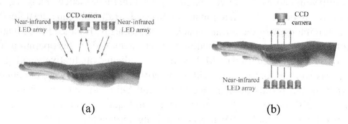

(a)   (b)

Fig. 1. Two imaging modes of MultiVein: (a) the reflection mode, (b) the transmission mode

In this work, we designed a novel dual mode near-infrared scanner called MultiVein, which can run in the transmission mode or the reflection mode freely. The MultiVein has three distinguishing characteristics. 1) It can acquire reflected and transmitted DHV images in real time. The average acquisition speed was 24 fps. 2) The luminescent intensity of each LED lamp in the array was controllable. Then, the NIR illumination intensity was adjustable to be adapted to the surrounding imaging environments. It was a crucial factor to acquire high quality NIR images. 3) A specific and low-cost MOSFET unit was designed to drive each element in the LED array. It was helpful to provide suitable illumination for different scenarios e.g. palm thicknesses and hand postures.

2   The Related Work

The first apparatus for DHV biometrics was invented by Joseph Rice in 1987 [14]. Subsequently, various kinds of infrared imaging device have been emerged. The infrared DHV imaging devices can be classified roughly into two categories i.e. commercial products and custom-produced devices in terms of the application purposes. The VP-II

X Hand Vascular Scanner produced by Techsphere Co. Ltd was a successful product for DHV recognition [15].

For the research purposes in laboratory, the custom produced devices were needed. In 2006, Wang et al. developed a NEC thermal tracer to acquire thermal images of the dorsal hand veins [7]. They also investigated the imaging quality of FIR-based and NIR-based DHV imaging techniques. In 2007, Zhao et al. developed a NIR-based DHV imaging device that can run in the reflection mode [16]. It adopted a transmission light source to improve the intensity contrast of the DHV images. In 2015, Gruschina et al. designed a NIR-based DHV imaging device named VeinPLUS that can run in the transmission mode [17]. It adopted fifty 940 nm LED lamps as the transmission light source, but the illumination intensity cannot be adjusted. In 2018, Kauba et al. developed a NIR-based DHV imaging device that can run in the transmission mode and the reflection mode [13]. They investigated the influence factors e.g. ambient light, hand surface conditions, etc., and compared the image qualities of the two modes. However, the infrared images of thick palms were blurred due to the unbalanced illumination.

3   Design Scheme of MultiVein

3.1   Architecture and Actual Hardware Design of MultiVein

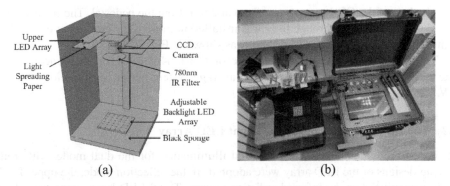

Fig. 2. (a) Schematic diagram of the set-up of MultiVein. (b) The actual hardware of MultiVein.

The schematic diagram of the set-up of MultiVein was illustrated in Fig. 2(a). There were two LED arrays i.e. the upper LED array and the adjustable backlight LED array mounted on the top side and the pedestal respectively. The upper LED array was utilized as the infrared radiation source in the reflection mode. It was divided into two groups located on both sides of the CCD camera. Each group contained 4 NIR LED lamps (HIR333C-A) that emit 850 nm infrared light. The two parallel connected sets of lamps were driven by a 100 mA constant current source. They provided constant infrared illumination in the reflection mode. The reflected infrared light was captured by a CCD camera mounted on the top side. Two light spreading papers were placed under the upper LED arrays respectively. It was helpful to reduce the specularly reflected infrared light.

A black sponge was mounted on the pedestal. It was helpful to keep the background black.

The infrared radiation source of the transmission mode was the adjustable backlight LED array mounted on the pedestal. It contained 25 NIR LED lamps (HIR333C-A) which were arranged as 5 rows and 5 columns. The emitted infrared light with wavelength of 850 nm penetrated palms in the transmission mode. It was noted that each lamp in the backlight LED array was driven by an independent N-channel MOSFET unit. When MultiVein running in the transmission mode, the microcontroller (STC8G2K64S4) produced 25 separated PWM signals to drive the gate ports of the corresponding MOSFET channels. Each MOSFET unit switched on and off quickly with a different duty cycle to control the illumination intensity of each lamp. Figure 3 shown the driving circuit of the 25 lamps in the adjustable backlight LED array.

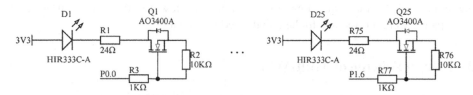

Fig. 3. The driving circuit of 25 channels in the backlight LED array.

The lens of the CCD camera was fixed at 25cm from the pedestal. The focal length was 6 mm. An IR pass-through filter was installed in front of the lens to cut out visible light. The actual hardware of MultiVein was shown in Fig. 2(b).

The specification of MultiVein: image resolution is 640 * 480 pixel, image acquisition rate is 24 fps, the interface is USB UVC, average system power consumption is about 3W.

3.2 The Driving Design of the Backlight LED Array

In order to provide suitable Near-Infrared illumination for the dual modes, different driving designs of the LED array were adopted. In the reflection mode, the upper LED array was utilized as the infrared radiation source. The 8 LED lamps were turned on or turned off simultaneously. The backlight LED array mounted on the pedestal did not work in the reflection mode. The appropriate half intensity range can be estimated roughly according to the following principle.

Let θ denote the beam angle of the lamp, h denotes the detection distance between the hand back and the LED lamp (h $\approx$ 20 mm), d represent the pitch between the LED lamps (d = 11 mm), then the beam angle θ obeyed with the following relationship:

$$\tan\left(\frac{180° - \theta}{2}\right) = \frac{h}{0.5d} \tag{1}$$

The default value of θ was 30°.

In the transmission mode, the on-off state and drive voltage level of each lamp in the backlight LED array can be adjusted to obtain optimum exposure. Whether the

LED lamp was activated or not depending on a switch circuit. As shown in Fig. 4, four activating examples i.e. arrow shape, diamond shape, box shape, times sign shape were illustrated. It demonstrated that the selective on-off state of each LED lamp can be controlled expediently and flexibly.

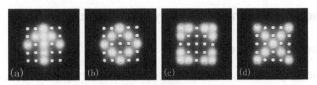

Fig. 4. Four selective activation examples of the LED lamps array. (a) arrow shape activation, (b) diamond shape activation, (c) box shape activation, (d) times sign shape activation.

The driving voltage level of each lamp in the backlight LED array can also be controlled. In practice, the voltage values were determined by pulse width modulation (PWM) technology. Let I denote luminous intensity of a LED lamp, it can be calculated by the following equation:

$$I = \frac{D \times E_e}{25}. \tag{2}$$

where D represented duty cycle of the PWM. It ranged from 0 to 25. Ee is luminous intensity of a LED lamp when the current is set to 20 mA. For the HIR333C-A LED lamp, Ee = 15 mW/sr. An empirical driving voltage setting scheme was shown in Fig. 5. The square represented the space location of the lamp, and the digit value in each square represented luminous intensity of the corresponding lamp. Figure 5(a) demonstrated the values of luminous intensity for left hand, while Fig. 5(b) shown the values of luminous intensity for right hand. It meant that higher driving voltage level was adopted when detecting the center of palm, whereas lower drive voltage level was selected for imaging the thinner parts of the hand. Therefore, luminous intensity of the LED lamp can be adjusted in terms of practical conditions.

2.4	4.2	5.4	5.4	4.2
2.4	8.4	13.2	9.6	6
2.4	9.6	15	12	12
2.4	15	15	15	15
15	15	15	15	15

(a)

4.2	5.4	5.4	4.2	2.4
6	9.6	13.2	8.4	2.4
12	12	15	9.6	2.4
15	15	15	15	2.4
15	15	15	15	15

(b)

Fig. 5. An empirical driving voltage setting scheme. The unit is mW/sr. The luminous intensity of each LED lamp for imaging (a) the left hand, (b) the right hand respectively.

Parameter adjustment method: Through previewing the DHV image, the exposure of each area on the hand in the image was observed. The driving level of the corresponding LED was adjusted downwards in the overexposed area and upwards in the unexposed area.

4   Experiments and Image Quality Assessment

4.1   Image Acquisition Experiments

Image acquisition experiments were carried out to validate the performance of MultiVein. We recruited 45 volunteers to collect the NIR dorsal hand vein images. In each imaging mode, 5 NIR images of left hand and right hand for each subject were collected. Thus, a total of 900 images were collected to build MultiVein dataset. Figure 6 demonstrated four example NIR images in MultiVein dataset. The original image size was 640 × 480. Figure 6(a) and Fig. 6(b) shown the reflection and transmission NIR images of right hand respectively. Figure 6(c) and Fig. 6(d) shown the corresponding images of left hand respectively. It could be observed that the transmission images displayed the vein patterns clearer in visual.

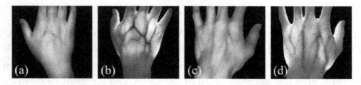

Fig. 6. The example NIR images acquired from a subject using MultiVein. (a) the reflection image of right hand, (b) the transmission image of right hand, (c) the reflection image of left hand, (d) the transmission image of left hand.

It was also noted that more texture characteristics could be observed from the transmission images. It was benefited from the flexibility of illumination adjustment, and the ability to transmit light to reveal deeper veins.

4.2   Qualitative Evaluation of Image Quality

The quality of images acquired by MultiVein was evaluated qualitatively by making comparison with the transmission images selected from an open dataset named Vein-PLUS [17]. As shown in Fig. 7(a), the transmission image in PROTECTVein displayed the hand vein network with acceptable contrast, but the black shadow in the lower part raised difficulties for the subsequent image processing. As shown in Fig. 7(b), the transmission image acquired by MultiVein disclosed the vein network more clear, and has better texture contrast in visual. It was due to the efficiency of flexible illumination adjustment of the backlight LED array. The illumination intensity was high to avoid underexposure in the thick palm area, whereas it was low when detecting the thin area.

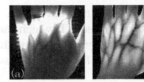

Fig. 7. The comparison of the transmission NIR image selected from VeinPLUS dataset and MultiVein dataset. (a) a transmission NIR image in VeinPLUS dataset. (b) a transmission NIR image acquired by MultiVein.

4.3   Quantitative Evaluation of Image Quality

In order to make quantitative evaluation of the NIR image quality, we conducted a statistic analysis in terms of four indices i.e. Q_m, Q_d [18], Q_{t1} and Q_{t2} [19]. Here, Q_m and represented the intensity uniformity of a ROI region, Q_d represented the clarity degree of a ROI region. Q_{t1} and Q_{t2} represented the mean gray score and gray variance score of a ROI region respectively.

Prior to make the quantitative evaluation, we extracted the ROI region denoted as F using the method presented in our previous work [20]. The size of the ROI region was expressed as H × W (H and W was set to 200). Then, the ROI region was divided into N × N square blocks denoted as F_n. n represented the index number of each block. The index Q_m can be obtained as follows:

$$Q_m = Min\left(\frac{Max(M(n)) - Min(M(n))}{Mean(M(n))}, 1\right). \tag{3}$$

where, M is the average gray value of the blocks. The smaller Q_m meant the more uniform intensity of the ROI region.

The computational process of Q_d was as follows. First, a blurred image K was obtained by filtering the ROI region F using Gaussian loss-filter G. The maximum difference values between each center pixel and its 8 neighborhoods of F and K were calculated respectively as follows:

$$\begin{cases} T(i,j) = Max(abs(F(i,j) - F(i+k,j+l))) \\ T'(i,j) = Max(abs(K(i,j) - K(i+k,j+l))) \end{cases}. \tag{4}$$

Then, the maximum difference value was taking as the value of the center pixel. The index Q_d can be calculated as follows:

$$Q_d = \frac{abs\left(\sum_{i=0}^{H-1}\sum_{j=0}^{W-1} T(i,j) - \sum_{i=0}^{H-1}\sum_{j=0}^{W-1} T'(i,j)\right)}{\sum_{i=0}^{H-1}\sum_{j=0}^{W-1} T(i,j)}. \tag{5}$$

The higher Q_d meant the more clarity of the ROI region.

Let M_0 denote the optimal mean gray value of F, which was computed as the average value in terms of the sum of the maximum gray value and the minimum gray value of all images in the database. M_0 was different for various dataset. The score of the mean gray can be defined as follows:

$$Q_{t1} = \left[1 - \left|\frac{M - M_0}{M_0}\right|\right] \times 100\%. \tag{6}$$

The higher Q_{t1} meant the more uniform gray score of the ROI region.

The calculation of Q_{t2} was essentially the normalization of variance of ROI region. The score of the gray variance can be obtained as follows:

$$Q_{t2} = \frac{Var - Var_{min}}{Var_{max} - Var_{min}} \times 100\%. \tag{7}$$

where Var represented the variance of ROI region, Var_{min} and Var_{max} were the minimum and maximum value of the gray variance.

Two kinds of quantitative comparisons were carried out. First, we made a comparison among different single images in terms of Q_m and Q_d. Figure 8 illustrated the ROI regions that were extracted from four representative datasets. Figure 8(a) shown ROI-1 which was extracted from the DF reflection image Dataset [21], while Fig. 8(b) presented ROI-2 which was extracted from MultiVein reflection image dataset. As shown in Fig. 8(c) and Fig. 8(d), the two transmission ROI regions denoted as ROI-3 and ROI-4, were extracted from VeinPLUS dataset [14] and MultiVein transmission image dataset respectively. The values of Q_m and Q_d of these ROI regions were listed in Table 1.

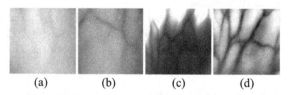

(a)   (b)   (c)   (d)

Fig. 8. The ROI regions extracted from four representative datasets. (a) ROI-1 extracted from DF reflection image Dataset, (b) ROI-2 extracted from MultiVein reflection image dataset, (c) ROI-3 extracted from VeinPLUS dataset, (d) ROI-4 extracted from MultiVein transmission image dataset.

Table 1. The Q_m and Q_d of the ROI regions in Fig. 8

Index	Reflection ROI images		Transmission ROI images	
	ROI-1	ROI-2	ROI-3	ROI-4
Q_m	0.2278	0.3814	1.0000	0.7323
Q_d	0.3096	0.4763	0.2058	0.6201

For the reflection ROI regions, the Q_m of ROI-1 was 0.2278 that is less than that of ROI-2 (0.3814). It meant that ROI-1 has better brightness uniformity than ROI-2. However, the Q_d of ROI-2 performed better than ROI-1. It reflected that ROI-2 has better texture detail with slightly higher background blur. For the transmission ROI images, ROI-4 has better quality than ROI-3 in terms of both Q_m and Q_d. It was due to the suitable illumination provided by the flexible luminescent intensity adjustment of each LED lamp in the backlight LED array. It was noted that the brightness uniformity of the reflection images was better than that of the transmission images, whereas the texture detail and intensity contrast of the transmission images was better than that of the reflection images.

Second, we made quantitative comparisons with the NIR reflection dorsal hand vein images collected from different dataset. The compared dataset included DF dataset containing 365 reflection images provided by our team [20], DHV dataset containing 3677 reflection images provided by Jilin University [21], NCUT dataset containing 2040 reflection images provided by North China University of Technology [22], and MultiVein dataset containing 450 reflection images. The mean and standard deviation of the four indices were listed in Table 2. It can be seen that the reflection images acquired by MultiVein had superior quality in terms of Q_m, Q_{t1} and Q_{t2}. It meant that the brightness uniformity, intensity consistency and intensity contrast of the reflection images in MultiVein dataset performed better. The Q_d indicated clarity degree or contour sharpness of objects. The NIR reflection images in MultiVein dataset had slightly lower Q_d than that of NCUT dataset, but performed better than the NIR reflection images in DF and DHV dataset. Overall, the NIR reflection images acquired by MultiVein shown superior quality than the NIR reflection images in the other three datasets, that were acquired by different NIR imaging devices.

Table 2. The mean and standard deviation of the indices of four NIR dorsal hand vein reflection image dataset.

Dataset	Index (Mean/SD)			
	Q_m	Q_d	Q_{t1}	Q_{t2}
DF reflection image dataset [20]	0.62/0.17	0.32/0.05	66.99/7.81	58.74/15.09
DHV reflection image dataset [21]	0.67/0.13	0.45/0.08	78.65/8.56	50.91/39.00
NCUT reflection image dataset [22]	0.51/0.06	**0.62/0.02**	84.17/4.12	50.07/29.71
MultiVein reflection image dataset	**0.33/0.10**	0.57/0.03	**86.79/5.60**	**75.25/26.26**

5 Conclusions

In this work, we developed a novel dual mode near-infrared imaging device called MultiVein, which can acquire NIR dorsal hand vein images in reflection mode and transmission mode in real time. The self-produced scanner has capability of infrared illumination adjustment by controlling the on-off state and driving voltage level of the LED lamps flexibly. Qualitative and quantitative evaluations of image quality were carried out by comparing the NIR dorsal hand vein images with the images in three available datasets. The images acquired by MultiVein had superior quality on the whole. It was believed that MultiVein will be a promising tool for DHV biometrics and health care. In the following work, we will investigate deeply the intrinsic mechanism between infrared light and biological tissues, aiming to further enhance the image quality. In addition, the adaptability of MultiVein to deal with more changes in the ambient environment or hand postures will be investigated, that is beneficial to improve the accuracy of personal recognition and health analysis.

Acknowledgments. This work was supported partly by National Natural Science Foundation of China (No. 61471225).

References

1. Jia, W., et al.: A survey on dorsal hand vein biometrics. J. Pattern Recogn. **120**, 108122 (2021)
2. Kumar, A., Prathyusha, K.V.: Personal authentication using hand vein triangulation and knuckle shape. J. IEEE Trans. Image Process. **18**(9), 2127–2136 (2009)
3. Kauba, C., Prommegger, B., Uhl, A.: Combined fully contactless finger and hand vein capturing device with a corresponding dataset. J. Sensors **19**(22), 5014 (2019)
4. Castro-Ortega, R., et al.: Zernike moment invariants for hand vein pattern description from raw biometric data. J. Electron. Imaging **28**(5), 053019 (2019)
5. Shao, H., Zhong, D., Du, X.: A deep biometric hash learning framework for three advanced hand-based biometrics. J. IET Biometrics **10**(3), 246–259 (2021)
6. Gade, R., Moeslund, T.B.: Thermal cameras and applications: a survey. Mach. Vis. Appl. **25**(1), 245–262 (2013). https://doi.org/10.1007/s00138-013-0570-5
7. Wang, L., Leedham, G.: Near-and far-infrared imaging for vein pattern biometrics. In: 2006 IEEE International Conference on Video and Signal Based Surveillance, pp. 52–58. IEEE Press, Sydney (2006)
8. Wang, L., Leedham, G.: A thermal hand vein pattern verification system. In: International Conference on Pattern Recognition and Image Analysis, pp. 58–65. LNIP, Bath (2005)
9. Wang, L., Leedham, G., Cho, S.-Y.: Infrared imaging of hand vein patterns for biometric purposes. J. IET Comput. Vis. **1**(3–4), 113–122 (2007)
10. Zhang, D., Guo, Z., Gong, Y.: Multispectral biometrics systems. In: Multispectral Biometrics, pp. 23–35. Springer, Cham (2016). https://doi.org/10.1007/978-3-319-22485-5_2
11. Chen, K., Zhang, D.: Band selection for improvement of dorsal hand recognition. In: 2011 International Conference on Hand-Based Biometrics, pp. 1–4. IEEE Press, Hong Kong (2011)
12. Wang, J., et al.: Hand vein recognition based on improved template matching. J. Int. J. Bioautom. **18**(4), 337–348 (2014)
13. Kauba, C., Uhl, A.: Shedding light on the veins-reflected light or transillumination in hand-vein recognition. In: 2018 International Conference on Biometrics (ICB), pp. 283–290. IEEE Press, Gold Coast (2018)
14. Rice, J.: Apparatus for the Identification of Individuals. Google Patents, Washington (1987)
15. Techsphere Hand Vascular Scanner Hand Vascular Pattern Recognition. http://www.vascularscanner.com/

16. Zhao, S., Wang, Y., Wang, Y.: Extracting hand vein patterns from low-quality images: a new biometric technique using low-cost devices. In: Fourth International Conference on Image and Graphics (ICIG 2007), pp. 667–671. IEEE Press, Chengdu (2007)
17. Gruschina, A.: VeinPLUS: a transillumination and reflection-based hand vein database. arXiv preprint arXiv:1505.06769 (2015)
18. Wang, C., et al.: Quality assessment on near infrared palm vein image. In: 2017 32nd Youth Academic Annual Conference of Chinese Association of Automation (YAC), pp. 1127–1130. IEEE Press, Hefei (2017)
19. Sheng, M.-Y., et al.: Quantitative assessment of hand vein image quality with double spatial indicators. In: 2011 International Conference on Multimedia Technology, pp. 642–645. IEEE Press, Hangzhou (2011)
20. Guo, Z., et al.: A novel algorithm of dorsal hand vein image segmentation by integrating matched filter and local binary fitting level set model. In: 2020 7th International Conference on Information Science and Control Engineering (ICISCE), pp. 81–85. IEEE Press, Changsha (2020)
21. Liu, F., et al.: A recognition system for partially occluded dorsal hand vein using improved biometric graph matching. J. IEEE Access. **8**, 74525–74534 (2020)
22. Huang, D., et al.: Local feature approach to dorsal hand vein recognition by centroid-based circular key-point grid and fine-grained matching. Image Vis. Comput. **58**, 266–277 (2017)

Multi-stream Convolutional Neural Networks Fusion for Palmprint Recognition

Qing Zhou, Wei Jia[✉], and Ye Yu

School of Computer Science and Information Engineering, Hefei University of Technology,
Hefei 230009, China
2020171213@mail.hfut.edu.cn, {jiawei,yuye}@hfut.edu.cn

Abstract. In recent years, researchers have carried out palmprint recognition study based on deep learning, and proposed a variety of methods based on deep learning. In these methods, convolution neural networks (CNN) were directly applied to the original ROI image of palmprint for training and recognition. In fact, after processing, palmprint can have other representations, such as directional representation, and magnitude representation, etc. However, researchers have not investigated the problem that applied CNNs to other representations of palmprint for recognition. In this paper, we propose a novel framework of multi-stream CNNs fusion for palmprint recognition. In this framework, palmprint are firstly processed into other different representations. Next, CNNs are applied to different palmprint representations for recognition, and then, the information fusion is conducted to effectively improve the recognition accuracy. Under this framework, we propose a concrete implementation, i.e., three-stream CNNs fusion for palmprint recognition. We evaluate the proposed method on five palmprint database. Experimental results show that the recognition accuracy of the proposed method is obviously better than some classical traditional methods and deep learning methods.

Keywords: Palmprint recognition · Multi-stream convolutional neural networks · Fusion

1 Introduction

In the past twenty years, researchers have proposed many effective palmprint recognition methods, which can be divided into two categories i.e., traditional methods and deep learning methods [1–3]. Among the traditional methods, directional coding methods and local texture descriptor methods have achieved very high recognition accuracy, and they are the two most commonly used traditional methods. The representative direction coding methods mainly include Competitive Code [4], Ordinal Code [5], and Robust Line Orientation Code (RLOC) [6], etc. The typical local descriptor methods mainly include Histogram of Oriented Lines (HOL) [7] and Local Line Directional Pattern (LLDP) [8].

Researchers have proposed some deep learning methods, which explore convolution neural networks (CNNs) for palmprint recognition [9–13]. However, these methods

W. Deng et al. (Eds.): CCBR 2022, LNCS 13628, pp. 72–81, 2022.
https://doi.org/10.1007/978-3-031-20233-9_8

have the following problem: CNN only directly uses the original ROI image of palm-print for training and recognition. Here, we define the original ROI image as original representation (OR). In fact, after processing, palmprint images can have other representations, such as directional representation (DR), and magnitude representation (MR), etc. However, researchers have not investigated the problem that applied CNNs to other representations of palmprint for recognition.

In this paper, we propose a novel framework of multi-stream CNNs fusion (MSC-NNF) for palmprint recognition. In this framework, palmprint images are firstly processed into other different representations. Next, CNNs are applied to different palmprint representations for recognition, and then, the information fusion is conducted to effectively improve the recognition accuracy. Under this framework, we propose a concrete implementation, i.e., three-stream CNNs fusion (TSCNNF) for palmprint recognition. In TSCNNF, the DR and MR of palmprint are extracted by using the modified finite radon transform (MFRAT) [6–8]. We then use CNNs to perform recognition on three representations including OR, DR and MR, and make information fusion using different fusion strategy.

The main contributions of this paper are as follows.

(1) We propose a novel framework of MSCNNF for palmprint recognition. It is the first time that CNNs are used to recognize different representations of palmprint, and information fusion is adopted to improve the recognition accuracy.
(2) Under the framework of MSCNNF, we propose TSCNNF for palmprint recognition, which is one of concrete implementation of MSCNNF.

2 Related Work

Some representative deep learning methods are introduced as follows. Genovese et al. [9] proposed the method of PalmNet, a CNN that uses a method to tune palmprint specific filters through an unsupervised procedure based on Gabor responses and Principal Component Analysis (PCA). Zhong et al. [10] proposed an end-to-end method for open-set 2D palmprint recognition by applying CNN with a novel loss function. Matkowski et al. [11] proposed End-to-End Palmprint Recognition Network (EE-PRnet) consists of two main networks, i.e., ROI Localization and Alignment Network and Feature Extraction and Recognition Network. Zhao et al. [12] presented a joint constrained least-square regression (JCLSR) model with a deep local convolution feature for palmprint recognition. Liu et al. [13] proposed a generalizable deep learning-based framework for the contactless palmprint recognition, in which the network is based on a fully convolutional network that generates deeply learned residual features. Jia et al. [2, 3] evaluated the performance of 17 classical CNNs and 20 CNNs based on neural architecture search (NAS) for palmprint recognition.

3 Methodology

3.1 Multi-stream CNNs Fusion Framework

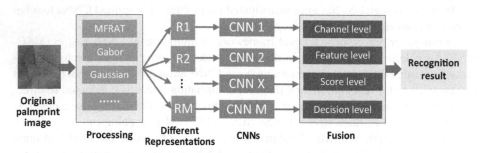

Fig. 1. The diagram of multi-stream CNNs fusion framework

In this subsection, we will introduce the proposed framework of MSCNNF, as shown in Fig. 1. The main ideas and steps of MSCNNF are as follows:

Step 1: For the original ROI image of palmprint, we use some filters or tools, such as Gabor filters and MFRAT, to extract other representations of palmprint. In Fig. 1, these representations are denoted as R1, R2, …, RM. M means that there are M representations of palmprint.
Step 2: On different representations, different CNNs models (or a same CNN model) are applied for training and recognition.
Step 3: Information fusion using different fusion strategy is conducted to improve the recognition accuracy, and then the final recognition result is obtained.

3.2 Three-Stream CNNs Fusion for Palmprint Recognition

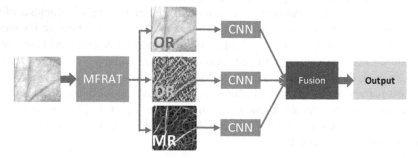

Fig. 2. The diagram of three-stream CNNs fusion

Under the framework of MSCNNF, we propose TSCNNF, which is a concrete implementation of MSCNNF. The main steps of MSCNNF are as follows:

- **Step 1:** Given a OR image, MFRAT is used to extract DR and MR, as shown in Fig. 2. The detail of MFRAT can be found in [6–8]. MFRAT accumulates the pixel values of line segments passing through the center point in 12 directions. Using winner-take-all rule, the MFRAT can extract DR and MR of palmprint. MFRAT has an important parameter, p, which is used to determine the size of MFRAT.
- **Step 2:** After step 1, palmprint has three representations including OR, DR and MR. In the work of [3], ProxylessNAS [14] is proved to be a CNN based on neural architecture search with good palmprint recognition ability. In this paper, we use ProxylessNAS as the backbone network to recognize different representations of palmprint.
- **Step 3:** Information fusion based on different fusion strategy is used to fuse the different recognition ability obtained different representations. In this paper, four fusion strategies are explored, which will be introduced as follows.

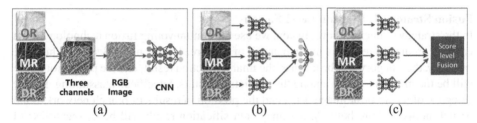

Fig. 3. Three fusion strategies used in TSCNNF. (a) The diagram of channel fusion, (b) The diagram of feature splicing, (c) The diagram of matching score level fusion.

Fusion Strategy 1: Channel Fusion
The channel fusion technology splices the OR, DR and MR into a three-channel RGB image, which is used as the input of the pre-training ProxylessNAS model. Usually, the input of the pre-training model is three-channel RGB images, while the palmprint OR is a single-channel grayscale image. Therefore, we use the OR, DR and MR as the three channels of RGB image to form one RGB image, which can meet the input requirements of pre-training model. At the same time, the new RGB image contains the information of OR, DR and MR, which improves the information of features and helps to improve the recognition accuracy. Figure 3(a) shows the diagram of channel fusion. Here, we named the channel fusion as $TSCNNF_C$.

Fusion Strategy 2: Feature Splicing
As shown in Fig. 3(b), for three branch recognition networks (OR, DR, and MR), the whole connection layer of the penultimate layer of each branch network is spliced, and finally the prediction results are obtained through a linear layer. In fact, the feature splicing in this paper belongs to feature layer fusion. Here, we named the fusion of feature splicing as $TSCNNF_F$.

Fusion Strategy 3: Matching Score Level Fusion

In the strategy of matching score level fusion, we use the Max and Sum rules to fuse the matching scores obtained from three branch recognition networks (OR, DR, and MR), as shown in Fig. 3(c). We take the probability value of each network prediction category as the matching score. Assume that the prediction scores of the ProlessxyNSA applied to the OR, DR and MR are S_o, S_d, and S_m, respectively. The scores using the Max and Sum rules are denoted as S_{max} and S_{sum}, which can be obtained by the following formulas.

$$S_{max} = Max(S_o, S_d, S_m) \tag{1}$$

$$S_{sum} = Sum(S_o, S_d, S_m) = \lambda(S_o, S_d, S_m) \tag{2}$$

where $\lambda = 1/3$. Here, we named the matching score fusion using Max rule and Sum rule as *TSCNNF$_S$-max* and *TSCNNF$_S$-sum*, respectively.

Fusion Strategy 4: Decision Level Fusion

In the strategy of decision level fusion, we use maximum voting fusion technology. That is, if the prediction results of more than half of the three branch networks are of the same category, the category will be taken as the final prediction result, and the prediction score will be the maximum score among the prediction results. Specifically, assuming that the category of a palmprint image is C_i, and the prediction results of branch network 1 and branch network 2 are both C_i, the image classification result will be C_i regardless of the prediction result of branch network 3. If the prediction results of three branches are different, the branch with the highest score among the prediction scores will be taken as the prediction result. We name the fusion method of maximum voting as *TSCNNF$_D$*, and the prediction score of each type of maximum voting fusion is:

$$TSCNNF_D = \begin{cases} Max(S_o, S_m), & ifP(S_o) = P(S_m) \\ Max(S_o, S_d), & ifP(S_o) = P(S_d) \\ Max(S_m, S_d), & ifP(S_m) = P(S_d) \\ Max(S_o, S_m, S_d), & otherwise \end{cases} \tag{3}$$

where $P(\bullet)$ represents the category of prediction.

4   Experiments

4.1   Palmprint Databases and Experimental Configuration

The proposed method is evaluated on five palmprint databases including the Hong Kong Polytechnic University palmprint database II (PolyU II) [15], the blue band of the Hong Kong Polytechnic University Multispectral (PolyU M_B) palmprint database [16], Hefei University of Technology (HFUT I) palmprint database [17], Hefei University of Technology Cross Sensor (HFUT CS) palmprint database [18], and Tongji University palmprint (TJU-P) database [19]. Table 1 lists the details of five databases.

In the experiments, all palmprint databases are divided into the training set and the test set. All palmprint images collected in the first session are taken in the training set,

Table 1. The details of palmprint database used for evaluation

Database name	Type	Individual number	Palm number	Session number	Session interval	Image number of each palm	Total image number
PolyU II	Palmprint	193	386	2	2 months	10×2	7752
PolyU M_B	Palmprint	250	500	2	9 days	6×2	6000
HFUT I	Palmprint	400	800	2	10 days	10×2	16000
HFUT CS	Palmprint	100	200	2	10 days	$10 \times 2 \times 3$	12000
TJU	Palmprint	300	600	2	61 days	10×2	12000

and all images collected in the second session are taken as the testing set. The batch size is set to 4, and the initial learning rate is set to 5×10^{-2}. With the increase of iterations, the learning rate drops 10 times every 100 iterations, and 500 iterations are trained. The Loss function uses cross entropy, and the optimizer uses Adam. All the experiments are done on a PC, which is configured with 3.6 GHz CPU and 32 GB RAM, and the GPU is configured with NVIDIA GeForce RTX 2080 Ti dual graphics card.

We conduct both identification and verification experiments. In identification experiment, the statistical value, i.e., accurate recognition rate (ARR) is exploited to evaluate the identification performance, which is rank 1 identification rate. We also conduct the verification experiment. The statistical value i.e., Equal Error Rate (EER), is used for performance evaluation.

4.2 Experiments of Different Values of p in MFRAT

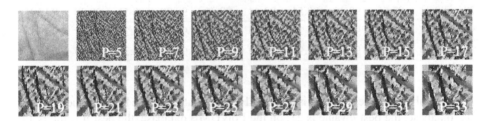

Fig. 4. The DRs extracted by MFRAT with different values of p

In MFRAT, different values of p will affect the scale of DR and MR extraction. Figures 4 and 5 show the DR and MR obtained by different p values. Different scales of DR and MR have certain influence on the recognition rate. Therefore, we conduct experiments on different scales of DR and MR in different palmprint databases. Table 2 lists ARRs according to different p values on five palmprint databases, and Table 3 lists the corresponding EERs. It can be seen that the best p value is 17 on the PolyUII database; on

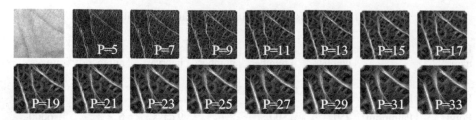

Fig. 5. The MRs extracted by MFRAT with different values of p

Table 2. The ARRs (%) on DR and MR extracted by different p values on five databases

	PolyUII		HFUT I		HFUT CS		TJU		PolyU MB	
p	MR	DR	MR	DR	MR	DR	MR	DR	MR	DR
5	97.02	97.76	97.88	97.78	98.95	98.92	98.46	97.89	99.23	99.16
7	97.08	97.88	98.07	97.94	99.03	98.98	98.50	97.94	99.42	99.33
9	97.11	97.98	98.48	98.15	99.15	99.07	98.65	98.06	99.48	99.57
11	97.28	98.03	99.05	98.44	99.22	99.19	98.79	98.19	99.61	99.64
13	98.66	98.43	99.33	98.89	99.27	99.32	98.95	98.33	99.78	99.77
15	99.13	98.99	**99.55**	**99.46**	99.40	99.48	99.03	98.44	99.94	99.89
17	**99.77**	**99.51**	99.42	99.42	99.55	99.54	99.12	98.65	**99.97**	**99.93**
19	99.47	99.15	99.35	99.36	99.62	99.69	99.23	98.71	99.81	99.91
21	99.45	98.37	99.11	99.18	**99.80**	**99.86**	**99.30**	**98.82**	99.60	99.82
23	99.09	98.11	98.89	98.99	99.77	99.79	99.19	98.77	99.54	99.75
25	98.78	97.97	98.76	98.80	99.72	99.66	99.11	98.73	99.54	99.66
27	98.76	97.67	98.47	98.67	99.61	99.58	99.02	98.67	99.33	99.51
29	98.31	97.55	98.35	98.54	99.44	99.43	98.88	98.51	99.30	99.50
31	98.05	97.47	98.32	98.21	99.29	99.35	98.75	98.38	99.17	99.38
33	97.80	97.21	98.15	97.98	99.10	99.21	98.71	98.33	99.05	99.15

HFUT database, the best p value is 15; on HFUT CS database, the best p value is 21; on TJU database, the best p value is 21; on the PolyUMB database, the best p value is 17. It can be seen from Table 5 that both DR and MR can be used in deep learning methods to obtain good recognition accuracy.

Table 3. The EERs (%) on DR and MR extracted by different p values on five databases

	PolyUII		HFUT I		HFUT CS		TJU		PolyU MB	
p	MR	DR	MR	DR	MR	DR	MR	DR	MR	DR
5	0.1217	0.0867	0.1196	0.1134	0.0345	0.0260	0.0645	0.0977	0.0131	0.0297
7	0.1114	0.0803	0.1152	0.1115	0.0312	0.0253	0.0640	0.0962	0.0104	0.0273
9	0.1045	0.0742	0.1098	0.1063	0.0293	0.0237	0.0629	0.0935	0.0097	0.0211
11	0.0965	0.0678	0.0904	0.1038	0.0285	0.0225	0.0611	0.0922	0.0080	0.0201
13	0.0788	0.0566	0.0816	0.0975	0.0274	0.0211	0.0585	0.0901	0.0070	0.0194
15	0.0621	0.0556	**0.0744**	**0.0828**	0.0257	0.0192	0.0568	0.0886	0.0021	0.0180
17	**0.0485**	**0.0336**	0.0799	0.0835	0.0245	0.0188	0.0550	0.0860	**0.0016**	**0.0173**
19	0.0505	0.0417	0.0803	0.0837	0.0231	0.0174	0.0536	0.0845	0.0065	0.0176
21	0.0518	0.0570	0.0833	0.0882	**0.0209**	**0.0159**	**0.0526**	**0.0801**	0.0081	0.0188
23	0.0698	0.0644	0.1001	0.0923	0.0214	0.0167	0.0542	0.0832	0.0089	0.0198
25	0.0736	0.0745	0.1039	0.0990	0.0220	0.0179	0.0552	0.0847	0.0090	0.0200
27	0.0745	0.0911	0.1100	0.1005	0.0233	0.0183	0.0570	0.0856	0.0122	0.0223
29	0.0806	0.0989	0.1123	0.1032	0.0251	0.0201	0.0602	0.0878	0.0127	0.0225
31	0.0852	0.1044	0.1125	0.1057	0.0269	0.0209	0.0617	0.0894	0.0139	0.0265
33	0.0897	0.1139	0.1137	0.1102	0.0300	0.0222	0.0623	0.0901	0.0146	0.0300

4.3 Experimental Results on Five Databases

We conducted experiments on five palmprint databases with the proposed method. In order to compare the performance with other classical methods, we also conduct comparative experiments. We compare the recognition accuracy with four classic traditional methods, including Competitive Code, Ordinal Code, RLOC, and LLDP. We also compare the recognition accuracy with three important deep learning methods including PalmNet [9], EfficientNet [20] and MobileNet_V3 [21]. Table 4 lists the experimental results. In Table 4, we also list the highest recognition rates of ProlessxyNAS in three different representations of palmprint, including OR, DR and MR, and we list the recognition results of the proposed method with different fusion strategies including $TSCNNF_C$, $TSCNNF_F$, $TSCNNF_S$-max, $TSCNNF_S$-sum and $TSCNNF_D$. In different fusion strategies, $TSCNNF_C$, $TSCNNF_S$-max, and $TSCNNF_D$ have achieved very promising recognition results. In five databases, the ARRs of $TSCNNF_C$, $TSCNNF_S$-Max, and $TSCNNF_D$ are all 100%, and the EERs they obtained are also very low. On five databases, $TSCNNF_D$ has achieved the highest ARR and the lowest EER. From Table 4, the recognition performance of $TSCNNF_D$ is obviously better than the classical traditional methods and deep learning methods.

Table 4. The recognition performances (ARR(%), EER(%)) of different methods on five palmprint databases

	PolyUII		HFUT I		HFUT CS		TJU		PolyU MB	
	ARR	EER	ARR	EER	ARR	EER	ARR	EER	ARR	EER
Competitive Code [4]	100	0.0259	99.78	0.2355	99.96	0.0743	99.85	0.2305	100	0.0044
Ordinal Code [5]	100	0.0514	99.84	0.2901	100	0.0497	99.97	0.1501	100	0.0072
RLOC [6]	100	0.0265	99.89	0.1835	100	0.0409	99.65	0.3485	100	0.0339
LLDP [8]	100	0.0516	99.31	0.5011	100	0.1994	99.65	0.4009	100	0.0033
PalmNet [9]	100	0.8380	100	0.0655	92.45	4.0974	100	0.0115	100	0.0047
EfficientNet [20]	97.39	0.3522	99.41	0.0507	96.55	0.5099	99.89	0.0022	100	0.0002
MobileNet_V3 [21]	97.35	0.5741	98.67	0.1734	95.20	0.5334	99.37	0.0552	100	0.0011
ProlessxyNAS + OR	98.63	0.1728	99.68	0.0407	99.78	0.0217	99.75	0.0187	100	0.00003
ProlessxyNAS + MR	99.77	0.0485	99.55	0.0744	99.80	0.0209	99.30	0.0526	99.97	0.0016
ProlessxyNAS + DR RR	99.51	0.0336	99.46	0.0828	99.86	0.0159	98.82	0.0801	99.93	0.0173
$TSCNNF_C$	100	0.0004	100	0.0006	100	0.0015	100	0.0002	100	0
$TSCNNF_F$	100	0.0004	99.92	0.0192	100	0.0100	100	0.0003	100	0
$TSCNNF_S$-max	100	0.0015	100	0.0021	100	0.0091	100	0.0010	100	0
$TSCNNF_S$-sum	99.98	0.0026	99.89	0.0189	99.98	0.0107	99.97	0.0070	100	0
$TSCNNF_D$	**100**	**0**	**100**	**0.0001**	**100**	**0.0008**	**100**	**0.0002**	**100**	**0**

5   Conclusions

In this paper, we proposed MSCNNF for palmprint recognition, which extracts deep information from multiple representations of palmprint. We then proposed a concrete implementation, i.e., TSCNNF for palmprint recognition, which uses ProxylessNAS as the backbone network and extracts deep information from OR, DR, and MR. Then, different fusion strategies are used to improve the recognition performance. We evaluated the proposed TSCNNF with different fusion strategies on five palmprint databases. Among different fusion strategies, $TSCNNF_C$, $TSCNNF_S$-Max, and $TSCNNF_D$ have achieved very promising recognition results. In five databases, the ARRs of $TSCNNF_C$, $TSCNNF_S$-Max, and $TSCNNF_D$ are all 100%, and the EERs they obtained are also very low. On five databases, $TSCNNF_D$ has achieved the highest ARR and the lowest EER. The recognition performance of $TSCNNF_D$ is obviously better than the classical traditional methods and deep learning methods.

Acknowledgments. This work is partly supported by the grant of the National Science Foundation of China, No. 62076086.

References

1. Fei, L., Lu, G., Jia, W., Teng, S., Zhang, D.: Feature extraction methods for palmprint recognition: a survey and evaluation. IEEE Trans. Syst. Man Cybernetics Syst. **49**, 346–363 (2018)
2. Jia, W., Gao, J., Xia, W., Zhao, Y., Min, H., Lu, J.T.: A performance evaluation of classic convolutional neural networks for 2D and 3D palmprint and palm vein recognition. Int. J. Autom. Comput. **18**, 18–44 (2021)
3. Jia, W., Xia, W., Zhao, Y., Min, H., Chen, Y.X.: 2D and 3D palmprint and palm vein recognition based on neural architecture search. Int. J. Autom. Comput. **18**, 377–409 (2021)
4. Kong, A., Zhang, D.: Competitive coding scheme for palmprint verification. In: Proceedings of the 17th ICPR, pp. 520–523 (2004)
5. Sun, Z.N., Tan, T.N., Wang, Y.H., Li, S.Z.: Ordinal palmprint representation for personal Identification. In: Proceedings of CVPR, pp. 279–284 (2005)
6. Jia, W., Huang, D.S., Zhang, D.: Palmprint verification based on robust line orientation code. Pattern Recogn. **41**, 1504–1513 (2008)
7. Jia, W., Hu, R.X., Lei, Y.K., Zhao, Y., Gui, J.: Histogram of oriented lines for palmprint recognition. IEEE Trans. Syst. Man Cybernetics Syst. **44**, 385–395 (2013)
8. Luo, Y.T., et al.: Local line directional pattern for palmprint recognition. Pattern Recogn. **50**, 26–44 (2016)
9. Genovese, A., Piuri, V., Plataniotis, K.N.: Scotti, F: PalmNet: Gabor-PCA convolutional networks for touchless palmprint recognition. IEEE Trans. Inf. Forensics Secur. **14**, 3160–3174 (2019)
10. Zhong, D., Zhu, J.: Centralized large margin cosine loss for Open-Set deep palmprint recognition. IEEE Trans. Circuits Syst. Video Technol. **30**, 1559–1568 (2020)
11. Matkowski, W.M., Chai, T., Kong, A.W.K.: Palmprint recognition in uncontrolled and uncooperative environment. IEEE Trans. Inf. Forensics Secur. **15**, 1601–1615 (2020)
12. Zhao, S., Zhang, B.: Joint constrained least-square regression with deep convolutional feature for palmprint recognition. IEEE Trans. Syst. Man Cybernetics Syst. (2021)
13. Liu, Y., Kumar, A.: Contactless palmprint identification using deeply learned residual features. IEEE Trans. Biometrics Behav. Identity Sci. **2**, 172–181 (2020)
14. Cai, H., Zhu, L., Han, S.: Proxylessnas: direct neural architecture search on target task and hardware. In: 7th International Conference on Learning Representations, ICLR (2019)
15. Zhang, D., Kong, W.K., You, J., Wong, M.: Online palmprint identification. IEEE Trans. Pattern Anal. Mach. Intell. **25**, 1041–1050 (2003)
16. Zhang, D., Guo, Z., Lu, G., Zhang, L., Zuo, W.: An online system of multispectral palmprint verification. IEEE Trans. Instrum. Meas. **59**, 480–490 (2010)
17. Jia, W., et al.: Palmprint recognition based on complete direction representation. IEEE Trans. Image Process. **26**, 4483–4498 (2017)
18. Jia, W., Hu, R.X., Gui, J., Zhao, Y., Ren, X.M.: Palmprint recognition across different devices. Sensors **12**, 7938–7964 (2012)
19. Zhang, L., Li, L., Yang, A., Shen, Y., Yang, M.: Towards contactless palmprint recognition: a novel device, a new benchmark, and a collaborative representation based identification approach. Pattern Recogn. **69**, 199–212 (2017)
20. M. Tan and Q. V. Le. EfficientNet: rethinking model scaling for convolutional neural networks. In 36th International Conference on Machine Learning, ICML 2019, pp. 10691–10700 (2019)
21. Howard, A. et al. Searching for mobileNetV3. In Proceedings of the IEEE International Conference on Computer Vision (ICCV), pp. 1314–1324 (2019)

Multi-view Finger Vein Recognition Using Attention-Based MVCNN

Weili Yang, Junduan Huang, Zhuoming Chen, Junhong Zhao,
and Wenxiong Kang$^{(\boxtimes)}$

School of Automation Science and Engineering, South China University of
Technology, Guangzhou, China
auwxkang@scut.edu.cn

Abstract. Finger vein images are susceptible to finger posture variation and inappropriate lighting due to the contact-less imaging method and the special imaging principle, which can cause the imaging area to shift and the vein texture to vanish. However, the algorithms cannot directly handle these issues because there are no reference images in single-view imaging. To this end, this paper uses three multi-view finger vein imaging methods to capture finger vein image sets for identity recognition, and three multi-view finger vein datasets are constructed for the first time. To efficiently exploit the complementary information in each multi-view image set, we propose VW-MVCNN, an attention-based multi-view neural network that embeds a View-Wise attention module with MVCNN to mine the identity information in each view and dynamically fuse them to improve accuracy. Extensive experiments are performed on the three datasets to validate the superiority of the proposed VW-MVCNN, and the advantages and disadvantages of the three multi-view finger vein imaging methods are discussed. The code and datasets will be released at https://github.com/SCUT-BIP-Lab/LFMB-MVFV.

Keywords: Multi-view finger vein · Fusion · Attention · VW-MVCNN

1 Introduction

Finger vein biometrics has received a lot of attention in recent years due to its high security [1–4]. Its imaging principle is based on the absorption property of deoxygenated hemoglobin to near-infrared (NIR) light. When NIR light is irradiated to the finger, the vessels can absorb most light while other tissues absorb less, allowing the image sensor to determine the vein textures of corresponding vessels. However, some factors influence the performance of finger vein-based biometric systems: finger posture variation and inappropriate lighting. The finger posture inevitably changes for its contact-less imaging method, resulting in

---

Member, IEEE.

W. Deng et al. (Eds.): CCBR 2022, LNCS 13628, pp. 82–91, 2022.
https://doi.org/10.1007/978-3-031-20233-9_9

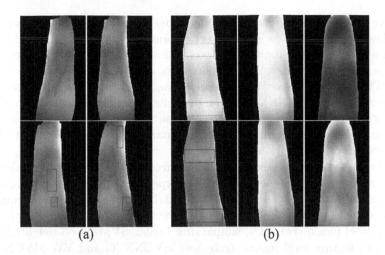

(a)   (b)

Fig. 1. (a) The imaging area shifting caused by posture variation, (b) The vein texture vanishing caused by inappropriate lighting.

a shift of the imaging area on the finger and, thus, a reduction of the common imaging area in two sample images. As shown in Fig. 1(a), the above two images serve as references, and the two new captured images are shown below. The red boxes represent the shifted-out vein textures, while the green boxes represent the newly shifted-in vein textures. As shown in Fig. 1(b), the inappropriate lighting causes vein textures in some finger vein images to vanish. In the first column, the light is absorbed very little by the joint fluid at the finger joints, causing strong light to be scattered in this area, and therefore the image contrast is poor. The red boxes represent vein textures that disappear at the finger joints, and the green boxes represent the vein textures that normally appear under proper lighting; the second column represents slender fingers, usually female fingers, which are not only slender in size but also have thin vessels. Thus the entire image is easily overexposed; in the third column, which are thicker fingers, the tissues inside the fingers can absorb more light, so the whole image is darker, and the vein texture contrast is insufficient.

Most finger vein biometric systems employ single-view imaging, but it is challenging to solve the problems caused by finger posture variation and inappropriate lighting with only a single vein image because the algorithms cannot intuitively realize that the image has imaging area shifted, as well as overexposure or underexposure, without a reference image. Only by comparing multiple images can the algorithm discover additions and deletions on the vein images more efficiently.

Multi-view finger vein recognition refers to the recognition of an individual(finger) using multi-view data from the same individual(finger), where the multi-view data is a multi-view finger vein image set captured under different conditions, such as different view angles, different lighting, and so on. In this paper, we adopt three different multi-view finger vein imaging methods and use multi-view finger vein image sets for verification and identification. And we propose an attention-based multi-view recognition neural network to extract the complementary information in the multi-view images and fuse them more efficiently. The proposed View-Wise attention-based Multi-View Convolution Neural Network (VW-MVCNN), which mines the complementary information of each view based on the content of current input multi-view images and dynamically assigns the fusion weight to the feature map of each view to achieve efficient multi-view information fusion.

We conducted extensive experiments on three multi-view finger vein datasets. First, we performed single-view recognition experiments and used an image quality assessment strategy to select the best quality finger vein image from each multi-view image set for recognition. Then, for multi-view recognition, there are two score-level fusion strategies: simple sum fusion, SVM-based weighted fusion [5], and two feature-level fusion strategies: MVCNN [6] and VW-MVCNN, are employed, and the experimental results show that the proposed VW-MVCNN is superior. We analyze the advantages and disadvantages of different multi-view imaging approaches and verify the feasibility of recognition using multi-view finger vein image sets. The main contributions of this paper are as follows:

1) For the first time, we adopt three different multi-view imaging methods and construct three multi-view finger vein datasets to facilitate multi-view finger vein recognition research. And we will release the three multi-view finger vein datasets for research purposes.
2) We propose VW-MVCNN, an attention-based multi-view recognition neural network that can input a multi-view finger vein image set into the network and predict the identity of this image set. The attention mechanism can mine complementary information between images and dynamically predict each view's fusion weight, effectively fusing the multi-view information to improve identity recognition accuracy.
3) We conducted extensive experiments to analyze the characteristics of different multi-view imaging methods. We conducted single-view recognition and various multi-view fusion recognition experiments, respectively, and the experimental results illustrate the effectiveness of the three multi-view imaging methods and the proposed VW-MVCNN.

The rest of this paper is organized as follows: Sect. 2 describes the details of the proposed approach, and Sect. 3 reports the experiments evaluated. Finally, we draw our conclusion in Sect. 4.

2   Proposed Method

This section first introduces the three multi-view finger vein imaging methods and corresponding multi-view finger vein datasets, then presents the attention-based multi-view recognition network VW-MVCNN.

2.1   Multi-view Imaging Approaches

Single-view imaging is widely used in finger vein biometric systems. Still, it is difficult to solve the problem of imaging area shifting caused by finger posture variation, as well as inappropriate lighting for different fingers. To this end, we adopt three different multi-view imaging approaches for each finger and finally establish three multi-view finger vein datasets to address these problems and improve recognition accuracy. Figure 2 shows the three multi-view imaging approaches and some example images of one same finger. These multi-view imaging approaches include 1. Multi-angle views imaging method, capturing multiple finger vein images with multiple cameras surrounding the finger; 2. Multi-finger-rotation views imaging method, capturing image sequences of the finger under longitudinal rotation with a single camera; and 3. Multi-illumination views imaging method, capturing multiple images of the finger under different light intensities with a single camera. The first two multi-view finger vein imaging approaches are intended to address the problem of imaging area shifting caused by finger posture variation, which can be avoided by capturing the finger at different viewing angles. The device and dataset of the multi-angle views imaging method are presented in [7,8], which can capture all the vein patterns on the finger quickly and conveniently but requires six cameras in hardware, and it is more costly and bulky. The multi-finger-rotation views imaging method and the multi-illumination views imaging method are less costly and more compact. For the multi-finger-rotation views imaging method, the finger is longitudinally rotated.

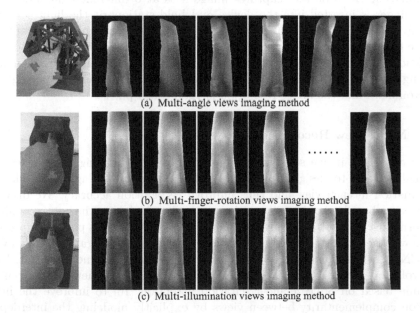

(a) Multi-angle views imaging method

(b) Multi-finger-rotation views imaging method

(c) Multi-illumination views imaging method

Fig. 2. The three multi-view imaging approaches and some example images of one same finger.

Because movement is relative, this is equivalent to the finger being stationary while the camera rotates around the finger, thus capturing different views of the vein patterns on the finger. However, because this multi-view imaging process requires the finger to rotate, it is less user-friendly. In the multi-illumination views imaging method, the NIR light quickly switches between multiple light intensities while the camera synchronously captures finger vein images at each light intensity. This multi-view imaging approach is more user-friendly but only addresses the problem of inappropriate lighting and does not address the issue of finger posture variation. It is worth stating that the latter two multi-view imaging approaches can be applied directly to existing systems without hardware changes, only requiring modifications to the imaging control logic.

Each of the three datasets acquired a kind of multi-view finger vein image set of the same 668 fingers, containing the index and middle fingers of each volunteer's right and left hands. The multi-angle views dataset is a subset of the LFMB-3DFB dataset [7], which only contains multi-view finger vein images. Each finger is inserted into the device 10 times, yielding 6 finger vein images with different angle views each time. During the 10 insertions, the fingers are rotated randomly in the longitudinal direction with an angle within $\pm 80°$. The multi-finger-rotation views dataset captures image sets during finger rotation. Each finger is inserted into the device in a fixed posture (approximately $-30°$ of the normal finger posture), then slowly rotated to around $+30°$, with the camera capturing images at about 80 fps during the rotation, and so on 3 times, with the number of images captured ranging from 90~250 each time. The multi-illumination views dataset captures image sets at 6 different light intensities. Each finger is inserted into the device and held stationary, the light source is quickly switched to 6 levels of light intensity, the finger vein images are captured at the corresponding light intensities, and so on for 10 iterations. During the 10 insertions, the fingers are rotated randomly in the longitudinal direction with an angle within $\pm 30°$. All three datasets are taken in the same indoor lighting environment, and the image resolution is 1280×800 pixels.

2.2   Multi-view Recognition Network

After capturing image sets with different multi-view imaging approaches, the critical issue is to design an effective fusion algorithm to aggregate identity information in each view and thus improve recognition accuracy. We draw on multi-view-based 3D object recognition methods, which have the best recognition performance of 3D object recognition algorithms [6,9]. In this paper, we propose a View-Wise attention-based Multi-View Convolution Neural Network (VW-MVCNN), which combines a View-Wise attention module and the Multi-View Convolution Neural Network (MVCNN) [6]. We design a View-Wise attention module based on Squeeze-and-Excitation attention [10] to improve the information complementarity between views by explicitly modeling the interdependencies between the embedding of each view. Because some textures disappear and new ones appear in other views, so images in different views have different identity information, and the View-Wise attention mechanism can automatically predict the fusion weights of each view based on the identity information to improve the complementarity of identity information among views in each image set. The proposed VW-MVCNN network is shown in Fig. 3. A multi-view finger vein image set $\{I_i, i = 1 \cdots n\}$ that captured from one finger using one of the three multi-view imaging methods is fitted into VW-MVCNN, where n is the number of views or images, each image I_i extracts an embedding $E_i \in \mathbb{R}^{w \times h \times c}$ by a weight-sharing feature encoder $F(\cdot, \theta)$. Then all embeddings $\{E_i, i = 1 \cdots n\}$ comprises a global views embedding $E \in \mathbb{R}^{w \times h \times c \times n}$. In the View-Wise attention module, the global embedding $E \in \mathbb{R}^{w \times h \times c \times n}$ is first reduced to $f \in \mathbb{R}^{1 \times 1 \times c \times n}$ using a global average pooling then predicts a fusion weight vector $W \in \mathbb{R}^{1 \times n}$ using two Fully Connected layers (FC layers) and ReLU activation functions, allowing information to flow across views. Each element of the fusion weight vector W is multiplied with the corresponding view of the global embedding E to obtain a recalibrated global views embedding $E' \in \mathbb{R}^{w \times h \times c \times n}$, E' is then transmitted via a view-pooling layer that employs element-wise maximum operation across channels as in MVCNN [6], to produce a single, compact feature. This feature then goes through two FC layers for classification, where the first FC layer has a ReLU function, and its output is used as the identity feature to calculate matching scores, and the second FC layer is to predict the category probabilities and normalize them using Softmax.

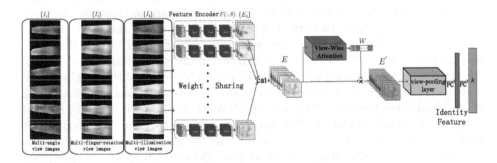

Fig. 3. The VW-MVCNN Network.

3 Experiments

In this section, we conducted subject-independent verification and subject-independent close-set identification tasks [7] on single-view and multi-view data. The structure of the single-view network is shown in Fig. 4, which is based on MobileNet V2 [11] and consists of a feature encoder and a classifier head. Both are the same structure as the corresponding modules of MVCNN and VW-MVCNN. The feature encoder consists of a convolution layer and three Inverted Residuals Blocks from MobileNet V2. The classifier head consists of two FC layers. For the multi-illumination views and multi-finger-rotation views methods, there are more common textures among views, and we use an entropy-based image quality assessment method [12] to select the best quality finger vein image in each image set for recognition, which can be seen as the upper bound for single-view recognition performance: $Entropy = -\sum_{i=0}^{255} P(i) \log_2(P(i))$, where $P(i)$ is the probability of gray-value i appearing on the image. In the comparison experiments of multi-view recognition, we compare two score-level fusion methods and two feature-level fusion methods, i.e., simple sum fusion, SVM-based weighted-sum fusion [5], MVCNN, and VW-MVCNN.

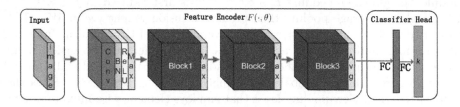

Fig. 4. The single-view network based on MobileNetV2.

3.1 Experimental Settings

The three multi-view finger vein datasets are divided into training, validation, and testing subsets, respectively, in the ratio of 5:2:3, with corresponding finger numbers of 334, 134, and 200. And the finger indexes are the same in the three subsets, as are the finger indexes of intra- and inter-pairs in the validation and testing subsets. The metrics for the verification are EER, TAR@FAR = 0.01, and TAR@FAR = 0.001, while the identification are mAP, Rank1 and Rank5. All experiments are performed using 1080Ti and Pytorch, and the weighted sum of cross-entropy loss and center loss is used as loss functions in the training of the single-view network, MVCNN, and VW-MVCNN, with a weight ratio of 1:0.005. The total epochs are 500, and batch size = 64. The Adam optimizer with a weight decay of $1 \times e^{-4}$ is employed. The learning rate was initially set to lr = $1 \times e^{-3}$, and reduced by a factor of 2 at 300 and 400 epochs, respectively. The images are resized to 256×160 pixels, and the identity feature is set to 256 dimensions and is used to calculate cosine distance.

Table 1. Single-view finger vein recognition results of the multi-angle views dataset.

Multi-angle views	EER (%)	TAR@FAR = 0.01	TAR@FAR = 0.001	mAP	Rank1	Rank5
0 View	8.82	0.5967	0.2679	0.4671	0.7191	0.9115
60 View	11.65	0.5259	0.2200	0.3765	0.6160	0.8902
120 View	7.74	0.6748	0.3298	0.4871	0.7490	0.9347
180 View	**6.75**	**0.7340**	**0.4733**	**0.5978**	**0.8292**	**0.9614**
240 View	9.51	0.6059	0.2388	0.4225	0.6695	0.9003
300 View	8.91	0.5881	0.2664	0.4169	0.6674	0.9064

Table 2. Single-view finger vein recognition results of the multi-illumination views dataset.

Multi-illumination views	EER (%)	TAR@FAR = 0.01	TAR@FAR = 0.001	mAP	Rank1	Rank5
Light 1	4.14	0.8892	0.6823	0.8168	0.9585	0.9833
Light 2	3.44	0.9261	**0.7874**	**0.8501**	**0.9831**	**0.9974**
Light 3	**2.99**	**0.9264**	0.7400	0.8419	0.9799	0.9958
Light 4	3.63	0.8860	0.6575	0.8171	0.9678	0.9917
Light 5	4.02	0.8781	0.6442	0.7811	0.9638	0.9932
Light 6	5.23	0.8311	0.5435	0.7222	0.9309	0.9821
Selected Light	**2.45**	**0.9334**	**0.7997**	**0.8635**	0.9824	0.9966

Table 3. Single-view finger vein recognition results of the multi-finger-rotation views dataset.

Multi-finger- rotation views	EER (%)	TAR@FAR = 0.01	TAR@FAR = 0.001	mAP	Rank1	Rank5
Single image	2.19	0.9467	0.8250	0.4001	0.8175	**0.9967**
Selected image	**1.81**	**0.9626**	**0.8656**	**0.4076**	**0.8275**	0.9958

3.2   Single-view Recognition Experiments

Table 1 shows the results of single-view recognition on the multi-angle views dataset. 0 View refers to the finger ventral view, and 180 View refers to the finger dorsal view. Because the finger was randomly rotated within ±80° during data collection, all results are less than ideal. The best results are obtained at 180° View, which obtains an EER of 6.75% and an mAP of 0.5978. This is because the dorsal finger vein image contains both the vein pattern and the dorsal finger knuckle pattern. Table 2 shows the results of the multi-illumination views dataset, Light 1 − 6 corresponds to each level of light intensity, and Selected Light corresponds to the selection of the best image quality from six light intensity vein images using the image quality assessment algorithm. Light 3 obtains the best EER of 2.99%, and Light 2 obtains the best mAP of 0.8501. When the best quality images are selected, the EER falls to 2.45%, and the mAP rises to 0.8635. Table 3 shows the results of the multi-finger-rotation views dataset. Single Image uses all the images of the finger rotation image sequence to train the single-view recognition network, that is, a lot of data enhancement is done. Compared with the results in Table 2, it is clear that this data augmentation improves recognition accuracy. Selected Image corresponds to the selection of the best image quality from each image sequence. The recognition performance is improved further, obtaining an EER of 1.81% and an mAP of 0.4076. The above results show that ensuring proper lighting and finger posture is a viable strategy to improve the performance of single-view finger vein recognition.

Table 4. Multi-view finger vein fusion results of the multi-angle views dataset.

Fusion method	EER (%)	TAR@FAR = 0.01	TAR@FAR = 0.001	mAP	Rank1	Rank5
Sum	2.69	0.9350	0.7189	0.8644	0.9890	0.9986
SVM-Weighted Sum	2.61	0.9341	0.7359	0.8692	0.9895	0.9977
MVCNN	0.89	0.9917	**0.9704**	0.9834	**0.9995**	0.9995
VW-MVCNN	**0.77**	**0.9934**	0.9640	**0.9842**	0.9988	**1.0000**

Table 5. Multi-view finger vein fusion results of the multi-illumination views dataset.

Fusion method	EER (%)	TAR@FAR = 0.01	TAR@FAR = 0.001	mAP	Rank1	Rank5
Sum	1.41	0.9846	0.9152	0.9260	0.9975	0.9991
SVM-Weighted Sum	1.35	0.9885	0.9327	0.9443	0.9984	0.9991
MVCNN	1.26	0.9929	**0.9511**	0.9673	0.9986	0.9991
VW-MVCNN	**1.24**	**0.9955**	**0.9511**	**0.9775**	**0.9991**	0.9991

3.3 Multi-view Recognition Comparison Experiments

Tables 4, 5, and 6 show the results of four multi-view fusion strategies: simple sum fusion, SVM-based weighted-sum fusion, MVCNN, and VW-MVCNN. The multi-angle views dataset obtains the most significant improvement in multi-view fusion compared to single-view recognition because each view in this imaging method captures the vein textures in different regions on the finger, resulting in a high complementarity between images. The multi-view fusion results on the multi-illumination views dataset and multi-finger-rotation views dataset are similar, but the multi-view fusion on the multi-illumination views dataset improves more than the corresponding single view recognition, indicating that the multi-illumination views imaging method yields vein images with richer complementary information and also indicating the importance of appropriate lighting. The recognition performance of the simple sum fusion and SVM-based weighted-sum fusion on multi-finger-rotation views dataset does not improve, and only when using MVCNN and VW-MVCNN is there an obvious improvement. MVCNN and VW-MVCNN have better recognition performance in all three tables, indicating that feature layer fusion is more efficient. VW-MVCNN, in particular, achieves the best experimental results across all three datasets, with EER of 0.77%, 1.24%, and 1.37%, and mAP of 0.9842, 0.9775, and 0.4207, respectively.

Table 6. Multi-view finger vein fusion results of the multi-finger-rotation views dataset.

Fusion method	EER (%)	TAR@FAR = 0.01	TAR@FAR = 0.001	mAP	Rank1	Rank5
Sum	1.87	0.9620	0.8561	0.4076	0.8258	0.9958
SVM-Weighted Sum	1.86	0.9633	0.8554	0.4072	0.8242	0.9975
MVCNN	1.58	0.9785	0.8937	**0.4210**	0.8417	**1.0000**
VW-MVCNN	**1.37**	**0.9817**	**0.9063**	0.4207	**0.8467**	**1.0000**

4 Conclusion

In this paper, we adopt three multi-view finger vein imaging methods and constructed three multi-view finger vein datasets containing image sets of the same finger. To complement and fuse identity information in the multi-view image set more effectively, we propose VW-MVCNN, which combines a View-Wise attention module and MVCNN. We conducted single-view recognition and multi-view fusion recognition experiments on three datasets. The results show that the proposed multi-view finger vein imaging methods and VW-MVCNN effectively improve identity recognition performance.

Acknowledgements. This work was supported by the National Natural Science Foundation of China (No. 61976095) and the Natural Science Foundation of Guangdong Province, China (No. 2022A1515010114).

References

1. Kang, W., et al.: Study of a full-view 3D finger vein verification technique. tifs **15**, 1175–1189 (2020)
2. Zhang, Z., et al.: Study on reflection-based imaging finger vein recognition. TIFS **17**, 2298–2310 (2022)
3. Huang, J., et al.: FVT: finger vein transformer for authentication. TIM **71**, 1–13 (2022)
4. Tang, S., et al.: Finger vein verification using a Siamese CNN. IET Biom. **8**, 306–315 (2019)
5. Gutschoven, B., et al.: Multi-modal identity verification using support vector machines (SVM). FUSION (2000): THB3/3-THB3/8 vol 2
6. Su, H., et al.: Multi-view convolutional neural networks for 3D shape recognition. In: ICCV (2015)
7. Yang, W., et al.: LFMB-3DFB: a large-scale finger multi-biometric database and benchmark for 3D finger biometrics. IJCB, pp. 1–8 (2021)
8. Yang, W., et al.: A novel system and experimental study for 3D finger multi-biometrics. TBIOM (2022)
9. Chen, S., et al.: MVT: multi-view vision transformer for 3D recognition. BMVC (2021)
10. Hu, J., Li, S., Sun, G.: Squeeze-and-excitation networks. In: CVPR 2018 (2018)
11. Sandler, M., et al.: MobileNetV2: inverted residuals and linear bottlenecks. In: CVPR, pp. 4510–4520 (2018)
12. Yang, W., et al.: FVRAS-Net: an embedded finger-vein recognition and AntiSpoofing system using a unified CNN. TIM **69**, 8690–8701 (2020)

Selective Detail Enhancement Algorithm for Finger Vein Images

Mingze Sun, Jiahao Li, Huabin Wang[✉], Yujie Xu, and Liang Tao

Anhui Provincial Key Laboratory of Multimodal Cognitive Computation, School of Computer Science and Technology, Anhui University, Hefei, China
wanghuabin@ahu.edu.cn

Abstract. In near-infrared finger vein images, the contrast between vein texture and skin is low, and traditional algorithms based on enhancement filters and grayscale stretching are difficult to effectively enhance the vein structure, and it is easy to introduce noise. Therefore, a selective enhancement algorithm for finger vein images based on adaptive guided filtering is proposed. Firstly, a gradient operator weighted guided filter with better edge-preserving ability is proposed to decompose the vein structure of finger vein images, and obtain smooth layer and detail layer. Secondly, a selective weighting factor is designed for vein detail layer enhancement while reducing noise interference. Finally, the enhanced detail layer is fused with the smooth layer to obtain an enhanced image of finger veins. The experimental results show that the proposed algorithm can effectively improve the quality of finger vein images. In six popular image quality evaluation indicators such as information entropy (IE) and peak signal-to-noise ratio, the image recognition rate after enhancement is also improved due to mainstream algorithms.

Keywords: Fingervein enhancement · Gradient operator · Guided filtering

1 Introduction

With the rapid development of the information age, people pay more and more attention to information security. Biometric-based identification has gradually become a research hotspot. Among various biometric identification algorithms, fingerprint recognition has higher requirements on the humidity and cleanliness of fingers [1]; Due to the limitation of hardware conditions of iris acquisition equipment, it is difficult to popularize widely [2]; The extraction of voiceprint features is susceptible to environmental factors [3]. So finger vein identification has been widely used in the public domain and personal identity due to its advantages of living body identification, convenient collection, high security, real-time detection, and anti-counterfeiting [4]. The main process of finger vein recognition includes finger vein image acquisition, preprocessing, feature extraction, feature matching and recognition. Among them, preprocessing is the primary link. Affected by

This work was supported in part by the Natural Science Foundation of Anhui Province under Grant 1908085MF209,and the National Undergraduate Training Program for Innovation and Entrepreneurship under grant number 202210357082.

factors such as acquisition hardware, ambient lighting, and finger posture, the quality of the collected finger vein images is not high, which in turn affects the recognition rate.

In order to solve the problems of low contrast in finger vein images, inconspicuous structure of finger vein network details, local absence, and large noise, scholars at home and abroad have studied image enhancement algorithms. [5] proposed an enhancement algorithm to improve histogram equalization and Retinex algorithm, which can effectively enhance grayscale images, but the improvement of image information entropy is not obvious. [6] proposed a blur enhancement image algorithm, which improves the image contrast through blur enhancement rather than linear increase, but it is sensitive to noise, which leads to a decrease in the performance of the algorithm. [7] proposed a fusion image enhancement algorithm based on Laplacian pyramid directional filter bank is proposed, which overcomes the defect that wavelet cannot mine edge quality and information, so that image texture details can be fully preserved. [8] proposed an image enhancement algorithm combining local pixel grouping and principal component analysis, which improved the denoising ability of the algorithm. The above algorithm can effectively enhance the quality of grayscale images, but the contrast between the texture of vein images and the skin is not high, and it is easy to introduce noise when using the same strategy for enhancement. Therefore, the vein image should be decomposed first to obtain the detail layer containing the vein texture and the smooth layer of the skin area. The introduction of noise can be effectively avoided by separately enhancing the detail layer.

Guided filters were first proposed by He and can be used for texture detail decomposition of finger vein images [9]. It can keep the edge smooth like a bilateral filter and retain more details near the edge, and it has a wide range of applications in the field of image processing, such as edge enhancement, image smoothing, dehazing, etc. LI By introducing the edge -perceived factor into the existing guidance image filter (GIF), weighted the weighted guidance filter (WGIF), which proposed the weighted guidance filter (WGIF), which improved the local filtering-based algorithm [10]. The edge preservation smoothing technology is affected by the halo artifact. The weight factor of WGIF based on the local variance difference penalizes the normalization factor of GIF, which improves the edge preservation effect, but the edge information reflected locally is limited, and the area edge with large variance. The intensity is not necessarily large; moreover, the regularization factor is fixed and does not apply to all images. Long proposed an improved weighted guided filtering algorithm based on the Log edge operator [11], using the absolute assignment response of the local Log (Laplacian-of-Gaussian) operator to replace the local area variance, and the regularization factor takes the value of 0.1 times the maximum value of the Log image, which improves the robustness and universality of the algorithm [12]; however, when the width of the edge is smaller than the width of the Log operator, details may be lost.

Since the normalization factor l of the guided filtering is a fixed value, the difference of texture changes of different window pixels is not considered. If the normalization factor l is selected too large, it may lead to blurred edges. In this paper, based on WGIF, combined with the advantage that the gradient operator can more accurately reflect the intensity of pixel changes, the weight factor is improved, the penalty effect of the weight factor is strengthened, and the edge protection ability of the filter is improved. In this paper, the finger vein image is first decomposed based on the improved weighted guided filter to obtain the smooth layer and the detail layer, and an adaptive weight factor is designed to selectively enhance the detail layer. Finger vein image. The proposed algorithm can retain and highlight more vein texture details while reducing noise, and achieve better enhancement effect.

The main contributions of this paper are as follows:

1. The algorithm for adaptive segmentation and selective detail enhancement of finger vein images is proposed. By segmenting the image of the detail layer of finger vein texture, and designing the edge weight factor to select the vein texture area in the detail layer that needs to be enhanced, the vein structure can be enhanced and the introduction of noise can be avoided.
2. The weighted guided filtering algorithm improved by gradient operator is proposed. Designing the gradient operator and calculating the regularization factor can more accurately reflect the intensity of pixel changes, enhance the penalty effect on the regularization factor, and improve the edge-preserving ability of the finger vein image.

2 Relevant Work

2.1 Guided Filtering

First save the collected vein image, use guided filtering as the local linear model image filter, set the guiding images as G, the image to be filtered as F, and the output image as O. The edge-preserving effect of the guided filter is expressed as follows:

$$F(p) = O(p) + e(p) \tag{1}$$

The local linear model is as follows:

$$O(p) = a_{p'}G(p) + b_{p'}, \forall p \in \Omega_{\zeta 1}(p') \tag{2}$$

Among them, $\Omega_{\zeta 1}(p')$ represents a square window with the pixel p' as the center and the radius size is $\zeta 1$. In this window, the values of ap' and bp' are fixed. Derive both sides of the above equation to get:

$$\nabla O = a_{p'} \nabla G \tag{3}$$

If G has a gradient, then O also has a similar gradient, so guided filtering has edge-preserving properties. Determine the two parameters a and b by minimizing the cost function (3), as follows:

$$M(a_{p'}, b_{p'}) = \sum_{p \in \Omega_{\zeta 1}(p')} ((a_{p'}G(p) + b_{p'} - F(p))^2 + \lambda a_{p'}^2) \tag{4}$$

The first term is the fidelity term, which ensures that the local linear model is established while minimizing the difference between F and O; the second term is the regularization term, and l is the regularization factor to prevent the coefficient a from being too large.

2.2 Weighted Guided Filtering

Since the normalization factor λ of the guided filtering is a fixed value, the difference of texture changes of different window pixels is not considered. If the normalization factor λ is selected too large, it may lead to blurred edges. To this end, Li proposed a algorithm to adaptively adjust the normalization factor λ based on local variance: weighted guided filtering [13]. Let the guiding image be G, $G,\sigma_{G,1}2(p')$ is the variance in a local window with a radius of 1×1 centered on p', and the edge weight factor is defined as follows:

$$\Gamma_G(p') = \frac{1}{T}\sum_{p=1}^{T}\frac{\sigma_{G,1}^2(p') + \varepsilon}{\sigma_{G,1}^2(p) + \varepsilon} \tag{5}$$

Among them, the regularization factor ε is a constant, and the value is usually $(0.001 \times R)^2$, R is the gray value range, T is the total number of image pixels, and p traverses all pixels of the image. Generally, the edge weight factor Γ of an edge region or a pixel with a sharp pixel change is greater than 1, while the edge weight factor Γ of a smooth region or a pixel with a gentle pixel change is less than 1. The prominent edge weight factor Γ of the weighted guided filter has a regulating effect on a, making it more stable and having a better protection effect on the edge.

3 Selective Detail Enhancement Algorithm for Finger Vein Images

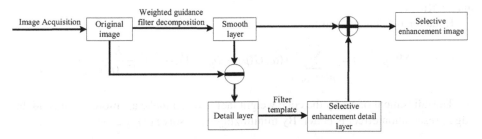

Fig. 1. Framework for Selective detail enhancement algorithm

Figure 1 shows the framework for selective detail enhancement algorithm. Firstly, the weight factor of the weighted guided filtering is optimized by the gradient operator, and the gradient operator weighted guided filtering with better edge-preserving ability is obtained. The filter is used to filter and decompose the finger vein image, and the smooth layer and the detail layer are obtained. Secondly, an adaptive filter weight template is designed to filter the detail layer image to obtain a selectively enhanced detail layer, which can enhance the vein structure and avoid noise enhancement. Finally, the enhanced detail layer is combined with the smooth layer to obtain an enhanced image of finger veins.

3.1 Weighted Guided Filtering Improved by Gradient Operator

The weight factor of the weighted guided filter (WGIF) penalizes the guided filter (GIF) and improves the edge preservation effect, but the edge information reflected locally is limited, and the edge strength of the area with large variance may also be small; Also, the regularization factor ε is fixed and does not apply to all images. Long proposed an improved weighted guided filtering algorithm of the Log edge operator, using the absolute assignment response of the local Log (Laplacian-of-Gaussian) operator to replace the local area variance, and the regularization factor value is 0.1 times the maximum value of the Log image, which improves the generality of the algorithm [11]; however, when the width of the edge is smaller than the width of the Log operator, details may be lost.

Based on the above shortcomings, this paper proposes to replace the edge weight factor based on local variance with the gradient operator response, and proposes a gradient weighted guided filter (GWGIF). The regularization factor ε is 0.1 times the maximum gradient value, which can be more accurate. It reflects the intensity of pixel changes, enhances the penalty effect on the normalization factor, and improves the edge-preserving ability. The edge weight factor improved by the gradient operator is defined as follows:

$$\Gamma_G(p') = \frac{1}{T} \sum_{p=1}^{T} \frac{\nabla f(p') + \varepsilon_{\nabla f}}{\nabla f(p) + \varepsilon_{\nabla f}} \tag{6}$$

where $\nabla f(p')$ represents the gradient of pixel p', and $\varepsilon \nabla f$ takes the value of $0.1 \times \max(\nabla f(p'))$.

Equation (4) changes into:

$$M(a_{p'}, b_{p'}) = \sum_{p \in \Omega_{\zeta 1}(p')} ((a_{p'}G(p) + b_{p'} - F(p))^2 + \frac{\lambda}{\Gamma_G(p')} a_{p'}^2) \tag{7}$$

The adjustment of $a_{p'}$ by the edge weight factor Γ can make $a_{p'}$ more stable, and the edge preservation effect is better. By minimizing M to solve (7), we get:

$$a_{p'} = \frac{\mu_{G \otimes F, \zeta 1}(p') - \mu_{G, \zeta 1}(p') \mu_{F, \zeta 1}(p')}{\sigma_{G, \zeta 1}^2(p') + \frac{\lambda}{\Gamma_G(p')}} \tag{8}$$

$$b_{p'} = \mu_{F, \zeta 1}(p') - a_{p'} \mu_{G, \varsigma 1}(p') \tag{9}$$

where $\otimes$ represents the dot product of two matrices, $\mu_{G \otimes X}$, $\mu_{G \otimes X}$, $\zeta 1(p')$, $\mu_{G, \zeta 1}(p')$, $\mu_{X, \zeta 1}(p')$ represent the mean values of matrices $G \otimes X$, G, X in a local rectangular window with radius $\zeta 1$, respectively.

When the input image is used as the guide image, that is, when $G = X$, the guide filter has the function of edge preservation, and Eq. (8) can be changed to:

$$a_{p'} = \frac{\sigma_{G, \zeta 1}^2(p')}{\sigma_{G, \zeta 1}^2(p') + \frac{\lambda}{\Gamma_G(p')}} \tag{10}$$

where $\sigma 2_{G,\zeta 1}(p')$ is the variance of a window of radius $\zeta 1$ centered on p'. Each window will solve the corresponding a_p, b_p, , so it is necessary to calculate the average $(\overline{a}_p, \overline{b}_p)$ of multiple a_p, b_p:

$$\overline{a}_p = \frac{1}{|\Omega_{\zeta 1}(p')|} \sum_{p' \in \Omega_{\zeta 1}(p')} a_{p'} \tag{11}$$

$$\overline{b}_p = \frac{1}{|\Omega_{\zeta 1}(p')|} \sum_{p' \in \Omega_{\zeta 1}(p')} b_{p'} \tag{12}$$

where $|\Omega_{\zeta 1}(p')|$ is the base of $\Omega_{\zeta 1}(p')$.

3.2 Selective Detail Enhancement

First, the global detail enhancement is performed on the filtered and decomposed image for comparison. Through formula (1), we can obtain F as the input image, O as the filtered image, and e as the detail and noise of the filtered part of the image. Therefore, what detail enhancement has to do is to enlarge the filtered detail part by a certain factor and add it back to the filtered output:

$$O_{enh}(p) = F(p) + \theta e(p) \tag{13}$$

where θ is the magnification factor.

The above global enhancement can indeed enhance the details of the image, but e contains the details and noise filtered out in the original image, Therefore, when e is amplified by θ, the noise contained in it is inevitably amplified. Therefore, this paper proposes a selective detail enhancement algorithm:

$$O_{enh}(p) = F(p) + \eta(p)\theta e(p) \tag{14}$$

where η is calculated by Γ in formula (5), which is used as a filter enhancement template to select the part of e that needs to be enhanced. In this way, selective detail enhancement has stronger denoising ability than global detail enhancement.

In Fig. 2, from left to right, the original image and the selective enhancement results are shown. It is not difficult to see that the selective enhancement has improved the visual effect of the image to a certain extent.

(a) original image   (b) detail enhancement

Fig. 2. Selective detail enhancement effect of finger vein image

After the above analysis, this paper proposes an improved weighted guided filtering finger vein image enhancement algorithm (GWFIF) based on gradient operator. Firstly, the input finger vein image I is filtered with a weighted guided filter improved by gradient operator, and the detail layer D and smooth layer S of the finger vein image are obtained. The detail layer provides the texture information of the finger vein image, and the smooth layer reflects the finger vein image. Approximate contour information and light intensity of vein images. Finally, the template is obtained according to the Γ calculated by formula (5), the image details are selectively enhanced, and added back to the smooth layer to obtain the selectively enhanced image ISE. The steps of global enhancement and selective enhancement of finger vein images are shown in Table 1.

Table 1. Selective detail enhancement algorithm for finger vein image

Input: Finger Vein Image I
Output: Selectively Enhanced Image ISE
1. Calculate the normalization factor Γ according to formulas (6)–(11). The normalization factor Γ can enhance the image details
2. Filter the finger vein image I(x, y) through the weighted guided filter improved by the gradient operator to obtain the detail layer D(x, y) and the smooth layer S(x, y)
3. Obtain the Γ of the template by formula (5), and then use the template Γ to filter the noise according to formula (14), adjust the amplification factor, selectively amplify the texture information of the detail layer, and obtain the selectively enhanced detail layer $D_e(x, y)$
4. Add $D_e(x, y)$ back to the smoothing layer D(x, y) to get the finger vein image ISE(x, y) with selective detail enhancement

4 Experimental Results and Analysis

In this section, we will conduct a comparison experiment of finger vein image enhancement effect on three popular finger vein databases: FV-PolyU database [14] and FV-TJ database [15]. Comparison Experiment of Image Quality Evaluation Index After Enhancement, Comparison experiment of recognition rate before and after finger vein image enhancement. To evaluate the effectiveness of the proposed algorithm in this paper.

4.1 Experimental Environment

Desktop: DESKTOP-67SPAU4; CPU: Intel(R) Core(TM) i5-7500 CPU @3.40GHz 3.41GHz; running memory: 16G; operating system: win10 64-bit; programming environment: MATLAB R2019b.

4.2 Analysis of Venous Enhancement Effect

In order to verify the effectiveness of the algorithm in this chapter, experiments are compared with the following image enhancement algorithms. [16] proposed a algorithm for image enhancement through image or video fusion (EUIVF), and [17] proposed fusion enhancement algorithms based on fused images (MF, PM, WV), filter-based algorithms (WGIF), and the selective detail enhancement algorithm(SDE) proposed in this paper. This section analyzes the image enhancement effect of each algorithm from both subjective and objective perspectives. Due to space limitations, this section selects three groups of representative images from each database as examples for subjective visual analysis (Fig. 3). And choose standard deviation (SD), average gradient (AG), spatial frequency (SF), information entropy (IE), peak signal-to-noise ratio (PSNR), natural image quality (Natural image quality, NIQE) six popular image quality Evaluation parameters are used as objective quality evaluation indicators, as shown in Tables 2 and 3.

Figure 3 shows the comparison charts of the enhancement effect of the algorithm proposed in this paper in the FV-PolyU database and the FV-TJ database. The first column of images is the original image, Columns 2–6 are the images enhanced by the contrast algorithm respectively, and the seventh column is the renderings after using the enhancement algorithm proposed in this chapter. By observing the original image and the enhanced images obtained by using various algorithms, it can be found that EUIVF has a poor effect on finger vein image enhancement, which is caused by the low contrast of the finger vein image itself; MF, PM, and WV effectively suppress noise and improve the brightness of the image, but the contrast of the image is not improved, resulting in an unclear image; WGIF effectively suppresses the noise of the image and improves the image contrast, but the edge of the image texture is blurred; the selective detail enhancement algorithm (SDE) proposed in this paper is effective. It suppresses noise, improves image contrast and clarity to a certain extent, and enriches texture detail information. The finger vein images enhanced by the enhancement algorithm have better visual effects.

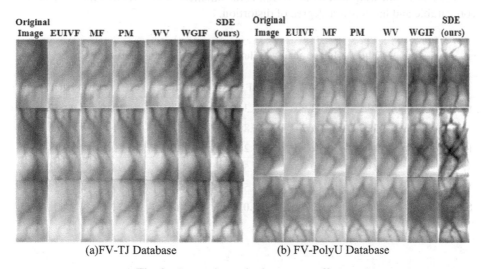

(a)FV-TJ Database   (b) FV-PolyU Database

Fig. 3. Comparison of enhancement effects

Ten images are randomly selected from each group of databases for objective quality evaluation and comparison experiments, see Table 2 and Table 3. The AG, SF and IE of the image enhanced by the GWGIF-based enhancement algorithm are significantly higher than other algorithms. The higher the AG, the higher the clarity of the image, which proves that GWGIF-Selective improves the clarity of the original image. The higher the SF, the richer the edge structure and detail information of the enhanced image, which proves that GWGIF-Selective can enrich the information of the fine edge structure. The higher the IE, the more information the GWGIF-Selective algorithm contains than the source image. The low value of GWGIF-Selective is due to the fact that the filter template has passed some noise, which affects the amplification factor of the detail layer. PSNR and NIQE are also comparable, the larger the PSNR value, the better the image quality. The smaller the NIQENIQE, the better the texture details of the image are in line with the visual habits of the human eye, the smaller the distortion, and the better the quality. Through the above analysis, it is objectively verified that the GWGIF-based finger vein image enhancement algorithm (GWGIF-Selective) can effectively improve the quality of the original image.

Algorithm analysis: The selective detail enhancement based on GWGIF has achieved ideal results in the evaluation of various indicators. In the SD comparison experiment, GWGIF-Selective is the highest, indicating that the gray level dispersion of the image enhanced by this algorithm is higher. In the comparative experiments of IE, SF, AG and NIQE, the image enhancement algorithm based on GWGIF has the highest value, which shows that the grayscale variation range of the image enhanced by the two algorithms has been improved, and the texture change information of the image has been enriched. Contains more useful information. In the NIQE comparison experiment, GWGIF-Selective has a lower value and better effect. In the PSNR comparison experiment, WGIF has better effect, indicating that its distortion is the smallest, and GWGIF-Selective is also comparable and has a lower degree of distortion.

Table 2. Image quality evaluation of FV-PolyU Database

	SD	AG	SF	PSNR	IE	NIQE
EUIVF	30.15	1.32	2.35	13.24	6.53	11.22
MF	32.74	2.24	3.88	16.48	6.71	7.66
PM	44.00	1.90	3.26	17.12	7.06	10.58
WV	41.27	2.02	3.53	17.61	6.98	10.56
WGIF	54.03	3.30	5.54	**28.64**	**7.49**	**7.57**
SEA (ours)	**56.11**	**3.77**	**7.01**	25.46	7.24	8.02

Table 3. Image quality evaluation of FV-TJ Database

	SD	AG	SF	PSNR	IE	NIQE
EUIVF	23.58	1.71	3.70	12.66	6.47	9.71
MF	24.80	2.94	5.49	15.30	6.54	7.84
PM	37.14	2.36	4.70	15.00	7.00	10.80
WV	36.53	2.61	5.15	15.93	7.07	9.89
WGIF	44.35	4.57	8.29	**25.18**	7.42	**7.13**
SEA (ours)	**48.11**	**5.14**	**10.26**	22.09	**7.48**	7.88

4.3   Comparison Experiment of Recognition Rate

In the experiments in this section, in order to verify the effectiveness of the algorithm in this chapter, the recognition rate comparison experiments were carried out on the FV-TJ and FV-Polyu databases respectively. First, the algorithm LBP [18], HOG [19], block WLD [20], WLBP, and LDP algorithms are used to obtain the recognition rate of the original data set Then use the algorithm mentioned in the paper to enhance the original database. Then find the recognition rate of the enhanced dataset.

LBP and HOG are widely used local descriptors, which are simple to calculate and robust to illumination, but are susceptible to noise. WLD is a robust, simple and efficient local feature descriptor. The LDP algorithm is very similar to the LBP algorithm, but it obtains the neighborhood gray value of the center pixel after convolution and summation with the Kirsch operator. Since the edge gradient value is more stable than the pixel gray value, the LDP algorithm is more robust to noise. The use of Gabor transform, LBP, and spatial region histogram in the LGBP algorithm makes the algorithm robust to illumination changes and misregistration. Comparing the results of running various algorithms on the original dataset and the enhanced dataset for each group, we find that our selective detail enhancement has very good results for the FV-Polyu datasets, However, in the FV-TJ dataset, only a few algorithms have improved the recognition rate or equal error rate, and these algorithms are all algorithms with complex calculations, many factors to consider, and many optimization factors. The reason for the analysis is that we observed the FV-TJ original image data set and found that the original image of the data set is clear enough, and all algorithms on the original image of the data set have a recognition rate of more than 99%. We will difficult to enhance it to get the desired effect. The recognition results on the FV-Polyu dataset are most algorithms improve the recognition rate or increase the equal error rate. We can conclude that when the original image is not clear enough, the recognition rate of our enhancement algorithm is the best compared to the experiment, but when the original image is clear enough, its effect is slightly lacking. Looking at Tables 4 and 5, we can find that the recognition rate and the equal error rate are almost improved for several feature extraction algorithms based on the enhanced dataset. It is proved that the algorithm proposed in this paper is effective in enhancing finger vein images.

Table 4. Comparison of experimental results on the FV-Polyu database

	RR (%) (before)	EER (%) (before)	RR (%) (after)	EER (%) (after)
LBP	98.82	1.7094	98.61	**1.6026**
HOG	99.25	1.7094	**99.47**	**1.4540**
WLD	99.04	1.9113	**99.04**	**1.4957**
WLBP	98.40	1.8162	**99.68**	**1.3095**
LDP	95.09	4.2735	**97.76**	**2.4645**
AVGRAGE	98.12	2.2840	**98.92**	**1.6652**

Table 5. Comparison of experimental results on FV-TJ database

	RR (%) (before)	EER (%) (before)	**RR (%) (after)**	**EER (%) (after)**
LBP	100	0.0025	99.84	0.1563
HOG	100	0.0098	**100**	**0**
WLD	99.69	0.2888	**99.84**	0.3125
WLBP	100	0.1563	**100**	**0.1563**
LDP	99.69	0.3125	**99.69**	**0.3125**
AVGRAGE	99.87	0.1540	**99.88**	0.1875

5   Conclusion

This paper firstly analyzes the traditional guided filtering theory, analyzes the shortcomings of the traditional guided filtering, and uses the gradient algorithm to improve the original normalization factor, and obtains an improved weighted guided filter (GWGIF) based on the gradient operator. GWGIF does not add new parameters, nor does it change the linear complexity of the original filter, which can more accurately reflect the pixel point changes of the image edge and texture information, and improve the edge preservation ability of the filter. Using GWGIF to filter finger vein images with unclear texture, high noise and low contrast can obtain a smooth layer closer to the general outline of the finger vein and a detailed layer with more texture information and less noise. The selective detail enhancement algorithm filters the noise through the filter template and selectively enlarges the detail layer, which can better describe the changes of the vein edge structure, enrich the texture detail information, and improve the image quality, and the algorithm is robust and universal.

References

1. Zhou, X., Hu, A., Li, G., et al.: A robust radio-frequency fingerprint extraction scheme for practical device recognition. IEEE Internet Things J. **8**(14), 11276–11289 (2021)
2. Peng, C., Jiang, H., Qu, L.: Deep convolutional neural network for passive RFID tag localization via joint RSSI and PDOA fingerprint features. IEEE Access **9**, 15441–15451 (2021)
3. Nguyen, K., Fookes, C., Ross, A., et al.: Iris recognition with off-the-shelf CNN features: a deep learning perspective. IEEE Access **6**, 18848–18855 (2018)
4. Zeng, C., Ma, C., Wang, Z., et al.: A review of speaker recognition research under the framework of deep learning. Comput. Eng. Appl. **56**(7), 8–16 (2020)
5. Du, M.: Research on Feature Extraction Algorithm of Finger Vein Image. Anhui University, Anhui (2020)
6. Liu, H., Tang, Q., Jie, Y.: Application of improved histogram equalization and Retinex algorithm in gray image enhancement. Chin. J. Quantum Electron. **31**(5), 526–532 (2014)
7. Vlachos, M., Dermatas, E.: Fuzzy segmentation for finger vessel pattern extraction of infrared images. Pattern Anal. Appl. **18**(4), 901–919 (2014). https://doi.org/10.1007/s10044-014-0413-7
8. Jin, H., Yang, X., Jiao, L., et al.: Image Enhancement via Fusion Based on Laplacian Pyramid Directional Filter Banks. DBLP 3656 (2005)
9. Tang, H., Muda, A.K., Choo, Y.H., et al.: Historic document image de-noising using principal component analysis (PCA) and local pixel grouping (LPG). Adv. Intell. Syst. Comput. **557**, 77–87 (2017)
10. He, K., Sun, J., Tang, X.: Guided image filtering. IEEE Trans. Pattern Anal. Mach. Intell. **35**(6), 1397–1409 (2013)
11. Li, Z., Zheng, J., Zhu, Z., et al.: Weighted guided image filtering. IEEE Trans. Image Process. **24**(1), 120–129 (2015)
12. Long, P., Lu, H.: Improved weighted guided filtering algorithm for LoG edge operator. Comput. Appl. **35**(9), 2661–2665 (2015)
13. Marr, D., Hildreth, E.: Theory of edge detection. Proc. R. Soc. Lond. Ser. B Biol. Sci. **207**(1167), 187–217 (1980)
14. Kumar, A., Zhou, Y.: human identification using finger images. IEEE Trans Image Process. **21**(4), 2228–2244 (2011)
15. Liu, S., Yang, J.: Finger vein recognition based on fuzzy directional energy features. Electron. Des. Eng. **22**(8), 123–125, 130 (2014)
16. Chiang, J.Y., Chen, Y.C.: Underwater image enhancement by wavelength compensation and dehazing. IEEE Trans. Image Process. **21**(4), 1756–1769 (2012)
17. Fu, X., Zeng, D., Huang, Y., et al.: A fusion-based enhancing algorithm for weakly illuminated images. Signal Process. **129**, 82–96 (2016)
18. Xiao, B.: Research on Finger Vein Recognition Technology. Southeast University, Jiangsu (2017)
19. Dalal, N., Triggs, B.: Histograms of oriented gradients for human detection. In: IEEE Computer Society Conference on Computer Vision and Pattern Recognition, pp. 886–893 (2005)
20. Li, S.: Image Feature Extraction under Complex Lighting. Chang'an University, Xi'an (2018)

SP-FVR: SuperPoint-Based Finger Vein Recognition

Xianjing Meng[(✉)] and Shuai Yuan

School of Computer Science and Technology, Shandong University of Finance
and Economics, Jinan 250014, People's Republic of China
xianjing.meng@sdufe.edu.cn

Abstract. Among existing finger vein recognition methods, the
keypoint-based method has gained much attention owning to its
deformation-tolerance. However, the adopted keypoint descriptors may
be insufficient in keypoint quantity and descriptor distinctiveness, since
they are generally artificially-designed and sensitive to the poor quality of the finger vein images. To address the above-mentioned problem,
an automatically-learned keypoint-based method utilizing fully convolutional neural networks (FCNNs), called SuperPoint-based finger vein
recognition (SP-FVR), is proposed in this paper. We first adjust the
finger vein images by pertinent intensity correction, noise removal and
resizing. Then, we locate and learn the keypoint descriptors utilizing
the SuperPoint model. Finally, the keypoints are matched by a bilateral
strategy. Experiments on the HKPU and SDU-MLA databases demonstrate the effectiveness of the proposed method in real applications, the
EERs are 0.0025 and 0.0138, with the FRRs-at-0-FAR of 0.0218 and
0.0890, respectively.

Keywords: Finger vein recognition · Keypoint · SuperPoint ·
Biometrics

1 Introduction

Finger vein recognition is competitive among the prevalent biometrics owning to
its security and convenience, therefore has been widely accepted and increasingly
adopted in commercial applications [1]. However, its performance is still limited
by the quality and deformation problems [2] brought by the non-contact capturing under Near Infrared Rays (NIRs) and non-rigidity of the fingers. Extensive
research works [3] have been proposed to deal with the problems, which can
be roughly categorized as local pattern-based method, Region of Interest (ROI)
-based method, keypoint-based method and vessel-based method.

Among the existing methods, this paper pays attention to the keypoint-
based method, since it is comparatively advantageous in many aspects [4]. The
local pattern-based method is mainly based on pixel-level features, such as Local
Binary Pattern (LBP), Local Line Binary Pattern (LLBP) and many high-order

W. Deng et al. (Eds.): CCBR 2022, LNCS 13628, pp. 104–113, 2022.
https://doi.org/10.1007/978-3-031-20233-9_11

or learning-based variants [5]. The local patterns are fine in granularity and dense, however, are relatively low in determinability and sensitive to deformations. The ROI-based method mainly refers to recognition of whole finger ROIs based on machine learning algorithms. Typical methods are recognition based on Linear Discriminant Analysis (LDA), Principal Component Analysis (PCA) and Convolutional Neural Networks (CNNs) [6]. This kind of method can extract features automatically, but is sensitive to image quality and deformations. Moreover, additional images are required to train the transformation matrix, which are not practical is real applications. The vessel-based method is based on the vasculature structures spread in the images, thus the vessel segmentation is prerequisite. Due to the low contrast and obscure image quality, the vessels segmented may be problematic and affect the following recognition [7]. Hence, the vessel segmentation methods are stressed and researched attentively by the researchers. However, we think the vessel-based method still needs further improvements [8]. The keypoint-based method is mainly based on descriptors extracted from structurally meaningful or geometrically explicable positions, such as cross or end points of vessels and extreme points. Comparing to other methods, the advantages of the keypoint-based method can be summarized as follows: (a) High distinctiveness, the descriptors extracted in keypoint-based method are large in scope and relatively high in discriminability. (b) Deformation-tolerance, the descriptors are usually tolerant to rotation and translations, etc., which are harmful to other methods. (c) Coarse granularity and small templates, the keypoints are localized in typical positions, thus are coarse and small in templates, which can save storage space and matching time. (d) Avoidance of vessel segmentation, keypoints can be automatically extracted, thus avoid the error propagation of the vessel segmentation. (e) Relevance to vessel structures, the distribution of the keypoints is in accordance with the vessel topologies, hence their matching results can be further refined in the guidance of the position relationships.

However, the keypoint-based method is not thoroughly explored, which may be caused by the following reasons: (a) affected by the image quality, the quantity and stability of the keypoint descriptors are always questionable. (b) the descriptors are generally artificially-designed, which are not pertinent in representativeness. (c) the similarity of main vessel can bring inter-class resemblances, which may introduce false pairings. To deal with the above-mentioned problems, we learn the keypoints using Fully Convolutional Neural Networks (FCNNs). A conventional framework called SuperPoint is introduced to finger vein recognition, which automatically learn the keypoint descriptors to improve intra-class similarities and suppress inter-class resemblances.

The proposed method is composed of three main stages. First, the finger vein images is pre-processed by illumination inhomogeneity correction, bias removal and scale adjusting. Then, the keypoints are localized and described by the FCNNs-based SuperPoint model. Finally, the descriptors are matched with a bilateral matching strategy. Extensive experiments have been conducted on the HKPU and SDU-MLA databases, the EERs are 0.0025 and 0.0138, respectively, which demonstrate the effectiveness of the proposed method. We also provide the FRRs-at-0-FAR, which are usually adopted in commercial scenarios. The values are 0.0218 and 0.0890, respectively, which also present the applicability of the proposed method in real applications.

Our method have the following contributions. First, a finger vein recognition framework based on automatically learned keypoints is designed, which achieves high performance and is applicable in high security applications. Second, the learning strategy is introduced to the keypoint-based finger vein recognition, which is novel and provides new directions in improving finger recognition performance. Finally, effective pre-processing strategies are introduced to deal with the influences brought by the image quality and deformations, etc.

The remaining of this paper is organized as follows. Section 2 presents the proposed method. Section 3 demonstrates the experimental results and its effectiveness. This paper concludes with a discussion of future research consideration in Sect. 4.

2   Proposed Method

The proposed finger vein recognition is a systematic framework, which consists of three main stages including pre-processing, feature extraction, matching and false pairing removal. In this part, each stage is elaborated to make our method reproducible.

2.1   Pre-processing

The finger vein images suffer from severe image quality problems, such as low intensity contrast and blurry vessel margin, etc, which can be seen in Fig. 1a. These quality problems make the finger vein images different from the natural ones and limit the recognition performance. To improve the image quality, illumination inhomogeneity correction, noise removal and scale adjusting are applied.

In this paper, an image I is defined as Eq. (1):

$$I = b \cdot Img + n \tag{1}$$

here, Img represents the original 'pure' image. b denotes the additive or multiplicative noise, and n is defined as the random noise. According to this model, we take b as additive model and estimate it using a Gaussian-like convolution with the template t of $ones(11, 11)$ [9] (Fig. 1b), thus the image after bias removal can be defined as Eq. (2) (Fig. 1c):

$$rimg = I - conv2(I, t) \tag{2}$$

then, the noise is restrained by the average filtering of template size 3×3. Finally, the image is enhanced by histogram equalization resized to 192×128 by nearest interpolation, which can be seen in Fig. 1(d). Though the pre-processing strategy seems artificial, it is highly effective in promoting the performance in the proposed keypoint-based recognition. The reason might be the acquiring of the perfect images with distinct, smooth and precise location edges. The effectiveness is graphically illustrated in Fig. 2.

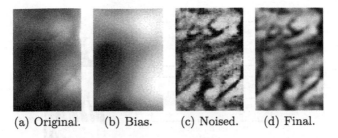

(a) Original.   (b) Bias.   (c) Noised.   (d) Final.

Fig. 1. Demo images in the pre-processing procedure. (a) The ROI extracted from original finger vein iamges; (b) The estimated bias; (c) Image after bias removal; (d) The final image after pre-processing.

(a) Before pre-processing.   (b) After pre-processing.

Fig. 2. Matching comparison before and after pre-processing. There is only 1 keypoint matching pair in the genuine matching (a), while the number is boosted to 31 in the same matching after pre-processing.

2.2 Keypoint Extraction and Description

In order to provide robust features for the finger vein image description, we involve the automatically learned keypoint extracted by Superpoint network [10], which demonstrates good performance for integrating robust structural information during keypoint detection. The Superpoint model is a FCNN framework that consists of keypoint localization and description, which can be seen in Fig. 3.

In the whole framework, the single encoder layer is shared to reduce the dimensionality of the image, which include a series of convolutional layers, max-pooling layers, rectified linear units (ReLUs) for activation and batch normalization (BN) to get a informative feature map. Through three max-pooling layers, the image with size $W \times H$ is transformed to image sized $W_c \times H_c$ with $W_c = W/8, H_c = H/8$. Hence, the encoder maps the input image I to an intermediate tensor with smaller spatial dimension and greater channel depth.

The decoders are keypoint decoder for keypoint localization and descriptor decoder for keypoint depiction. The keypoint decoder transform the input of size $W_c \times H_c \times 65$, which corresponds to local, non-overlapping 8×8 grid regions of pixels and an extra "pointness" channel. After a channel-wise softmax, the grid regions are reshaped to size of $W \times H$. The descriptor decoder computes

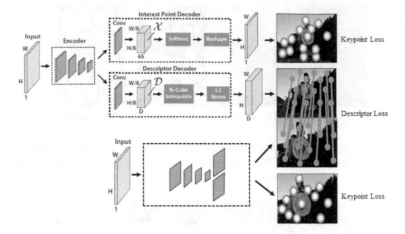

Fig. 3. The flowchart of the SuperoPoint model.

the input of size $W_c \times H_c \times 256$ and outputs a tensor sized $W \times H \times 256$. A model similar to Universal Correspondence Network(UCN) [3] is first utilized to output a semi-dense grid of descriptors, then Bicubic interpolation of the descriptors is performed, and a dense map of L_2-normalized fixed length descriptors is obtained.

The final loss is the weighted sum of keypoint detector and descriptor, the details can be referred in literature [1]. In this paper, the model is not re-trained or fine-tuned in limits of the lack of finger vein samples and ground truths. Hence, we adopt the pre-trained Superpoint model in the proposed method with careful pre- and post-processing strategies. The parameters in this model are all remained unchanged.

2.3 Matching

Two images are matched according to the similarity of descriptors calculated by the Euclidian distances. Descriptors a and b from the two images A and B are matched successfully if and only if the scores of a and b is *threshold* times higher than a with other descriptors in image B and the scores of b and a is *threshold* times higher than b with other descriptors in image A. The final matching score is defined as the number of matching pairs.

3 Experimental Results

In this section, the experimental databases and settings are first introduced. Then, the experimental results in verification and identification modes are presented with parameters and each functional components analyzed. The comparison with state-of-the-art methods is also provided.

Table 1. Component analysis on the PolyU and SDU-MLA database.

Method	HKPU Database			SDUMLA database		
	EER	FRR-at-0-FAR	RR	EER	FRR-at-0-FAR	RR
No pre-processing	0.0970	0.8397	0.6793	0.0998	0.8842	0.6787
Proposed method	0.0025	0.0218	0.9983	0.0138	0.0890	0.9792

3.1 Experimental Databases

The proposed method is evaluated on the HKPU and SDU-MLA databases, respectively. The first session of the HKPU database [11] is utilized in this paper, which includes 1,872 ($156 \times 2 \times 6$) images, and is captured from the index and middle fingers from the left hand of 156 volunteers, with each finger contributing 6 images. The second session is not conventionally adopted in literature, because not all the volunteers showed up in this session. The images in this database are various in intra-class deformations due to the uncontrolled capturing. Thus, the ROI is correspondingly segmented using methods segmented in literature [12]. The SDU-MLA database [13] consists of 3,816 ($106 \times 6 \times 6$) images, which are captured from 106 volunteers. Each of the volunteers contributes the index, middle and ring fingers of both hands, with 6 images of each finger. Images in this database are more complex in deformations and quality, we extract the ROI using a different method from literature [14].

3.2 Evaluation Protocols

The proposed method is tested in both the verification and identification modes. In the verification mode, the genuine and imposter finger vein images are fully matched. Consequently, there are $312 \times C_6^2$ genuine matchings and $312 \times 6 \times 311 \times 6/2$ imposter matchings on the HKPU database, $636 \times C_6^2$ genuine matchings and $636 \times 6 \times 635 \times 6/2$ imposter matchings on the SDU-MLA database, respectively. According to the score distribution, the Equal Error Rate (EER), False Reject Rate (FRR) at zero False Accept Rate (FAR) (FRR-at-0-FAR) are provided. In the identification mode, the real identity authentication is simulated, i.e., to find the finger of which each image belongs to. In the experiment, each finger vein images is utilized as the probe, then a template is randomly selected from the remaining ones. Hence, there are 312×6 probes and $312 \times 6 \times 312$ matcings on the HKPU database, 636×6 probes and $636 \times 6 \times 636$ matchings on the SDU-MLA database. The rank-1 recognition rate is mainly tested, the average rank-1 recognition rate of ten repeated experiments is provided. The Receiver Operating Characteristic (ROC) is also illustrated to further depict the performance.

3.3 Performance Analysis

In this part, the performance of the proposed method is first analyzed in comparison to recognition without pre-processings. The threshold in matching is also

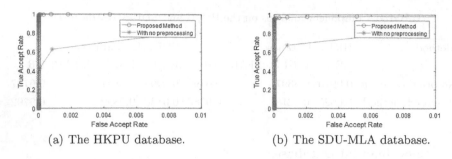

(a) The HKPU database.   (b) The SDU-MLA database.

Fig. 4. ROC curves for the two databases.

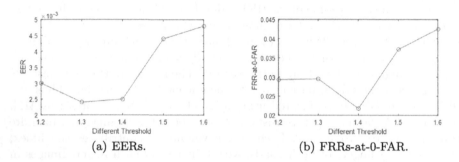

(a) EERs.   (b) FRRs-at-0-FAR.

Fig. 5. Analysis of threshold in matching on the HKPU database.

illustrated. The EERs, FRRs-at-0-FAR and Recognition Rates (RRs) on the HKPU and SDU-MLA databases are tabulated in Table 1, with the ROC curves illustrated in Fig. 4. From the results, we can figure out that the EERs on the two databases are 0.0025 and 0.0138, respectively and the FRRs-at-0-FAR of the proposed method are 0.0218 and 0.0890, respectively. The results demonstrate the effectiveness of the proposed method, the FRRs-at-0-FAR also show the applicability of our method in real applications. The average RRs of ten repeated experiments on the two databases are also provided, which are 99.83% and 97.92% with variances of $\pm5.3584e7$ and $\pm3.5588e6$, respectively. The method with no pre-processing is compared, the EERs are 0.0970 and 0.0998, the FRRs-at-0-FAR are 0.8397 and 0.08842, the average RRs are $0.6397(\pm6.4177e5)$ and $0.6787(\pm2.6026e5)$, respectively. It is obvious that the pre-processing strategies are beneficial and effective.

The parameter of threshold in matching is tested on the HKPU database, the results of EERs and FRRs-at-0-FAR is provided in Fig. 5. The thresholds are from 1.2 to 1.6 with step of 0.1, from the results, we can figure out that the proposed method is stable, we take the threshold of 1.4 in compromise of the two evaluation criterions.

We also compare the proposed method with typical pre-processings adopted in keypoint-based methods on the HKPU database, the results are tabulated in Table 2. The pre-processing techniques includes histogram equalization [15],

Table 2. The performance comparison with typical pre-processing techniques on the HKPU database.

Method	EER	FRR-at-0-FAR
Histogram equalization [15]	0.0623	0.8579
Intensity correction [9]	0.0583	0.8393
Vessel segmentaion [16]	0.0094	0.1951
Chief curvature extraction [17]	0.0418	0.5021
Intensity correction [4]	0.0429	0.9848
Proposed method	0.0025	0.0218

Table 3. The performance comparison with the keypoint-based methods on the HKPU and SDU-MLA database.

Method	HKPU database		SDU-MLA database	
	EER	FRR-at-0-FAR	EER	FRR-at-0-FAR
Pang et al. [15]	0.1081	0.9274	0.1473	0.9340
Kim et al. [9]	0.0105	0.1079	0.0532	0.2853
Peng et al. [16]	0.0235	0.4359	0.0624	0.5259
Matsuda et al. [17]	0.0379	0.7600	0.0715	0.4785
Liu et al. [2]	0.0501	0.5199	–	–
Meng et al. [4]	0.0114	0.1169	0.0585	0.2875
Proposed Method	0.0025	0.0218	0.0138	0.0890

- the results are not provided in the original paper.

bias removal-based intensity correction [4,9], vessel segmentation [16] and chief curvature extraction [17]. Here, the vessel segmentation method is adopted from our previous work of retinal vasculature segmentation [18]. From Table 2, we can figure out that all the pre-processing strategies are helpful in improving the recogniton performance. The proposed method is superior than other methods, especial for the evaluation criterion of FRR-at-0-FAR. The vessel segmentation based pre-processing is second best, with EER and FRR-at-0-FAR of 0.0094 and 0.1951, it might be brought by the enhancement of the vessel edges.

3.4   Comparison with State-of-the-Art Keypoint-Based Methods

In this part, we compared the proposed method with the existing keypoint-based methods, which consists of the Scale Invariant Feature Transform (SIFT) descriptor-based method and its variants [4,9,15,16], methods based on the minutiae matching [2] and the deformation-tolerant-based feature point matching (DT-FPM) [17], the results are tabulated in Table 3. From the table, one can figure out that the minutiae of cross overs and end points are unsatisfactory with the EER of 0.0501 and FRR-at-0-FAR of 0.5199, respectively. It may caused by the segmentation errors of the vessels. The artificially designed keypoints of

SIFT and DT-FPM also perform unsatisfactory with the EERs of 0.1081 and 0.0379, FRRs-at-0-FAR of 0.9274 and 0.7600 on the HKPU database, EERs of 0.1473 and 0.0715, FRRs-at-0-FAR of 0.9340 and 0.4785 on the SDU-MLA database, respectively, due to the image quality problem. From the work of Kim et al., Peng et al., and Meng et al., we can figure out that the preprocessings are effective to improve the keypoint-based recognition performance. The proposed method is designed utilizing the learning-based keypoints and typical prepro-cessing strategies are proposed, thus the performance is acceptable with EER and FRR-at-0-FAR of 0.0025 and 0.0218 on the HKPU database, 0.0138 and 0.0890 on the SDU-MLA database, respectively.

4 Conclusion and Discussion

Our method introduce automatically learned keypoints into finger vein recog-nition, a systematic recognition framework based on the FCN-based model of SuperPoint is proposed. Our method is demonstrated to be effective with EERs of 0.0025 and 0.0138 on the HKPU and SDU-MLA databases, respectively. In the keypoint-based recognition, unsatisfactory image quality is a big challenge which limits the performance. A targeted pre-processing is designed for vessel enhancement and scale adjusting. The results tabulated in Table demonstrates the effectiveness of the operations. There are also defects in our work, for exam-ple, the parameters are not carefully fine-tuned for better performances. What's more, typical keypoint positions should not be confined in corner points, hence our next work will focus on multiple keypoints learning.

Acknowledgments. This work is supported by the Natural Science Foundation of China under Grant Nos. 61801263 and 61976123, Taishan Young Scholars Program of Shandong Province and the Key Development Program for Basic Research of Shandong Province (ZR2020ZD44).

References

1. Jain, A.K., Ross, A., Prabhakar, S.: An introduction to biometric recognition. IEEE Trans. Circuits Syst. Video Technol. **14**(1), 4–20 (2004)
2. Liu, F., Yang, G., Yin, Y., Wang, S.: Singular value decomposition based minutiae matching method for finger vein recognition. Neurocomputing **145**, 75–89 (2014)
3. Shaheed, K., Mao, A., Qureshi, I., Kumar, M., Hussain, S., Zhang, X.: Recent advancements in finger vein recognition technology: methodology, challenges and opportunities. Inf. Fusion **79**, 84–109 (2022)
4. Meng, X., Xi, X., Yang, L., Yin, Y.: Finger vein recognition based on intensity inhomogeneity correction and scale invarint feature transform. J. Nanjing Univ. Natrual Sci. **54**(1), 1–10 (2018)
5. Lu, Y., Xie, S., Wu, S.: Exploring competitive features using deep convolutional neural network for finger vein recognition. IEEE Access **7**, 35113–35123 (2019)
6. Zeng, J., et al.: Finger vein verification algorithm based on fully convolutional neural network and conditional random field. IEEE Access **8**, 65402–65419 (2020)

7. Yang, L., Yang, G., Yin, Y., Xi, X.: Finger vein recognition with anatomy structure analysis. IEEE Trans. Circuits Syst. Video Technol. **28**(8), 1892–1905 (2017)
8. Yang, W., Hui, C., Chen, Z., Xue, J.-H., Liao, Q.: FV-GAN: finger vein representation using generative adversarial networks. IEEE Trans. Inf. Forensics Secur. **14**(9), 2512–2524 (2019)
9. Kim, H.-G., Lee, E.J., Yoon, G.-J., Yang, S.-D., Lee, E.C., Yoon, S.M.: Illumination normalization for SIFT Based finger vein authentication. In: Bebis, G., et al. (eds.) ISVC 2012. LNCS, vol. 7432, pp. 21–30. Springer, Heidelberg (2012). https://doi.org/10.1007/978-3-642-33191-6_3
10. DeTone, D., Malisiewicz, T., Rabinovich, A.: Superpoint: self-supervised interest point detection and description. In: Proceedings of the IEEE Conference on Computer Vision and Pattern Recognition Workshops, pp. 224–236 (2018)
11. Kumar, A., Zhou, Y.: Human identification using finger images. IEEE Trans. Image Process. **21**(4), 2228–2244 (2011)
12. Meng, X., Xi, X., Yang, G., Yin, Y.: Finger vein recognition based on deformation information. Sci. China Inf. Sci. **61**(5), 1–15 (2018)
13. Yin, Y., Liu, L., Sun, X.: SDUMLA-HMT: a multimodal biometric database. In: Sun, Z., Lai, J., Chen, X., Tan, T. (eds.) CCBR 2011. LNCS, vol. 7098, pp. 260–268. Springer, Heidelberg (2011). https://doi.org/10.1007/978-3-642-25449-9_33
14. Meng, X., Yang, G., Yin, Y., Xiao, R.: Finger vein recognition based on local directional code. Sensors **12**(11), 14937–14952 (2012)
15. Pang, S., Yin, Y., Yang, G., Li, Y.: Rotation invariant finger vein recognition. In: Zheng, W.-S., Sun, Z., Wang, Y., Chen, X., Yuen, P.C., Lai, J. (eds.) CCBR 2012. LNCS, vol. 7701, pp. 151–156. Springer, Heidelberg (2012). https://doi.org/10.1007/978-3-642-35136-5_19
16. Peng, J., Wang, N., Abd El-Latif, A.A., Li, Q., Niu, X., Finger-vein verification using Gabor filter and sift feature matching. In: Eighth International Conference on Intelligent Information Hiding and Multimedia Signal Processing, vol. 2012, pp. 45–48. IEEE (2012)
17. Matsuda, Y., Miura, N., Nagasaka, A., Kiyomizu, H., Miyatake, T.: Finger-vein authentication based on deformation-tolerant feature-point matching. Mach. Vis. Appl. **27**(2), 237–250 (2016)
18. Meng, X., Yin, Y., Yang, G., Han, Z., Yan, X.: A framework for retinal vasculature segmentation based on matched filters. Biomed. Eng. Online **14**(1), 1–20 (2015)

TransFinger: Transformer Based Finger Tri-modal Biometrics

Zhuolin Zhao[1,2], Haigang Zhang[1(✉)], Zhibin Chen[2], and Jinfeng Yang[1]

[1] Institute of Applied Artificial Intelligence of the Guangdong-Hong Kong-Macao Greater Bay Area, Shenzhen Polytechnic, Shenzhen, Guangdong, China
zhg2018@sina.com

[2] School of Electronic and Information Engineering, University of Science and Technology Liaoning, Anshan, Liaoning, China

Abstract. Finger is a very competent biometric carrier, which contains many valuable biometric features (fingerprint, finger-vein and finger-knuckle-print). Exploring multi-modal biometric fusion recognition of fingers is very meaningful for improving the security and stability of finger feature expression. Due to the differences in the expression of different modal features, the interaction mode and fusion strategy between different modalities are the key to finger multi-modal biometrics. Recently, we note that Transformer exhibits strong performance in natural language processing and computer vision. In this paper, a Transformer based finger tri-modal fusion and recognition framework, termed TransFinger, is proposed, where Transformer attention is employed to calculate the interaction response among the three modalities of the finger, and from this, the channel and spatial attentions of different modalities are generated. To the best of our knowledge, it is the first to apply Transformer attention to implement the fusion and recognition of finger biometrics. At the same time, with only minor changes, the TransFinger framework has good generalization for the number of fused modalities. Simulation results have demonstrated the effectiveness of the proposed finger tri-modal fusion and recognition framework.

Keywords: Finger biometrics · Multi-modal fusion · Transformer

1 Introduction

Fingers contain rich biological modalities, and the uni-modal features have played an important role in identity identification for a long time [1]. Studies in recent years have shown that, except of fingerprint(FP), the finger-vein(FV) and

This work was supported by the Shenzhen Science and Technology Program (No. RCBS20200714114940262), National Natural Science Foundation of China (No. 61806208 and 62076166).

finger-knuckle-print(FKP) also have outstanding identity identification capabilities. Although finger uni-modal biometric recognition is widely used, it also exposes some insurmountable problems. Affected by the deficiencies of biometric features, acquisition conditions and external operating environment, the finger uni-modal biometric features can not meet the needs of high-reliability identification in practical applications in terms of universality, stability and practicality. For example, from a technical perspective, FP and FKP features are easy to forge and destroy, while FV feature is of poor quality and severely affected by noise. From a biological perspective, the FP texture of some people is too shallow to extract accurate representation information; some people's FP and FKP features are occluded and damaged due to some diseases of the finger epidermis, such as ringworm. The above embarrassing disadvantages of finger uni-modal features have promoted the development of finger multi-modal features recognition technology [2].

FP is located on the palmar end of the finger, FV inside the finger, FKP on the back side of finger joint, which are close to each other but do not interfere with each other, as shown in Fig. 1. In addition, FP, FV and FKP modal features all belong to the "linetype" structure and are similar in feature expression. Such advantages make it reasonable and portable to implement the finger-based multi-modal biometric fusion and recognition. Our research team has experienced long-term exploration in the fusion recognition of finger trimodal features. Using granular computing as a methodology, we build the basic fusion framework of finger trimodalities [3,4]. However, granular computing based method requires large storage space and consumes a lot of computing resources, which is disadvantageous for the real applications of the finger biometric fusion recognition model. Using coding strategy to fusion finger trimodalities is another work [5], where the coding method often plays a decisive role. However, coding results are highly targeted and prone to failure.

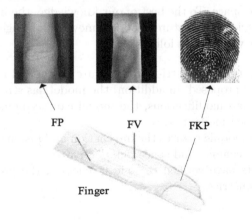

Fig. 1. Finger tri-modal biometric features

Deep learning technologies represented by convolutional neural networks (CNN) [6] have been widely developed, and they have shown better performance than traditional methods in the fields of pattern recognition, object detection, and semantic segmentation. There are some methods using CNN as the feature backbone for tri-modal feature fusion of fingers [2,7]. The common practice is to implement the tri-modal feature aggregation of fingers in the middle layer of CNN feature extraction, and then use the subsequent feature extractor to achieve final recognition. Graph Convolutional Neural Networks [8] show strong performance when dealing with non-Euclidean data. By constructing the feature subgraphs of the three modalities of the finger and merging them into the full graph of the finger features, the fusion and recognition of the three modal features of the finger will be converted into the reconstruction relationship between the subgraph and the full graph [9]. No matter it is a CNN-based or GCN-based finger trimodal fusion method, feature alignment and fusion strategy are the key factors that must be considered.

Unlike the CNN feature extraction structure, the Vision Transformer (ViT) completely relies on the attention mechanism to solve computer vision problems [10]. In the ViT algorithm, the entire image is divided into small image blocks, and then the linear embedding sequence of these small image blocks is sent to the network as the input of the Transformer [11], and then the training of image classification is performed by means of supervised learning. The success of Transformer in computer vision motivates us to apply it to finger trimodal feature fusion. Different from the self-attention mechanism in ViT, we adopt Transformer attention to realize the interactive response between different finger biometric modalities. In this paper, a Transformer based finger tri-modal features fusion and recognition framework, termed TransFinger, is proposed. The main feature fusion module (TransFusion) consists of Transformer Channel Attention (TCA) and Transformer Spatial Attention (TSA), where TCA realizes attention response in the dimension of visual feature channel of three modalities of finger, while TSA determines the influence relationship of different modalities in the dimension of feature space. To the best of our knowledge, there are no published Transformer-based tri-modal feature fusion framework for fingers. And the main contributions of our work are as follows:

- A general Transformer based tri-modal feature fusion and recognition framework for fingers is proposed. In addition, the model has strong generalization and with only small modifications, the model can accommodate changes in the number of fused modalities.
- The TransFusion module realizes the interaction and fusion of different modal features from the channel and space perspectives.
- Simulation results have verified the effectiveness of the proposed finger tri-modal fusion biometrics.

2   Related Work

2.1   Finger Unimodal Biometrics

FP recognition has a long history of development and tends to mature. The FP image acquisition device is relatively simple and stable, which makes it has strong practicality. FP recognition technology can be roughly classified into three categories, feature engineering based approach [1,12], code based approach[5,13] and the deep learning based method [2,14]. Different from the FP feature, the FV is located in the subcutaneous tissue of the finger, which makes it difficult to be worn out and polluted. The FV features have strong stability and discrimination, and are less affected by external influences. The method of FV collection is transmission imaging of Near-infrared source. In addition, the FV belongs to living characteristics, which makes it is not easy to be forged. We divide the FV recognition methods into two categories, the traditional recognition method [15,16] and the deep learning based methods [17]. The FKP features are located on the back surface around the finger joint, which has rich texture information and high discriminability. The knuckle pattern is not easy to wear and is an ideal biometric feature. The works of Woodard and Flynn validated the uniqueness of the FKP pattern and laid the foundation for the development of FKP recognition technology [18].

2.2   Finger Multi-modal Biometrics

There are four levels of fusion in a multimodal biometric system, pixel level, feature level, matching score level and decision level [2]. The fusion at the pixel level, also called as sensor fusion, refers to direct fusion of multi-modal images acquired by sensors. Since large differences exist between different modal images in content, noise, etc., it is unstable and infeasible to make fusion for the tri-modal biometrics of fingers at pixel level. The fusion at matching level and decision level are respectively based on the matching results and the recognition results of the uni-modal biometric features. Although these strategies are easy to implement on the system, there are many inherent defects, such as strong algorithm dependence, low efficiency and limited recognition performance. More critically, the fusion at matching layer or decision layer ignores the discriminating power of multi-modal biometrics. Therefore, such fusion strategy is not optimal in nature. The fusion at feature level aims to extract more accurate feature information by performing a series of processing on the biometric images, which is a relatively reasonable choice compared with other fusion strategies [4,19]. As mentioned above, finger multi-modal fusion recognition on the feature layer can be divided into artificial feature-based fusion [3,5], CNN-based fusion [2,7], and GCN-based fusion [9,19].

3   Transformer Based Fusion and Recognition Framework

In this section, we present the proposed Transformer based feature fusion framework, named TransFinger. Figure 2 shows the TransFinger framework for finger

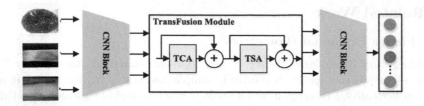

Fig. 2. TransFinger framework. TCA represents the Transformer Channel Attention, while TSA is the Transformer Spatial Attention.

tri-modal features fusion and recognition. We implement finger tri-modal feature extraction using three independent CNN branches. Then, the extracted features are fed to the Transformer-based fusion module (TransFusion) to realize the interactive response of different modal features. It can be obtained that

$$f(FP), f(FV), f(FKP) = \Theta(Conv_1(FP), Conv_2(FV), Conv_3(FKP)) \tag{1}$$

where $Conv_i(\cdot)$, $i = 1, 2, 3$, represents the convolutional feature extraction blocks, $\Theta(\cdot)$ represents the TransFusion module, and f represents the tri-modal features after fusion. We use the concatenation operation to achieve tri-modal feature aggregation of fingers, and then, through another convolution feature extraction and output decision function, the feature recognition results can be obtained as

$$s = \sigma(Conv(\circledast(f(FP), f(FV), f(FKP)))) \tag{2}$$

where $\circledast(\cdot)$ is the concatenation operation, and $\sigma(\cdot)$ represents the Softmax activation function. The following is a detailed introduction to the TransFusion module.

3.1 Transformer Attention

The Vision Transformer (ViT) [10] implements the global interaction among image patches in a self-attention manner. Generally, For the features x in vector form with dimension of $h \times s$, it is first to create the query-key-value triplets through corresponding feature maps, such that

$$q = x \cdot W^q, \quad k = x \cdot W^k, \quad v = x \cdot W^v \tag{3}$$

where h and s represent the number and dimension of features x respectively, and W^q, W^k and W^v are the corresponding learnable map matrices with dimension of $s \times p$. Then the query vectors q is used to find its correlation with the key features k, while the value embedding holds the status of the current form of the input feature. The attention-based interaction output x' can be obtained as

$$x' = \sigma \left(\frac{qk^T}{\sqrt{d^k}} \right) v \tag{4}$$

where d^k represents the dimension of q, and $d^k = p$.

In addition, the Multi-Head Attention (MHA) operation can better improve the model performance, where the input visual features are divided into low-dimensional feature vectors by equal scale, and finally the feature reconstruction is realized by the oncatenation operation, such that

$$x' = \circledast \left(\sigma \left(\frac{q_i k_i^T}{\sqrt{d_i^k}} \right) v_i \right), i = 1, 2, \cdots, n \tag{5}$$

where n is equal to the number of self-attention heads. q_i, k_i and v_i are calculated by the corresponding low-dimensional map matrices W_i with dimensional of $h \times (s/n)$. Meanwhile, $d_i^k = s/n$.

3.2 TransFusion

We hope to explore the interactive responses between different modalities with the help of attention mechanism to achieve deep fusion of multi-modal features of fingers. TransFusion consists of two parts, in which the Transformer Channel Attention (TCA) refers to obtain the channel attentions, and the Transformer Spatial Attention (TSA) is applied to calculate the spatial attentions.

After the first convolutional feature extraction blocks, we can obtain the tri-modal feature expression of the finger, F_{fp}, F_{fv} and F_{fkp}. The dimension of the feature is marked as $[C, H, W]$, where C is the channel number and (H, W) represents the dimension of single channel feature. In TCA, combining the $MaxPool$ and $AvgPool$ operations, we can obtain the high-level vector-wise representation for finger tri-modalities with dimension of $2C \times 1$. After the feature mapping operation (MAP), the feature dimension is converted to the same dimension as the number of channels ($C \times 1$). For the calculation of channel attentions for FP features, k, q and v can be obtained as

$$\begin{aligned} F'_{fp} = g\left(F_{fp}\right), F'_{fv} = g\left(F_{fv}\right), F'_{fkp} = g\left(F_{fkp}\right) \\ v = k = F'_{fp}, \quad q_1 = F'_{fv}, \quad q_2 = F'_{fkp} \end{aligned} \tag{6}$$

where $g(\cdot)$ represents the feature dimension transformation operation mentioned above.

Then the channel attentions of FP features can be obtained as

$$v_{fp} = s \left[s\left(\frac{q_1 k^T}{\sqrt{d_k}} \right) + s\left(\frac{q_2 k^T}{\sqrt{d_k}} \right) \right] v \tag{7}$$

where $s(\cdot)$ represents the $Sigmoid$ function. Different from the original Transformer attention, the $Softmax$ activation function is replaced with $Sigmoid$ function in TCA module. In addition, in order to ensure the dominance of the corresponding finger unimodal features, and encourage the network to selectively focus on adding complimentary information to the "source" features, a residual branch is added as shown in Fig. 2. Then we can get the attention interaction features for FP modality as

$$TCA\,(fp) = F_{fp} + g'\,(v_{fp}) \tag{8}$$

where $g'\,(\cdot)$ is the inverse operation of $g\,(\cdot)$.

Similarly, we can also obtain the feature outputs for F_{fv} and F_{fkp} after TCA responses. At the same time, the multi-head attention strategy can also be considered when calculating the attention interaction features (Fig. 3).

TSA computes transformer attention from the spatial perspective. Through the addition operation of the channel dimension, we can express the finger uni-modal features with a single channel with dimension of $H \times W$. The *Reshape* operation converts the channel features to vector form with dimension of $HW \times 1$. The calculation of spatial attentions in TSA are very similar to TCA, expect that another *Reshape* operation is applied to convert the vector features to channel features. In addition, TSA also considers residual operations. Specifically we can get the output features after TransFusion module for FP modality as

$$F_{fp} = TSA\,(TCA\,(fp)) + TCA\,(fp) \tag{9}$$

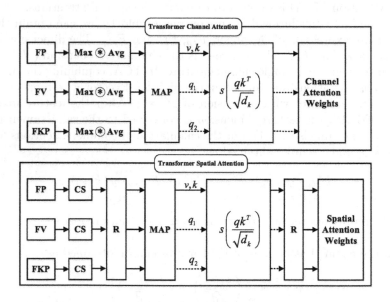

Fig. 3. TransFusion module. **MAP** represents the dimension conversion operation, **CS** represents the channel sum operation, and **R** represents the reshape operation.

4   Simulation Results

In this section, we present the simulation results for the proposed transformer based finger tri-modal fusion and recognition framework. The applied finger trimodal database is constructed from 585 fingers. For one finger, there are 10 FP, FV and FKP images respectively, and the total number of the images in the database is 17550. The training set, validation set, and test set are allovated as the ratio of 8:1:1. The experiments are performed on the Pytorch architecture of the Ubuntu 16.04 system equipped with the A100-SXM4-40G GPU. ResNet50 is applied as the feature extraction backbone, while the TransFusion module is inserted between the second and third residual blocks. The batchsize is set to 128, and the learning rate is set to 0.0001. We train the TransFinger model based on Adam optimizer within 1000 epochs.

We compare the performance of the proposed TransFinger framework with other feature fusion methods for finger tri-modal biometrics. The representative of the traditional feature fusion algorithm, the local coding algorithm [5] participates in the performance comparison. CNN based fusion method [2] directly concatenates the trimodal features together. In addition, the graph based fusion methods are also taken into consideration. Connection fusion uses the original node sequence to fuse graphs [9]. Competitive fusion refers to setting a competitive strategy to achieve node feature ranking, thereby guiding the matching of corresponding nodes. In contrast, The eigenvector centrality fusion considers the structural information of the graph to achieve node alignment [9]. In addition, Crystal fusion [19] integrates the tri-modal features of the finger from the input layer, and Score fusion [20] realizes the weighted output of decision information at the decision layer.

We use recognition accuracy (ACC) and equal error rate (EER) as evaluation metrics. Table 1 presents the comparison results. The TransFinger framework achieves the highest recognition accuracy (99.7%) and the smallest EER (0.094×10^{-2}). The recognition time of a single sample is also shown in Table 1. Although the fastest recognition speed is not achieved, the recognition efficiency of TransFinger framework can meet the needs of real-time applications.

Table 1. Comparison results for finger tri-modal fusion and recognition.

Method	ACC (%)	EER (%)	Times (ms)
Local Coding [5]	99.0	0.201	42.5
CNN [2]	98.9	0.289	50.2
Connection_Fusion [9]	98.3	0.300	59.3
Score_Fusion [20]	96.4	0.394	49.7
Crystal_Fusion [19]	96.1	0.414	**37.4**
Competitive_Fusion [9]	99.3	0.186	51.3
Eigenvector_Fusion [9]	99.6	0.167	77.3
TransFinger	**99.7**	**0.094**	53.6

Additionally, TransFinger is suitable for bi-modal fusion and recognition of finger biometrics after minor modifications. Taking the fusion of FP and FV features as examples, the channel attention weights of FP features only depend on the attentional interaction of FP and FV features, that is $v_{fp} = s\left(qk^T/\sqrt{d_k}\right)v$. Table 2 presents the simulation results for finger bi-modal feature fusion and recognition. On the one hand, due to the lack of the assistance of one modal feature, the recognition accuracy and equal error rate of the bi-modal fusion and recognition of the finger are both reduced. On the other hand, the TransFinger framework proposed in this paper still performs the best. Besides, among the finger tri-modal features, the recognition based on the vein feature tends to outperform the other two modalities. This conclusion has been verified in several works [2,9,16]. Table 2 also shows the same results. Finger bi-modal recognition accuracy involving FV features is higher than the fusion recognition of FP and FKP features.

Table 2. Simulation results for finger bi-modal fusion and recognition, where P, V and K represent FP, FV and FKP features respectively.

Method	ACC (%)			EER (%)		
	P+V	V+K	P+K	P+V	V+K	P+K
Local Coding [5]	98.5	98.6	98.2	0.210	0.211	0.218
CNN [2]	98.1	98.0	97.8	0.301	0.302	0.312
Connection_Fusion [2]	97.6	97.7	97.2	0.311	0.311	0.321
Score_Fusion [20]	96.0	96.0	95.8	0.404	0.408	0.414
Crystal_Fusion [19]	95.3	95.2	95.0	0.524	0.528	0.536
Competitive_Fusion [9]	98.4	98.3	98.1	0.254	0.259	0.268
Eigenvector_Fusion [9]	99.0	98.8	98.2	0.256	0.261	0.278
TransFinger	**99.2**	**99.2**	**99.0**	**0.188**	**0.198**	**0.205**

5   Conclusion

In this paper, we propose a Transformer-based framework, termed TransFinger, for tri-modal fusion and recognition of fingers, which is the first work to apply Transformer attention to finger biometric fusion. The TransFusion module is applied to realize the attention interaction and feature fusion of tri-modal features of fingers, which includes channel attention (TCA) and spatial attention (TSA). The simulation experiments have verified the effectiveness of the TransFinger framework. It is worth mentioning that, with only minor changes, TransFinger can realize the bi-modal fusion recognition of fingers. In future work, we will continue to explore feature fusion strategies based on Transformer attention from two aspects of fusion accuracy and fusion efficiency.

References

1. Zhao, Q., Zhang, L., Zhang, D., et al.: Adaptive pore model for fingerprint pore extraction. In: 2008 19th International Conference on Pattern Recognition, pp. 1–4. IEEE (2008)
2. Wang, L., Zhang, H., Yang, J.: Finger multimodal features fusion and recognition based on CNN. In: 2019 IEEE Symposium Series on Computational Intelligence (SSCI), pp. 3183–3188. IEEE (2019)
3. Yang, J., Zhong, Z., Jia, G., et al.: Spatial circular granulation method based on multimodal finger feature. J. Electr. Comput. Eng. **2016**, 1–7 (2016)
4. Yang, J., Zhang, X.: Feature-level fusion of fingerprint and finger-vein for personal identification. Pattern Recogn. Lett. **33**(5), 623–628 (2012)
5. Li, S., Zhang, H., Shi, Y., et al.: Novel local coding algorithm for finger multimodal feature description and recognition. Sensors **19**(9), 2213 (2019)
6. Gu, J., Wang, Z., Kuen, J., et al.: Recent advances in convolutional neural networks. Pattern Recogn. **77**, 354–377 (2018)
7. Wen, M., Zhang, H., Yang, J.: End-to-end finger trimodal features fusion and recognition model based on CNN. In: Feng, J., Zhang, J., Liu, M., Fang, Y. (eds.) CCBR 2021. LNCS, vol. 12878, pp. 39–48. Springer, Cham (2021). https://doi.org/10.1007/978-3-030-86608-2_5
8. Zhang, S., Tong, H., Xu, J., et al.: Graph convolutional networks: a comprehensive review. Comput. Soc. Netw. **6**(1), 1–23 (2019)
9. Qu, H., Zhang, H., Yang, J., Wu, Z., He, L.: A generalized graph features fusion framework for finger biometric recognition. In: Feng, J., Zhang, J., Liu, M., Fang, Y. (eds.) CCBR 2021. LNCS, vol. 12878, pp. 267–276. Springer, Cham (2021). https://doi.org/10.1007/978-3-030-86608-2_30
10. Dosovitskiy, A., Beyer, L., Kolesnikov, A., et al.: An image is worth 16 × 16 words: transformers for image recognition at scale. arXiv preprint arXiv:2010.11929 (2020)
11. Vaswani, A., Shazeer, N., Parmar, N., et al.: Attention is all you need. In: Advances in Neural Information Processing Systems, vol. 30 (2017)
12. Kaur, M., Singh, M., Girdhar, A., et al.: Fingerprint verification system using minutiae extraction technique. World Acad. Sci. Eng. Technol. **46**, 497–502 (2008)
13. Masmoudi, A.D., Masmoudi, D.S.: Implementation of a fingerprint recognition system using LBP descriptor. J. Test. Eval. **38**(3), 369–382 (2010)
14. Zeng, F., Hu, S., Xiao, K.: Research on partial fingerprint recognition algorithm based on deep learning. Neural Comput. Applicat. **31**(9), 4789–4798 (2019)
15. Ojala, T., Pietikainen, M., Maenpaa, T.: Multiresolution gray-scale and rotation invariant texture classification with local binary patterns. IEEE Trans. Pattern Anal. Mach. Intell. **24**(7), 971–987 (2002)
16. Liu, F., Yang, G., Yin, Y., et al.: Singular value decomposition based minutiae matching method for finger vein recognition. Neurocomputing **145**, 75–89 (2014)
17. Liu, W., Li, W., Sun, L., et al.: Finger vein recognition based on deep learning. In: 2017 12th IEEE Conference on Industrial Electronics and Applications (ICIEA), pp. 205–210. IEEE (2017)
18. Woodard, D.L., Flynn, P.J.: Finger surface as a biometric identifier. Comput. Vis. Image Understand. **100**(3), 357–384 (2005)

19. Zhao, Z., Ye, Z., Yang, J., Zhang, H.: Finger crystal feature recognition based on graph convolutional network. In: Feng, J., Zhang, J., Liu, M., Fang, Y. (eds.) CCBR 2021. LNCS, vol. 12878, pp. 203–212. Springer, Cham (2021). https://doi.org/10.1007/978-3-030-86608-2_23
20. Patil, V.H., Dhole, M.R.S.S.A.: An efficient secure multimodal biometric fusion using palm print and face image. Int. J. Appl. Eng. Res. **11**(10), 7147–7150 (2016)

Face Detection, Recognition
and Tracking

A Survey of Domain Generalization-Based Face Anti-spoofing

Fangling Jiang[1], Yunfan Liu[2], Bing Liu[1], Xiaoliang Chen[3], and Qi Li[2(✉)]

[1] School of Computer Science, University of South China, Hengyang 421001, China
jfl@usc.edu.cn
[2] CRIPAC, NLPR, CASIA, Beijing 100190, China
qli@nlpr.ia.ac.cn
[3] SoundAI Technology Co., Ltd., Beijing 100190, China

Abstract. In recent years, remarkable research attention has been attracted to improve the generalization ability of face anti-spoofing methods, and domain generalization techniques have been widely exploited for adapting face anti-spoofing models to unseen testing scenarios. In this paper, we present a comprehensive survey on domain generalization-based face anti-spoofing methods. Specifically, we propose a taxonomy for existing methods and conduct a thorough review on these methods by comparing and analyzing their motivations, highlights, and common technical characteristics. Afterward, we introduce commonly used datasets and evaluation metrics, and also analyze the performance of existing methods to uncover key factors affecting the generalization performance. Finally, we conclude this survey with a forecast on promising future research directions.

Keywords: Face anti-spoofing · Domain generalizaiton · Unseen testing scenarios · Generalied feature learning

1 Introduction

With the rapidly growing application of face recognition systems in financial transaction and social security, face anti-spoofing, an important technique which aims to protect the identity verification process from presentation attacks, has been receiving increasing attention due to its theoretical significance and practical value. Most conventional face anti-spoofing methods, no matter based on hand-crafted features or spatial and temporal features learned with deep neural networks, assume that the training and testing data have identical and independent distributions (i.e., the *i.i.d.* assumption). However, this assumption does not hold in many practical applications of face anti-spoofing due to the large variation in image acquisition scenes, capturing devices, and manufacturing processes.

Intuitively, it is extremely difficult, if not impossible, to collect training data which could cover all possible variations of the potential presentation attack in real world applications, and thus the gap between the distribution of training and test data would always exist. Consequently, due to such data discrepancy, directly applying the decision boundary learned with training data to testing images, which are usually unavailable during training, would inevitably produce incorrect classification results and lead to a dramatic performance drop (see Fig. 1(a)). Therefore, improving the generalization performance on unseen testing scenarios is critical for the development of practical face anti-spoofing methods.

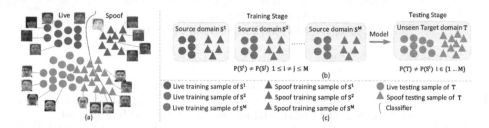

Fig. 1. Illustration of (a) the gap between the distribution of training and testing data, (b) problem definition of domain generalization-based face anti-spoofing. $P(X)$ refers to the data distribution of domain X, and (c) explanation of all notations included.

As one of the most effective potential techniques for solving this problem, domain generalization [1] aims to learn a model that could be well-generalized to testing domains unseen during the training process from one or several different but related source domains. Since the goal of improving generalization performance on unseen testing scenarios is largely consistent with that of face anti-spoofing (see Fig. 1(b)), domain generalization was first introduced to this field in [2] and has been extensively explored in subsequent work, which is summarized in Table 1. Due to the remarkable breakthrough made and the great number of studies proposed in domain generalization-based face anti-spoofing, in this paper, we present a comprehensive survey of research in this field to summarize existing approaches and forecast promising future research directions. To the best of our knowledge, this is the first literature review of face anti-spoofing methods focusing on their generalization ability on unseen testing scenarios, where most previous surveys mainly center on discussing conventional methods that do not consider the domain discrepancy.

The rest of this article is organized as follows. In Sect. 2, we review existing methods in this field and present a taxonomy for systematic summarization and comparison. In Sect. 3, we introduce commonly used datasets and evaluation metrics, and also analyze the performance of existing methods to uncover important factors affecting the generalization performance. Afterward, we discuss potential research directions in Sect. 4, aiming to inspire more related work targeting the improvement of the generalization performance of face anti-spoofing in the future. Finally, we draw some conclusions in Sect. 5.

2   Methodologies

In this section, we review existing domain generalization-based face anti-spoofing methods in detail by comparing and analyzing their motivations, highlights, and common technical characteristics. Table 1 gives an overview and a taxonomy of these methods. It is worth noting that all these methods are categorized according to their main innovations.

Table 1. Overview of domain generalization-based face anti-spoofing methods.

Category	Method	Year	Highlights
Domain alignment	MLDG [2]	2018	Minimize the MMD distance
	MADDG [3]	2019	Multi-adversarial shema, dual-force triplet mining constraint, depth constraint
	DAF [4]	2020	Class-conditional domain discriminator module with a gradient reversal layer, temporal domain-invariant feature learning
	SSDG [5]	2020	Single-side adversarial learning, asymmetric triplet loss
	DRDG [6]	2021	Sample and feature reweighting, depth constraint
	SDFANet [7]	2021	Local-region and global image alignment, domain attention strategy, multi-scale attention fusion
	CDA [8]	2022	Conditional domain adversarial, parallel domain regularization
	CSD-S [9]	2022	Single-side adversarial learning, asymmetric triplet loss, low-rank decomposition
Meta-learning	RFM [10]	2020	Meta-learning regularized by depth constraint
	D^2AM [11]	2021	Pseudo domain labels
	FAS-DR-BC [12]	2021	Meta-teacher, bi-level optimization
	PDL-FAS [13]	2021	Pseudo-domain labels, depth loss
	ANR [14]	2021	Adaptive feature normalization, inter-domain compatible and inter-class separable loss
	DBMNet [15]	2021	Two meta-learners regularized by a triplet loss and a depth loss, respectively
	HFN+MP [16]	2022	Learnable meta pattern extractor, bi-level meta optimization
Disentangled representation learning	DR-MD-Net [17]	2020	Disentangle liveness features from subject discriminative features
	VLAD-VSA [18]	2021	Domain-shared and domain-specific visual words separation, centroid adaptation
	DASN [19]	2021	Suppress spoof-irrelevant factors, doubly adversarial learning
	SSAN [20]	2022	Content and style representation separation, enhance liveness-related style features and suppress domain-specific ones
	Unknown Cam [21]	2022	Camera-invariant feature learning, feature decomposition, feature discrimination augmentation
Data augmentation	LMFD-PAD [22]	2022	Learnable frequency filters, hierarchical attention module
Physical cues supervision	UAPG [23]	2020	Depth, material and reflection guided proxy tasks, uncertainty-aware attention

2.1   Domain Alignment-Based Methods

Most existing domain generalization-based face anti-spoofing methods fall into this category, where domain-invariant features are learned by minimizing the distribution discrepancies among source domains. Based on the specific technique adopted for aligning the source domains, these methods could be further divided into two sub-categories: maximum mean discrepancy minimizing based approaches and domain adversarial learning based approaches.

Li et al. [2] first introduce domain generalization to face anti-spoofing. They design a regularization term that minimizes the maximum mean discrepancy (MMD) distance among different domains to improve the generalization ability of learned features. Different from [2], most methods [3–9,19] are based on the idea of domain adversarial learning [24]. Shao et al. [3] propose an adversarial learning scheme between a shared feature generator and multiple domain discriminators to align the marginal distributions among different domains and learn domain-invariant features. Considering the rich diversity of spoof face images, some work [4,5,8,9] proposes to handle the distribution of live and spoof face images in greater detail. Jia et al. [5] align the distributions of live face images by single-side adversarial learning, and separate the spoof face images of each domain while aggregating the real ones of all domains by an asymmetric triplet loss. Low-rank decomposition is used to extend the work of [5] to improve the robustness of the live and spoof face classifier in [9]. Furthermore, Jiang et al. [8] align the conditional distribution of both live and spoof faces from different domains to learn domain-invariant conditional features. Moreover, [6,7] propose to perform refined feature alignments by giving different attention during domain adversarial training to samples, features, and regions of images.

Generally, features that are invariant to source domain shift could also be more generalized to the target domain. However, the generalization performance of existing methods on unseen target domains is still difficult to guarantee when the differences between the source-target and source-source domain shift are large. In face anti-spoofing, there are many factors that affect domain discrepancies, and the data on the current training set is usually limited, so this is a problem worthy of further study.

2.2   Meta-Learning-Based Methods

Meta-learning, which is known as learning-to-learn and aims to learn general knowledge from episodes sampled from related tasks, is a commonly used learning strategy to improve the generalization ability of models in domain generalization-based face anti-spoofing. Existing work has been studied from the aspects of feature learning [10,14,15], supervision information [11–13] and input data [16].

From the perspective of feature learning, episodes are usually built according to unseen testing scenarios of face anti-spoofing. $M - 1$ of the M source domains are used as the meta-train set, and the remaining one is used as the meta-test set to simulate domain shift. After building episodes, Shao et al. [10]

and Jia et al. [15] exploit a depth loss and a triplet loss to regularize the optimization process of meta-learners. Liu et al. [14] propose to adaptively select feature normalization methods to learn domain-invariant features. Considering domain labels usually are unknown in application, Chen et al. [11,13] generate pseudo-domain labels by feature clustering during meta-learning instead of using domain labels. Qin et al. [12] train a teacher to learn how to supervise the live and spoof classifier performing better rather than using handcrafted labels as supervision information. Besides, meta-learning is also used to construct a learnable network to automatically extract generalized input patterns for generalization performance improvement of face anti-spoofing [16].

2.3 Disentangled Representation Learning-Based Methods

It is a challenging task to force all learned features to be domain-invariant in face anti-spoofing due to the diversity of various influencing factors such as identities, spoof faces, acquisition environments, and acquisition devices. Intuitively, aligning part of all learned features that have a large impact on generalization performance and ignoring other features is a more feasible idea, and disentangled representation learning is an effective way to alleviate this problem. Disentangled representation learning-based face anti-spoofing methods generally decompose features into two parts: domain-shared features and domain-specific features, in which domain-shared features are encouraged to be domain-invariant and domain-specific features containing information about various influencing factors are suppressed.

Some work focuses on dealing with the negative impact of a single impact factor on generalization performance. The identity and camera discriminative features are disentangled from liveness features in [17] and [21] to improve the generalization ability of learned features. Other methods take into account a variety of spoof-irrelevant factors such as identity, acquisition environments, and acquisition devices. Kim et al. [19] present a doubly adversarial learning framework to suppress these spoof-irrelevant factors and then enhance the generalization ability on unseen domains for face anti-spoofing. In [18], the learned entire VLAD features are separated into domain-shared and domain-specific features, and only the domain-shared features are enforced to be domain-invariant. Besides, wang et al. [20] disentangle style features from content features, and design a contrastive learning loss to enhance liveness-related style features while suppressing the domain-specific ones.

2.4 Others

In addition to the above three categories, researchers have also tried to improve the generalization performance of face anti-spoofing from other perspectives. Fang et al. [22] extract frequency maps by learnable frequency filters as inputs from a data augmentation aspect. Physical cues such as depth, material, and reflection maps are used to supervise the face anti-spoofing model learning generalized features across domains in [23].

Table 2. Commonly used datasets for domain generalization-based face anti-spoofing.

Dataset	Year	Subjects	Samples	Acquisition Scenarios	Acquisition Devices	Presentation Attacks
CASIA-MFSD [25]	2012	50	600	Indoor scenario	Low- and normal-quality USB cameras, high-quality Sony NEX-5 camera	Cut, warped, flat photos; Replayed videos (iPad)
Replay-Attack [26]	2012	50	1200	Two illumination conditions	Macbook webcam	Printed photos (Triumph Adler DCC 2520 color laser printer); Replayed photos and videos (iPhone 3GS, iPad)
MSU-MFSD [27]	2015	35	280	Indoor scenario	Macbook air webcam, Nexus 5	Printed photos (HP Color Laserjet CP6015xh printer); Replayed videos (iPad Air, iPhone 5S)
OULU-NPU [28]	2017	55	5940	Three scenarios with background and illumination variations	Frontal cameras of six types of smartphones	Printed photos (Canon image PRESS C6011, PIXMA iX6550 printers); Replayed videos (Dell UltraSharp 1905FP, MacBook Retina)

3   Datasets and Evaluation

Datasets. OULU-NPU, CASIA-MFSD, Replay-Attack, and MSU-MFSD are commonly used datasets in domain generalization-based face anti-spoofing. An overview of the characteristics of these datasets is provided in Table 2. It is clear that these datasets have large differences in acquisition devices, acquisition scenarios, and manufacturing processes of face artifacts, which causes the domain shift among different datasets and further brings challenges to the generalization of face anti-spoofing models. Most domain generalization-based face anti-spoofing methods follow the evaluation protocols in [3] for measuring the performance of benchmark approaches. These protocols are based on the idea of Leave-One-Out, where only one dataset is considered as the unseen target domain and the rest as source domains. Considering the high cost of building a dataset in face anti-spoofing, we hope to learn generalized models using as few source domains as possible. Therefore, the generalization ability of state-of-the-art face anti-spoofing methods is also evaluated on limited source domains.

Although domain generalization-based face anti-spoofing has made great progress in recent years, there is still a gap between the academic experimental setting and the practical application environment, due to the difference in sample quantity and data distribution. To better simulate the practical application scenario, Costa-Paz et al. [20,29] aggregate more than ten existing face anti-spoofing datasets together and design protocols in terms of acquisition devices, acquisition scenarios, and types of face artifacts to evaluate the generalization performance of face anti-spoofing models.

Table 3. Comparison of state-of-the-art face anti-spoofing methods on four testing sets. 'O', 'C', 'I', and 'M' are abbreviations for OULU-NPU, CASIA-MFSD, Replay-Attack, and MSU-MFSD, respectively.

Method	Year	O&C&I to M		O&M&I to C		O&C&M to I		I&C&M to O		AVG
		HTER (%)	AUC (%)	HTER (%)	AUC (%)	HTER (%)	AUC (%)	HTER (%)	AUC (%)	HTER (%)
MLDG [2]	2018	23.91	84.81	32.75	74.51	36.55	68.54	25.75	79.52	29.74
MADDG [3]	2019	17.69	88.06	24.50	84.51	22.19	84.99	27.89	80.02	23.07
DR-MD-Net [17]	2020	17.02	90.10	19.68	87.43	20.87	86.72	25.02	81.47	20.65
DAF [4]	2020	15.42	91.13	17.41	90.12	15.87	91.72	14.72	93.08	15.86
RFM [10]	2020	13.89	93.98	20.27	88.16	17.30	90.48	16.45	91.16	16.98
SSDG-R18 [5]	2020	7.38	97.17	10.44	95.94	11.71	96.59	15.61	91.54	11.29
SDA [30]	2021	15.40	91.80	24.50	84.40	15.60	90.10	23.10	84.30	19.65
D^2AM [11]	2021	12.70	95.66	20.98	85.58	15.43	91.22	15.27	90.87	16.10
DRDG [6]	2021	12.43	95.81	19.05	88.79	15.56	91.79	15.63	91.75	15.67
FAS-DR-BC [12]	2021	11.67	93.09	18.44	89.67	11.93	94.95	16.23	91.18	14.57
ANR [14]	2021	10.83	96.75	17.85	89.26	16.03	91.04	15.67	91.90	15.10
DASN [19]	2021	8.33	96.31	12.04	95.33	13.38	86.63	**11.77**	94.65	11.38
DBMNet [15]	2021	7.86	96.54	14.00	94.58	16.42	90.88	17.59	90.92	13.97
VLAD-VSA [18]	2021	4.29	98.25	**8.76**	95.89	7.79	**97.79**	12.64	94.00	**8.37**
SDFANet [7]	2021	**4.28**	97.59	12.56	93.63	**6.14**	97.30	12.26	94.29	8.81
SGDA [31]	2022	10.80	95.30	20.50	87.40	11.30	95.00	19.50	87.90	15.53
LMFD-PAD [22]	2022	10.48	94.55	12.50	94.17	18.49	84.72	12.41	**94.95**	13.47
SSAN-R [20]	2022	6.67	**98.75**	10.00	96.67	8.88	96.79	13.72	93.63	9.82
CDA-R18 [8]	2022	6.19	97.90	10.20	94.87	16.00	89.59	13.33	93.66	11.43
HFN+MP [16]	2022	5.24	97.28	9.11	96.09	15.35	90.67	12.40	94.26	10.53
CSD-S [9]	2022	5.00	97.58	10.00	**96.85**	12.07	94.68	13.45	94.43	10.13

Table 4. Error Rate (%) of different types of unseen attacks on the protocol O&C&I to H, where 'H' represents the HQ-WMCA [32] dataset, and 'O', 'C', and 'I' are abbreviations for OULU-NPU, CASIA-MFSD, and Replay-Attack, respectively.

	Glass	Mannequin	Rigid Mask	Flexible Mask	Paper Mask	Wig	Tattoo	Makeup
SSDG-R18	93.44	24.63	76.14	96.62	7.22	100	94.74	94.29

Evaluation Metrics. Most existing methods are both qualitatively and quantitatively evaluated based on previously mentioned protocols. Commonly used quantitative evaluation metrics are Area Under Curve (AUC) ratio and Half Total Error Rate (HTER) [26], where HTER is the average of False Rejection Rate (FRR) and False Acceptance Rate (FAR). Some visualization tools such as t-SNE [33] and Grad-CAM [34] are used to explore the decision-making process of the learned model and qualitatively measure the overall performances.

Performance Analysis. To uncover the important factors affecting the generalization performance of face anti-spoofing models, we conduct extensive experiments on existing methods on four protocols and throughly analyze their performance (shown in Table 3). Generally, over the course of four years, the generalization performance has been significantly improved on all four protocols, although there is still plenty of room for continuous improvement.

Each of the four datasets in the protocols has its own characteristics. In consequence, the domain shift among the four protocols is different. According to Table 3, the state-of-the-art performance for each protocol is achieved by different methods. In other words, existing methods are still incapable of learning completely domain-invariance features for mitigating the gap between domains, and the difference between source-source and source-target domain shift is an important factor affecting the generalization performance. For instance, we regard HQ-WMCA as the target domain and focus on evaluating the impact of domain shift caused by unseen presentation attack instruments. The comparison results on the protocol O&C&I to H are shown in Table 4. Although SSDG-R18 achieves a lower HTER in the protocol O&C&I to M, the model learned from source domains O&C&I still has extremely high error rates for most types of unseen attacks from the HQ-WMCA dataset. Open set domain generalization could be an effective way to solve this problem.

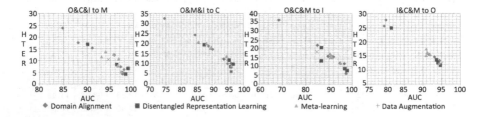

Fig. 2. Performance comparison among different types of methods.

Moreover, we could also conclude that the reduction of source domains leads to a sharp decline in performance. This indicates that both the scale and diversity of training data are important for improving the generalization performance of face anti-spoofing. Relatively speaking, disentangled representation learning and domain alignment-based methods achieve better overall performance than other categories of methods, as shown in Fig. 2. This indicates that suppressing domain-specific features and finely enforcing domain-shared ones to be domain-invariant is an effective way to improve the generalization ability for face anti-spoofing.

4   Future Research Directions

Though lots of efforts have been made on domain generalization-based face anti-spoofing as surveyed, there still remain many open problems. Here we summarize some challenges and future research directions in this field.

1) **Small-scale dataset.** Most existing face anti-spoofing datasets are small in scale and have limited diversity in the patterns of presentation attacks, and collecting a large-scale dataset covering diverse live and spoof face

images is extremely difficult and prohibitively expensive. However, it has been proved that finetuning models trained on large-scale datasets to downstream tasks can improve the generalization ability, and thus large-scale pretraining, self-supervised, semi-supervised, and few-shot domain generalization are worth investigating for face anti-spoofing. Besides, learning to generate novel domains to increase the diversity of source domains would be a promising direction.

2) **Interpretability.** Face anti-spoofing methods are usually used in scenarios with high-security requirements, but we still lack an understanding of learned features and the decision-making behavior of models. Exploring interpretable domain generalization-based face anti-spoofing methods is an urgent need for practical applications of face anti-spoofing.

3) **Heterogeneous approaches.** As shown in Sect. 3, most evaluation protocols currently are homogeneous. The source-source domain shift and source-target domain shift are similar. In practical applications, the unseen target domain is unpredictable. The source-target domain shift may be large different from the source-source one. It would be interesting to see more work on datasets, evaluation protocols, and algorithms for heterogeneous domain generalization-based face anti-spoofing.

5 Conclusion

In this paper, we present a comprehensive survey on existing studies in domain generalization-based face anti-spoofing. Specifically, the problem definition, techniques, datasets, evaluation metrics, performance analysis, and future research directions are discussed in detail. We hope this survey could provide a valuable summarization for researchers who are interested in face anti-spoofing and inspire more future work to promote the development of this field.

Acknowledgments. This work is funded by the Beijing Municipal Natural Science Foundation (Grant No. 4222054), the Natural Science Foundation of Hunan Province (Grant No. 2022JJ30481), the Natural Science Foundation of China (Grant No. 62076240).

References

1. Wang, J., Lan, C., Liu, C., Ouyang, Y., Qin, T.: Generalizing to unseen domains: a survey on domain generalization, arXiv preprint arXiv:2103.03097 (2021)
2. Li, H., He, P., Wang, S., Rocha, A., Jiang, X., Kot, A.C.: Learning generalized deep feature representation for face anti-spoofing. TIFS **13**(10), 2639–2652 (2018)
3. Shao, R., Lan, X., Li, J., Yuen, P.C.: Multi-adversarial discriminative deep domain generalization for face presentation attack detection. In: CVPR, pp. 10023–10031 (2019)
4. Saha, S., et al.: Domain agnostic feature learning for image and video based face anti-spoofing. In: CVPR Workshops, pp. 802–803 (2020)

5. Jia, Y., Zhang, J., Shan, S., Chen, X.: Single-side domain generalization for face anti-spoofing. In: CVPR, pp. 8484–8493 (2020)
6. Liu, S., et al.: Dual reweighting domain generalization for face presentation attack detection, arXiv preprint arXiv:2106.16128 (2021)
7. Zhou, L., Luo, J., Gao, X., Li, W., Lei, B., Leng, J.: Selective domain-invariant feature alignment network for face anti-spoofing. TIFS **16**, 5352–5365 (2021)
8. Jiang, F., Li, Q., Liu, P., Zhou, X., Sun, Z.: Adversarial learning domain-invariant conditional features for robust face anti-spoofing, arXiv preprint arXiv:2205.22027 (2022)
9. Liu, M., Mu, J., Yu, Z., Ruan, K., Shu, B., Yang, J.: Adversarial learning and decomposition-based domain generalization for face anti-spoofing. PRL **155**, 171–177 (2022)
10. Shao, R., Lan, X., Yuen, P.C.: Regularized fine-grained meta face anti-spoofing. In: AAAI, vol. 34, no. 07, pp. 11974–11981 (2020)
11. Chen, Z., et al.: Generalizable representation learning for mixture domain face anti-spoofing, arXiv preprint arXiv:2105.02453 (2021)
12. Qin, Y., Yu, Z., Yan, L., Wang, Z., Zhao, C., Lei, Z.: Meta-teacher for face anti-spoofing. TPAMI (2021)
13. Kim, Y.E., Lee, S.-W.: Domain generalization with pseudo-domain label for face anti-spoofing, arXiv preprint arXiv:2107.06552 (2021)
14. Liu, S., et al.: Adaptive normalized representation learning for generalizable face anti-spoofing. In: ACM MM, pp. 1469–1477 (2021)
15. Jia, Y., Zhang, J., Shan, S.: Dual-branch meta-learning network with distribution alignment for face anti-spoofing. TIFS **17**, 138–151 (2021)
16. Cai, R., Li, Z., Wan, R., Li, H., Hu, Y., Kot, A.C.: Learning meta pattern for face anti-spoofing. TIFS **17**, 1201–1213 (2022)
17. Wang, G., Han, H., Shan, S., Chen, X.: Cross-domain face presentation attack detection via multi-domain disentangled representation learning. In: CVPR, pp. 6678–6687 (2020)
18. Wang, J., et al.: VLAD-VSA: cross-domain face presentation attack detection with vocabulary separation and adaptation. In: ACM MM, pp. 1497–1506 (2021)
19. Kim, T., Kim, Y.: Suppressing spoof-irrelevant factors for domain-agnostic face anti-spoofing. IEEE Access **9**, 86966–86974 (2021)
20. Wang, Z., et al.: Domain generalization via shuffled style assembly for face anti-spoofing, arXiv preprint arXiv:2203.05340 (2022)
21. Chen, B., Yang, W., Li, H., Wang, S., Kwong, S.: Camera invariant feature learning for generalized face anti-spoofing. TIFS **16**, 2477–2492 (2021)
22. Fang, M., Damer, N., Kirchbuchner, F., Kuijper, A.: Learnable multi-level frequency decomposition and hierarchical attention mechanism for generalized face presentation attack detection. In: WACV, pp. 3722–3731 (2022)
23. Wu, J., Yu, X., Liu, B., Wang, Z., Chandraker, M.: Uncertainty-aware physically-guided proxy tasks for unseen domain face anti-spoofing, arXiv preprint arXiv:2011.14054 (2020)
24. Ganin, Y., Lempitsky, V.: Unsupervised domain adaptation by backpropagation. In: International Conference on Machine Learning. PMLR, pp. 1180–1189 (2015)
25. Zhang, Z., Yan, J., Liu, S., Lei, Z., Yi, D., Li, S.Z.: A face antispoofing database with diverse attacks. In: ICB, pp. 26–31 (2012)
26. Chingovska, I., Anjos, A., Marcel, S.: On the effectiveness of local binary patterns in face anti-spoofing. In: International Conference of Biometrics Special Interest Group, pp. 1–7 (2012)

27. Wen, D., Han, H., Jain, A.K.: Face spoof detection with image distortion analysis. TIFS **10**(4), 746–761 (2015)
28. Boulkenafet, Z., Komulainen, J., Li, L., Feng, X., Hadid, A.: OULU-NPU: a mobile face presentation attack database with real-world variations. In: FG, pp. 612–618 (2017)
29. Costa-Pazo, A., Jiménez-Cabello, D., Vázquez-Fernández, E., Alba-Castro, J.L., López-Sastre, R.J.: Generalized presentation attack detection: a face anti-spoofing evaluation proposal. In: ICB, pp. 1–8 (2019)
30. Wang, J., Zhang, J., Bian, Y., Cai, Y., Wang, C., Pu, S.: Self-domain adaptation for face anti-spoofing, arXiv preprint arXiv:2102.12129 (2021)
31. Kim, Y.-E., Nam, W.-J., Min, K., Lee, S.-W.: Style-guided domain adaptation for face presentation attack detection, arXiv preprint arXiv:2203.14565 (2022)
32. Heusch, G., George, A., Geissbühler, D., Mostaani, Z., Marcel, S.: Deep models and shortwave infrared information to detect face presentation attacks. TBIOM **2**(4), 399–409 (2020)
33. Van der Maaten, L., Hinton, G.: Visualizing data using t-SNE. JMLR **9**, 2579–2605 (2008)
34. Selvaraju, R.R., Cogswell, M., Das, A., Vedantam, R., Parikh, D., Batra, D.: Grad-cam: visual explanations from deep networks via gradient-based localization. In: ICCV, pp. 618–626 (2017)

An Empirical Comparative Analysis of Africans with Asians Using DCNN Facial Biometric Models

Jawad Muhammad[1,2]([⊠]), Yunlong Wang[1,2], Leyuan Wang[1,2],
Kunbo Zhang[1,2], and Zhenan Sun[1,2]

[1] School of Artificial Intelligence, University of Chinese Academy of Sciences,
Beijing 100049, China
[2] Research on Intelligent Perception and Computing, National Laboratory of Pattern
Recognition, Institute of Automation, Chinese Academy of Sciences,
Beijing 100190, China
{jawad,yunlong.wang,leyuan.wang}@cripac.ia.ac.cn, kunbo.zhang@ia.ac.cn,
znsun@nlpr.ia.ac.cn
http://www.cripacsir.cn/

Abstract. Recently, the problem of racial bias in facial biometric systems has generated considerable attention from the media and biometric community. Many investigative studies have been published on estimating the bias between Caucasians and Asians, Caucasians and Africans, and other racial comparisons. These studies have reported inferior performances of both Asians and Africans when compared to other races. However, very few studies have highlighted the comparative differences in performance as a function of race between Africans and Asians. More so, those previous studies were mainly concentrated on a single aspect of facial biometrics and were usually conducted with images potentially captured with multiple camera sensors, thereby compounding their findings. This paper presents a comparative racial bias study of Asians with Africans on various facial biometric tasks. The images used were captured with the same camera sensor and under controlled conditions. We examine the performances of many DCNN-based models on face detection, facial landmark detection, quality assessment, verification, and identification. The results suggested higher performance on the Asians compared to the Africans by most algorithms under the same imaging and testing conditions.

Keywords: Racial bias · Face recognition · African biometric · Other-race effect

1 Introduction

There have been numerous contributions to the algorithmic fairness of facial biometric systems (FBS). These studies can be broadly categorised into research on (1) bias estimation and (2) bias mitigation [1,2]. The works on bias estimation concentrate on analyzing the effects of various covariates on the performance

W. Deng et al. (Eds.): CCBR 2022, LNCS 13628, pp. 138–148, 2022.
https://doi.org/10.1007/978-3-031-20233-9_14

of the FBS, such as demographics (race, sex, age, etc.), subject-specific (pose, expression, aging, make-up, use of accessories), and environmental factors (such as illumination, occlusion, resolution) [3]. In contrast, mitigation studies propose methods for suppressing the effects of these covariates. This research focuses on the estimation aspect. Contributions in the estimation study typically involve analyzing the performance differences and outcomes as a function of a specific covariate differentiation. Study on the demographic covariates is the most popular among researchers. This is because of the obvious sociological factors associated with system integrity and fairness among various demographic groups. As facial biometric systems are being adopted and deployed for critical tasks directly affecting individuals' lives, demographic bias is becoming more prevalent in these deployed systems. The American Civil Liberties Union (ACLU) recently conducted a study and reported that Amazon's Rekognition Tool misclassified photos of almost 40% of the non-Caucasian U.S. members of Congress as criminals [4]. These and many reported events have once again highlighted the need for a more inclusive bias estimation study to help policymakers and administrators make informed decisions on accepting a specific facial biometric system. This paper presents a comparative demographic study of African vs. Asian subjects by considering both the data-driven and scenario-driven factors. The specific contributions of this paper are summarised as follows:

1. A comparative performance racial bias study is presented. Unlike the existing racial bias estimation studies that mainly concentrate on Caucasian-related analysis with other races on face recognition, this study presents an analysis of Africans with Asians on face detection, facial landmark detection, quality assessment, verification, and identification.
2. We have established that under controlled imaging conditions, facial biometrics algorithms are more accurate on Asians than on Africans.

The remaining part of this paper is organized as follows: In Sect. 2, a review of some related work on previous racial bias studies is presented. Section 3 describes the comparative racial bias study in detail, followed by the performance results with discussions, and the conclusion will be provided at the end.

2   Related Work

2.1   Racial Bias Studies

The recent social injustice movement has motivated many researchers leading to a growing number of bias-related studies published. Empirical analysis on the effect of race, gender or age demographic covariates for various Facial Processing Tasks (FPT's) has equally been published [4,6–11]. Some of this analysis concentrates on FTPs such as verification, identification, age/gender classification, and landmark detection. In [7], some of the popular commercial facial classification systems were evaluated on the widely used face datasets (IJB-A, Adience and PPB), and it was found that the misclassification error of lighter skin subjects was much lower than that of the darker skin subjects with the lighter skin having only a maximum of 0.8% error rate. In contrast, darker skin has up to a maximum error rate of 34.7%. Similarly, in [9], the results reported indicate that the face recognition rate of the African race was among the lowest in all the other race categories considered by the researchers. In another study in [10], the authors experimentally concluded that subject of black race and female cohort consistently shows lower matching accuracies.

Researchers have established that people easily recognise faces from their race rather than faces from other races (known as other race effects) and that these effects have been observed in the developed face recognition algorithms [14]. In [15], the researchers fused five western and east Asian algorithms to investigate the fusion results. They establish that, at the low false acceptance rate required for most security applications, the western algorithms recognise Caucasian faces more accurately than Asian faces. Equally, the Asian algorithms recognise Asian faces more accurately than Caucasian faces, thereby affirming the 'other race effect' characteristics in the computational algorithms. NIST [6] evaluated the face verification performance of about 106 commercially deployed algorithms and reported that the false positive rates of subjects of African and Asian descent are much higher than that of other races. However, in the same study, it was found that the false positives of the subjects of Asian descent were lower for the algorithms developed in China. The problem is that this research cannot be reproduced as both the dataset and the algorithms studied are not publicly available. In [12], the recognition performance of six algorithms (3 commercial, 2 trainable and 1 no-trainable) was investigated on the subsets of various demographic cohorts(black, white and Hispanic), and they established that the results of the female black under the age group 18–30 consistently shows lower accuracies. However, they propose the concept of dynamic face matcher whereby a different classifier will be used for each demographic cohort, and that use of a demographically balanced dataset can help mitigate potential bias. Nevertheless, this research employs old algorithms as it was conducted before the deep learning era. Other researchers have previously established similar trends. [13] concluded that the algorithms show some performance differences as a function of the race of the face. The concept of yoking was coined by [5], which involves constraining imposter pairs distribution so that they are all demographically comparable.

2.2   DCNN Models

Over the years, various deep learning methods of facial representation have been proposed. The deep learning methods typically adopt a Convolutional Neural Network (CNN) to process the face images in their entirety (irrespective of the number of image channels) using a very large number of images. These methods can be broadly categorized as either closed-set recognition (classification) problems or open-set recognition (metric learning) problems [16]. In the closed set recognition problem, the testing identities must be included in the training set, and the model can be formulated as multi-class with each identity as a class. While in the open set, the testing identities are not included in the training set, and the model only learns the embedding that can be generally used to differentiate between identities [17]. This makes the face recognition task such as verification, identification and clustering easier. In this paper, due to our requirement criteria for evaluating the model's generalization on the Asian and African cohorts, the embedding-based models were employed, such as Facenet [18], SphereFace [16], lightCNN [19] and Arcface [20]. In Facenet, the face image was projected into an embedding of compact euclidian space to which distances between any two embeddings correspond to the measure of their corresponding face similarity [18]. The parameters of the embeddings were learnt directly from the samples of the training face images using the euclidian margin-based triplet loss function. In SphereFace, instead of the euclidian margin, an angular margin-based loss function was employed for the training [16]. The angular margin function modified the softmax function by manipulating its decision boundaries, thereby making the softmax boundaries more stringent in differentiating classes than in the normal softmax function. For the ArcFace, an additive angular margin was used to enhance the discrimination of the extracted embedding features [20]. The extracted embedding has a clear geometric interpretation due to its correspondence to the geostatic distance on the hyperspace. In lightCNN, the embedding was generated through Max-Feature-Map (MFM) operations which produce a compact representation of the input face image [19].

3   The Study

3.1   Database Generation and Pre-processing

For a fair comparative analysis, we collected images of an equal number of subjects from Africans and Chinese. The two races' images were captured using the same camera sensor. The African images were captured in Nigeria as part of our ongoing African database collection project. The Chinese images were captured in Shandong, China. For each subject, multiple still images were captured in a single session. During the capturing exercise, some subjects were asked to use eyeglasses, and an optional illumination light source was also used. The images were then sorted, and numerically duplicate images were removed. Two images were considered numerical duplicates if the two images' correlation coefficient was greater than 0.9. Using this criterion, many still images were discarded. After processing, the database comprises 251 African and 251 Chinese subjects, with 112 Chinese males, 139 Chinese females, 131 African males and 120 African females. There are 1978 Chinese and 2614 African face images. The images were then cropped and aligned using the five-point alignment [21]. The alignment involves rotating the faces so that the two eyes are in a horizontal line, and the normalisation involves scaling the faces such that the horizontal distance between the two eyes is fixed at 60 and the vertical distance between the eye's centre and the mouth is fixed at 80. The aligned image was then resized to 144×144.

3.2   The Models

The comparative evaluations were performed using some selected pre-trained models from open source SOTA algorithms. For the face detection experiments, the models conbsidered are: S3FD[1], MTCNN[2], DSFD[3] and YOLO-Face[4]. For the face recognition experiments, the models considered are: SphereFace[5], lightCNN-29V2[6], ArcFace-model-r100-ii[7], and models (CASIA-Softmax, Balanced-Softmax and Global-Softmax) downloaded from[8]. The model Balanced-Softmax was trained with the BUPT-Balancedface database which has an equal number of subjects for all the race cohorts it contains and the Global-Softmax model was trained with BUPT-Globalface database that has same distribution as the population distribution of the world. For the quality assurance experiments, the models considered are Serfiq [23] and Patch model [24] All the models were downloaded and intentionally adopted unsupervised without fine-tuning on any of the datasets. This is necessary for assessing the comparative performance of the models on the two datasets.

3.3   Dataset Visualisation

Since both the two datasets were captured with the same camera sensor, it is important to analyze the two datasets through visualization on a 2-D plane. Specifically, we employ the t-SNE dimension reduction technique [25] to reduce the dimension of the image intensities and their corresponding extracted features using the lightCNN-29V2 and ArcFace-model-r100-ii model into 2-D data points. The results are shown in Fig. 1 for the complete dataset distribution and Fig. 2 for the gender distribution in the datasets. Some important observations from these visualizations: First, the two datasets have no distinctive distribution regarding either the image intensities or the extracted features. This confirmed that a few image variations exist among the two datasets that can substantially skew generated results. Secondly, the gender distribution using the image intensities for the Chinese dataset is relatively more distinctive and could be easier to classify than the Africans. However, the visualization for the gender distribution using the extracted features shows that the lightCNN-29V2 extracted features are gender distinctive, while that of the ArcFace-model-r100-ii model is slightly less distinctive.

---

[1] https://github.com/weiliu89/caffe/tree/ssd.
[2] https://github.com/kpzhang93/MTCNN_face_detection_alignment.
[3] https://github.com/Tencent/FaceDetection-DSFD.
[4] https://github.com/sthanhng/yoloface.
[5] https://github.com/wy1iu/sphereface.
[6] https://github.com/AlfredXiangWu/LightCNN.
[7] https://github.com/deepinsight/insightface.
[8] http://www.whdeng.cn/RFW/model.html.

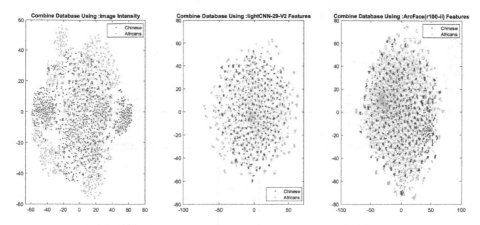

Fig. 1. Dataset Visualisations using image intensities (left), lightCNN-29V2 model (middle) and ArcFace-model-r100-ii model (right)

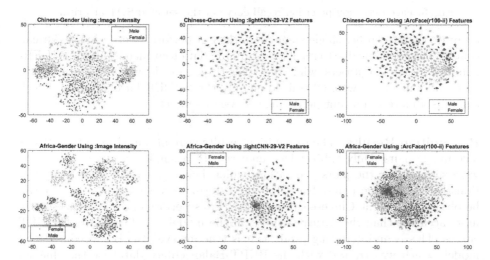

Fig. 2. Gender Distribution Visualisations using image intensities (left), lightCNN-29V2 model (middle) and ArcFace-model-r100-ii model (right) for Chinese (Top row) and Africans (Bottom row)

3.4 Face Detection Results

Face detection results differentiation as a function of race has not been exhaustively studied and reported in the previous racial bias investigations of any demographic combinations. As such, in this paper, we generate comparative results of the relative performances of these algorithms on the Chinese and the African database cohorts. The precision-recall curve results are shown in Fig. 3 with the average precisions (AP). The MTCNN model, a multi-stage network, is less

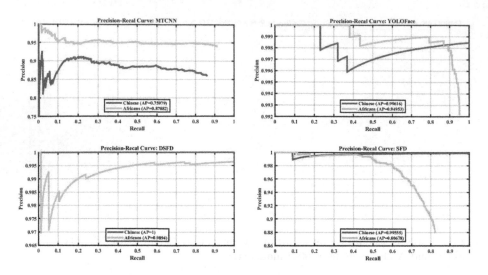

Fig. 3. Face detection precision-recall curve of the selected SOT algorithms

accurate than the other single-stage networks but performs better in the African cohort. This could be due to its diverse training data that includes both WIDER-Face and Celeb-A datasets, while the other three models, which perform better on the Asian cohort, were all trained on only the WIDER-Face database, which contains a more significant percentage of Asian subjects.

Recognition Results. The recognition results were obtained from the subject face image pairs. Only subject face images with a similarity of less than 80% were selected for the pairs generation, which helps to reduce results duplications of the genuine pairs. The DET curve results are shown in Fig. 4. It can be observed that the Chinese subsets algorithm's performances are consistently more accurate than the Africans across all the models, as depicted in the DET curves. This is an interesting result as it is true for even the Balanced-Softmax model, which was trained with the BUPT-Balancedface database that has an equal number of subjects for all the race cohorts, and the Global-Softmax model that was trained with BUPT-Globalface database, which has the same distribution as the population distribution of the world. To qualitatively visualize the recognition results, the worst performing pairs by each of the algorithms and their corresponding scores on the African and Chinese cohorts are shown in Fig. 5 and Fig. 6 respectively are used.

Identification Results. The one-to-many identification results were obtained using all the selected images of both datasets and only images with fixed quality. Considering a maximum rank of 5, the Cumulative Match Curve (CMC) results for these two image categories are shown in Fig. 7. It can be observed that there

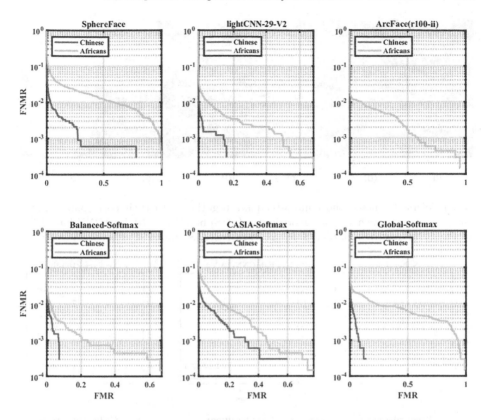

Fig. 4. DET curves of various algorithms on the Chinese and African pairs

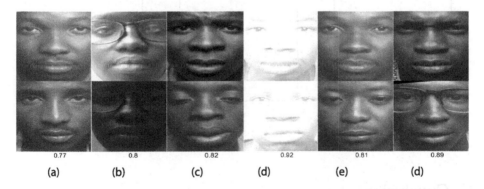

Fig. 5. Worst African cohort imposter pairs together with their corresponding similarity scores for each of the algorithms : (a) SphereFace; (b) lightCNN-29-V2; (c) ArcFace(r100-ii); (d) Balanced-Softmax; (e) CASIA-Softmax; (f) Global-Softmax

exists a consistent lower performance gap between the results of the Africans against the Chinese across most of the algorithms except the LightCNN algorithm, in which the gap is below at lower ranks and above at the upper ranks.

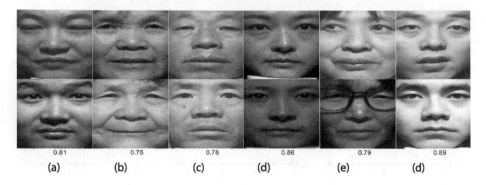

Fig. 6. Worst Chinese cohort imposter pairs together with their corresponding similarity scores for each of the algorithms : (a) SphereFace; (b) lightCNN-29-V2; (c) ArcFace(r100-ii); (d) Balanced-Softmax; (e) CASIA-Softmax; (f) Global-Softmax

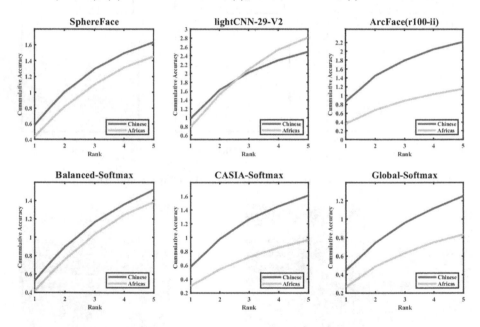

Fig. 7. CMC curves of the various algorithms on the two race cohort

4   Conclusion

In this paper, a comprehensive comparative analysis of African vs. Asian facial biometrics using various pre-trained models has been presented. We have established that under constant imaging and testing conditions, the results on the Asian faces are relatively better than that of the Africans. This correlates with other works in the literature that established the relatively poor performance of algorithms on Africans compared with Caucasians.

References

1. Gong, S., Liu, X., Jain, A.K.: Mitigating face recognition bias via group adaptive classifier. arXiv preprint arXiv:2006.07576 (2020)
2. Wang, M., Deng, M.: Mitigating bias in face recognition using skewness-aware reinforcement learning. In: Proceedings of the IEEE/CVF Conference on Computer Vision and Pattern Recognition, pp. 9322–9331 (2020)
3. Drozdowski, P., Rathgeb, C., Dantcheva, A., Damer, N., Busch, C.: Demographic bias in biometrics: a survey on an emerging challenge. IEEE Trans. Technol, Soc (2020)
4. Singer, N.: Amazon's facial recognition wrongly identifies 28 lawmakers, a.c.l.u. says, 2020–02-23 2018. http://www.nytimes.com/2018/07/26/technology/amazon-aclu-facial-recognition-congress.html
5. Cavazos, J.G., Phillips, P.J., Castillo, C.D., O'Toole, A.J.: Accuracy comparison across face recognition algorithms: Where are we on measuring race bias? Behavior, and Identity Science, IEEE Transactions on Biometrics (2020)
6. Patrick, G., Mei, N., Kayee, H.: Face recognition vendor test (frvt) part 3: Demographic effects. National Institute of Standards and Technology, Report NISTIR 8280 (2019)
7. Buolamwini, J., Gebru, T.: Gender shades: intersectional accuracy disparities in commercial gender classification. In: Conference on fairness, accountability and transparency, Conference Proceedings, pp. 77–91 (2018)
8. Du, M., Yang, F., Zou, N., Hu, X.: Fairness in deep learning: a computational perspective, arXiv preprint arXiv:1908.08843 (2019)
9. Wang, M., Deng, M., Hu, J., Tao, X., Huang, Y.: Racial faces in the wild: Reducing racial bias by information maximization adaptation network. In: Proceedings of the IEEE International Conference on Computer Vision, Conference Proceedings, pp. 692–702 (2019)
10. Wang, M., Deng, W.: Mitigate bias in face recognition using skewness-aware reinforcement learning, arXiv preprint arXiv:1911.10692 (2019)
11. Nagpal, S., Singh, M., Singh, R., Vatsa, M., Ratha, N.: Deep learning for face recognition: pride or prejudiced? arXiv preprint arXiv:1904.01219 (2019)
12. Klare, B.F., Burge, M.J., Klontz, J.C., Bruegge, R.W.V., Jain, A.K.: Face recognition performance: role of demographic information. IEEE Trans. Inf. Forens. Secur. 7(6), 1789–1801 (2012)
13. Cavazos, J.G., Phillips, P.J., Castillo, C.D., O'Toole, A.J.: Accuracy comparison across face recognition algorithms: where are we on measuring race bias?" arXiv preprint arXiv:1912.07398 (2019)
14. Furl, N., Phillips, P.J., O'Toole, A.J.: Face recognition algorithms and the other-race effect: computational mechanisms for a developmental contact hypothesis. Cognitive Science 26(6), 797–815 (2002)
15. Phillips, P.J., Jiang, F., Narvekar, A., Ayyad, J., O'Toole, A.J.: An other-race effect for face recognition algorithms. ACM Trans. Appl. Perception (TAP) 8(2), 1–11 (2011)
16. Liu, W., Wen, Y., Yu, Z., Li, M., Raj, B., Song, L.: Sphereface: deep hypersphere embedding for face recognition. In: Proceedings of the IEEE Conference on Computer Vision and Pattern Recognition, Conference Proceedings, pp. 212–220 (2017)
17. Sun, Y., Wang, X., Tang, X.: Deep learning face representation from predicting 10,000 classes", in Proceedings of the IEEE Conference on Computer Vision and Pattern Recognition, pp. 1891–1898 (2014)

18. Schroff, F., Kalenichenko, D., Philbin, J.: Facenet: a unified embedding for face recognition and clustering. In: Proceedings of the IEEE Conference on Computer Vision and Pattern Recognition, Conference Proceedings, pp. 815–823 (2015)
19. Wu, X., He, R., Sun, Z., Tan, T.: A light cnn for deep face representation with noisy labels. IEEE Trans. Inf. Forens. Secur. **13**(11), 2884–2896 (2018)
20. Deng, J., Guo, J., Xue, N., Zafeiriou, S.: Arcface: additive angular margin loss for deep face recognition. In: Proceedings of the IEEE Conference on Computer Vision and Pattern Recognition, Conference Proceedings, pp. 4690–4699
21. Sun, Y., Wang, X., Tang, X.: Deep convolutional network cascade for facial point detection. In: Proceedings of the IEEE Conference on Computer Vision and Pattern Recognition, pp. 3476–3483 (2013)
22. Yang, S., Luo, P., Loy, C.-C., Tang, X.: Wider face: a face detection benchmark. In: Proceedings of the IEEE Conference on Computer Vision and Pattern Recognition, pp. 5525–5533 (2016)
23. Terhorst, P., Kolf, J.N., Damer, N., Kirchbuchner, F., Kuijper, A.: Ser-fiq: unsupervised estimation of face image quality based on stochastic embedding robustness. In: Proceedings of the IEEE/CVF Conference on Computer Vision and Pattern Recognition, pp. 5651–5660 (2020)
24. Wong, Y., Chen, S., Mau, S., Sanderson, C., Lovell, B.C., Patch-based probabilistic image quality assessment for face selection and improved video-based face recognition. In: CVPR: WORKSHOPS. IEEE 2011, pp. 74–81 (2011)
25. Visualizing data using t-sne: v. d. Maaten, L., Hinton, G. J. Mach. Learn. Res. **9**, 2579–2605 (2008)
26. O'Toole, A.J., Phillips, P.J., An, X., Dunlop, J.: Demographic effects on estimates of automatic face recognition performance. Image Vision Comput. **30**(3), 169–176 (2012)

Disentanglement of Deep Features for Adversarial Face Detection

Bo Yan, Quanwei Wu, and Yi Wang[✉]

Dongguan University of Technology, Dongguan, China
{2112015047,wangyi}@dgut.edu.cn

Abstract. Existing adversarial face detectors are mostly developed against specific types of attacks, and limited by their generalizability especially in adversarial settings. In this paper, we propose a new detection strategy based on a dual-classifier driven deep-feature disentanglement model for detecting different types of adversarial faces. Experimental results over adversarial examples and face forgery attacks show that the proposed detection method is effective with better generalizability and more adversarially robust comparing with previous methods.

1 Introduction

Deep Neural Networks (DNNs) are widely used in biometric applications such as face recognition, makeup transfer and face editing [1–3]. Despite of the positive usage, recent study in adversarial machine learning [4–6] and face forgery [7–9] show that high-performing biometric systems can be easily fooled by malicious inputs that are intentionally generated on DNN-based models. Figure 1 shows typical examples of adversarial face.

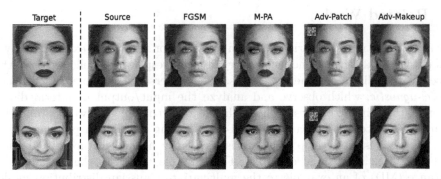

Fig. 1. Illustration of adversarial faces generated by different types of attacks.

For example, FGSM [4] generates additive adversarial perturbations that are imperceptible to human eyes. The resulting *adversarial example* often looks indifference to the original source image but fools a face recognition system for the target person. *Physical attacks* such as Adv-Patch [10] can be printed out and used in the real world. However, physical implementable samples such as Adv-Patch, Adv-Glasses and Adv-Hat are often noticeable to humans and not transferrable. Makeup Presentation Attack (M-PA) for impersonation can be either performed by a makeup artist or synthesized by face forgery techniques that often involve a GAN architecture [7,11]. Such globally synthesized images can results in unnatural facial expressions. State-of-the-art (SOTA) methods such as Adv-Makeup [8] proposes to blend fine-grained makeup transfer and adversarial learning schemes to generate more imperceptible and transferrable attacks under both digital and physical scenarios.

Existing adversarial face detection methods are developed against specific attacks and can be defeated under a different threat model [12]. For instance, it was found that existing face forgery detectors that are designed to classify GAN synthesized images such as Deepfakes [13] and makeup transfers [7] are not *adversarially robust* [6]. We are inspired from the recent explanatory study of adversarial examples that there exist *highly predictive but non-robust features* in standard machine learning datasets contributing not only to good generalization but also adversarial vulnerability of DNNs [5]. Accordingly, we propose to exploit the predictive inconsistency between robust and non-robust features of DNNs for adversarial face detection of different attack types as shown in Fig. 1.

Our main contributions are: 1) We design a supervised deep feature disentanglement model with the variation auto-encoder (DD-VAE) to construct predictive inconsistency between two classifiers for robust and non-robust features of a dataset; 2) We propose a simple yet effective method based on the dual-classifier prediction inconsistency that can detect adversarial faces generated on different types of attacks; 3) We evaluate the detection performance with benchmark datasets to show that the proposed detection scheme is effective with better generalizability and more adversarial robust comparing with previous methods.

2   Related Work

We review existing adversarial detection methods for adversarial examples, physical patch-based attacks, and face forgery attacks, respectively, followed by VAE-based feature disentanglement methods. Most adversarial example detectors are *model-agnostic*, which observe and analyze the input/output or intermediate-layer feature characteristics without the need of changing network properties or internal states of the base model [14–17]. Along this line, a popular detection strategy is to develop some statistics of the normal feature distribution and test it on adversarial examples. For example, [15] uses the Mahalanobis distance (MD) of an example to the multivariate Gaussian distribution model developed in the deep feature space. [16] introduces local intrinsic dimensionality (LID) to describe the distribution of adversarial examples. [17] advanced the generalization capabilities and detection performance by incorporating sensitivity inconsistency detection (SID) between normal and adversarial examples against the decision boundary transformation. Most of these methods directly apply a detection on the input example and its intermediate-layer layers without interpretation of the features. As the distribution varies between attacks, they are generally limited to the transferability of adversarial detection [18].

Compared with the L_p norm bounded adversarial examples in the digital world, physical attacks are more practical in real-world by attaching an adversarial patch to an object or wearing an adversarially-made subject such as Adv-Hat and Adv-Glasses. However, the physical implementable samples are usually rather noticeable. The detection methods often involve locating the region of adversarial patch and mitigating patch attacks. For instance, [19] proposed a *Jujutsu* detector develops a better locating method by leveraging the salient features in the saliency map and a guided feature transfer method for adversarial detection. PatchGuard++ [20] moves a sliding window of mask over the feature map and takes the inconsistent masked prediction as an attack indicator. These methods leverage the corrupted region or features by the adversarial patch for detection and thus their performance depends on the patch and sample quality.

Face forgery or face manipulation include makeup transfers [8], M-PA [7], and Deepfake attacks [13]. The detection methods try to learn the intrinsic characteristics in real and forgery faces but often suffer from generalization issues [9,12,21]. That is, the performance significantly reduces when applied to forgery generated by unseen attacks. For example, most Deepfake detectors distinguish GAN synthesized fake videos based on training a DNN model. Recent study shows that even the top three winning entries of the DeepFake Detection Challenge (DFDC) can be easily bypassed in different attack scenarios including a proper design of universal adversarial perturbations that are highly transferrable across detectors [12].

Disentangled representation learning is conventionally used to factorize the input data x into distinct information factors of variations [22], and is recently studied to explain the root cause of adversarial example [5]. Accordingly, feature disentanglement models are proposed for adversarial detection in the latent space of VAE. [23] separates the latent representation z into face content and liveness features for anti-spoofing. [24] conjectures that the adversarial inputs are tied to some vulnerable features susceptible to adversarial perturbation and proposes a minmax game to train a VAE with two latent feature spaces. [25] proposes an input-space class-disentanglement model with a class-dependent VAE and applies it to adversarial example detection. Most of these methods are based on a variant of VAE to encourage some disentanglement on z. However, the learned latent factors in z are often exceedingly abstract and their correspondence to the underlying task can be obscure, which largely affects the reconstruction hence the detection performance. Moreover, direct disentanglement on z cannot be easily adapted to detect unseen attacks which tend to have different latent distribution characteristics and thus is limited by generalizability.

3   Methodology

We propose an indirect approach different from the existing VAE-based methods by involving a dual-classifier to guide the latent disentanglement. Figure 2 depicts

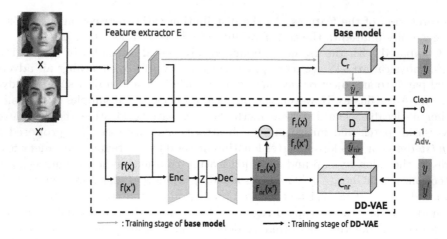

Fig. 2. The proposed framework for adversarial face detection based on DD-VAE.

a framework of the proposed adversarial detection method with a side network auxiliary to the base model of face recognition.

3.1 Supervised Feature Disentanglement

The proposed DD-VAE model is trained on a synthetic dataset consisting pairwise images of the original face x and its adversarial sample x'. Note that x' can also be a Deepfake or AdvMakeup image generated from other type of attacks. We use concatenated deep features of x and x' from the last convolution layer of the base model to form the input vector, denoted by $\mathbf{f}_d = [f(x), f(x')]$, to a simple VAE module [22] where the encoder and decoder are two fully connected layers, respectively. We found empirically in our context that such a simple structure serve almost equally well comparing with a more sophisticated one.

We are inspired by the phenomenon of vulnerable dense mixtures in the hidden layers where conventional clean training process using SGD biases the model towards learning non-robust networks [26]. Thus, we propose to encourage the VAE to disentangle *non-robust* features which are more "universal" and sensitive to the adversarial inputs across the dataset. In doing this, we introduce a dual-classifier structure to guide the disentanglement of VAE.

We adopt the classic objective function of VAE to minimize the reconstruction error with independent latent variables of z by

$$L_{\text{VAE}}(\mathbf{f}_d) = \|\mathbf{f}_d - \text{Dec}(\text{Enc}(\mathbf{f}_d, \sigma), \varphi)\|_2 + \text{KL}(q(z)\|p(z)) \tag{1}$$

where σ, φ are the Gaussian parameters assumed for the latent distribution. Denote the VAE reconstruction by $\mathbf{f}_{nr} = \text{Dec}(\text{Enc}(\mathbf{f}_d, \sigma), \varphi)$. We label $\mathbf{f}_{nr}(x)$ with the source class y and $\mathbf{f}_{nr}(x')$ with the target class y' for the pairwise normal and adversarial samples, respectively. The supervised non-robust data are then fed to the auxiliary classifier C_{nr}.

On the other hand, we subtract the disentangled non-robust feature $\mathbf{f}_{nr}$ from the original deep feature vectors $\mathbf{f}_d$ to obtain more robust features, denoted by $\mathbf{f}_r = \mathbf{f}_d - \mathbf{f}_{nr}$. To enforce the consistency of learning on robust data, we assign the source label y to the pair $\mathbf{f}_r(x)$ and $\mathbf{f}_r(x')$ since the base classifier C_r is expected to produce the same predictive results for x and x' on their robust features $\mathbf{f}_r(x)$ and $\mathbf{f}_r(x')$, respectively. We can further enhance the prediction consistency of C_r by aligning the pairwise robust features of normal and adversarial samples by minimizing their distance in the feature space, e.g.,

$$\mathcal{L}_{\texttt{dist}}(\mathbf{f}_r) = \|\mathbf{f}_r(x), \mathbf{f}_r(x')\|_2 \tag{2}$$

Note that the base model parameters are pre-trained with the original data (x, y) and fixed throughout the DD-VAE training stage. Thus, the base classifier C_r can be regarded as deploying a regularization to guide the VAE-based feature disentanglement in the auxiliary branch. Putting it altogether, the objective function of the proposed DD-VAE model is therefore

$$\mathcal{L}_{\texttt{total}} = \mathcal{L}_{\texttt{VAE}} + \mathcal{L}_{\texttt{CE}}(C_{nr}(\mathbf{f}_{nr}), \mathbf{y}_{nr}) + \mathcal{L}_{\texttt{CE}}(C_r(\mathbf{f}_r), \mathbf{y}_r) + \alpha \cdot \mathcal{L}_{\texttt{dist}} \tag{3}$$

where $\mathbf{y}_{nr} = [y, y']$, $\mathbf{y}_r = [y, y]$ and $\mathcal{L}_{\texttt{CE}}(\cdot)$ is the cross-entropy loss function. Unless otherwise specified, the hyper-parameter $\alpha = 1$. The training process of supervised disentanglement iterates until the DD-VAE model is converged on the overall objective function.

3.2   Detection on Predictive Inconsistency

In the dual-classifier model, a normal sample x is likely to induce the same predictive results for its supervised information is the same on C_r and C_{nr}. Whereas an adversarial input x' tends to induce inconsistent prediction results, i.e., $\hat{y}_r \neq \hat{y}_{nr}$, for different supervised information is given to the disentangled robust and non-robust features. The design is verified in Fig. 3 where the consistency rate of dual-classifier predictions is measured by counting the percentage of $\hat{y}_r = \hat{y}_{nr}$ on clean x and its adversarial samples x' generated by various types of attacks. It can be seen that the consistency rate shoots up to 98.5% for clean samples x and drops sharply for adversarial faces of all types to below 10%. In practice, we deploy a simple network D with two fully-connected layers for adversarial face detection based on prediction inconsistency of the dual-classifier outputs.

4   Performance Evaluations

4.1   Experimental Settings

In this section, we evaluate the proposed scheme in comparison with other adversarial detectors on different types of adversarial face attacks including various methods of adversarial examples, SOTA makeup transfers and GAN-synthesized images from benchmark datasets. For the base model, we train a FaceNet model [1] on the clean dataset of normal examples. The learning rate of the DD-VAE model is set to 0.001.

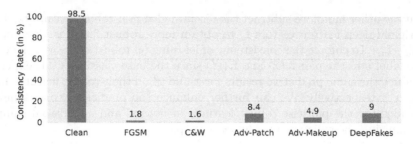

Fig. 3. Dual-classifier prediction consistency on clean and adversarial samples.

4.2   Adversarial Example Detection

We use 334 clean faces from the LADN dataset [11] to generate adversarial examples on the base model with five popular attack methods provided in the *advertorch* library[1]. In particular, we use PGD to construct pairwise examples with the clean faces for training the proposed DD-VAE framework. For each type of attack, we generate 3340 adversarial examples for test. The adversarial perturbation in l_∞ norm is set to 8/255. For C&W and DeepFool, the learning rate is set to 0.01. The attack iteration is set to 100. The proposed method is compared with other intermediate-layer feature-based adversarial detection schemes of MD [15], LID [16], SID [17] as introduced in Sect. 2. We measure the adversarial detection accuracy in terms of AUC and TPR at less than 5% FPR. The results are summarized in Table 1. The proposed method outperforms the comparing methods in all cases, especially for the optimization-based attacks of C&W and DeepFool. It demonstrates that our method has better *generalizability* on unseen attacks that are significantly different from those used for training the detector model.

Table 1. Detection accuracy of adversarial examples generated by different attacks.

Method	FGSM		PGD		BIM		C&W		DeepFool	
	TPR	AUC	TPR	AUC	TPR	AUC	TPR	AUC	TPR	AUC
LID	86.22	96.96	87.00	97.53	94.07	98.62	22.78	64.44	25.19	64.90
MD	89.11	94.33	87.32	95.23	96.10	97.58	39.57	79.35	45.12	70.11
SID	98.15	99.13	83.81	96.79	89.60	96.27	40.63	82.17	33.15	73.77
Proposed	**98.88**	**99.31**	**99.69**	**99.95**	**98.78**	**99.63**	**66.47**	**92.71**	**52.72**	**76.31**

4.3   Face Forgery Detection

As introduced in Sect. 2, existing face forgery detectors can be easily bypassed by unseen attacks and adversarial learning [8,9,12]. In this section, we evaluate our

---

[1] https://github.com/BorealisAI/advertorch.

detection performance on Adv-Makeup [8] which combines GAN synthesized makeup transfer with adversarial perturbations. In particularly, Adv-Makeup captures the eye shadow region to train a specific makeup generator to create a tattoo eye shadow and paste it to the target's eye region. Thus, it can also be regarded as a special case of local patch-based attacks. An example of Adv-Makeup is shown in Fig. 1. To the best of our knowledge, there is not yet published work on adversarial detection of this type of attacks. Therefore, we compare our method with advanced detection methods for adversarial examples and patched-based attacks, respectively. We perform the evaluation of adversarial face detection on the LADN dataset where ten random attacks are generated for each clean face to obtain in total 3340 adversarial faces using Adv-Makeup. Figure 4 plots the total accuracy of detecting both clean and adversarial faces by the four comparing methods where PATCHGUARD++ [20] and Jujutsu [19] are designed for detecting patch-based attacks and SID is the second best forming method for adversarial sample detection in Table 1. The proposed method achieves the highest detection rate of 98.8% for the SOTA attack of Adv-Makeup.

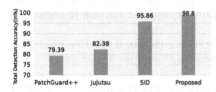

Fig. 4. Adv-Makeup Detection.

Table 2. FaceForgery++ Detection.

Attacks	N.Textues	D.Fakes	Adv-D.Fakes
Xception	83.32	94.01	5.29
F3-Net	91.44	97.46	2.10
Proposed	**94.56**	**98.23**	**97.50**

We also performed evaluations on two face manipulation methods of NeuralTextures (N.Textures) and DeepFakes (D.Fakes) with 67080 training samples and 14820 test samples from FaceForensics++ [13]. We compare our method with two face forgery detection models, namely F3-Net [27] and Xception [13]. Table 2 shows that our method is also highly effective on detecting GAN synthesized faces. We then generate adversarial perturbation with the PGD attack on F3-Net and add it to the DeepFake synthetically-generated images (Adv-D.Fakes). Test results show that both DeepFake detectors are defeated on Adv-D.Fakes while the proposed DD-VAE based detector is much more *adversarial robust* with a detector rate remaining as high as 97.50%.

5   Conclusion

Previous methods for adversarial face detection are mostly developed with respect to a specific type of attacks, and can be defeated under a new threat model. In this paper, we propose a new detection strategy based on deep-feature disentanglement with a VAE by constructing predictive inconsistency of a dual classifier model on adversarial faces. The proposed indirect approach of exploiting robust and non-robust features overcomes limitations of conventional disentangled feature learning in the latent space. We evaluate the proposed method on various attacks including adversarial examples and face forgery attacks. Experimental results show that our approach is more effective with better generalizability and adversarial robust comparing with previous methods.

Acknowledgments. The work was supported in part by NFSC Grant No. 61876038 Dongguan Science and Technology of Social Development Program under Grant 20221800905182, and Characteristic Innovation Projects of Guangdong Colleges and Universities (Grant No. 2021KTSCX134).

References

1. Schroff, F., Kalenichenko, D., Philbin, J.: FaceNet: a unified embedding for face recognition and clustering. In: IEEE Conference Computer Vision and Pattern Recognition Work, pp. 815–823 (2015)
2. Liu, M., et al.: STGAN: a unified selective transfer network for arbitrary image attribute editing. In: IEEE Conference Computer Vision and Pattern Recognition, pp. 3668–3677 (2019)
3. Hu, S., et al.: Protecting facial privacy: generating adversarial identity masks via style-robust makeup transfer. In: IEEE Conference Computer Vision and Pattern Recognition, pp. 15014–15023 (2022)
4. Goodfellow, I.J., Shlens, J., Szegedy, C.: Explaining and Harnessing Adversarial Examples. In: International Conference on Learning Representations (2015)
5. Ilyas, A., Santurkar, S., Tsipras, D., Engstrom, L., Tran, B., Madry, A.: Adversarial examples are not bugs, they are features. Adv. Neural. Inf. Process. Syst. **32**, 125–136 (2019)
6. Carlini, N., Farid, H.: Evading deepfake-image detectors with white-and black-box attacks. In: IEEE Conference Computer Vision and Pattern Recognition, pp. 2804–2813 (2020)
7. Rathgeb, C., Drozdowski, P., Busch, C.: Makeup presentation attacks: review and detection performance benchmark. IEEE Access **8**, 224958–224973 (2020)
8. Yin, B., et al.: Adv-Makeup: a new imperceptible and transferable attack on face recognition. In: International Joint Conference on Artificial Intelligence, pp. 1252–1258 (2021)
9. Jia, S., Ma, C., Yao, T., Yin, B., Ding, S., Yang, X.: Exploring frequency adversarial attacks for face forgery detection. In: IEEE Conference Computer Vision and Pattern Recognition, pp. 4103–4112 (2022)
10. Brown, T.B., Mané, D., Roy, A., Abadi, M., Gilmer, J.: Adversarial Patch. CoRR (2017)
11. Gu, Q., Wang, G., Chiu, M.T., Tai, Y.W., Tang, C.K.: LADN: local adversarial disentangling network for facial makeup and de-makeup. In: International Conference on Computer Vision, pp. 10480–10489 (2019)
12. Neekhara, P., Dolhansky, B., Bitton, J., Ferrer, C.C.: Adversarial threats to Deep-Fake detection: a practical perspective. In: IEEE Conference Computer Vision and Pattern Recognition, pp. 923–932 (2021)

13. Rossler, A., Cozzolino, D., Verdoliva, L., Riess, C., Thies, J., Niessner, M.: Face-Forensics++: learning to detect manipulated facial images. In: International Conference on Computer Vision, pp. 1–11 (2019)
14. Huang, B., Wang, Y., Wang, W.: International Joint Conference on Artificial Intelligence, Macau, China, pp. 4689–4696
15. Lee, K., Lee, K., Lee, H., Shin, J.: A simple unified framework for detecting out-of-distribution samples and adversarial attacks. In: Conference on Neural Information Processing Systems, vol. 31, pp. 7167–7177 (2018)
16. Ma, X., et al.: Characterizing adversarial subspaces using local intrinsic dimensionality. In: International Conference on Learning Representations (2018)
17. Tian, J., Zhou, J., Li, Y., Duan, J.: Detecting adversarial examples from sensitivity inconsistency of spatial-transform domain. In: AAAI Conference on Artificial Intelligence, pp. 9877–9885 (2021)
18. Carlini, N., Wagner, D.: Towards evaluating the robustness of neural networks. In: IEEE Symposium on Security and Privacy, San Jose, CA, USA, IEEE, pp. 39–57 (2017)
19. Chen, Z., Dash, P., Pattabiraman, K.: Turning your strength against you: detecting and mitigating robust and universal adversarial patch attack. arXiv Prepr. **1**(1) (2021)
20. Xiang, C., Mittal, P.: PatchGuard++: efficient provable attack detection against adversarial patches. Int. Conf. Learn. Represent. Work., pp. 1–6 (2021)
21. Chen, S., Yao, T., Chen, Y., Ding, S., Li, J., Ji, R.: Local relation learning for face forgery detection. In: AAAI Conference Artificial Intelligence, pp. 1081–1088 (2021)
22. Kingma, D.P., Welling, M.: Auto-encoding variational Bayes. In: International Conference on Learning Representations, pp. 1–14 (2014)
23. Zhang, K.-Y., Yao, T., Zhang, J., Tai, Y., Ding, S., Li, J., Huang, F., Song, H., Ma, L.: Face anti-spoofing via disentangled representation learning. In: Vedaldi, A., Bischof, H., Brox, T., Frahm, J.-M. (eds.) ECCV 2020. LNCS, vol. 12364, pp. 641–657. Springer, Cham (2020). https://doi.org/10.1007/978-3-030-58529-7_38
24. Joe, B., Hwang, S.J., Shin, I.: Learning to disentangle robust and vulnerable features for adversarial detection. arXiv Prepr. (2019)
25. Yang, K., Zhou, T., Zhang, Y., Tian, X., Tao, D.: Class-disentanglement and applications in adversarial detection and defense. Adv. Neural. Inf. Process. Syst. **19**, 16051–16063 (2021)
26. Allen-Zhu, Z., Li, Y.: Feature purification: how adversarial training performs robust deep learning. In: IEEE Annual Symposium on Foundations of Computer Science, pp. 977–988 (2022)
27. Qian, Y., Yin, G., Sheng, L., Chen, Z., Shao, J.: Thinking in frequency: face forgery detection by mining frequency-aware clues. In: Vedaldi, A., Bischof, H., Brox, T., Frahm, J.-M. (eds.) ECCV 2020. LNCS, vol. 12357, pp. 86–103. Springer, Cham (2020). https://doi.org/10.1007/978-3-030-58610-2_6

Estimation of Gaze-Following Based on Transformer and the Guiding Offset

Sheng Gao, Xiao Sun$^{(\boxtimes)}$, and Jia Li

Hefei University of Technology, Hefei, China
sunx@hfut.edu.cn

Abstract. Gaze-following is a challenging task in computer vision. With the help of gaze-following, we can understand what other people are looking and predict what they might do. We propose a two-stage solution for the gaze point prediction of the target person. In the first stage, the head image and head position are fed into the gaze pathway to predict the guiding offset, then we generate the multi-scale gaze fields with the guiding offset. In the second stage, we concatenate the multi-scale gaze fields with full image and feed them into the heatmap pathway to predict a heatmap. We leverage the guiding offset to facilitate the training of gaze pathway and we add the channel attention module. We use Transformer to capture the relationship between the person and the predicted target in the heatmap pathway. Experimental results have demonstrated the effectiveness of our solution on GazeFollow dataset and DL Gaze dataset.

Keywords: Gaze-following · Vision transformer · Guiding offset · Saliency

1 Introduction

The task of gaze-following is to detect the target that a given person is looking at [1]. It has a very important role in understanding human-human interaction. We can infer the intention of a person by the person-to-person focus, or determine the region of interest of a person by the focus of the person in the scenario, and infer what attracts the consumers' attention most (such as ingredients of the food). Gaze-following is also being widely used in the medical field and assisted driving. In the medical field, gaze-following is used to facilitate some patients through gaze-based interactive systems. In driving, gaze-following can detect whether the driver is fatigued and whether he/she is concentrating. Though the gaze-following is crucial, it is also challenging for the following reasons: firstly, it needs to handle different scenarios (such as the scene is too dark); secondly, inferring the gaze point requires the depth information of the scene.

Despite the importance of this topic, only a few works have explored the problem in recent years [2, 4, 9, 10]. Early work on gaze-following usually simplifies the setting, for example, limiting the scope (e.g., people only follow each other [8]), restricting the situation (e.g., using the camera to capture the face for better head pose estimation [6]), or using complex inputs (multiple images [11]). [1] is the first to propose a study of gaze-following in general natural scenes. After that, Lian et al. [2] has proposed a

© The Author(s), under exclusive license to Springer Nature Switzerland AG 2022
W. Deng et al. (Eds.): CCBR 2022, LNCS 13628, pp. 158–168, 2022.
https://doi.org/10.1007/978-3-031-20233-9_16

two-stage solution from the perspective of mimicking the gaze-following behavior of the third perspective. And more work is starting to pay attention to depth information [4].

The main contributions of this paper can be summarized in the following three points: i) we treat the head position as a key point and the gaze point as another key point to be predicted. To obtain the relationship between head position and gaze point, we predict the guiding offset and use it to generate an attention map. ii) we add channel attention module in the first stage, which facilitates the process of channel feature changes in the head image. Iii) we employ Transformer for gaze-following and we prove that Transformer is significant for gaze-following.

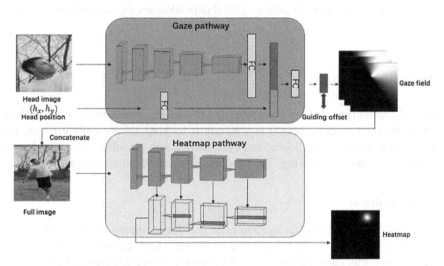

Fig. 1. We show the architecture of our model for gaze-following. In the gaze pathway, the guiding offset is predicted, which is then encoded into multi-scale gaze fields. We concatenate the multi-scale gaze fields with full image and use them to predict a heatmap to get the final gaze point through the heatmap pathway.

2   Related Work

Gaze-Following. Gaze-following is to estimate what a person is looking at in a picture. [2] proposes a two-stage solution for predicting the gaze point of a target person in a scene by imitating the human gaze behavior. A depth map is used for tackling a complex scene [4]. [9] introduces a numerical coordinate regression to calculate the gaze target point. [19] proposes a method for following gaze in video by predicting where a person is looking even if the object is in a different frame. [20] integrates local binocular spatial attention mechanism and global binocular spatial attention mechanism. [14] presents a novel model for single-user 2D gaze estimation in a retail environment. [17] uses human gaze to identify informative regions of images for the interaction.

Saliency. The saliency detection focuses on predicting fixation map during an observer is free viewing an image. [12] predicts the 2D viewing saliency map for a given frame. Previous works about saliency prediction combine the features from different levels to model a bottom-up, top-down architecture [7]. [18] proposes a new saliency model to reuse existing neural networks.

Attention Mechanism. The channel attention [5] Squeeze the feature map to get the global features at the channel level, and then perform the Excitation operation on the global features. It can learn the relationship between each channel and gets the weights of different channels. Transformer is able to reflect complex spatial transformations and captures feature dependencies over long distances to obtain a global feature representation. [15] uses self-attention to capture global dependencies and convolution to extract local details.

3 Proposed Method

Based on the human gaze behavior, we propose a two-stage solution to solve this problem. When people infer where a person in a picture is looking, they usually estimate their viewing area from the person's head and eyes, then reason the salient object in that area to predict where they are looking. The network architecture shows in Fig. 1.

3.1 Gaze Pathway

The gaze pathway takes head image and head position as inputs for the guiding offset prediction, as shown in Fig. 2. We feed the head image into ResNext-50 [3] for feature extraction. To focus more on the most informative channel features and suppress the less important features, we add the channel attention module [5] to ResNext-50. Then we concatenate head features with head position features encoded by several fully connected layers for the guiding offset prediction. Firstly, the guiding offset provides both the direction features and distance features of gaze point. We can use distance to determine the relative size of objects. Secondly, we can use the guiding offset to supervise the learning of the gaze pathway, which is more robust when training. Eventually, the predicted guiding offset will be used to generate the multi-scale gaze fields, which will be further used for heatmap regression in the heatmap pathway.

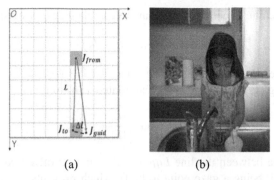

(a)   (b)

Fig. 2. Example of guiding offset in the image space. (a) The ground truth guiding offset placed at the position of keypoint J_{from} points to its adjacent keypoint J_{to}. The inferred guiding offset points to the position of a proposal pixel J_{guid}. Δl is the distance from J_{guid} to J_{to}.. (b) shows the image corresponding to (a). The keypoint J_{from} is head position, the keypoint J_{to} is ground truth gaze point, J_{guid} is predicted gaze point.

3.2 Gaze Field

Once the guiding offset is estimated, we can get the predicted gaze point. The gaze point may be along with the direction of the guiding offset and the ground truth gaze point will be around with the predicted gaze point. Suppose there is a point P $= (p_x, p_y)$, the probability that the point P is the gaze point should be proportional to the angle θ between the line L_{HP} and the predicted guiding offset, here H $= (h_x, h_y)$ is the head position, as shown in Fig. 3. The smaller the θ is, the higher the probability that the point is a gaze point. We use the cosine function to describe the mapping from angle to probability value. We refer to the probability distribution of points that are gaze points without considering the scene content as the gaze field. Thus, the gaze field is a probability map and the value of each point shows the probability of that point being the gaze point. The gaze field has the same size with the scene image.

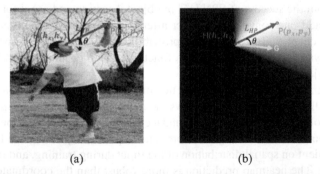

(a)   (b)

Fig. 3. (a) is full image, (b) is gaze field that corresponds to (a). The red line indicates the gaze direction of the boy within the image, and the blue dot indicates the head position. The gaze field measures the probability of each point being a gaze point, which calculated by cosine function between the line direction of L_{HP} and the predicted guiding offset G. (Color figure online)

Particularly, the line direction of L_{HP} can be calculated as follows:

$$L = (p_x - h_x, p_y - h_y) \tag{1}$$

Given an image, we denote the guiding offset as $G = (g_x, g_y)$, then the probability of the point P being the gaze point can be calculated as follows:

$$\text{Sim}(P) = \max(\frac{\langle L, G \rangle}{|L||G|}, 0) \tag{2}$$

When the angle between the line L_{HP} and the guiding offset exceeds 90°, we set the probability of P being a gaze point to be 0, which prevents the predicted guiding offset from being opposite to the true gaze direction. If the predicted guiding offset is accurate, then the probability distribution is sharp along the guiding offset; otherwise, the probability change is smooth.

In practice, we generate the multi-scale gaze fields with different sharpness. Specifically, we control the sharpness of the gaze field in the following way:

$$\text{Sim}(P, \gamma) = [\text{Sim}(P)]^\gamma \tag{3}$$

We choose three different γ to represent the decay rate in the Eq. 3 and our experiments verify the effectiveness of the multi-scale gaze fields. The gaze field is sharper when γ is larger. Considering the decay rate and effective field of view, we set $\gamma_1 = 5$, $\gamma_2 = 2$, $\gamma_3 = 1$ respectively, which means the angle is about 30°, 45°, 60°.

3.3 Heatmap Pathway

We concatenate the full image with the multi-scale gaze fields and feed them into the heatmap pathway for heatmap regression. The index of the point corresponding to the maximum value of the heatmap is considered to be the coordinate of the ground truth gaze point. We use Conformer-S/16 [15] as the backbone for the heatmap pathway. To deal with the different scales of object in the scene content, we fuse multi-scale features. We borrow from the success of FPN [16] in object detection and use it for the heatmap pathway. We add one convolutional layer after the output of FPN and get a heatmap with only one channel. To calculate the probability of each pixel, our last layer in the heatmap pathway is a Sigmoid activation function, which ensures the probability is in the range [0, 1].

Our reasons for predicting probability heatmap rather than the coordinate of the gaze point are as follows: i) the heatmap allows the network to output the image directly by using the convolutional network entirely, and it effectively captures the strong correlation between key points. ii) predicting the coordinate requires fully connected layers, which heavily dependent on spatial distribution of the input during training, and impair spatial generalization. The heatmap prediction is more robust than the coordinate estimation, which means that the gaze point prediction based on heatmap can still be correct, even if some entries in the heatmap are not accurately predicted. Iii) the gaze point is usually multimodal and heatmap regression satisfies the multimodal prediction.

Following [13], by centering a Gaussian kernel at the position of gaze point, we generate the heatmap of ground truth gaze point as follows, $g = (g_x, g_y)$ and $H(i, j)$ are the ground truth gaze point and its heatmap. σ is the variance of Gaussian kernel and we empirically set $\sigma = 3$.

$$H(i, j) = \frac{1}{\sqrt{2\pi}\sigma} e^{-\frac{(i-g_x)^2 + (j-g_y)^2}{2\sigma^2}} \tag{4}$$

Transformer is able to reflect complex spatial transformations and captures feature dependencies over long distances to obtain a global feature representation, we choose Conformer-S/16 as our backbone, as shown in Table 1. If the network is too deep, the extracted features for small objection might disappear, so we reduce the depth of Conformer-S/16. When we combine Conformer-S/16 with FPN, we drop stage c5 and choose stage c1 where output is 56×56 instead. The reasons we choose 56×56 are as follows: i) if the size of feature map is too large, it will increase the computational cost. ii) c1 and c2 are the same size, which avoids feature map error when upsampling.

Table 1. Architecture of Conformer-S/16.

Stage	c1	c2	c3	c4	c5
Output	112×112 56×56	56×56	28×28	14×14	7×7

3.4 Training

The inputs of our network are head image, head position and full image. Practically, head image and head position are used for the first stage and the full image is used for the second stage. The head image and full image are resized to 224×224, and the head position is the coordinate when the full image size is normalized to 1×1. The output of the first stage is the guiding offset and the output of the second stage is a heatmap with size 56×56, and the value of the heatmap is the probability of the point being a gaze point.

The guiding offset loss uses L1 loss and lists as follows, L_i and G_i are $i - th$ ground truth of the guiding offset and the predicted guiding offset, and n is batch size.

$$L_g = -\frac{1}{n} \sum_{i=1}^{n} |L_i - G_i| \tag{5}$$

The binary cross entropy loss (BCE Loss) is employed for heatmap prediction and it is achieved by the following equation, Y_i and X_i are the $i - th$ entry of ground truth heatmap and predicted heatmap, N is heatmap size 56×56.

$$L_h = -\frac{1}{N} \sum_{i=1}^{N} Y_i \log X_i + (1 - Y_i) \log(1 - X_i) \tag{6}$$

The whole loss function is summed by guiding offset loss and heatmap loss:

$$L = L_g + L_h \tag{7}$$

4 Experiments

We conduct several experiments to demonstrate the effectiveness of our method. We first introduce the dataset and experimental details and then we analyze the results of performance and ablation study.

4.1 Dataset and Evaluation Metric

Dataset. We adopt the GazeFollow dataset [1] and DL Gaze dataset [2] to validate our method. The entire dataset contains 130,339 people and 122,143 images, including various activities of people in everyday scenes. 4,782 people of the dataset are used for testing and the rest for training. The DL Gaze dataset contains kind of activities of 16 volunteers in 4 scenes which include working office, laboratory, library and corridor in the building. There are 86 videos, 95,000 frames (30 fps) in total. Each frame contains one gaze point.

Evaluation Metric. These metrics are employed to evaluate the difference between the ground truth and our prediction. We use the **Area Under Curve (AUC)** criteria to evaluate the quality of our predicted heatmap. We report **L2 distance (Dist)**: The Euclidean distance between our predicted gaze point and the average of ground truth annotations. We also report the **minimum L2 distance (MDist)** between our predicted gaze point and all ground truth annotations. The full image size is normalized to 1×1.

4.2 Performance

We compare our proposed method with the following state-of-the-art gaze-following methods:

Lian et al. [2]: They propose a two-stage solution for gaze-following. They predict gaze direction and encode it into multi-scale gaze direction fields. Then they concatenate it with full image to generate a heatmap for gaze point.

Jeong et al. [4]: The network uses three-stage deep neural networks to tackle such complex scenes considering the depth information of the image. They calculate the gaze point from the generated heatmap.

Chen et al. [10]: A human-centric relationship inference module is designed, and they build a network with three pathways to predict the gaze target.

Jin et al. [9]. The network structure provides shared scene features and they introduce a numerical coordinate regression to calculate the gaze target point.

Tu et al. [21]. Their work redefines the Human-Gaze-Target detection task as detecting human head locations and their gaze targets simultaneously.

Table 2. Performance comparison on the GazeFollow dataset.

Methods	AUC	Dist	MDist
Lian et al. [2]	0.906	0.145	0.081
Jeong et al. [4]	0.908	0.139	0.077
Chen et al. [10]	0.908	0.136	0.074
Jin et al. [9]	0.919	0.126	0.076
Tu et al. [21]	0.917	0.133	0.069
One human	0.924	0.096	0.040
Our	**0.923**	0.142	0.080

Table 3. Performance comparison on the DL Gaze dataset.

Methods	Dist
Recasens et al. [1]	0.203
Lian et al. [2]	0.169
Chen et al. [10]	0.152
Our	0.151

The experiment results in Table 2 and Table 3 show that our model outperforms some baselines in some evaluation metrics on different datasets. We have the following findings: (1) On GazeFollow dataset, our model achieves an AUC of 0.923, and it outperforms all baselines, which means we can predict a better heatmap. (2) On DL Gaze dataset, our model achieves a Dist of 0.151, and it performs the best which proves that our model can also perform well on the Dist metric. (3) On GazeFollow dataset, our model achieves a Dist of 0.142, which does not perform very well, maybe because of the lack of depth information. (4) Performance on DL Gaze is worse than that on GazeFollow, which shows the challenge of applying gaze-following in reality.

4.3 Ablation Study

In order to evaluate the effectiveness of every component of different inputs and network. We design the following baselines:

Full image + CNN: We directly feed the full image into the heatmap pathway for heatmap regression. And the heatmap pathway uses ResNet-50 as backbone.

Full image + Transformer: We directly feed the full image into the heatmap pathway for heatmap regression. But the heatmap pathway uses Conformer-S/16 as backbone.

The experiment results are listed in Table 4. We can summarize the following two conclusions: First, we can see that Transformer works better than CNN, which shows its superiority for gaze-following. Especially, Transformer is more useful in generating

Table 4. The results of ablation study

Methods	AUC	Dist	MDist
Full image + CNN	0.849	0.212	0.146
Full image + Transformer	0.886	0.189	0.143
Our model	**0.923**	0.142	0.080

heatmaps. Second, with a gaze pathway to predict guiding offset and generate the multi-scale gaze fields, our method greatly outperforms full image with Transformer, which further validates that it is reasonable for our model to mimic the human gaze behavior and generate multi-scale gaze fields with guiding offset.

We also verify the effect of both the original and the modified Conformer-S/16 on our model. Our modified Conformer-S/16 achieves an AUC of 0.923 while the original Conformer-S/16 only achieves an AUC of 0.915, which proves that our modified Conformer-S/16 performs better.

4.4 Analysis

Here we show several examples of success and failure, as shown in Fig. 4. The first two examples prove our model can predict well, some other peaks can predict the gaze point correctly even if the position of heatmap maximum is not right. These results show that using the gaze pathway to simulate the human perspective is able to distinguish people in the image, as it produces different outputs for different people in the same image. The last two examples show that our method may identify less accurately, perhaps because of the image scene is too complex or lack of image depth information.

Fig. 4. The first two show successful cases and the last two show failed cases. The blue dot in full image represent the ground truth gaze point. (Color figure online)

We want to evaluate the performance when our model predicts inaccurately. So, we introduce the maximum L2 distance between our predicted gaze point and all ground truth annotations on the GazeFollow dataset. It can represent the worst result of our model. Our method achieves 0.274, and Lian et al. achieves 0.287. We can conclude that our model works better when some scenes are difficult to predict. This also means that our model predicts stable results.

5 Conclusion

Gaze-following is a challenging task in computer vision. In this paper, we propose a two-stage solution with the help of human gaze behavior. In the first stage, we predict the guiding offset based on the head image and head position. Then we use the guiding offset to generate the multi-scale gaze fields. After that, the multi-scale gaze fields are concatenated with the full image as priori feature, and feed them into the heatmap pathway which is mainly composed of Transformer in the second stage. Finally, we get a heatmap. This study contributes to our understanding of the role of the guiding offset and the channel attention module. It also shows that Transformer is helpful for gaze-following. Experimental results on GazeFollow dataset and DL Gaze dataset have demonstrated the advantage and performance improvement of our model for gaze-following.

Acknowledgments. This work is supported by the General Programmer of the National Natural Science Foundation of China (61976078, 62202139), the National Key R&D Programme of China (2019YFA0706203) and the Anhui Provincial Natural Science Foundation (2208085QF191).

References

1. Recasens, A., Khosla, A., Vondrick, C., Torralba, A.: Where are they looking? Advances in neural information processing systems, 28 (2015)
2. Lian, D., Yu, Z., Gao, S.: Believe it or not, we know what you are looking at! In Asian Conference on Computer Vision, pp. 35–50. Springer (2018)
3. Xie, S., Girshick, R., Doll´ar, P., Tu, Z., He, K.: Aggregated residual transformations for deep neural networks. In: Proceedings of the IEEE Conference on Computer Vision and Pattern Recognition, pp. 1492–1500 (2017)
4. Jeong, J.E., Choi, Y.S.: Depth-enhanced gaze following method. In: Proceedings of the 36th Annual ACM Symposium on Applied Computing, pp. 1090–1093 (2021)
5. Hu, J., Shen, L., Sun, G.: Squeeze-and-excitation networks. In: Proceedings of the IEEE conference on computer vision and pattern recognition, pp. 7132–7141 (2018)
6. Krafka, K., et al.: Eye tracking for everyone. In: Proceedings of the IEEE Conference on Computer Vision and Pattern Recognition, pp. 2176–2184 (2016)
7. Judd, T., Ehinger, K., Durand, F., Torralba, A.: Learning to predict where humans look. In: 2009 IEEE 12th International Conference on Computer Vision, pp. 2106–2113. IEEE (2009)
8. Marin-Jimenez, M.J., Zisserman, A., Eichner, M., Ferrari, V.: Detecting people looking at each other in videos. Int. J. Comput. Vis. **106**(3), 282–296 (2014)
9. Jin, T., Lin, Z., Zhu, S., Wang, W., Hu, S.: Multiperson gaze-following with numerical coordinate regression. In: 2021 16th IEEE International Conference on Automatic Face and Gesture Recognition (FG 2021), pp. 01–08. IEEE (2021)

10. Chen, W., et al.: Gaze estimation via the joint modeling of multiple cues. IEEE Trans. Circuits Syst. Video Technol. **32**(3), 1390–1402 (2021)
11. Park, H.S., Shi, J.: Social saliency prediction. In: Proceedings of the IEEE Conference on Computer Vision and Pattern Recognition, pp. 4777–4785 (2015)
12. Leifman, G., Rudoy, D., Swedish, T., Bayro-Corrochano, E., Raskar, R.: Learning gaze transitions from depth to improve video saliency estimation. In: Proceedings of the IEEE International Conference on Computer Vision, pp. 1698–1707 (2017)
13. Pfister, T., Charles, J., Zisserman, A.: Flowing convnets for human pose estimation in videos. In: Proceedings of the IEEE International Conference on Computer Vision, pp. 1913–1921 (2015)
14. Pathirana, P., Senarath, S., Meedeniya, D., Jayarathna, S.: Single-user 2d gaze estimation in retail environment using deep learning. In: 2022 2nd International Conference on Advanced Research in Computing (ICARC), pp. 206–211. IEEE (2022)
15. Peng, Z., et al.: Conformer: local features coupling global representations for visual recognition. In: Proceedings of the IEEE/CVF International Conference on Computer Vision, pp. 367–376 (2021)
16. Lin, T.-Y., Doll'ar, P., Girshick, R., He, K., Hariharan, B., Belongie, S.: Feature pyramid networks for object detection. In: Proceedings of the IEEE Conference on Computer Vision and Pattern Recognition, pp. 2117–2125 (2017)
17. MohebAli, R., Toroghi, R.M., Zareian, H.: Human action recognition using attention mechanism and gaze information. In: Mediterranean Conference on Pattern Recognition and Artificial Intelligence, pp. 3–17. Springer (2022)
18. Kümmerer, M., Theis, L., Bethge, M.: Deep gaze i: boosting saliency prediction with feature maps trained on imagenet. arXiv preprint arXiv:1411.1045 (2014)
19. Recasens, A., Vondrick, C., Khosla, A., Torralba, A.: Following gaze in video. In: Proceedings of the IEEE International Conference on Computer Vision, pp. 1435–1443 (2017)
20. Dai, L., Liu, J., Zhaojie, J.: Binocular feature fusion and spatial attention mechanism based gaze tracking. IEEE Trans. Hum.-Mach. Syst. **52**(2), 302–311 (2022)
21. Tu, D., Min, X., Duan, H., Guo, G., Zhai, G., Shen, W.: End-to-end human-gaze-target detection with transformers. arXiv preprint arXiv:2203.10433 (2022)

Learning Optimal Transport Mapping of Joint Distribution for Cross-scenario Face Anti-spoofing

Shiyun Mao, Ruolin Chen, and Huibin Li[✉]

School of Mathematics and Statistics, Xi'an Jiaotong University, Xi'an 710049, China
`huibinli@xjtu.edu.cn`

Abstract. Face anti-spoofing (FAS) under different scenarios is a challenging and indispensable task for a real face recognition system. In this paper, we propose a novel cross-scenario FAS method by learning the optimal transport mapping of joint distributions under the unsupervised domain adaption framework, namely OTJD-FAS. In particular, given the training and testing real or fake face samples from different scenarios (i.e., source and target domains), their deep CNN features are firstly extracted and the labels of the test samples are firstly predicted by an initial binary classifier. Then, the gap of joint distributions (i.e., in the product space of deep features and their corresponding labels) between training and testing sets is measured by the Wasserstein distance and their optimal transport mapping is learned. Finally, an adaptive cross-entropy loss for classification and cross-entropy loss of testing labels are employed for the final FAS. Extensive experimental results demonstrated on the MSU-MFSD, CASIA-FASD and Idiap REPLAY-ATTACK databases under cross-scenario setting show that aligning joint distributions is more effective than the widely used only aligning marginal distributions based methods and the proposed method can achieve competitive performance for cross-scenario FAS.

Keywords: Face anti-spoofing · Joint distribution · Optimal transport mapping · Domain adaptation

1 Introduction

Face anti-spoofing (FAS), specifically face presentation attack detection technology aims to determine whether a user before a given face recognition system is a real or fake person. Generally, photo printing, video replay, and face mask are three types of typical face presentation attack schemes. In the past two decades, various FAS methods have been proposed including both traditional methods and deep learning based methods. Traditional methods based on handcraft descriptors [1,2] can be further classified into texture-based, motion-based, and image analysis-based methods. Subsequently, hybrid (handcrafted + deep learning) [3,4] and end-to-end deep learning-based methods [5–7] have also been proposed.

© The Author(s), under exclusive license to Springer Nature Switzerland AG 2022
W. Deng et al. (Eds.): CCBR 2022, LNCS 13628, pp. 169–179, 2022.
https://doi.org/10.1007/978-3-031-20233-9_17

However, due to the variations of lighting, facial appearance, or camera quality, the performance of most FAS methods will be significantly reduced under the cross-scenario settings. In light of this, researchers begin to focus on improving the cross-scenario capabilities of deep FAS models by using the tools of domain adaptation (DA) and domain generalization (DG). In most DA methods, the distributions of source and target features are matched in a learned feature space, by using Maximum Mean Discrepancy (MMD) [8,9], Correlation Alignment (CORAL) [10] or Kullback-Leiber divergence (KL) [11]. Besides, another promising direction is based on the adversarial training [12], where a discriminator (domain classifier) is trained to distinguish between the source and target representations. However, in some scenarios, the target domain data cannot be obtained in advance. The basic idea of DG is to assume that there is a potential generalization feature space between the given source domains and unseen target domains. By aligning multiple source domain data to learn a common feature space, the model trained in the source domains can been well generalized to other unseen target domains.

Different from the existing DA based methods which try to aligning the marginal distributions in the feature spaces between source domain and target domain, in this paper, we consider the joint distribution of both data features and labels. The main idea of this paper is to find an optimal transport mapping (i.e., transfer plan) from the product space (both features and labels) of source domain to that of target domain, under which the distribution inconsistency is measured by the Wasserstein distance [16]. By minimizing this metric, the joint distribution of the features and labels of the training samples can be mapped into a new space where those transformed source-domain joint distribution and target-domain joint distribution can be well aligned. At the same time, we train a classifier on the transformed joint distribution of the source domain and use it for the final FAS in target domain. Experimental results evaluated on current popular FAS datasets demonstrate the effectiveness of our proposed method.

The remainder of this paper is organized into five sections. Section 2 briefly reviews related works for cross-scenario FAS, while Sect. 3 introduces the details of our proposed method. Section 4 presents datasets and experimental results, and Sect. 5 summarizes the whole paper.

2   Related Works

Domain adaptation techniques are used to mitigate the data distribution differences between source and target domains. For most cases, the distributions of source and target features are matched in a learned feature space. If these features have similar distributions, the classifier trained on the features of the source domain samples can also be generalized to classify the target domain samples. Several DA methods based on metric learning were proposed to match the distributions of source and target features in a learned feature space for cross-domain FAS. ADDA [14] sought to minimize an approximate domain discrepancy distance through an adversarial objective with respect to a domain discriminator. DRCN [24] learned a shared encoded representation for both: (i) supervised classification of labeled source data and (ii) unsupervised reconstruction of unlabeled target data. DupGAN [25] employed a novel GAN architecture with a dual adversarial discriminator, which can achieve domain-invariant representation and domain transformation. Li et al. [13] used the unsupervised domain adaptation learning framework to learn a mapping function to align the PCA embedded eigenspaces between source and target domains by minimizing their MMD. DR-UDA [27] proposed ML-Net to learn a discriminative feature representation by using the labeled source domain face images via metric learning. Besides, they added UDA-Net and DR-Net to optimize the source and target domain encoders jointly and specific domains by reconstructing the source and target domain face images from the common feature space respectively. In addition, Jia et al. [15] proposed a domain adaptation network with domain-invariant feature space via marginal distribution alignment (target domain labels are not given) and conditional distribution alignment (some target domain labels are given) across source and target domains. Recently, OCKD [28] introduced a teacher-student framework to improve the cross-domain performance of FAS with one-class domain adaptation. GDA [30] proposed to directly fit the target data to the models, i.e., stylizes the target data to the source-domain style via image translation, and further feeds the stylized data into the well-trained source model for classification.

In addition, domain generalization helps to learn generalized feature representations from multiple source domains without accessing the target data. AMEL [29] proposed an Adaptive Mixture of Experts Learning (AMEL) framework, which exploits the domain-specific information to adaptively establish the link among the seen source domains and unseen target domains to further improve the generalization. Concretely, Domain-Specific Experts (DSE) were designed to investigate discriminative and unique domain-specific features as a complement to common domain-invariant features. Besides, Dynamic Expert Aggregation (DEA) was proposed to adaptively aggregate the complementary information of each source expert based on the domain relevance to the unseen target domain. And combined with meta-learning, these modules work collaboratively to adaptively aggregate meaningful domain-specific information for various unseen target domains. DRLM [31] proposed domain dynamic adjustment meta-learning (D2AM) without using domain labels, which iteratively divides mixture domains via discriminative domain representation and trained a generalizable face anti-spoofing with meta-learning. Besides, they designed a domain feature based on Instance Normalization and proposed a domain representation learning module to extract discriminative domain features for clustering. Moreover, they additionally utilized maximum mean discrepancy (MMD) to align the distribution of sample features to a prior distribution to reduce the side effect of outliers on clustering performance, which improves the reliability of clustering.

In order to solve cross-scenario FAS problem, we propose to use the joint distribution of features and labels when measuring the distance between source domain and target domain, so that the label information of source domain can be fully utilized. In particular, inspired by [17], we learn the optimal transport mapping of joint distributions for the cross-scenario FAS.

3   Proposed Method

Our proposed method is mainly based on the theory of regularized discrete optimal transport and the overview of the method is introduced in Fig. 1.

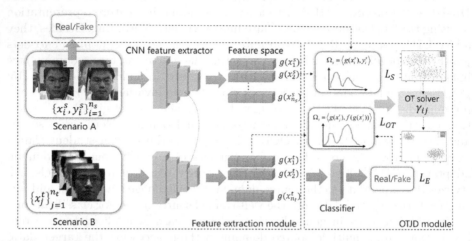

Fig. 1. An overview of the proposed method. Given the training and testing real or fake face samples from different scenarios (i.e., source and target domains), their deep CNN features are firstly extracted and the labels of the test samples are predicted by an initial binary classifier. Then, the gap of joint distributions (i.e., in the product space of deep features and their corresponding labels) between training and testing sets is measured by the Wasserstein distance and their optimal transport mapping is learned. Finally, source domain classification loss L_S, optimal transport loss L_{OT}, and target domain entropy loss L_E are employed for the final FAS.

3.1   Discrete Optimal Transport with Entropy Regularization

Given training samples (source domain) $\{x_i^s\}_{i=1}^{n_s}$ and test samples (target domain) $\{x_i^t\}_{i=1}^{n_t}$, where x_i^s and $x_i^t \in \mathbb{R}^d$ denote the feature vectors of each face sample from source and target domains respectively, the feature distributions of training and test samples can be written as

$$\mu_s = \sum_{i=1}^{n_s} p_i^s \delta_{x_i^s}, \mu_t = \sum_{i=1}^{n_t} p_i^t \delta_{x_i^t}, \tag{1}$$

where $\delta_{x_i^s}$ and $\delta_{x_i^t}$ are the Dirac functions at location x_i^s and x_i^t respectively. p_i^s and p_i^t are the probability masses associated with i-th data sample and belong to the probability simplex, $\sum_{i=1}^{n_s} p_i^s = \sum_{i=1}^{n_t} p_i^t = 1$. The probability coupling set between these two distributions can be defined as

$$\Pi = \{\gamma \in (\mathbb{R}^+)^{n_s \times n_t} | \gamma \mathbf{1}_{n_t} = \mu_s, \gamma^\mathsf{T} \mathbf{1}_{n_s} = \mu_t\}, \tag{2}$$

where $\mathbf{1}_d$ is the d-dimension vectors of ones. Then, the discrete formulation of the optimal transport problem is:

$$\gamma_0 = arg \min_{\gamma \in \Pi} \langle \gamma, \boldsymbol{C} \rangle_F, \tag{3}$$

where $\langle \cdot, \cdot \rangle_F$ is the Frobenius matrix norm. $\boldsymbol{C} \geq 0$ is the cost matrix.

To solve the problem more efficiently, the entropy regularized version of the above optimal transport problem is proposed [18] and can be formulated as follows:

$$\gamma_0^\lambda = arg \min_{\gamma \in \Pi} \langle \gamma, \boldsymbol{C} \rangle_F + \lambda \Omega_s(\gamma), \tag{4}$$

where $\Omega_s(\gamma) = \sum_{i,j} \gamma(i,j) log \gamma(i,j)$ computes the negative entropy of γ.

3.2   Learning Optimal Transport of Joint Distributions for FAS

Denote $g : x \rightarrow z$ as an feature embedding function, where each input face sample is mapped into the feature space Z, and $f : z \rightarrow y$ as a classifier which maps the feature space to the label space on target domain. The cost associated to this space can be expressed as a weighted combination of the costs in the product space of features and labels, that is:

$$d(g(x_i^s), y_i^s; g(x_j^t), f(g(x_j^t))) = \lambda_0 \parallel g(x_i^s) - g(x_j^t) \parallel^2 + \lambda_1 L_t(y_i^s, f(g(x_j^t))), \tag{5}$$

for i-th source and j-th target element, the first term in Eq. (5) compares the compatibility of the embeddings for source and target domains, while the second term $L_t(\cdot, \cdot)$ is a classification loss, which considers the classifier f learned in target domain and its regularity with respect to the labels available in source domain. Parameters λ_0 and λ_1 are two scalar values weighing the contributions of distance terms. Then, the regularized optimal transport loss L_{OT} with joint distributions can be formulated as follows:

$$L_{OT} = \sum_i \sum_j \gamma_{ij} d(g(x_i^s), y_i^s; g(x_j^t), f(g(x_j^t))) + \lambda_2 \Omega_s(\gamma). \tag{6}$$

It can be noted that the formula reported in Eq. (6) depends only on the classifier learned in target domain. The loss in source domain (L_S) can be combined in (6). The form of L_S is as follows:

$$L_S = \frac{1}{n^s} \sum_i L_s(y_i^s, f(g(x_i^s))). \tag{7}$$

The classification loss function for source domain (L_S) and target domain (L_T) can be any general twice-differentiable loss function. For FAS problem, we choose the adaptive cross-entropy (AdaCE) loss. The forms of AdaCE losses in source domain and target domain are formulated as follows:

$$L_s(y_i^s, f(g(x_i^s))) = (1 - e^{-CE(x_i^s, y_i^s)})^\beta CE(x_i^s, y_i^s), \tag{8}$$

$$L_t(y_i^s, f(g(x_j^t))) = (1 - e^{-CE(x_j^t, y_i^s)})^\beta CE(x_j^t, y_i^s), \tag{9}$$

where $CE(\cdot,\cdot)$ is the cross-entropy loss. The forms of AdaCE losses are to add modulation factors $(1 - e^{-CE(x_i^s, y_i^s)})^\beta$ and $(1 - e^{-CE(x_i^t, y_i^t)})^\beta$ for source and target domains respectively. The AdaCE loss can adaptively adjust the weights of cross-entropy loss according to classification accuracy in each batch.

In addition, we employ the entropy minimization principle to make the classifier adaptively adjust its parameters to further adapt to the distribution of target domain. This process is performed by minimizing the following equation:

$$L_E = \mathbb{E}_{x \sim X_t} \sum_{k=1}^{K} f(g(x)) log f(g(x)), \tag{10}$$

where K denotes the total number of sample classes in target domain.

Overall, the final objective function of the proposed approach can be formulated as follows:

$$L_{total} = L_{OT} + \lambda_3 L_S + \lambda_4 L_E, \tag{11}$$

where λ_3 and λ_4 are the balance parameters.

4   Experimental Results

4.1   Databases

MSU-MFSD Database [21]. It consists of 280 videos of real and fake faces of 55 subjects. The face videos are captured by two types of cameras (Laptop camera and Android phone camera) with resolutions of 640×480 and 720×480, respectively. The MSU-MFSD contains mainly two different spoofing attacks, printed photo attack and replay video attack. It is also divided into training and testing subsets based on different subjects. **CASIA-FASD Database** [20]. It consists of 600 videos of real and attack attempts of 50 different subjects. Compared with Idiap REPLAY-ATTACK database, CASIA-FASD uses more face acquisition devices with different quality levels (Sony NEX-5 with the resolution 1280×720, two different USB cameras with the resolution 640×480). The spoofing types include: warped photo attack, cut photo attack, and replaying attack. **Idiap REPLAY-ATTACK Database** [19]. It consists of 1200 videos of both real and attack attempts of 50 different subjects taken by the webcam on a MacBook with the resolution 320×240. The videos were captured under two conditions: 1) the controlled condition with a uniform background and the fluorescent light; 2) the adverse condition with the complex background and natural lighting. Spoofing attack was launched by using Canon PowerShot to capture face videos and the high-resolution videos were displayed using iPad 1 (1024×768), iPhone 3GS (480×320) and paper as the spoofing medium. Figure 2 shows some examples of these three databases.

4.2   Experimental Setting

In this paper, we use MTCNN algorithm [22] for face detection and alignment. All detected face images are normalized to $256 \times 256 \times 3$ and then resized to

Fig. 2. Examples of real (first row) and fake (second row) faces from the MSU-MFSD (M), CASIA-FASD (C) and Idiap REPLAY-ATTACK (I) databases. It is easy to find that there are large cross-scenario differences, such as lighting, background, resolution and so on.

$224 \times 224 \times 3$. We implement our OTJD-FAS method on PyTorch platform and use ResNet-18 [23] pre-trained on ImageNet as our backbone. Specifically, we utilize all the convolutional layers of ResNet-18 as the backbone of the feature extractor. Our model is trained with only single-scale face images by using Adam optimizer with weight decay of 5e-4 and using mini-batch sizes of $m_s = m_t = 180$ for two domains (90 samples per class in source mini-batch) on a single NVIDIA RTX 3090 GPU. The hyper parameters $\beta, \lambda_0, \lambda_1, \lambda_2, \lambda_3$ and λ_4 are set to 2, 0.001, 0.0001, 0.01, 0.2 and 0.02 respectively. For fair comparison of cross-scenario FAS, we use the Half Total Error Rate (HTER) metric, which is the average of False Acceptance Rate (FAR) and False Rejection Rate (FRR).

4.3 Experimental Results

We randomly select one dataset as source domain for training and another dataset as target domain for testing. Therefore, there are a total of six test tasks: $C \rightarrow I, C \rightarrow M, I \rightarrow C, I \rightarrow M, M \rightarrow C, M \rightarrow I$. In this case, all labeled images in source domain and unlabeled images in target domain are used for training. Since our main contribution is to introduce a new joint distribution mapping method between source and target domains, we compare the state-of-the-art DA based FAS methods by using Generative Adversarial and MMD methods. The comparison results are shown in Table 1.

Table 1. Performance comparisons of the proposed method and other related DA based FAS methods. $*$ indicates that we reproduced the method proposed in our experimental setting.

Method	$C \rightarrow I$	$C \rightarrow M$	$I \rightarrow C$	$I \rightarrow M$	$M \rightarrow C$	$M \rightarrow I$	Average
ADDA [14]	41.8	36.6	49.8	35.1	39.0	35.2	39.58
DRCN [24]	44.4	27.6	48.9	42.0	28.9	36.8	38.10
DupGAN [25]	42.4	33.4	46.5	36.2	27.1	35.4	36.83
Li et al. [13]	39.2	14.3	**26.3**	33.2	10.1	33.3	26.10
ML-Net [27]	43.3	14.0	45.4	35.3	37.8	**11.5**	31.22
Jia et al. [15]$*$	28.1	24.2	40.9	28.7	17.4	14.4	25.62
OTJD-FAS	**28.0**	**13.8**	37.2	**26.3**	**6.50**	19.4	**21.87**

From Table 1, we can find that by aligning the joint distributions between source and target domains using the optimal transport mapping can make fully use of the label information, and our proposed method is effective for cross scenario FAS. All other related DA based FAS methods only consider the differences of feature distributions between source and target domains. Our proposed OTJD method outperforms the state-of-the-art methods in four out of six test tasks and achieves the best average results. The differences in the experimental results of different cross-datasets indicate that the unknown attack types on the test set will affect the performance to a certain extent.

In Fig. 3, we also plot the t-SNE [26] to visualize the feature embedding quality of source and target domains learned by OTJD-FAS method. The first two visualizations show the effect learned by ResNet18-SourceOnly method (denoted as SourceOnly) and OT method [32], which only considering the feature distributions when measuring distances between source and target domains. The last one is based on OTJD-FAS. As shown in Fig. 3, the samples from source domain and target domain are scattered for the SourceOnly model, and the embeddings do not well-aligned the distributions. For OT based method, the source domain samples are separated, however, the target domain samples are still not separated, which illustrates the necessity of measuring the distance of joint distributions. In OTJD-FAS model visualization, the source and target domain samples can be perfectly aligned with each other, which indicates that by utilizing OTJD-FAS, we can find an embedding that can both align the source and target distributions and also maximize the difference between classes.

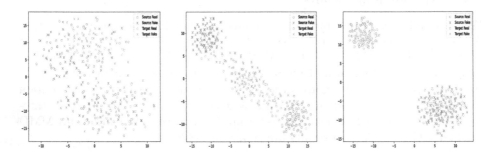

Fig. 3. The t-SNE embeddings of samples from MSU-MFSD (source) and CASIA-FASD (target) for the SourceOnly classifier, OT based method [32] and the proposed OTJD method. The effectiveness of transporting and aligning joint distributions (OTJD) is obviously better than that of marginal distributions (OT).

Ablation Study. To further show the effectiveness of the proposed method, we perform ablation study experiments under the domain adaptation setting to investigate the performance obtained for each network component. The experimental procedures are as follows: four types of models are trained for comparisons, namely the Baseline model (with only source domain classification loss), the Baseline+OT model (with source domain classification loss and OT loss), the

Table 2. Evaluation of the different components of the proposed method for cross-scenario testing (HTER) in a domain adaptation setting.

Method	$C \to I$	$C \to M$	$I \to C$	$I \to M$	$M \to C$	$M \to I$	Average
Baseline	43.2	20.0	55.2	33.3	18.5	28.9	33.18
Baseline+OT [32]	42.9	19.2	45.4	29.2	18.3	24.6	29.93
Baseline+OTJD	30.5	17.2	44.4	26.3	17.2	23.1	26.45
OTJD-FAS	**28.0**	**13.8**	**37.2**	**26.3**	**6.5**	**19.4**	**21.87**

Baseline+OTJD model (with source domain classification loss and OTJD loss), and OTJD-FAS model (with source domain classification loss, target domain entropy loss and OTJD loss).

It can be seen that all the components are useful for our OTJD-FAS method. OT method can improve cross-scenario FAS by aligning the feature distribution of source and target domains compared to the baseline method. In addition, since OTJD-FAS method considers the joint distribution of features and labels when measuring the distances between source and target domains, it achieves better cross-scenario experimental results than OT method. OTJD-FAS method aims to mitigate and reduce the joint distribution inconsistencies between face samples collected under different conditions. Besides, entropy loss allows for low density separation between target domain data classes, so that adding entropy loss can improve cross-scenario experimental results. All the components play key roles in learning a common representation between the source and target domains. Summarizing, this ablation study shows that the individual components bring complimentary information to achieve the best classification results.

5   Conclusion

In this paper, we introduce a novel cross-scenario deep face anti-spoofing method by learning the optimal transport mapping of feature-label joint distributions. In particular, we propose to use the Wasserstein distance and regularized joint distribution optimal transport mapping to measure and reduce the distribution inconsistency between face samples collected under different conditions. Comprehensive experimental results show the effectiveness and the advantagement of our proposed method over most DA methods based on metric learning. In the future, we will try to extend the proposed method to 3D faces and use it to detect 3D mask attacks.

References

1. Komulainen J, Hadid A, Pietikäinen M: Context based face anti-spoofing. In: In: IEEE Sixth International Conference on Biometrics, pp. 1–8 (2013)
2. Patel, K., Han, H., Jain, A.K.: Secure face unlock: spoof detection on smartphones. IEEE Trans. Inf. Forensics Secur. **11**, 2268–2283 (2016)

3. Rehman, Y.A.U., Po, L.M., Komulainen, J.: Enhancing deep discriminative feature maps via perturbation for face presentation attack detection. Image Vis. Comput. **94**, 103858 (2020)
4. Khammari, M.: Robust face anti-spoofing using CNN with LBP and WLD. IET Image Proc. **13**, 1880–1884 (2019)
5. Liu, Y., Jourabloo, A., Liu, X.: Learning deep models for face anti-spoofing: binary or auxiliary supervision. In: CVPR, pp. 389–398 (2018)
6. Yu Z, Zhao C, Wang Z, et al.: Searching central difference convolutional networks for face anti-spoofing. In: CVPR, pp. 5295–5305 (2020)
7. Zhang, S., Liu, A., Wan, J., et al.: Casia-surf: a large-scale multi-modal benchmark for face anti-spoofing. IEEE Trans. Biometrics Beh. Identity Sci. **2**, 182–193 (2020)
8. Pei, Z., Cao, Z., Long, M., et al.: Multi-adversarial domain adaptation. In: AAAI (2018)
9. Rahman, M.M., Fookes, C., Baktashmotlagh, M., Sridharan, S.: On minimum discrepancy estimation for deep domain adaptation. In: Singh, R., Vatsa, M., Patel, V.M., Ratha, N. (eds.) Domain Adaptation for Visual Understanding, pp. 81–94. Springer, Cham (2020). https://doi.org/10.1007/978-3-030-30671-7_6
10. Sun, B., Saenko, K.: Deep CORAL: correlation alignment for deep domain adaptation. In: Hua, G., Jégou, H. (eds.) ECCV 2016. LNCS, vol. 9915, pp. 443–450. Springer, Cham (2016). https://doi.org/10.1007/978-3-319-49409-8_35
11. Zhuang, F., Cheng, X., Luo, P., et al.: Supervised representation learning: transfer learning with deep autoencoders. In: Twenty-Fourth International Joint Conference on Artificial Intelligence (2015)
12. Tzeng, E., Hoffman, J., Saenko, K., et al.: Adversarial discriminative domain adaptation. In: CVPR, pp. 7167–7176 (2017)
13. Li, H., Li, W., Cao, H., et al.: Unsupervised domain adaptation for face anti-spoofing. ITFS **13**, 1794–1809 (2018)
14. Tzeng E, Hoffman J, Saenko K, et al.: Adversarial discriminative domain adaptation. In: CVPR, pp. 7167–7176 (2017)
15. Jia, Y., Zhang, J., Shan, S., et al.: Unified unsupervised and semi-supervised domain adaptation network for cross-scenario face anti-spoofing. Pattern Recogn. **115**, 107888 (2021)
16. Cuturi, M., Doucet, A.: Fast computation of wasserstein barycenters. In: International Conference on Machine Learning. PMLR, pp. 685–693 (2014)
17. Damodaran, B.B., Kellenberger, B., Flamary, R., Tuia, D., Courty, N.: DeepJDOT: deep joint distribution optimal transport for unsupervised domain adaptation. In: Ferrari, V., Hebert, M., Sminchisescu, C., Weiss, Y. (eds.) ECCV 2018. LNCS, vol. 11208, pp. 467–483. Springer, Cham (2018). https://doi.org/10.1007/978-3-030-01225-0_28
18. Cuturi, M.: Sinkhorn distances: lightspeed computation of optimal transport. In: Advances in Neural Information Processing Systems, pp. 2292–2300 (2013)
19. Chingovska, I., Anjos, A., Marcel, S.: On the effectiveness of local binary patterns in face anti-spoofing. BIOSIG, pp. 1–7 (2012)
20. Zhang, Z., Yan, J., Liu, S., et al.: A face antispoofing database with diverse attacks. In: ICB, pp. 26–31 (2012)
21. Wen, D., Han, H., Jain, A.K.: Face spoof detection with image distortion analysis. TIFS **10**, 746–761 (2015)
22. Zhang, K., Zhang, Z., Li, Z., et al.: Joint face detection and alignment using multitask cascaded convolutional networks. IEEE Signal Process. Lett. **23**, 1499–1503 (2016)

23. He, K., Zhang, X., Ren, S., et al.: Deep residual learning for image recognition. In: CVPR, pp. 770–778 (2016)
24. Ghifary, M., Kleijn, W.B., Zhang, M., Balduzzi, D., Li, W.: Deep reconstruction-classification networks for unsupervised domain adaptation. In: Leibe, B., Matas, J., Sebe, N., Welling, M. (eds.) ECCV 2016. LNCS, vol. 9908, pp. 597–613. Springer, Cham (2016). https://doi.org/10.1007/978-3-319-46493-0_36
25. Hu, L., Kan, M., Shan, S., et al.: Duplex generative adversarial network for unsupervised domain adaptation. In: CVPR, pp. 1498–1507 (2018)
26. Van der Maaten, L., Hinton, G.: Visualizing data using t-SNE. J. Mach. Learn. Res. **9**, 2579–2605 (2008)
27. Wang, G., Han, H., Shan, S., Chen, X.: Unsupervised adversarial domain adaptation for cross-domain face presentation attack detection. TIFS **16**, 56–69 (2021)
28. Li, Z., Cai, R., Li, H., Lam, K.-Y., Hu, Y., Kot, A.C.: One-class knowledge distillation for face presentation attack detection. TIFS **17**, 2137–2150 (2022)
29. Zhou, Q., et al.: Adaptive mixture of experts learning for generalizable face anti-spoofing. ACM MM (2022)
30. Zhou, et al.: Generative domain adaptation for face anti-spoofin. In: ECCV (2022)
31. Chen, Z., et al.: Generalizable representation learning for mixture domain face anti-spoofing. In: AAAI, pp. 1132–1139 (2021)
32. Flamary, R., Courty, N., Tuia, D., et al.: Optimal transport for domain adaptation. IEEE Trans. Pattern Anal. Mach. Intell. **39**, 1853–1865 (2016)

MLFW: A Database for Face Recognition on Masked Faces

Chengrui Wang, Han Fang, Yaoyao Zhong, and Weihong Deng[✉]

Beijing University of Posts and Telecommunications, Beijing, China
{crwang,zhongyaoyao,whdeng}@bupt.edu.cn

Abstract. As more and more people begin to wear masks due to current COVID-19 pandemic, existing face recognition systems may encounter severe performance degradation when recognizing masked faces. To figure out the impact of masks on face recognition model, we build a simple but effective tool to generate masked faces from unmasked faces automatically, and construct a new database called Masked LFW (MLFW) based on Cross-Age LFW (CALFW) database. The mask on the masked face generated by our method has good visual consistency with the original face. Moreover, we collect various mask templates, covering most of the common styles appeared in the daily life, to achieve diverse generation effects. Considering realistic scenarios, we design three kinds of combinations of face pairs. The recognition accuracy of SOTA models declines 5%–16% on MLFW database compared with the accuracy on the original images. MLFW database can be viewed and downloaded at http://whdeng.cn/mlfw.

Keywords: Face recognition · Masked face dataset

1 Introduction

COVID-19 pandemic forces people to start wearing masks to prevent themselves from the disease. However, a mask will occlude a part region of a face, and change the facial features that can be obtained by face recognition models. This raises concerns about whether a face recognition model can work well on masked faces [1–3], especially when the model has never seen any masks during the training process. In order to maintain the security of face recognition, the most important method in the contactless authentication, it is urgent to come up with a credible approach to evaluate the performance of face recognition models on the masked faces.

Recently, lots of works focus on generating masked face images and constructing related datasets. Anwar *et al.* [4] present an opensource tool to mask faces and create a large dataset of masked faces. Wang *et al.* [5] propose three types of masked face datasets. Du *et al.* [6] use 3D face reconstruction to add the mask templates on the UV texture map of the non-masked face. Cabani *et al.* [7] provide a fine-grained dataset for detecting people wearing masks and those not

© The Author(s), under exclusive license to Springer Nature Switzerland AG 2022
W. Deng et al. (Eds.): CCBR 2022, LNCS 13628, pp. 180–188, 2022.
https://doi.org/10.1007/978-3-031-20233-9_18

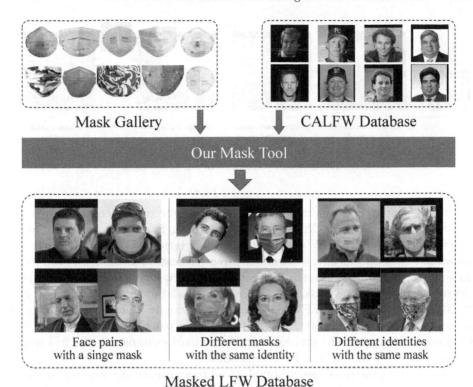

Mask Gallery   CALFW Database

Our Mask Tool

| Face pairs with a singe mask | Different masks with the same identity | Different identities with the same mask |

Masked LFW Database

Fig. 1. With the mask tool, we remake the face images in CALFW database with masks in a gallery, and construct a new database, Masked LFW (MLFW) database, which shares the face verification protocol and the same identities in LFW database.

wearing masks. However, existing tools usually transform the whole mask to generate masked faces, resulting in unrealistic generation effect to a certain extent. In addition, there lacks a specialized dataset to verify the performance of face recognition models.

Face identification and face verification are the basic paradigms in face recognition. Face identification accesses the identity of a query image through finding the most similar face in a gallery, while face verification attempts to verify whether two given face images have the same identity. The protocol of face verification makes it easy to construct a persuasive database used for verifying the performance of face recognition models on masked faces. Labeled Faces in the Wild (LFW) database [8] is a widely-used benchmark for face verification, which evaluates the performance of face recognition models in the unconstrained scenarios, and has attracted a lot of researchers. Beyond that, several databases have been proposed based on LFW for special scenarios [9–12]. Particularly, Cross-Age LFW [10] (CALFW) database adds age intra-class variation into the positive pairs of the original LFW database, which better simulates the situation of face verification in the real world.

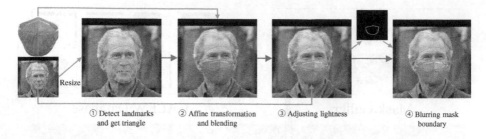

① Detect landmarks   ② Affine transformation   ③ Adjusting lightness   ④ Blurring mask
and get triangle   and blending   boundary

Fig. 2. The main procedure of our mask tool.

In this paper, we reinvent the CALFW database and construct a new database called Masked CALFW (MLFW) through adding masks to some selected images of CALFW database. The illustration of MLFW database is shown in Fig. 1. Specifically, we consider three verification scenarios, 1) two faces have the same identity but wear different masks, 2) two faces have different identities but wear the same mask, 3) one face has a mask but the other does not. For the 6,000 face pairs in CALFW database, we randomly divide them into three subsets, which contain 3,000, 1,500 and 1,500 face pairs respectively according to different scenarios. The division reflects the hard examples in the real world and increases the difficulty of face verification.

To construct the database, we build a tool to automatically generate masked faces from unmasked faces. In the process of wearing mask, the tool divides both mask and face into multiple triangles separately according to landmarks, and adds each patch of mask to the correlative facial patch through affine transformation, which produces a appropriate fit between mask and face. Besides, the tool adjusts the brightness of mask and smooths the edge between mask and face to make mask look more consistent with face. For achieving diverse generation effects, we construct a mask gallery which contains various pre-processed masks and propose a method to interfere with the mask position.

The main contributions of this paper are as follows:

- We provide a tool to automatically generate masked face from unmasked face, which achieves real and diverse generation effects.
- Based on the proposed tool, we build a masked version called MLFW to evaluate the performance of face recognition model on masked faces.

2   Mask Tool

2.1   Main Procedure

In this section, we detail the main procedure of our mask tool. The brief illustration is shown in Fig. 2, which consists of four steps.

Detect Landmarks and Get Triangles. Given input face image I_f, we firstly resize I_f to I_f' of larger size $H_t \times W_t$, which aims to reduce aliasing in the output masked face, and detect landmarks of I_f' through a 68-points detector [13]. Then, according to specific landmarks set on I_m, we extract 14 patches from both I_f' and I_m, and calculate a transformation matrix for each pair of patches.

Affine Transformation and Blending. After that, we project the mask I_m to I_f' to generate the masked face image I_o' based on the affine transformation.

Adjusting Lightness. Next, we calculate the average value of L-channel on the center facial region of I_f to adjust the L-channel of mask in I_o' under the control of weight α.

Blurring Mask Boundary. Furthermore, in order to further reduce the visual inconsistency, we apply Gaussian Blur to blur the boundary between mask and face in I_o' with kernel size β. Finally, we resize I_o' to the output size.

The visual difference of masked face generated under different parameters are shown in Fig. 3. In this work, $H_t \& W_t, \alpha$ and β are set to 500, 0.6 and 5, respectively.

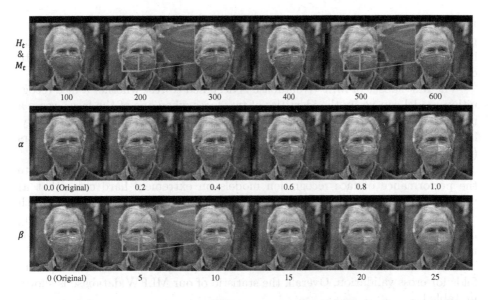

Fig. 3. Mask faces generated under different parameters $H_t \& W_t$ (top), α (center) and β (bottom).

2.2   Generation Variety

To achieve various generation effect, we simulate different mask position on the nose through perturbing the top landmark of the face, and perturbing the top landmark of the mask to change the shape of mask. Some examples are shown in Fig. 4. In addition, the mask templates used to generate masked face are randomly selected from the mask gallery.

Fig. 4. The example mask faces generated under landmark perturbation.

3   MLFW Database

With the help of the mask tool, we construct MLFW database based on CALFW database, and the main process can be described into the following steps.

Dividing Faces into Three Subsets. CALFW database contains 6,000 face pairs (3,000 positive pairs and 3,000 negative pairs). We spilt the 6,000 pairs into three subsets, which contain 3,000, 1,500, 1,500 face pairs separately, to construct our MLFW database.

The first subset of MLFW database is designed to test whether a face recognition model can verify the identities of two faces when one of the faces wears a mask. Therefore, we only add mask to one face image of each face pair. Specially, in this subset, the number of positive pairs is the same as that of negative pairs (1,500 positive pairs and 1,500 negative pairs).

The second and third subsets of MLFW database are designed to evaluate the performance of face recognition models on extremely hard cases that a) two faces with the same identity wear different masks and b) two faces with different identities wear the same mask, respectively. Compared with adding masks randomly, experimental results show that the accuracy of SOTA models is further reduced by at least 2% with our elaborate strategy.

In addition, our MLFW dataset has been equally divided into 10 separate folds for cross validation. Overall, the statistic of our MLFW database is shown in Table 1.

Table 1. Statistic of our MLFW database. *Mask count* represents the count of masked faces in each face pair.

Mask count	Positive pair	Negative pair
1	1500	1500
2	1500	1500

Fig. 5. Examples of masked faces generated by our mask tool.

Table 2. Comparison of verification accuracy (%) on MLFW database, as well as LFW [8], SLLFW [9], TALFW [12], CPLFW [11], and CALFW [10] databases using six high-performanced deep face recognition models. The models [A-F] are A) Private-Asia R50 ArcFace [14], B) CASIA-WebFace R50 CosFace [15], C) VGGFace2 R50 ArcFace [16], D) MS1MV2 R100 Arcface [17], E) MS1MV2 R100 Curricularface [18], F) MS1MV2 R100 SFace [19].

	LFW [8]	SLLFW [9]	TALFW [12]	CPLFW [11]	CALFW [10]	MLFW
A	99.50	98.00	69.97	84.12	91.12	74.85
B	99.50	98.40	49.48	87.47	92.43	82.87
C	99.60	98.80	55.37	91.77	93.72	85.02
D	99.77	99.65	64.48	92.50	95.83	90.13
E	99.80	99.70	69.32	93.15	95.97	90.60
F	99.82	99.68	64.47	93.28	95.83	90.63

Generating Masked Faces. With the support of 31 mask templates, we generate the MLFW database according to the aforementioned settings. For each face image in MLFW database, we provide the masked image of original size 250×250, and the landmarks used for alignment. Pairing information is also stored and we use different suffixes, such as _0001 and _0002, to distinguish the same original image of different masks. The examples of masked faces generated by our tool are shown in Fig. 5.

4   Baseline

To evaluate the recognition performance on Masked LFW (MLFW) database, we select six opensourced SOTA deep face recognition methods as follows: (1) ResNet50 model trained on a private asia face dataset [14] with ArcFace [17], (2) ResNet50 model trained on CASIA-WebFace database [15] with CosFace [20], (3) ResNet50 model trained on VGGFace2 database [16] with ArcFace [17], (4) ResNet100 model trained on MS1MV2 database [21] refined by insightface with [17], (5) ResNet100 model trained on MS1MV2 database [21] with CurricularFace [18], (6) ResNet100 model trained on MS1MV2 database [21] with SFace [19].

In addition to the face verification performance (%) on MLFW database, we also report accuracy (%) on Labeled Faces in the Wild (LFW) database [8], Similar-looking LFW (SLLFW) database [9], Transferable Adversarial LFW database [12], Cross-pose LFW (CPLFW) and Cross-age LFW (CALFW) for comprehensive evaluation.

As shown in Table 2, the accuracy of SOTA model on MLFW database is about 5%–16% lower than that on CALFW database, which demonstrates that SOTA methods also can not be directly used to recognize masked faces.

5   Conclusion

In this paper, we aim to investigate the performance of face recognition models on masked faces. To this end, we have introduced a mask generation tool and built a test dataset, MLFW database. Finally, we have demonstrated that the recognition performance of face recognition models declines significantly on the masked face dataset.

Acknowledgments. This work was supported by the National Natural Science Foundation of China under Grants 61871052 and 62192784.

References

1. Zhu, Z., et al.: Masked face recognition challenge: the WebFace260m track report. arXiv preprint arXiv:2108.07189 (2021)
2. Deng, J., Guo, J., An, X., Zhu, Z., Zafeiriou, S.: Masked face recognition challenge: the insightface track report. arXiv preprint arXiv:2108.08191 (2021)
3. Boutros, F., et al.: MFR 2021: masked face recognition competition. In: 2021 IEEE International Joint Conference on Biometrics (IJCB). IEEE (2021)
4. Anwar, A., Raychowdhury, A.: Masked face recognition for secure authentication. arXiv preprint arXiv:2008.11104 (2020)
5. Wang, Z., et al.: Masked face recognition dataset and application. arXiv preprint arXiv:2003.09093 (2020)
6. Du, H., Shi, H., Liu, Y., Zeng, D., Mei, T.: Towards NIR-VIS masked face recognition. IEEE Signal Process. Lett. **28**, 768–772 (2021)
7. Cabani, A., Hammoudi, K., Benhabiles, H., Melkemi, M.: MaskedFace-Net-a dataset of correctly/incorrectly masked face images in the context of covid-19. Smart Health (2021)
8. Huang, G.B., Mattar, M., Berg, T., Learned-Miller, E.: Labeled faces in the wild: a database for studying face recognition in unconstrained environments (2008)
9. Deng, W., Hu, J., Zhang, N., Chen, B., Guo, J.: Fine-grained face verification: FGLFW database, baselines, and human-DCMN partnership. Pattern Recogn. **66**, 63–73 (2017)
10. Zheng, T., Deng, W., Hu, J.: Cross-Age LFW: a database for studying cross-age face recognition in unconstrained environments. arXiv preprint arXiv:1708.08197 (2017)
11. Zheng, T., Deng, W.: Cross-Pose LFW: a database for studying cross-pose face recognition in unconstrained environments, Tech. Rep. Beijing University of Posts and Telecommunications (2018)
12. Zhong, Y., Deng, W.: Towards transferable adversarial attack against deep face recognition. IEEE Trans. Inf. Forensics Secur. **16**, 1452–1466 (2020)
13. Bulat, A., Tzimiropoulos, G.: How far are we from solving the 2D & 3D face alignment problem? (and a dataset of 230,000 3D facial landmarks). In: International Conference on Computer Vision (2017)
14. Wang, Q., Zhang, P., Xiong, H., Zhao, J.: Face.evoLVe: a high-performance face recognition library. arXiv preprint arXiv:2107.08621 (2021)
15. Yi, D., Lei, Z., Liao, S., Li, S.Z.: Learning face representation from scratch. arXiv preprint arXiv:1411.7923 (2014)

16. Cao, Q., Shen, L., Xie, W., Parkhi, O.M., Zisserman, A.: VGGFace2: a dataset for recognising faces across pose and age. In: 13th IEEE International Conference on Automatic Face & Gesture Recognition (2018)
17. Deng, J., Guo, J., Xue, N., Zafeiriou, S.: ArcFace: additive angular margin loss for deep face recognition. In: Proceedings of the IEEE Conference on Computer Vision and Pattern Recognition (2019)
18. Huang, Y., et al.: CurricularFace: adaptive curriculum learning loss for deep face recognition. In: Proceedings of the IEEE/CVF Conference on Computer Vision and Pattern Recognition (2020)
19. Zhong, Y., Deng, W., Hu, J., Zhao, D., Li, X., Wen, D.: SFace: sigmoid-constrained hypersphere loss for robust face recognition. IEEE Trans. Image Process. **30**, 2587–2598 (2021)
20. Wang, H., et al.: CosFace: large margin cosine loss for deep face recognition. In: Proceedings of the IEEE Conference on Computer Vision and Pattern Recognition (2018)
21. Guo, Y., Zhang, L., Hu, Y., He, X., Gao, J.: MS-Celeb-1M: a dataset and benchmark for large-scale face recognition. In: Leibe, B., Matas, J., Sebe, N., Welling, M. (eds.) ECCV 2016. LNCS, vol. 9907, pp. 87–102. Springer, Cham (2016). https://doi.org/10.1007/978-3-319-46487-9_6

Multi-scale Object Detection Algorithm Based on Adaptive Feature Fusion

Yue Xu[1,2,3], Fengsui Wang[1,2,3]($\boxtimes$), Zhenglei Xie[1,2,3], and Yunlong Wang[1,2,3]

[1] School of Electrical Engineering, Anhui Polytechnic University, Wuhu 241000, China
fswang@ahpu.edu.cn
[2] Anhui Key Laboratory of Detection Technology and Energy Saving Devices, Wuhu 241000, China
[3] Key Laboratory of Advanced Perception and Intelligent Control of High-End Equipment, Ministry of Education, Wuhu 241000, China

Abstract. Aiming at the problem that each detection feature layer of the single-shot multibox detector (SSD) algorithm does not perform feature fusion and the detection effect is poor, an adaptive feature fusion SSD model is proposed. Firstly, the location of the shallow feature map and the multi-scale receptive field on the deep feature map are added, and the scaling and adaptive fusion of different scale feature maps are carried out to improve the representation ability of detail information. Secondly, the feature layer of the same scale can provide different ranges of feature information, transfer the specific features with detailed information to the abstract features with semantic information, and use the global average pool to guide learning and expand the expression ability of features. After training and testing on the PASCAL VOC data set, the detection accuracy reaches 80.6% and the detection speed reaches 60.9 fps, which verifies the robustness and real-time performance of the algorithm.

Keywords: Object detection · SSD algorithm · Adaptive fusion · Multi-scale receptive field

1 Introduction

In recent years, object detection technology has attracted more and more attention [1]. Multi-scale detection is also the focus of object detection. Detection of objects at different scales requires that the detection network is robust to scale. Therefore, multi-scale object feature learning is the key to improve detection performance.

In order to improve the detection network ability to locate the object, this paper proposes an adaptive feature fusion multi-scale detection algorithm (AFF-SSD). The algorithm is based on the SSD network structure. Firstly, the multi-scale position information fusion module is used to construct a new network branch, and the characteristics of different layers are integrated and adjusted to the same resolution, so that the network can adaptively learn the details of the position of the object and strengthen the feature extraction ability. Then the feature refinement enhancement module is used for back-end fusion, and the feature weight in the channel is changed to improve the scale invariance of the feature and obtain better detection results. Finally, the comparison experiment and ablation experiment show the effectiveness of the proposed algorithm. The object recognition accuracy in PASCAL VOC is 80.6%, and the detection speed also meets the real-time requirements.

2   Related Works

Many scholars have studied how to better achieve multi-scale object detection, and have summarized and analyzed from the aspects of network structure, training method and algorithm process. SSD [2] is a typical multi-scale feature map detection network, which predicts objects on feature maps of different receptive fields. SNIP [3] draws on the idea of multi-scale training and uses the image pyramid as the input of the model to process the context area around the bounding box at an appropriate scale, but only part of the training is chosen, and the inference speed is slow. TridentNet [4] is a scale-aware object detection network, which uses dilated convolution to construct a parallel three-branch network, and the weights of the three branches are shared, which reduces the risk of parameter overfitting. FPN [5] establishes a feature pyramid structure, which distributes objects of different sizes to different layers for prediction. This top-down unidirectional fusion is widely used in Faster RCNN [6], YOLOv3 [7], Cascade RCNN [8], and other models. However, direct fusion reduces the multi-scale representation ability, and the down-sampling process loses the highest-level pyramid feature information, so many versions are iterative after the FPN is proposed. Among them, PANet [9] is a pyramid attention network for image restoration, which distances features and shortens information paths from multi-scale feature pyramids, creating top-down path enhancements. Bi-FPN [10] adds some jump connections on the basis of PANet, constructed a module by fusing top-down and bottom-up, and stacked repeatedly to enhance information fusion. DyFPN [11] introduces the original FPN, but each layer contains convolutions with different kernel sizes filter to expand the receptive field to integrate more useful information. Although these feature fusion methods are effective, they also increase the time complexity of detection.

3   Proposed Method

In this section, an object detection model based on adaptive fusion and feature refinement is proposed. The overall framework and the details of each module are described in detail.

3.1   Network Framework

In view of the shortcomings of the SSD model, this paper uses the Position Information Fusion Module (PIFM) to collect the texture, edge, and other details of the top-level feature map, and learns the feature weights of the three layers of conv3_3, conv4_3 and conv6 respectively, and calculates the correlation of pixels in the feature map of different layers. Then the Feature Refinement Enhancement Module (FREM) is used to fuse the information of the middle and end of VGG16 to obtain more receptive fields and more expressive features, the frame structure is shown in Fig. 1. The input image outputs multi-scale feature map through each convolution layer in the AFF-SSD network, and uses the predicted convolution layer to transform the feature map. Finally, the object of the original image is located and detected.

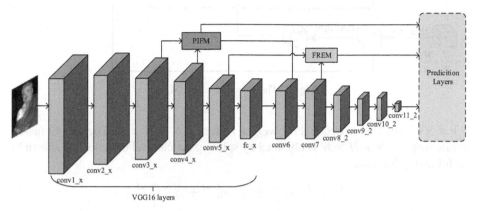

Fig. 1. AFF-SSD network structure.

3.2 PIFM Framework

When the network gradually deepens, the receptive field gradually changes, and the language expression ability also increases, but it will also reduce the resolution of the image. Many details become more blurred after convolution operation of multi-layer networks. The shallow neural network has small receptive field and strong expression ability of detail features, but the extracted feature semantics is weak. Therefore, in order to obtain strong semantic features, the SSD algorithm uses the conv4_3 layer of the main feature network, and introduces another convolution layer to classify and localize objects. However, the effective information of conv4_3 is less, and the information fusion between multi-layer feature maps is not considered, so the detection accuracy is low. PIFM is designed to adaptively learn the position weight of each scale feature map fusion. The structure is shown in Fig. 2, which is composed of feature scaling and adaptive fusion.

The AFF-SSD algorithm extracts the feature maps of conv3_3 and conv6 in VGG16 respectively. The conv6 layer is obtained by convolution to expand the receptive field, which can enhance the target's localization ability. In the figure, $C \times 2H \times 2W$, $C \times H \times W$ and $C \times H/2 \times W/2$ are from the characteristics of conv3_3, conv4_3 and conv6, respectively. Firstly, adjust conv6 to the same number of channels as conv4_3 by one-dimensional convolution, and then resize is used to the same size by interpolation. At this time, conv3_3 to conv4_3 only needs to carry out convolution with convolution kernel size of 3 and step size of 2, so as to obtain the feature map of the same size and channel. Then the three-level feature of $C \times H \times W$ is input into the convolution of 1

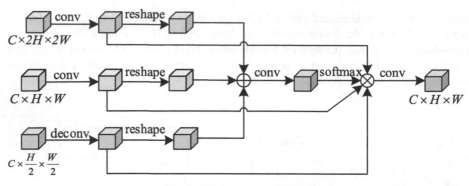

Fig. 2. The structure of PIFM

$\times 1 \times N$ (N set 256) to obtain three weight vectors of $N \times H \times W$. The weight fusion feature map of $3N \times H \times W$ is obtained by splicing the channel direction, as shown in the following formula:

$$y_{ij}^l = \alpha_{ij}^l \cdot x_{ij}^{1 \to l} + \beta_{ij}^l \cdot x_{ij}^{2 \to l} + \gamma_{ij}^l \cdot x_{ij}^{3 \to l} \tag{1}$$

$$\alpha_{ij}^l = \frac{e^{\lambda_{\alpha_{ij}}^l}}{e^{\lambda_{\alpha_{ij}}^l} + e^{\lambda_{\beta_{ij}}^l} + e^{\lambda_{\gamma_{ij}}^l}} \tag{2}$$

x^l denotes the l-layer feature, where $l \in (\{1, 2, 3\})$, y_{ij}^l represents the (i, j) vector of the output feature map y^l between channels, $x_{ij}^{n \to l}$ represents the feature vector at the location (i, j) of the feature map from n to l, α, β, γ is a learning parameter representing the importance of each layer feature map, α_{ij}^l, β_{ij}^l, γ_{ij}^l represents the value at the location (i, j), satisfying:

$$\alpha_{ij}^l + \beta_{ij}^l + \gamma_{ij}^l = 1 \tag{3}$$

Next, the weight vector of $3 \times H \times W$ is obtained by convolution of the above weight fusion map with $1 \times 1 \times 3$, which is normalized by softmax operation, and the obtained three weight vectors are multiplied and added to the three feature maps to obtain the fused $C \times H \times W$ feature map. Finally, 3×3 convolution is used to obtain the predictive output layer with 512 channels. PIFM calculates the correlation of feature pixels from different layers, and combines three feature maps of different scales into a new feature map after conversion to produce better semantic prediction, which makes up for the decrease of detection accuracy caused by the decrease of convolution layer.

3.3 FREM Framework

Spatial path has rich spatial information and detail information, learning complex non-linear mapping in image space; the context path provides a large receptive field to encode context information. The feature map of conv5_3 layer in VGG16 is obtained by convolution of conv4_3, which is the output of spatial path. The conv7 layer is the output of the context path that the feature graph information is converted from the last FC of VGG16. The features of these two paths are different at the level of feature representation, so a FREM module is proposed to optimize the features of each stage. The network frame is shown in Fig. 3.

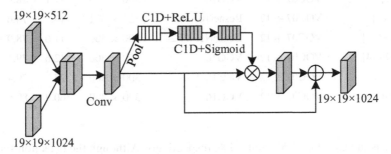

Fig. 3. The structure of FREM

Firstly, the conv5_3 and conv7 feature maps are superimposed by concatenating, and the channel dimension is adjusted by convolution. At the same time, the Batch Normalization layer and the Rectified Linear Unit are used to generate the weight vector to strengthen the refinement of the underlying characteristics by high-level information. Then, the global average pooling compressed spatial information is used to guide the feature learning, and the 1×1 convolution is used for nonlinear excitation to avoid the loss of detail information caused by dimension reduction. The intermediate feature map is obtained by sigmoid function activation. Finally, it is combined with the weight vector to generate the output feature map through element-by-element multiplication and addition operations. This method not only retains the spatial information of the original image, but also reduces the interference of useless information.

4 Experiment

The training set used in the experiment is a joint training set consisting of PASCAL VOC2007 training set and VOC2012 training set and verification set, with a total of 16551 graphs, of which 90% is the training set and 10% is the verification set.

4.1 Experimental Results

In order to test the performance of AFF-SSD algorithm, it is compared with some classical algorithms. The test results are shown in Table 1.

SSD* is a model obtained from the original SSD algorithm through data enhancement and reproduction. The table shows that the proposed target detection algorithm based on multi-scale location information fusion and feature refinement and enhancement has good performance in speed and detection accuracy. Compared with the two-stage algorithm Faster R-CNN [6], AFF-SDD improves the detection accuracy by 7.4%; compared with FD-SSD [14] and ESSD [15] models with backbone network VGG16, the detection

Table 1. The comparison results of different algorithms

Methods	Dataset	Backbone	Input size	FPS	mAP (%)
Faster R-CNN [6]	VOC07 + 12	VGG16	600 × 1000	7	73.2
SSD* [2]	VOC07 + 12	VGG16	300 × 300	77.1	78.6
DSSD [12]	VOC07 + 12	Resnet101	321 × 321	13.6	78.6
DF-SSD [13]	VOC07 + 12	DenseNet-s-32–1	300 × 300	11.6	78.9
FD-SSD [14]	VOC07 + 12	VGG16	300 × 300	12.6	79.1
ESSD [15]	VOC07 + 12	VGG16	300 × 300	25	79.4
AAF-SSD (ours)	VOC07 + 12	VGG16	300 × 300	60.9	80.6

accuracy is increased by 1.5% and 1.1%, respectively. Although the detection speed of the AF-SSD model is lower than that of the SSD model, it still meets the requirements of real-time detection.

4.2 Experimental Results

To make the effectiveness of the final algorithm AAF-SSD more intuitive, several pictures are in Fig. 4 below.

Fig. 4. Visualization result diagram

From the visual image of the detection effect, the confidence score of the algorithm is higher and the target location is more accurate. The original SSD* algorithm has the problem of missed detection of buses, which cannot effectively identify the problem of occlusion. The AFF-SSD algorithm mines the correlation between different feature layers through multi-scale position information fusion module, and fuses position information for the feature layer of small target detection to improve the positioning ability of the object.

4.3 Ablation Experiment

To compare the specific performance of the model by adding modules to the SSD* model, the ablation experiment is carried out by using the control variable method. The same data set and experimental environment are set to independently verify the influence of PIFM and FREM on the detection performance. The AFF-SSD model with PIFM alone is 80.4%, and the AF-SSD model with FREM alone is 80.0%. When PIFM and FREM are added at the same time, the detection accuracy reaches 80.6%.

5 Conclusion

In order to effectively use context information for multi-scale object detection, this paper proposes an adaptive feature fusion AF-SDD model. Firstly, conv3_3 with strong position information and conv6 with large receptive field are used to combine these two layers with conv4_3 for feature scaling, and the local positioning information and global semantic information are adaptively fused to improve the positioning and recognition ability of the model for the object. Secondly, in order to optimize the information of feature map, spatial path and context path are combined to enhance texture details. AFF-SSD algorithm not only ensures the real-time detection of speed, but also effectively improves the detection of different scale problems on PASCAL VOC dataset. In the follow-up work, the model will continue to be optimized, and the network structure with stronger feature extraction ability will be tried to maintain the detection accuracy.

Acknowledgments. This work was supported by the Natural Science Foundation of Anhui Province, China (Grand No. 2108085MF197 and Grand No.1708085MF154), the Natural Science Foundation of the Anhui Higher Education Institutions of China (Grant No. KJ2019A0162), the Open Research Fund of Anhui Key Laboratory of Detection Technology and Energy Saving Devices, Anhui Polytechnic University (Grant No. DTESD2020B02), the National Natural Science Foundation Pre-research of Anhui Polytechnic University (Xjky2022040), and the Graduate Science Foundation of the Anhui Higher Education Institutions of China (Grant No. YJS20210448 and YJS20210449).

References

1. Fang, L.P., He, H.J., Zhou, G.M.: Research overview of object detection methods. J. Comput. Eng. Appl. **54**, 11–18 (2018)
2. Liu, W., Anguelov, D., Erhan, D., et al.: SSD: single shot multibox detector. In: 14th European Conference on Computer Vision, Amsterdam, Netherlands, pp. 21–37 (2016)
3. Singh, B., Davis, L.S.: An analysis of scale invariance in object detection – SNIP. In: 2018 IEEE Conference on Computer Vision and Pattern Recognition, Salt Lake City, USA, pp. 3578–3587 (2018)

4. Li, Y., Chen, Y., Wang, N., et al.: Scale-aware trident networks for object detection. In: 2019 IEEE/CVF International Conference on Computer Vision, Seoul, Korea (South), pp. 6054–6063 (2019)
5. Lin, T.-Y., Dollár, P., Girshick, R., et al.: Feature pyramid networks for object detection. In: 2017 IEEE Conference on Computer Vision and Pattern Recognition. Honolulu, HI, USA, pp. 936–944 (2017)
6. Ren, S., He, K., Girshick, R., et al.: Faster R-CNN: towards real-time object detection with region proposal networks. IEEE Trans. Pattern Anal. Mach. Intell. **39**, 1137–1149 (2017)
7. Redmon, J., Farhadi, A.:YOLOv3: an incremental improvement. J. Comput. Vis. Pattern Recogn. arXiv:1804.02767 (2018)
8. Cai, Z., Vasconcelos, N.: Cascade R-CNN: delving into high quality object detection. In: 2018 IEEE/CVF Conference on Computer Vision and Pattern Recognition, Salt Lake City, UT, USA, pp. 6154–6162 (2018)
9. Liu, S., Qi, L., Qin, H., Shi, J., et al.: Path aggregation network for instance segmentation. In: 2018 IEEE/CVF Conference on Computer Vision and Pattern Recognition, Salt Lake City, UT, USA, pp. 8759–8768 (2018)
10. Tan, M., Pang, R., Le, Q.V.: EfficientDet: scalable and efficient object detection. In: 2020 IEEE/CVF Conference on Computer Vision and Pattern Recognition, Seattle, USA, pp. 10781–10790 (2020)
11. Zhu, M., Han, K., Yu, C., et al.: Dynamic feature pyramid networks for object detection. J. arXiv:2012.00779 (2020)
12. Fu, C.-Y., Liu, W., Ranga, A., et al.: DSSD: deconvolutional single shot detector. J. arXiv: 1701.06659 (2017)
13. Zhai, S., Shang, D., Wang, S., et al.: DF-SSD: an improved SSD object detection algorithm based on denseNet and feature fusion. J. IEEE Access **8**, 24344–24357 (2020)
14. Yin, Q., Yang, W., Ran, M., et al.: FD-SSD: an improved SSD object detection algorithm based on feature fusion and dilated convolution. J. Signal Process. Image Commun, **98**, 116402 (2021)
15. Zheng, L., Fu, C., Zhao, Y.: Extend the shallow part of single shot multibox detector via convolutional neural network. In: Tenth International Conference on Digital Image Processing, pp. 287–293. IEEE, International Society for Optics and Photonics (2018)

Sparsity-Regularized Geometric Mean Metric Learning for Kinship Verification

Yunhao Xu and Junlin Hu$^{(\boxtimes)}$

School of Software, Beihang University, Beijing, China
hujunlin@buaa.edu.cn

Abstract. Kinship verification through face images is a challenging research problem in biometrics. In this paper, we propose a sparsity-regularized geometric mean metric learning (SGMML) method to improve the well-known geometric mean metric learning (GMML) method and apply it to kinship verification task. Unlike GMML method that utilizes a linear map with fixed dimension, our SGMML method is capable of automatically learning the best projection dimension by employing the sparsity constraints on Mahalabios metric matrix. The proposed SGMML can effectively tackle the over-fitting problem and the data mixing up problem in the projected space. We conduct experiments on two benchmark kinship verification datasets, and experimental results demonstrate the effectiveness of our SGMML approach in kinship verification.

Keywords: Metric learning · Geometric mean · Sparsity regularization · Kinship verification

1 Introduction

Kinship verification through face images is a challenging research problem. The goal of this task is to distinguish whether there is a kinship by giving two different human face images. Compared with traditional DNA paternity testing methods, facial image-based kinship verification technique has the advantages of high efficiency and convenience. It has many real-world applications such as social media analysis, missing children search, image automatic annotation and so on. With more attention paid to facial kinship verification, it has made gratifying achievements in various aspects [1–4]. However, kinship verification by facial images in real-life scenarios is still very challenging, as facial images may change considerably due to variations in expression, pose, age and make-up. Figure 1 lists four types of kinship images sampled from KinFaceW-I dataset [1].

In this paper, we follow the metric learning-based framework [5–7] that have made brilliant achievements in the field of kinship verification, and use the geometric mean metric learning (GMML) [8] method to learn Mahalabios distance between two facial images to distinguish their kin-relationship. The difficulty of kinship verification with GMML method is the selection of the new mapping

W. Deng et al. (Eds.): CCBR 2022, LNCS 13628, pp. 197–204, 2022.
https://doi.org/10.1007/978-3-031-20233-9_20

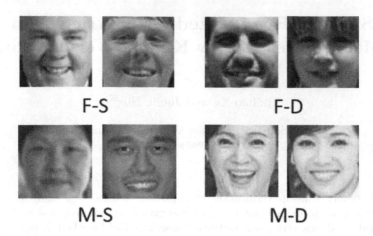

F-S   F-D

M-S   M-D

Fig. 1. Four types of kinship images from KinFaceW-I [1] dataset including Father-Son (F-S), Father-Daughter (F-D), Mother-Son (M-S), and Mother-Daughter (M-D).

space dimension. To address this problem, we propose a sparsity-regularized geometric mean metric learning (SGMML) method for kinship verification, where the best mapping dimension is determined by making the Mahalabios matrix sparse. To demonstrate the superiority of our SGMML method, we compare it with the original GMML method on KinFaceW-I and KinFaceW-II [1] datasets and analyze the importance of sparse regularization. Experimental results show that our SGMML method can bring an improvement in terms of the mean verification accuracy ranging from 1.5% to 2.8% compared to GMML method.

2   Proposed Method

This section first introduces some notations on Mahalanobis metric learning. Then we review geometric mean metric learning (GMML) and sparsity regularization. Finally, we formulate our SGMML method for kinship verification.

2.1   Notations

In this paper, matrices are denoted as boldface capital letters and vectors are denoted as boldface lower case letters. Let $X = (x_1, x_2, ..., x_n) \in \mathbb{R}^{d \times n}$, where d is the dimension of each data point, n is the number of data points. Corresponding to any positive semidefinite matrix $M \in \mathbb{R}^{d \times d}$, the Mahalanobis distance of data points x_i and x_j is the map $d_M : \mathbb{R}^d \times \mathbb{R}^d \to \mathbb{R}$ given by

$$d_M(x_i, x_j) = \sqrt{(x_i - x_j)^T M (x_i - x_j)}. \tag{1}$$

According to matrix decomposition theorem, if M is a positive semidefinite matrix, there exists a matrix $L \in \mathbb{R}^{k \times d}$, such that $M = L^T L$. Then we get

$$
\begin{aligned}
d_M^2(x_i, x_j) &= (x_i - x_j)^T M(x_i - x_j) \\
&= (x_i - x_j)^T L^T L(x_i - x_j) = (Lx_i - Lx_j)^T(Lx_i - Lx_j).
\end{aligned} \tag{2}
$$

There are many Mahalanobis metric learning algorithms that can be used to estimate the parameters of M such as logistic discriminant metric learning [10], learning with side information [11], distance metric learning through the maximization of the jeffrey divergence [12], etc. In this paper, we exploit the GMML [8] method and improve it by sparsity regularization to obtain M as GMML enjoys several very attractive properties like geometric attraction of Riemannian geometry, fast computational speed and closed-form solution.

2.2   GMML

Let $\mathcal{S} = \{(i,j) | x_i \text{ and } x_j \text{ are in the same class}\}$ be pairwise index sets of similar pairs and let $\mathcal{D} = \{(i,j) | x_i \text{ and } x_j \text{ are in different classes}\}$ be pairwise index sets of dissimilar pairs. $|\mathcal{S}|$ and $|\mathcal{D}|$ are the sizes of sets $\mathcal{S}$ and $\mathcal{D}$, respectively. The main idea of geometric mean metric learning (GMML) is to find a matrix M under the constraint that minimizes the distances between similar points using M and the distances between dissimilar points using M^{-1}. The optimization problem of GMML is formulated as

$$
\min_M \frac{1}{|\mathcal{S}|} \sum_{(i,j) \in \mathcal{S}} d_M^2(x_i, x_j) + \frac{1}{|\mathcal{D}|} \sum_{(i,j) \in \mathcal{D}} d_{M^{-1}}^2(x_i, x_j). \tag{3}
$$

There are two intuitions that support the objective function (3): the distance $d_M^2(x_i, x_j)$ increases monotonically in M, whereas the distance $d_{M^{-1}}(x_i, x_j)$ decreases monotonically in M; and the gradients of d_M and $d_{M^{-1}}$ point in nearly opposite directions.

We can further express the objective function (3) in terms of trace as

$$
\begin{aligned}
\min_M \frac{1}{|\mathcal{S}|} &\sum_{(i,j) \in \mathcal{S}} \text{tr}(M(x_i - x_j)(x_i - x_j)^T) \\
&+ \frac{1}{|\mathcal{D}|} \sum_{(i,j) \in \mathcal{D}} \text{tr}(M^{-1}(x_i - x_j)(x_i - x_j)^T),
\end{aligned} \tag{4}
$$

where $\text{tr}(A)$ denotes the trace of a matrix A. Let S and D be the similarity and dissimilarity matrices of similar points and dissimilar points as

$$
\begin{aligned}
S &= \frac{1}{|\mathcal{S}|} \sum_{(i,j) \in \mathcal{S}} (x_i - x_j)(x_i - x_j)^T , \\
D &= \frac{1}{|\mathcal{D}|} \sum_{(i,j) \in \mathcal{D}} (x_i - x_j)(x_i - x_j)^T.
\end{aligned} \tag{5}
$$

Then the optimization formulation (4) of GMML can be rewritten as follows

$$\min_{\boldsymbol{M}} J(\boldsymbol{M}) = \text{tr}(\boldsymbol{M}\boldsymbol{S}) + \text{tr}(\boldsymbol{M}^{-1}\boldsymbol{D}). \tag{6}$$

According to the Theorem 3 of GMML [8], the cost function $J(\boldsymbol{M})$ in (6) is both strictly convex and strictly geodesically convex. Therefore, it is enough to set the following gradient to zero to obtain the global minimum:

$$\frac{\partial J(\boldsymbol{M})}{\partial \boldsymbol{M}} = \boldsymbol{S} - \boldsymbol{M}^{-1}\boldsymbol{D}\boldsymbol{M}^{-1} = 0. \tag{7}$$

Then, we can get the following equation:

$$\boldsymbol{M}\boldsymbol{S}\boldsymbol{M} = \boldsymbol{D}. \tag{8}$$

Equation (8) is a Riccati equation whose unique solution is the midpoint of the geodesic connecting $\boldsymbol{S}^{-1}$ and $\boldsymbol{D}$. Therefore we get the closed-form solution as

$$\boldsymbol{M} = \boldsymbol{S}^{-\frac{1}{2}} \left(\boldsymbol{S}^{\frac{1}{2}} \boldsymbol{D} \boldsymbol{S}^{\frac{1}{2}} \right)^{\frac{1}{2}} \boldsymbol{S}^{-\frac{1}{2}}. \tag{9}$$

2.3 Sparsity Regularization

Given the Mahalanobis distance as defined in equation (2), $\boldsymbol{M} = \boldsymbol{L}^T \boldsymbol{L}$, and $\boldsymbol{L} \in \mathbb{R}^{k \times d}$ maps feature points from the original space to the projected space. In most cases, $k \leq d$, but the best projection dimension k is unknown. A common practice is to specify k in advance based on experience, however this is not easy to find the optimal projection dimension. If k is set too large, there are two drawbacks: over-fitting and high computational cost, as it provides extra degrees of freedom for metric adjustment. On the other hand, setting k too small may lead to poor discrimination between different classes because the data points will be mixed together in the projected space. Therefore, a principled method is needed to automatically learn the best value of k to improve the accuracy and reduce the computational cost.

Let $\boldsymbol{W} = \boldsymbol{L}\boldsymbol{L}^T \in \mathbb{R}^{k \times k}$, where $\boldsymbol{W}_l$ represents the l-th row vector of $\boldsymbol{W}$. We can easily obtain the following equation

$$\boldsymbol{W}_l \equiv 0 \iff \boldsymbol{L}_l \equiv 0, \tag{10}$$

where $\boldsymbol{L}_l$ represents the l-th row in $\boldsymbol{L}$. Each all-zero row in $\boldsymbol{L}$ represents a one-dimensional zero subspace and the projection of data points in this dimension is zero. If we can find all all-zero rows, we can determine the optimal dimension k for the projection. The all-zero row in $\boldsymbol{W}$ implies imposing the all-zero row constraint on $\boldsymbol{W}$. According to [9], the number of all-zero rows in $\boldsymbol{W}$ can be maximized by minimizing the $\text{tr}(\boldsymbol{L}\boldsymbol{L}^T)$.

Algorithm 1: Sparsity-Regularized Geometric Mean Metric Learning

---

Input: X, $\mathcal{S} = \{(i,j)\}$, $\mathcal{D} = \{(i,j)\}$, η

   Compute the similarity and dissimilarity matrices:

$$S = \sum_{(i,j)\in\mathcal{S}} (x_i - x_j)(x_i - x_j)^T$$

$$D = \sum_{(i,j)\in\mathcal{D}} (x_i - x_j)(x_i - x_j)^T$$

   Compute Mahalanobis metric matrix:

$$M = (S + \eta I)^{-\frac{1}{2}} \left((S + \eta I)^{\frac{1}{2}} D (S + \eta I)^{\frac{1}{2}} \right)^{\frac{1}{2}} (S + \eta I)^{-\frac{1}{2}}$$

Return: M

2.4 SGMML

To learn the best projection dimension of M, we employ sparsity regularization term on GMML method, and propose our sparsity-regularized geometric mean metric learning (SGMML) method. The objective function of our SGMML is formulated as

$$\min_{M} J(M) = \text{tr}(MS) + \text{tr}(M^{-1}D) + \eta\,\text{tr}(LL^T), \tag{11}$$

where η is a hyper-parameter that determines the sparsity of Mahalanobis metric matrix M.

According to the operation rules of matrix trace, $\text{tr}(W) = \text{tr}(LL^T) = \text{tr}(L^T L) = \text{tr}(M)$. Then we obtain the following formula

$$\begin{aligned} \min_{M} J(M) &= \text{tr}(MS) + \text{tr}(M^{-1}D) + \eta\,\text{tr}(M) \\ &= \text{tr}(M(S + \eta I)) + \text{tr}(M^{-1}D). \end{aligned} \tag{12}$$

This objective function is also strictly convex and strictly geodesically convex on the SPD manifold as the objective function of GMML. Therefore, we can obtain the global minimum of objective function (12) by setting its gradient to zero. The objective function $J(M)$ in (12) can be solved as (6) and the closed-form solution can be calculated by

$$M = (S + \eta I)^{-\frac{1}{2}} \left((S + \eta I)^{\frac{1}{2}} D (S + \eta I)^{\frac{1}{2}} \right)^{\frac{1}{2}} (S + \eta I)^{-\frac{1}{2}}. \tag{13}$$

3 Experiments

3.1 Datasets and Settings

To evaluate the performance of our SGMML method for kinship verification, we compare SGMML with GMML method on two benchmark kinship face datasets: KinFaceW-I [1] and KinFaceW-II [1]. In KinFaceW-I, each related kinship image

Table 1. The mean verification accuracy (%) of two methods using three features on KinFaceW-I dataset.

Method	Feature	F-S	F-D	M-S	M-D	Mean
GMML	HOG	80.11	73.15	71.96	72.41	74.41
	DSIFT	78.85	73.50	71.94	74.13	74.61
	LBP	77.21	69.80	68.08	73.70	72.20
SGMML	HOG	83.02	74.67	74.15	77.10	**77.24**
	DSIFT	81.40	74.20	75.20	73.60	**76.10**
	LBP	81.40	73.53	70.25	72.13	**74.33**

Table 2. The mean verification accuracy (%) of two methods using three features on KinFaceW-II dataset.

Method	Feature	F-S	F-D	M-S	M-D	Mean
GMML	HOG	79.20	72.00	73.40	69.80	73.60
	DSIFT	80.40	70.60	73.80	73.40	74.55
	LBP	77.00	73.20	72.40	69.40	73.00
SGMML	HOG	81.40	73.60	75.40	71.00	**75.35**
	DSIFT	81.40	74.20	75.20	73.60	**76.10**
	LBP	79.60	76.40	73.20	71.60	**75.20**

pair was collected from different photos. In KinFaceW-II, each related kinship image pair was captured from the same photo. Each dataset contains four kinship relationships: Father-Son (F-S), Father-Daughter (F-D), Mother-Son (M-S) and Mother-Daughter (M-D). Figure 1 shows four pairs of face images selected from the KinFaceW-I dataset.

In our experiments, we use the cropped face images of size 64×64, and convert them into gray-scale images. For each face image, we follow the settings as in [6], and extract histograms of oriented gradients (HOG) feature [13], dense scale invariant feature transform (DSIFT) feature [15] and local binary patterns (LBP) feature [14] respectively, and then use principal component analysis (PCA) technique to reduce the dimensions of these features to 200. Following the setting in [1,5,6], we mark the true kinship pairs as similar samples, and the images of each parent with randomly selected children who are not their true children as dissimilar samples. We adopt 5-fold cross-validation, and the final evaluation index is the mean verification accuracy for each type of kinship.

3.2 Results and Analysis

To ensure the invertibility of S and D in GMML and SGMML methods, we add a small matrix λI to S and D respectively, where we set $\lambda = 10^{-4}$ in our experiments. Table 1 and Table 2 report the mean verification accuracy of our SGMML method and original GMML method on two datasets, in which the

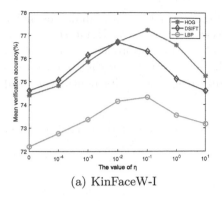
(a) KinFaceW-I

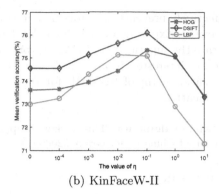
(b) KinFaceW-II

Fig. 2. The mean verification accuracy (%) of our SGMML method with the increase of η on (a) KinFaceW-I and (b) KinFaceW-II dataset, respectively.

parameter of the sparsity regularization term in SGMML method is empirically set as $\eta = 0.1$. It can be observed that our SGMML method significantly outperforms GMML method (more than 1.5%) on the KinFaceW-I and KinFaceW-II datasets, especially for the HOG feature in the KinFaceW-I dataset, SGMML improves the performance of GMML by 2.8%. The reason is that a stronger constraint on $\mathrm{tr}(\boldsymbol{M})$ will make $\boldsymbol{M}$ more sparse, while a smaller constraint on $\mathrm{tr}(\boldsymbol{M}^{-1})$ also means that $\boldsymbol{M}$ is more sparse.

We further evaluate the effects of the sparsity regularization term (i.e., parameter η) to SGMML. When the $\eta = 0$, GMML is a special case of SGMML. Figure 2 plots the curves of the mean verification accuracy (%) with the increase of η on KinFaceW-I and KinFaceW-II datasets, respectively. The mean verification accuracy increases first and then begins to decrease when η is larger than 0.1. The reason is that a suitable η can make the Mahalabios matrix $\boldsymbol{M}$ sparse and find the best projection dimension, however the large η leads to $\boldsymbol{S} + \eta \boldsymbol{I}$ being far away from $\boldsymbol{S}$. The final result is no longer the approximation of geometric mean metric between $\boldsymbol{S}$ and $\boldsymbol{D}$, but the approximation of geometric mean metric between $\boldsymbol{I}$ and $\boldsymbol{D}$. We can see from Fig. 2 that our SGMML obtains the best performance when η is near to 0.1, so we set it as 0.1 in our experiments.

Throughout experimental results in Table 1, Table 2 and Fig. 2, we can see that our SGMML performs better than GMML for kinship verification. These experimental results show that our proposed SGMML method is able to adaptively learn the best projection dimension of $\boldsymbol{M}$.

4   Conclusion

This paper has presented a sparsity-regularized geometric mean metric learning (SGMML) method for kinship verification via face images. The proposed SGMML method automatically determines the best dimension of the projected space by exploiting sparsity regularization on Mahalabios metric matrix, which effectively prevents data mixing and over-fitting problems in Mahalabios metric learning. Experimental results on KinFaceW-I and KinFaceW-II datasets demonstrate the superiority of SGMML compared to GMML approach. In future work, we are interested in adaptively selecting hyper-parameter of the sparsity regularization term of SGMML for further improving the performance of kinship verification.

Acknowledgments. This work was supported by the National Natural Science Foundation of China under Grant 62006013.

References

1. Lu, J., Zhou, X., Tan, Y.-P., Shang, Y., Zhou, J.: Neighborhood repulsed metric learning for kinship verification. IEEE Trans. Pattern Anal. Mach. Intell. **36**(2), 331–345 (2014)
2. Zhou, X., Hu, J., Lu, J., Shang, Y., Guan, Y.: Kinship verification from facial images under uncontrolled conditions. In: ACM International Conference on Multimedia, pp. 953–956 (2011)
3. Zhou, X., Jin, K., Xu, M., Guo, G.: Learning deep compact similarity metric for kinship verification from face images. Inf. Fusion **48**, 84–94 (2019)
4. Qin, X., Tan, X., Chen, S.: Trisubject kinship verification: understanding the core of A family. IEEE Trans. Multimedia **17**(10), 1855–1867 (2015)
5. Lu, J., et al.: The FG 2015 kinship verification in the wild evaluation. In: IEEE International Conference and Workshops on Automatic Face and Gesture Recognition, pp. 1–7 (2015)
6. Lu, J., Hu, J., Tan, Y.-P.: Discriminative deep metric learning for face and kinship verification. IEEE Trans. Image Process. **26**(9), 4269–4282 (2017)
7. Hu, J., Lu, J., Tan, Y.-P., Yuan, J., Zhou, J.: Local large-margin multi-metric learning for face and kinship verification. IEEE Trans. Circuits Syst. Video Technol. **28**(8), 1875–1891 (2018)
8. Zadeh, P., Hosseini, R., Sra, S.: Geometric mean metric learning. In: International Conference on Machine Learning, pp. 2464–2471 (2016)
9. Jiang, N., Liu, W., Wu, Y.: Order determination and sparsity-regularized metric learning adaptive visual tracking. In: IEEE Conference on Computer Vision and Pattern Recognition (2012)
10. Guillaumin, M., Verbeek, J., Schmid, C.: Is that you? Metric learning approaches for face identification. In: IEEE International Conference on Computer Vision, pp. 498–505 (2009)
11. Xing, E.P., Jordan, M.I., Russell, S.J., Ng, A.Y.: Distance metric learning with application to clustering with side-information. In: Advances in Neural Information Processing Systems, pp. 521–528 (2003)
12. Nguyen, B., Morell, C., Baets, B.D.: Supervised distance metric learning through maximization of the Jeffrey divergence. Pattern Recogn. **64**, 215–225 (2017)
13. Dalal, N., Triggs, B.: Histograms of oriented gradients for human detection. In: IEEE Conference on Computer Vision and Pattern Recognition, pp. 886–893 (2005)
14. Ahonen, T., Hadid, A., Pietikainen, M.: Face description with local binary patterns: application to face recognition. IEEE Trans. Pattern Anal. Mach. Intell. **28**(12), 2037–2041 (2006)
15. Lowe, D.G.: Distinctive image features from scale-invariant keypoints. Int. J. Comput. Vision **60**(2), 91–110 (2004)

YoloMask: An Enhanced YOLO Model for Detection of Face Mask Wearing Normality, Irregularity and Spoofing

Zhicheng Cao, Wenlong Li, Heng Zhao, and Liaojun Pang[✉]

School of Life Science and Technology, Engineering Research Center of Molecular and Neuro Imaging, Ministry of Education, Xidian University, Xi'an 710126, Shaanxi, China
ljpang@mail.xidian.edu.cn

Abstract. Wearing of surgical face masks has become the new norm of our daily life in the context of the COVID-19 pandemic. Under many conditions at various public places, it is necessary to check or monitor whether the face mask is worn properly. Manual judgement of mask wearing not only wastes manpower but also fails to monitor it in a way of all-time and real-time, posing the urge of an automatic mask wearing detection technology. Earlier automatic mask wearing methods uses a successive means in which the face is detected first and then the mask is determined and judged followingly. More recent methods take the end-to-end paradigm by utilizing successful and well-known CNN models from the field of object detection. However, these methods fail to consider the diversity of face mask wearing, such as different kinds of irregularity and spoofing. Thus, we in this study introduce a comprehensive mask wearing detection dataset (named as *Diverse Masked Faces*) by distinguishing a total of five different classes of mask wearing. We then adapt the YOLOX model for our specific task and further improve it using a new composite loss which merges the CIoU and the alpha-IoU losses and inherits both their advantages. The improved model is referred as *Yolo-Mask*. Our proposed method was tested on the new dataset and has been proved to significantly outperform other SOTA methods in the literature that are either successive or end-to-end.

Keywords: Face mask wearing detection · Deep learning · YOLO · Spoofing · Irregularity

1 Introduction

Wearing of surgical face masks (also known as medical masks) has long proven to be an effective intervention to control virus transmission during outbreaking of influenza pandemics or other respiratory diseases [1,2]. As the COVID-19 pandemic continues to infect more population worldwide [3], face mask wearing has become a new norm of our society. Studies [4,5] have shown that proper

W. Deng et al. (Eds.): CCBR 2022, LNCS 13628, pp. 205–213, 2022.
https://doi.org/10.1007/978-3-031-20233-9_21

wearing of masks can effectively reduce the transmission risk of the SARS-CoV-2 virus. Regardless of the type, environment or wearer, face masks can ensure a dual preventive function. The mask can physically block the transmission of pathogens to the air through saliva droplets – which plays a significant role in preventing virus infected people from spreading the virus to the surrounding environment, and they can also reduce the probability of disease caused by virus inhalation on uninfected people. As a result, most countries have issued face mask wearing regulations during the pandemic to curb it from spreading.

On the other side, with a large population being required to wear face masks at various public places, the task of face mask wearing detection has also emerged. For example, customers are usually checked or reminded whether the face mask is worn properly before entrance into public venues such as restaurants, cinemas, shopping malls, subway stations and other buildings. In face of such a large population group, it inflicts a huge burden of the business owners and other public service providers and it consumes a lot of manpower to manually check the mask wearing situation [6]. It also depletes the physical strength and stamina of the personnel at public places. What's more, Manual checking of face masks at public places introduces the risk of the inspection personnel being exposed to the virus and increases probability of cross-infection [7]. Therefore, how to use machines to automatically and accurately detect the wearing of masks in public places has become an increasingly important research topic, and many AI-based methods for mask wearing detection have been proposed in the last three years.

Since automatic detection of face mask wearing is essentially a special task of object detection, researchers have applied all kinds of objection detection methods to solve this specific problem [8]. Traditional object detection methods (such as the VJ method [9], HOG [10], DPM [11]) heavily rely on the manual design of features and the degree of automation of feature learning is quite low. Deep learning-based methods (i.e., deep neural networks [12]), on the contrary, can automatically extract low-level features such as image edge and texture, and represent higher-level semantic features.

Object detectors based on deep learning can be divided into two main types: one-stage object detectors and two-stage object detectors. In a two-stage object detector, deep features are used to propose the so-called region proposals, and these features are then used during the classification and bounding box regression of object candidates. Two-stage methods can achieve high detection accuracy but are generally slow. Since there are many inference steps per image, the detection speed is not as fast as a one-stage detector. Besides, Two-stage or multi-stage detectors are usually not end-to-end trainable. Examples of two-stage detector includes the region convolutional neural network (R-CNN) [13], and its improved variants of Fast R-CNN [14] and Faster R-CNN [15], Mask R-CNN [16], and the latest evolved version, Granulated RCNN (G-RCNN) [17]. Single-stage detectors instead predict bounding boxes on an input image without the step of proposing candidate boxes. The detection process therefore consumes less time and can be implemented in real-time. Single-stage object detectors prioritize inference speed and are very fast, but perform relatively more poorly in recognizing irregularly shaped objects or groups of small objects. Some of the most popular single-stage object detection algorithms are YOLO v1 [18], SSD [19], RetinaNet [20], and the latest YOLOX algorithm [21].

Due to the advantages of deep learning-based detection models over traditional detection methods, so far, most face mask detection algorithms utilize deep neural networks. Generally speaking, these deep learning-based face task wearing methods can be divided into two categories: the successive methods and the end-to-end methods [8]. The successive methods divide the mask wearing detection task into a succession of sub-tasks of face detection, mask detection and wearing classification, etc. [22]. The end-to-end methods on the contrary usually take an object detection approach [23,24]. We in this research take the end-to-end approach by treating the mask wearing detection problem as a multi-class object detection task. To ensure a fast detection speed, we design a one-stage detector in stead of a two-stage detector. Furthermore, in view of the fact that most research works do not consider diverse cases of mask wearing (usually only 2–3 cases), we in this paper identify 5 different wearing cases and treat it as a five-class object detection problem after collecting our own dataset. Such a practice is much more beneficial in many real-world applications.

2 Methodology

2.1 Network Structure

The detailed network structure of YoloMask is illustrated in Fig. 1. Similar to YOLOX, YoloMask consists of four main modules: the input, the backbone, the neck and the predictor. The input image is set to be a fixed size of 416*416 in the three channels of R,G and B. The backbone is chosen to be CSP-DarkNet, an improved variant of DarkNet [25] which is inspired by CSPNet [26]. More specifically, the backbone module consists of units of CBS, Focus, CSP and SPP. The CBS unit is a basic building block which is a cascaded connection of convolution, batch normalization and SiLU activation [27]; The SPP unit is a CBS unit processed by the spatial pyramid pooling (SPP) technique [28] and then followed by another CBS unit; The CSP unit comprises paralleled CBS units of different numbers that are concatenated and then followed by an additional CBS unit; The Focus unit samples the feature maps first and then is followed by another CBS unit.

The neck of YoloMask is built using the feature pyramid network (FPN) and the path aggregation netowrk (PAN) [29] techniques. Such a form of neck is meant for fusion of feature information at different scales. During prediction, similar to YOLOX, we also use the technique of "Decoupled Head" which is an improvement on other models of the YOLO series such as YOLO v3-v5. This decoupled head separates classification and localization into paralleled branches yielding a higher detection performance as well as faster convergence of the model. It should be noted that an IoU branch is added to the regression branch. For our specific model of YoloMask, the decoupled outputs are in the size of 52*52*5, 52*52*1 and 52*52*4 for the classification, IoU and regression branches at the first scale, respectively.

Data augmentation strategies such as Mosaic and MixUp are also included to boost the model performance. Anchor-free technique is also involved by reducing the predictions for each location from 3 to 1 and making them directly predict four values, i.e., the height and width and the two offsets of the predicted box.

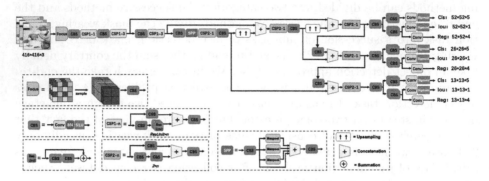

Fig. 1. The overall network structure of our mask wearing detection model, YoloMask. Zoom-in is recommended to see more details.

The technique of multi-positives is also utilized which assigns the center 33 area as positives rather than selects only the center location as the positive sample for each object [30]. The multi-positives trick alleveates the issue of positive/negative sample imbalance during training. A simplified version of the advanced label assignment technique of OTA [31], i.e., SimOTA, is used which treats the assigning procedure as an Optimal Transport (OT) problem and takes a dynamic top-k strategy to get an approximate solution.

2.2 Loss Function

Following the design of the network structure, we further improve its performance by introducing a new composite loss, alpha-CIoU, which merges the CIoU [32] and the alpha-IoU [33] losses and inherits both their advantages.

CIoU benefits the detection performance by considering the distance between the predicted and ground-truth box centers as well as the width-to-height ratio, on top of the intersection over union ratio as previous IoU losses did. It is calculated as

$$CIoU = IoU - \frac{\rho^2(b, b^{gt})}{c^2} - \eta v, \tag{1}$$

where ρ denotes the Euclidean distance between the centers of the predicted and ground-truth bounding boxes, and c is the diagonal length of the smallest rectangle that encloses the two boxes. v measures the consistency of the aspect ratio and is weighted by a trade-off parameter η, which are given by $v = \frac{4}{\pi^2} \left[atan(\frac{w^{gt}}{h^{gt}}) - atan(\frac{w}{h}) \right]^2$ and $\eta = \frac{v}{1-IoU+v}$, respectively.

As a family of power IoU loss, alpha-IoU generalizes IoU losses by adding an power index, i.e., $\mathcal{L}_{\alpha-IoU} = 1 - IoU^{\alpha}$. Then, taking advantages of the two losses above, alpha-IoU can be defined as

$$\mathcal{L}_{\alpha-IoU} = 1 - IoU^{\alpha} + \frac{\rho^{2\alpha}(b, b^{gt})}{c^{2\alpha}} + (\eta v)^{\alpha}. \tag{2}$$

3   Experiments and Analysis

3.1   Dataset and Setup

Current datasets of face mask wearing detection usually make a distinction between a worn mask and no mask being worn, but fail to comprehensively consider and distinguish among irregular cases of mask wearing such as a worn mask but with exposed nose, a worn mask but with exposed mouth, and spoofing masks (e.g., cloth, scarfs, hands, as shown in Fig. 2). Such a lack of differentiation between normal and abnormal mask wearing fails to ensure the efficiency of the mask and the security of public health as expected. Hence, we take liberty to prepare our own dataset (named as *Diverse Masked Faces*) which in total include five cases of mask wearing: the face without any mask (labelled as 'face_alone'), the face with a mask worn (labelled as 'face_mask'), the face with the nose exposed (labelled as 'nose_out'), the face with the mouth exposed (labelled as 'mouth_out'), and the face with mask spoofing (labelled as 'spoof').

Fig. 2. Samples of our prepared dataset (Diverse Masked Faces) in all the five different cases. The last two correspond to the spoofing case by either a scarf or hand.

During making of our own dataset, we collect face images from the MAFA face occlusion dataset [34] and the WIDER Face dataset [35]. The images for the face_alone case are mainly selected from the WIDER Face dataset. The images for the face_ mask, nose_out, mouth_out and spoof cases are mainly selected from the MAFA dataset. All the five cases of faces are manually labelled by ourselves with the help of the LabelImg tool [36]. A total number of 2548 images are included in our dataset which consists of 4288 labelled faces with or without masks. The dataset is then divided into the training subset and the test subset at a ratio of faces roughly being equal to 7:3 (3116 for training and 1172 for testing to be specific). The dataset is summarized in Table 1.

The training and parameter settings of YoloMask and YOLOX-s are basically the same as those of the original YOLOX model. The MS COCO dataset is used to pre-train the weights and the batchsize is set to 4. The cosine annealing with warmup is used for the learning rate which is reset to 0.000625 due to a different batchsize. A total of 65 epochs are trained where the mosaic and mixup data enhancement are turned off in the last 15 epochs.

3.2   Performance Evaluation

We compare our method YoloMask against other four up-to-date methods in the literature which represent the successive methods or the end-to-end methods. As seen in Table 2, the mean average precision (mAP) of our method at different IoU values and the F1 score are significantly higher than the three other methods of MTCNN+MobileNet, Faster R-CNN and SSD, as well as the foundation model of YOLOX-s that this paper is based. Moreover, our model has a smaller number of parameters and FLOPs than all the end-to-end methods but is larger than the successive method of MTCNN+MobileNet, indicating a low complexity of our model. Nonetheless, our method achieves the largest FPS of 55.5 than all the other methods, demonstrating the speed advantage of our model. Some of the mask wearing detection results are presented in Fig. 3.

Table 1. Summary of the self-prepared dataset, Diverse Masked Faces.

Class of mask wearing	No. of images	No. of faces	Training size	Testing size
face_alone	800	2099	1569	530
face_mask	796	1139	796	343
nose_out	314	337	238	99
mouth_out	147	167	119	48
Spoofing	491	546	394	152
Total	2548	4288	3116	1172

Table 2. Comparison of detection performance between our proposed method of Yolo-Mask and other SOTA methods in the literature, in terms of mean average precision, F1-score, model complexity and speed, as well as method classification. Note that the F1-score is calculated as the macro F1-score at the 0.75 IoU.

METRICS	MTCNN+MobileNet [22]	Faster RCNN [23]	SSD [24]	YOLO v3 [37]	YOLOX-s [21]	YoloMask (Ours)
mAP(IoU = 0.5)	0.607	0.858	0.879	0.834	0.892	**0.904**
mAP(IoU = 0.75)	0.277	0.718	0.735	0.717	0.783	**0.784**
mAP(IoU = 0.5:0.95)	0.321	0.582	0.597	0.575	0.624	**0.632**
F1-score	0.505	0.601	0.764	**0.776**	0.759	0.773
Parameters	**3.06 M**	28.32 M	24.01 M	61.55M	8.98 M	8.98 M
GFLOPs	**1.14**	908.11	61.21	65.55	11.26	11.26
FPS	0.3	11.9	49.1	47.5	55.5	**55.5**
Method category	Successive	End-to-end	End-to-end	End-to-end	End-to-end	**End-to-end**
Detector stages	Two stages	Two stages	One stage	One stage	One stage	**One stage**

4 Summary

In order to alleviate the physiological and economical burdens of mask wearing enforcement, we in this research studied automatic detection of mask wearing using an end-to-end approach with a single-stage detector. We introduced a new mask wearing detection dataset (named as Diverse Masked Faces) which comprehensively considered the normality, irregularity and spoofing during mask wearing. We further proposed an enhanced detection model (referred as YoloMask) which was adapted for the specific task of mask detection and was improved by designing a new composite loss of alpha-CIoU. We tested the proposed method on the new dataset and experimental results proved that overall it significantly

Fig. 3. Sample detection outputs of all different methods on the dataset in all five mask wearing cases. From top to the bottom are the detection results by MTCNN+MobileNet, Faster R-CNN, SSD, YOLO v3, YOLOX-s, and our own Yolo-Mask, respectively. Zoom-in recommended for viewing of details.

outperformed all other state-of-the-art methods in the literature in terms of accuracy and detection speed.

Acknowledgments. We greatly acknowledge the financial supports from the Natural Science Foundation of China (NSFC No. 61906149), the Natural Science Basic Research Program of Shaanxi (Program No. 2021JM-136), the Natural Science Foundation of Chongqing (cstc2021jcyj-msxmX1068), the Xi'an Science and Technology Program (No. 21RGSF0011) and the Fundamental Research Funds for the Central Universities (No. QTZX22072).

References

1. BalAzy, A., Toivola, M., Adhikari, A., Sivasubramani, S.K., Reponen, T., Grinshpun, T.: Do n95 respirators provide 95 viruses, and how adequate are surgical masks? Am. J. Infect. Control **34**(2), 51–57 (2006)
2. MacIntyre, C.R., Cauchemez, S., Dwyer, D.E., Seale, H., Cheung, P., Ferguson, N.M.: Face mask use and control of respiratory virus transmission in households. Emerg. Infect. Dis. **15**(2), 233–241 (2009)
3. WHO: The WHO coronavirus (COVID-19) dashboard [EB/OL] (2022). https://covid19.who.int/
4. Feng, S., Shen, C., Xia, N., Song, W., Fan, M., Cowling, B.J.: Rational use of face masks in the covid-19 pandemic. Lancet Resp. Med. **8**(5), 434–436 (2020)
5. Abboah-Offei, M., Salifu, Y., Adewale, B., Bayuo, J., Ofosu-Poku, R., Opare-Lokko, E.B.A.: A rapid review of the use of face mask in preventing the spread of covid-19. Int. J. Nurs. Stud. Adv. **3**, 100013 (2021)
6. Spitzer, M.: Masked education? the benefits and burdens of wearing face masks in schools during the current corona pandemic. Trends Neurosci. Educ. **20**, 100138–100138 (2020)
7. Sabetian, G., et al.: Covid-19 infection among healthcare workers: a cross-sectional study in Southwest Iran. Virol. J. **18**(1), 58 (2021)
8. Wang, B., Zheng, J., Chen, C.L.P.: A survey on masked facial detection methods and datasets for fighting against covid-19. IEEE Trans. Artif. Intell. **3**(3), 323–343 (2022)
9. Viola, P., Jones, M.: Rapid object detection using a boosted cascade of simple features. In: 2001 CVPR, vol. 1, pp. 511–518 (2001)
10. Dalal, N., Triggs, B.: Histograms of oriented gradients for human detection. In: 2005 CVPR, vol. 1, pp. 886–893 (2005)
11. Felzenszwalb, P., McAllester, D., Ramanan, D.: A discriminatively trained, multi-scale, deformable part model. In: 2008 CVPR, pp. 1–8 (2008)
12. Bengio, Y., Courville, A., Vincent, P.: Representation learning: a review and new perspectives. IEEE Trans. Pattern Anal. Mach. Intell. **35**(8), 1798–1828 (2013)
13. Girshick, R., Donahue, J., Darrell, T., Malik, J.: Rich feature hierarchies for accurate object detection and semantic segmentation. In: 2014 CVPR, pp. 580–587 (2014)
14. Girshick, R.: Fast r-cnn. In: 2015 ICCV, pp. 1440–1448 (2015)
15. Ren, S., He, K., Girshick, R., Sun, J.: Faster r-cnn: towards real-time object detection with region proposal networks. IEEE TPAMI **39**(6), 1137–1149 (2017)
16. He, K., Gkioxari, G., Dollár, P., Girshick, R.: Mask r-cnn. In: 2017 ICCV, pp. 2980–2988 (2017)
17. Pramanik, A., Pal, S.K., Maiti, J., Mitra, P.: Granulated rcnn and multi-class deep sort for multi-object detection and tracking. IEEE Trans. Emerg. Topics Comput. Intell. **6**(1), 171–181 (2022)

18. Redmon, J., Divvala, S., Girshick, R., Farhadi, A.: You only look once: unified, real-time object detection. In: CVPR, pp. 779–788 (2016)
19. Liu, W., et al.: SSD: single shot multibox detector. In: Leibe, B., Matas, J., Sebe, N., Welling, M. (eds.) ECCV 2016. LNCS, vol. 9905, pp. 21–37. Springer, Cham (2016). https://doi.org/10.1007/978-3-319-46448-0_2
20. Lin, T.Y., Goyal, P., Girshick, R., He, K., Dollár, P.: Focal loss for dense object detection. IEEE Trans. Pattern Anal. Mach. Intell. **42**(2), 318–327 (2020)
21. Ge, Z., Liu, S., Wang, F., Li, Z., Sun, J.: YOLOX: exceeding yolo series in 2021 (2021)
22. Yang, Q., Lan, Z.: Mask wearing specification detection based on cascaded convolutional neural network. In: 7th International Conference on Systems and Informatics, pp. 1–6 (2021)
23. Zhao, Y., Geng, S.: Object detection of face mask recognition based on improved faster RCNN. In: bin Ahmad, B.H., Cen, F. (eds.) 2nd International Conference on Computer Vision, Image, and Deep Learning, vol. 11911, pp. 145–152. International Society for Optics and Photonics, SPIE (2021)
24. Nithin, A., Jaisharma, K.: A deep learning based novel approach for detection of face mask wearing using enhanced single shot detector (ssd) over convolutional neural network (cnn) with improved accuracy. In: 2022 International Conference on Business Analytics for Technology and Security (ICBATS), pp. 1–5 (2022)
25. Redmon, J., Farhadi, A.: Yolov3: an incremental improvement. arXiv e-prints (2018)
26. Wang, C.Y., Liao, H.Y.M., Wu, Y.H., Chen, P.Y., Hsieh, J.W., Yeh, I.H.: CSP-Net: a new backbone that can enhance learning capability of cnn. In: 2020 CVPR Workshops, pp. 1571–1580 (2020)
27. Elfwing, S., Uchibe, E., Doya, K.: Sigmoid-weighted linear units for neural network function approximation in reinforcement learning. Neural Netw. **107**, 3–11 (2018)
28. He, K., Zhang, X., Ren, S., Sun, J.: Spatial pyramid pooling in deep convolutional networks for visual recognition. IEEE TPAMI **37**(9), 1904–16 (2014)
29. Liu, S., Qi, L., Qin, H., Shi, J., Jia, J.: Path aggregation network for instance segmentation. In: 2018 CVPR, pp. 8759–8768 (2018)
30. Tian, Z., Shen, C., Chen, H., He, T.: Fcos: fully convolutional one-stage object detection. In: 2019 ICCV, pp. 9626–9635 (2019)
31. Ge, Z., Liu, S., Li, Z., Yoshie, O., Sun, J.: Ota: optimal transport assignment for object detection. In: 2021 CVPR, pp. 303–312 (2021)
32. Zheng, Z., Wang, P., Liu, W., Li, J., Ye, R., Ren, D.: Distance-iou loss: faster and better learning for bounding box regression. In: AAAI Conference on Artificial Intelligence, pp. 12993–13000 (2020)
33. HE, J., Erfani, S., Ma, X., Bailey, J., Chi, Y., Hua, X.S.: \alpha-iou: a family of power intersection over union losses for bounding box regression. In Ranzato, M., Beygelzimer, A., Dauphin, Y., Liang, P., Vaughan, J.W. (eds.) NIPS, vol. 34, pp. 20230–20242. Curran Associates, Inc. (2021)
34. Ge, S., Li, J., Ye, Q., Luo, Z.: Detecting masked faces in the wild with lle-cnns. In: 2017 CVPR, pp. 426–434 (2017)
35. Yang, S., Luo, P., Loy, C.C., Tang, X.: Wider face: a face detection benchmark. In: 2016 CVPR, pp. 5525–5533 (2016)
36. Tzutalin: Labelimg (2015). https://github.com/tzutalin/labelImg Git code
37. Singh, S., Ahuja, U., Kumar, M., Kumar, K., Sachdeva, M.: Face mask detection using YOLOv3 and faster R-CNN models: COVID-19 environment. Multimedia Tools Appl. **80**, 1–16 (2021)

Gesture and Action Recognition

Adaptive Joint Interdependency Learning for 2D Occluded Hand Pose Estimation

Pingping Wu, Lunke Fei$^{(\boxtimes)}$, Shuping Zhao, Peipei Kang, Shaohua Teng, and Xiaozhao Fang

School of Computer Science and Technology, Guangdong University of Technology, Guangzhou, China
flksxm@126.com

Abstract. Hand pose estimation based on 2D RGB images has drawn increasing research interest due to its many practical applications, such as Human-Computer Interaction (HCI) and Virtual Reality (VR). However, most existing methods focus on learning hand structure and key point representations, which cannot well exploit the joint interdependency of 2D occluded hand pose estimation. In this paper, we propose an adaptive joint interdependency learning network (AJIL) for 2D occluded hand pose estimation by adaptively learning hand joint interdependency, including three sub-networks. First, a cascade multi-task mask-learning subnetwork is used to learn hand pose structure. Then, a modified transformer encoder is designed to exploit the high spatial relationship between the hand joints. Lastly, the joint correlation is obtained from the multi-view hand pose images via 21 long short-term memory (LSTM). Extensive studies on three widely used datasets including the CMU Panoptic Hand, Large-Scale Multiview Hand Pose, and also our newly established pen-holding hand pose (PHHP) images dataset which is conducted to evaluate our proposed method. Experimental results show that our proposed method can achieve a very competitive 2D hand pose estimation performance when compared with the baseline models.

Keywords: Hand pose estimation · 2D occluded hand pose estimation · Hand joint interdependency learning

1 Introduction

Hand pose estimation, which aims to understand the activities of human hands, is a longstanding and interesting problem with a variety of practical applications such as Human-Computer Interaction (HCI), Virtual Reality (VR), and robotics. Over the past decades, a number of hand pose estimation methods have been proposed, including the 2D RGB [1,2], video-based [3], depth-based [4], and 3D estimation methods [5]. While these methods with depth and 3D information have achieved competitive pose estimation performance, they usually require expensive equipment and special shooting environments, making

© The Author(s), under exclusive license to Springer Nature Switzerland AG 2022
W. Deng et al. (Eds.): CCBR 2022, LNCS 13628, pp. 217–225, 2022.
https://doi.org/10.1007/978-3-031-20233-9_22

them less effective for practical applications. For this reason, existing studies focus most on 2D-based hand pose estimation.

In recent years, there have been many methods proposed for 2D hand pose estimation, such as the mask-pose cascaded CNN (MPC) [1], optimized convolutional pose machine (OCPM) [6], and nonparametric structure regularization machine (NSRM) [2]. Unlike the human body pose, human hands are very flexible, making 2D hand poses easily self-occluded. While the DCNN-based methods such as CPM [7], and MPC [1] are capable of learning good feature representations, they usually fail to obtain geometric constraints among joints, resulting in joint inconsistency in the final prediction. How to fix the joint inconsistency problem for 2D hand pose estimation remains an unsolved and interesting topic.

In this paper, we propose a new architecture called the adaptive joint interdependency learning (AJIL) method for 2D occluded hand pose estimation. Specifically, we first use an image segmentation learning network, usually the U-net, to learn the hand pose mask representation, and then engineer the limb's structure learning module to further extract the hand pose limbs features representation [8,9]. Third, in the key-points learning module, we make good use of the transformer encoder to focus on key-point detection. Finally, the key-points maps combining the salient maps of hand pose and limbs are learned by the optional multi-view pose module for refining the confidence maps. Experimental results on three hand pose benchmark datasets clearly show the effectiveness of our proposed method.

2   Occluded Hand Pose Estimation Network

In this section, we first present the overall framework of the proposed network and then elaborate on the two components of the proposed network.

2.1   Overview of the Occluded Hand Pose Estimation Network

Figure 1 shows the basic framework of the proposed occluded hand pose estimation network, which mainly consists of two sub-networks: hand-limbs mask learning (HLML) and adaptive joint interdependency learning (AJIL). For the hand-limbs mask learning sub-network, we first use the image segmentation network to obtain the hand mask map, and then jointly learn the limb structure by combining input images and hand mask maps. For the AJIL sub-network, to adaptively learn the key points correlation information, we design a key point learning module to extract the high-dimensional spatial information between joints and use a multi-view pose module to refine the key-points confidence maps (KCM) based on the multi-view message. Finally, 21 key points and 20 limbs are automatically depicted, as shown in Fig. 1. In the following, we detail the implementations of the two sub-networks.

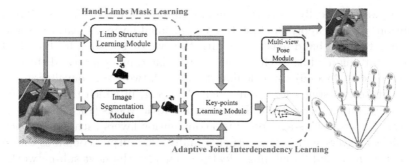

Fig. 1. The overall framework of the occluded hand pose estimation network, which represent hand pose as 21 keypoints, 20 limbs, and 6 limb mask maps.

2.2 Hand-limb Masks Learning Sub-network

Figure 2 shows the basic idea of the hand-limb mask learning (HLML) sub-network, which aims to extensive exploit the discriminative mask feature from hand pose images. It is recognized that key-points learning is based on the hand region from the noisy image, where the hand position is the crucial information for estimation. Due to this, our HLML sub-network uses the multi-task model to focus on the synthetic mask area. To accurately locate the hand mask, we process the images by using an image segmentation module, e.g., U-net, instead of a normal VGG backbone module. Furthermore, inspired by the NSRM [2], we learn the hand limb structure by 5 convolution layers with 7×7 kernel and 2 convolution layers with 1×1 kernel. After that, we apply cross-entropy loss to the hand mask map and the limb mask maps for restraining the mask learning process.

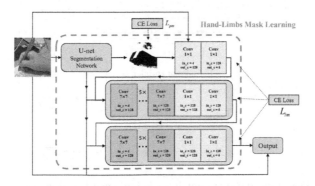

Fig. 2. The hand-limb mask learning network.

Let $G \in R^{c \times w \times h}$ be the DNN-based feature maps, where w and h represents the width and height of the input images and c denotes the channel number. For the U-net, we empirically resize the original input color images into $3 \times 520 \times 520$. In addition, we only apply the first 18 convolutional layers as feature extraction layers to obtain the hand mask map with the size of $1 \times 46 \times 46$. For the limb structure learning module, we first combine the hand mask map and the original image (resized to 46×46) and calculate them with two 1×1 convolution blocks. Then, we take two stages for 6 limb mask learning, in which the 6 limb masks shown in Fig. 1 are represented as Limb Probabilistic Masks (LPM) (more details in NSRM [2]), and each stage contains 5 convolution layers with 7×7 kernel and 2 convolution layers with 1×1 kernel. Finally, the output combines one hand mask feature map and 6 limb-mask feature maps for the next sub-network.

2.3 Adaptive Joint Interdependency Learning Sub-network

2D hand pose images usually contain self-occlusion, making the conventional DCNNs less effective for occlusion information learning and also less generalization capability. To address this, we design an adaptive joint interdependency learning method (AJIL) to adaptively learn the key-points correlation information and multi-views image correlation information. Figure 3 shows the pipeline of the AJIL sub-network, which consists of one transformer encoder for key-points correlation learning and 21 LSTMs for multi-view hand key points learning. Following the common practice of pose estimation, we represent the ground true KCM of the hand key-point as a 2D Gaussian centering around the labeled key-point with standard deviation σ_{KCM}. In addition, we apply the sum-of-squared-error loss (MSE) for hand pose estimation to the output of the hand key points.

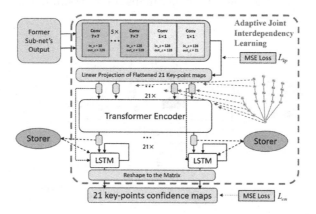

Fig. 3. Detail of adaptive joint interdependency learning sub-network.

Specifically, to learn the critical feature from the digital image, we get a feature map $G \in R^{10 \times 46 \times 46}$ for the AJIL through the former sub-network. We also exploit 5 convolution layers with 7×7 kernel and 2 convolution layers with

1×1 kernel for generating 21 key-point maps, where one map represents only one key point. Then, we flatten the 21 key-point feature maps G_n into vector V_n, which will be downscaled to the num_dim (a hyperparameter) dimension by linear projection. Subsequently, V_n is fed into the transformer encoder to learn the relationship between the key points. After this process, we still get 21 one-dimensional vectors V_n. Each one-dimensional vector V_k is then fed to an LSTM module respectively. After training in the LSTM module, we obtained vectors with the same dimensionality as before. Finally, we reshape the vectors into matrices and merge them into 21 key point confidence maps.

In order to learn the relationship of multi-angle images M_n, we store the key point vector V_n' of the same gesture in different shooting angle images for the subsequent training. For instance, when a view of an image, like M_2, is trained, the Storer will extract the vector V_1' of M_1 and feed them into the LSTM for training simultaneously. In addition, V_n without a transformer encoder training will also engage in the training of LSTM. Moreover, if there is no multi-angle image for a certain gesture, we will use the copied V_k' instead.

2.4 Loss Function

To better learn the discriminative mask feature, we apply the cross-entropy loss as the constraint to train the hand-limb mask learning module, i.e.,

$$L_{pm} = L_{lm} = \sum_{g \in G} \sum_{p \in I} S^*(p \mid g) \log \hat{S}(p \mid g) + (1 - S^*(p \mid g)) \log(1 - \hat{S}(p \mid g)), \quad (1)$$

where $S^*(p \mid g)$ is the representation of ground true of the hand-limb masks at Pixel p, and Group g, and $\hat{S}(p \mid g)$ is the prediction of the hand-limb masks at Pixel p, and Group g. The detail of $S^*(p \mid g)$ is as follow:

$$S^*(p \mid g) = \exp\left(-\frac{\mathcal{D}(p, \overline{p_i p_j})}{2\sigma_{PCK}^2}\right), \quad (2)$$

where $\mathcal{D}(p, \overline{p_i p_j})$ is the distance between the pixel p and the line segment $\overline{p_i p_j}$, and σ_{KCM} is a hyper parameter to control the spread of the Gaussian.

In addition, we apply the sum-of-squared-error loss to restrict the output of the AJIL method, as follows:

$$L_{cm} = L_{kp} = \sum_{k=1} \sum_{p \in I} \left\| C^*(p \mid k) - \hat{C}(p \mid k) \right\|_2^2, \quad (3)$$

where $\hat{C}(p \mid k)$ is the predition of the key points and $C^*(p \mid k)$ is defined as follows:

$$C^*(p \mid k) = \exp\left\{-\frac{\|p - p_k^*\|_2^2}{2\sigma_{PCK}^2}\right\}. \quad (4)$$

Finally, the overall loss function is a weighted sum of the hand-limbs loss and the loss of the key-point maps, as follows:

$$Loss = L_{cm} + \lambda_1 L_{pm} + \lambda_2 L_{lm} + \lambda_3 L_{kp}, \quad (5)$$

where L_{cm} is for the key-points confidence maps as well as L_{kp}, L_{pm} is for the hand pose map, and L_{lm} is for the six limb maps, and λ_n are the hyperparameters to control the relative weight of the intermediate supervision.

3   Experiment

In this section, we evaluate the proposed hand pose estimation network on two public datasets and also our newly established PHHP image dataset. To better evaluate the proposed method, we compare the proposed method with three baseline hand pose estimation methods such as CPM [7], NSRM [2], and Attention Lightweight Hand Pose Estimation (ALHP) [10] in terms of the Probability of Correct Key-point within a Normalized Distance Threshold [11] (PCK). For a fair comparison, all experiments are conducted under the same PyTorch framework and similar Adam optimizer. In addition, all methods were performed under the same platform with two GTX 3080 graphics cards (including 8,960 CUDA cores), AMD 5800X CPU, 64GB RAM, and 500GB hard disk drive. For the proposed method, we initialize the parameters with the Xavier and the learning rate, the num_dim and batch size of our method are empirically set to 1E-6, 529, and 32, respectively. In addition, we set the λ_1, λ_2 and λ_3 as 0.03, 0.06, and 0.4 respectively.

3.1   Dataset Settings

In this experiment, we first select the CMU [12] dataset and LSM [13] dataset to evaluate the effectiveness of the proposed method. Then, we mix the other two datasets with the PHHP datase (our newly established dataset) to conduct the experiments, since our study focuses on the hand pose estimation under serious occluded and complex backgrounds. For each dataset, we use 80% of the samples as the training set, 10% as validation, and 10% as the test set. Lastly, we cropped all images as well as the flipped samples into the sizes of 520×520 pixels. Table 1 tabulates the detailed information of the evaluated dataset setting.

Table 1. The detail of the evaluated dataset setting.

Datasets	Instances	Training (80%)	Validation (10%)	Testing (10%)
CMU [12]	14,817	11,853	1,481	1,481
LSM [13]	20,690	16,552	2,069	2,069
CMU+PHHP	16,782	13,425	1,678	1,678
LSM+PHHP	22,662	18,129	2,266	2,266

3.2 Estimation Results

Table 2 tabulates the PCKs of different methods on the different datasets, where the σ_{KCM} is set to the value ranging in 0–1 and the 5 PCKs with the largest changes are reported. From Table 2, we can see that our proposed method can achieve obviously better average PCKs than the other baseline models such as the CPM [7], NSRM [2], and ALHP [10] on all datasets. This is because our proposed network efficient segmentation networks, multi-task restricted learning, and cascade learning, such as a better PCK can be obtained. Moreover, our proposed AJIL further utilizes a transformer encoder for adaptive learning the hand pose key points instead of only learning the hand structure information.

Table 2. The PCKs of different methods on the CMU [12], LSM [13], CMU+PHHP, and LSM+PHHP datasets.

CMU dataset [12]							CMU+PHHP dataset					
σ_{KCM}	0.04	0.06	0.08	0.1	0.12	Ave	0.1	0.12	0.14	0.16	0.18	Ave
CPM [7]	55.25	73.23	81.45	85.97	88.8	76.94	53.1	65.28	73.76	80.23	86.19	71.71
NSRM [2]	59.3	76.19	83.59	87.54	90.18	79.36	53.71	66.71	74.31	82.18	87.83	72.95
ALHP [10]	60.81	76.98	84.29	88.1	90.96	80.23	54.28	67.56	75.11	82.69	88.12	73.55
AJIL	62.95	77.92	85.54	88.64	91.23	**81.26**	54.89	67.83	76.41	83.56	88.94	**74.33**
LSM Dataset [13]							LSM+PHHP Dataset					
σ_{KCM}	0.06	0.08	0.1	0.12	0.14	Ave	0.14	0.16	0.18	0.2	0.22	Ave
CPM [7]	65.71	72.54	78.38	83.21	85.89	77.15	63.66	74.39	82.27	88.84	91.93	80.22
NSRM [2]	66.14	73.9	78.85	85.43	87.29	78.32	64.8	76.43	86.55	89.21	91.99	81.8
ALHP [10]	67.45	75.71	79.71	86.84	88.04	79.55	65.54	77.81	87.17	90.61	92.62	82.75
AJIL	67.98	76.92	82.13	87.9	91.53	81.29	66.78	79.49	88.24	91.79	94.12	84.08
AJIL+	68.2	76.98	83.23	88.5	92.43	**83.7**	67.66	80.46	88.27	92.32	94.35	**84.61**

In addition, we also explore the performance of different methods on the mixed datasets, including the CMU+PHHP and LSM+PHHP, such that they contain more occluded hand pose images. As can be seen in Table 2, our proposed AJIL method shows higher PCKs than the four compared methods, demonstrating the promising effectiveness of the proposed method. Moreover, on the LSM and LSM+PHHP datasets, we use 4 multi-view images as a frame to train the network (referred to as AJIL+) and report the estimation results in Table 2. It can be seen that the performance of the AJIL method can be further improved by combining the multi-view images over the AJIL method. The possible reason is that the modified LSTM module can adaptively learn the same characteristics information from multi-view images.

4 Conclusion

In this paper, we present an efficient end-to-end hand pose estimation network consisting of two subnetworks: HLML and AJIL. We first use a segmentation network to learn the hand pose mask and the hand-limb mask. Then, we adaptively learn the hand key points correlation by transformer encoder and the relationship between the multi-view images by 21 LSTM models. We evaluate our proposed network on two public datasets and one newly established pen-holding hand pose image dataset and the experimental results show that the proposed network achieves better hand pose performance than the baseline networks. For future work, it seems to be an interesting direction to apply our method to other pose estimation applications such as occluded human pose estimation.

Acknowledgments. This work was supported in part by the Guangzhou Science and technology plan project under Grant 202002030110, and in part by the National Natural Science Foundation of China under Grant 62176066 and Grant 62106052.

References

1. Wang, Y., Peng, C., Liu, Y.: Mask-pose cascaded cnn for 2d hand pose estimation from single color image. IEEE Trans. Circ. Syst. Video Technol. **29**(11), 3258–3268 (2018)
2. Chen, Y., et al.: Nonparametric structure regularization machine for 2D hand pose estimation. In Proceedings of the IEEE/CVF Winter Conference on Applications of Computer Vision, pp. 381–390 (2020)
3. Khaleghi, L., Moghaddam, A. S., Marshall, J., Etemad, A.: Multi-view video-based 3D hand pose estimation. arXiv preprint arXiv:2109.11747 (2021)
4. Ren, P., Sun, H., Hao, J., Wang, J., Qi, Q., Liao, J.: Mining multi-view information: a strong self-supervised framework for depth-based 3D hand pose and mesh estimation. In Proceedings of the IEEE/CVF Conference on Computer Vision and Pattern Recognition, pp. 20555–20565 (2022)
5. Cheng, W., Park, J.H., Ko, J.H.: HandFoldingNet: a 3D hand pose estimation network using multiscale-feature guided folding of a 2D hand skeleton. In: Proceedings of the IEEE/CVF International Conference on Computer Vision, pp. 11260–11269 (2021)
6. Pan, T., Wang, Z., Fan, Y.: Optimized convolutional pose machine for 2D hand pose estimation. J. Visual Commun. Image Represent. **83**, 103461 (2022)
7. Wei, S.E., Ramakrishna, V., Kanade, T., Sheikh, Y.: Convolutional pose machines. In: Proceedings of the IEEE Conference on Computer Vision and Pattern Recognition, pp. 4724–4732 (2016)
8. Fei, L., Zhao, S., Jia, W., Zhang, B., Wen, J., Xu, Y.: Toward efficient palmprint feature extraction by learning a single-layer convolution network. IEEE Trans. Neural Netw. Learn. Syst. (2022)
9. Fei, L., Zhang, B., Zhang, L., Jia, W., Wen, J., Wu, J.: Learning compact multifeature codes for palmprint recognition from a single training image per palm. IEEE Trans. Multimedia **23**, 2930–2942 (2020)
10. Santavas, N., Kansizoglou, I., Bampis, L., Karakasis, E., Gasteratos, A.: Attention! a lightweight 2d hand pose estimation approach. IEEE Sens. J. **21**(10), 11488–11496 (2020)
11. Simon, T., Joo, H., Matthews, I., Sheikh, Y.: Hand keypoint detection in single images using multiview bootstrapping. In: Proceedings of the IEEE Conference on Computer Vision and Pattern Recognition, pp. 1145–1153 (2017)

12. Joo, H., et al.: Panoptic studio: a massively multiview system for social motion capture. In Proceedings of the IEEE International Conference on Computer Vision, pp. 3334–3342 (2015)
13. Gomez-Donoso, F., Orts-Escolano, S., Cazorla, M.: Large-scale multiview 3D hand pose dataset. Image Vision Comput. **81**, 25–33 (2019)

Contrastive and Consistent Learning for Unsupervised Human Parsing

Xiaomei Zhang[1], Feng Pan[3], Ke Xiang[3], Xiangyu Zhu[1(✉)], Chang Yu[1,2],
Zidu Wang[1,2], and Zhen Lei[1,2]

[1] CBSR&NLPR, CASIA, Beijing, China
{xiaomei.zhang,xiangyu.zhu,chang.yu,zlei}@nlpr.ia.ac.cn,
wangzidu2022@ia.ac.cn
[2] School of Artificial Intelligence, University of Chinese Academy of Sciences,
Beijing, China
[3] Zhejiang Sunny Optical Intelligence Technology Co., Ltd., Yuyao, China
{fpan,xiangke}@sunnyoptical.com

Abstract. How to learn pixel-level representations of human parts without supervision is a challenging task. However, despite its significance, a few works explore this challenge. In this work, we propose a contrastive and consistent learning network (C^2L) for unsupervised human parsing. C^2L mainly consists of a part contrastive module and a pixel consistent module. We design a part contrastive module to distinguish the same semantic human parts from other ones by contrastive learning, which pulls the same semantic parts closer and pushes different semantic ones away. A pixel consistent module is proposed to obtain spatial correspondence in each view of images, which can select semantic-relevant image pixels and suppress semantic-irrelevant ones. To improve the pattern analysis ability, we perform a sparse operation on the feed-forward networks of the pixel consistent module. Extensive experiments on the popular human parsing benchmark show that our method achieves competitive performance.

Keywords: Unsupervised human parsing · Part contrastive module · Pixel consistent module

1 Introduction

Human parsing aims to assign a class label to each pixel of the human body in an image. Various applications make use of it, including human behavior analysis, clothing style recognition and retrieval, clothing category classification and so on. However, most works focus on supervised methods. A major drawback of supervised methods is that they need pixel-wise semantic labels for every image in a dataset. These datasets are a labor-intensive process that spends significant amounts of time and money. To remedy this situation, weakly-supervised methods employ weaker forms of supervision, *e.g.*, image-level labels [1], bounding boxes [2] and scribbles [3], and semi-supervised methods use partially labeled

W. Deng et al. (Eds.): CCBR 2022, LNCS 13628, pp. 226–236, 2022.
https://doi.org/10.1007/978-3-031-20233-9_23

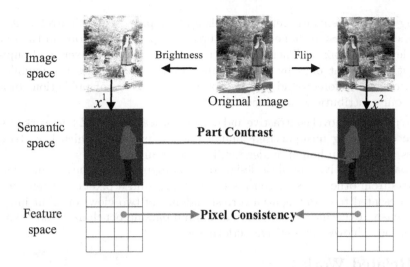

Fig. 1. An illustration of the proposed contrastive and consistent learning method for unsupervised human parsing. In this method, two views are randomly augmented from an image, and the parts with different semantics of two views are encouraged to be contrastive, and the pixels with the same semantics from the corresponding features of the two views are encouraged to be consistent.

examples to train the module. Although above methods can reduce labor consumption, training networks still rely on some form of supervision.

In this paper, we deal with this problem by introducing a novel unsupervised human parsing approach, which does not need annotated training data. More concretely, we aim to learn pixel-level representations for unsupervised human parsing by contrastive and consistent learning that consists of a part contrastive module and a pixel consistent module.

The major challenge of unsupervised human parsing is to identify part semantics. The insight of our part contrastive module is to leverage part-level representations to learn part semantics. Recently, self-supervised representation learning methods [4–6] show how to obtain the classification of images with unlabeled training data. They compute features to capture the category of a whole image, thus they cannot meet the need for the classification of parts in human parsing. Therefore, we use multiple high-level features, capturing the semantic characteristic of each human part. According to the characteristics, each pixel is assigned to its corresponding category. Figure 1 shows our motivation that the same categories (*e.g.*, upper-body) is distinguished from the other categories (*e.g.*, lower-body) by contrastive loss. In this way, the same semantic parts are pulled closer and different semantic ones are pushed away.

The part-level representations cannot be effective for dense pixel classification, because they ignore the spatial correspondence. To amend this problem, we design a pixel consistent module. As shown in Fig. 1 that the pixels with the same semantics from the corresponding features of the two views are encouraged to be consistent. The module extracts the spatial correlation in each view of images, aiming to select semantic-relevant pixels and suppress semantic-irrelevant ones. Specifically, we first reshape input features into patches and obtain the semantic relevance of pixels. Then, we select semantic-relevant pixels and suppress semantic-irrelevant ones by a sparse operation, which makes the module pay attention to the foreground and improves the accuracy of prediction. In summary, our contributions are threefold:

1. We propose a novel contrastive and consistent learning (C^2L) network to solve the challenging unsupervised human parsing problem, which has attracted less attention in human understanding community.
2. A part contrastive module is designed to distinguish the same semantic human parts from other ones by contrastive learning, and a pixel consistent module is presented to obtain spatial correspondence of two views of input images.
3. Extensive experiments on a popular human parsing benchmark show that our method achieves competitive performance.

2   Related Work

Unsupervised Human Parsing. There have only been a few attempts in the literature to tackle human parsing under a fully unsupervised setting. Hung *et al.* [7] learned part features that are semantically consistent across images and achieved good results in their paper. Lorenz *et al.* [8] presented a method to disentangle object shape and appearance to obtain a part modeling result. Liu *et al.* [9] followed the above methods [8] to disentangle object shape and appearance and proposed a self-supervised part classification loss. Different from the above methods, our C^2L does not require predefined constraints, *e.g.*, saliency map [7], elliptical assumption of the shape of human parts [8] and background cut [9]. We are more interested in learning a model that can predict part-level semantic information without supervision.

Contrastive Learning. Contrastive learning [4,10,11] has been developing rapidly, which learns representations to discriminate positive image pairs (constructed from different augmentations of the same images) from dissimilar, negative image pairs. Varied strategies are proposed to choose appropriate negative pairs. In MoCo [4,5], a memory buffer and a momentum encoder were designed to provide negative samples. In SimCLR [10,11], the negative samples were the large training mini-batches. Some papers [12,13] designed methods to alleviate the bias issue caused by incorrect (false) negative images by modifying the contrastive loss function. PC^{2}Seg [14] sampled the negative examples strategically rather than changing the loss function. Compared with these attempts, we choose semantic inconsistent features as negative pairs.

3   Proposed Method

3.1   Overall Framework

In this paper, we propose a new network called Contrastive and Consistent Learning (C^2L) that aims to assign every pixel a label with unlabeled training

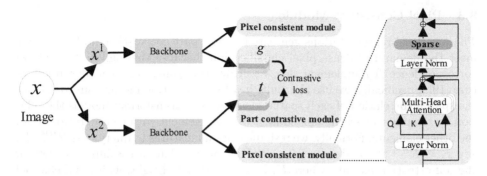

Fig. 2. Architecture of the proposed contrastive and consistent learning for unsupervised human parsing.

data. Specifically, as shown in Fig. 2, given an input image, the random photometric transforms generate two views. These views are sent into the backbone network, *e.g.*, ResNet [15] or any other convolutional neural network to obtain original features, and then we send these features to the part contrastive module and the pixel consistent module, respectively. The part contrastive module can distinguish the same semantic human parts from other ones, at the level of the global feature. The pixel consistent module can obtain spatial correspondence between pixels to adaptively aggregate semantically consistent pixels, improving the accuracy of the prediction.

3.2 Part Contrastive Module

The part contrastive module uses a 1×1 *conv* to reduce the channel number of original features and a group convolutional layer to decrease the computation, and then reshapes them to $g = \{g_0, \ldots, g_k\}$ and $t = \{t_0, \ldots, t_k\}$. We define a set of encoded keys $t_0, \ldots, t_k$ for each encoded query g_i. The encoded keys and queries are generated from different views of the input image, respectively. However, here each key and query no longer represents the whole view, and encodes a human part of a view. The positive key t_+ encodes the same part of the two views, which is one of the N feature vectors from another view of the same image. Note that N usually corresponds to the number of labels in a dataset. Hungarian-matching [16] is the sampling strategy to ensure that the positive key t_+ encodes the same semantic part with encoded query g_i. While the negative keys t_- encode the other parts of the different view. We use a contrastive loss function InfoNCE [17], it can pull g_i close to the positive key t_+ while pushing it away from other negative keys t_-:

$$\mathcal{L}_r = \sum_{i=0}^{k} -log \frac{\exp(g_i \cdot t_+/\tau)}{\exp(g_i \cdot t_+/\tau) + \sum_{t_-} \exp(g_i \cdot t_-/\tau)}, \tag{1}$$

where τ denotes a temperature hyper-parameter as in [18].

3.3   Pixel Consistent Module

The part-level representations generated by the part contrastive module cannot meet the demand of dense pixel classification, because they ignore the spatial correspondence. To implement this, we utilize the transformer encoder architecture [19]. Specifically, we use the multi-head self-attention mechanism to extract the spatial correlation of each spatial element. The transformer models the relation by refining the feature embeddings of each element with consideration to all the other elements. Formally, we reshape original features to query $Q \in R^{HW \times C}$, key $K \in R^{HW \times C}$, and value $V \in R^{HW \times C}$ which denote the input triplets of the self-attention module, where H, W and C denote height, width and channel number of the original features m, respectively. We do not use the fixed positional embeddings in the network. Then, the spatial correspondence $F \in R^{HW \times C}$ is obtained through the standard multi-head self-attention layer, with the whole process defined as $F = multi(m)$. Through end-to-end training on a human parsing dataset, the spatial correlation is obtained.

However, some works [20,21] have suggested that performing selection of spatial correlation is critical for pattern analysis. Therefore, we employ a sparse operation on the feed-forward networks (FFNs) in the transformer encoder. We begin with a brief review of sparse code algorithms. Sparse code [22] aims to learn a useful sparse representation of any given data. The mathematical representation of the general objective function for this problem can help:

$$\min_{\alpha \in R^k} \frac{1}{2} \|x - D\alpha\|_2^2 + \lambda \|\alpha\|_1, \tag{2}$$

where $x \in R^{HW \times C}$ is the given data, $D \in R^{HW \times k}$ is the decoder matrix, λ is a regularization parameter. In general, we have $k < C$, and the loss function should be small if D is "good" at representing the signal x. It is well known that L_1 loss penalty yields a sparse solution α and $\alpha \geq 0$. To prevent D from being arbitrarily large (which would lead to arbitrarily small values of α), it is common to constrain its columns $(d_i)_{j=1}^k$ to have an L_2 norm less than or equal to one. We call c the convex set of matrices verifying this constraint:

$$c = \{D \in R^{HW \times k} s.t. \forall j = 1, \ldots, k, d_j^T d_j \leq 1\}. \tag{3}$$

We perform pixel consistent operations on the feed-forward networks (FFNs) by extending the original sparse code to a spatial correlation. The spatial correlation (the outputs of the multi-head self-attention layer F) is the input of the sparse code. Thus the pixel consistent loss is defined as:

$$\mathcal{L}_c = \min_{\alpha \in R^k} \frac{1}{2} \|F - D\alpha\|_2^2 + \lambda \|\alpha\|_1, \tag{4}$$

Then, the $D\alpha$ is the output of sparse code, and it connects with the outputs of the multi-head self-attention layer by short connections as the output of our pixel consistent module.

Algorithm 1. C^2L pseudocode

P_i^1, P_i^2 : random photometric augmented version
G_i : random geometric augmented version
f_θ : the backbone
S_σ, C_τ: the pixel consistent module and the part contrastive module, respectively
for $(x_i) \sim \mathcal{D}$ do
$\qquad y_{i,:}^1, g_{i,:}^1 \leftarrow S_\sigma/C_\tau(G_i(f_\theta(P_i^1(x_i))))$
$\qquad y_{i,:}^2, g_{i,:}^2 \leftarrow S_\sigma/C_\tau(f_\theta(G_i(P_i^2(x_i))))$
end for
$\mu^1, z^1 \leftarrow BatchKMeans(y_{ip}^1 : i \in [N], p \in [HW])$
$\mu^2, z^2 \leftarrow BatchKMeans(y_{ip}^1 : i \in [N], p \in [HW])$
for $(x_i) \sim \mathcal{D}$ do
$\qquad y_{i,:}^1, g_{i,:}^1 \leftarrow S_\sigma/C_\tau(G_i(f_\theta(P_i^1(x_i))))$
$\qquad y_{i,:}^2, g_{i,:}^2 \leftarrow S_\sigma/C_\tau(f_\theta(G_i(P_i^2(x_i))))$
$\qquad \mathcal{L}_r \leftarrow \mathcal{L}_{contrastive}(g_{i,:}^1, g_{i,:}^2)$
$\qquad \mathcal{L}_{view} \leftarrow \mathcal{L}_{clust}(y_{i,:}^1, \mu^1, z^1) + \mathcal{L}_{clust}(y_{i,:}^2, \mu^2, z^2)$
$\qquad \mathcal{L}_c \leftarrow \mathcal{L}_c$
$\qquad \mathcal{L}_{total} \leftarrow \mathcal{L}_{view} + \mathcal{L}_r + \mathcal{L}_c$
$\qquad f_\theta, S_\sigma, C_\tau \leftarrow backward(\mathcal{L}_{total})$
end for

3.4   Pseudo Code of C^2L

Algorithm 1 provides the pseudo code of C^2L for this unsupervised method. We follow PiCIE [23], for each image x_i in the dataset. We randomly sample two photometric transformations, P_i^1 and P_i^2. And then, P_i^1 and P_i^2 are sent into the backbone f_θ and the geometric transformations G_i in different order to improve the robustness of the network. Finally, features are sent into pixel consistent module S_σ and part contrastive module C_τ, respectively. This yields two features for each pixel p in each image x_i:

$$y_{i,:}^1, g_{i,:}^1 \leftarrow S_\sigma/C_\tau(G_i(f_\theta(P_i^1(x_i)))), y_{i,:}^2, g_{i,:}^2 \leftarrow S_\sigma/C_\tau(f_\theta(G_i(P_i^2(x_i)))), \quad (5)$$

We employ clustering separately in the two views to get two sets of pseudo-labels and centroids:

$$\mu^1, z^1 = \arg\min_{z,\mu} \sum_{i,p} \left\| y_{ip}^1 - \mu_{yip} \right\|^2, \mu^2, z^2 = \arg\min_{z,\mu} \sum_{i,p} \left\| y_{ip}^2 - \mu_{yip} \right\|^2, \quad (6)$$

Given these two sets of centroid and pseudo-labels, the features are adhered to the clustering labels in a cluster loss [23]. Now that we have two views, we want this to be true in each view:

$$\mathcal{L}_{view} \leftarrow \mathcal{L}_{clust}(y_{i,:}^1, \mu^1, z^1) + \mathcal{L}_{clust}(y_{i,:}^2, \mu^2, z^2), \quad (7)$$

Overall, the total loss for our C^2L can be formulated as:

$$\mathcal{L}_{total} \leftarrow \mathcal{L}_{view} + \alpha\mathcal{L}_r + \beta\mathcal{L}_c, \quad (8)$$

where α and β are the weight to balance the two terms. α is set to 0.5 and β is set to 0.3, which is validated by experiments.

Table 1. Ablation study for every module. The baseline is PiCIE. Pacm denotes our part contrastive module. Picmnosparse denotes our pixel consistent module without the sparse code operation. Picm denotes our pixel consistent module.

#	Baseline	Pacm (ours)	Picmnosparse (ours)	Picm (ours)	mIoU (%)
1	✓				9.62
2	✓	✓			12.33
3	✓	✓	✓		14.61
4	✓	✓		✓	16.27

4   Experiments

4.1   Datasets and Evaluation Metrics

ATR dataset [24] contains 7700 multi-person images with challenging poses and viewpoints (6000 for training, 700 for validation and 1000 for testing). In this paper, we merge the ground truth to the upper-body, lower-body and background, respectively, evaluating performance. Evaluation metrics for ATR, following supervised human parsing [25,26], the performance is evaluated in terms of mean pixel Intersection-over-Union (mIoU).

4.2   Implementation Details and Baseline

For all experiments, we use the Feature Pyramid Network [27] with ResNet-18 [15] backbone pre-trained on ImageNet [28]. The fusion dimension of the feature pyramid is 128 instead of 256. Following PiCIE [23], the cluster centroids are computed with mini-batch approximation with GPUs using the FAISS library [29]. For the baseline, we do not use image gradients as an additional input when we use ImageNet-pretrained weight. For optimization, we adopt Adam. As for the crop size of the dataset, we resize images to 320×320 as the input size. The mini-batch size for k-means is 192, and the batch size for training and testing is 96.

The baseline is PiCIE [23] which is an explicit clustering method. PiCIE clusters the feature vectors of given images and uses the cluster assignment as labels to train the network. Since the size of images explodes the number of feature vectors to cluster, PiCIE applies mini-batch k-means to first compute the cluster centroids, assign labels, and then train the network.

4.3   Ablation Study

Ablation of Each Module. We conduct ablation studies with Resnet-18 as our backbone and report all the performance on the ATR validation set. For starters, we evaluate the performance of the baseline (PiCIE), as the result in Tabel 1 (#1). To verify the effect of the part contrastive module, we remove the pixel consistent module in Fig. 2. The experiment result is shown in Table 1 (#2). This modification improves the performance to 12.33%(2.71%↑) with negligible

Table 2. Ablation study for weight α and β. $\alpha = 0.5$ and $\beta = 0.3$ achieve the best prediction.

α	mIoU (%)	Acc. (%)	$\beta(\alpha = 0.5)$	mIoU (%)	Acc. (%)
0.0	9.62	34.58	0.0	15.17	68.44
0.3	12.01	58.60	**0.3**	**16.27**	**71.32**
0.5	**12.33**	**69.30**	0.5	16.06	69.02
0.7	12.06	65.21	0.7	15.33	68.51
1.0	11.63	52.13	1.0	15.32	68.05

additional parameters. We further evaluate the role of the pixel consistent module. As for this module, we replace its sparse code with normal FFNs. The result is shown in Table 1 (#3), obtaining the performance of 14.61%. We add sparse code to the pixel consistent module, the accuracy has been further improved to achieve 16.27%. Compared with the baseline, C^2L achieves a great improvement.

Ablation of Hyper-Parameters. Table 2 examines the sensitivity to hyper-parameters of C^2L. The hyper-parameter α, β in Eq. (8) serve as the weight to balance the contrastive loss and sparse code loss. We report the results of different α, β in the left and right of Table 2, respectively. We first conduct experiments to obtain the best α. In the left of Table 2, it shows a trend that the segmentation performance improves when we increase the α. when $\alpha = 0.5$, the performance achieves the best result. As shown in the right of Table 2, when $\beta = 0$, our C^2L without sparse code operation. By increasing β, $\beta = 0.3$ achieves the best prediction.

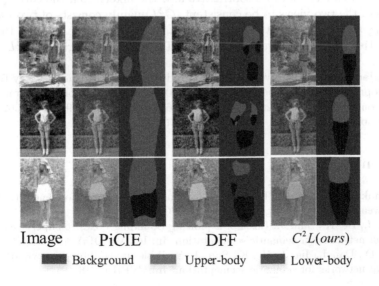

| Image | PiCIE | DFF | C^2L(ours) |

■ Background   ■ Upper-body   ■ Lower-body

Fig. 3. Qualitative comparison results on ATR for unsupervised human parsing.

Table 3. The quantitative comparison of unsupervised human parsing on ATR.

Method	mIoU (%)	Acc. (%)
PiCIE [23]	9.62	34.58
DFF [30]	12.63	56.15
$C^2L(Ours)$	16.27	71.32

4.4   Comparison on Unsupervised Human Parsing

The unsupervised human parsing from unlabeled images is a challenge that has not been well explored. DFF [30] proposes to use non-negative matrix factorization upon the CNN features to obtain the semantic concepts, which need to optimize on the whole datasets during inference to keep semantic consistency.

To visualize the part segmentation result, we show some resulting images from ATR in Fig. 3. We can find that our method can correctly segment most parts. What's more, the foreground can be extracted from the complex background. This is because our part contrastive module can distinguish the same human parts from other ones by contrastive learning and our pixel consistent module obtains spatial correspondence in each view of images to improve foreground extracting. Results in Table 3 validate the effectiveness of our method.

5   Conclusion

In this paper, we propose contrastive and consistent learning (C^2L), a novel unsupervised human parsing method. It encourages human parts with different semantics of two views to be contrastive and the pixels from the corresponding features of the two views to be consistent. C^2L mainly consists of two modules, including a part contrastive module and a pixel consistent module. Both the quantitative and qualitative results demonstrate the superiority of C^2L.

Acknowledgement. This work was supported in part by the National Key Research & Development Program (No. 2020YFC2003901), Chinese National Natural Science Foundation Projects (No. 62206280, 62176256, 61876178, 61976229 and 62106264), the Youth Innovation Promotion Association CAS (No. Y2021131).

References

1. Pathak, D., Krahenbuhl, P., Darrell, T.: Constrained convolutional neural networks for weakly supervised segmentation. In: ICCV. (2015)
2. Dai, J., He, K., Sun, J.: Boxsup: exploiting bounding boxes to supervise convolutional networks for semantic segmentation. In: ICCV (2015)
3. Lin, D., Dai, J., Jia, J., He, K., Sun, J.: Scribblesup: scribble-supervised convolutional networks for semantic segmentation. In: CVPR (2016)

4. He, K., Fan, H., Wu, Y., Xie, S., Girshick, R.: Momentum contrast for unsupervised visual representation learning. In: CVPR (2020)
5. Chen, X., Fan, H., Girshick, R., He, K.: Improved baselines with momentum contrastive learning. arXiv preprint arXiv:2003.04297 (2020)
6. Wang, X., Zhang, R., Shen, C., Kong, T., Li, L.: Dense contrastive learning for self-supervised visual pre-training. In: CVPR (2021)
7. Hung, W.C., Jampani, V., Liu, S., Molchanov, P., Yang, M.H., Kautz, J.: Scops: self-supervised co-part segmentation. In: CVPR (2019)
8. Lorenz, D., Bereska, L., Milbich, T., Ommer, B.: Unsupervised part-based disentangling of object shape and appearance. In: CVPR (2019)
9. Liu, S., Zhang, L., Yang, X., Su, H., Zhu, J.: Unsupervised part segmentation through disentangling appearance and shape. In: CVPR (2021)
10. Chen, T., Kornblith, S., Norouzi, M., Hinton, G.: A simple framework for contrastive learning of visual representations. In: ICML (2020)
11. Chen, T., Kornblith, S., Swersky, K., Norouzi, M., Hinton, G.: Big self-supervised models are strong semi-supervised learners. arXiv preprint arXiv:2006.10029 (2020)
12. Chuang, C.Y., Robinson, J., Yen-Chen, L., Torralba, A., Jegelka, S.: Debiased contrastive learning. arXiv preprint arXiv:2007.00224 (2020)
13. Huynh, T., Kornblith, S., Walter, M.R., Maire, M., Khademi, M.: Boosting contrastive self-supervised learning with false negative cancellation. arXiv preprint arXiv:2011.11765 (2020)
14. Zhong, Y., Yuan, B., Wu, H., Yuan, Z., Peng, J., Wang, Y.X.: Pixel contrastive-consistent semi-supervised semantic segmentation. In: ICCV (2021)
15. He, K., Zhang, X., Ren, S., Sun, J.: Deep residual learning for image recognition. In: CVPR (2016)
16. Kuhn, H.W.: The Hungarian method for the assignment problem. NRL **2**(1–2), 83–97 (1955)
17. Oord, A.V.d., Li, Y., Vinyals, O.: Representation learning with contrastive predictive coding. arXiv preprint arXiv:1807.03748 (2018)
18. Wu, Z., Xiong, Y., Yu, S.X., Lin, D.: Unsupervised feature learning via non-parametric instance discrimination. In: CVPR (2018)
19. Vaswani, A., et al.: Attention is all you need. In: NeurIPS (2017)
20. Donoho, D.L.: Compressed sensing. TIT **52**(4), 1289–1306 (2006)
21. Wright, J., Yang, A.Y., Ganesh, A., Sastry, S.S., Ma, Y.: Robust face recognition via sparse representation. TPAMI **31**(2), 210–227 (2008)
22. Mairal, J., Bach, F., Ponce, J., Sapiro, G.: Online dictionary learning for sparse coding. In: ICML (2009)
23. Cho, J.H., Mall, U., Bala, K., Hariharan, B.: Picie: unsupervised semantic segmentation using invariance and equivariance in clustering. In: CVPR (2021)
24. Liang, X., et al.: Deep human parsing with active template regression. TPAMI **37**(12), 2402–2414 (2015)
25. Li, T., Liang, Z., Zhao, S., Gong, J., Shen, J.: Self-learning with rectification strategy for human parsing. In: CVPR (2020)
26. Yuan, Y., Chen, X., Wang, J.: Object-contextual representations for semantic segmentation. In: Vedaldi, A., Bischof, H., Brox, T., Frahm, J.-M. (eds.) ECCV 2020. LNCS, vol. 12351, pp. 173–190. Springer, Cham (2020). https://doi.org/10.1007/978-3-030-58539-6_11
27. Lin, T.Y., Dollar, P., Girshick, R., He, K., Hariharan, B., Belongie, S.: Feature pyramid networks for object detection. In: CVPR (2017)

28. Jia, D., Wei, D., Socher, R., Li, L.J., Kai, L., Li, F.F.: Imagenet: a large-scale hierarchical image database. In: CVPR (2009)
29. Johnson, J., Douze, M., Jégou, H.: Billion-scale similarity search with gpus (2017)
30. Collins, E., Achanta, R., Süsstrunk, S.: Deep feature factorization for concept discovery. In: Ferrari, V., Hebert, M., Sminchisescu, C., Weiss, Y. (eds.) Computer Vision – ECCV 2018. LNCS, vol. 11218, pp. 352–368. Springer, Cham (2018). https://doi.org/10.1007/978-3-030-01264-9_21

Dynamic Hand Gesture Authentication Based on Improved Two-Stream CNN

Wenwei Song[1,2], Linpu Fang[1], Yihong Lin[1,2], Ming Zeng[1], and Wenxiong Kang[1,2,3(✉)]

[1] School of Automation Science and Engineering, South China University of Technology, Guangzhou 510641, China
auwxkang@scut.edu.cn
[2] Pazhou Lab, Guangzhou 510335, China
[3] Guangdong Enterprise Key Laboratory of Intelligent Finance, Guangzhou 510705, China

Abstract. Recently, dynamic hand gesture (DHG) has been discovered to be a promising biometric trait containing both physiological and behavioral characteristics simultaneously. DHGs are recorded by videos, so the authentication process is a challenging fine-grained video understanding task. Fully exploring physiological and behavioral characteristics to capture the fine-grained spatiotemporal identity features is the key to DHG authentication. Thus, in this paper, we propose to use the classic two-stream CNN for video understanding-based DHG authentication due to their explicit spatial (static) and temporal (dynamic) information modeling ability. Through analyzing prior two-stream CNN-based authentication methods in depth, we find five improvable aspects and propose the corresponding enhancement strategies. Comprehensive experiments on the SCUT-DHGA dataset show that the improved two-stream CNN can significantly outperform existing SOTA DHG authentication methods.

Keywords: Biometrics · Dynamic hand gesture authentication · Two-stream CNN · Video understanding

1 Introduction

With the great development of intelligent devices, it is urgent to develop easy-to-use and secure user authentication methods for access control. Traditional knowledge-based authentication methods such as passwords cannot meet the requirement of convenience and security due to the increases of memory burden and the risks of malicious attacks [1]. In recent years, biometric authentication methods have been proposed as effective alternatives to traditional knowledge-based counterparts and have been extensively used in various products such as intelligent phones and laptops. Biometric authentication methods utilize distinctive biometric traits to verify users' identities. Since the biometric traits are unique and unforgettable, they can bring users a more secure and user-friendly experience.

Among existing biometric traits, DHGs are very promising. Compared with physiological characteristic dominated traits, such as faces, fingerprints, irises, finger veins, *etc.*, DHGs can provide stronger resistance to spoofing attacks with the help of behavioral characteristics. Moreover, DHGs also contain abundant physiological

W. Deng et al. (Eds.): CCBR 2022, LNCS 13628, pp. 237–246, 2022.
https://doi.org/10.1007/978-3-031-20233-9_24

characteristics, such as hand shape and skin textures. The physiological and behavioral characteristics are highly complementary, thus making DHG authentication more accurate and more secure.

DHG authentication systems mainly use three kinds of acquisition devices to capture hand gestures currently, including inertial measurement units [2,3], touch screens [4,5], and cameras [1,6,7]. The inertial measurement unit and the touch screen require users to contact the devices physically, so the intrusive data collection manners significantly reduce the user-friendliness of DHG authentication. Also, the captured hand gestures are usually represented as trajectories of fingers' movements. Thus, a large number of physiological characteristics are lost, which is not conducive to taking full advantage of the DHGs. The video-based DHG authentication system uses a camera to obtain gesture videos. This non-contact way is more user-friendly. Besides, DHG videos retain plentiful physiological and behavioral characteristics. Therefore, video-based DHG authentication is more desirable.

Video-based DHG authentication methods are mainly divided into two categories: trajectory analysis-based methods and video understanding-based methods. The trajectory analysis-based methods first estimate the motion trajectories of hand keypoints [1,6,8,9] from videos with hand pose estimation algorithms [10] and then extract behavioral features from these motion trajectories. The video understanding-based methods directly extract features from videos that contains sufficient physiological and behavioral characteristics. The physiological characteristics are embedded in each frame, while behavioral characteristics are embodied in successive adjacent frames. Considering that video understanding based-methods can obtain richer identity features, in this paper, we focus on the video understanding-based DHG authentication.

For video understanding-based DHG authentication, the key is to distill fine-grained spatiotemporal identity features. Wu *et al.* [7] first extracted the silhouette covariance descriptor from DHG videos to verify users; however, the performance of this hand-crafted feature extraction method is not satisfactory. Wu *et al.* [11] afterward adopted a powerful two-stream convolutional neural network (TS-CNN) [12]) to extract features, resulting in significant performance improvement. Recently, Liu *et al.* [13] released a large-scale DHG authentication dataset called SCUT-DHGA, and proposed the DHGA-net based on I3D (a 3D CNN) [14], to benchmark this dataset. The results demonstrate that the DHGA-net is significantly superior to the TS-CNN in terms of EER (Error Equal Rate). Whereas, the interpretability of 3D CNNs is worse than two-stream CNNs since they jointly learn the physiological and behavioral characteristics, hardly figuring out the effects of the two parts.

In this paper, to fully unleash the potential of two-stream CNNs in DHG authentication, we analyze them in depth and then adopt five strategies to improve them. The results on the SCUT-DHGA dataset indicate that our enhanced two-stream CNN can not only achieve significant performance improvement compared with the TS-CNN but also can outperform the DHGA-net by a large margin.

2   The Proposed Method

2.1   Analyses of the Two Stream CNN-Based DHG Authentication Method

Through careful analyses of the two stream CNN-based DHG authentication method (TS-CNN) [11], we think it mainly has five improvable drawbacks. (1) **Hand gesture videos are underutilized:** The TS-CNN uses the single RGB image/depth map and single optical flow image broken up from videos as training samples to train the spatial and temporal branches, respectively, which greatly increases the difficulty of network learning. (2) **An inefficient optical flow is used:** The extraction of optical flow is very time-consuming and storage-demanding. Moreover, the optical flow is often pre-calculated offline, which cannot achieve adaptive behavior/motion representation learning according to specific tasks. (3) **An obsolete backbone is adopted:** The TS-CNN uses the classical AlexNet as the backbone for image feature extraction. However, the AlexNet not only has a larger number of model parameters but also performs worse than current advanced network architectures, such as the ResNet. (4) **A suboptimal loss function is selected:** DHG authentication can be regarded as a metric learning task. The TS-CNN uses the Softmax loss as the supervision signal to train the model, which has been proved that it is less effective in some metric learning tasks, such as face authentication [15]. (5) **The information fusion strategy is not fully explored:** Reasonable fusion of physiological and behavioral information is significant for improving hand gesture authentication performance. The TS-CNN only uses the intermediate-fusion strategy, which may not be the best choice currently, as it is challenging to achieve satisfactory feature fusion.

2.2   Improved Two-Stream CNN

For the first drawback of the TS-CNN, we use multiple video frames jointly to derive a global feature representation of a DHG video via average pooling on the temporal dimension, which can help reduce ambiguities among samples, resulting in more robust and discriminative identity features. For the second drawback, we use the PA (Persistence of Appearance) proposed in [16] to replace the optical flow as the behavior representation. The PA is computationally efficient and can be trained in an end-to-end fashion. For the third and fourth drawbacks, we adopt more advanced ResNet and AM-Softmax [15] as the backbone and loss function. Combining the above strategies, we redesign the two streams of the TS-CNN based on the work of Zhang *et al.* [16]. The enhanced architecture is shown in Fig. 1 where the spatial and temporal streams are mainly used to encode the physiological and behavioral information of hand gestures, respectively.

As shown in Fig. 1, we first obtain the input data for the two streams by a sparse sampling scheme proposed in the TSN [17]. Specifically, a DHG video is uniformly divided into N segments, each of which contains m (we set m as four in this paper) adjacent frames, resulting in N snippets $\{\{\mathbf{I}_{S_1}^1, \mathbf{I}_{S_1}^2, \mathbf{I}_{S_1}^3, \mathbf{I}_{S_1}^4\}, ..., \{\mathbf{I}_{S_N}^1, \mathbf{I}_{S_N}^2, \mathbf{I}_{S_N}^3, \mathbf{I}_{S_N}^4\}\}$. These snippets will be used to calculate behavior representation PA through the PA module in the temporal stream, and the first frame of each snippet $\{\mathbf{I}_{S_1}^1, ..., \mathbf{I}_{S_N}^1\}$ will be used as the inputs of the spatial stream.

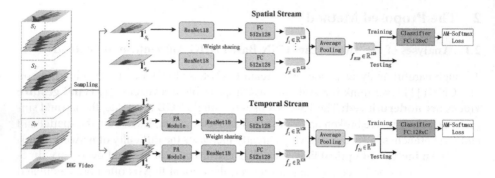

Fig. 1. Overview of our proposed improved two-stream CNNs.

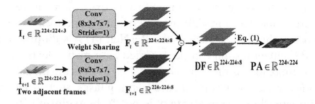

Fig. 2. Illustration of the PA module.

For the spatial stream, each frame is first encoded by a ResNet18 that outputs a 512-dim feature vector after the global average pooling (GAP) layer. This 512-dim feature vector is then transformed to a 128-dim feature vector by a fully-collected (FC) layer. The final physiological feature of a DHG in the spatial stream is represented as the average of all feature vectors. For the temporal stream, it works the same as the spatial stream except for the PA module. Figure 2 illustrates the working scheme of the PA module. It represents the motion between two adjacent frames as a single-channel PA map. Given two adjacent frames I_t and I_{t+1}, the PA module first obtains their corresponding low-level feature maps F_t and F_{t+1} through a lightweight convolution layer. Then, it calculates the difference between F_t and F_{t+1}, obtaining the difference feature map DF. Finally, it transforms DF into a single-channel PA map as follows:

$$PA(x,y) = \sqrt{\sum_{i=1}^{M}(DF(x,y,i))^2} \tag{1}$$

where $DF(x,y,i)$ represents the value of pixel (x,y) on the i-th channel of the DF, M is the channel numbers of DF, which is set to eight in this paper. For a snippet with m adjacent frames, the PA module calculates the PA map between every two adjacent frames and stacks the obtained $(m-1)$ PA maps together as the input to the ResNet18 in the temporal stream. Finally, both branches are trained under the supervision of the AM-Softmax loss [15]. In the testing stage, the cosine distance between the query feature and the registered DHG feature is calculated to measure their similarity. If the distance is smaller than the pre-defined threshold, the user is accepted, otherwise rejected.

2.3 Two-Stream Information Fusion

The raw RGB frames and the stacked PA maps contain physiological and behavioral information, respectively. The two kinds of information are complementary and can be merged to improve performance. Thus, it is significant to explore a reasonable fusion strategy for the two-stream information.

In this paper, we comprehensively investigate three mainstream fusion strategies, including early fusion, intermediate fusion, and late fusion, to address the fifth drawback to some extent. For the early fusion, the original RGB frames and stacked PA maps are concatenated together and then sent to the backbone for identity feature extraction. For the intermediate fusion, the information fusion is performed after the FC layer, and the final identity feature is the weighted sum of the two feature vectors, f_{RGB} and f_{PA}, extracted from the spatial and temporal streams. For the late fusion, we first calculate the cosine distance of the two DHG features for each stream individually and then obtain the final distance by the weighted sum of the two distances.

3 Experiments

3.1 Dataset and Settings

We conduct extensive experiments on the large-scale SCUT-DHGA dataset [13], which is the only publicly available dynamic hand gesture authentication dataset that contains RGB videos, to demonstrate the effectiveness of our proposed method. The SCUT-DHGA dataset contains 29,160 DHG videos collected from 193 subjects. Videos from 143 subjects are divided into the training set, while videos from the other 50 subjects are divided into the test set. The videos in the test set are collected across two stages with an average interval of about one week, resulting in two test settings, *i.e.*, single-session and cross-session authentication. In the single-session authentication, the registered and query video both come from the first stage, while in the cross-session authentication, they come from two different stages.

In this paper, we focus on two main test protocols of the SCUT-DHGA dataset: *MG* and *UMG*. For the *MG* protocol, models are trained with videos from the six DHG types and are tested using videos from the same six DHG types. For the *UMG* protocol, the models are trained with videos from five DHG types and are tested using videos from the one remaining DHG type. Therefore, both the *MG* and *UMG* have six test settings, corresponding to six gesture types, respectively.

3.2 Implementation Details

We follow the common practice to initialize the backbone (ResNet18) using the weights pretrained on the ImageNet dataset. We also initialize the PA module using the weights pretrained on the Something-Something-V2 dataset. All networks are optimized by Adam. The weight decay factor and learning rate are set to 1e–7 and 1e–5, respectively. When training the spatial and temporal stream networks, we set the mini-batch size to 45 and 32, respectively. We adopt online data augmentations during training, including random rotation ($\pm 15°$) and color jittering (± 0.3). We also dropout the DHG video features, f_{RGB} and f_{PA}, by a probability of 0.5. The spatial and temporal streams are trained for 50 and 200 epochs, respectively. Finally, all experiments are implemented using Pytorch on an Nvidia GTX1080Ti GPU.

Table 1. Comparisons between our proposed improved two-stream CNN and the baseline DHGA-net. The inputs to the spatial and temporal streams are the sampled RGB frames and PA maps, respectively.

Setting	Single session EER(%)			Cross session EER (%)		
	DHGA-net	Spatial stream	Temporal stream	DHGA-net	Spatial stream	Temporal stream
UMG_{-g_1}	2.53	0.13	1.10	13.40	4.40	7.16
UMG_{-g_2}	2.84	0.18	1.07	13.87	3.09	5.22
UMG_{-g_3}	2.00	0.36	0.49	10.84	3.78	4.89
UMG_{-g_4}	1.82	0.71	0.76	8.20	2.78	3.44
UMG_{-g_5}	2.04	0.18	0.49	10.96	3.09	3.84
UMG_{-g_6}	2.36	0.13	2.02	13.60	4.04	6.93
Average	2.27	0.28	0.99	11.81	3.53	5.25

3.3 Performance of the Two Single Streams

We first evaluate the performance of the spatial and temporal streams of our proposed improved two-stream CNN. The comparison with the baseline DHGA-net proposed for benchmarking the SCUT-DHGA dataset [13] is shown in Table 1. The results manifest that both spatial and temporal streams significantly outperform the DHGA-net. In the single session, the average EER of the DHGA-net is 2.27% under the UMG, while the spatial and temporal streams can achieve 0.28% and 0.99% average EERs, decreasing the average EERs by 1.99% and 1.28% respectively. In the cross session, the average EER of the DHGA-net is 11.81% under the UMG, while the spatial and temporal streams can achieve 3.53% and 5.25% average EERs, decreasing the average EERs by 8.28% and 6.56%, respectively. It can not only demonstrate the effectiveness of our improvement strategies but also can justify the feasibility of both physiological and behavioral characteristics for DHG authentication. Besides, the results also show that the performance of the spatial stream is better than that of the temporal stream. The reasons are two-fold. First, the behavioral characteristic understanding involves extracting fine-grained spatiotemporal features, which is more difficult than the physiological characteristic understanding. Second, the representation of behavioral characteristics (PA) is not optimal and needs further improvement.

3.4 Impact of Local Feature Number

To verify the impact of the local feature number (i.e., the number of segments, N, in Fig. 1) on the performance of the spatial and temporal streams, we conduct comprehensive comparison experiments under the MG. The comparison results are shown in Fig. 3. We can see that the results of both streams have the same trend. When N is fixed during training, the average EER will decrease to saturation with the increase of N in testing. This can prove that the combination of multiple local features is very crucial for authentication performance improvement, but too many local features will cause information redundancy and can not contribute to a significant boost. When the N in testing

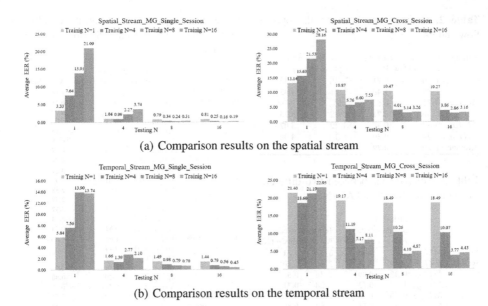

(a) Comparison results on the spatial stream

(b) Comparison results on the temporal stream

Fig. 3. Comparison results of different local feature number.

is small (for example, less than or equal to 4) and less than the N in training, the average EER becomes significantly larger with the increase of N during training. The reason is that the training process makes the networks only discriminative for features that combine enough local information. When the N in testing is relatively large (for example, 8 or 16) and greater than the N in training, the N during training will have a significant impact on the authentication performance. For example, setting N to 1 during training will cause a considerable EER increase. It is because minimal local features have very limited discriminative information, making networks hard to train. These results clearly demonstrate the effectiveness of the first improvement strategy for the first drawback of the TS-CNN.

3.5   Impact of Behavior Representation

The results in Table 1 demonstrate the effectiveness of the PA (the temporal stream). Here, we compare the PA with the optical flow to further demonstrate its superiority in behavior representation by replacing the optical flow with PA maps in the temporal stream. In this paper, we adopt the same method as the TS-CNN for optical flow extraction offline. The comparison results under the MG setting are shown in Table 2. The results show that the PA can achieve a lower EER than the optical flow for most DHG categories, and the PA's average EER is lower than the optical flow by 0.50% and 0.76% in single session and cross session. We attribute the success of the PA to its ability to adaptively generate decent behavior representations for hand gesture authentication. In addition, it is important to mention that the PA can be derived online and is therefore more suitable for deployment in authentication systems than the optical flow.

Table 2. Comparisons between the optical flow and PA.

Setting	Single session EER (%)		Cross session EER (%)	
	Optical Flow	PA	Optical Flow	PA
MG_g_1	1.56	**0.71**	7.36	**5.33**
MG_g_2	1.82	**1.40**	5.71	**4.42**
MG_g_3	0.71	**0.53**	**3.87**	3.98
MG_g_4	1.36	**0.71**	4.62	**3.73**
MG_g_5	0.84	**0.56**	3.22	**3.07**
MG_g_6	1.44	**0.80**	4.36	**4.04**
Average	1.29	**0.79**	4.86	**4.10**

Table 3. Comparisons between two different backbones: ResNet18 and AlexNet.

Setting		EER (%)			
		Spatial stream		Temporal stream	
		AlexNet	**ResNet18**	AlexNet	**ResNet18**
Single session	MG_g_1	1.42	**0.18**	3.33	**0.71**
	MG_g_2	0.89	**0.31**	2.80	**1.40**
	MG_g_3	0.93	**0.09**	2.44	**0.53**
	MG_g_4	1.29	**0.53**	3.24	**0.71**
	MG_g_5	0.76	**0.18**	1.91	**0.56**
	MG_g_6	0.84	**0.18**	3.84	**0.80**
	Average	1.02	**0.24**	2.93	**0.79**
Cross session	MG_g_1	7.78	**4.09**	12.64	**5.33**
	MG_g_2	6.64	**3.27**	11.38	**4.42**
	MG_g_3	7.04	**2.93**	10.82	**3.98**
	MG_g_4	5.93	**2.58**	12.42	**3.73**
	MG_g_5	6.73	**2.49**	9.56	**3.07**
	MG_g_6	7.09	**3.47**	11.73	**4.04**
	Average	6.87	**3.14**	11.43	**4.10**

Table 4. Comparisons among three different loss functions: Softmax, Softmax+Center, AM-Softmax.

Setting			EER (%)		
			Softmax	Softmax+Center	**AM-Softmax**
Spatial stream	Single session	MG_g_1	0.91	0.58	**0.18**
		MG_g_2	0.84	0.62	**0.31**
		MG_g_3	0.84	0.36	**0.09**
		MG_g_4	1.16	**0.27**	0.53
		MG_g_5	0.89	0.36	**0.18**
		MG_g_6	0.87	0.31	**0.18**
		Average	0.92	0.41	**0.24**
	Cross session	MG_g_1	10.13	8.49	**4.09**
		MG_g_2	14.13	10.38	**3.27**
		MG_g_3	10.24	5.51	**2.93**
		MG_g_4	9.76	5.53	**2.58**
		MG_g_5	9.44	4.71	**2.49**
		MG_g_6	9.98	6.24	**3.47**
		Average	10.61	6.81	**3.14**
Temporal stream	Single session	MG_g_1	0.73	**0.62**	0.71
		MG_g_2	1.64	**1.07**	1.40
		MG_g_3	1.04	**0.44**	0.53
		MG_g_4	0.78	**0.58**	0.71
		MG_g_5	0.73	**0.36**	0.56
		MG_g_6	1.47	1.20	**0.80**
		Average	1.07	**0.71**	0.79
	Cross session	MG_g_1	12.27	10.20	**5.33**
		MG_g_2	10.16	9.18	**4.42**
		MG_g_3	9.31	6.60	**3.98**
		MG_g_4	7.56	4.98	**3.73**
		MG_g_5	5.07	4.33	**3.07**
		MG_g_6	8.96	8.36	**4.04**
		Average	8.89	7.27	**4.10**

3.6 Impact of Backbone

The backbone has a significant impact on image feature extraction. In this section, we compare our adopted RestNet18 with the AlexNet used in the TS-CNN. The comparison results under the MG are listed in Table 3. It indicates that the ResNet18 can consistently outperform the AlexNet by large margins for both spatial and temporal streams due to its more rational design and more powerful non-linear representation capability in hand gesture authentication.

3.7 Impact of Loss Function

The loss function is vital for model optimization. In this section, we compare three loss functions, including Softmax, Softmax plus Center [18], and AM-Softmax. The comparison results under the MG are shown in Table 4. It shows that both the Softmax plus Center and AM-Softmax can significantly outperform the Softmax, which proves the importance of adding constraints to decrease intra-class variation. Moreover, our adopted AM-Softmax loss function also significantly outperforms Softmax plus Center in the cross-session. Overall, our adopted AM-Softmax performs best.

3.8 Comparisons Among Different Two-Stream Information Fusion Methods

We compare three different two-stream information fusion methods, including early fusion, intermediate fusion, and late fusion, under the UMG. We first verify the per-

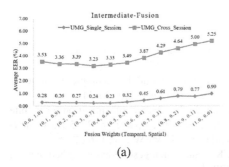 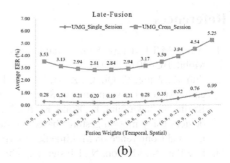

(a)   (b)

Fig. 4. Results of intermediate-fusion and late-fusion with different fusion weights.

formance of the intermediate-fusion and late-fusion with different fusion weights. The results in Fig. 4 show that setting the weight of the temporal stream to be smaller than the weight of the spatial stream is good for both intermediate fusion and late fusion. This is in line with our expectations because the performance of the spatial stream is better than that of the temporal stream, as shown in Table 1. Thus, it is very reasonable to give the spatial stream a higher weight. Finally, when the weights are set to 0.3 and 0.7 for the temporal and spatial stream, both intermediate-fusion and late-fusion can achieve relatively good results. Thus, we adopt this weight setting for the intermediate-fusion and late-fusion in subsequent experiments to compare with the early-fusion, and the results are listed in Table 5. We can find that the late-fusion can perform best because it can make a comprehensive evaluation according to the similarities of physiological and behavioral characteristics by setting an appropriate fusion weight based on their actual performance.

Table 5. Comparisons among three different two-stream information fusion methods.

Setting	Single session EER (%)			Cross session EER (%)		
	Early-fusion	Intermediate-fusion	Late-fusion	Early-fusion	Intermediate-fusion	Late-fusion
UMG_g_1	0.51	0.18	**0.13**	3.71	4.02	**3.47**
UMG_g_2	0.69	0.18	**0.13**	4.29	2.84	**2.44**
UMG_g_3	0.89	0.22	**0.09**	**2.67**	3.98	3.51
UMG_g_4	0.73	**0.53**	0.58	2.76	2.27	**1.82**
UMG_g_5	0.31	0.13	**0.13**	2.53	2.33	**1.98**
UMG_g_6	0.53	0.22	**0.13**	4.20	3.91	**3.67**
Average	0.61	0.24	**0.20**	3.36	3.23	**2.81**

4   Conclusion

In this paper, we first analyze the authentication-oriented TS-CNN in depth, expecting to fully unleash the potential of two-stream CNNs in DHG authentication. We then propose the improved two-stream CNNs for DHG authentication by enhancing the TS-CNN from five aspects. The extensive results on the SCUT-DHGA dataset demonstrate the effectiveness of the introduced methods.

Acknowledgments. This work was supported by the National Natural Science Foundation of China under Grant 61976095.

References

1. Aumi, M.T.I., Kratz, S.G.: Airauth: evaluating in-air hand gestures for authentication. In: MobileHCI 2014 (2014)
2. Sun, Z., Wang, Y., Qu, G., Zhou, Z.: A 3-d hand gesture signature based biometric authentication system for smartphones. Secur. Commun. Netw. **9**, 1359–1373 (2016)
3. Karita, S., Nakamura, K., Kono, K., Ito, Y., Babaguchi, N.: Owner authentication for mobile devices using motion gestures based on multi-owner template update. In: 2015 IEEE International Conference on Multimedia & Expo Workshops (ICMEW), pp. 1–6 (2015)
4. Sae-Bae, N., Memon, N., Isbister, K., Ahmed, K.: Multitouch gesture-based authentication. IEEE Trans. Inf. Forensics Secur. **9**, 568–582 (2014)
5. Shen, C., Zhang, Y., Guan, X., Maxion, R.: Performance analysis of touch-interaction behavior for active smartphone authentication. IEEE Trans. Inf. Forensics Secur. **11**, 498–513 (2016)
6. Tian, J., Qu, C., Xu, W., Wang, S.: Kinwrite: handwriting-based authentication using kinect. In: NDSS (2013)
7. Wu, J., Christianson, J., Konrad, J., Ishwar, P.: Leveraging shape and depth in user authentication from in-air hand gestures. In: 2015 IEEE International Conference on Image Processing (ICIP), pp. 3195–3199 (2015)
8. Nugrahaningsih, N., Porta, M., Scarpello, G.: A hand gesture approach to biometrics. In: Murino, V., Puppo, E., Sona, D., Cristani, M., Sansone, C. (eds.) ICIAP 2015. LNCS, vol. 9281, pp. 51–58. Springer, Cham (2015). https://doi.org/10.1007/978-3-319-23222-5_7
9. Wang, X., Tanaka, J.: Gesid: 3D gesture authentication based on depth camera and one-class classification. Sensors (Basel, Switzerland) **18**, 3265 (2018)
10. Gu, J., Wang, Z., Ouyang, W., Zhang, W., Li, J., Zhuo, L.: 3D hand pose estimation with disentangled cross-modal latent space. In: 2020 IEEE Winter Conference on Applications of Computer Vision (WACV), pp. 380–389 (2020)
11. Wu, J., Ishwar, P., Konrad, J.: Two-stream cnns for gesture-based verification and identification: Learning user style. In: 2016 IEEE Conference on Computer Vision and Pattern Recognition Workshops (CVPRW), pp. 110–118 (2016)
12. Simonyan, K., Zisserman, A.: Two-stream convolutional networks for action recognition in videos. In: NIPS (2014)
13. Liu, C., Yang, Y., Liu, X., Fang, L., Kang, W.: Dynamic-hand-gesture authentication dataset and benchmark. IEEE Trans. Inf. Forensics Secur. **16**, 1550–1562 (2021)
14. Carreira, J., Zisserman, A.: Quo vadis, action recognition? a new model and the kinetics dataset. In: 2017 IEEE Conference on Computer Vision and Pattern Recognition (CVPR), pp. 4724–4733 (2017)
15. Wang, F., Cheng, J., Liu, W., Liu, H.: Additive margin softmax for face verification. IEEE Signal Process. Lett. **25**, 926–930 (2018)
16. Zhang, C., Zou, Y., Chen, G., Gan, L.: Pan: persistent appearance network with an efficient motion cue for fast action recognition. In: Proceedings of the 27th ACM International Conference on Multimedia, pp. 500–509 (2019)
17. Wang, L., Xiong, Y., Zhe Wang, Yu., Qiao, D.L., Tang, X., Van Gool, L.: Temporal segment networks for action recognition in videos. IEEE Trans. Pattern Anal. Mach. Intell. **41**, 2740–2755 (2019)
18. Wen, Y., Zhang, K., Li, Z., Qiao, Yu.: A discriminative feature learning approach for deep face recognition. In: Leibe, B., Matas, J., Sebe, N., Welling, M. (eds.) ECCV 2016. LNCS, vol. 9911, pp. 499–515. Springer, Cham (2016). https://doi.org/10.1007/978-3-319-46478-7_31

Efficient Video Understanding-Based Random Hand Gesture Authentication

Huilong Xie[1,2], Wenwei Song[1,2], and Wenxiong Kang[1,2,3](✉)

[1] School of Automation Science and Engineering, South China University of
Technology, Guangzhou 510641, China
[2] Pazhou Lab, Guangzhou 510335, China
[3] Guangdong Enterprise Key Laboratory of Intelligent Finance,
Guangzhou 510705, China
auwxkang@scut.edu.cn

Abstract. Hand gesture is an emerging biometric trait that is receiving increasing attention. In recent years, there have emerged several video understanding-based hand gesture authentication methods. However, their parameter number is too large to be deployed directly on mobile devices. Thus, we introduce the advanced Knowledge Distillation via Knowledge Review (KDKR) to compress the Temporal Difference Symbiotic Neural Network (TDS-Net). Compared with the teacher model, whose average equal error rates are 2.846% and 6.953% in single and cross sessions, the parameter number of the student model is reduced by 77.29%, while the average equal error rates only increase by 1.757% and 4.229%, respectively. Besides, we investigate some attention modules in depth to improve the KDKR and obtain a suitable fusion method in the KDKR for random hand gesture authentication networks.

Keywords: Dynamic hand gesture authentication · Video understanding · Knowledge distillation · Attention mechanism

1 Introduction

Various authentication methods have emerged with the rapid development of the Internet. Unlike conventional knowledge-based and token-based authentication methods, biometrics-based authentication methods mainly use biometric characteristics for verification. At present, biometric authentication methods can be divided into two categories. One is physiological characteristics-based authentication represented by face authentication, iris authentication, vein authentication, and fingerprint authentication. The other is behavioral characteristics-based authentication represented by gait authentication, voice authentication, and gesture authentication. Technologies such as iris authentication, fingerprint authentication, and face authentication that utilize physiological characteristics are relatively mature and have been successfully applied in production and life. In current biometric authentication methods, understanding behavioral characteristics is more challenging than understanding physiological characteristics.

W. Deng et al. (Eds.): CCBR 2022, LNCS 13628, pp. 247–256, 2022.
https://doi.org/10.1007/978-3-031-20233-9_25

However, they have great potential and deserve our study due to their high-security property.

Hand gesture authentication methods mainly include trajectory-based methods [1] and vision-based methods. Trajectory-based gesture authentication methods require wearing relevant devices (i.e., smart watch) to capture the movement signal of the hand gesture trajectory or the electric signal of the muscle [2]. In contrast, vision-based gesture authentication methods only need to be performed in front of an RGB or other modal camera, such as hand gesture authentication networks developed based on 3D convolutional neural networks [3] and hand gesture authentication networks developed based on two-stream convolutional neural networks [4], which directly use hand gesture video as input and obtain identity information for authentication.

The random hand gesture authentication studied in this paper is an authentication method that includes both physiological and behavioral characteristics, which is more secure yet more challenging than the authentication method only based on physiological characteristics. The random hand gesture authentication not only needs to understand physiological characteristics, such as hand shape, finger length [5], palm area shape [6], and palm print, but also behavioral characteristics, such as finger movement habit, speed, and acceleration. Also, with the current ravages of COVID-19, our contactless methods of authentication is superior to contacted methods of authentication such as fingerprint recognition.

As shown in Fig. 1, the flowchart details the process of hand gesture authentication. It can be divided into enrolling and verifying phases. In the enrolling phase, the users should perform hand gestures in front of the camera. Then the hand gesture videos are fed to the trained feature extractor to obtain the corresponding identity features, which will be saved to the feature gallery. In the verifying phase, users need to perform hand gestures like that in the enrolling phase to obtain the identity features, which are treated as probes to be compared with their claimed identity features in the feature gallery. The system accepts the user if the distance between two features is lower than a given threshold. Otherwise, it rejects the user.

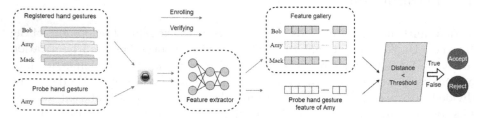

Fig. 1. Hand gesture authentication flowchart.

Deep convolution neural networks have many parameters and require substantial computational resources. However, random hand gesture authentication models usually need to be deployed on mobile devices which often have limited computational resources. We can use model compression to improve model efficiency and realize the model for real-time random hand gesture authentication on mobile devices.

The current model compression methods mainly include model pruning, network decomposition, weight sharing, weight quantization, and knowledge distillation. In this paper, we focus on knowledge distillation considering its practicality, efficiency, and most importantly the potential to be useful. The pioneering work of knowledge distillation [7] uses teacher networks to generate soft targets, thus providing richer information to student networks than hard targets. In recent years, many knowledge distillation variants have been proposed to alleviate the demand for computational resources in deep convolutional neural networks. Romero et al. [8] extend this idea to the hidden layer features of the network for learning. Kim et al. [9] use the student network for self-supervised learning. Mirzadeh et al. [10] use teacher assistants to resolve model size differences between student and teacher models. The Knowledge Distillation via Knowledge Review (KDKR) is a general distillation framework that uses cross-stage connection paths to obtain guidance for fusion knowledge from the teacher network, which is more suitable for our work.

In this paper, we use a knowledge distillation approach to compress the TDS-Net and obtain a more lightweight student network. The main contributions of our work are three-fold: (1) We balance computational cost and model performance by using knowledge distillation to lighten the TDS-Net. (2) We redesign the attention-based fusion module of the KDKR to further improve distillation performance. (3) We conduct extensive ablation experiments to justify the rationality of the module's redesign.

2   The Proposed Method

2.1   Analyses of the TDS-Net

The TDS-Net is a customized video understanding model for random hand gesture authentication [4], which has two branches, the ResNet branch and the Symbiotic branch, respectively. The input of the TDS-Net is raw RGB video, and the behavioral cues mainly come from the inter-frame difference maps. The inter-frame difference maps directly encode movement trends of hand gestures, providing explicit guidance for the model. They are obtained by the Interframe Subtraction-Channel Averaging unit (ISCA), defined as

$$IS_i^j(x,y,t) = I_i^j(x,y,t+1) - I_i^j(x,y,t), \tag{1}$$

$$CA^j(x,y,t) = \frac{1}{C}\sum_{i=1}^{C} IS_i^j(x,y,t), \tag{2}$$

where i represents the i-th channel, j represents the j-th feature, t represents the t-th frame image, and C represents the total number of channels.

The ResNet branch of the TDS-Net uses the ResNet18 [11] to get physiological information of hand gestures. In contrast, the Symbiotic branch is a lightweight convolutional network attached to the ResNet branch to get behavioral information from the inter-frame difference map. There are lateral connections between the two branches. The ResNet branch transforms the obtained physiological features into inter-frame difference maps containing behavioral characteristics through the ISCA. It then transmits them to the Symbiotic branch to provide high-level semantic inter-frame difference information. The Symbiotic branch provides the gradient information to the ResNet branch during the network training process. The two branches can complement each other for better performance.

The TDS-Net also performs the fusion module of the information in the two branches at the top of the network, *i.e.*, the behavioral feature $\mathbf{B} = (b_1, b_2, ..., b_{128})^T$ and the physiological feature $\mathbf{P} = (p_1, p_2, ..., p_{128})^T$ are fused. The feature fusion module adaptively fuses the physiological and behavior information based on behavioral energy (BE-Fusion). The BE-Fusion module quantifies the response intensity of features by feature energy to measure the importance of both information and fuses the information of the two branches by weighted concatenation, which can be defined as

$$
\begin{aligned}
\widehat{\boldsymbol{F}}_{BE} &= \frac{\left[\widehat{\boldsymbol{P}}^T, \boldsymbol{B}^T\right]^T}{\sqrt{\lambda^2 + E_B}} \\
&= \frac{1}{\sqrt{\lambda^2 + E_B}} \left(\frac{\lambda p_1}{\|\boldsymbol{P}\|_2}, \frac{\lambda p_2}{\|\boldsymbol{P}\|_2}, \dots, \frac{\lambda p_{128}}{\|\boldsymbol{P}\|_2}, b_1, b_2, \dots, b_{128} \right)^T,
\end{aligned}
\tag{3}
$$

where $\widehat{\boldsymbol{P}} = \frac{\lambda P}{\|\boldsymbol{P}\|_2}$ is the normalized physiological feature vector output from the ResNet branch, and $\lambda > 0$ is a hyperparameter, and $E_B = \boldsymbol{B}^T \boldsymbol{B}$ is the energy intensity of the feature vector $\boldsymbol{B}$ output from the Symbiotic branch.

2.2 Distillation Architecture for Hand Gesture Authentication Networks

This subsection introduces the KDKR [12] and uses it for hand gesture authentication model compression. In the knowledge distillation framework, the teacher network adopts the TDS-Net. The ResNet branch of the TDS-Net has more parameters, and we employ the MobilenetV2 [13] to replace the ResNet branch. Also, since the Symbiotic branch has fewer parameters, we retain its structure. We can obtain the final student network through the above modifications. The knowledge distillation architecture of the random hand gesture authentication network is shown in Fig. 2.

The KDKR framework fuses features at different levels in the student network through the attention-based fusion (ABF) module, which can realize the transmission of distilled knowledge at different levels, and measures the feature differences between the student and teacher networks through the hierarchical context loss (HCL) module, which can enable the flow of knowledge from the teacher network to the student network for guided learning called distillation loss, defined as

$$
\mathcal{L}_{\text{dis}} = \mathcal{D}\left(\mathbf{F}_s^n, \mathbf{F}_t^n\right) + \sum_{i=n-1} \mathcal{D}\left(\mathcal{U}\left(\mathbf{F}_s^i, \mathbf{F}_s^{i+1,n}\right), \mathbf{F}_t^i\right),
\tag{4}
$$

where $\mathbf{F}_s^i$ denotes the feature of the i-th stage in the student network, and $\mathbf{F}_t^i$ denotes the feature of the i-th stage in the teacher network, and $\mathcal{U}(,)$ is a module for fusing different levels of features, and $\mathcal{D}(,)$ is a module for measuring feature differences. The $\mathcal{U}(,)$ and $\mathcal{D}(,)$ correspond to the ABF and HCL modules in Fig. 2, respectively.

In our experiments, the training loss is the sum of the distillation loss and the task-specific loss, and only the student network is involved in the inference process. So it brings no additional computational cost and is cost-free at the test time. For the random hand gesture authentication task, the task-specific loss is $\mathcal{L}_{AM}$ [14] and the training loss function is defined as

$$\mathcal{L} = \mathcal{L}_{AM} + \lambda \mathcal{L}_{dis}, \tag{5}$$

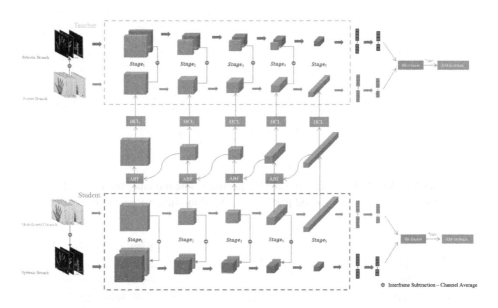

Fig. 2. Knowledge distillation architecture for the TDS-Net.

where λ is a hyperparameter used to balance these two losses.

The detailed structure of the ABF module is shown in Fig. 3(a). First, the higher-level features are resized to the same shape as the lower-level features. Second, two different feature maps are concatenated along the channel dimension and generate two $H \times W$ spatial attention maps through two 1×1 convolutions. After that, the two spatial attention maps are multiplied with their corresponding feature maps of the two levels. Finally, these two weighted feature maps are added to generate one fused feature map. The ABF module can get different spatial attention maps according to the input feature maps to achieve adaptive feature fusion. The design of this feature fusion strategy is more flexible and can achieve a better feature fusion performance.

However, the spatial attention module has the limitation that it cannot obtain the information on the channel dimension. To address this deficiency, we develop alternative designs for the ABF module. To test whether the channel attention mechanism is beneficial to the knowledge distillation performance for our random hand gesture authentication network, we employ three attention modules, the SE [15], CA [16], and CBAM [17], to replace the spatial attention module in the original ABF module, respectively, as shown in the green dashed box part of Fig. 3(a). The detailed structure of the SE, CA, and CBAM are shown in Figs. 3(b), 3(c), and 3(d), respectively. And we also try to use addition (*add*) and separation(*sep*) to replace concatenation (*cat*), as shown in the red box part in Fig. 3(a). By redesigning the ABF module in two places, we fully verify the rationality of the fusion module and obtain a variant of the ABF module suitable for random gesture authentication tasks.

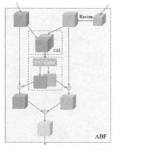

(a) The detailed structure of the ABF module. The red and green dashed boxes are the two improved parts of the ABF module, respectively.

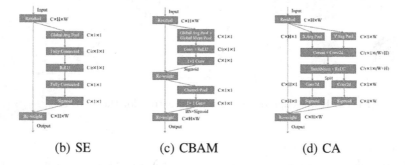

(b) SE   (c) CBAM   (d) CA

Fig. 3. The detailed structure of the ABF module and three lightweight attention mechanisms. The (b), (c), and (d) are detailed attention mechanism structures that will replace the spatial attention mechanism in the ABF module shown as the green dashed box in (a). (Color figure online)

3   Experiments

3.1   Dataset and Settings

The SCUT-DHGA dataset [3] is the largest dataset available for the hand gesture authentication task, collected from 193 subjects. In the dataset, each subject makes six different gestures, each repeated ten times, and each hand gesture video contains 64 frames. Fifty subjects' two-session hand gestures are recorded with an average interval of one week. A total of 29,160 video sequences are captured. Figure 2 shows an example of feeding a hand gesture video to the network.

In identity verification experiments, the experimental configuration can be divided into *subject-dependent* and *subject-independent* settings according to whether the subjects to be verified appear during the training process. In this paper, we adopt the more challenging *subject-independent* setting, *i.e.*, the subjects to be verified do not appear during the training process. We adopt the data from 50 subjects with two sessions as the test set, which results in two test settings: single and cross sessions. The remaining 143 subjects are used as the training set. At the same time, we focus on the more secure, more user-friendly random hand gesture authentication, in which the registered gesture types can be different from the probe ones.

In Table 1, we design two sets of contrast experiments. We demonstrate the performance of the KDKR by comparing the experimental results of *Teacher* and *Student1* (*Student2*) and the training efficiency of the KDKR by comparing the experimental results of *Baseline* and *Student1*. Then we introduce the notations in the Table 1. We employ $G_i(i = 1, 2, ..., 6)$ to denote a randomly selected batch of hand gesture videos that do not contain the $Gesture_i$ category, of which 20-frame segments are randomly selected to train the model [4]. At test time, the enrolled gesture category is $Gesture_i$ and the probe gesture categories are the rest of the five gesture types. We employ *Teacher* to denote TDS-Net, which is used as the teacher network in the knowledge distillation framework. We employ *Baseline* to denote the student network trained directly on the SCUT-DHGA dataset without pre-training using the ImageNet dataset and without the knowledge distillation framework. In contrast, we employ *Student1* and *Student2* to denote the student networks trained within the knowledge distillation framework. The student network is a convolutional neural network that uses the backbone of the lightweight MobileNetV2 to replace the backbone of the ResNet branch of TDS-Net. The width of the MobileNetV2 backbones of *Baseline* and *Student1* is 1.0. While for *Student2*, except for the width of MobileNetV2 backbone is 0.75, the other structures are the same as that of *Student1*.

3.2   Implementation Details

We use the Adam optimizer for network training. For the TDS-Net training, the backbone network is pre-trained using the ImageNet dataset and fine-tuned for 100 epochs in the SCUT-DHGA dataset with an initial learning rate of 1e−5, decayed by 0.45 every 50 epochs. In the knowledge distillation experiments, the student networks are optimized by Adam and trained for 100 epochs. The initial learning rate is 0.02 and decays by 0.1 every 20 epochs. Random rotation within $\pm15°$ and color jittering related to luminance, contrast, and saturation are used to augment the data. All experiments are implemented on an NVIDIA GTX3090 GPU using Pytorch.

3.3 Performance of Knowledge Distillation

The remarkable performance of knowledge distillation can be seen from Table 1. Compared with *Baseline*, the average equal error rate of *Student1* is decreased by 16.625% in single session and 17.120% in cross session. We think that the significant performance improvement of *Student1* compared to *Baseline* is due to the additional guidance brought by the KDKR. Guided by the advanced knowledge of the teacher network, the student network can learn more and perform better. At the same time, random hand gesture authentication in cross session has a higher equal error rate than in single session, reflecting the effect of time on hand gesture authentication.

At the same time, we count the parameter number of *Teacher*, *Student1*, and *Student2* in Table 1. We can find that compared with *Teacher*, the parameter number of *Student1* (*Student2*) is reduced by 77.29% (84.89%), while the average equal error rates in single and cross sessions only increase by 1.757% (2.881%) and 4.229% (5.25%), respectively. Through knowledge distillation, the parameter number of the network is significantly reduced while ensuring a decent reduction in network accuracy, making the hand gesture authentication network somewhat qualified for deployment on mobile devices.

Table 1. Performance of single session and cross session hand gesture authenticated networks. The evaluation index of both $G_i(i = 1, 2, ..., 6)$ and *Average* is the equal error rate (EER) (%). The *Param* in the last row counts each model's parameter number(M).

Setting	Single session				Cross session			
	Teacher	Baseline	Student1	Student2	Teacher	Baseline	Student1	Student2
G_1	3.178	22.452	5.55	6.868	5.74	27.234	11.508	12.38
G_2	3.91	23.716	5.072	7.488	5.126	28.7	9.694	10.874
G_3	2.04	15.434	3.666	4.692	6.772	22.336	10.932	11.84
G_4	3.63	21.95	5.33	6.094	8.806	33.148	11.892	12.394
G_5	2.138	23.68	3.636	4.506	7.572	29.002	12.16	13.674
G_6	1.878	20.136	4.362	4.716	7.7	29.36	10.816	12.056
Average	2.846	21.228	4.603	5.727	6.953	28.302	11.182	12.203
Params	11.45	2.6	2.6	1.73	11.45	2.6	2.6	1.73

3.4 Ablation Experiments for ABF Module

As shown in Table 2, we can find that using CBAM and replacing *cat* with *add* will result in the best knowledge distillation in the G_1 setting compared to the original structure (Baseline+cat). We think that each channel of the feature map encodes different knowledge. By introducing the channel attention mechanism and cooperating with the spatial attention mechanism, it can comprehensively reflect what and where the model needs to focus on and further improve the performance of the ABF module.

Table 2. Changes in the average equal error rate for other attentional designs of the ABF module compared to the original structure (Baseline+cat) in single and cross sessions.

	cat	add	sep
Baseline	0.000%	−1.333%	−1.694%
CBAM	−0.682%	**−1.788%**	−1.620%
CA	−0.413%	−0.211%	−1.059%
SE	−0.627%	+0.118%	−0.554%

4 Conclusion

In this paper, we focus on random hand gesture authentication in which the registered and probe hand gestures can be different. To better enable the hand gesture authentication model to be deployed on mobile devices, we use the KDKR to compress the model. And the experiments show that the improved ABF module is much better than the original design, with a significant reduction in the parameter number of the compressed model and a slight increase in the equal error rate.

Acknowledgments. This work was supported by the National Natural Science Foundation of China under Grant 61976095.

References

1. Ducray, B., Cobourne, S., Mayes, K., Markantonakis, K.: Comparison of dynamic biometrie security characteristics against other biometrics. In: 2017 IEEE International Conference on Communications (ICC), pp. 1–7 (2017)
2. Yu, X., Zhou, Z., Xu, M., You, X., Li, X.: Thumbup: identification and authentication by smartwatch using simple hand gestures. IN: 2020 IEEE International Conference on Pervasive Computing and Communications (PerCom), pp. 1–10 (2020)
3. Liu, C., Yang, Y., Liu, X., Fang, L., Kang, W.: Dynamic-hand-gesture authentication dataset and benchmark. IEEE Trans. Inf. Forensics Secur. **16**, 1550–1562 (2021)

4. Song, W., Kang, W., Yang, Y., Fang, L., Liu, C., Liu, X.: TDS-Net: towards fast dynamic random hand gesture authentication via temporal difference symbiotic neural network. In: 2021 IEEE International Joint Conference on Biometrics (IJCB), pp. 1–8 (2021)
5. Aumi, M.T.I., Kratz, S.G.: Airauth: evaluating in-air hand gestures for authentication. In: MobileHCI 2014 (2014)
6. Wu, J., Christianson, J., Konrad, J., Ishwar, P.: Leveraging shape and depth in user authentication from in-air hand gestures. In: 2015 IEEE International Conference on Image Processing (ICIP), pp. 3195–3199 (2015)
7. Hinton, G.E., Vinyals, O., Dean, J.: Distilling the knowledge in a neural network. arXiv abs/1503.02531 (2015)
8. Romero, A., Ballas, N., Kahou, S.E., Chassang, A., Gatta, C., Bengio, Y.: FitNets: hints for thin deep nets. CoRR abs/1412.6550 (2015)
9. Kim, K., Ji, B., Yoon, D., Hwang, S.: Self-knowledge distillation with progressive refinement of targets. In: 2021 IEEE/CVF International Conference on Computer Vision (ICCV), pp. 6547–6556 (2021)
10. Mirzadeh, S.I., Farajtabar, M., Li, A., Levine, N., Matsukawa, A., Ghasemzadeh, H.: Improved knowledge distillation via teacher assistant. In: AAAI (2020)
11. He, K., Zhang, X., Ren, S., Sun, J.: Deep residual learning for image recognition. In: 2016 IEEE Conference on Computer Vision and Pattern Recognition (CVPR), pp. 770–778 (2016)
12. Chen, P., Liu, S., Zhao, H., Jia, J.: Distilling knowledge via knowledge review. In: 2021 IEEE/CVF Conference on Computer Vision and Pattern Recognition (CVPR), pp. 5006–5015 (2021)
13. Sandler, M., Howard, A.G., Zhu, M., Zhmoginov, A., Chen, L.C.: MobileNetv 2: Inverted residuals and linear bottlenecks. In: 2018 IEEE/CVF Conference on Computer Vision and Pattern Recognition, pp. 4510–4520 (2018)
14. Wang, F., Cheng, J., Liu, W., Liu, H.: Additive margin softmax for face verification. IEEE Sig. Process. Lett. **25**, 926–930 (2018)
15. Hu, J., Shen, L., Albanie, S., Sun, G., Wu, E.: Squeeze-and-excitation networks. IEEE Trans. Pattern Anal. Mach. Intell. **42**, 2011–2023 (2020)
16. Hou, Q., Zhou, D., Feng, J.: Coordinate attention for efficient mobile network design. In: 2021 IEEE/CVF Conference on Computer Vision and Pattern Recognition (CVPR), pp. 13708–13717 (2021)
17. Woo, S., Park, J., Lee, J.-Y., Kweon, I.S.: CBAM: convolutional block attention module. In: Ferrari, V., Hebert, M., Sminchisescu, C., Weiss, Y. (eds.) ECCV 2018. LNCS, vol. 11211, pp. 3–19. Springer, Cham (2018). https://doi.org/10.1007/978-3-030-01234-2_1

Multidimension Joint Networks for Action Recognition

Wanhao Jia[✉], Yi Jin, and Hui Tian

School of Computer and Information Technology, Beijing Jiaotong University, Beijing 100044,
China
{21125178,yjin}@bjtu.edu.cn, tianhui@cmict.chinamobile.com

Abstract. Motion types, spatial and temporal features are two crucial elements
of information for video action recognition. 3D CNNs boast good recognition
performance but are computationally expensive and less competitive on temporal
feature extraction. 2D CNNs are computationally cheap and more adaptive to
temporal features but can not achieve promising performance. In this work, we
design a multidimension joint (MJ) module which can be embedded into 2D CNNs
and strike the balance between computational cost and performance. To this end,
we propose a spatio-temporal features and motion changes extraction module
which includes two paths: Spatio-temporal joint (STJ) path and Temporal motion
enhance (TME) path. The STJ path utilizes 3D CNNs to describe spatio-temporal
representation. The TME path calculates feature-oriented temporal differences,
which is used to enhance motion-sensitive channels.

Keywords: Action recognition · Multidimension Networks · Spatio-temporal
enhancement

1 Introduction

Action recognition, a key branch in video understanding, has been a growing demand
in video-related applications. Traditional human action recognition is more scene-based
[11, 12] in which action is not time dependent. With developing technology, temporal-
related action recognition has recently become a focus for research.

The mainstream of existing methods are 3D CNN based framework and 2D CNN
based framework. 3D CNNS have been shown to be effective in spatio-temporal modeling [4, 20, 22], but spatio-temporal modeling can not capture enough information
contained in the video. The two-stream network was designed to take spatial information and optical flow as temporal information into account [3, 18, 19], which enhanced
performance remarkably. However, the cost of computating optical flow is very high,
therefore traditional two-stream networks are not friendly for real-world applications. 3D
CNNs have problems such as slow convergence and heavy computations, more importantly, 3D CNNs often lack specific consideration in the temporal dimension, the points
mentioned above would also limit the network usage on real-world applications.

W. Deng et al. (Eds.): CCBR 2022, LNCS 13628, pp. 257–266, 2022.
https://doi.org/10.1007/978-3-031-20233-9_26

Based on the above observation, we design an effective multidimension joint (MJ) module which can be embedded into 2D CNNs and strike the balance between computational cost and performance. Instead of generating another type of input to train the network, we model the motion within the network based on the level of the features, which greatly reduces the computational effort.

Inspired by the Temporal Difference Network(TDN), we obtain the change of motion information through subtraction operation between adjacent feature maps, thus eliminating the need to calculate optical flow data, which can well counteract the shortcoming of 3D CNNs being insensitive to temporal features. Meanwhile, 3D CNNs can use the field of view to extract information with a wider span from the feature time dimension. Therefore, in order to further reduce the computation and enhance the utilization of long time series information, our multidimensional joint module contains two paths: a) Spatio-temporal joint (STJ) path which is implemented by three dimensional convolution kernels to describe spatio-temporal representation. b) Temporal motion enhance (TME) path which focuses on local motion modeling, we present a light-weight and low-resolution difference module to supply a single RGB with motion patterns via lateral connections.

To demonstrate the effectiveness of our model, we implement it with ResNets and perform experiments on Something-Something datasets. In summary, our main contribution lies in the following two aspects:

1) We propose a multidimension joint module that works in a plug-and-play manner, which is able to extract appropriate spatio-temporal patterns and motion information to recognize actions.
2) We have conducted extensive experiments and shown our competitive performances on Something-SomethingV2 dataset.

2 Related Works

In this section, we discuss related work based on 2D and 3D CNN frameworks, where TDN [2] and ACTION-Net [1] inspired us to propose the Multidimension Joint Network (MJN).

The framework based on 3D CNN has the capability of spatio-temporal modeling and improves the performance of video action recognition [6, 22]. I3D [3] inflated the ImageNet pre-trained 2D kernels to 3D kernels for capturing spatio-temporal information. SlowFast network [5] involves a slow branch and a fast branch to model slow and fast motions respectively. 3D CNN-based methods contain a large number of parameters, which causes various problems, such as easily overfitting [6] and difficulties in convergence [23]. Although recent studies [17, 23] have shown that 3D convolution can be factored, thereby reducing the computational burden to some extent, the computational burden is still much larger compared to 2D CNN-based frameworks.

Recently, several studies have proposed to embed modules into 2D CNNs. These modules are able to model the motion and temporal information. For example, TSM [15] firstly introduced temporal modeling to 2D CNN-based frameworks, in which a shift operation for a part of channels was embedded. MFNet [13], TEINet [16] and

TEA [14] were proved to be effective on the ResNet architecture. STM [10] proposed a block for modeling the spatio-temporal and motion information instead of the ordinary residual block. GSM [21] leverages group spatial gating to control interactions in spatial-temporal decomposition. TDN [2] presents a video-level motion modeling framework with the proposed temporal difference module, with a focus on capturing both short-term and long-term temporal structure for video recognition.

The combination of spatio-temporal features and motion features can be understood similarly as the two-stream architecture [19], ACTION-Net [1] models the motion inside the network based on the feature level rather than generating another type of input, such as optical flow [9], for training the network, which significantly reduces computations. Inspired by SENet [8], the channel-wise features are extracted based on the temporal domain to characterize the channel interdependencies for the network. Correspondingly, a neural architecture equipped with such a module is dubbed ACTION-Net. ACTION comprises three components for extracting aforementioned features: (1) Spatio-Temporal Excitation (STE), (2) Channel Excitation (CE) and (3) Motion Excitation (ME).

3 Design of Multidimension Joint Networks

In this section, we are going to introduce technical details for our proposed Multidimension Joint Networks (MJN) together with Multidimension Joint Module (MJM). As the MJM consists of two sub-modules: Spatio-Temporal Joint (STJ) module and Temporal Motion Enhance (TME) module, we firstly introduce these two sub-modules respectively and then give an overview on how to integrate them to an MJM. Notations used in this section are: N (batch size), T (number of segments), C (channels), H (height), W (width) and r (channel reduce ratio). It should be noticed that all tensors outside the MJM are 4D (N × T, C, H, W). We first reshape the input 4D tensor to 5D tensor (N, T, C, H, W) before feeding to the MJ in order to enable the operation on specific dimension inside the MJ. The 5D output tensor is then reshaped to 4D before being fed to the next 2D convolutional block.

3.1 Spatio-Temporal Joint (STJ)

STJ is efficiently designed for exciting spatio-temporal information by utilizing 3D convolution. To achieve this, STJ generates a spatio-temporal mask $M \in R^{N \times T \times 1 \times H \times W}$.

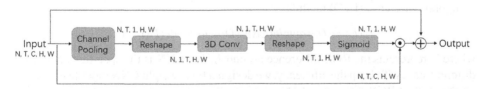

Fig. 1. Spatio-Temporal Joint (STJ) Module structure

that is used for element-wise multiplying the input $X \in R^{N \times T \times C \times H \times W}$ across all channels. As illustrated in Fig. 1, given an input $X \in R^{N \times T \times C \times H \times W}$, we first average the input tensor across channels in order to get a global spatio-temporal tensor $F \in R^{N \times T \times 1 \times H \times W}$ with respect to the channel axis. Then we reshape F to $F' \in R^{N \times 1 \times T \times H \times W}$ to be fed to a 3D convolutional layer K with kernel size $3 \times 3 \times 3$, which can be formulated as.

$$F_o' = K * F' \tag{1}$$

We finally reshape F_o' back to $F_o \in R^{N \times T \times 1 \times H \times W}$ and feed it to a Sigmoid activation in order to get the mask $M \in R^{N \times T \times 1 \times H \times W}$, which can be represented as.

$$M = \delta(F_o) \tag{2}$$

The final output can be interpreted as.

$$Y = X + X \odot M \tag{3}$$

Compared to the conventional 3D convolutional operation, STJ is much more computationally efficient as the input feature F' is averaged across channels. Each channel of the input tensor X can perceive the importance of spatio-temporal information from a refined feature excitation $\delta(F_o)$.

3.2 Temporal Motion Enhance (TME)

Temporal Difference Module has been explored by TDN [2] previously, which aims to model motion information by calculating adjacent feature maps difference based on the feature level instead of the pixel level. Different from TDN that proposed a short-term and long-term temporal modeling for extracting motion, we only use the short-term temporal modeling to extract local motion and rely on STJ to extract long-term global motion.

As illustrated in Fig. 2(b), the motion information is modeled by adjacent frames. Given the feature $F \in R^{N \times T \times C \times H \times W}$, we squeeze the number of channels for F by a scale ratio r (r = 16 in this work), which can be interpreted as.

$$F_r = K_1 * F \tag{4}$$

where K_1 is a 1×1 2D convolutional layer and $F_r \in R^{N \times T \times \frac{C}{r} \times H \times W}$, after sampling the key frames I_i in feature maps F_r, we extract several temporal RGB difference in a local window centered at I_i, and then stack them along channel dimension $D(I_i) = [D_{-2}, D_{-1}, D_1, D_2]$. Based on this representation, we present an efficient form of Local Temporal Difference (LTD) module:

$$H(I_i) = Upsample(CNN(Downsample(D(I_i)))) \tag{5}$$

where D represents the RGB difference around I_i, and CNN is the specific network for different stages. To keep the efficiency, we design a light-weight CNN module to operate on the stacked RGB difference $D(I_i)$. It generally follows a low-resolution processing strategy: (1) downsample RGB difference by half with an average pooling, (2) extract motion features with a 2D CNN, (3) upsample motion features to match RGB features. The final features will concat and get unsqueezed by another 1×1 2D convolutional layer to keep the same shape with STJ output.

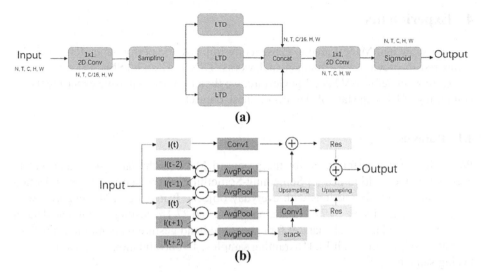

(a)

(b)

Fig. 2. Temporal Motion Enhance (TME) Module (a) consists of one sub-module (b) Local Temporal Difference (LTD) module.

3.3 Multidimension Joint Networks (MJN)

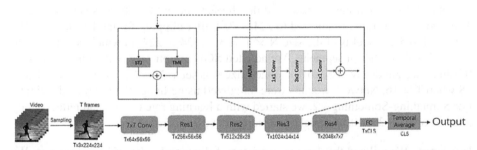

Fig. 3. Multidimension Joint Network structure for ResNet-50 [7]. The size of output feature map is given for each layer (CLS refers to number of classes and T refers to number of segments). The input video is firstly split into T segments equally and then one frame from each segment is randomly sampled [24]. The Multidimension Joint module is inserted at the start in each residual block.

The overall Multidimension Joint Module(MJM) takes the element-wise addition of two excited features generated by STJ and TME respectively (see multidimension joint module block in Fig. 3). By doing this, the output of the MJM can perceive information from a spatio-temporal perspective and motion. Figure 3 shows the MJN architecture for ResNet-50, wherein the MJM is inserted at the beginning in each residual block. It does not require any modification for original components in the block.

4 Experiments

We first show that MJN is able to consistently improve the performance for 2D CNNs compared to previous two fundamental works TSN [24] and TSM [15] on datasets Something-Something V2 and EgoGesture, we then perform extensive experiments for comparing MJN with state-of-the-arts on these datasets.

4.1 Datasets

We evaluated the performance for the proposed MJN on the large-scale and widely used action recognition dataset Something-Something V2, which is a large collection of humans performing actions with everyday objects. It includes 174 categories with 168,913 training videos, 24,777 validation videos and 27,157 testing videos, and dataset EgoGesture is a large-scale dataset for egocentric hand gesture recognition, it involves 83 classes of gestures with 14,416 training samples, 4,768 validation samples and 4,977 testing samples.

4.2 Implementation Details

Training. We perform experiments on video action recognition tasks according to the same strategy mentioned in TSN [24]. Given an input video, we first divide it into T segments of equal length. Then we randomly selected one frame from each segment to obtain a clip with T frames. The size of the shorter side of these frames is fixed to 256. The size of each frame is adjusted to 224×224 after clipping for model training. The input fed to the model is of the size $N \times T \times 3 \times 224 \times 224$, in which N is the batch size, T is the number of segments. We adopted SGD as optimizer with a momentum of 0.9 and a weight decay of 5×10^{-4}. Batch size was set as $N = 64$ when $T = 8$ and $N = 48$ when $T = 16$. Network weights were initialized using ImageNet pretrained weights. For Something-Something V2, we started with a learning rate of 0.01 and reduced it by a factor of 10 at 30, 40, 45 epochs and stopped at 50 epochs.

Inference. We utilized the three-crop strategy following [5, 10, 25] for inference. We firstly scaled the shorter side to 256 for each frame and took three crops of 256×256 from scaled frames. We randomly sampled from the full-length video for 10 times. The final prediction was the averaged Softmax score for all clips.

4.3 Comparisons with the State-of-the-Art

We compare our approach with the state-of-the-art on Something-Something V2 and EgoGesture, which is summarized in Table 1. MJN outperforms these two 2D CNN counterparts, TSN and TSM, on both two datasets (Table 2).

   TSN effectively models long-range temporal dynamics by learning from multiple segments of one video in an end-to-end manner, but it is worth noticing that TSN does not contain any component that is able to model the temporal information, instead, it relies excessively on computationally expensive Optical Flow features. By employing

Table 1. Comparisons with the state-of-the-arts on Something-Something V2 and EgoGesture

Method	Backbone	Pretrain	Plug-and-play	Something V2		EgoGesture	
				Top-1	Top-5	Top-1	Top-5
TRN [24]	BNInception	ImageNet		48.8	77.6	–	–
TSN[24]	ResNet-50	Kinetics	✓	27.8	57.6	83.1	98.3
TSM[15]	ResNet-50	Kinetics	✓	58.7	84.8	92.1	98.3
TEINet[16]	ResNet-50	ImageNet	✓	62.4	–	–	–
STM[10]	ResNet-50	ImageNet		62.3	**88.8**	–	–
MJN	ResNet-50	ImageNet	✓	**62.5**	87.3	**93.1**	**98.5**

Table 2. Accuracy and model complexity on EgoGesture dataset. All methods use ResNet-50 as backbone and 8 frames input for fair comparison.

Method	FLOPs	ΔFLOPs	Param	Top-1
TSN	33 G	–	23.68 M	83.1
TSM	33 G	–	23.68 M	92.1
STJ	33.1 G	+ 0.1G(+0.3%)	23.9 M	92.6
TME	34.75 G	+ 1.75G(+5.3%)	26.7 M	92.9
MJN	34.89 G	+ 1.89G(+5.7%)	28.12 M	**93.1**

a temporal shift operation to a part of channels, TSM introduced temporal modeling, in which a shift operation for a part of channels was embedded into 2D CNNs, which significantly improves the 2D CNN baseline compared to TSN. However, TSM still lacks explicit temporal modeling. By adding the MJ module to TSN, MJN takes spatio-temporal modeling and temporal motion modeling into account. It can be noticed that the Top-1 accuracy of MJN is improved by 3.8% to Something-Something V2 dataset, and the superiority of MJN on EgoGesture is quite impressive.

4.4 Ablation Study

In this section, we investigate the design of our MJN with respect to efficacy of STJ and TME. We carry out ablation experiments using 8 frames as the input on the EgoGesture dataset for inspecting these two aspects.

Results show that each module is able to improve the performance for 2D CNN baselines provided by TSN and TSM with limited added computational cost. Concretely, STJ adds negligible extra computation compared to TSM by averaging channels globally and averaging spatial information globally yet it renders useful information to the network. TME adds more computation and parameters to the network than STJ yet it is acceptable. It captures temporal differences on the spatial domain among adjacent frames over the time and achieves better performance compared to STJ. When integrating all these two sub-modules, it can be seen that the MJN achieves the highest accuracy and increases 1.0% Top-1 accuracy together with increasing 5.7% FLOPs.

5 Conclusion

We target at designing a module to be inserted to 2D CNN models for video action recognition and introduce a novel MJmodule that utilizes multipath excitation for spatio-temporal features and motion features. The proposed module could be leveraged by any 2D CNN to build a new architecture MJN for video action recognition. We show that MJN achieves consistently improvements compared to 2D CNN counterparts with limited extra computations introduced.

Acknowledgement. This work was supported by China Mobile Joint Fund Project of Ministry of Education (MCM20200203), and National key research and development program of China (2020YFB2103801).

References

1. Wang Z, She Q, Smolic A. Action-net: multipath excitation for action recognition. In: Proceedings of the IEEE/CVF Conference on Computer Vision and Pattern Recognition, pp. 13214–13223 (2021)
2. Wang L, Tong Z, Ji B, et al.: TDN: temporal difference networks for efficient action recognition. In: Proceedings of the IEEE/CVF Conference on Computer Vision and Pattern Recognition, pp. 1895–1904 (2021)
3. Carreira, J., Zisserman, A.: Quo vadis, action recognition? A new model and the kinetics dataset. In: Proceedings of the IEEE Conference on Computer Vision and Pattern Recognition, pp. 6299–6308 (2017)
4. Chen, Y., Kalantidis, Y., Li, J., Yan, S., Feng, J.: A 2-nets: double attention networks. In: Advances in Neural Information Processing Systems, pp. 352–361 (2018)
5. Feichtenhofer, C., Fan, H., Malik, J., He, K.: SlowFast networks for video recognition. In: Proceedings of the IEEE International Conference on Computer Vision, pp. 6202–6211 (2019)
6. Hara,K., Kataoka, H., Satoh, Y.: Can spatiotemporal 3D CNNs retrace the history of 2D CNNs and ImageNet? In: Proceedings of the IEEE Conference on Computer Vision and Pattern Recognition, pp. 6546–6555 (2018)
7. He, K., Zhang, X., Ren, S., Sun, J.: Deep residual learning for image recognition. In: Proceedings of the IEEE Conference on Computer Vision and Pattern Recognition, pp. 770–778 (2016)
8. Hu, J., Shen, J., Sun. G.: Squeeze-and-excitation networks. In: Proceedings of the IEEE Conference on Computer Vision and Pattern Recognition, pp. 7132–7141 (2018)
9. Ilg, E., Mayer, N., Saikia, T., Keuper, M., Dosovitskiy, A., Brox, T.: FlowNet 2.0: evolution of optical flow estimation with deep networks. In: Proceedings of the IEEE Conference on Computer Vision and Pattern Recognition, pp. 2462–2470 (2017)

10. Jiang, B., Wang, M., Gan, W., Wu, W., Yan, J.: STM: spatiotemporal and motion encoding for action recognition. In: Proceedings of the IEEE International Conference on Computer Vision, pp. 2000–2009 (2019)
11. Kay, W., et al.: The kinetics human action video dataset. arXiv preprint arXiv:1705.06950 (2017)
12. Kuehne, H., Jhuang, H., Garrote, E., Poggio, T., Serre, T.: HMDB: a large video database for human motion recognition. In: 2011 International Conference on Computer Vision, pp. 2556–2563. IEEE (2011)
13. Lee, M., Lee, S., Son, S., Park, G., Kwak, N.: Motion feature network: fixed motion filter for action recognition. In: Ferrari, V., Hebert, M., Sminchisescu, C., Weiss, Y. (eds.) ECCV 2018. LNCS, vol. 11214, pp. 392–408. Springer, Cham (2018). https://doi.org/10.1007/978-3-030-01249-6_24
14. Li, Y., Ji, B., Shi, X., Zhang, J., Kang, B., Wang, L.: TEA: temporal excitation and aggregation for action recognition. In: Proceedings of the IEEE/CVF Conference on Computer Vision and Pattern Recognition, pp. 909–918 (2020)
15. Lin, J., Gan, C., Han, S.: TSM: temporal shift module for efficient video understanding. In: Proceedings of the IEEE International Conference on Computer Vision, pp. 7083–7093 (2019)
16. Liu, Z., et al.: TEINet: towards an efficient architecture for video recognition. In: AAAI, pp. 11669–11676 (2020)
17. Qiu, Z., Yao, T., Mei, T.: Learning spatio-temporal representation with pseudo-3d residual networks. In: Proceedings of the IEEE International Conference on Computer Vision, pp. 5533–5541 (2017)
18. Shi, L., Zhang, Y., Cheng, J., Lu, H.: Two-stream adaptive graph convolutional networks for skeleton-based action recognition. In: Proceedings of the IEEE Conference on Computer Vision and Pattern Recognition, pp. 12026–12035 (2019)
19. Simonyan, K., Zisserman, A.: Two-stream convolutional networks for action recognition in videos. In Advances in Neural Information Processing Systems, pp. 568–576 (2014)
20. Stroud, J., Ross, D., Sun, C., Deng, J., Sukthankar, R.: D3D: distilled 3d networks for video action recognition. In: The IEEE Winter Conference on Applications of Computer Vision, pp. 625–634 (2020)
21. Sudhakaran, S., Escalera, S., Lanz, O.: Gate-shift networks for video action recognition. In: Proceedings of the IEEE/CVF Conference on Computer Vision and Pattern Recognition, pp. 1102–1111 (2020)
22. Tran, D., Bourdev, L., Fergus, R., Torresani, L., Paluri, M.: Learning spatiotemporal features with 3D convolutional networks. In: Proceedings of the IEEE International Conference on Computer Vision, pp. 4489–4497 (2015)
23. Tran, D., Wang, H., Torresani, L., Ray, J., LeCun, Y., Paluri, M.: A closer look at spatiotemporal convolutions for action recognition. In Proceedings of the IEEE conference on Computer Vision and Pattern Recognition, pp. 6450–6459 (2018)
24. Wang, L., Xiong, Y., Wang, Z., Qiao, Y., Lin, D., Tang, X., Van Gool, L.: Temporal segment networks: towards good practices for deep action recognition. In: Leibe, B., Matas, J., Sebe, N., Welling, M. (eds.) ECCV 2016. LNCS, vol. 9912, pp. 20–36. Springer, Cham (2016). https://doi.org/10.1007/978-3-319-46484-8_2
25. Wang, X., Girshick, R., Gupta, A., He, K.: Non-local neural networks. In: Proceedings of the IEEE Conference on Computer Vision and Pattern Recognition, pp. 7794–7803 (2018)
26. Yang, C., Xu, Y., Shi, J., Dai, B., Zhou, B.: Temporal pyramid network for action recognition. In: Proceedings of the IEEE/CVF Conference on Computer Vision and Pattern Recognition, pp. 591–600 (2020)

27. Zolfaghari, M., Singh, K., Brox, T.: ECO: efficient convolutional network for online video understanding. In: Ferrari, V., Hebert, M., Sminchisescu, C., Weiss, Y. (eds.) ECCV 2018. LNCS, vol. 11206, pp. 713–730. Springer, Cham (2018). https://doi.org/10.1007/978-3-030-01216-8_43
28. Jin, Y., Lu, J., Ruan, Q.: Coupled discriminative feature learning for heterogeneous face recognition. IEEE Trans. Inf. Forensics Secur. **10**(3), 640–652
29. Zhang, Y., Jin, Y., Chen, J., Kan, S., Cen, Y., Cao, Q.: PGAN: part-based nondirect coupling embedded GAN for person. IEEE MultiMedia **27**(3), 23–33

Multi-level Temporal-Guided Graph Convolutional Networks for Skeleton-Based Action Recognition

Kunlun Wu[(✉)] and Xun Gong

School of Computing and Artificial Intelligence, Southwest Jiaotong University,
Chengdu, China
wukunlun@my.swjtu.edu.cn, xgong@swjtu.edu.cn

Abstract. Skeleton-based action recognition is a crucial and challenging task, which has promoted remarkable progress in diverse fields. Nevertheless, how to capture long-range temporal relationships remains a challenging problem, which is vital to reducing the ambiguity of indistinguishable actions. Towards this end, we propose a novel Multi-Level Temporal-Guided Graph Convolutional Network (ML-TGCN) to tackle the above problem. We leverage the multi-level temporal-guided mechanism to learn diverse temporal receptive fields for mining the discriminative motion patterns. Moreover, most current approaches cannot effectively explore the comprehensive spatial topology due to the skeleton graph is heuristically predefined, thus we propose a cross-space GCN to capture global context and maintain strengths of GCNs (i.e., hierarchy and local topology) jointly beyond the physical connectivity. The experimental results on the challenging datasets *NTU RGB+D* and *Kinetics-Skeleton* verify that ML-TGCN can achieve state-of-the-art performance.

Keywords: Skeleton-based action recognition · Multi-level temporal-guided · Graph convolutional network

1 Introduction

With the prosperity achieved in deep learning and computer vision, action recognition has accomplished better development in recent years and already applicated in various fields, such as human-computer interaction, eldercare, video surveillance and healthcare assistance. Current action recognition baselines can be categorized into video-based and skeleton-based. Rapid developments in 3D depth cameras such as Microsoft Kinect and Intel RealSense sensors, besides, human pose estimation algorithms make it more convenient to obtain 2D or 3D skeleton coordinates quickly and accurately. The skeleton-based action recognition methods have received more attention for their excellent topology-based representation and robustness to the environmental changes. Nowadays, the most dominative method to achieve skeleton-based action recognition has become Graph Neural Networks (GNNs), especially, GCNs have been investigated to be

W. Deng et al. (Eds.): CCBR 2022, LNCS 13628, pp. 267–275, 2022.
https://doi.org/10.1007/978-3-031-20233-9_27

very effective in modeling non-Euclidean data. ST-GCN [1] is the first model that uses the spatial-temporal skeleton graph for action recognition. Latter, diverse variants based on ST-GCN have boosted the recognition performance. Despite the fact that ST-GCNs have made remarkable progress, the structural constraints have limited the expressive ability of GCNs.

For ST-GCNs [1–3], the topology of the spatial graph represents the physical connection and is pre-designed for all layers, which can hinder the expressive ability due to the limited spatial-temporal receptive field. Particularly, message propagation can only flow along a fixed path when graph links are directed. Numerous studies have shown that the relationship between body joints not associated in the spatial graph is still crucial for recognition, such as "dancing" that left hand is apart from right hand. To better guide the encoder about where and when to focus on jointly, we attempt to overcome the aforementioned limitations by introducing a novel Multi-Level Temporal-Guided Graph Convolutional Network to jointly learn discriminative local-global spatiotemporal features. Intuitively, diverse temporal levels are determined by the size of the corresponding temporal segment, which can allow the model to learn fine-grained features of highly similar relations and effectively reduce the ambiguity of indistinguishable actions. Furthermore, the proposed cross-space GCN learns global context and local information by capturing the dependencies of non-local joints in the spatial graph. To summarize, the main contributions of this work lie in three folds:

- We propose a novel Multi-Level Temporal-Guided Mechanism (ML-TGM) to capture diverse temporal receptive fields, which can significantly improve recognition performance on hard samples, i.e., reducing the ambiguity of highly similar actions.
- With the aim to capture the optimal spatial topology, we develop an effective cross-space GCN to learn global context and local information simultaneously, allowing the model can mine relationships between the joints that are far away from each other in the anatomy-based graph.
- The experimental results on two large-scale datasets *NTU RGB+D* [4] and *Kinetics-Skeleton* [1] indicate our ML-TGCN can exceed state-of-the-art.

2 Methodology

In this section, we mainly illustrate the proposed method in two core parts. First, we present the proposed ML-TGM in detail. Subsequently, we analyze the drawbacks of traditional GCNs and introduce the principle of cross-space GCN.

2.1 Multi-level Temporal-Guided Mechanism

As previously emphasized in Sect. 1, understanding long-term temporal dependencies is vital for efficient relations modeling, especially for indistinguishable actions. Therefore, we propose a Multi-level Temporal-guided Mechanism (ML-TGM) to accomplish the above goal. As shown in Fig. 1, we first use a hierarchical backbone, i.e., several layers of regular ST-GCN, to obtain the general

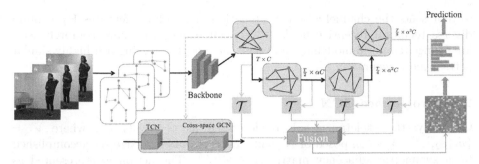

Fig. 1. Conceptual diagram of our ML-TGCN. The skeleton-based features are fed into multi-level temporal-guided GCN to extract long-range spatial-temporal relationships. The module of each level consists of the temporal convolution and the proposed cross-space GCN. Eventually, the fused multi-level features are utilized for action recognition.

features representation $\mathbf{F}_g \in \mathbb{R}^{T \times C}$. Then, the model learns multi-level temporal dependencies via the proposed mechanism. Each level consists of a temporal convolution and $\times K$ cross-space GCN, which corresponds to the different receptive fields. Earlier levels mine the fine-grained behaviour features with more temporal series, whereas the latter levels learn a coarse representation with fewer series, we leverage the interaction of different levels to guide our model for understanding long-range temporal relations. Moreover, to better model network hierarchy, temporal features merging is the essential one, thus we adopt a transformation function $\mathcal{T}$ to ensure the representation of different levels can obtain a unified feature representation $\mathbf{F}_u \in \mathbb{R}^{T \times C_m}$, which attempts to resample the series across temporal dimensions. Specifically, we accomplish it by utilizing an interpolate function and a linear mapping to the richer semantic space. We denotes the representation of each level as $\mathbf{F}^{(n)} \in \mathbb{R}^{\frac{T}{2^{n-1}} \times \alpha^{n-1}C}$, α is the channel-wise scale factor. The transformed features $\mathbf{F}_{\mathcal{T}}^{(n)} \in \mathbb{R}^{T \times C_m}$ via the function $\mathcal{T}$ can be denoted as:

$$\mathbf{F}_{\mathcal{T}}^{(n)} = Interpolation(\mathbf{F}^{(n)} \Theta^{(n)}) \tag{1}$$

$\Theta^{(n)}$ is the feature transformation at each level. Intuitively, earlier levels have lower semantics, whereas the latter levels have higher semantics. To balance the interaction of them, we adopt a trainable weight $\lambda^{(n)}$ at each level for exploring the appropriate relationships. The transformed features can be described as:

$$\tilde{\mathbf{F}}_{\mathcal{T}}^{(n)} = \lambda^{(n)} \mathbf{F}_{\mathcal{T}}^{(n)} \tag{2}$$

Here, the temporal length of all the refined representations is the same. Eventually, we merge the features at each level along the channel dimension to get the multi-level temporal representation, which can be formulated as follows:

$$\tilde{\mathbf{F}}_{\mathcal{T}} = \tilde{\mathbf{F}}_{\mathcal{T}}^{(1)} \oplus \tilde{\mathbf{F}}_{\mathcal{T}}^{(2)} \oplus ... \oplus \tilde{\mathbf{F}}_{\mathcal{T}}^{(n)} \tag{3}$$

$\oplus$ represents the channel-wise concatenation. The refined features $\tilde{\mathbf{F}}_T$ contain diverse temporal receptive fields, which can benefit the more comprehensive long-range temporal modeling and boost the model to distinguish highly similar actions more accurately.

2.2 Cross-space GCN

Generally, the skeleton graph is described as $G = (\mathcal{V}, \mathcal{E})$, where $\mathcal{V} = \{v_1, v_2, ..., v_N\}$ is composed of N joints, $\mathcal{E}$ represents the edge set accomplished by a symmetric adjacency matrix $A \in \mathbb{R}^{N \times N}$. The action is represented as graph sequences $X \in \mathbb{R}^{T \times N \times C}$, and the original input is defined by features X and graph structure A jointly. Existing GCN-based approaches mostly model the skeleton data by a spatial GCN and temporal convolution, which typically introduce incremental modules to enhance the expressiveness ability. However, the formed spatial-temporal receptive fields are pre-defined heuristically and distant nodes have weak information interaction. Therefore, we attempt to merge multi-scale structural features to learn higher-order polynomials of the adjacency matrix for mining global relations. The regular multi-scale formulation can be denoted as:

$$X' = \sum_{k=0}^{K} \widehat{D}^{(k)^{-\frac{1}{2}}} \widehat{A}^{(k)} \widehat{D}^{(k)^{-\frac{1}{2}}} XW \tag{4}$$

where K is the number of scales for aggregation, $\widehat{A}^{(k)}$ is the adjacency matrix of $\mathbf{A}$ at k^{th} scale, $D^{(k)}$ is the diagonal degree matrix of $\widehat{A}^{(k)}$ and W is the trainable linear transformation. Many investigations have verified that ordinary multi-scale mechanisms still concentrate more on the local region due to cyclic walks. The self-loops can create more space for cycles, resulting in the bias of the receptive field. To solve the above problem, we modify the above formulation to suppress redundant dependencies. Specifically, we propose a mechanism ϕ to reformulate the adjacency matrix at each scale, which can be formulated as:

$$\widehat{A}^{(k)} = \mu \widehat{A}^{(k)} + (\mu - 1)\widehat{A}^{(k-1)} + I \tag{5}$$

$\mu \in [0, 1]$ is a learnable parameter and I is the identity matrix, self-loops I is essential for learning the k-hop relationships and accelerating convergence.

In real scenarios, the performed actions always have complex cross-space connectivity, thus we attempt to make a more exhaustive feature interaction. Specifically, current methods treat the spatial aggregation as the fusion along the channel dimension, i.e., each channel shares the same human topology, but actually different channels have independent spatial context and should have the trainable adjacency matrix respectively. Therefore, we further modify graph convolution along the channel dimension. To be specific, we split channels into G groups, each channel in a group shares the joint-level learnable adjacency matrix. The model refines features by the operation Φ, which can be denoted as:

$$\widehat{F} = \psi(\widehat{A}_{1,:,:}^c F_{:\lfloor \frac{C}{G} \rfloor,:} || \widehat{A}_{2,:,:}^c F_{\lfloor \frac{C}{G} \rfloor:\lfloor \frac{2C}{G} \rfloor,:} || ... || \widehat{A}_{i,:,:}^c F_{\lfloor \frac{(i-1)C}{G} \rfloor:\lfloor \frac{iC}{G} \rfloor,:}) \qquad 1 \le i \le G \tag{6}$$

where $F \in \mathbb{R}^{C \times N}$ is the transformed feature by using the mechanism ϕ, $\widehat{A}^c \in \mathbb{R}^{G \times N \times N}$ is the grouped adjacency matrix, $\|$ and ψ is the channel-wise concatenation and shuffle operation. The combination of ϕ and Φ forms the proposed cross-space GCN, with the aim to enhance the features interaction of different joints and explore the optimal spatial topology beyond the physical connectivity.

3   Experiments

3.1   Datasets

NTU RGB+D. *NTU RGB+D* is the widely used and extensive dataset of 3D joint coordinates. It contains 56880 human action video sequences in 60 classes. The publishers of *NTU RGB+D* recommend two benchmarks: Cross-Subject (*X-Sub*) and Cross-View (*X-View*). This dataset is composed of two benchmarks: 1) Cross-subject (*X-Sub*): The volunteers of each subset perform 40320 actions for training, and the complement subset contains 16560 clips for evaluation. 2) Cross-view (*X-View*): This benchmark includes 37920 and 18960 clips for forming the train and evaluation set respectively. These videos are captured by three *Kinetic* depth sensors of equal height but different viewpoints. Each skeleton graph of *NTU RGB+D* consists of 25 body key points denoted by 3D coordinates.

Kinetics-Skeleton. *Kinetic-Skeleton* dataset contains about 300,000 video clips in 400 classes collected from the Internet. The captured skeleton information contains 18 body joints, along with their 2D coordinates and confidence score. Different from *NTU RGB+D*, skeleton sequences are not provided by the depth cameras but estimated by the publicly available *OpenPose* toolbox. There are 240,436 samples for training and 19794 samples for testing. Following the conventional evaluation method, Top-1 and Top-5 accuracies are reported.

3.2   Implementation Details

All experiments are conducted on four RTX 3080 TI GPUs with the PyTorch deep learning framework. We trained our models for a total of 140 epochs with batch size 32 and SGD as optimizer on *NTU RGB+D*, while on *Kinetics-Skeleton* we trained our models for a total of 80 epochs, with batch size 128. The learning rate is set to 0.1 at the beginning and then reduced by a weight decay of 10 at the epochs 60, 90, 120 and 45, 55, 70 for *NTU RGB+D* and *Kinetics-Skeleton* respectively. Moreover, we preprocessed the data with the same procedure used in [3]. In all of these experiments, we use the standard cross-entropy loss for optimization.

3.3   Ablation Studies

We analyze the proposed module by experiments on the *X-View* benchmark of *NTU RGB+D* dataset. The Top-1 accuracy of classification is used as the evaluation criterion. For this ablation study, we verify the performance of ML-TGM and cross-space GCN. Moreover, we visualize the learned skeleton graph and corresponding adjacency matrix for a more convincing explanation.

The Effectiveness of ML-TGM. Here we focus on verifying the benefits of applying the proposed ML-TGM. From Fig. 2, we can see the accuracy of ML-TGM with different levels. The proposed ML-TGM can be viewed as the general temporal modeling when we only use a single level, and the experimental results indicate that the recognition performance can actually obtain the improvement when we utilize ML-TGM. Based on the intuition of the effectiveness and efficiency, we adopt 4 levels in our ML-TGCN. Furthermore, we make a comparison of the strong baseline (left) and ML-TGM (right) to verify the performance on the hard classes. As shown in Fig. 3, we visualize the normalized confusion matrix to show the accuracy of each hard class, and especially use red rectangles to mark classes with significant improvement, which indicates that ML-TGM can reduce the ambiguity of highly similar actions (*reading and writing*, etc.) indeed.

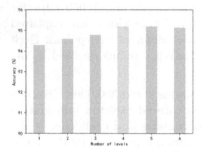

Fig. 2. The effectiveness of ML-TGM with different levels.

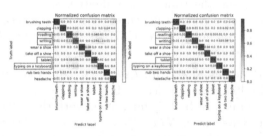

Fig. 3. The normalized confusion matrix of the strong baseline and ML-TGCN.

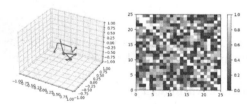

Fig. 4. The learned skeleton graph and corresponding adjacency matrix.

Table 1. The comparison of cross-space GCN and existing GCNs.

Method	Accuracy (%)
ST-GCN [1]	93.6
2s AGCN [3]	94.1
2s AGCN (Non-Local) [3]	94.4
MS-G3D [5]	94.9
Cross-space GCN	$\mathbf{95.2^{\uparrow 1.6}}$

The Performance of Cross-Space GCN. To analyze the region of space that the model focuses on when performing actions, we visualize the learned skeleton graph and corresponding adjacency matrix. As shown in Fig. 4, we randomly select a test sample of "fall down" class in *NTU RGB+D* dataset, and the learned skeleton graph (left) shows that the model pays more attention on hands, knees and hips, which indicates that our model focuses actually on the action-related region. Moreover, in the learned adjacency matrix (right), we can also observe that the model actually learns global relationships, e.g., the feet and hands are apart from each other, whereas the corresponding value of the adjacency matrix is non-zero. The above result indicates that cross-space GCN captures global context beyond the physical connectivity indeed. To further verify the

Table 2. The comparisons with our ML-TGCN on *NTU RGB+D* dataset.

Datasets	Approaches	Top-1 (%)
NTU RGB+D (X-Sub)	ST-GCN [1]	81.5
	STGR-GCN [6]	86.9
	AS-GCN [2]	86.8
	2s-AGCN [3]	88.5
	DGNN [7]	89.9
	MS-G3D [5]	91.5
	Ta-CNN++ [8]	90.7
	SMotif-GCN+TBs [9]	90.5
	ML-TGCN	**91.5**
NTU RGB+D (X-View)	ST-GCN [1]	88.3
	STGR-GCN [6]	92.3
	AS-GCN [2]	94.2
	2s-AGCN [3]	95.1
	DGNN [7]	96.2
	MS-G3D [5]	95.2
	Ta-CNN++ [8]	95.1
	SMotif-GCN+TBs [9]	96.1
	ML-TGCN	**96.6**

Table 3. The comparisons with our ML-TGCN on *Kinetic-Skeleton* dataset.

Datasets	Approaches	Top-1 (%)	Top-5 (%)
Kinetic-Skeleton	ST-GCN [1]	30.7	52.8
	AS-GCN [2]	34.8	56.8
	2s-AGCN [3]	36.1	58.7
	DGNN [7]	36.9	59.6
	MS-G3D [5]	38.0	60.9
	MST-GCN [10]	38.1	60.8
	Hyper-GNN [11]	37.1	60.0
	SMotif-GCN+TBs [9]	37.8	60.6
	ML-TGCN	**38.5**	**61.2**

superiority of cross-space GCN, we make comparisons with other state-of-the-art methods and adopt the same temporal model for a fair comparison. From Table. 1, we can observe that cross-space outperforms the baseline 1.6% and have a competitive performance compared with other state-of-the-art methods.

3.4 Comparison with the State-of-the-Art

We compare our method with state-of-the-art algorithms on *NTU RGB+D (X-View)* and *NTU RGB+D (X-Sub)* respectively to verify the excellent performance of our proposed ML-TGCN. As shown in Table. 2, we report the Top-1 accuracy of these methods on both cross-subject and cross-view benchmarks of the *NTU RGB+D* dataset. For *NTU RGB+D (X-Sub)*, we can observe that ML-TGCN has a competitive performance compared with state-of-the-art methods. For example, ML-TGCN outperforms Ta-CNN++ [8] 0.8% and MST-GCN [10] 1.6% respectively. For *NTU RGB+D (X-View)*, we can also see a clear superiority as reported previously. For *Kinetic-Skeleton*, the same as current state-of-the-art methods, we leverage Top-1 and Top-5 accuracy as our evaluation metrics. As shown in Table. 3, ML-TGCN also has an obvious improvement in recognition accuracy, e.g., our model has a 0.8% performance gain compared with [9]. The above experimental results demonstrate the superiority of our ML-TGCN.

4   Conclusions

In this work, we innovatively present a Multi-Level Temporal-Guided Mechanism (ML-TGM) to capture long-range temporal relationships, which can significantly improve the recognition accuracy of indistinguishable actions, i.e., the proposed model can effectively reduce the ambiguity of highly similar actions. Moreover, we propose a cross-space GCN to capture the global context and enhance local information jointly beyond physical connectivity, with the aim to explore the optimal spatial topology. The combination of them forms a novel network called Multi-Level Temporal-Guided Graph Convolutional Network (ML-TGCN). Experimental results on two challenging datasets *NTU RGB+D* and *Kinetics-Skeleton* indicate our approach can achieve the known state-of-the-art.

References

1. Yan, S., Xiong, Y., Lin, D.: Spatial temporal graph convolutional networks for skeleton-based action recognition. In: Thirty-second AAAI conference on artificial intelligence (2018)
2. Li, M., Chen, S., Chen, X., Zhang, Y., Wang, Y., Tian, Q.: Actional-structural graph convolutional networks for skeleton-based action recognition. In: Proceedings of the IEEE/CVF Conference on Computer Vision and Pattern Recognition, pp. 3595–3603 (2019)
3. Shi, L., Zhang, Y., Cheng, J., Lu, H.: Two-stream adaptive graph convolutional networks for skeleton-based action recognition. In: Proceedings of the IEEE/CVF Conference on Computer Vision and Pattern Recognition (2019) 12026–12035

4. Shahroudy, A., Liu, J., Ng, T.T., Wang, G.: NTU RGB+D: a large scale dataset for 3d human activity analysis. In: Proceedings of the IEEE Conference on Computer Vision and Pattern Recognition, pp. 1010–1019 (2016)
5. Liu, Z., Zhang, H., Chen, Z., Wang, Z., Ouyang, W.: Disentangling and unifying graph convolutions for skeleton-based action recognition. In: Proceedings of the IEEE/CVF Conference on Computer Vision and Pattern Recognition, pp. 143–152 (2020)
6. Li, B., Li, X., Zhang, Z., Wu, F.: Spatio-temporal graph routing for skeleton-based action recognition. Proc. AAAI Conf. Artif. Intell. **33**, 8561–8568 (2019)
7. Shi, L., Zhang, Y., Cheng, J., Lu, H.: Skeleton-based action recognition with directed graph neural networks. In: Proceedings of the IEEE/CVF Conference on Computer Vision and Pattern Recognition, pp. 7912–7921 (2019)
8. Xu, K., Ye, F., Zhong, Q., Xie, D.: Topology-aware convolutional neural network for efficient skeleton-based action recognition. Proc. AAAI Conf. Artif. Intell. **36**, 2866–2874 (2022)
9. Wen, Y.H., Gao, L., Fu, H., Zhang, F.L., Xia, S., Liu, Y.J.: Motif-GCNs with local and non-local temporal blocks for skeleton-based action recognition. IEEE Trans. Pattern Anal. Mach. Intell. (2022)
10. Chen, Z., Li, S., Yang, B., Li, Q., Liu, H.: Multi-scale spatial temporal graph convolutional network for skeleton-based action recognition. Proc. AAAI Conf. Artif. Intell. **35**, 1113–1122 (2021)
11. Hao, X., Li, J., Guo, Y., Jiang, T., Yu, M.: Hypergraph neural network for skeleton-based action recognition. IEEE Trans. Image Process. **30**, 2263–2275 (2021)

Research on Gesture Recognition of Surface EMG Based on Machine Learning

Linjie Liu, Na Zhang, and Ke Li$^{(\boxtimes)}$

Center for Intelligent Medical Engineering, School of Control Science and Engineering,
Shandong University, Jinan 250000, People's Republic of China
`kli@sdu.edu.cn`

Abstract. Gesture recognition pertains to recognizing meaningful expressions of motion by human, it is utmost important in medical rehabilitation, robot control as well as prosthesis design. Compared with gesture recognition based on machine vision, the gesture recognition based on wearable device, especially wearable surface electromyogram (sEMG) signal acquisition equipment, has more important theoretical and practical application prospects. However, there are still many urgent problems in sEMG signals, involving the signal acquisition and recognition accuracy of multi-channel sEMG signals, to be solved. For these problems, we designed a wearable sEMG armband with convenient acquisition and high precision to record sEMG signals and then done the gesture recognition based on deep learning method. Firstly, sEMG signals are classified, denoised and extracted features, and then extended data by sliding window. Then, Convolutional Neural Networks (CNN) and Multilayer Perceptron (MLP) were constructed to classify the 9 predefined gestures. The result showed that both methods achieve high offline recognition rate. The average gesture recognition accuracy of CNN is 99.47%; The average gesture recognition accuracy of MLP is 98.42%.

Keywords: Surface EMG · Hand gesture recognition · CNN · MLP

1 Introduction

Hand is an important part of the human body, many things in daily life have to complete relying on the hand. Hand function is delicate and complex [1, 2], and it is difficult to recover after injury or hemiplegia, which seriously affect the normal life of patients [3, 4]. The traditional rehabilitation therapy is mainly based on one-to-one rehabilitation training between therapist and patient. In this process, patients' subjective participation is low but the cost is high, so many patients cannot get effective treatment. However, clinical data shows that the repeated active motor intention of hemiplegic patients can accelerate the recovery of injured motor nerves and help shorten the recovery time.

This study was supported by the National Natural Science Foundation of China (62073195), in part by the National Key Research and Development Program (2020YFC2007904), and in part by the Key Research & Development Programs of Guangdong Province (2020B0909020004) and Shandong Province (2019GSF108164, 2019GSF108127, 2019JZZY021010).

W. Deng et al. (Eds.): CCBR 2022, LNCS 13628, pp. 276–283, 2022.
https://doi.org/10.1007/978-3-031-20233-9_28

Decoding human motion intentions from surface EMG signals is an important method to realize prosthesis control [5]. Therefore, in order to better apply sEMG signals to human-computer interface control, decoding and recognizing hand motion patterns from sEMG signals has received extensive attention in recent years [6, 7].

In the early stage, the domestic research on EMG signal was mainly through the use of multiple electrodes to detect the EMG signal of specific muscle tissue including radial wrist flexor, ulnar wrist extensor, superficial flexor digitorum, palmaris longus and so on [8, 9]. But in this study, we designed a novel sEMG armband using 5 equidistant placed Delsys sEMG sensors to collect sEMG signals from subjects' forearm. The armband simplifies the acquisition process of sEMG signals and makes it more convenient for users to wear. Meanwhile, two machine learning methods, convolutional neural network and multi-layer perceptron were selected as classifiers in this experiment in order to achieve a high classification rate and lay the foundation for prosthetic hand control.

2 Signal Acquisition and Processing

2.1 Experimental Preparation

9 healthy right-handed subjects (5 males and 4 females) with an average age of 23.3 years were recruited for the experiment. Each subject was given an informed consent prior to the experiment. The experimental procedures were approved by the Institutional Review Board of Shandong University and were in accordance with the Declaration of Helsinki (Fig. 1).

Nine common gestures were selected in the experiment, involving single finger movements, multiple fingers movements and grasping movements. Single finger movements include thumb opposite palm (TOP), index finger bending (IFB), middle finger bending (MFB) and ring finger bending (RFB); Multi-finger movements include pinching the index finger and thumb (TIP), keeping the five fingers together (KFT) and bending the three fingers (TFB) which is index finger, middle finger and ring finger; Grasping movements include clenching fist (CF) and cylinder grasping (CG), as shown in Fig. 2.

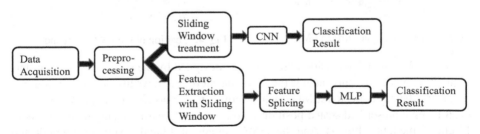

Fig. 1. Experimental process.

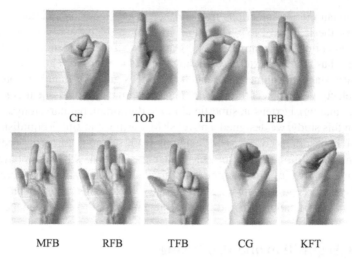

CF   TOP   TIP   IFB

MFB   RFB   TFB   CG   KFT

Fig. 2. The nine predefined gestures.

2.2 sEMG Acquisition

In this study, we designed a novel sEMG armband using 5 equidistant placed Delsys sEMG sensors to collect surface EMG signals from subjects' forearms (Fig. 4), and the sampling frequency was 1000 Hz. To ensure sEMG signal quality, the corresponding arm skin of subjects were cleansed with a scrub and disinfected with 75% alcohol before wearing the armband, and then, which was placed at the position from about 1/3 of the left forearm to the elbow joint (Fig. 3).

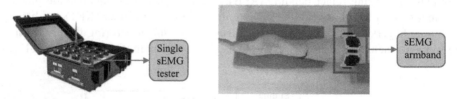

Fig. 3. Delsys Trigno surface EMG
tester

Fig. 4. Position of the EMG armband

The sEMG signal acquisition program was designed by the software LabView. The acquisition process mainly include the following steps. First, we used a test procedure to check whether the collected sEMG signals were normal or not. Next, Subjects were asked to sit using a prescribed seated position with their left forearm placing on a mat about 15 cm on the table (Fig. 4). And the sEMG signals of 9 hand gestures were collected in random order. There were 243 trials (9 hand gestures, 9 subjects, 3 times for one trial) in the experiment. One trial included 3 s of gesture forming time, 77 s of gesture holding time, and 3 s of gesture recovery time, as shown in Fig. 5. In order to facilitate the experiment of subjects, every trial has corresponding prompt tone, and the subjects can be also familiar with the experimental process before the formal experiment. 30-s rest was set between trials for subjects to prevent muscle fatigue.

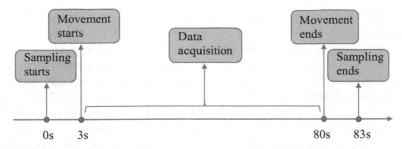

Fig. 5. Single experiment process

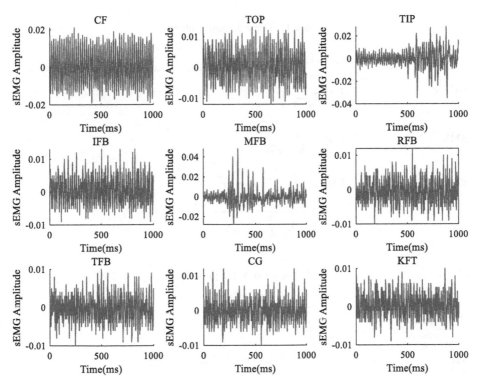

Fig. 6. Raw sEMG signals

2.3 Feature Extraction

The data in the gesture holding time was used to the further research. The raw sEMG signals of 9 hand motions during 1-s gesture holding time from one representative subject are shown in Fig. 6. The sEMG signals should be preprocessed before feature extraction. In this study, a Butterworth bandpass filter (10-Hz–450-Hz) was used to filter the sEMG signals, and a 50 Hz odd notch filter was used to eliminate the specific power frequency interference. Meanwhile, in order to expand the amount of data and facilitate the training of neural network, the data in the gesture holding time was extracted via sliding window method with 200-ms window width and 200-ms sliding distance. The data after sliding window processing was directly input into the CNN network for classification, and the features of the data are automatically extracted by the convolution layer.

Similarly, 9 time domain features were extracted via sliding window method in the phase of feature extraction, including mean value (MEAN), root mean square value (RMS), variance (VAR), standard deviation (SD), mean absolute value (MAV), number of zeros crossing (ZC), waveform length (WL), number of slope sign changes (SSC) and Willison amplitude (WAMP), as shown in Table 1. The window width and sliding distance are the same as above. Then the 9 features were sequentially arranged as the MLP network's input for training.

Table 1. 9 time domain features.

Feature	Formula
MEAN	$\bar{x} = \frac{1}{N} \sum_{k=1}^{N} x_k$
RMS	$RMS = \sqrt{\frac{1}{N} \sum_{k=1}^{N} x_k^2}$
VAR	$VAR = \frac{1}{N-1} \sum_{k=1}^{N} (x_k - \bar{x})^2$
SD	$SD = \sqrt{\frac{1}{N-1} \sum_{k=1}^{N} (x_k - \bar{x})^2}$
ZC	$ZC = \sum_{i=1}^{N} [\text{sgn}(-x_k \times x_{k+1}) \text{ and } |x_k - x_{k+1}| \geq a]$
WL	$WL = \sum_{k=1}^{N} |x_{k+1} - x_k|$
SSC	$SSC = \sum_{i=1}^{n-2} f[(x_i - x_{i-1}) \times (x_i - x_{i+1})]$
WAMP	$WAMP = \sum_{k=1}^{N} f(|x_k - x_{k+1}|)$

(*continued*)

Table 1. (*continued*)

Feature	Formula
MAV	$MAV = \frac{1}{N} \sum\limits_{k=1}^{N} |x_k|$

3 Classifier Design

3.1 CNN Design

The model of the classification method based on CNN is shown in Fig. 7. The model consists of an input layer, an output layer and two convolution blocks. Every convolution block has a convolution layer (3×3 convolution kernel) and a down-sampling layer (2×2 convolution kernel), which had 32 filters in the first convolution block, but 64 filters in the second convolution block. Besides, we added the dropout layer after two convolutional layers to prevent overfitting. The softmax function were used in output layer to achieve 9 classification problems. Adam optimizer and cross entropy loss function were selected in this CNN design.

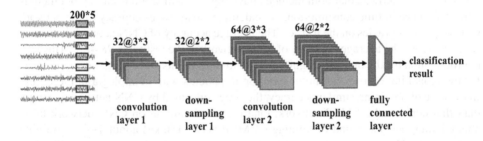

Fig. 7. The model of CNN

3.2 MLP Design

The model of the classification method based on MLP is shown in Fig. 8. The model consists of one input layer, three hidden layers and one output layer, and the number of three hidden layer nodes are 64, 32 and 16 respectively. In addition, the layers are fully connected with each other in this model, and data labels adopts a form of One-Hot Encoding. Similar to the classification model design based on CNN, Adam optimizer and cross entropy loss function were used in the MLP classification model design.

The parameters of the two networks including the kernel size, the number of layers and hidden nodes were determined by experiment.

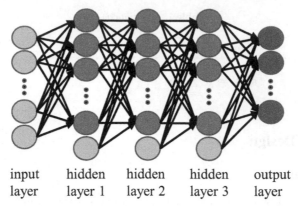

input   hidden   hidden   hidden   output
layer   layer 1   layer 2   layer 3   layer

Fig. 8. The model of MLP

4 Experimental Results and Analysis

The data from 9 gestures of 9 subjects who met the experimental requirements were analyzed and classified by two kinds of networks which were built with Python's keras library. We used about 80% of the data as the train set and the remaining 20% as the test set. The results showed that both methods have high classification accuracy but there is a big difference in time consumption. We calculate the average accuracy of the network by taking 10 accuracies on the test set. The average accuracy of CNN network in the test set is 99.47%. The average accuracy of MLP network in the test set is 98.42%. This lays the foundation for the online recognition of hand movements and is of great significance for the rehabilitation of hand motor function in patients with hemiplegia in the future. In the case of obtaining similar accuracy, the time consumed by CNN network is longer than that consumed by MLP network. One round of training on CNN network takes about 1 min, but one round of training on MLP network takes about 1−s. A training process of CNN is shown in Fig. 9 and a training process of MLP is shown in Fig. 10.

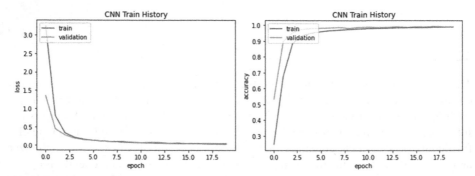

Fig. 9. A training process of CNN

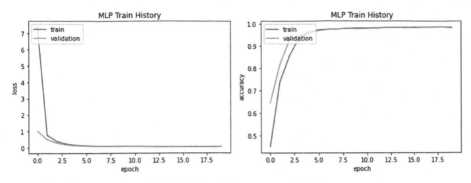

Fig. 10. A training process of MLP

5 Conclusion

This paper realizes the high accuracy classification of array sEMG signals. In this paper, a convenient EMG armband is designed to collect the sEMG signal of forearm. The method of machine learning is used to realize the off-line gesture recognition based on sEMG, and the high accuracy is achieved, which lays the foundation for the precise control of prosthesis control.

References

1. Göran, L.: Nerve injury and repair - a challenge to the plastic brain. J. Periph. Nerv. Syst. **8**(4), 209–226 (2003)
2. Overduin, S.A., Avella, A., Roh, J., et al.: Modulation of muscle synergy recruitment in primate grasping. J. Neurosci. **28**, 880 (2008)
3. Langhorne, P., Coupar, F., Pollock, A.: Motor recovery after stroke: a systematic review. J. Lancet Neurol. **8**, 741–754 (2009)
4. Johnston, S.C., Mendis, S., Mathers, C.D.: Global variation in stroke burden and mortality: estimates from monitoring, surveillance, and modelling. J. Lancet Neurol. **8**, 345–354 (2009)
5. Parajuli, N., Sreenivasan, N., Bifulco, P., et al.: Real-time EMG based pattern recognition control for hand prostheses: a review on existing methods, challenges and future implementation. J. Sensors **19**(20), 4596 (2019)
6. Balbinot, G., Li, G., Wiest, M.J., et al.: Properties of the surface electromyogram following traumatic spinal cord injury: a scoping review. J. Neuroeng. Rehabil. (2021)
7. Kumar, D.K., Jelfs, B., Sui, X., et al.: Prosthetic hand control: a multidisciplinary review to identify strengths, shortcomings, and the future. J. Biomed. Signal Process. Control (2019)
8. Su, Z.Y., Liu, H.D., Qian, J.W., Zhang, Z., Zhang, L.W.: Hand gesture recognition based on sEMG signal and convolutional neural network. Int. J. Pattern Recognit Artif Intell. **35**, 19 (2021)
9. Wang, F., Jin, J., Gong, Z., Zhang, W., Tang, G., Jia, Z.: Gesture Recognition Based on sEMG and Support Vector Machine. 2021 IEEE International Conference on Robotics, Automation and Artificial Intelligence (RAAI), pp. 24–28 (2021)

Affective Computing
and Human-Computer Interface

Adaptive Enhanced Micro-expression Spotting Network Based on Multi-stage Features Extraction

Zhihua Xie$^{(\boxtimes)}$, Sijia Cheng, Xiaoyu Liu, and Jiawei Fan

Key Lab of Optic-Electronic and Communication, Jiangxi Science and Technology
Normal University, Nanchang, China
xie_zhihua68@aliyun.com

Abstract. When micro-expressions are mixed with normal or macro-expressions, it becomes increasingly challenging to spot them in long videos. Aiming at the specific time prior of *Micro-expression* (ME)s, a ME spotting network called *AEM-Net* (Adaptive Enhanced ME Detection Network) is proposed. The network improves the spotting performance in the following four aspects. First, the multi-stage channel feature extraction module is proposed to extract feature information of different depths. Then, an attention spatial-temporal module was used to obtain salient and discriminative micro-expression segments while suppressing the generation of excessively long or short suggestions. Thirdly, a ME-NMS (Non-Maximum Suppression) network is developed to reduce redundancy and decision errors. Finally, two spotting mechanisms named anchor_based and anchor_free are combined in our method. Extensive experiments have done on prevalent CAS(ME)^2 and the SAMM-Long ME databases to evaluate the spotting performance. The results show that the AEM-Net achieves an impressive performance, which outperforms other state-of-the-art methods.

Keywords: Micro-expression · Spotting · Attention mechanism · Spatial-temporal features

1   Introduction

Micro-expressions (MEs), which can be applied in teaching, sales, national security, psychology, crime detection and so on, are involuntary facial movements that occur spontaneously when individual encounters certain emotion but try

Z. Xie—This work is supported by the National Nature Science Foundation of China (No. 61861020), the Jiangxi Province Graduate Innovation Special Fund Project (No. YC2021-X06).

to suppress facial expressions [1]. Nowadays, MEs analysis plays a vital role in analyzing people's hidden emotions in various situations.

The duration of MEs is very short (generally no more than 500 ms, the precise length definition varies) [2], and the intensities of involved muscle movements are subtle [3]. For real-world applications, although MEs and macro-expressions (MaEs) do not occur at simultaneously, a video may contain one or more expression clips. In other words, the function of the spotting is to find as many correctly predicted onset frame and offset frame as possible and keep the intersection over union (IoU) of ground truths (GTs) and proposals not lower than the specified threshold (shown in Fig. 1). This work aimed to explore the ME spotting algorithm.

At present, ME spotting in long videos is still a worthwhile research topic with attractive attentions. However, several challenges remain unresolved. (1) The existing ME spotting samples are very limited. Without abundant data, the deep neural network will fully "drain" the training data and over-absorb the information from the training set, resulting in performance degradation in testing set. (2) Because of the subtle movements of MEs, it is difficult to find out MEs integrally in long video sequences. In other words, it is difficult to determine the boundaries of MEs. (3) The temporal extent of expression varies dramatically compared to the size of objects in an image - from a fraction of 0.04 s to 4 s. The significant distinction in duration also makes it very challenging to locate MEs and MaEs.

In order to cope with the above three difficulties to a certain extent, we proposed an adaptive enhanced micro-expression spotting network based on specific prior of ME. The main contributions are summarized as follows:

- We proposed a multi-stage channel feature extraction module, named Prelayer, which is capable of fusing multi stage of optical flow modal information and RGB modal information and alleviating the problem of insufficient samples.
- The anchor-based and anchor-free mechanisms were together used in the ME positioning task in order to better locate the micro expression boundary.
- A new post-processing network about MEs, named ME-NMS (Non-Maximum Suppression), is proposed to enhance the spotting accuracy of an extremely short fragment.

2   Related Works

In MEs spotting, the duration of the ME can be located by sliding the time window. Deep learning is used to perform ME localization at the first time in [4], which exploits 2D convolution to extract spatial features, 1D convolution to extract temporal features, and the network module to generate clip proposals in the time domain. Moilanen et al. [5] adopts local binary patterns (LBP) to extract feature differences between each frame of the video sequence to analyze the changes in facial motion. Davison et al. [6,7] spots MEs by histograms of oriented gradients. They represents all sequences detected within 100 frames

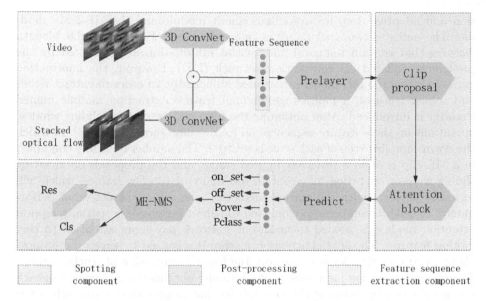

Fig. 1. The backbone of AEM-Net (Adaptive Enhanced Micro-Expression Detection Network) consists of four parts: the multi-stage channel feature extraction module (Prelayer), the clip proposal module, the position suppression and adaptive deep feature enhancement module (Attention block), and the ME-NMS module.

as true positives, including blinks and fixations. Meanwhile, motion sequences that were detected but not encoded, were classified as false positives. Patel et al. [8] proposed a method to compute optical flow vectors over a small scope and integrate them into the incorporated spatial-temporal region to determine the onset and offset times. Tran et al. [9] constructed a multiscale benchmark based on a sliding window multiscale assessment to fairly and better evaluate micro-expression identification methods. Wang et al. [10] implemented the same approach to spot micro-expressions in $CAS(ME)^2$. SOFTNet [11] proposed a multi-scale model to predict a score, which captures the possibility of a frame in an expression interval. Taking the location task as a regression problem, and promoting the learning efficiency by introducing pseudo tags. LSSNet [12] compared the effect of localization frames or segments, they also introduced a position suppression module, which is similar to a non-local neural network [13], which aims to suppress too long and too short proposals.

The AEM-Net proposed in this paper is an improvement on the work of LSSNet.

3   Method

3.1   Network Architecture

The proposed AEM-Net mainly consists of four parts, which are the multi-stage channel feature extraction module, the clip proposal module, position suppression and adaptive deep feature enhancement module and the ME-NMS module. The entire network structure is shown in Fig. 1. Firstly, the fixed-length features that contain temporal and spatial information are extracted by the pre-trained inflated 3D convolution network (I3D). However, the information extracted from the I3D model is not fused sufficiently. In order to extract richer and robust features, a multi-stage channel feature extraction module named Prelayer is introduced. After obtaining the features, we perform sliding window operations on these feature sequences on four scales (shown in Fig. 3), in which the down-sampling step of each scale is set to 2. The number of frames contained in a ME clip is often a relatively limited range, and the proposals obtained by sliding window operation may contain too many or too few frames, which will seriously interfere with the normal prediction and affect the detection performance. In order to suppress too long and too short proposals, a spatial-temporal attention module is needed to make our network pay more attention to tiny motion features. The spatial attention mechanism is used to screen the proposals in a certain range, so as to improve the feature expression of crucial regions. The channel attention mechanism automatically obtains the importance of each feature channel by learning the network so that automatically strengthen the important features and suppress the non-important features. Finally, the ME-NMS module is used to search local optimal candidate segments to suppress the false detection of candidate duration, so as to obtain a more reliable prediction.

3.2 Modules

3.2.1 Multi-stage Channel Feature Extraction

In order to extract richer and more robust features, we design a multi-stage channel feature extraction module, which function is to obtain and fuse informations in different depth and stage. The detail structure of the module is shown in Fig. 2. Specifically, we use three one-dimensional convolutional layers with the same number of convolutional kernels and different number of channels to convolute the spatio-temporal and the optical flow features from the I3D model. The unsuitable parameter of the convolutional layer will cause the offset of the estimated mean value, so we add a max pooling layer to reduce the offset error and retain more facial textures after each convolutional layer. Then, the feature sequences after max pooling operation are fused to obtain a richer feature representation. In addition, a convolutional layer with 1 * 7 kernels is set to not only reduce the dimensions and the number of parameters but also to extract informations in a different scale.

3.2.2 Clip Proposal Network

The anchor-based and anchor-free methods are jointly implemented to generate precise proposals for detection. The anchor-based module selects the closest-matched anchor and regresses the boundary step by step. The proposed anchor-free module regresses the distances from the center of an action instance to its boundaries.

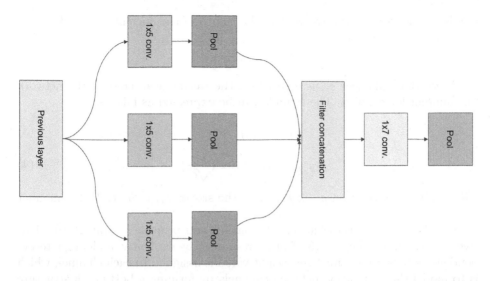

Fig. 2. The structure of multi-stage channel feature extraction, each convolution kernel is set up with 380, 640 and 1020 filters respectively to capture multi-stage channel feature.

The length of MaEs and MEs in the CAS(ME)^2 dataset ranges from 3 to 117 frames. To be exact, the length of MEs ranges from 8 to 16, and the length of MaEs ranges from 3 to 117. In view of attributes of MaEs and MEs, it is necessary to ensure that the generated proposals are between 2 and 128. However, the generated feature sequence is too large when the proposal scale is set to 2, which will lead to considerable computational complexity. Therefore, the case of scale 2 is discarded. In addition, five ratios [0.5, 0.75, 1, 1.5, 2] are set for the anchor of each scale, so we finally selected four scales from 2^3 to 2^6 as the anchor template. A convolutional layer with stride $s_i = 2$ is used to reduce the temporal length at each hierarchy. Suppose the regression output of layer i is l_i, r_i is the number of ratios of anchors, and the frame number of the sliding window is s_w. The number of anchors can be defined as follows:

$$n = r_i * s_w / l_i \qquad (1)$$

3.2.3 Spatio-temporal Attention Block

In order to pay more attention on short-term samples, we build an attention module. Firstly, building a location suppression module to suppress the too-long and too-short proposals. Secondly, setting up the channel-wise feature recalibrating module to increase the attention of the network to short time samples and enhances the performance of the network to spot MEs.

Assuming that the length of the sliding window is sw, the sampling frequency of this sliding window is f, the strides of the current layer are s_i, the input of sliding windows is $[bs, c_i, t_i]$, where bs is the batch size, c_i is the channel number. The formula that represents the length of the current proposals t_i can be expressed as follows:

$$t_i = \frac{s_w}{f \times s_i} \tag{2}$$

A position enhancer e_{ij} is used to set the weight of interest of the network for different length of t_i. The formula can be expressed as follows:

$$e_{ij} = \varphi_{ij} \times \rho_{ij} \tag{3}$$

$$w_{ij} = Softmax(\frac{e_{ij}}{\sqrt{c_i}}) \tag{4}$$

where the size of position ρ_{ij} is $[bs, s_i, t_i]$, the size of φ_{ij} is $[bs, t_i, 1]$, the number of ρ_{ij} is c_i.

We also focus on the channel relationship and propose a strategy to adaptively recalibrates channel-wise feature responses by explicitly modeling interdependencies between channels. A weight value is assigned to each channel, which is to model the correlation between channels by forming a bottleneck structure and output the same number of weights as the input channels.

In addition, due to the inconsistent length of the one-dimensional data samples, we used layer normalization. We added a dropout operation to prevent overfitting and further explored the setting of the drop ratio. The operation can be expressed:

$$\gamma_{ijl-1} = \gamma_{ijl-1} * r^{drop} \tag{5}$$

$$o_{ij} = \gamma'_{ij} \odot w_{ij} \tag{6}$$

γ_{ijl-1} are neurons in the neural network, set r^{drop} of the neurons stop working.

3.2.4 ME-NMS Module

In this paper, in order to further reduce category decision errors, we introduce ME-NMS module which is more suitable for ME spotting. In the post-processing process, we set the box with the highest score as the to-be-selected first, then arrange the candidate boxes according to their scores from the highest to the lowest, intersecting the current candidate segment with the union of the previous n best candidate, and those with scores lower than a threshold γ are discarded (γ is set to 0.2), so that the false detection samples can be screened out. Because the micro-expression duration is extremely short and susceptible to interference, we set the threshold of MEs based on the micro-expression prior. Owing to this operation, our multi-scale localization process to locate MEs more accurately.

Taking into account a video sequence, the anchor-based spotting module predicts anchors at each time position, for anchor-free, considering a temporal location a_j ($j \in \{0, ..., t-1\}$) at feature map F_i, we can map it back onto the input sequence:

$$J' = s_i / 2 + a_j * s_i \tag{7}$$

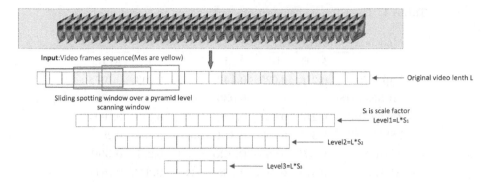

Fig. 3. Clip proposal network, which constructed of four scales of ME clip spotting

Since the length of micro-expressions in the CAS(ME)^2 dataset is between 3 and 16, considering the mapping mechanism, we set a threshold for micro-expression localization in the post-processing process to filter candidate clips:

$$f(i)_{off} - f(i)_{on} = l_{max} + s_w / 2 = 23 \qquad (8)$$

where l_{max} is the number of frames of the longest micro-expression video clip, and s_w is the slider box size of layer2. When the duration of the obtained candidate segment is greater than this threshold, the candidate segment will be taken as our final result.

4 Experiment

In our experiments, the TV-L1 optical flow operator is captured to extract the motion-related information for ME. Then, the I3D network, which is used to set fixed sliding windows, is constructed to extract the fixed-length features from the extracted optical flow and the original image. Finally, we add the multi-stage channel feature extraction module in front of the clip proposal network to make the network more sensitive to tiny motion features, and further, integrate the spatio-temporal information to alleviate the problem of insufficient samples. Three groups of comparative experiments are carried to test the performance of AEM-net. To keep the fairness, we adopt the popular F1-score metric for micro-expression spotting [14].

4.1 Experimental Results and Analysis

We compared the performance of AEM-Net with some recently proposed methods, the baseline we referred to is on two public ME long video datasets, CAS(ME)^2 [15] and SAMM-LV [16]. To keep the fairness, we adopt the popular F1-score metric for micro-expression spotting. The comparison results are shown in Table 1, demonstrating how the AEM-Net approach greatly improves

Table 1. The F1-score comparisons with other advanced methods

Models	CAS(ME)^2			SAMML-LV		
	MaE	ME	ALL	MaE	ME	ALL
Yap [17]	0.216	0.025	0.142	0.192	0.043	0.107
MESNet [18]	–	–	0.036	–	–	0.088
Zhang [19]	0.213	0.022	0.140	0.07	0.133	0.100
LSSNet [12]	0.368	0.050	0.314	**0.314**	0.191	0.286
AEM-Net	**0.377**	0.095	**0.325**	0.311	0.297	**0.300**
AEM-SE	0.315	**0.104**	0.286	0.260	**0.315**	0.264

Bold fonts indicate the best results

Table 2. Different spotting method effect on micro-expression spotting

	F1_score_macro	F1_score_micro	F1_score
Anchor-free (Af)	0.219	0.000	0.194
Anchor-based (Ab)	0.341	0.060	0.295
Ab+Af	**0.351**	**0.093**	**0.315**

Bold fonts indicate the best results

the performance of micro-expression localization. AEM-SE is a network in which the attention module of channel features is added to AEM-Net. From Table 1, we see that AEM-Net significantly improves spotting performance and AEM-SE make the network pay more attention to detail features but weaken the attention to structural features.

Results in Table 2 compare the effects of MEs spotting with the anchor-based method, the anchor-free method, and the anchor-based + anchor-free method.

The results show that the combine of two mechanisms improves the accuracy of MaEs localization and the MEs localization.

To further verify the contribution of multi-stage channel feature extraction module (Prelayer), the ablation experiments on this module are conducted on CAS(ME)^2. The spotting results are listed in Table 3. As seen in Table 3, compared to a network without Prelayer(Non pre), our network optimize the localization performance.

The impact of ME-NMS on network spotting performance is demonstrated in Table 4. The NMS method stands for the same post-processing method without adding a threshold of MEs, NMS-Nom is using the traditional NMS algorithm. ME-NMS enables a certain enhancement effect of micro-expression spotting performance by setting a prior thresholds that fit micro-expressions.

Table 3. The performance of adding Pre_Layer

	F1_score_macro	F1_score_micro	F1_score
Pre_layer	**0.351**	**0.093**	**0.315**
Non_pre	0.325	0.049	0.275

Bold fonts indicate the best results

Table 4. Performance of ME-NMS

	F1_score_macro	F1_score_micro	F1_score
NMS	**0.351**	0.086	0.312
ME-NMS	**0.351**	**0.093**	**0.315**
NMS_Nom	0.312	0.051	0.272

Bold fonts indicate the best results

5 Conclusions

In this paper, a Prelayer model is developed for ME spatial-temporal feature fusion, aiming to improve the processing of micro-motion samples. This work combines the anchor-free mechanism with the anchor-based mechanism to accurately locate the onset and offset frames of expressions, avoiding a prior biases regarding localization and duration. Moreover, the ME-NMS module is integrated to further reduces a prior-based false-positive micro-expression samples. In addition, channel attention and spatial attention jointly enhance the adaptive learning of key areas and deep features of the network. Comprehensive experiments demonstrate the effectiveness of our method. AEM-Net is capable of improving localized ME and MaE instances with various duration. It achieves promising performance on CAS(ME)^2 and SAMM-LV dataset. Meaningful feature learning and action localization in an end-to-end ME spotting framework are promising directions for future research. Besides, we will also further study the bio-informatics principle of micro-expressions and further improve the performance of ME spotting.

References

1. Porter, S., Brinke, L.: Reading between the lies: identifying concealed and falsified emotions in universal facial expressions. Psychol. Sci. **19**(5), 508–514 (2008)
2. Ekman, P., Friesen, W. V.: Nonverbal leakage and clues to deception. Psychiatry **32**(1), 88–106 (1969)
3. Porter, S., Brinke, L.: Reading between the lies identifying concealed and falsified emotions in universal facial expressions. Psychol. Sci. **19**(5), 508–514 (2008)
4. Zhang, Z., Chen, T. H., Liu, G., Fu, X.: SMEconvnet: a convolutional neural network for spotting spontaneous facial micro-expression from long videos. IEEE Access **6**(71), 143–171 (2018)
5. Antti, M., Guoying, Z., Matti, P.: Spotting rapid facial movements from videos using appearance-based feature difference analysis. In: International Conference on Pattern Recognition, pp. 1722–1727 (2014)

6. Adrian, D.K., Moi, Y.H., Cliff, L.: Micro-facial movement detection using individualised baselines and histogram based descriptors. In: International Conference on Systems, Man, and Cybernetics, pp. 1864–1869 (2015)
7. Adrian, D., Walied, M., Cliff, L., Choon, N.C., Moi, Y.H.: Objective micro-facial movement detection using FACS-based regions and baseline evaluation. In: International Conference on Automatic Face and Gesture Recognition (FG), pp. 642–649 (2018)
8. Devangini, P., Guoying, Z., Matti, P.: Spatiotemporal integration of optical flow vectors for micro-expression detection. In: International Conference on Advanced Concepts for Intelligent Vision Systems, pp. 369–380 (2015)
9. Thuong, T.K., Xiaopeng, H., Guoying, Z.: Sliding window based micro-expression spotting: a benchmark. In: International Conference on Advanced Concepts for Intelligent Vision Systems, pp. 542–553 (2017)
10. Sujing, W., Shuhuang, W., Xingsheng, Q., Jingxiu, L., Xiaolan, F.: A main directional maximal difference analysis for spotting facial movements from long-term videos. Neurocomputing 382–389 (2017)
11. Genbing, L., See, J., Laikuan, W.: Shallow optical flow three-stream CNN for macro-and micro-expression spotting from long videos. In: ICIP, pp. 2643–2647 (2021)
12. Wangwang, Y., Jingwen, J., Yongjie, L.: LSSNET: a two-stream convolutional neural network for spotting macro-and micro-expression in long videos. In: ACM Conference on Multimedia, pp. 4745–4749 (2021)
13. Xiaolong, W., Girshick, R., Gupta, A., Kaiming, H.: Non-local neural networks. In: IEEE Conference on Computer Vision and Pattern Recognition, pp. 7794–7803 (2018)
14. Li, J., Soladie, C., Seguier, R., Wang, S.-J., Yap, M.H.: Spotting micro-expressions on long videos sequences. In: IEEE International Conference on Automatic Face and Gesture Recognition, pp. 1–5 (2019)
15. Qu, F., Wang, S.J., Yan, W. J., Li, H., Wu, S., Fu, X.: CAS(ME) 2: a database for spontaneous macro-expression and micro-expression spotting and recognition. IEEE Trans. Affect. Comput. 9(4), 424–436 (2017)
16. Yap, C., Kendrick, C., Yap, M.: SAMM long videos: a spontaneous facial micro-and macro-expressions dataset. In: 2020 15th IEEE International Conference on Automatic Face and Gesture Recognition, pp. 194–199 (2020)
17. Yap, C., Yap, M., Davison, A., Cunningham, R.: 3D-CNN for facial micro- and macro-expression spotting on long video sequences using temporal oriented reference frame. arXiv:2105.06340 (2021)
18. Wang, S., He, Y., Li, J., Fu, X.: MESNet: a convolutional neural network for spotting multi-scale micro-expression intervals in long videos. IEEE Trans. Image Process. 3956–3969 (2021)
19. Zhang, L., et al.: Spatio-temporal fusion for macro-and micro-expression spotting in long video sequences. In: 2020 15th IEEE International Conference on Automatic Face and Gesture Recognition, pp. 245–252 (2022)

Augmented Feature Representation with Parallel Convolution for Cross-domain Facial Expression Recognition

Fan Yang[1,2], Weicheng Xie[1,2(✉)], Tao Zhong[1,2], Jingyu Hu[1,2], and Linlin Shen[1,2]

[1] Computer Vision Institute, School of Computer Science and Software Engineering, Shenzhen University, Shenzhen, China
{yangfan2021n,zhongtao2021n,2110276105}@email.szu.edu.cn
[2] Shenzhen Institute of Artificial Intelligence and Robotics for Society, Guangdong Key Laboratory of Intelligent Information Processing, Shenzhen University, Shenzhen, China
{wcxie,llshen}@szu.edu.cn

Abstract. Facial expression recognition (FER) has made significant progress in the past decade, but the inconsistency of distribution between different datasets greatly limits the generalization performance of a learned model on unseen datasets. Recent works resort to aligning feature distributions between domains to improve the cross-domain recognition performance. However, current algorithms use one output each layer for the feature representation, which can not well represent the complex correlation among multi-scale features. To this end, this work proposes a parallel convolution to augment the representation ability of each layer, and introduces an orthogonal regularization to make each convolution represent independent semantic. With the assistance of a self-attention mechanism, the proposed algorithm can generate multiple combinations of multi-scale features to allow the network to better capture the correlation among the outputs of different layers. The proposed algorithm achieves state-of-the-art (SOTA) performances in terms of the average generalization performance on the task of cross-database (CD)-FER. Meanwhile, when AFED or RAF-DB is used for the training, and other four databases, i.e. JAFFE, SFEW, FER2013 and EXPW are used for testing, the proposed algorithm outperforms the baselines by the margins of 5.93% and 2.24% in terms of the average accuracy.

Keywords: Domain generalization · Parallel convolution · Facial expression recognition · Self-attention

1 Introduction

Facial expression recognition (FER) is beneficial to understand human emotions and behaviors, which is widely applied in emotional computing, fatigue detec-

© The Author(s), under exclusive license to Springer Nature Switzerland AG 2022
W. Deng et al. (Eds.): CCBR 2022, LNCS 13628, pp. 297–306, 2022.
https://doi.org/10.1007/978-3-031-20233-9_30

tion and other fields. Over the last decade, people have proposed deep learning architectures and collected a large number of datasets, which greatly facilitates the study of FER. However, people interpret facial expressions differently, their annotations to the dataset are inevitably subjective. This leads to a relatively large domain shift between different datasets, and the difference in the collection scenes and object styles will also greatly increase this shift gap, which will greatly impair the performance of the model on unseen datasets.

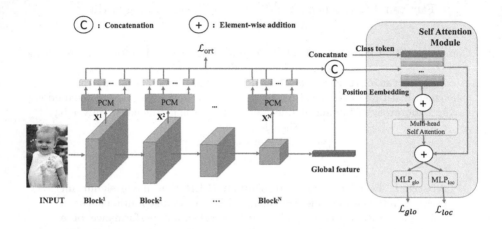

Fig. 1. An overview of our algorithm. N denote the number of blocks. X_i denote the feature maps output by $Block^i$. PCM denotes the Parallel Convolution Module in Fig. 2 (b). Both MLP_{glo} and MLP_{loc} consist of a fully connected layer.

Recently, many works try to learn domain-invariant features to reduce this domain shift. Chen et al. [2] argue that some local features in facial expressions are beneficial to Cross-Domain Facial Expression Recognition (CD-FER) because these local features are easier to transfer across different datasets, can represent more detailed information that is beneficial to fine-grained adaptation. However, these CD-FER algorithms employ unique output block for the feature representation of each layer, even the fusion of these outputs is unable to sufficiently encode the complex correlation among them.

In this work, we introduce a simple yet effective structure that only needs to use parallel convolution operations from different layers to extract rich hierarchical information. These features can help improve the generalization performance of the network on unseen datasets without affecting the discriminative performance on the source domain. Compared with other methods with unique convolution output, the proposed parallel convolution module augment the feature representation, and better capture the correlation among different scales of features from various layers, which is critical for the transferability ability of a recognition network.

Our main contributions are summarized as follows

- We introduce a novel parallel convolution to augment the feature representation of each layer, and a specific orthogonal loss to enhance the independence of branches for representing different semantics.
- We propose a hierarchical feature representation based on the multi-head self-attention module for cross-database FER, by modeling the complex correlation of the features from different layers with the combinations of multiple-scale features.
- By comparing the state of the arts on the task of cross-database FER, our method achieve state-of-the-art performances in terms of the average generalization performance.

2 Proposed Method

In this section, we introduce the proposed framework in Fig. 1, which mainly consists of three parts, i.e. a backbone network for representing the global discriminative features, a parallel convolution module in Sect. 2.1 used to extract features at different levels, and a multi-head self-attention module in Sect. 2.2 used to capture the correlation information between global discriminative and auxiliary features.

2.1 Parallel Convolution Module (PCM)

While one convolution output can effectively encode the expression hidden semantics with highly nonlinear representation, e.g. local variation of geometry structure and texture, it may not work well for the representation of the in-the-wild expression samples, which often include largely occluded or posed faces [2]. This challenge motivates us to construct multiple convolution outputs to represent the complex semantics implied in these samples.

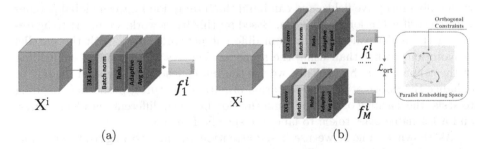

(a)   (b)

Fig. 2. (a) Original: One feature representation (b) Ours: Parallel Convolution Module (PCM). M denote the number of Parallel Feature Outputs of each network block.

Specifically, we introduce a parallel structure in Fig. 2(b) to capture multi-branch features for each block of the backbone network, which is formulated as follows

$$f_j^i = \phi(\sigma(Norm(Conv(X^i)))) \tag{1}$$

where i and j denote the depth of blocks and number of parallel features, respectively. σ and ϕ denote Relu activation function and the adaptive average pooling layer, respectively. There are two merits to using such a structure. First, parallel features can be generated by adding only a few network parameters, which does not sacrifice the training speed of the network; The second is that convolution can well capture the local information of features, such local information is more transferable for the task of FER.

In order to reduce the entanglement among the outputs of the parallel convolution, so as to enable each parallel output to learn specific semantic and improve the generalization ability of the feature representation, we further introduce the regularization term of orthogonalization as follows

$$\mathcal{L}_{ort} = -\frac{1}{B} \sum_{i=1}^{B} \sum_{m=1}^{M} \sum_{n=1}^{M} (f_m^i)^T f_n^i \tag{2}$$

where f_m^i denotes the m-th parallel feature from the i-th block for each sample.

2.2 Multi-head Self-attention Module (MSH)

It is revealed in [1] that the features extracted by the network become more task-specific as the depth of the neural network increases. That is, the shallow layers often represent some relatively similar features which may have better transferability, while the deep layers will encode the features for specific tasks. Based on this, as shown in Fig. 1, we design a cascaded module to leverage hierarchical features from different depths to help improve its generalization ability.

Visual transformers (ViT) [3] can well capture global information in images with global receptive fields, and can build the interaction between global patches with the self-attention mechanism. Based on this framework, we resort to aggregating the multi-scale features from different network blocks with the parallel convolution, rather than using the sequence features of split patch embedding in the original ViT. Specifically, we use the multi-head self-attention module to enhance the information representation of parallel features, positional encoding to assist the learning of positional information between different parallel features, and a learnable class token to label the specific features.

As shown in Fig. 1, we use a self-attention module to augment the information of parallel features. Since the classification token summarizes the global information of other features, and it does not depend on the input information, thus can avoid the preference for a certain parallel information and help the model to improve its generalization performance.

Formally, we first concatenate all features as follows

$$F = ((f^1 \oplus f^2 \oplus ... f^M) \oplus f^g \oplus f^c) + f^p \qquad (3)$$

where M denotes the number of parallel features for each layer, f^g denotes the global feature and the f^c is a learnable classification token. Matrices f^i, f^g, f^c are with the dimension of $(B, M \times D)$, where B and D denote the batch size and the feature dimension, respectively. Matrix f^p is a learnable embedding with the dimension of $(B, (M+2) \times D)$ for describing the location information of the features. Then, we use a multi-head attention module to capture the key features, while integrating information from all features. Specifically, we transformed the feature F into queries q, keys k and values v as follows

$$[q, k, v] = F[W_q, W_k, W_v] \qquad (4)$$

To aggregate these features, the attention weights are adjusted as follows

$$A = \varepsilon(\frac{qk^T}{\sqrt{d}}) \qquad (5)$$

where ε denote the Softmax function, and d denote the dimension of feature. Finally, the output of self-attention can be obtained as follows

$$F' = Av + F \qquad (6)$$

where v is the value in Eq. (4).

2.3 Joint Training Loss

Based on the features with the self-attention model, i.e. F' in Eq. (6), the classification probabilities are formulated as follows

$$p_{i,c}^{loc} = \varepsilon(MLP_{loc}(F'_{loc})) \qquad (7)$$

$$p_{i,c}^{glo} = \varepsilon(MLP_{glo}(F')) \qquad (8)$$

where F'_{loc} is the feature output by the self attention module of $f^1 \oplus f^2 \oplus ... f^M$ in Eq. (3) and is a part of F'. Finally, the two classification losses in Fig. 1 are then formulated as follows

$$\mathcal{L}_{loc} = -\frac{1}{B} \sum_{i=1}^{B} \sum_{c=1}^{K} y_{i,c} log(p_{i,c}^{loc}) \qquad (9)$$

$$\mathcal{L}_{glo} = -\frac{1}{B} \sum_{i=1}^{B} \sum_{c=1}^{K} y_{i,c} log(p_{i,c}^{glo}) \qquad (10)$$

where K denotes the number of expression classes. $p_{i,c}^{loc}$ and $p_{i,c}^{glo}$ are the predicted probabilities of the c-th class specific to the local and global branches. The total loss is then formulated as follows

$$\mathcal{L} = \mathcal{L}_{glo} + \lambda\mathcal{L}_{loc} + \gamma\mathcal{L}_{ort} \qquad (11)$$

where λ and γ are set as 1 in this work.

3   Experimental Results

3.1   Implementation Details

We use six mainstream facial expression datasets for the evaluation, follow the protocol as [2], and use the IResNet50 pretrained on the MS-Celeb-1M [13] as the backbone. The setting of the parameters specific to the newly added layers follow the Xavier algorithm [12]. For the parallel convolution in Fig. 2(b), M is set as 5, the feature dimension of each parallel convolution output, i.e. D, is set to 16. For global feature representation, i.e. f^g in Eq. (3), another convolution operation and pooling layer are performed to encode a feature vector with the dimension of $N \times D = 64$.

Table 1. Comparison of cross-database performances. The results are reproduced by our implementation with exactly the same source dataset, backbone network and pre-trained model. The best and 2nd best performances are labeled with bold and underline. * or † denotes the results that are implemented by us or cited from [2].

Method	Source set	JAFFE	SFEW	FER2013	EXPW	Mean	Reference
Baseline*	RAF	52.58	51.60	**57.89**	70.09	58.04	-
ICID† [14]	RAF	50.57	48.85	53.70	69.54	55.66	Neurocomputing2019
LPL† [15]	RAF	53.05	48.85	55.89	66.90	56.17	CVPR2017
FTDNN† [16]	RAF	52.11	47.48	55.98	67.72	55.82	SIBGRAPI2017
SAFN† [17]	RAF	**61.03**	**52.98**	55.64	64.91	58.64	CVPR2019
AGRA* [2]	RAF	58.68	51.37	57.49	<u>70.73</u>	<u>59.53</u>	TPAMI2021
Ours*	RAF	<u>59.15</u>	<u>52.75</u>	<u>57.82</u>	**71.42**	**60.28**	-
Baseline*	AFED	57.74	47.25	46.55	49.50	50.26	-
ICID† [14]	AFED	57.28	44.27	46.92	52.91	50.34	Neurocomputing2019
LPL† [15]	AFED	61.03	<u>49.77</u>	49.54	55.26	53.9	CVPR2017
FTDNN† [16]	AFED	57.75	47.25	46.36	52.89	51.06	SIBGRAPI2017
SAFN† [17]	AFED	64.79	49.08	48.89	<u>55.69</u>	<u>54.61</u>	CVPR2019
AGRA* [2]	AFED	**65.25**	48.16	<u>49.73</u>	51.56	53.67	TPAMI2021
Ours*	AFED	<u>62.44</u>	**52.29**	**51.43**	**58.62**	**56.19**	-

3.2   Comparison with the State of the Arts

To study the generalization performance of our method on unseen datasets, we use RAF [7] or AFED [2] as source domain dataset, and JAFFE, SFEW2.0 [4], FER2013 [5] and EXPW [6] are used as target datasets, while only the source domain dataset are used for the training. The results are shown in Table 1.

Table 1 shows that our method achieved the best performances among six state-of-the-art algorithms in terms of the mean accuracy. For each target dataset, our algorithm either achieves the best performance, or ranks the 2nd. Meanwhile, compared with the baseline, the proposed algorithm achieved the improvement of 2.24% or 5.93% when RAF or AFED is used as source dataset. Specifically, our algorithm appears to be more effective than the competitors on the target datasets with larger number of samples, e.g. FER2013 and EXPW.

3.3 Algorithm Analysis

In this section, we first perform ablation study in Table 2 to analyze the role of each module, where we can see from the 1st and 2nd rows that PCM help the model achieve an improvement of 4.56% over the baseline in terms of the average generalization performance. It is revealed in the 2nd–4th rows that using only the self-attention mechanism may affect the generalization ability. It pays attention to the features that help improve the discrimination performance on the original domain, while affecting the generalization performance on the target domain. The learnable classification token with a fixed position can effectively integrate features between different levels, and it is not biased towards a certain feature, thus can help the model improve the generalization ability.

Table 2. The results of ablation study. CLS-token denotes a learnable embedding for integrating information of different features in Eq. (3). OrtLoss is the regularization loss in Eq. (2)

Backbone	PCM	MSH	CLS-token	OrtLoss	JAFFE	SFEW	FER2013	EXPW	Mean
IResNet50	✗	✗	✗	✗	57.74	47.25	46.55	49.50	50.26
IResNet50	✔	✗	✗	✗	**63.84**	48.16	49.73	57.66	54.84
IResNet50	✔	✔	✗	✗	56.80	47.25	49.93	56.75	52.68
IResNet50	✔	✔	✔	✗	61.97	47.93	**52.38**	**60.29**	55.64
IResNet50	✔	✔	✔	✔	62.44	52.29	51.43	58.62	56.19

Table 3. Parameter sensitivity analysis for the parallel convolution based on the training of AFED. 1* denotes one parallel branch with the feature dimension being the dimension sum of features from the five parallel branches.

Backbone	M	JAFFE	SFEW	FER2013	EXPW	Mean
IResNet50	1	61.03	47.70	49.59	57.13	53.86
IResNet50	3	**62.91**	47.47	48.98	56.83	54.04
IResNet50	5	61.97	**47.93**	**52.38**	**60.29**	**55.64**
IResNet50	7	59.15	47.70	50.34	56.70	53.47
IResNet50	1*	60.56	45.87	49.23	55.40	52.76

In order to give insight into the features learned by our method during the training process. We visualize how the features of different domains evolve as training progresses. Specifically, we simultaneously input samples from different domains into the network to obtain features, use t-SNE to project them into the 2D space, and present the results in Fig. 3. It shows that the baseline model can separate the source samples, while it can not well distinguish the data of the target domain. As shown in the bottom row of Fig. 3, our algorithm obtain features that are still separable in the feature space. More importantly, samples from different domains are more concentrated compared with the baseline, which means that the learned features can be made have similar distributions in different domains, by better learning the complex correlation among features from different layers, thereby yielding more powerful generalization ability.

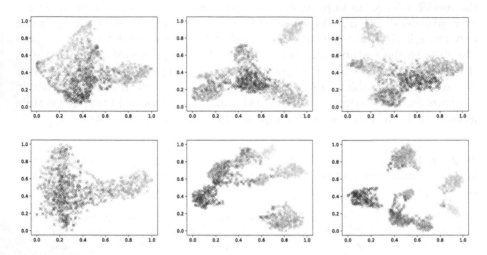

Fig. 3. Illustration of the feature distributions learned by IResNet (upper, baseline) and our algorithm (lower) at epochs of 1, 21 and 51 in the 1st-3rd columns, respectively. 'o' denotes the sample from the source domain (RAF-DB), 'x' denotes the sample from the target domain (SFEW2.0). Different colors represent different labels.

We also study the performance sensitivity against the number of Parallel Convolution branches, i.e. M in Fig. 2, the results are shown in Table 3. Table 3 shows that the setting of $M = 5$ achieves the best average performance. While too few parallel outputs can not sufficiently capture the rich hierarchical information among different layers, too many outputs increase the possibility of feature entanglement, which may decrease the cross-database generalization performance. To study whether the improvement is resulted from the dimensional ascension by the parallel convolution, we evaluate the performance of a specific setting, i.e. the feature dimension is set as the same as that of the proposed convolution, in the last row of Table 3. These results show that the improvements are not resulted from the mere dimensional ascension.

In order to give insight into the working mechanism of the proposed parallel convolution, we visualize the heatmaps output by the parallel convolution in Fig. 4, where the heatmaps with the similar semantics are gathered in the same column with an alignment. Figure 4 shows that the heatmaps in the same column appear with the similar semantic, while the outputs of different parallel branches shows with diverse and independent semantics. When the parallel convolution is performed, semantic alignment is actually not employed. In this case, the random combinations of independent semantics can thus enhance the feature representation ability for in-the-wild circumstances with complex semantics.

Original   Parallel 1   Parallel 2   Parallel 3   Parallel 4   Parallel 5

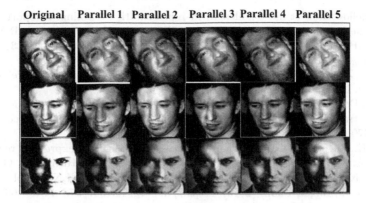

Fig. 4. Visualization of heatmaps from the outputs of parallel convolution branches.

4   Conclusion

In this work, we introduce a parallel convolution to augment the feature representation ability for in-the-wild expressions with complex semantics, and an additional regularization loss to let each branch independently respond to a semantic. Based on multiple combinations of the outputs from the parallel convolution, a self attention is followed to encode the correlations among multiple layers. Experimental results on cross-database FER show that our algorithm can better capture the complex correlations among multiple layers, and largely outperforms the state of the arts in terms of the cross-domain generalization performance. In our future work, we will give insight into the working mechanism of the parallel convolution for the generalization ability improvement. Other paradigms in addition to ViT will be investigated to test the generality of the proposed parallel convolution and the specific regularization loss.

Acknowledgements. The work was supported by the Science and Technology Project of Guangdong Province under grant no. 2020A1515010707, Natural Science Foundation of China under grants no. 62276170, 91959108, the Science and Technology Innovation Commission of Shenzhen under grant no. JCYJ20190808165203670.

References

1. Yosinski, J., et al.: How transferable are features in deep neural networks?. In: Advances In Neural Information Processing Systems, vol. 27 (2014)
2. Chen, T., et al.: Cross-domain facial expression recognition: a unified evaluation benchmark and adversarial graph learning. IEEE Trans. Pattern Anal. Mach. Intell. (2021)
3. Vaswani, A., et al.: Attention is all you need. In: Advances in Neural Information Processing Systems, vol. 30 (2017)
4. Dhall, A., et al.: Static facial expression analysis in tough conditions: Data, evaluation protocol and benchmark. In: 2011 IEEE International Conference on Computer Vision Workshops (ICCV Workshops). IEEE (2011)

5. Goodfellow, I.J., et al.: Challenges in representation learning: a report on three machine learning contests. In: Lee, M., Hirose, A., Hou, Z.-G., Kil, R.M. (eds.) ICONIP 2013. LNCS, vol. 8228, pp. 117–124. Springer, Heidelberg (2013). https://doi.org/10.1007/978-3-642-42051-1_16
6. Zhang, Z., et al.: From facial expression recognition to interpersonal relation prediction. Int. J. Comput. Vision **126**(5), 550–569 (2018)
7. Li, S., Deng, W.: Reliable crowdsourcing and deep locality-preserving learning for unconstrained facial expression recognition. IEEE Trans. Image Process. **28**(1), 356–370 (2018)
8. Yan, K., Zheng, W., Cui, Z., Zong, Y.: Cross-database facial expression recognition via unsupervised domain adaptive dictionary learning. In: Hirose, A., Ozawa, S., Doya, K., Ikeda, K., Lee, M., Liu, D. (eds.) ICONIP 2016. LNCS, vol. 9948, pp. 427–434. Springer, Cham (2016). https://doi.org/10.1007/978-3-319-46672-9_48
9. Zheng, W., et al.: Cross-domain color facial expression recognition using transductive transfer subspace learning. IEEE Trans. Affect. Comput. **9**(1), 21–37 (2016)
10. Ganin, Y., Lempitsky, V.: Unsupervised domain adaptation by backpropagation. In: International Conference on Machine Learning. PMLR (2015)
11. Piratla, V., Netrapalli, P., Sarawagi, S.: Efficient domain generalization via common-specific low-rank decomposition. In: International Conference on Machine Learning. PMLR (2020)
12. Glorot, X., Bengio, Y.: Understanding the difficulty of training deep feedforward neural networks. In: Proceedings of the Thirteenth International Conference on Artificial Intelligence and Statistics. JMLR Workshop and Conference Proceedings (2010)
13. Guo, Y., Zhang, L., Hu, Y., He, X., Gao, J.: MS-Celeb-1M: a dataset and benchmark for large-scale face recognition. In: Leibe, B., Matas, J., Sebe, N., Welling, M. (eds.) ECCV 2016. LNCS, vol. 9907, pp. 87–102. Springer, Cham (2016). https://doi.org/10.1007/978-3-319-46487-9_6
14. Ji, Y., et al.: Cross-domain facial expression recognition via an intra-category common feature and inter-category distinction feature fusion network. Neurocomputing **333**, 231–239 (2019)
15. Li, S., Deng, W., Du, J.P.: Reliable crowdsourcing and deep locality-preserving learning for expression recognition in the wild. In: Proceedings of the IEEE Conference on Computer Vision and Pattern Recognition (2017)
16. Zavarez, M.V., Berriel, R.F., Oliveira-Santos, T.: Cross-database facial expression recognition based on fine-tuned deep convolutional network. In: 2017 30th SIBGRAPI Conference on Graphics, Patterns and Images (SIBGRAPI). IEEE (2017)
17. Xu, R., et al.: Larger norm more transferable: an adaptive feature norm approach for unsupervised domain adaptation. In: Proceedings of the IEEE/CVF International Conference on Computer Vision (2019)

Hemispheric Asymmetry Measurement Network for Emotion Classification

Ruofan Yan, Na Lu$^{(\boxtimes)}$, Xu Niu, and Yuxuan Yan

School of Automation Science and Engineering, Xi'an Jiaotong University, Xi'an 710049, China
lvna2009@xjtu.edu.cn

Abstract. Electroencephalogram (EEG) based emotion recognition has received considerable attention from many researchers. Methods based on deep learning have made significant progress. However, most of the existing solutions still need to use manually extracted features as the input to train the network model. Neuroscience studies suggest that emotion reveals asymmetric differences between the left and right hemispheres of the brain. Inspired by this fact, we proposed a hemispheric asymmetry measurement network (HAMNet) to learn discriminant features for emotion classification tasks. Our network is end-to-end and reaches the average accuracy of 96.45%, which achieves the state-of-the-art (SOTA) performance. Moreover, the visualization and analysis of the learned features provides a possibility for neuroscience to study the mechanism of emotion.

Keywords: Deep learning · Convolution neural network · EEG · Emotion recognition

1 Introduction

Emotion carries unique biological information, which integrates people's perceptions and behaviors. The analysis and recognition of emotions has become an interdisciplinary research topic, and received an increasing amount of applications in disease monitoring [1], task workload estimation [2] etc. Traditional emotion recognition methods based on facial expressions, voice tones, and body posture [3] can be camouflaged and thus are not reliable enough. In contrast, EEG signal is spontaneously generated by the human nervous system, which can very well reflect emotional states and is extremely hard to forge.

Deep learning approaches for EEG emotion classification have shown great potential in this field which [4, 5] can be divided into two categories: extracted features based methods and end-to-end methods. Zheng and Lu [6] extracted differential entropy (DE) [7] as EEG features, and used deep belief networks (DBN) for classification. These methods require handcrafted features and expert knowledge. On the other hand, end-to-end network has been proposed to promote the algorithm performance in real-time scenarios. In [5] a LSTM-based deep recursive neural network (RNN) was proposed to automatically learn the features from the original EEG signals. But the performance of end-to-end networks still needs to be improved. The interpretability of deep learning solutions is also a concern and has not been solved in previous studies. To develop a more efficient end-to-end network solution for EEG emotion classification, a prior knowledge incorporated dual channel network is developed which measures the hemispheric asymmetry during emotion movement.

The main contributions of this study are as follows: (a) We proposed an end-to-end HAMNet, omitting the manual denoising and feature extraction in traditional methods, which obtains SOTA performance in emotion classification. (b) A dual channel mirror structure is applied to process EEG data to incorporate the spatial discrepancy between the two brain hemispheres. (c) We visualized the temporal and spatial EEG features, and spotted some inspiring discoveries in the field of neuroscience.

2 Related Work

In the past decade, correlations between emotion and EEG has been extensively researched and demonstrated. Neuroscience research shows that emotion-producing mechanisms are related to the asymmetry between the hemispheres of the brain [8]. The EEG signals in different frequency bands and channels have enclosed informative features for different emotions. Previous researches suggest that signals in gamma-band (roughly 30–100 Hz) are strongly related to emotional cognition [9, 10].

Duan et al. [11] implemented DE to represent emotional state representations. The combination of DE on symmetrical electrodes (Differential asymmetry, DASM; and rational asymmetry, RASM) [7] was also considered as emotional features. Besides, to smooth the feature sequence, the moving average filter and linear dynamic system (LDS) approach were applied.

Although researchers have focused on the asymmetry between the hemispheres of the brain and extracted features that contain mismatched information, these methods usually require prior knowledge, manual feature extraction and some feature smoothing methods. In [12], Niu et al. proposed a novel knowledge-driven feature component interpretable network (KFCNet) to solve the motor imagery classification problem. Band-pass linear-phase digital finite impulse response filters are applied to initialize the temporal convolution kernels. Inspired by the above methods, we designed filter banks in gamma band, and embed prior knowledge into convolution layer to train an emotion classification model.

3 Method

In this section we will introduce the architecture of HAMNet, data mirroring, and the two-step training strategy of pre-traning and fine-tuning. Architecture of HAMNet is shown in Fig. 1 where BN means batch normalization and PA means power calculation. Parameters of each layer are illustrated in the figure. Specifically, HAMNet includes a mirrored data input layer, two parallel convolution layers, a power calculation layer, a relational metric layer, a classification layer, and a softmax layer. Layers in the orange dotted box is the single channel network for pre-training, and the module in the blue dotted box is the parallel network for fine-tuning.

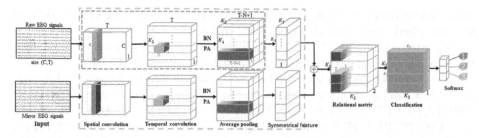

Fig. 1. Architecture of the HAMNet

3.1 Network Structure

Firstly, the raw EEG data trial $X_R \in R^{C \times T}$ is mirrored in the channel dimension, denoted as $X_M \in R^{C \times T}$. C represents the number of electrodes, and T represents the number of sampling points. They are both used as the parallel depthwise input samples. The details of mirror processing will be discussed in Sect. 3.2. The first layer of HAMNet implements spatial filtering and achieves the effect of spatial source separation through spatial convolution.

The second parallel convolutional layer shares the same parameters, which are initialized by the FIR filter bank designed by windowed inverse Fourier transform, in analogy to temporal filtering. The pass band of FIR filters ranges from 40 Hz to 76 Hz, and each filter bandwidth is 2 Hz. A total of 18 sets of filters are used.

For a discrete signal sequence $\{x_1, x_2, ...x_n\}$ in a specific frequency band, the Fourier transform of each point is denoted as X_k, $k = \{1, 2, ...n\}$, the average power spectral density (PSD) can be formulated as

$$PSD = \frac{\sum_{k=1}^{n} |X_k|^2}{n}. \tag{1}$$

Through batch normalization (BN), average power calculation (PA) and pooling layer, it is equivalent to obtain the PSD of the samples and the symmetric mirror samples. Then the obtained symmetric features are concatenated and fed to the following relational metric learning layer.

The relational metric layer performs a convolution operation on the concatenated input to automatically measure the relationship between the two symmetric samples. This layer can implicitly learn the difference between the original EEG distribution and its symmetric distribution. Therefore, the asymmetry of motion EEG distribution can be considered. The output of the relation between the symmetric samples are further fed to the classification layer. The final emotion labels are given by the classification layer and the softmax layer. Cross-entropy loss is used to update the network.

3.2 Mirror Data Processing

The input to HAMNet is composed of the original EEG sequence and its mirror version. Based on the EEG mirror processing, a symmetric version of a specific emotion signal distribution can be obtained. The relation comparison between the original distribution and its mirror distribution can shed new light on the emotion classification considering the hemispheric asymmetry of emotion EEG signal.

We symmetrically flip the original samples to get the mirror samples according to the electrode position. Electrodes are configured according to ESI NeuroScan System with 62 channels in total as shown in Fig. 2. The data in the middle column (FPZ, FZ, FCZ, CZ, CPZ, PZ, POZ, OZ) does not change, and the 27 pairs of electrode channels (FP1, F7, F3, FT7, FC3, T7, P7, C3, TP7, CP3, P3, O1, AF3, F5, F7, FC5, FC1, C5, C1, CP5, CP1, P5, P1, PO7, PO5, PO3, and CB1 of the left hemisphere, and FP2, F8, F4, FT8, FC4, T8, P8, C4, TP8, CP4, P4, O2, AF4, F6, F8, FC6, FC2, C6, C2, CP6, CP2, P6, P2, PO8, PO6, PO4, and CB2 of the right hemisphere) are mirrored respectively. The amount of input data has been doubled in this way.

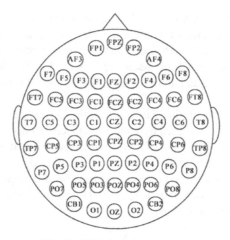

Fig. 2. ESI NeuroScan system

3.3 Pre-training and Fine-Tuning

Two stages of training is adopted. Pre-training only takes the raw EEG data as input through single-branch convolutional network (branch in the orange dotted box), and directly sends the output to the pooling and classification layers. Then fine-tuning operation feeds both the original and mirrored data into the overall HAMNet network with the two branches altogether. The parameters of pre-training result for spatial convolution are loaded as its initialization. The temporal convolutional layers are frozen in the fine-tuning stage.

4 Experiments

In this section, we firstly introduce the emotion dataset and the details of the experiment settings. Then we compare our results with baselines, visualize the learned features and discuss the results.

4.1 Dataset

SEED [6] from Shanghai Jiaotong University is a collection of EEG emotion data provided by BCMI Labs. The dataset contains EEG signals of subjects watching movie clips labeled as positive, negative, and neutral. The experiment provides 15 movie clips of four minutes each. Each experiment has 15 trials. 15 subjects each performed three experiments with a one-week interval between each experiment. There are raw data and feature extraction data in the dataset, we choose the raw data in this research. EEG signals are downsampled to 200 Hz, and cropped by second to generate the samples.

4.2 Experimental Setting

We adopt five-fold cross-validation method on each experiment[13]. There are about 680 samples per fold. We take the average classification accuracy (ACC) of 3 experiments across all subjects as a metric to evaluate model performance. In the network, K_1 is set as 16, K_2 is set as 18, and N is set as 41. Adam optimization is employed to minimize the loss function. The learning rate is set as 10^{-4} in pre-training and changes to 0.5×10^{-4} while fine-tuning. We set the first-moment decay term and the second-moment decay term to 0.9 and 0.999 respectively. 800 epochs are iterated in pre-training and 600 epochs are iterated in fine-tuning with a batch size of 100. Pytorch is used for coding. A computer server with a CPU E5–2643 of 3.40 GHz and a GPU of NVIDIA Quadro NVS315 was used.

4.3 Experiment Results

The performance comparison of our method with traditional methods and multiple deep network-based solutions were conducted on SEED dataset. The method in [10] was the first one using DE and DASM as emotion-related features, and training a SVM as the classifier. The method in [6] proposed a deep belief network (DBN) with DE features extracted from part of channels. In [14] which was published in 2022, the raw EEG signals were converted into a four-dimensional space-spectral-temporal representation, and then the 4D-ann network adopted spectral and spatial attention mechanisms to adaptively assign weights to different brain regions and frequency bands. Li et al. [15] proposed a novel bi-hemispheric discrepancy model (BiHDM) in 2020 which considered the asymmetric differences between two hemispheres and achieved excellent performance. We use ACC to compare our model with the above four baseline models, as shown in Table 1.

Table 1. The classification accuracy of different methods on SEED.

Method	SVM [10]	DBN [6]	BiHDM [15]	4D-ANN [14]	**HAMNet**
Feature	DE	DE	Raw data	Raw data	Raw data
ACC(%)	84.22	86.65	93.12	96.10	**96.45**

The ACC of our model reaches 96.45%, which achieves the state-of-the-art performance on the SEED dataset comparing with the baseline models. The ACC of the pre-training network was 93.53%, which increased by 2.92% after fine-tuning, which has well demonstrated the effectiveness of our two-step training strategy. Figure 3 shows the average accuracy on each subject. An obvious improvement with fine-tuning can be observed.

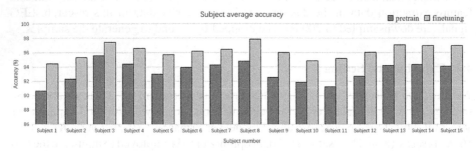

Fig. 3. ACC of HAMNet on each subject

4.4 Visualization of the Learned Temporal Features

To visualize the features learned from the time convolution layer based on FIR bandpass filters, we visualized the convolution kernels trained on Subject 4, as shown in Fig. 4. Compared with the initial filter curve, the learned filters with axis offset shows the adaptability of time domain learning, indicating effective information in narrow bands.

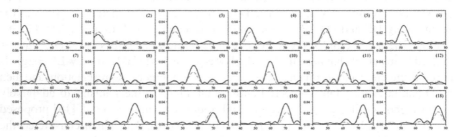

Fig. 4. Illustration of the amplitude-frequency maps of 18 filter banks after Fourier transform. The blue dotted line represents the initial filter state, and the red solid line depicts the filters learned by the temporal layer.

For some filters, the main lobe amplitude of the curve increases, and the side lobe amplitude decreases. Therefore the spectrum leakage phenomenon is reduced, indicating the performance has been automatically improved.

4.5 Visualization of the Learned Spatial Features

Figure 5 shows the brain topographic map of the kernels in the parallel spatial convolution layers of Subject 4. The number of spatial convolution kernels was set to 16. The two edge electrodes of CB1 and CB2 were removed due to insignificance. By comparing the brain maps corresponding to the original data and the mirror data, we can observe that the two features are almost symmetric, and the phenomenon of event-related synchronization and event-related desynchronization occurs. From the dark areas, it can be observed that the frontal lobe, temporal lobe and central area of the brain contain important information related to emotion recognition.

Original data

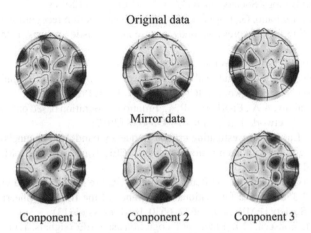

Mirror data

Conponent 1   Conponent 2   Conponent 3

Fig. 5. Illustration of the brain topographic map. The black dots in the figure represent the positions of 60 electrodes, and the red and blue colors represent the positive and negative weights respectively. The darker the color, the greater the absolute value is.

5 Conclusion

In this paper, inspired by the research on emotion generation mechanism in neuroscience, we proposed an emotion classification method based on symmetric channel deep learning model. The proposed HAMNet is an end-to-end network, which does not need to extract features manually, saves computation, and has a better performance than the current mainstream emotion classification methods. The processing speed of emotion recognition reaches about 1 s, providing a possible solution for real-time classification. In addition, our model uses band-pass filters to embed emotional band prior knowledge into the convolution layer to initialize parameters. Based on the results, we visualized and analyzed the temporal and spatial learned features, and verified the effectiveness of asymmetric differences in the cerebral hemisphere in emotion classification tasks. Besides, the features learned by our model are interpretable after visualization, which provides the possibility for neuroscience scientists to study the mechanism of emotion.

Acknowledgement. This work is supported by National Natural Science Foundation of China grant 61876147.

References

1. Ali, M., Mosa, A.H., Machot, F.A., Kyamakya, K.: EEG-based emotion recognition approach for e-healthcare applications. In: 2016 Eighth International Conference on Ubiquitous and Future Networks (ICUFN), pp. 946–950. IEEE Press (2016)
2. Kothe, C.A., Makeig, S.: Estimation of task workload from EEG data: new and current tools and perspectives. In: 2011 Annual International Conference of the IEEE Engineering in Medicine and Biology Society, pp. 6547–6551. IEEE Press (2011)
3. Kessous, L., Castellano, G., Caridakis, G.: Multimodal emotion recognition in speech-based interaction using facial expression, body gesture and acoustic analysis. J. Multimodal User Interf. 3(1), 33–48 (2010)
4. Yang, Y., Wu, Q., Qiu, M., Wang, Y., Chen, X.: Emotion recognition from multi-channel EEG through parallel convolutional recurrent neural network. In: 2018 International Joint Conference on Neural Networks (IJCNN), pp. 1–7. IEEE Press (2018)
5. Alhagry, S., Fahmy, A.A., El-Khoribi, R.A.: Emotion recognition based on EEG using LSTM recurrent neural network. Emotion 8(10), 355–358 (2017)
6. Zheng, W.L., Lu, B.L.: Investigating critical frequency bands and channels for EEG-based emotion recognition with deep neural networks. IEEE Trans. Autonom. Mental Dev. 7(3), 162–175 (2015)
7. Shi, L.C., Jiao, Y.Y., Lu, B.L.: Differential entropy feature for EEG-based vigilance estimation. In: 2013 35th Annual International Conference of the IEEE Engineering in Medicine and Biology Society (EMBC), pp. 6627–6630. IEEE Press (2013)
8. Alarcao, S.M., Fonseca, M.J.: Emotions recognition using EEG signals: a survey. IEEE Trans. Affect. Comput. 10(3), 374–393 (2017)
9. Keil, A., Müller, M.M., Gruber, T., et al.: Effects of emotional arousal in the cerebral hemispheres: a study of oscillatory brain activity and event-related potentials. J. Clin. Neurophysiol. 112(11), 2057–2068 (2001)
10. Balconi, M., Lucchiari, C.: Consciousness and arousal effects on emotional face processing as revealed by brain oscillations. a gamma band analysis. Int. J. Psychophysiol. 67(1), 41–46 (2008)
11. Duan, R.N., Zhu, J.Y., Lu, B.L.: Differential entropy feature for EEG-based emotion classification. In: 6th International IEEE/EMBS Conference on Neural Engineering. IEEE 2013, pp. 81–84 (2013)
12. Niu, X., Lu, N., Kang, J.H., Cui, Z.Y.: Knowledge-driven feature component interpretable network for motor imagery classification. J. Neural Eng. 19(1), 016032 (2022)
13. Zheng, W.L., Zhu, J.Y., Lu, B.L.: Identifying stable patterns over time for emotion recognition from EEG. J. IEEE Trans. Affective Comput. 10(3), 417–429 (2017)
14. Xiao, G., Shi, M., Ye, M., et al.: 4D attention-based neural network for EEG emotion recognition. J. Cogn. Neurodyn. 2022, 1–14 (2022). https://doi.org/10.1007/s11571-021-097 51-5
15. Li, Y., Wang, L., Zheng, W., et al.: A novel bi-hemispheric discrepancy model for EEG emotion recognition. IEEE Trans. Cogn. Dev. Syst. 13(2), 354–367 (2020)

Human Action Recognition Algorithm of Non-local Two-Stream Convolution Network Based on Image Depth Flow

Bo Li[1], Pan Pan[2], Xin Feng[2(✉)], and Yongxin Ge[3]

[1] Department of Criminal Science Technology, Chongqing Police College, Chongqing,
China
[2] College of Computer Science and Engineering,
Chongqing University of Technology, Chongqing, China
panpan9314@2020.cqut.edu.cn,xfeng@cqu.edu.cn
[3] Chongqing University, Chongqing, China
yongxinge@cqu.edu.cn

Abstract. Action recognition has wide prospects in the field of video surveillance. At present, the popular Temporal Segment Networks (TSN) has been applied to action recognition and has achieved good results. However, TSN uses RGB images as the input of CNN, which can be easily affected by the illumination, complex backgrounds, and local occlusion, resulting in poor robustness and low recognition accuracy. In this paper, we design a two-stream network for action recognition by adding a depth flow to fuse with the original RGB image, which we term as the depth flow TSN (D-TSN). In addition, to increase the receptive fields of both the spatial and temporal CNN flows for recognizing actions with long-term dependencies, we further propose an N-TSN model by embedding a non-local attention module into the shallow layer of the network. Experiments show that both the proposed D-TSN and N-TSN models achieve superior performance to the original TSN method on the widely used action recognition dataset.

Keywords: Human action recognition · Depth image · Temporal Segment Network (TSN) · Non-local module

1 Introduction

With the rapid development of artificial intelligence, human action recognition has been widely used in hospital monitoring systems, virtual reality enhancement, etc. It has become an important technology in smart medical care, smart public security, and other key projects and has become a current research hotspot [1,2].

Algorithms based on Convolution Neural Network (CNN) [3] are widely used in action recognition. Currently, there are two mainstream network frameworks. One is the 3D-CNN, which directly takes video information as input [4]. The other is the two-stream CNN that takes images and optical flow features as input [5]. However, these two networks can only capture short-distance temporal dependencies in the video, and they usually require intensive sampling of video segments to capture long-distance temporal dependencies. However, it will not only increase computational overhead but also limit their ability to capture long-distance temporal dependencies when the length of temporal dependencies is longer than the number of frames of video segments. In 2016, Wang Limin et al. proposed a new time-domain segmentation network model based on the two-stream network model: the TSN model (Temporal Segment Networks) [6]. Based on the two-stream network framework, TSN combines a sparse time sampling strategy to divide each video into three segments and randomly selects one RGB image and two optical flow images from each segment as an input. Thus, the long time sequence video can be processed better and the action recognition rate is higher.

This paper designs a new action recognition algorithm based on the TSN two-stream network framework. Firstly, in order to overcome the difficulties of the 3D-CNN network for action recognition, such as gradient explosion and parameter over-fitting, the three-dimensional video recognition is converted to frame-by-frame sequential image recognition. In particular, we explicitly extract a depth flow from the video segment and fuse it with the spatial flow to construct a two-stream depth flow TSN network, which we term as D-TSN. In addition, to overcome the shortage of local attention based CNN for long-term action recognition, we further propose to apply a non-local attention module to globally assign different weights for different feature flows, and a non-local TSN model (N-TSN) is finally established to make the network have higher recognition performance.

2   Related Work

2.1   Two-Stream Convolution Neural Network

The two-stream CNN network model achieves human action recognition by capturing the spatial and temporal information of the video and fusing the video information from two dimensions. It has two types of inputs: RGB and optical flow. For RGB images, one frame is randomly selected from each video, and for optical flow images, it is obtained by stacking the optical flow displacement fields of consecutive frames. The two-stream network model takes as input a randomly selected frame from each video and its adjacent frames of optical flow images. Compared with the traditional 3D convolution network, the two-stream network decomposed the video information from two dimensions and used two independent CNNs to process the information of different dimensions, which reduced the input scale, reduced the amount of calculation and achieved good pedestrian recognition performance.

2.2   TSN Network

Although the 3D convolution network and two-stream network algorithms perform well for short-distance timing dependencies in videos, they perform poorly for long-distance timing dependencies [4,7]. Therefore, traditional algorithms mostly adopt dense sampling of videos, which reduces the computational efficiency of the algorithm. However, the ability of such methods to capture long-distance timing dependencies is still limited. It is difficult to effectively process videos with long action time ranges.

For this reason, the TSN network uses the sparse sampling strategy to process the video information [6]. During training, TSN learns to tune the parameters according to the entire video information. In the inference stage, compared with the classical two-stream network, TSN only needs to sample a short-term video segment from the whole video for classification, which is more efficient. In addition to RGB image and optical flow image, TSN also uses RGB-Diff image and distorted optical flow image as input. The RGB-Diff image contains the RGB difference information between adjacent frames, while the distorted optical flow image uses the camera displacement information to supplement the optical flow information to obtain the optical flow image with more time motion information.

3   Method

In this paper, RGB image and depth flow image are selected as input to train two independent CNNs, namely the spatial flow and the depth flow, and the recognition results are obtained by integrating the two networks. Meanwhile, the video processing mode of the TSN network framework is adopted to sample the video with a sparse sampling strategy, which not only ensures the global information integrity of the video but also improves the network efficiency.

3.1   D-TSN Network Based on Depth Flow Fusion

Model Framework. In this paper, a new D-TSN network is designed by combining the advantages of the two-stream network and the TSN network. On the basis of the original spatial flow, a new depth flow is added as the input of the two-stream frame. The D-TSN is defined as:

$$D - TSN(T_1, T_2, ...T_k) = H(G(F(T_1; W), F(T_2; W), ...F(T_k; W)))   \quad (1)$$

where T_1, T_2,...,T_k refers to the 1st, 2nd ....,k-th video segments, k represents the number of video segments after video division. $F(T; W)$ represents the specific score of each action after the segment T is input into the CNN with parameter W. The function G indicates that the scores of K segments are combined to produce a single stream of the entire video's specific score. In this paper, the average method of function G is selected. The H function represents the fusion of a spatial flow network and a depth flow network. SoftMax is used to get the score of input video for each category so as to predict the video action category. The D-TSN network is shown in Fig. 1.

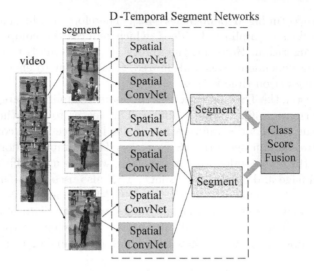

Fig. 1. D-TSN network

Loss Function. The difference between the network prediction and ground-truth is represented by the loss function. D-TSN and TSN have similar model architectures, so the loss function is also similar, which is expressed by the following formula:

$$L(y, G) = -\sum_{i=1}^{C} y_i \left(G_i - log \sum_{j=1}^{C} e^{G_j} \right) \tag{2}$$

where, y_i is the correct class identification of category i, C is the total number of actional categories, and G_i refers to the score of each category corresponding to a single stream in the whole video. Here, the average function is used as an aggregation function to fuse the scores of each segment.

In order to improve the training speed of the model, the small-batch stochastic gradient descent algorithm is selected in this paper to optimize the parameters of the model, and the gradient of parameters related to the model loss function can be expressed as the following:

$$\frac{\partial L(y, G)}{\partial W} = \frac{\partial L}{\partial G} \frac{\partial G}{\partial W} \tag{3}$$

$$G = g(F(T)) \tag{4}$$

$g(.)$ is the average function, and the gradient of the model can be obtained by combining Eqs. (3) and (4):

$$\frac{\partial L(y, G)}{\partial W} = \frac{\partial L}{\partial G} \frac{\partial G}{\partial W} = \frac{\partial L}{\partial G} \frac{\partial G}{\partial F(T)} \frac{\partial F(T)}{\partial W} = \frac{\partial L}{\partial G} \sum_{k=1}^{K} \frac{\partial G}{\partial F(T_k)} \frac{\partial F(T_k)}{\partial W} \tag{5}$$

The model divides the video into three segments, so $K = 3$. The network learns parameters in the whole video, not only for a single segment, which makes the parameters more accurate for discriminating video action categories and improves the robustness of the whole network.

3.2 N-TSN Network Based on Visual Attention Mechanism

To address the problem that traditional CNN based action recognition networks have local characteristics and can only capture dependencies for distant pixel points through increasing the size of the convolutional kernel, we apply the non-local module [9] to introduce the global attention for long-term action recognition and propose a new non-local TSN model, denoted as N-TSN, and the N-TSN model framework is shown in Fig. 2.

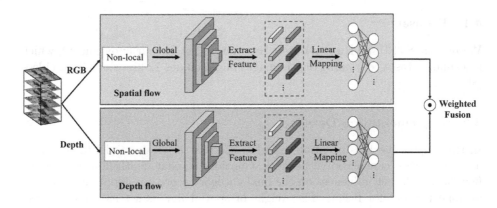

Fig. 2. N-TSN model

In the N-TSN model, the non-local module is first used to process the input image to obtain the global information of the image. At this time, the size of the output image remains unchanged. Then, the output image and the corresponding depth image are input to the spatial flow and depth flow CNN for automatic learning and feature extraction. The probability distribution of the video action category is obtained by feature linear mapping, and the output of the two streams is fused by weighted fusion as the final prediction result. The N-TSN is defined as:

$$N - TSN(T_1, T_2, ...T_k) = H(G(F(N(T_1; W)), F(N(T_2; W)), ...F(N(T_k; W))))$$
(6)

where, $N(T; W)$ represents the image of the same size as the original input obtained for each video segment after the non-local module. The N-TSN model does not change the main network of the D-TSN model but captures the non-local attention information of the input data in the shallow network through the non-local module, and then inputs the data into the CNN layer, which captures the local dependencies layer by layer to extract the input features, and finally uses the SoftMax activation function to get the output. The loss function of the N-TSN model is similar to that of the D-TSN model. Cross entropy is used to represent classification loss, which is defined as Eq. (7):

$$L(y, N) = -\sum_{i=1}^{C} y_i (N_i - log \sum_{j=1}^{C} e^{N_j})$$ (7)

Here, N_i refers to the score of each category corresponding to a single stream of the entire video in the N-TSN model, and the average method is adopted as the aggregation function.

4 Experiments

4.1 Dataset

We use the SYSU 3D Human-object Interaction Set for our experiments, which is a small dataset containing depth images and includes 12 kinds of action videos [8].

4.2 Implementation Details

In this paper, the BN-Inception model is used as the basic model to construct a single-stream convolutional network. Considering that depth flow and spatial flow have different influences on the final category score, we adopt the weighted average method for fusion. The weight of spatial flow is set as 1 and that of depth flow is set as 1.2. For the N-TSN model, we use the RGB image or depth image after angle cropping and scale dithering as the input. For all experiments, we use recognition accuracy to evaluate our method.

4.3 Results and Analysis

D-TSN. As shown in Table 1, compared to the single-stream CNN with input RGB and depth images, the fused two-stream CNN achieves a higher accuracy of 91.6%. After analysis, we found that compared to RGB images, depth images contain more key feature information, and this depth information acts as a complement to spatial information, which makes the network performance improve. However, compared to optical flow images, which contain inter-frame motion information that can be used as input for the temporal dimension, depth images do not contain temporal information, so the accuracy of depth images + RGB images is lower compared to optical flow images + RGB images. However, since the SYSU dataset used is a small dataset, the network performs better, but in fact, adding only one depth stream does not improve the overall accuracy of the network greatly, so we consider the following new approach to add the non-local module to improve the recognition accuracy.

Table 1. Recognition accuracy of D-TSN algorithm on SYSU dataset

Algorithm	Input	Accuracy %
TSN	RGB	84.50
TSN	Depth	86.15
TSN	Flow + RGB	91.34
D-TSN	RGB	87.11
D-TSN	Depth	88.34
D-TSN	Depth + RGB	**91.60**

N-TSN. We conducted experiments on N-TSN based on the D-TSN, and the experimental results are shown in Table 2. After using the non-local module, the recognition accuracy of the network for RGB images and depth images is improved compared to that without the module. This proves that using the non-local module to capture non-local dependencies in images can improve the recognition accuracy.

A post-embedded comparative experiment was conducted in order to study the influence of the embedded position of a non-local module on the recognition results. That is, the embedding position of a non-local module was added into the deep layer of CNN. The results show that embedding non-local modules into the deep layer (post-embedding) of the network main body does not perform as well as embedding the shallow layer (front-embedding), so we finally adopt the method of embedding non-local modules into the shallow layer of the network main body to build the N-TSN model. Finally, we conducted fusion experiments on two single-flow CNNS with non-local modules, and the accuracy of the final N-TSN model was shown in Table 3.

Table 2. Recognition accuracy on SYSU dataset by post-embedded N-TSN.

Algorithm	Input	
	RGB	Depth
TSN	84.50	86.15
D-TSN	87.11	88.34
N-TSN (front embedding)	89.05	88.78
N-TSN (post embedding)	88.03	88.51

Table 3. Comparison of recognition accuracy of different two-stream networks on SYSU dataset.

Algorithm	Input	Accuracy %
HON4D [10]	Depth	79.2
HFM [11]	Depth + RGB	76.7
MPCCA [12]	Depth + RGB	80.7
MTDA [13]	Depth + RGB	84.2
JOULE [8]	Depth + RGB	84.9
TSN [6]	Flow + RGB	91.34
D-TSN	Depth + RGB	91.60
N-TSN (front embedding)	Depth + RGB	**92.63**

Compared with the existing mainstream algorithms, the accuracy of the two-stream network with RGB image and depth image fusion is better than that of the single-stream network. The result of the N-TSN model reached 92.63%, which is improved compared with the original TSN and D-TSN models. This proves that the non-local module can improve the performance of the network.

5 Conclusion

In this paper, we construct a new non-local N-TSN network action recognition algorithm, which combines RGB image spatial flow with depth flow and uses a non-local module to capture long-term dependencies. For action recognition in complex scenes, it is still a research point to explore new image modalities and accurately extract the spatial-temporal information contained in videos.

Acknowledgement. This work was supported by the Science and Technology Research Project of Chongqing Education Commission (No. KJQN202001710), the Construction Project of Chongqing Key Laboratory of Toxicology and Drug Analysis(No. 201833), the National Natural Science Foundation of China (Grant No. 62176031), and the Fundamental Research Funds for the Central Universities (Grant No. 2021CDJQY-018).

References

1. Hinton, G.E., Salakhutdinov, R.: Reducing the dimensionality of data with neural networks. Science **313**, 504–507 (2006)
2. Luo, H.L., Wang, C.J., Lu, F.: An overview of video action recognition. J. Commun. **39**(06), 169–180 (2018)
3. Cao, C., et al.: Skeleton-based action recognition with gated convolutional neural networks. IEEE Trans. Circuits Syst. Video Technol. **29**, 3247–3257 (2019)
4. Ji, S., et al.: 3D convolutional neural networks for human action recognition. IEEE Trans. Pattern Anal. Mach. Intell. **35**, 221–231 (2013)

5. Simonyan, K., Zisserman, A.: Two-stream convolutional networks for action recognition in videos. In: NIPS (2014)
6. Wang, L., et al.: Temporal segment networks: towards good practices for deep action recognition. arXiv abs/1608.00859 (2016)
7. Peng, X., et al.: Bag of visual words and fusion methods for action recognition: comprehensive study and good practice. arXiv abs/1405.4506 (2016)
8. Hu, J., et al.: Jointly learning heterogeneous features for RGB-D activity recognition. IEEE Trans. Pattern Anal. Mach. Intell. **39**, 2186–2200 (2017)
9. Wang, X., et al.: Non-local neural networks. In: 2018 IEEE/CVF Conference on Computer Vision and Pattern Recognition, pp. 7794–7803 (2018)
10. Oreifej, O., Liu, Z.: HON4D: histogram of oriented 4D normals for activity recognition from depth sequences. In: 2013 IEEE Conference on Computer Vision and Pattern Recognition, pp. 716–723 (2013)
11. Cao, L., et al.: Heterogeneous feature machines for visual recognition. In: 2009 IEEE 12th International Conference on Computer Vision, pp. 1095–1102 (2009)
12. Cai, Z., et al.: Multi-view super vector for action recognition. In: 2014 IEEE Conference on Computer Vision and Pattern Recognition, pp. 596–603 (2014)
13. Zhang, Y., Yeung, D.-Y.: Multi-task learning in heterogeneous feature spaces. In: AAAI (2011)

Synthetic Feature Generative Adversarial Network for Motor Imagery Classification: Create Feature from Sampled Data

Huan Luo, Na Lu$^{(\boxtimes)}$, Xu Niu, and Xuecai Zhou

Xi'an Jiaotong University, Xi'an 710049, Shaanxi, People's Republic of China
lvna2009@xjtu.edu.cn

Abstract. Motor imagery (MI) classification based on deep learning (DL) has made great progress. These methods heavily rely on sufficient training samples, which makes a great challenge for MI classification due to the difficulty of collecting brain signals. Generative adversarial network (GAN) has been an efficient tool to augment data. However, it is difficult to generate EEG samples from Gaussian noise by existing GANs. Also, the two-phase processing (augmentation and classification) in GANs causes computational inefficiency. In addition, EEG signal carries important private information which must be protected appropriately and has been disregarded in previous studies. To address these issues, Synthetic Feature Generative Adversarial Network (SF-GAN) is proposed combining data augmentation and classification. The input Gaussian noise of the generator is replaced by EEG samples and the generator generates features instead of raw data. A classifier interacting with the generator is incorporated. The performance of SF-GAN was verified by extensive experiments. It has been observed that the distribution of the synthetic features covers the distribution of real features which can be directly used as the augment input to the classifier instead of raw data and well protect data privacy.

Keywords: EEG privacy · Motor imagery · Generative adversarial network · Synthetic feature · Data augmentation

1 Introduction

Brain-computer interface (BCI) establishes a direct connection between the brain and external devices. During human mental movement, neurons in the cerebral cortex generate low electrical currents. In different mental activities of human brain, the activated neurons are different, so the generated electrical signals are different. In BCI, the voltage fluctuation recorded by electrodes attached to the scalp are called Electroencephalography (EEG), which are widely used for analysis and classification. In recent years, the motor imagery (MI) paradigm has been widely used in rehabilitation, military and other fields, constructing interaction between the brain intention and the action of external devices.

W. Deng et al. (Eds.): CCBR 2022, LNCS 13628, pp. 324–331, 2022.
https://doi.org/10.1007/978-3-031-20233-9_33

Although deep learning-based MI classification methods have made great progress, they are heavily limited by insufficient data. Therefore, some data augmentation methods were developed to augment training data, the most popular of which are generative adversarial network (GAN) [1] and variational autoencoder (VAE) [2]. VAE consists of an encoder and a decoder, where the encoder constructs the latent variable probability distribution from the original data probability distribution, and the decoder reconstructs the approximate probability distribution of the original data from the latent variable probability distribution. But due to the non–stationarity of EEG signals, the decoder tends to reconstruct Gaussian noise rather than non-Gaussian useful parts in EEG signal, which limits the application of VAE in BCI.

GAN can generate MI EEG data from Gaussian noise. But traditional GAN-based data augmentation methods have three issues. Firstly, Gaussian noise with a fixed mean and variance is difficult to generate pseudo-EEG signals with weak spatial correlation, which makes the generation task too difficult. Thus, the generator has very poor ability compared with the discriminator in MI task, which easily leads to model collapse in GAN. Secondly, privacy protection of sensitive EEG data is seriously disregarded so far. Moreover, the majority of GAN methods for classification are divided into two phases: (1) train generators with real data to generate synthetic data; (2) train classifiers with real data and synthetic data. This two-phase process is relatively inefficient and time-consuming.

To addressing the above issues (insufficient generation ability of generator, privacy protection and low efficiency caused by two phases), we propose Synthetic Feature Generative Adversarial Network (SF-GAN). In SF-GAN, we use multiple subjects' EEG samples as the generator input and the generator only needs to generate synthetic features, which greatly improves the generator ability and protects data privacy by hiding the data details at the same time. Moreover, besides the discriminator, a classifier interacting with the generator is incorporated too, which can not only improve the generator's ability, but also efficiently obtains a good classification performance directly after training the SF-GAN.

2 Related Work

In 2014, Goodfellow et al. first proposed Generative Adversarial Networks (GAN) [1], the core of which is to design a generator (G) and a discriminator (D) that compete each other. Generator and discriminator finally converge to an equilibrium through iterative optimization, so that the generator can generate synthetic samples that obey approximately the real data distribution without relying on any prior knowledge. In the same year, Mirza et al. proposed Conditional GAN (cGAN) [3], which uses one-hot to encode labels and connects the one-hot labels to the samples of input discriminator and the noise of input generator, to consider the label information of the dataset. Radford et al. proposed Deep Convolutional GAN (DCGAN) [4] to alleviate the model collapse problem. This method cancels all the pooling layers and adds the Batch Normalization layers. The generator uses the deconvolution for upsampling. As an improvement of cGAN, Auxiliary Classifier GAN (ACGAN) [5] was proposed by Augustus et al., which extended the function of the discriminator to distinguish authenticity and categories. Moreover, the

Wasserstein GAN (WGAN) [6] was proposed replacing the JS divergence with the Earth mover distance estimation to enhance the stability and robustness of the training process. Gulrajani *et al.* introduced a gradient penalty loss [7] on WGAN, called Improved WGAN, achieving faster convergence speed and higher quality of synthetic data.

The application of GAN in BCI is a relatively new research direction, and its potential to generate synthetic EEG data remains to be further explored. In 2018, Kay *et al.* proposed EEG-GAN [8] to generate synthetic EEG signals. Roy *et al.* proposed MEEEG-GAN [9] to generate MI EEG signals, in which generator and discriminator constructed from bidirectional long short-term memory neurons in 2020. In 2021, Fangzhou *et al.*u sed CycleGAN [10] to generate surrogate MI EEG data of stroke patients. Sooner, Jiaxin *et al.* proposed Att-LGAN [11] and MoCNN [11] for MI dataset augmentation and classification, achieving best results.

Although GAN has important applications in BCI, we must provide privacy guarantee to prevent EEG data from illegal disclosure when actually using personal sensitive data [12]. In other words, we must guarantee synthetic samples can't deduce individual data when capturing global information of the training set. This research direction might also become a hot spot in the future.

3 Proposed Method

As mentioned, the proposed method mainly adopted the strategy of using multiple subjects' EEG samples as the generator input and generator generating synthetic features, which greatly reduces the difficulty of the EEG generation task and protects data privacy. Besides the discriminator, a classifier interacts with the generator too, which can not only improve the generator's ability, but also the efficiency.

As shown in Fig. 1, SF-GAN includes a Data-sampling generator, a Feature extractor, an Authenticity discriminator, and a Category discriminator. The data-sampling generator generates synthetic features. The feature extractor extracts the real features of the real data. The two discriminators decide the authenticity and categories of given features, respectively. Through their confrontation and collaboration, the generator can generate synthetic features that are different from the real features but obey its overall distribution (reducing the generation difficulty and protecting the privacy). Meanwhile, after training the SF-GAN, the feature extractor and category discriminator together form a highly accurate and efficient classifier.

3.1 Dataset and Preprocessing

In this study, we used the BCI competition IV dataset 2a [13] for discussion and experiments. The EEG data for this dataset were recorded from 9 subjects who performed 4 motor imagery tasks, namely (0) left hand, (1) right hand, (2) both feet, and (3) tongue. In our experiments, we only consider the 22-EEG channels' signal of subjects 1, 2, 3, 5, 6, 7, 8, 9 with a sampling frequency of 250 Hz and a length of 4s. We used 4-fold cross validation on two sessions of each subject.

We only perform minimal preprocessing on the dataset [14]. The raw signal is bandpass filtered to 4–38 Hz to remove the noise caused by eye movements, muscle activity and other interference. We then performed electrode-wise exponential moving standardization with a decay factor of 0.999.

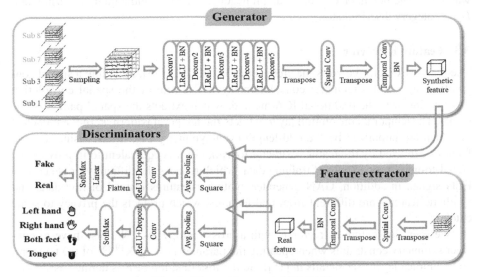

Fig. 1. The architecture of SF-GAN

3.2 Data-Sampling Generator

Experiments [11, 15] have shown that the quality of the MI EEG signals of subjects 1, 3, 7, and 8 is better than others for their higher accuracy in the classification task. Thus, in the SF-GAN, we choose to get the input of the generator from sampling the training data of these four subjects. Other subjects can also be employed. For example, we could randomly sample one from the signals of left-hand task from each subject to generate synthetic features labeled left-hand. The first half of the generator uses deconvolution layers to construct pseudo-data, and the second half imitates the feature extractor to extract synthetic features. Due to the introduction of multiple subjects' EEG information, the overall distribution of synthetic features covers the overall distribution of real features, which expands the decision boundary of classification.

We jointly train the generator with the authenticity discriminator and the category discriminator so that it can generate realistic and easily-classified synthetic features. Assuming that the real EEG signal is denoted as $X \in \mathbb{R}^{C \times T} \sim P$, where C is the number of channels and T is the sequence length. If there are m subjects and each subject has n samples, the j-th EEG sample of the i-th subject is represented as $x_i^j, X_i \sim P_i$. Suppose the sampling result from subjects 1, 3, 7, 8 is

$X_s = \left[X_1 = x_1^{j_1}, X_3 = x_3^{j_2}, X_7 = x_7^{j_3}, X_8 = x_8^{j_4} \right] \sim P_s = P(X_1, X_3, X_7, X_8)$. The loss of the generator is defined as:

$$\mathcal{L}_G = - \underset{X_s \sim P_s}{\mathbb{E}} \left[\log(D_1(G(X_s))) + \sum Y \log(D_2(G(X_s))) \right]. \tag{1}$$

where Y = one-hot label, G = data-sampling generator, D_1 = authenticity discriminator, D_2 = category discriminator.

3.3 Feature Extractor

The feature extractor borrows the architecture of KFCNet [15], including a spatial convolution layer and a temporal convolution layer. The role of the spatial convolution layer is similar to the traditional ICA method, which extracts the spatial pattern of the signal. The temporal convolution layer extracts the temporal pattern, kernel parameters of which are initialized by the odd-length even-symmetry FIR filters. Using the real features extracted by the feature extractor to train GAN is equivalent to improving the signal-to-noise ratio (SNR) of training data, which reduces the difficulty of generation EEG signal. In addition, GAN generates synthetic features instead of raw data, and synthetic features are different from real features, which protects the privacy to some extent.

We train the feature extractor F with a cross-entropy loss. We also have to consider symmetry constraints when updating the parameters $W \in \mathbb{R}^{19 \times 51}$ of the temporal convolutional layer (See details in [15]). So the loss function of F is defined as:

$$\mathcal{L}_F = - \underset{X \sim P}{\mathbb{E}} \left[\sum Y \log(D_2(F(X))) \right] + \mathcal{L}_{sc}. \tag{2}$$

where symmetry loss $\mathcal{L}_{sc}$ (See details in [15]) is:

$$\mathcal{L}_{sc} = \frac{10^6}{19 \times 51} \sum_{f=1}^{19-1} \left[\sum_{n=0}^{51-1} \left| \|W_{f,n}\| - \|W_{f,51-1-n}\| \right| \right]. \tag{3}$$

3.4 Discriminators

Synthetic features and real features are input to two discriminators. The Authenticity discriminator D_1 consists of an average pooling layer, a classification convolutional layer, and a fully connected layer. The Category discriminator D_2 consists of an average pooling layer and a classification convolutional layer. The final predicted label is determined by voting on the output of the classification convolutional layer [15].

The loss functions of training D_1 and D_2 are formulated respectively as

$$\mathcal{L}_{D_1} = - \underset{X_s \sim P_s}{\mathbb{E}} \left[\log(1 - D_1(G(X_s))) \right] - \underset{X \sim P}{\mathbb{E}} \left[\log(D_1(F(X))) \right] + \lambda \mathcal{L}_{gp}, \tag{4}$$

$$\mathcal{L}_{D_2} = - \underset{X_s \sim P_s}{\mathbb{E}} \left[\sum Y \log(D_2(G(X_s))) \right] - \underset{X \sim P}{\mathbb{E}} \left[\sum Y \log(D_2(F(X))) \right], \tag{5}$$

where $\lambda = 10$, $\mathcal{L}_{gp}$ is the gradient penalty loss [7] that regulates the model optimization, $\mathcal{L}_{gp} = \underset{\hat{X} \sim \hat{P}}{\mathbb{E}} \left[\left(\nabla_{\hat{X}} D_1 \left(\hat{X} \right)_2 - 1 \right)^2 \right]$, $\hat{X}$ is a random sample between synthetic features and real feature.

4   Experiments and Comparisons

In our experiments, we used the KFCNet pretrained model to initialize the parameters of the feature extractor to speed up the training process. We repeated the experiment 4 times for each subject, and performed 4-fold cross validation in each experiment. We recorded the highest average 4-fold accuracy in the 4 experiments.

On BCIC IV-2a dataset, we compared the performance of KFCNet without data augmentation and SF-GAN (like KFCNet with data augmentation) for each subject, and the result is shown in Table 1. It is obvious that using the SF-GAN data augmentation method, the classification accuracy of each subject has been significantly improved. The average accuracy of KFCNet for all subjects is 83.66%, while accuracy of SF-GAN can reach 86.02%, which demonstrates the effectiveness of our method for data augmentation. This also proves that the synthetic features generated by SF-GAN are of high quality, which facilitates classification.

Table 1. Comparison of the results of KFCNet and SF-GAN on BCIC IV-2a dataset (%).

Method	KFCNet	SF-GAN
S1	92.71	**94.27**
S2	62.50	**68.21**
S3	94.44	**95.14**
S5	83.68	**86.81**
S6	62.15	**66.32**
S7	98.44	**99.66**
S8	91.32	**93.75**
S9	84.03	84.03
Avg.	83.66	**86.02**

We also compared our SF-GAN with the state-of-the-art method Att-LGAN [11]. Figure 2 (left) shows the confusion matrix of Att-LGAN on the BCIC IV-2a dataset, and Fig. 2 (right) shows the confusion matrix of the SF-GAN method. By comparison, we find that the average accuracy of SF-GAN is about 86% which is higher than that of Att-LGAN with 83%, which demonstrates the superiority of the SF-GAN, outperforming the state-of-the-art GAN-based methods. These experiment results show the proposed algorithm outperforms the non-augmentation method and Att-LGAN.

In order to verify that the synthetic features are different from the real features (protecting privacy), and their overall distribution covers the overall distribution of the real features (expanding the decision boundary), we also use t-SNE [16] to reduce the features to 2 dimensions and visualize.

After using t-SNE to reduce the four classes of synthetic features and real features into 2 dimensions, as shown in the Fig. 3, we can clearly see that for each class of motor imagery task, almost every synthetic feature is different from the real feature. Moreover, the distribution of synthetic features covers larger region than the distribution of real features, which ensures that when using synthetic features and real features to train the classifier, the decision boundary of the classifier is expanded. So the performance of the model on the test set can be improved.

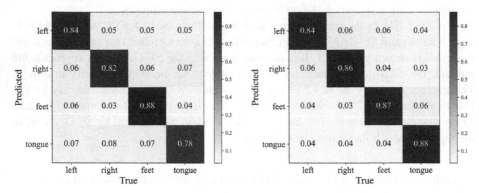

Fig. 2. The confusion matrix of Att-LGAN(left) and SF-GAN(right)

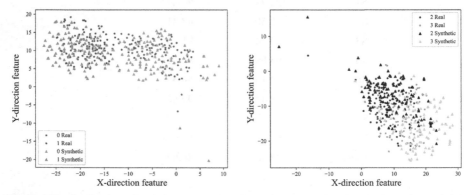

Fig. 3. The distribution of real features and synthetic features reduced to 2 dimensions of right hand vs left hand(left) and feet vs tongue(right)

5 Conclusion

This paper aimed to solve three challenges: GAN model collapse caused by insufficient capability of the generator compared with the discriminator; personal EEG data leakage; low efficiency of two-phase processing in GAN. We proposed SF-GAN where we use multiple subjects' EEG samples as the generator input and the generator only needs to generate synthetic features instead of raw data. Besides the discriminator, a classifier interacts with the generator in the meanwhile. We conducted experiments on BCIC IV-2a dataset, and demonstrated that our method outperforms non-augmentation method

(KFCNet) and the state-of-the-art GAN-based method (Att-LGAN). Furthermore, SF-GAN can protect personal privacy by only using intermediate features and expanding the decision boundary of MI classifier. The existing works in BCI field usually disregards the necessity of privacy protection. Therefore, we plan to further study privacy issues in EEG data with federated learning, differential privacy etc. in the future.

Acknowledgments. This work is supported by National Natural Science Foundation of China under Grant No. 61876147.

References

1. Goodfellow, I.J., et al.: Generative adversarial nets advances in neural information processing systems. In: Conference on Neural Information Processing Systems, pp. 2672–2680 (2014)
2. Kingma, D.P., Welling, M.: Auto-encoding variational Bayes. arXiv:1312.6114 [cs, stat.] (2014)
3. Mirza, M., Osindero, S.: Conditional generative adversarial nets. arXiv preprint arXiv:1411.1784 (2014)
4. Odena, A., Olah, C., Shlens, J.: Conditional image synthesis with auxiliary classifier gans. arXiv preprint arXiv:1610.09585 (2016)
5. Schons, T., Moreira, G., Silva, P., Coelho, V., Luz, E.: Convolutional network for EEG-based biometric. In: Mendoza, M., Velastín, S. (eds.) CIARP 2017. LNCS, vol. 10657, pp. 601–608. Springer, Cham (2018). https://doi.org/10.1007/978-3-319-75193-1_72
6. Arjovsky, M., Chintala, S., Bottou, L.: Wasserstein generative adversarial networks. In: Proceedings International Conference on Machine Learning, vol. 70, pp. 214–23 (2017)
7. Gulrajani, I., Ahmed, F., Arjovsky, M., Dumoulin, V., Courville, A.C.: Improved training of Wasserstein GANs. In: Conference on Neural Information Processing Systems, pp. 5767–5777 (2017)
8. Kay, G.H., Robin, T.S., Tonio, B.: EEG-GAN: generative adversarial networks for electroencephalographic (EEG) brain signals. arXiv:1806.01875 [cs, eess, q-bio, stat], June 2018. 00016 (2018)
9. RoY, S., Dora, S., Mccreadie, K., Prasad, G.: MIEEG-GAN: generating artificial motor imagery electroencephalography signals. In: International Joint Conference on Neural Networks, pp. 1–8. IEEE (2020)
10. Xu, F., et al.: Classification of left-versus right-hand motor imagery in stroke patients using supplementary data generated by CycleGAN. IEEE Trans. Neural Syst. Rehabil. Eng. **29**, 2417–2424 (2021)
11. Jiaxin, X., Siyu, C., Yongqing, Z., Dongrui, G., Tiejun, L.: Combining generative adversarial network and multi-output CNN for motor imagery classification. J. Neural Eng., 1741–2552 (2021)
12. Debie, E., Moustafa, N., Whitty, M.T.: A privacy-preserving generative adversarial network method for securing EEG brain signals. In: International Joint Conference on Neural Networks, p. 8 (2020)
13. Brunner, C., Leeb, R., Muller-Putz, G.R., Schlogl, A., Pfurtscheller, G.: 2008 BCI competition—Graz data set A (2008)
14. Schirrmeister, R.T., et al.: Deep learning with convolutional neural networks for EEG decoding and visualization Hum. Brain Mapp. **38**, 5391–5420 (2017)
15. Niu, X., Na, L., Kang, J., Cui, Z.: Knowledge-driven feature component interpretable network for motor imagery classification. J. Neural Eng. **19**, 016032 (2022)
16. Van der Maaten, L., Hinton, G.: Visualizing data using t-SNE J. Mach. Learn. Res. **9**(11) (2008)

Speaker and Speech Recognition

An End-to-End Conformer-Based Speech Recognition Model for Mandarin Radiotelephony Communications in Civil Aviation

Yihua Shi[1], Guanglin Ma[1,2], Jin Ren[1,3](✉), Haigang Zhang[1], and Jinfeng Yang[1]

[1] Institute of Applied Artificial Intelligence of the Guangdong-Hong Kong-Macao Greater Bay Area, Shenzhen Polytechnic, Shenzhen 518055, China
{yhshi,renjin666,zhanghg,jfyang}@szpt.edu.cn
[2] School of Computer Science and Software Engineering, University of Science and Technology Liaoning, Anshan 114051, China
[3] Shenzhen Institutes of Advanced Technology, Chinese Academy of Sciences, Shenzhen 518055, China

Abstract. In civil aviation radiotelephony communications, misunderstandings between air traffic controllers and flight crews can result in serious aviation accidents. Automatic semantic verification is a promising assistant solution to decrease miscommunication, thanks to advancements in speech and language processing. Unfortunately, existing general speech recognition models are ineffective when it comes to capturing contextual long-distance dependent local similarity features in radiotelephony communications. To address these problems, this paper proposes an end-to-end Conformer-based multi-task learning speech recognition model for Mandarin radiotelephony communications in civil aviation. The Conformer model improves local information capture while retaining the global information modeling capabilities of contextual long-distance dependencies, owing to the introduction of the convolution module to the Transformer model. Meanwhile, multi-task learning is used to further improve performance by combining connectionist temporal classification (CTC) and attention-based encoder-decoder (AED) models. The experimental results show that the proposed model can perform global and local acoustic modeling effectively, making it particularly suitable for extracting acoustic features of Mandarin civil aviation radiotelephony communications.

Keywords: Mandarin civil aviation radiotelephony communication · Automatic speech recognition · Multi-task learning · Conformer · End-to-end

1 Introduction

To keep the aircraft working safely and efficiently, air traffic controllers (ATCOs) and flight crews must have a clear and accurate understanding of each other's intentions via radiotelephony communications [1]. Only when both sides make timely, objective, and correct judgments in terms of terminology standardization, content integrity, and readback consistency, can instructions be delivered and executed in the right way [2]. In the human information perception range, the visual part accounts for more than 80%, the auditory part accounts for about 15%, and the rest is less than 5%. Since both the ATCOs (within the airport tower) and the flight crews (within the aircraft cockpit) are in a closed space with a limited field of view, the effective visual perception signals mainly consist of the radar scanning point and visual numbers on the dashboard of the data link system. Therefore, different from most scenarios, the sense of hearing has become the primary medium for real-time information perception in radiotelephony communications. Especially under the trend of the high-speed development of the domestic air transport industry and the dramatic growth of air traffic flow, the physical and mental pressure of ATCOs has increased significantly with the increase of control density [3]. Misunderstandings may occasionally arise, caused by environmental noise interference, fatigue, lack of concentration, and excessive tension [4]. However, in the event of an accident, the impact would be disastrous.

In recent years, with the rapid development of various technologies such as speech signal processing, natural language processing, and deep learning, it has gradually become possible to employ computers to realize automatic semantic verification between the ATCO's control instructions and the flight crew's readback instructions [3]. As is often the case, it is necessary to transcribe the speech signal into text through automatic speech recognition (ASR), and then perform text matching to realize semantic verification. Although this two-stage solution has the potential for integration into a one-stage framework, existing work still struggles to directly model speech recognition and text matching efficiently across modalities in an end-to-end manner. Therefore, the performance of speech recognition in the former stage is still an important foundation that affects the overall performance of the system, which is also the focus of this paper.

As a semi-artificial professional language, radiotelephony communications exhibit unique acoustic and linguistic characteristics in pronunciation, interactive mode, word selection, and sentence construction [5]. Unlike other languages, to reduce the uncertainty caused by the ambiguity of pronunciation and terminology, and avoid potential safety hazards caused by misunderstandings between the two sides, the Mandarin speech dataset for radiotelephony communications conforms to the civil aviation radio communication standard and has the following characteristics: (1) the pronunciation of words is special, for example, the *number 0* is pronounced as "*dòng*", and the *number 7* is pronounced as "*guǎi*"; (2) the language is standard with a clear sense of meaning, such as *approach* and *departure*; (3) compared with widely-used open-source Mandarin speech datasets, its transcripts are longer because a single sentence sample usually consists of control instruction from the ATCO and readback instruction from the flight crew; (4) ATCOs and flight crews are required to communicate in strict accordance with the format of "*the other side's call sign – one's own call sign - the content of the call*", where the similar sentence structure leads to the significant contextual long-distance dependent local similarity characteristics.

Unfortunately, from the perspective of phonetic and linguistic characteristics of civil aviation radiotelephony communications, it is difficult for existing ASR methods to effectively extract the significant contextual long-distance dependent local similarity features.

To solve the above issues, this paper proposes an end-to-end Conformer-based multi-task learning speech recognition model for Mandarin radiotelephony communications in civil aviation. By introducing the convolution module into the Transformer [6] model, the Conformer model [7] further enhances local information capture while retaining the global information modeling capability of contextual long-distance dependencies. Meanwhile, multi-task learning is performed jointly with the connectionist temporal classification (CTC) model and attention-based Encoder-Decoder (AED) model to further improve its performance. Experiments show that the Conformer-based multi-task learning speech recognition model proposed in this study can effectively perform the acoustic modeling of global and local information, making it suitable for extracting the acoustic features of the Mandarin speech dataset for civil aviation radiotelephony communications.

The rest of this paper is organized as follows. Section 2 introduces the related work. Section 3 describes the Conformer-based multi-task learning speech recognition model for civil aviation radiotelephony communications. Section 4 introduces the dataset and experimental settings and analyzes the experimental results. Finally, Sect. 5 concludes the work.

2 Related Work

As a classic representative of traditional acoustic models for speech recognition, Gaussian Mixture Model-Hidden Markov Model (GMM-HMM) consists of two parts. HMM [8] models the transition probability of speech states, and GMM [9] acoustically models the observation probability of the model based on the probability distribution of feature vectors. Although the GMM-HMM is simple in structure and fast in training, GMM ignores the contextual temporal information between frames. Furthermore, as a shallow model, it is difficult to learn deep nonlinear feature transformations. By introducing a deep neural network (DNN) to replace the original GMM module to realize the estimation of the observation probability, each output node of the DNN is employed to estimate the posterior probability of the corresponding state of the HMM under the given acoustic characteristics. The formed DNN-HMM [10] model only needs to train a single neural network, which can achieve better performance than GMM-HMM. Although DNN-HMM allows inter-frame feature splicing input to enhance temporal information to a certain extent, its modeling ability and flexibility on contextual temporal information are still insufficient. The above traditional speech recognition model is usually composed of multiple modules, including preprocessing, feature extraction, acoustic model, language model, pronunciation dictionary, and decoding search. Each sub-module is independently trained and optimized following its objectives, where the cascading accumulated errors among modules make it difficult for the local optimal solution of each sub-module to be consistent with the global optimal solution. In addition, strictly aligned annotations at the frame level are required to train the hybrid model, where the complicated data preparation work will increase the training difficulty of the entire system.

To address the above problems, end-to-end speech recognition models have gradually become a research hotspot in academia and industry in the past decade [11, 12]. The overall modeling of speech recognition is greatly simplified by integrating multiple original modules into a single system, which can be jointly optimized around a unified objective. The CTC model [13, 14] proposed by Graves et al. solves the unequal length problem of input and output sequences by introducing blank symbols, which can achieve end-to-end modeling without providing strict alignment information between speech frames and text characters in advance. On this basis, Graves proposes a recurrent neural network transducer (RNN-T) [15] model for streaming speech recognition, which breaks the original conditional independence assumption of CTC. By elaborately integrating the language model and acoustic model for joint optimization, it can generate low-latency real-time speech recognition results before receiving a complete speech sequence as input, making it popular in the industry. The "Listen, Attend and Spell" (LAS) [16] model jointly proposed by Carnegie Mellon University and Google is a representative of the AED model [17]. Without following the conditional independence assumption, the model predicts character probability distributions given acoustic sequences without considering prior alignment information. The data-driven learning paradigm allows the model to construct alignment associations between input and output sequences in a more free and flexible way.

As far as the speech recognition task of civil aviation radiotelephony communications is concerned, scholars at home and abroad have explored several works. Based on the DNN-HMM model, Liu et al. [18] improved the DNN into a convolutional deep neural network based on shared hidden layers and reach excellent cross-language speech recognition performance on the Mandarin and English speech datasets for radiotelephony communications. Qiu et al. [19] proposed a speech recognition model based on bidirectional long short-term memory network - connectionist temporal classification (BiLSTM-CTC), which achieved better recognition performance than the DNN-HMM model on the English speech dataset for radiotelephony communications. Zhou et al. [20] proposed a CNN-enhanced hybrid CTC-attention end-to-end speech recognition model, which achieved better recognition performance than the DNN-HMM model on the noisy Mandarin speech dataset for radiotelephony communications. Although the above work provides a basis for follow-up research, it is still difficult to effectively extract the significant contextual long-distance dependent local similarity features in the Mandarin speech dataset for civil aviation radiotelephony communications.

3 Speech Recognition Model for Mandarin Radiotelephony Communications in Civil Aviation

3.1 Multi-task Learning Speech Recognition Model

The Connectionist Temporal Classification (CTC) [13, 14] model aims to automatically learn many-to-one alignment mappings between frame-level acoustic feature input sequences and their corresponding label output sequences. Without providing strict alignment annotations at the frame level in advance like traditional speech recognition methods, CTC only needs sentence-level annotations composed of arbitrary fine-grained units such as phonemes, syllables, characters, or words to achieve end-to-end speech recognition. As an attention-based Encoder-Decoder (AED) model, the "Listen, Attend and Spell" (LAS) [16] model aims to simulate the human auditory perception process. Unlike the conditional independence assumption satisfied by the CTC model, the data-driven learning paradigm of LAS allows the model to construct aligned associations between input and output sequences in a more free and flexible manner.

In the CTC model, the posterior probability of the output sequence satisfies the conditional independence assumption, resulting in relatively weak inter-symbol correlation modeling, which requires a language model as an additional constraint to further improve performance. On the contrary, in the LAS model, its data-driven alignment learning allows the flexible modeling of contextual long-distance dependencies. However, due to the lack of monotonicity constraints like CTC, the alignment results learned by LAS are susceptible to noise interference. In addition, when the sequence length is larger, the attention-based model becomes more complex, and only relying on data-driven learning will increase the training difficulty [21]. In summary, although the CTC and LAS models have their strengths in speech recognition tasks, the features learned by the two are complementary and have the possibility of joint optimization. Therefore, inspired by the idea of multi-task learning, a joint CTC-attention model is proposed to further improve the model performance by learning from each other's strengths.

By introducing the multi-task training idea, the CTC objective function is considered as an additional training task. Through joint training and optimization with the LAS objective function, it is equivalent to the two models of CTC and LAS sharing the same encoder, and the decoding stage is jointly trained according to their respective objective functions. The training of the entire model benefits from the introduction of the monotonic alignment learning method between the input and output of the CTC, and its loss function is the weighted sum of the losses of the two models:

$$L_{MTL} = \lambda L_{CTC} + (1 - \lambda)L_{LAS} \tag{1}$$

where λ is a hyperparameter used to control the weights of the two tasks, $0 \leq \lambda \leq 1$.

The loss function of CTC can be expressed as formula (2),

$$
\begin{aligned}
L_{CTC} &= -\ln(P(y|x)) \\
&= -\ln\Big(\sum_{\pi_i \in \mathcal{B}^{-1}(y)} P(\pi_i|x) \Big) \\
&= -\ln\Big(\sum_{\pi_i \in \mathcal{B}^{-1}(y)} \prod_{t=1}^{T} P(\pi_i^t|x_t) \Big) \\
&= -\ln\Big(\sum_{\pi_i \in \mathcal{B}^{-1}(y)} \prod_{t=1}^{T} \hat{y}_{\pi_i^t}^t \Big), \quad \forall \pi_i \in L'^T
\end{aligned}
\tag{2}
$$

where $x = (x_1, x_2, \ldots, x_T)$ and $y = (y_1, y_2, \ldots, y_U)$ denote the frame-level acoustic feature input sequence and its corresponding label output sequence, respectively, $\pi_i = (\pi_i^1, \pi_i^2, \ldots, \pi_i^T)$ represents the ith possible path between x and y, $\hat{y}_{\pi_i^t}^t$ represents the probability that the model outputs the predicted label π_i^t at time step t, the new alphabet L' is an extension of the original alphabet L by introducing "*blank*", i.e. $L' = L \cup \{blank\}$, L'^T represents the set of all possible path sequences of length T defined on L', many-to-one mapping $\mathcal{B}: L'^T \mapsto L^U$ represents the operation of any possible path π_i by combining consecutive repeated characters and then removing blanks to finally obtain the label output sequence y, $\mathcal{B}^{-1}(y)$ is the set of all possible paths corresponding to the output sequence y.

The loss function of LAS can be expressed as formula (3),

$$
\begin{aligned}
L_{LAS} &= -\ln P(z|x) \\
&= -\sum_i \ln P(z_i|x, z_{<i}) \\
&= -\sum_i \ln(AttendAndSpell(z_{<i}, h)) \\
&= -\sum_i \ln(AttendAndSpell(z_{<i}, Listen(x)))
\end{aligned}
\tag{3}
$$

where $x = (x_1, x_2, \ldots, x_T)$ and $z = (z_1, z_2, \ldots, z_U, < EOS >)$. Denote the input acoustic feature sequence and the output sequence of transcribed text characters, respectively, $< EOS >$ is the sequence terminator, $Listen$ represents the operation of transforming an acoustic feature x. Into a higher-order representation $h = (h_1, h_2, \ldots, h_V)$, $V \leq T$, $AttendAndSpell$ represents the operation of predicting the probability distribution of characters at the current time step based on previously generated characters and higher-order representation h.

3.2 Conformer-Based Multi-task Learning Speech Recognition Model

In this section, we propose a Conformer-based multi-task learning speech recognition model for Mandarin radiotelephony communications in civil aviation. As shown in Fig. 1, the model consists of three parts. First, the acoustic features are sub-sampled to reduce dimensionality through the Convolution neural network (CNN) module. Subsequently, the dimensionality-reduced acoustic features are converted into hidden layer features by stacking twelve Conformer [7] modules. Finally, the entire model is optimized jointly with LAS and CTC. By introducing the convolution module into the Transformer model, the Conformer model enhances local information capture while retaining the global information modeling capability of contextual long-distance dependencies. The CNN module exploits the translation invariance in the temporal domain to capture the local similarity features in the dataset, and then the long-distance dependencies between local similarity features are established with the help of the Transformer's ability to model long-distance dependencies in context. Each Conformer module adds a multi-head self-attention module and a convolution module between the two feedforward neural networks. Finally, normalization is performed by the layer normalization module, and the first four modules are connected by residuals.

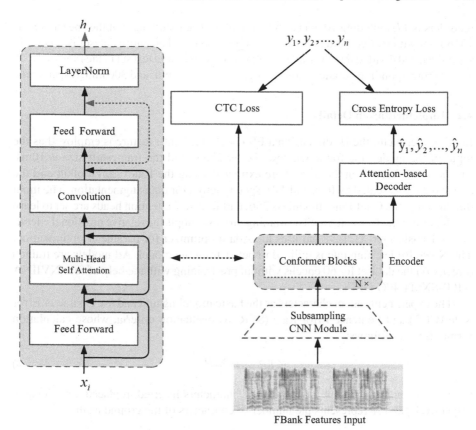

Fig. 1. The Conformer-based multi-task learning speech recognition model for Mandarin radiotelephony communications in civil aviation

4 Experiment and Result Analysis

4.1 Mandarin Speech Dataset for Civil Aviation Radiotelephony Communications

Concerning the actual recording data of civil aviation radiotelephony communications and related course materials, under the guidance of the first-line ATCOs and instructors of radiotelephony communication courses in civil aviation, a corpus was constructed, and professional ATCOs were selected to record the corpus in a quiet environment. In this way, the constructed dataset conforms to the phonetic and linguistic distribution characteristics of civil aviation radiotelephony communications in terms of call content, syntactic structure, speech control, pronunciation rules, and language standards. The Mandarin speech dataset for civil aviation radiotelephony communications is a para-phrase dataset, where each speech sample is composed of the ATCO's control instruction and the flight crew's readback instruction in series. In this way, the instruction can be executed correctly and efficiently in a double-checked manner.

The data storage format of the Mandarin speech dataset is WAV audio file, and the sampling frequency of each recording is 16 kHz, 16bit, and mono. The number of recorders is 17, including 10 males and 7 females. The total length of the speech data is 1516 min, with 641 corpora and 10971 recorded voices. The entire dataset is randomly scrambled and divided into the training set, validation set, and test set in the ratio of 7:1:2, and the corresponding durations are about 1074 min, 142 min, and 300 min, respectively.

4.2 Implementation Details

In this experiment, the 80-dimensional FBank (Filter bank) feature is employed as the input of the model, the frame window size is 25ms, and the frameshift size is 10ms. The acoustic features in the dataset are extracted using the Kaldi [22] toolkit, and the above dataset is scaled by 0.9x and 1.1x speed factors for data augmentation. The input dimension of the Conformer module is 256, and four self-attention heads are set to learn rich feature extraction patterns. The training process adopts the relative positional encoding in Transformer-XL [23] and uses the Adam optimizer for parameter optimization. The Noam [6] learning rate is utilized to better train the model. All models are trained directly on the dataset for 60 epochs without pre-training with the help of four NVIDIA A100-SXM4-40G GPUs.

The experiments adopt characters as the basic modeling unit and use Character Error Rate (CER) and Sentence Error Rate (SER) as evaluation criteria, whose calculation formulas are as follows:

$$CER = \frac{I+S+D}{N} \tag{4}$$

where I, S, and D represent the number of characters inserted, replaced, and deleted, respectively, and N represents the number of characters of the ground truth;

$$SER = \frac{F}{M} \tag{5}$$

where F is the number of sentences with transcription errors, and M is the total number of sentences.

4.3 Multi-task Learning Hyperparameter Selection

The optimal proportion of the multi-task learning weight λ in formula (1) is selected for the LSTM, Transformer, and Conformer, respectively, to verify the effectiveness of the proposed speech recognition model. Experiments are performed by setting a set of discrete values to explore the influence of the weight λ on model training. The specific value starts from $\lambda = 0.1$ and ends at $\lambda = 0.9$ with a step size of 0.1. The CER and SER performance of the three models are listed in Table 1. For the convenience of observation, the data in Table 1 is visualized as shown in Fig. 2. It can be seen from Fig. 2 that the value of λ has different effects on different models. Therefore, the two indicators of CER and SER are combined to select appropriate λ weights for different models, as shown in the λ weights corresponding to the bold performance results in Table 1.

Table 1. The effect of multi-task learning weight λ on various models

λ	LSTM	Transformer	Conformer
	CER/SER (%)	CER/SER (%)	CER/SER (%)
0.1	**3.11/5.58**	3.94/6.44	2.03/2.51
0.2	3.2/6.63	3.37/5.25	2.27/2.65
0.3	3.2/6.72	3.12/4.59	2.3/2.93
0.4	3.21/6.86	3.1/4.69	2.24/2.93
0.5	3.22/6.86	3.41/5.4	2.19/2.98
0.6	3.22/6.72	3.43/5.49	2.25/3.12
0.7	3.28/6.91	3.09/4.64	2.27/2.98
0.8	3.26/6.48	3.07/4.35	2.35/3.22
0.9	3.32/6.44	**2.94/4.12**	**1.98/2.89**

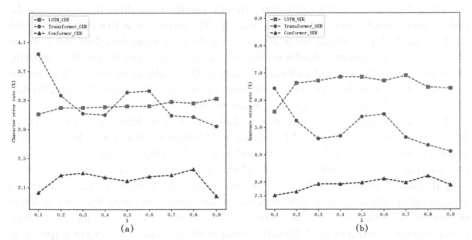

Fig. 2. The effect of multi-task learning weight λ on various models. (a) CER criteria. (b) SER criteria.

4.4 Comparative Experiment and Result Analysis

The LSTM, Transformer, and Conformer models are selected for single-task and multi-task learning to demonstrate the effectiveness of multi-task learning. The LSTM and Transformer models can be obtained by stacking their respective modules to replace the dashed box encoder part of the Conformer-based model in Fig. 1. The Noam [6] learning rate is employed to better train the Transformer and Conformer, and about 16,000 frames are selected for each batch of data for training.

The LSTM model employs five bidirectional LSTM modules for stacking. The input and hidden layer dimensions of the first layer are 1280 and 512, respectively, and the input and hidden dimensions of the other layers are 512. By summing the hidden layer features of the bidirectional LSTM output, the hidden layer feature dimension of the output remains constant. The Transformer model uses a twelve-layer Transformer module, each layer uses four self-attention heads, the input dimension of each layer is 256, and the relative positional encoding [23] in Transformer-XL is used, which are all consistent with the Conformer model parameter configuration.

Table 2. The performance comparison of three single-task or multi-task learning models

Model	LSTM	Transformer	Conformer
	CER/SER (%)	CER/SER (%)	CER/SER (%)
CTC	4.27/25.65	5.4/24.04	2.8/9.8
LAS	3.63/5.21	3.96/6.11	2.15/**2.65**
MTL	**3.11/5.58**	**2.94/4.12**	**1.98**/2.89

Table 2 shows the comparative experimental results of the three models for single-task or multi-task learning (MTL), respectively. The results show that considering both the CER and SER performance evaluation criteria, the Conformer-based multi-task learning speech recognition model achieves the best results in all experiments. By comparing the results of single-task and multi-task learning, the results of multi-task learning are generally better than those of single-task learning, which also verifies the effectiveness of the multi-task learning speech recognition model.

Compared with the Transformer model, the Conformer model outperforms the Transformer model in both CER and SER. Since the Conformer model introduces the convolution module into the Transformer model, it further enhances the capture of local information while retaining the global information modeling capability of contextual long-distance dependencies. As a paraphrase dataset, the Mandarin speech dataset for civil aviation radiotelephony communications has significant contextual long-distance dependent local similarity features. Therefore, the Conformer-based model can effectively extract global and local acoustic features of the dataset to further improve its performance.

4.5 Attention Visualization Analysis

Figure 3 shows the attention visualization comparison results of three multi-task learning speech recognition models based on LSTM, Transformer, and Conformer, respectively. The horizontal axis represents the acoustic feature sequence, and the vertical axis represents the corresponding text sequence of the speech transcription output. Among all the visualization results, the Conformer-based multi-task learning speech recognition model (Fig. 3(c)) performs the best in terms of the effectiveness of global and local information modeling, making it particularly suitable for extracting the significant contextual long-distance dependent local similarity features in the dataset.

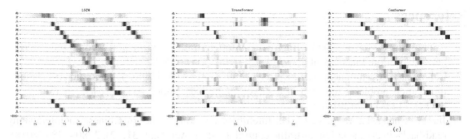

Fig. 3. Comparison of attention visualization of three multi-task learning models. (a) LSTM. (b) Transformer. (c) Conformer.

As shown in Fig. 3, the speech-text mapping alignments learned by the three multi-task learning models are mainly concentrated around the diagonal. From left to right, with the change of model types, the segmentation edges of the acoustic features of adjacent characters become clearer, and the overall color depth increases, indicating that the quality of the learned alignment relationship is gradually improved. It is worth noting that the Conformer-based model not only learns a relatively obvious alignment relationship backbone near the diagonal but also learns several contextual long-distance dependent local similarity features, helping it to achieve the best performance in all comparative experiments. Specifically, four of them are the most obvious, namely "*sān yāo dòng wǔ*" (三幺洞五) and "*jìn pǎo dào dòng liǎng zuǒ*" (进跑道洞两左) in Fig. 3(c). The attention visualization results also demonstrate that the contextual long-distance dependent local similarity features are of great value for the Mandarin speech dataset for civil aviation radiotelephony communications.

5   Conclusion

This paper proposes an end-to-end Conformer-based multi-task learning speech recognition model for Mandarin radiotelephony communications in civil aviation. By introducing the convolution module into the Transformer model, the Conformer model enhances local information capture while retaining the global information modeling capability of contextual long-distance dependencies. Meanwhile, multi-task learning is performed jointly with the CTC and AED to further improve its performance. Comparative experiments and attention visualization results show that the proposed model can effectively perform the acoustic modeling of global and local features, making it particularly suitable for extracting the significant contextual long-distance dependent local similarity features in the Mandarin speech dataset for radiotelephony communications in civil aviation.

Acknowledgments. This work was supported in part by the General Higher Education Project of Guangdong Provincial Education Department (No. 2020ZDZX3085), in part by China Postdoctoral Science Foundation (No. 2021M703371), in part by the Post-doctoral Foundation Project of Shenzhen Polytechnic (No. 6021330002K), and in part by Shenzhen Science and Technology Program (No. RCBS20200714114940262).

References

1. Prinzo, O.V., Morrow, D.G.: Improving pilot/air traffic control voice communication in general aviation. Int. J. Aviat. Psychol. **12**(4), 341–357 (2002)
2. Lahtinen, T.M., Huttunen, K.H., Kuronen, P.O., Sorri, M.J., Leino, T.K.: Radio speech communication problems reported in a survey of military pilots. Aviat. Space Environ. Med. **81**(12), 1123–1127 (2010)
3. Jia, G., Cheng, F., Yang, J., Li, D.: Intelligent checking model of Chinese radiotelephony read-backs in civil aviation air traffic control. Chin. J. Aeronaut. **31**(12), 2280–2289 (2018)
4. Lu, Y., Shi, Y., Jia, G., Yang, J.: A new method for semantic consistency verification of aviation radiotelephony communication based on LSTM-RNN. In: 2016 IEEE International Conference on Digital Signal Processing (DSP), pp. 422–426. IEEE Press, New York (2016)
5. Illman, P.E., Gailey, G.: Pilot's Radio communications Handbook, 6th edn. McGraw-Hill Professional (2012)
6. Vaswani, A., Shazeer, N., Parmar, N., et al.: Attention is all you need. In: NIPS 2017, pp. 6000–6010. Red Hook, New York (2017)
7. Gulati, A., Qin, J., Chiu, C.C., et al.: Conformer: convolution-augmented transformer for speech recognition. In: Proceedings Interspeech 2020, pp. 5036–5040 (2020)
8. Jelinek, F.: Continuous speech recognition by statistical methods. Proc. IEEE **64**(4), 532–556 (1976)
9. Juang, B.H.: Maximum-likelihood estimation for mixture multivariate stochastic observations of Markov chains. AT&T Techn. J. **64**(6), 1235–1249 (1985)
10. Hinton, G., Deng, L., Yu, D., et al.: Deep neural networks for acoustic modeling in speech recognition: the shared views of four research groups. IEEE Signal Process. Mag. **29**(6), 82–97 (2012)
11. Li, J.: Recent advances in end-to-end automatic speech recognition. arXiv preprint arXiv: 2111.01690 (2022)
12. Hannun, A.: The history of speech recognition to the year 2030. arXiv preprint arXiv: 2108.00084 (2021)
13. Graves, A., Fernandez, S., Gomez, F., Schmidhuber, J.: Connectionist temporal classification: labelling unsegmented sequence data with recurrent neural networks. In: 23rd International Conference on Machine Learning, pp. 369–376 (2006)
14. Graves, A.: Connectionist temporal classification. In: Supervised Sequence Labelling with Recurrent Neural Networks. Studies in Computational Intelligence. LNCS, vol. 385, pp. 61–93. Springer, Heidelberg (2012). https://doi.org/10.1007/978-3-642-24797-2_7
15. Graves, A.: Sequence transduction with recurrent neural networks. arXiv preprint arXiv: 1211.3711 (2012)
16. Chan, W., Jaitly, N., Le, Q., Vinyals, O.: Listen, attend and spell: a neural network for large vocabulary conversational speech recognition. In: 2016 IEEE International Conference on Acoustics, Speech, and Signal Processing (ICASSP), pp. 4960–4964 (2016)
17. Chorowski, J., Bahdanau, D., Serdyuk, D., Cho, K., Bengio, Y.: Attention-based models for speech recognition. In: 28th International Conference on Neural Information Processing Systems, pp. 577–585 (2015)
18. Liu, Y., Guo, X., Zhang, H., Yang, J.: An acoustic model of civil aviation's radiotelephony communication. In: 8th International Conference on Computing and Pattern Recognition (ICCPR 2019), pp. 315–319 (2019)
19. Qiu, Y., Jia, G., Yang, J., Liu, Y.: Speech recognition model of civil aviation radiotelephony communication based on BiLSTM. J. Sig. Process. **35**(02), 293–300 (2019). (in Chinese)

20. Zhou, K., Yang, Q., Sun, X., Liu, S., Lu, J.: Improved CTC-attention based end-to-end speech recognition on air traffic control. In: Cui, Z., Pan, J., Zhang, S., Xiao, L., Yang, J. (eds.) IScIDE 2019. LNCS, vol. 11936, pp. 187–196. Springer, Cham (2019). https://doi.org/10.1007/978-3-030-36204-1_15
21. Yu, D., Deng, L., Yu, K., Qian, Y.: Artificial Intelligence Speech Recognition Understanding and Practice. Publishing House of Electronics Industry, Beijing (2020).(in Chinese)
22. Povey, D., Ghoshal, A., Boulianne, G., et al.: The Kaldi speech recognition toolkit. In: 2011 IEEE Workshop on Automatic Speech Recognition and Understanding (ASRU 2011). IEEE Signal Processing Society (2011)
23. Dai, Z., Yang, Z., Yang, Y., Carbonell, J., Le, Q., Salakhutdinov, R.: Transformer-XL: attentive language models beyond a fixed-length context. In: 57th Annual Meeting of the Association for Computational Linguistics, pp. 2978–2988 (2019)

ATRemix: An Auto-tune Remix Dataset for Singer Recognition

Lifang Wang[1], Bingyuan Wang[2], Guanghao Tan[3], Wei-Qiang Zhang[4(✉)], Jun Feng[1], Bing Zhu[1], and Shenjin Wang[4]

[1] Key Laboratory of Media Audio and Video, Communication University of China, Beijing 100024, China
[2] School of Electronic Engineering and Computer Science, Peking University, Beijing 100871, China
[3] School of Information and Electronics, Beijing Institute of Technology, Beijing 100081, China
[4] Department of Electronic Engineering, Tsinghua University, Beijing 100084, China
wqzhang@tsinghua.edu.cn

Abstract. In recent years, with the development of video websites such as YouTube, TikTok, and Bilibili, a great number of auto-tune remix audios are produced every day. Auto-tune remix audios are usually made from existing famous audios. The original clips can be tuned to various remixes through professional editing techniques. In the creation process, the characteristics of the singer are usually maintained, thus the original materials can be traced by singer recognition methods. This paper mainly focuses on the research of auto-tune remix singer recognition. As this topic has not been discussed before, we create a dataset of auto-tune remix audios and attempt to recognize the identity of the singer. Firstly, we use an x-vector model trained on the TIMIT dataset, and then evaluate it on the ATRemix dataset. Secondly, ATRemix dataset used to train different models, and SubATRemix dataset used as a test set, which shows good performance.

Keywords: Music information retrieval · Auto-tune remix · Singer identification

1 Introduction

Auto-tune remix songs are created by clipping, merging, and tuning existing short audios, such as advertisements and sitcoms. The materials used for creation are usually not original. As the Internet is currently full of auto-tune remix songs, the issue of copyright protection has attracted great attention, both in the academic community and the industrial field. In a creation process, the original materials basically come from the same singer, and the characteristics of the singer are maintained through the creation process. As a result, we can identify and categorize auto-tune remixes by singer recognition methods. Our

W. Deng et al. (Eds.): CCBR 2022, LNCS 13628, pp. 348–355, 2022.
https://doi.org/10.1007/978-3-031-20233-9_35

goal is to solve the problem of singer recognition in auto-tune remix scenario. To promote our research, we proposed a high-quality, open-access Mandarin ATRemix dataset in this paper and validated it with different methods. Our submission can be seen at https://github.com/wlf03/ATRemix-master.git.

There are numerous datasets built for singer (speaker) recognition, covering a range from general [1] to different scenarios [2], different languages [3] and accents [4], different media [5,6] as well as different generation methods [7]. Meanwhile, as an emerging research area, datasets for music identification are on quick growth. Some of the latest works focus on the quantity [8], while others concentrate on specific scenes [9]. However, few have worked on the auto-tune remix, a special scene with extended varieties and more complex conditions. Auto-tune remix songs are created by professional editing, manually adjusted into high-quality, aesthetic songs through complex editing, sophisticated matching, and elaborate tuning. As the creation process depends on heavy labor from professionals, it is much harder to build such a dataset.

In this paper, we introduce the open-access ATRemix, which is a high-quality, brand-new singer recognition dataset. In this dataset, 110 Mandarin auto-tune remix audios without accompaniment are recreated from 11 famous singers' songs. All audios are created in a professional editing studio. The total duration of the recording is around 3.7 h, and all songs are segmented into 2482 sentence-level utterances by post-processing. And the data of different singers can be added continuously in the future. Although these auto-tune remix audios are changed greatly in key and rhythm, the tone always keeps the same. So, we consider this problem as an issue of the speaker identification.I-vector and x-vector [10] are typical speaker recognition systems and MFA-Conformer [11] achieves the best performance. We use these speaker recognition systems to validate the ATRemix and achieve comparatively great performance. ATRemix dataset provides a reference for large-scale dataset acquisition and a tentative study for optimizing automated high-volume generation.

The rest of this paper is organized as follows: Section 2 details the auto-tune remix creation pipeline and the Qualitative Characteristics. We introduce the details of the training model based on ATRemix as well as results and evaluation in Sect. 3. Finally, we conclude the paper in Sect. 4.

2 The Creation of ATRemix

2.1 Data Sources

Our data come from www.bilibili.com. This site is the most representative site for auto-tune remix audios. The singers of our dataset are all representations of the currently most popular ones on short video platforms, especially among the youth. According to Table 1, sources of material include commercials, TV dramas, talk shows, skits, etc. The source audios cover a wide variety of styles and are constantly updated, making the dataset highly expandable.

Table 1. Weights of different types of audios.

	Percentage	Total length (minute)
Advertising	9.12%	13.85
Film and television	27.34%	63.58
Live broadcast	17.62%	50.25
Skit	19.50%	33.88
News clip	26.42%	60.48

2.2   ATRemix Creation Pipeline

In this part, we mainly create a refined dataset of auto-tune remixes. In order to solve this problem, we apply the artificial synthesis to build a subset of website data for singer recognition. We follow the basic steps of industrial standards and focus on audio processing, regardless of the video components (Fig. 1).

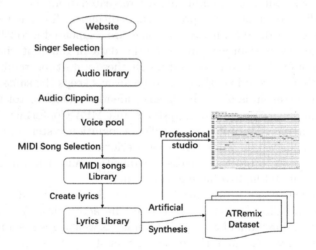

Fig. 1. Steps in building ATRemix dataset.

Step1: Singer Selection. To refine our model, we first create a human-voice subset of the original dataset. Short songs of 11 different singers are chosen from the website to form an audio library. The standards are as follows:

- Whether the source materials are vocal-based. In some cases, e.g., G0200280 (a dubbing actor) and G0300248 (a sitcom with accent), actors' tone can be heard clearly. However, in films and television dramas, e.g., G0900217 (a drama clip), the human voice is very difficult to hear.

- Whether the audio source is clear.
- Whether the audio library is comprehensive. Many singers have limited source materials, thus we have to splice their vowels and consonants to form a phone. However, other audio libraries like speaker G02 are more complete.
- Whether the tuned audio remains recognizable. In some cases, the original clip is tuned to an outrageous extent, which is unconducive to identify. As a result, we exclude materials with excessive techniques or personal Inspiration.

Step2: Audio Clipping. After selecting the representative auidos under each singer, we cut up materials of the same singer and tag the fragments as audio files according to Chinese syllables. As a result, a voice pool composed of audio clips is generated.

Following the standards on www.bilibili.com, we chop the audios manually by vocal pauses. The fragments are then annotated in Praat [11]. We have 11 singers' voice pools, which can be made into various songs through professional editing technology.

Step3: MIDI Song Selection. Besides original materials, target songs are also a major component in ATRemix creation. In our MIDI dataset, all songs are selected according to their quality and popularity in auto-tune remix applications.

Step4: Lyric Creation. Before audio synthesis, a MIDI song is selected. As auto-tune remix creators often change the content to a large extent, we then chop out the lyrics and refill them with our own compositions. The creation of lyrics is free, thus we can re-sing the song by using the fragments in the voice pool.

Step5: Artificial Synthesis. The synthesis phase, which is most challenging and creative, is the core process of our work. In this part, we use UTAU [12], a professional editing studio, to splice the tuned fragments in the voice pool of each singer. After selecting MIDI music and creating the lyrics, we match them with corresponding syllables in the singer's voice pool. The fragments are tuned in the previous step, so we fill them in our lyrics according to the MIDI notes. If a phone is not included, we slice the consonant and vowel from similar words to synthesize it. Due to quality issues, we only fit the pitches of syllables to the target song, without adding accompaniment or conducting post-mixing.

2.3   Audio Segmentation

After artificial synthesis, we segment the newly-created auto-tune remixes into smaller fragments for training the singer recognition system. All songs are first segmented into sentence-level utterances according to the lyrics. Then, to avoid the existence of ultra-long utterances in our final database, any utterance longer than 10 s is further segmented into shorter ones. Most fragments concentrate between 1–5 seconds. After dropping silent utterances, we obtain 2482 utterances with a total duration of around 3.7 h. According to Table 2, about 200 audio files are generated for each singer in the ATRemix dataset.

Table 2. Features of ATRemix dataset.

	Total number	Average length
Themes	11	20.19 m
Audios	110	2.02 m
Lyrics	2482	5.37 s

2.4 ATRemix: Qualitative Characteristics

As shown in Fig. 2, the creation of ATRemix dataset has changed the original song (the closest one) significantly in both time domain and speech spectrum. However, the auto-tune remix essentially retains the melody of target MIDI music.

Apart from the advantages of wide scenario coverage, rich variety, and timeliness, all the auto-tune remixes in our dataset are handmade. We allow the words in voice pools to *sing* according to most melodies by diminishing the interference from tuning. Basically only the pitch is changed, and the characteristics of the original voice, especially the tone, are retained to a greater extent. Therefore, we are able to achieve higher sound quality and fidelity.

3 Experiments

3.1 Data Processing

Training Data: The TIMIT dataset that consist of 6,300 sentences from 630 speakers, with each speaker has 10 sentences. The ATRemix dataset that contains 11 famous singers' songs, and each singer has 10 Mandarin auto-tune remix songs without accompaniment. After slicing, a total of 2482 utterances were obtained. The SubATRemix is a smaller ATRemix dataset, which contains 5 singers not seen in the ATRemix dataset, each singer has 1 song, a total of 50 utterances were obtained after segmentation.

Data Augmentation: Due to ATRemix as the training set is relatively small, We augmented the ATRemix data with noise, time shift, and time stretch, which based on the Kaldi CNCeleb recipe and combined them with the clean data. After the augmentation, 9928 utterances from 11 singers were generated to extract acoustic features.

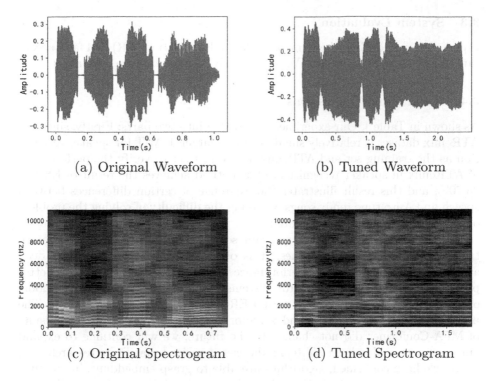

(a) Original Waveform

(b) Tuned Waveform

(c) Original Spectrogram

(d) Tuned Spectrogram

Fig. 2. Qualitative analysis of ATRemix dataset.

3.2 Network Configurations

We apply x-vector and i-vector [10], commonly used technique in speaker recognition to identify the singers in the ATRemix dataset. In addition to these, we use the MFA-Conformer [11] network for verification.

x-vector. The x-vector network contains multiple frame-level time delay neural network (TDNN) layers, a statistical pooling layer, two sentence-level fully-connected layers, and a layer of softmax.

i-vector. Since the GMM-UBM model cannot overcome the impact of channel interference information on speaker recognition. Dehak proposed i-vector based factor analysis technique. The i-vector contains not only speaker difference information, but also channel difference information.

MFA-Conformer. Convolution-augmented Transformer (Conformer) [13], a combination of CNNs and Transformers. The proposed Multi-scale Feature Aggregation Conformer (MFA-Conformer), whose structure follows the practical experience in end-to-end speech recognition and achieved state-of-the-art results.

3.3 System Evaluation

Equal error rate (EER): the error rate when false rejection (FR) and false acceptance (FA) at an equal point. We report EER for performance evaluation.

3.4 Results and Discussions

As shown in Table 3, Our experiment is divided into two parts: Firstly, since the ATRemix dataset is relatively small, we use a larger TIMIT for speaker recognition as the training set and ATRemix as the test set to verify the performance of ATRemix in speaker recognition. Our method achieves the result of EER = 25.70%, and this result illustrates the existence of certain differences between speech and Auto tune remix songs, verifying the difficulty of solving the problem of auto tune remix singer recognition.

Secondly, we use ATRemix as train set and SubATRemix as test set to train based on different baselines. It is observed that MFA-Conformer deep architecture achieves the best performance. Specifically, i-vector achieves better performance compared to x-vector systems, while the MFA-Conformer model obtained the best performance with EER = 4.00%. After augmentation, The performance of both i-vector and x-vector has improved, however the results of MFA-Conformer did not change. In the future, we will continue to expand our open-access Mandarin ATRemix dataset in order to facilitate research.

As we have confirmed, algorithms are able to grasp embeddings in an auto-tune remix and prone to imitate through extensive training. Meanwhile, currently synthesized remixes are fine-tuned to rival human-made Jinriki Vocaloid. However, if we chop remixes from other materials from the website and fit them into the model, themes are hard to identify, indicating that better models should be designed for the real condition.

Table 3. Comparison of results using different models.

Train set	Test set	x-vector	i-vector	MFA-Conformer
TIMIT	ATRemix	25.70	–	–
ATRemix	SubATRemix	13.89	8.33	**4.00**
Aug-ATRemix	SubATRemix	11.11	**2.78**	4.00

4 Conclusions

Wi have gradually entered the lives of the youth, and their influence cannot be underestimated. For the first time we have created an auto-tune remix dataset and tried to solve this problem using machine learning algorithms from existing music retrieval domain. Our work has demonstrated that the auto-tune remix singer recognition problem can be solved to a large extent.

Speaker recognition methods are fit for the artificial synthesis scenario, showing promising future. Meanwhile, current methods in relevant areas can be more directly applied to our dataset, indicating that the deep interaction between auto-tune remix and traditional realms is possible. As an audio type with most complex production, solving the problem of auto-tune remix singer recognition will not only offer new perspectives, but also help with difficulties in other music retrieval scenes methodologically.

Acknowledgements. This work was supported by the National Natural Science Foundation of China under Grant No. U1836219 and No. 62276153, and in part by a grant from the Guoqiang Institute, Tsinghua University.

References

1. Nagraniy, A., Chungy, J.S., Zisserman, A.: VoxCeleb: a large-scale speaker identification dataset. In: Proceedings INTERSPEECH, pp. 2616–2620 (2017)
2. Srivastava, S., Gopal, G., Bhardwaj, S.: Multi-scenario dataset for speaker recognition. J. Intell. Fuzzy Syst. **34**(3), 1385–1392 (2018)
3. Fan, Y., Kang, J.W., Li, L.T., et al.: CN-CELEB: a challenging Chinese speaker recognition dataset. In: Proceedings ICASSP, pp. 7604–7608 (2020)
4. Kalluri, S.B., Vijayasenan, D., Ganapathy, S., et al.: NISP: a multi-lingual multi-accent dataset for speaker profiling. In: Proceedings ICASSP, pp. 6953–6957 (2021)
5. Roth, J., Chaudhuri, S., Klejch, O., et al.: Ava active speaker: an audio-visual dataset for active speaker detection. In: Proceedings ICASSP, pp. 4492–4496 (2020)
6. Bost, X., Labatut, V., Linares, G.: Serial speakers: a dataset of TV series. In: Proceedongs LREC (2020)
7. Ismail, M., Memon, S., Dhomeja, L.D., et al.: Development of a regional voice dataset and speaker classification based on machine learning. J. Big Data **8**(1), 1–18 (2021)
8. Yesiler, F., Tralie, C., Correya, A., et al.: Da-TACOS: a dataset for cover song identification and understanding. In: Proceedings ISMIR, pp. 327–334 (2019)
9. Bayle, Y., Marsik, L., Rusek, M., et al.: Kara1k: a karaoke dataset for cover song identification and singing voice analysis. In: Proceedings ICASSP, pp. 177–184 (2017)
10. Yuan, X., Li, G., Han, J., et al.: Speaker identification based on Ivector and Xvector. J. Phys. Conf. Ser. **1827** (2021)
11. Zhang, Y., Lv, Z., Wu, H., et al.: MFA-conformer: multi-scale feature aggregation conformer for automatic speaker verification. arXiv:2203.15249 (2022)
12. Inoue, A., Fukumoto, M.: A proposal of creating ideal UTAU voice based on voice of the user's own key by interactive differential evolution. In: Proceedings CSII, pp. 56–59 (2019)
13. Gulati, A., Qin, J., Chiu, C.-C., et al.: Conformer: convolution-augmented transformer for speech recognition. In: Proceedings INTERSPEECH, pp. 5036–5040 (2020)

Low-Resource Speech Keyword Search Based on Residual Neural Network

Dafei Wang[1,2], Zhihua Huang[1,2(✉)], Hui Li[1,2], and Wenchen Liu[1,2]

[1] School of Information Science and Engineering, Xinjiang University, Urumqi 830017, China
{wdf,xdlh98,lwczf}@stu.xju.edu.cn, zhhuang@xju.edu.cn
[2] Key Laboratory of Signal Detection and Processing in Xinjiang Uygur Autonomous Region,
Xinjiang University, Urumqi 830017, China

Abstract. Low-resource speech keyword search is usually based on DTW template matching. However, this method has low precision and is sensitive to speaker or recording environment changes. This paper proposes a low-resource speech keyword search method based on image recognition. Bottleneck features are extract through a pre-trained model based on multi-language to generate similarity matrix images. ResNet is used to classify similarity matrix images. According to the image classification result, it is determined whether the speech keyword appears. This model does not require prior language knowledge and abundant corpus resources, so it is suitable for low-resource speech keyword search. We validate the performance of the model on different datasets. On SWS 2013, the model recall, accuracy, and F1 increased by 20.83%, 17.59%, and 19.18%, respectively. On QUESST 2014, they increased by 24.44%, 24.96%, and 24.70%, respectively. Experimental results show that the propose method is effective.

Keywords: Low resource · Speech keyword search · Bottleneck feature · Residual neural network

1 Introduction

The purpose of speech keyword search is to determine whether keywords appear in a speech document. This technology is widely used in speech document information search, speech monitoring, data mining [1], etc. At present, there are three categories of speech keyword search methods, which are filler mode-based [2, 3], template matching-based [4, 5], and large vocabulary continuous speech recognition-based [6]. However, these methods generally have poor noise robustness and low accuracy due to the lack of low-resource speech corpus or other factors [2–7].

The traditional low-resource speech keyword search method usually uses the feature vector of speech data to generate a frame-level similarity matrix. Then, keyword search is implemented by Dynamic Time Warping (DTW) template matching algorithm [8]. It can search keywords without abundant corpus resources but relies heavily on the template's versatility [9]. The accuracy of keyword search sharply drops when there is noise in the speech data or audio recorded by different people in changing record conditions [10].

W. Deng et al. (Eds.): CCBR 2022, LNCS 13628, pp. 356–363, 2022.
https://doi.org/10.1007/978-3-031-20233-9_36

With the development of deep learning, researchers started to apply deep learning to low-resource speech keyword search [11, 13]. In 2018, Dhananjay Ram et al. transformed the low-resource speech keyword search task into an image binary classification task [12, 14]. This approach has two stages: posterior features of speech keywords and speech documents are obtained in the first stage. These features are used to generate frame-level similarity matrix images. The second stage is to train a convolutional neural network (CNN) to classify similar matrix images and determine whether the keyword appears in the speech document according to the classification result [14].

However, the posterior features have poor robustness to noise and are sensitive to the change of speaker or recording environment [8]. The convolutional neural network will show apparent degradation when its layer number deepens. This paper proposes a low-resource speech keyword search method based on the combination of bottleneck features (BNF) and residual neural network (ResNet). The network structure flow is shown in Fig. 1.

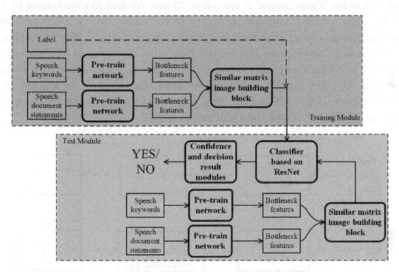

Fig. 1. Basic flowchart of low-resource speech keyword search based on BNF and ResNet

The structure of the paper is as follows. Section 2 describes the proposed model, including feature extraction, frame-level similarity matrix image construction, and residual neural network. Section 3 provides the experimental results and analysis. Finally, we conclude this work in Sect. 4.

2 Speech Keyword Search Method Based on BNF and ResNet

2.1 Bottleneck Feature Extraction

BNF are low-dimensional representations obtained from hidden bottleneck layers of the neural network. The number of hidden units in the bottleneck layer is smaller than in the other layers. The smaller network layer limits the flow of information in the network, allowing it to focus on the information required to optimize the final goal [18], which makes up for the disadvantage of posterior features.

Recently, a pre-trained network has been used to extract BNFs [21]. Its architecture is shown in Fig. 2. The pre-trained network includes multilingual training and single-language training [14]. Multilingual pre-trained networks can extract language-independent BNFs and enhance the versatility of keyword search models [21]. Therefore, this paper uses a multi-language pre-trained neural network to extract the BNFs. The pre-trained network is trained through corpus including 17 languages from the Babel Program, where the frame length of speech is 25 ms. We first get the output of 24 log filter banks. Then speech frames are applied to global mean normalization, and the first six values are passed through the discrete cosine transform (DCT) after Hamming window, resulting in a 144-dimensional vector. The processed speech data pass through the bottleneck network after global average normalization, then the network's output is downsampled. And they give the bottleneck network again after global average normalization to obtain the desired BNF [20]. This paper uses the Shennong feature extractor to extract the BNFs of keywords and speech documents.

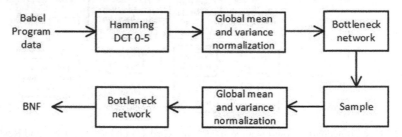

Fig. 2. Pre-trained neural network architecture for extracting BNFs

2.2 Image Construction

Similarity matrix images are constructed using BNFs of speech keywords and speech documents. Let the bottleneck feature of speech keywords be $Q = [q_1, q_2, q_3 \ldots, q_m]$ (m is the frame number of keywords). And let the BNF of the speech document be $T = [t_1, t_2, t_3 \ldots, t_n]$ (n is the frame number of the speech document). Given any two bottleneck feature vectors q_i and t_j, we compute a distance-like measure by taking the log of their dot product as follows:

$$S(q_i, t_j) = \log(q_i \cdot t_j) \tag{1}$$

We calculate the M × N dimensional distance matrix and apply range normalization. The formula is as follows:

$$s_{norm}(q_i, t_j) = -1 + 2(\frac{S(q_i, t_j) - s_{min}}{s_{max} - s_{min}}) \qquad (2)$$

We obtain a normalized frame-level similarity distance matrix with all values between -1 and 1. Among them $s_{min} = \min(s(q_i, t_j))$, $s_{max} = \max(s(q_i, t_j))$. The normalized frame-level similarity distance matrix is regarded as an image. The similarity matrix images are divided into two classes based on whether the speech keywords appear in the speech document. One class is the positive class where keywords appear, and the other is the negative class where keywords do not appear.

2.3 Residual Neural Networks

Deepening networks can learn the in-depth features of images and classify images more accurately. However, deepening the network is ease to cause network degradation, gradient disappearance, and gradient explosion problems. In 2015, Kaiming He et al. proposed the Residual Neural Network (ResNet) [15]. These problems are effectively solved by changing the learning objectives from the complete learning output to the learning residuals. We use the ResNet-34 network for low-resource speech keyword search. The network consists of four stacked residual blocks, including 33 convolutional layers, a max pooling layer of size 3 × 3, an average pooling layer, and a fully connected layer.

Keywords and documents to be detected are provided in the form of speech. Set the label according to whether the speech keyword appears. Labels are divided into two categories, one is that the keyword appears in the speech document, and the label is set to 1, and the other is that the keyword does not appear in the speech document, and the label is set to 0. First, we input the paired speech keywords and speech documents to the feature extraction network to obtain BNF. Then we get the frame-level similarity distance matrix by calculating the distance and normalization formulas. The generated frame-level similarity matrix images are grayscale, so the network is set to single-channel. Finally, we input the generated frame-level similarity matrix images and labels into the residual neural network to complete the model training.

3 Experimental Setup

3.1 Datasets

Spoken Web Search (SWS) 2013 dataset contains nine low-resource languages [16]. The training and evaluation each have 505 and 503 speech keywords. The train and evaluation datasets have different speakers and recording conditions. The search corpus [17] consists of 20 h of audio and 10762 utterances. For training, we randomly select 10,000 paired data from the training dataset, where the numbers of positive and negative classes are 5135 and 4865. To evaluate the performance of the model, we randomly select 501 sentence pairs from the evaluation dataset, where the numbers of positive and negative types are 246 and 255. Query by Example Search on Speech Task (QUESST)

2014 includes six low-resource languages [19]. The training and evaluation each have 560 and 555 speech keywords. The search corpus contains about 23 h of recordings, and the recording conditions and speakers differ from the training dataset. The number of speech pairs in the training dataset is 5471 for the positive class and 8052 for the negative class. The number of speech pairs in the evaluation dataset is 5213 for positive and 8048 for negative classes.

We set the threshold value as 0.5 in all experiments, with the experimental system being Ubuntu16.04, the CPU being Inter(R)Xeon(R)Gold5218 (2.30 GHz), and the GPU being Nvidia TeslaP100 (16 GB) server.

3.2 Comparison of the Impact of Different Pre-trained Network

We use multi-language and single-language pre-trained networks to extract the bottle-neck features of speech data in this section. The experiments compare the impact of different pre-trained networks on the keyword search model. The multi-language pre-trained network uses 17 languages from the IARPA Babel program, and the single-language pre-trained network uses the Fisher dataset. The setting of experimental parameters: Learning rate is 0.001, epoch size is 100, and batch size is 32.

Table 1. Comparing the influence of single-language and multi-language pre-trained neural networks for extracting bottleneck features

Methods (SWS2013)	Recall	Precision	F1
Single-language BNF + CNN	0.6829	0.6640	0.6733
Multi-language BNF + CNN	0.7195	0.7224	0.7209
Single-language BNF + ResNet34	0.8048	0.7471	0.7748
Multi-language BNF + ResNet34	0.8001	0.7606	0.7801

As in Table 1, the multi-language pre-trained model has better evaluation metrics combined with CNN-based classifiers. Furthermore, the multi-language pre-trained network performs slightly better than the single-language pre-trained network one when combined with ResNet34. The results show that the multi-language pre-trained network is more advantageous in extracting bottleneck features. Therefore, we choose the multi-language pre-trained network in the first stage.

3.3 Verification of the Impact of BNF and ResNet Speech Keyword Search Methods

To verify the effectiveness of our method, we performed ablation experiments on the SWS2013 dataset. We also explore the effects of ResNet and BNF on the performance of keyword search models. The experimental results are in Table 2.

Table 2. Performance comparison of different features and networks in the speech keyword search task

Methods (SWS2013)	Recall	Precision	F1
Posterior + CNN	0.5918	0.5847	0.5883
Multi-language BNF + CNN	0.7195	0.7224	0.7209
Posterior + ResNet34	0.6382	0.6487	0.6463
Multi-language BNF + ResNet34	0.8001	0.7606	0.7801

The baseline is the combination of posterior features and CNN. We replace posterior features with bottleneck features, resulting in 12.77%, 13.77%, and 13.26% improvements in the recall, accuracy, and F1. Experimental results show that the bottleneck feature is less sensitive to changing speaker and recording conditions, and the model has better retrieval performance. Further, we use ResNet34 as a classifier instead of CNN. Compared to the baseline, it brings some improvements in metrics. Therefore, our proposed model combined bottleneck features and ResNet34 and achieved the best performance, with 20.83%, 17.59%, and 19.18% improvement in the three indicators compared to the baseline.

Furthermore, to demonstrate the generalization of the proposed model, we experimented on QUESST2014 dataset, as shown in Table 3.

Table 3. Performance comparison of different features and networks in the speech keyword search task

Methods (QUESST 2014)	Recall	Precision	F1
Posterior + CNN	0.5557	0.5376	0.5465
Multi-language BNF + CNN	0.7377	0.7799	0.7518
Posterior + ResNet34	0.5680	0.5789	0.5733
Multi-language BNF + ResNet34	0.8001	0.7872	0.7935

The performance of the proposed model is still significantly improved compared with other reference models. The recall, accuracy, and F1 scores improved by 24.44%, 24.96%, and 24.70%. We can confirm that the model could achieve better retrieval performance on different datasets.

4   Conclusions

We propose a keyword search model apply for low-resource or even zero-resource speech. This method does not require resources such as pronunciation dictionaries, annotated corpora, etc., and requires only a few annotations to complete the model training for keyword search. When the speaker and the recording environment change, the method can still complete the keyword search task efficiently and accurately. In addition, we train the model in multiple languages and do not involve knowledge of the language itself. The model has strong versatility, and the trained model can complete the keyword search task of the target language without adjustment.

Acknowledgments. This research was funded by the Natural Science Foundation of Xinjiang Uygur Autonomous Region of China, Grant No. 2022D01C59, and National Key R&D Program of China, Grant No. 2018YFC0823402.

References

1. Rodriguez-Fuentes, L.J., Varona, A., Penagarikano, M., Bordel, G., Diez, M.: High-performance query-by-example spoken term detection on the SWS 2013 evaluation. In: 2014 IEEE International Conference on Acoustics, Speech and Signal Processing (ICASSP), pp. 7819–7823 (2014)
2. Yusuf, B., Gundogdu, B., Saraclar, M.: Low resource keyword search with synthesized Crosslingual exemplars. In: IEEE/ACM Transactions on Audio, Speech, and Language Processing, vol. 27, no. 7, pp. 1126–1135 (2019)
3. Gündoğdu, B., Sarı, L., Çetinkaya, G., Saraçlar, M.: Template-based Keyword Search with pseudo posteriorgrams. In: 2016 24th Signal Processing and Communication Application Conference (SIU), pp. 973–976 (2016)
4. Gündoğdu, B., Saraçlar, M.: Distance metric learning for posteriorgram based keyword search. In: 2017 IEEE International Conference on Acoustics, Speech and Signal Processing (ICASSP), pp. 5660–5664 (2017)
5. Audhkhasi, K., Rosenberg, A., Sethy, A., Ramabhadran, B., Kingsbury, B.: End-to-end ASR-free keyword search from speech. IEEE J. Sel. Top. Sign. Proces. **11**(8), 1351–1359 (2017)
6. Zhao, Z., Zhang, W.-Q.: End-to-end keyword search system based on attention mechanism and energy scorer for low resource languages. Neural Networks **139**, 326–334 (2021)
7. Fuchs, T.S., Segal, Y., Keshet, J.: CNN-based spoken term detection and localization without dynamic programming. In: ICASSP 2021–2021 IEEE International Conference on Acoustics, Speech and Signal Processing (ICASSP), pp. 6853–6857 (2021)
8. Deekshitha, G., Mary, L.: Multilingual spoken term detection: a review. Int. J. Speech Technol. **23**(3), 653–667 (2020)
9. Kishore, K.R., Sarkar, S., Rengaswamy, P., Rao, K.S.: Audio mining: unsupervised spoken term detection over an audio database. In: 2018 International Conference on Advances in Computing, Communications and Informatics (ICACCI), pp. 514–518 (2018)
10. Feng, S., Żelasko, P., Moro-Velázquez, L., et al.: Unsupervised acoustic unit discovery by leveraging a language-independent subword discriminative feature representation. In: ISCA Conference of the International Speech Communication Association (Interspeech), pp. 1534–1538 (2021)
11. San, N., et al.: Leveraging pre-trained representations to improve access to untranscribed speech from endangered languages. In: 2021 IEEE Automatic Speech Recognition and Understanding Workshop (ASRU), pp.1094–1101 (2021)
12. Ram, D., Miculicich, L., Bourlard, H.: CNN Based Query by Example Spoken Term Detection. In: ISCA Conference of the International Speech Communication Association (Interspeech), pp. 92–96 (2018)
13. Menon, R., Kamper, H., Quinn, J., Niesler, T.: Fast ASR-free and almost zero-resource keyword spotting using DTW and CNNs for humanitarian monitoring. In: ISCA Conference of the International Speech Communication Association (Interspeech), pp. 2608–2612 (2018)

14. Ram, D., Miculicich, L., Bourlard, H.: Neural network based end-to-end query by example spoken term detection. IEEE/ACM Trans. Audio, Speech, Lang. Processing **28**, 1416–1427 (2020)
15. He, K., Zhang, X., Ren, S., Sun, J.: Deep residual learning for image recognition. pp. 770–778 (2016)
16. Rodriguez-Fuentes, L.J., Penagarikano, M.: MediaEval 2013 spoken web search task: system performance measures (2013)
17. Naik, P., Gaonkar, M.N., Thenkanidiyoor, V., Dileep, A.D.: Kernel based matching and a novel training approach for CNN-based QbE-STD. In: 2020 International Conference on Signal Processing and Communications (SPCOM), pp. 1–5 (2020)
18. Menon, R., Kamper, H., Yilmaz, E., Quinn, J., Niesler, T.R.: ASR-free CNN-DTW keyword spotting using multilingual bottleneck features for almost zero-resource languages (2018)
19. Stoica, P.-D., Toma, Ş.-A., Ceaparu, M., Pura, M.L.: Spoken language detection experiments for Romanian. In: 2019 International Conference on Speech Technology and Human-Computer Dialogue (SpeD), pp. 1–6 (2019)
20. Silnova, A., et al.: BUT/Phonexia Bottleneck Feature Extractor. pp. 283–287 (2018)
21. Fer, R., Matějka, P., Grézl, F., Plchot, O., Veselý, K., Černocký, J.H.: Multilingually trained bottleneck features in spoken language recognition. Comput. Speech Lang. **46**, 252–267 (2017)

Online Neural Speaker Diarization with Core Samples

Yanyan Yue, Jun Du$^{(\boxtimes)}$, and Maokui He

University of Science and Technology of China, HeFei, China
{yyyue,hmk1754}@mail.ustc.edu.cn,jundu@ustc.edu.cn

Abstract. We propose an online neural diarization method based on TS-VAD, which shows remarkable performance on highly overlapping speech. We introduce online VBx to help TS-VAD get the target-speaker embeddings. First, when the amount of data is insufficient, only online VBx is executed to accumulate speaker information. Afterwards, a separate offline subsystem is utilized to extract i-vectors based on core samples for TS-VAD online decoding. Finally, we devise a speaker selection strategy that allows TS-VAD to handle an unknown number of speakers. We evaluate our system on AliMeeting dataset. The experimental results demonstrate that our online method can effectively handle high-degree overlapped audios.

Keywords: Online speaker diarization · TS-VAD · VBx · Core samples

1 Introduction

Speaker diarization, a task of segmenting recordings into homogeneous speaker-specific regions, i.e. "who spoke when" [1]. Good speaker diarization results are useful for applications such as speech transcription, dominant speaker detection, speech indexing and meeting summary [2,3].

A considerable amount of literature has been published on speaker diarization. These studies fall into two main categories, traditional clustering-based speaker diarization (CSD) approaches [4–6] and deep neural network-based approaches [7–11]. The former consists of separate sub-modules for segmentation, speaker embedding extraction, and clustering [1]. K-means [4], agglomerative hierarchical clustering (AHC) [5], spectral clustering(SC) [6], etc. are commonly used clustering algorithms. Clustering-based methods have achieved robust accuracy on many challenging sessions and cross-domain datasets [12]. However, the application of these approachs to highly overlapping speech is hindered by the assumption that a segment contains only one speaker. Recently, end-to-end neural speaker diarization (EEND) [7–9] and target-speaker speech activity detection (TS-VAD) [10,11] have attracted widespread attention. These neural network-based methods simultaneously predict the activity probability of each speaker in each frame, allowing to improve classification performance in high overlap regions. In the recent M2MeT challenge, the top three teams all chose TS-VAD as a baseline for handling high overlap meeting speech [13]. Although EEND and TS-VAD have achieved the state-of-the-art results on some datasets, there are still limitations in dealing with flexible number of speakers. Moreover, some researchers have tried to combine clustering-based methods with EEND to exploit the advantages of both, obtaining promising results [12,14].

The methods discussed above are all offline methods, whereas in practice we would like to be able to perform speaker diarization online. There is relatively little research on online diarization and most of it is based on extensions to existing offline algorithms. Some earlier studies used speaker adaptation to improve GMM-UBM-based systems into online systems [15,16]. For a couple of years, more and more clustering-based algorithms have been extended in an online fashion. In order to improve performance of chkpt-AHC, Zhang et al. [17] designed a graph-based reclustering process. [18] used the transformer transducer model for speaker turn detection and extracted turn-level embeddings. Due to the sparsity of speaker turns, the number of embeddings is relatively small even for longer speech durations, thus reducing the computational cost of spectral clustering. Our earlier work [19] implemented online processing in block manner based on variational Bayesian hidden Markov model with x-vector (VBx) [20]. By retaining the core samples, the classification accuracy of VBx on a small amount of data is improved. In addition, online diarization methods based on neural networks have been developed. Google proposed a fully supervised framework, UIS-RNN [21], to obtain better results than unsupervised online systems when annotation data are available. Subsequently, the performance of UIS-RNN was improved by proposing a different loss function and speaker turn modeling [22]. Futhermore, in [23], EEND is applied to the online system using the buffer mechanism. The authors compared four strategies for selecting data-filled buffers and yielded results comparable to those of the baseline system on DIHARD-II.

In this paper, we attempt to solve the challenging task of online diarization of high overlap speech. Our previous work [19], online VBx, showed superior performance on the AMI and DIHARD corpus. However, online VBx is ill-suited for processing audio with a high proportion of overlap. Therefore, we try to extend the TS-VAD [24] system, which performs well on overlapping data, to an online manner. Since the original TS-VAD was performed in chunks, TS-VAD can be considered an online system given the target speaker embeddings. In practice, however, it is difficult to obtain information about the participants in advance, and the target speaker embeddings are often obtained through an offline diarization system. Therefore, we propose a hybrid approach that combines online VBx with TS-VAD. When the amount of data is insufficient, we only perform online VBx to assign labels and accumulate speaker information. When a sufficient amount of data is expected to be available, we introduce the core samples module into the TS-VAD and use it to extract reliable i-vectors estimation. A selection strategy based on online VBx results is used to process an unknown number of speakers. We conducted experiments on AliMeeting Eval set and obtained better results than the baseline.

2 Related Work

2.1 The TS-VAD Model

Taking the customary speech features and target-speaker embeddings as input, TS-VAD predicts the frame-level activity probability for each speaker, which can be estimated by a neural network-based model. Let $O = \{o_1, o_2, ..., o_T\} \in \mathbb{R}^{T \times M}$ be the sequence of observed feature vectors, and $G = \{g_1, g_2, ..., g_P\} \in \mathbb{R}^{P \times V}$ be the i-vectors of P speakers. Firstly, the input feature sequence O is converted to frame-level embedding $E = \{e_1, e_2, ..., e_P\} \in \mathbb{R}^{T \times D}$ by 4 convolutional layers. The frame-level embedding is then concatenated with the target-speaker embedding G and fed into a speaker detection (SD) component consisting of 2-layer bidirectional LSTM with projection (BLSTMP). Finally, a BLSTMP processes the SD outputs and a linear layer produces the 2-class outputs for each speaker. TS-VAD is under a strong dependence on reliable i-vector estimation, which requires sufficiently good segmentation. The target-speaker embeddings are extracted with oracle speaker segments in the training stage and CSD results in the testing stage.

2.2 The Online VBx System

In this paper, we use the online VBx proposed in [19] as the front-end of TS-VAD to extract i-vectors. Online VBx is implemented through a block-wise approach. There are three dynamic memory modules in online VBx: the core samples module, the clustering samples module, and the global centroids module. For segment S_i, B samples are first drawn from the core samples by stratified sampling, and then these samples are fed into VBx with S_i to obtain the local clustering results. Due to the label ambiguity problem, constrained clustering of local centroids and global centroids is performed to match local labels with global labels. Finally, a time-decay based score function is used to update the core samples. This allows to take into account the effects of both temporal and spatial proximity.

3 Proposed Method

3.1 Overview

As mentioned before, to obtain the target speaker embeddings, many studies usually first obtain the initial diarization results using spectral clustering or VBx, which limits the extension of TS-VAD to online manner. Therefore, we introduce the online VBx as the front-end to TS-VAD to solve the problem of target speaker embeddings extraction as well as new speaker detection in online system. The most straightforward approach is to first use online VBx to get the initial diarization result whenever a segment arrives, then extract the i-vector with all the historical results, and finally perform TS-VAD to get the final label of the segment. Nevertheless, there are two major problems with this approach. One is the case that the computational complexity of extracting the i-vector increases with the audio duration. And the other is the i-vectors of the target speakers change frequently, which will affect the classification accuracy of TS-VAD. As a result, we divide the online diarization process into two stages as showed in Fig. 1.

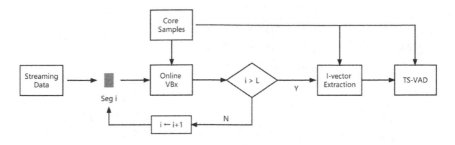

Fig. 1. Flowchart of online TS-VAD system incorporated with online VBx.

In an online system, data arrives dynamically. Reliable i-vectors estimation can not be achieved when the amount of data is small in the early stage. Therefore, we assume that there are few overlapping regions between speakers in the first few minutes of the meeting. At this point we only use online VBx to allocate labels while accumulating information about the speakers. That is, for a new segment S_i, if $i < L$, only online VBx is executed while the core samples are continuously updated. Here L is the pre-set sample size for online VBx only. After accumulating information of L samples, we use the core samples to extract the i-vectors. With the i-vectors, we can introduce TS-VAD to better handle overlapping segments.

3.2   Online TS-VAD with Core Samples

Core samples module is an important concept in online VBx. Extracting clustering samples from core samples improves the classification accuracy of VBx on a small amount of data. In addition, because only core samples are kept instead of all samples, memory consumption is reduced to some extent. In [19], core samples $\boldsymbol{X}^{\mathrm{core}} = \{\boldsymbol{X}_1^{\mathrm{core}}, \boldsymbol{X}_2^{\mathrm{core}}, ..., \boldsymbol{X}_C^{\mathrm{core}}\}$, $\boldsymbol{X}_c^{\mathrm{core}} = \{\boldsymbol{x}_{c,i_1}^{\mathrm{core}}, \boldsymbol{x}_{c,i_2}^{\mathrm{core}}, ..., \boldsymbol{x}_{c,i_N}^{\mathrm{core}}\}$, where $\boldsymbol{x}_{c,i_k}^{\mathrm{core}} \in \mathbb{R}^{D_1}$ is the x-vector corresponding to segment S_{i_k}. And in online TS-VAD, in addition to the x-vectors, the core samples store the fbanks of the corresponding samples as well as the diarization results of VBx, $\boldsymbol{S}^{\mathrm{core}} = \{\boldsymbol{X}^{\mathrm{core}}, \boldsymbol{F}^{\mathrm{core}}, \boldsymbol{R}^{\mathrm{core}}\}$. $\boldsymbol{F}^{\mathrm{core}}$ is similar to $\boldsymbol{X}^{\mathrm{core}}$, but $\boldsymbol{f}_{c,i_k}^{\mathrm{core}} \in \mathbb{R}^{T_{i_k} \times D_2}$, where T_{i_k} is the number of frames in segment S_{i_k} and D_2 is dimension of fbanks feature. And $\boldsymbol{R}^{\mathrm{core}}$ is the speaker distribution information generated by segments in the core samples module. As shown in Fig. 2, the core samples module has three main roles in online TS-VAD. Firstly, as with online VBx, clustering samples are sampled from $\boldsymbol{X}^{\mathrm{core}}$. Secondly, samples are taken from $\boldsymbol{F}^{\mathrm{core}}$ by stratified sampling and fed to TS-VAD for predicting. Thirdly, i-vectors are extracted according to

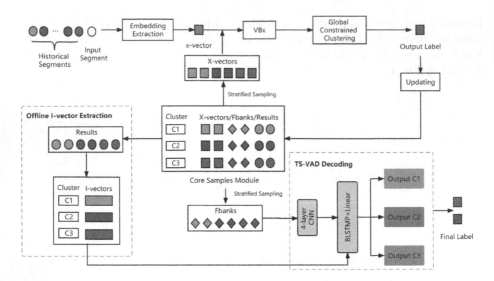

Fig. 2. Framework of online TS-VAD system with core samples. Assume that the number of output nodes P of TS-VAD is 3. For the input segment, online VBx assumes that only speaker $C3$ is speaking, while TS-VAD detects that both speaker $C2$ and speaker $C3$ are actively speaking.

R^{core}. We suppose that the maximum number of each class stored in the core samples is N and the maximum number of speakers in the dataset is C. The computational complexity of extracting the i-vector is $O(CN)$ regardless of the audio duration. In addition, the classification accuracy of the segments in the core samples is relatively high, so a reliable i-vector estimation can be obtained. And we find that frequent updates of the i-vector lead to a decrease in the final classification accuracy. Therefore we operate an additional offline subsystem to extract the i-vectors every t seconds based on the core samples.

One of the drawbacks of online VBx is that the number of predicted speakers is always higher than the actual number of speakers. And TS-VAD has limitations in handling flexible speakers. [11] designed a selection strategy to handle an unknown number of speakers in the testing phase. Assuming that the model can only handle P speakers, if the estimated number of speakers $\hat{P}$ is less than P, $P - \hat{P}$ i-vectors are randomly selected from the training set as irrelevant speaker information; if $\hat{P} > P$, the P speakers with the highest number of occurrences is selected from $\hat{P}$. We follow this strategy. When $\hat{P} < P$, the same processing is carried out. When $\hat{P} > P$, if the VBx output label of segment S_i is k, the corresponding i-vectors are selected firstly regardless of the number of times when speaker k appears, and then the most frequent $P - 1$ is selected from the remaining $\hat{P} - 1$ speakers.

4 Experiments

4.1 Experiment Setup

Clustering is carried out based on speech segments. We first use oracle boundary information to divide the audio into segments with a maximum length of 2 s. And the overlap between adjacent segments is 1 s. Online VBx is the same as in [19] except that the core samples module stores both x-vectors, fbanks, and VBx results. For TS-VAD, the training process follows [24]. The model is trained using AliMeeting, AISHELL4, and simulated data with CN-CELEB. The model parameters are updated using the Adam optimizer, and the learning rate is placed at 0.0001. The audio is cut into short segments with a window length of 8s and a window shift of 6 s, and the batch size is set to 128. The TS-VAD model is trained separately, with an output node number P of 4. In the testing phase of online TS-VAD, the sample size for the online VBx-only and the maximum number of stores allowed per class in the core samples are both set to 120. Moreover, the batch size is 32.

The experiments are conducted on the first channel of AliMeeting Eval set [25]. The number of speakers per audio is 2 to 4, and the duration is about 30 min. The dataset has a very high number of speech overlaps, with an average overlap rate of 34%. We employ the diarization error rate (DER) as evaluation metric, which is time weighted of false alarms (FA), miss errors (MISS) and speaker errors (SC). And no collar is considered for DER calculation.

4.2 Results

Table 1. DERs(%) results of online TS-VAD with different i-vectors update strategies.

I-vectors	FA	MISS	SC	DER
Historical Samples with t = 1	3.9	6.9	6.4	17.1
Historical Samples with t = 20	3.2	7.4	5.8	16.4
Core Samples with t = 1	3.8	7.0	6.7	17.5
Core Samples with t = 20	3.8	6.8	4.7	**15.3**

Superior performance of TS-VAD relies on reliable i-vectors estimation. Table 1 compares the impact of different i-vector update strategies on the performance of the online system. 'Historical Samples' and 'Core Samples' represent the extraction of i-vectors using VBx results from all historical samples and core samples respectively. And t means that i-vectors are updated every t seconds. It is worth noting that the performance of updating the i-vectors with historical samples containing more information is sub-optimal. This may be due to the presence of many misclassified segments in the historical samples, which interfered with the estimation of the i-vectors. In fact, the process of selecting core samples is also the process of discarding segments that have a higher probability of being misclassified. By contrast, updating i-vectors with core samples obtains a lower DER. Also, frequent updates of the i-vector can be expected to result in poorer results. Therefore, we extract i-vectors every 20 s using core samples, which not only achieves better performance, but also reduces computational costs.

Table 2 compares the results of different systems on the AliMeeting Eval set. By looking at the composition of the DER, it is observed that MISS is dominant in the DER of the offline and online VBx systems, which is consistent with the lack of capability of VBx to handle overlapping speech. By comparison with VBx, TS-VAD significantly reduces miss error. Despite the poor performance of online VBx, online TS-VAD still yields a DER of 15%, leading to the 37% relative diarization error rate reduction in relation to offline VBx. This suggests that it is sufficient to obtain relatively reliable i-vector estimation from the core samples.

Table 2. DERs(%) results on AliMeeting Eval set.

System	FA	MISS	SC	DER
Offline VBx	0.0	20.7	3.6	24.3
Offline TS-VAD	2.7	5.4	3.5	**11.6**
Online VBx	0.0	20.8	7.7	28.5
Online TS-VAD	3.8	6.8	4.7	**15.3**

Our experiments were performed on one NVIDIA Geforce RTX 3090 GPU. The average time taken to process a segment is 0.5 s, with online VBx taking 0.2 s and TS-VAD decoding taking 0.3 s.

5 Conclusion

In this paper, we propose an online neural speaker diarization method based on TS-VAD, where online VBx is introduced to obtain the target speaker embeddings. Specifically, we use online VBx to accumulate speaker information when the amount of data is not sufficient. We then extract i-vectors at intervals based on the core samples and apply them to the online decoding of TS-VAD. Additionly, a speaker selection strategy is used to process audios with flexible number of speakers. Actually, our approach can be extended to other neural network methods that require pre-fetching speaker embeddings. Experimental results suggest that our online system can efficiently process recodings with highly overlapping regions. Future work will be focused on the close integration of online VBx with TS-VAD.

Acknowledgements. This work was supported by the National Natural Science Foundation of China under Grant No. 62171427. This work was also funded by Ximalaya.

References

1. Park, T.J., Kanda, N., Dimitriadis, D., Han, K., Watanabe, S., Narayanan, S.: A review of speaker diarization: recent advances with deep learning. Comput. Speech Lang. **72**, 101317 (2022)
2. Vijayasenan, D., Valente, F., Bourlard, H.: An information theoretic approach to speaker diarization of meeting data. IEEE Trans. Audio Speech Lang. Process. **17**(7), 1382–1393 (2009)
3. Anguera, X., Bozonnet, S., Evans, N., Fredouille, C., Friedland, G., Vinyals, O.: Speaker diarization: a review of recent research. IEEE Trans. Audio Speech Lang. Process. **20**(2), 356–370 (2012)
4. Wang, Q., Downey, C., Wan, L., Mansfield, P.A., Moreno, I.L.: Speaker diarization with LSTM. In: 2018 IEEE International Conference on Acoustics, Speech and Signal Processing (ICASSP), pp. 5239–5243 (2018)
5. Garcia-Romero, D., Snyder, D., Sell, G., Povey, D., McCree, A.: Speaker diarization using deep neural network embeddings. In: 2017 IEEE International Conference on Acoustics, Speech and Signal Processing (ICASSP), pp. 4930–4934 (2017)
6. Lin, Q., Yin, R., Li, M., Bredin, H., Barras, C.: LSTM based similarity measurement with spectral clustering for speaker diarization. In: Interspeech 2019, pp. 366–370 (2019)
7. Fujita, Y., Kanda, N., Horiguchi, S., Nagamatsu, K., Watanabe, S.: End-to-end neural speaker diarization with permutation-free objectives (2019)
8. Fujita, Y., Kanda, N., Horiguchi, S., Xue, Y., Nagamatsu, K., Watanabe, S.: End-to-end neural speaker diarization with self-attention. In: 2019 IEEE Automatic Speech Recognition and Understanding Workshop (ASRU), pp. 296–303 (2019)
9. Horiguchi, S., Fujita, Y., Watanabe, S., Xue, Y., Nagamatsu, K.: End-to-end speaker diarization for an unknown number of speakers with encoder-decoder based attractors (2020)
10. Medennikov, I., et al.: Target-speaker voice activity detection: a novel approach for multi-speaker diarization in a dinner party scenario. In: Interspeech 2020, pp. 274–278 (2020)
11. He, M., Raj, D., Huang, Z., Du, J., Chen, Z., Watanabe, S.: Target-speaker voice activity detection with improved i-vector estimation for unknown number of speaker (2021)
12. Kinoshita, K., Delcroix, M., Tawara, N.: Integrating end-to-end neural and clustering-based diarization: getting the best of both worlds. In: ICASSP 2021– 2021 IEEE International Conference on Acoustics, Speech and Signal Processing (ICASSP), pp. 7198–7202 (2021)
13. Yu, F., et al.: Summary on the ICASSP 2022 multi-channel multi-party meeting transcription grand challenge. In: ICASSP 2022–2022 IEEE International Conference on Acoustics, Speech and Signal Processing (ICASSP), pp. 9156–9160 (2022)
14. Kinoshita, K., Delcroix, M., Iwata, T.: Tight integration of neural- and clustering-based diarization through deep unfolding of infinite gaussian mixture model. In: ICASSP 2022–2022 IEEE International Conference on Acoustics, Speech and Signal Processing (ICASSP), pp. 8382–8386 (2022)
15. Geiger, J.T., Wallhoff, F., Rigoll, G.: GMM-UBM based open-set online speaker diarization. In: Interspeech 2010, pp. 2330–2333 (2010)
16. Vaquero, C., Vinyals, O., Friedland, G.: A hybrid approach to online speaker diarization. In: Interspeech 2010, pp. 2638–2641 (2010)

17. Zhang, Y., et al.: Low-latency online speaker diarization with graph-based label generation (2021)
18. Xia, W., et al.: Turn-to-diarize: online speaker diarization constrained by transformer transducer speaker turn detection. In: ICASSP 2022–2022 IEEE International Conference on Acoustics, Speech and Signal Processing (ICASSP), pp. 8077–8081 (2022)
19. Yue, Y., Du, J., He, M., Yang, Y., Wang, R.: Online speaker diarization with core samples selection. In: Submitted for Interspeech 2022 (2022)
20. Landini, F., Profant, J., Diez, M., Burget, L.: Bayesian HMM clustering of x-vector sequences (VBx) in speaker diarization: theory, implementation and analysis on standard tasks. Comput. Speech Lang. **71**, 101254 (2021)
21. Zhang, A., Wang, Q., Zhu, Z., Paisley, J., Wang, C.: Fully supervised speaker diarization. In: ICASSP 2019–2019 IEEE International Conference on Acoustics, Speech and Signal Processing (ICASSP), pp. 6301–6305 (2019)
22. Fini, E., Brutti, A.: Supervised online diarization with sample mean loss for multi-domain data. In: ICASSP 2020–2020 IEEE International Conference on Acoustics, Speech and Signal Processing (ICASSP), pp. 7134–7138 (2020)
23. Xue, Y., et al.: Online streaming end-to-end neural diarization handling overlapping speech and flexible numbers of speakers (2021)
24. He, M., et al.: The USTC-Ximalaya system for the ICASSP 2022 multi-channel multi-party meeting transcription (M2MeT) challenge. In: ICASSP 2022–2022 IEEE International Conference on Acoustics, Speech and Signal Processing (ICASSP), pp. 9166–9170 (2022)
25. Yu, F., et al.: M2MeT: the ICASSP 2022 multi-channel multi-party meeting transcription challenge. In: ICASSP 2022–2022 IEEE International Conference on Acoustics, Speech and Signal Processing (ICASSP) (2022)

Pose-Unconstrainted 3D Lip Behaviometrics via Unsupervised Symmetry Correction

Xinyang Pian[1] and Jie Zhang[2]([✉])

[1] School of Artificial Intelligence, Beijing Technology and Business University,
Beijing 100048, China
[2] School of Automation and Electrical Engineering, University of Science and Technology
Beijing, Beijing 100083, China
zhangjie99@ustb.edu.cn

Abstract. Lip behavior in human speaking is a remarkable bio-modality with individual uniqueness and repeatability, which can be used for secure identity recognition. The dynamic lip modality in 3D point cloud sequences has depth cues. However, due to self-occlusion of the 3D lip, the single-view point cloud of a pose-unconstrainted speaking lip suffers missing local structure, which affects the accuracy of 3D lip behaviometrics. This paper proposes a pose-unconstrainted 3D lip behaviometrics method based on symmetry correction of lip point clouds. We construct an unsupervised neural network to capture the latent symmetry cue of a 3D lip under any pose and correct the structure of the lip point cloud. The improved point cloud sequence is fed into a spatiotemporal lip feature learning network for lip behaviometrics. The experiments on the public dataset S3DFM demonstrate that lip symmetry correction can improve the accuracy of the 3D lip behaviometrics by 2.65%.

Keywords: Lip behavior · Behaviometrics · Symmetry detection · Point cloud correction · Unsupervised learning

1 Introduction

Lip behavior has high informativeness and anti-forgery difficulty, which benefits broad application prospects in the fields, such as high-security behaviometrics and access control [1]. The current stage of 3D lip behaviometrics research uses 2D grayscale data to assist in learning constrained pose 3D point cloud features[2]. The 3D point cloud of non-frontal lips collected in a single view has the problem of missing local structures. Due to the symmetry of the 3D lip, the missing point cloud structure can be corrected or completed by the symmetrical counterpart. In a simple scene, the principal component analysis (PCA)[3] can be applied to determine the symmetry plane of an object. However, this method is very sensitive to small changes in geometry. The state-of-the-art symmetry detection method [3] is unsupervised global symmetric plane detection using Convolution Neural Network (CNN) on voxels. This method requires converting point clouds into voxel data and does not work well on the data with unclear symmetry.

To this end, we exploit the latent structural symmetry of 3D lips and automatically detect the symmetry planes of 3D lips in any pose based on point cloud feature learning. The symmetry-based lip point cloud inpainting improves the structural integrity and shape accuracy of 3D lip point cloud sequences. Based on this, a 4D spatiotemporal lip feature learning module is constructed for lip behaviometrics. The module automatically captures 3D spatial structure of the lip behavior sequence and behavioral dynamics in the time domain. Our contributions are as follows.

1) An unsupervised symmetry detection neural network for pose-unconstrained 3D lips is proposed. The network predicts a potential symmetry plane by learning the global features of an incomplete 3D lip point cloud.
2) A pose-unconstrained 3D lip behaviometrics framework based on point cloud correction is constructed. The method overcomes the influence of the speaker's lip pose changes, which extends the applicability of 3D lip behaviometrics.

2   Methodology

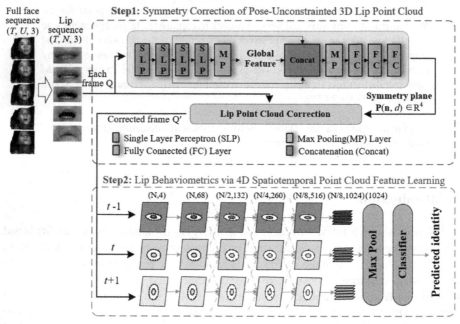

Fig. 1. The proposed framework has two parts: (1) symmetry correction module; (2) lip behaviometrics module. Our framework firstly corrects the symmetric structure of each 3D lip point cloud frame, and then the corrected lip point cloud sequences are fed into the spatiotemporal feature learning network for identity recognition.

2.1 Proposed Framework

We propose a symmetric correction method to improve the structure completeness of the lip point cloud. Figure 1 shows an overview of the proposed framework with two modules: symmetry correction module and identity recognition module.

First, a face point cloud sequence of T frames with each containing U points is pre-processed into a lip point cloud sequence with N points at each frame. Each point contains 3D coordinates $\mathbf{q}_i = (x_i, y_i, z_i)$, where $i \in \{1, \cdots, N\}$. Each lip point frame Q is fed to the symmetry correction module respectively. The global symmetry plane $\mathbf{P} = (\mathbf{n}, d)$ is obtained by the global symmetry prediction module, where $\mathbf{n} = (a, b, c)$ is the normal vector and d is the offset of the symmetry plane. The global symmetry plane is then used for symmetry correction. The corrected lip point cloud sequence is fed into the identity recognition module for spatiotemporal feature extraction and behaviometrics.

2.2 Symmetry-Aware Point Cloud Correction of Pose-Unconstrainted 3D Lips

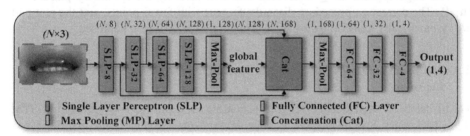

Fig. 2. The architecture of the symmetry detection network. The network learns hierarchical lip features by perceptrons and obtains global features by maximum pooling. The output is the symmetric plane parameters of the lip through the fully connected layer.

Symmetry Detection. The global symmetry prediction network consists of a multilayer perceptron (MLP) that learns the global features of each frame and predicts the global latent symmetry of the corresponding frame (as shown in Fig. 2).

The input point set Q passes through four levels of single layer perceptron (SLP), and the output features of i-th SLP are defined as a set of per-point features $SLPF_i$, where $i \in \{1 \cdots 4\}$. It can be expressed as below.

$$SLPF_i = \text{ReLU}(\text{SLP}(SLPF_{i-1})), \tag{1}$$

where $i \in \{2 \cdots 4\}$ is the index of the SLP layers.

We concatenate the first level, second level, and last level per-point features as lip global features $\mathbf{F} = \{SLPF_1, SLPF_2, SLPF_4\}$, where $SLPF_4$ feature aggregation is performed by max pooling and expanded to N per-points. The fully connected layer is then used to predict the parameters of the global symmetry plane $\mathbf{P} = (\mathbf{n}, d)$.

Point Cloud Correction. The set of corrected points $\mathbf{q}'_k \in Q'$ is obtained by applying the detected symmetry plane to each point $\mathbf{q}_k \in Q$. We represent a parametric correspondence line between the original point $\mathbf{q}_k$ and its possible corresponding point $\mathbf{q}'_k$ as Eq. (2), where t is the line parameter.

$$(x, y, z) = \mathbf{n} \cdot t + \mathbf{q}_k \tag{2}$$

The midpoint of the point pair satisfies Eq. (3).

$$\frac{\mathbf{q}_k + \mathbf{q}'_k}{2} = \mathbf{n} \cdot t + \mathbf{q}_k \tag{3}$$

Assume that the symmetric plane between the point correspondence is represented as Eq. (4), we can calculate the symmetrical point $\mathbf{q}'_k$ as Eq. (5).

$$\mathbf{n} \cdot (x, y, z) + d = 0 \tag{4}$$

$$\mathbf{q}'_k = \mathbf{q}_k - 2\frac{\mathbf{q}_k \cdot \mathbf{n} + d}{\|\mathbf{n}\|^2}\mathbf{n} \tag{5}$$

The original point set Q is divided into two parts by the symmetry plane $\mathbf{P} = (\mathbf{n}, d)$. The correction procedure discards the part with fewer points, and the rest part are symmetrically transformed by Eq. (5) to obtain the corrected point set.

2.3 Lip Behaviometrics Based on 4D Spatiotemporal Point Cloud Feature Learning

The lip behavior based identity recognition module uses PointNet++ [4] and PointLSTM [5] as backbones. Specifically, the architecture contains five stages. The first stage uses spatial grouping [5] to extract intra-frame features, and the second to fourth stages use spatiotemporal grouping and density-based sampling [5] to extract inter-frame features. The fifth stage extracts point-wise features and obtains global features by the max pooling layer. In the experiments, we investigate the architecture variants by placing PointLSTM layer in the stage 1, 2, 3 and 4, respectively, resulting in four variants called PointLSTM-raw, early, middle, and late, respectively.

2.4 Objective Function

The lip symmetry correction module is optimized using the Chamfer distance (CD)[6], where the CD is defined as

$$\mathcal{L}_s(Q, Q') = \sum_{\mathbf{q}_k \in Q} \min_{\mathbf{q}'_k \in Q'} \|\mathbf{q}_k - \mathbf{q}'_k\|_2^2 + \sum_{\mathbf{q}'_k \in Q'} \min_{\mathbf{q}_k \in Q} \|\mathbf{q}'_k - \mathbf{q}_k\|_2^2, \tag{6}$$

where Q' is the symmetric transformed point cloud, and Q is the original point cloud.

The lip behavior identity recognition module is trained using a cross-entropy loss function, supervised by the one-hot identity label $Y = \{y_1, y_2, \cdots y_M\}$, where M is the number of identities to be detected. This partial objective function can be defined as.

$$\mathcal{L}_I = -\frac{1}{M} \sum_{i=1}^M y_i \log \hat{y}_i, \tag{7}$$

where $y_i \in Y$, $\hat{y}_i$ denotes the probability that the input sample is of i-th identity.

3 Experiments

3.1 Implementation Details

The experiments were conducted on a machine with Intel (R) Core (TM) i9-10900X CPU @ 3.70GHz and NVIDIA GeForce RTX 2080Ti. The point cloud correction network was trained using Adaptive Momentum Estimation (Adam) with a learning rate of 1×10^{-4}, a weight decay of 1×10^{-4}, and a batch size of 128. The number of epochs is 100. The lip behavior recognition network was trained with the base learning rate of 1×10^{-4}, a weight decay of 0.005, and a batch size of 8. The number of epochs is 200, and the learning rate decayed with a rate of 0.1 when the training batch reaches 90, 160, and 180, respectively.

3.2 Dataset and Evaluation Indicators

In this paper, the Varying Pose (VP) subset in the public dataset - Speech-driven 3D Facial Motion (S3DFM-VP) [2] is used to verify the methods. S3DFM-VP collects multimodal data of 3D speaking faces in changing poses. There are 260 samples from 26 participants in the VP sub-dataset. The participants have different ages, genders, ethnicities, etc.

Indicators. We adopt two metrics including CD and mean symmetry plane error (*m*Err) to evaluate the symmetry detection module and identity recognition accuracy (Acc + Std) to assess the lip behaviometrics module. CD is defined as Eq. (6). *m*Err is defined as below.

$$mErr = \frac{1}{M} \sum_{i=1}^{M} \|\mathbf{P}_i - \mathbf{P}_i^{gt}\|, \tag{8}$$

where M is the number of samples, $\mathbf{P}_i$ and $\mathbf{P}_i^{gt}$ are the predicted and ground truth parameter vectors of the symmetry plane of the i-th sample.

$$Acc = \frac{TP + TN}{TP + TN + FP + FN}, \tag{9}$$

where True Positive (TP), True Negative (TN), False Positive (FP), and False Negative (FN) are obtained from confusion matrix.

3.3 Ablation Experiments

We classify the data based on the lip posture and obtain five classes, where classes I, II, III, IV and V represent increasing trends in the degree of attitude deviation. The sampling and N correspond to the downsampling method and the number of downsampling points for the input lip point cloud of the symmetry correction module. The ablation results are reported in Table 1.

From the results, we can see that the optimal average CD is achieved by the random sampling to 2048 points. In terms of *m*Err, the performance of 2048-point random sampling is comparable to that of the 1024-point random sampling. Thus, by balancing both performances, we set the random sampling of 2048 points as the optimal option.

Table 1. Comparison of different downsampling options and numbers of sampling points N. The results are mErr/CD ($\times 10^{-3}$ m). FP means Farthest Point sampling.

Sampling methods	N	Pose level					Average results
		I	II	III	IV	V	
Uniform	1024	0.14/0.20	0.24/0.29	1.42/0.25	1.47/0.26	1.06/0.35	0.87/0.27
Random		0.21/0.32	0.26/0.42	1.34/0.46	1.40/0.44	0.98/0.59	**0.84**/0.45
FP		0.18/0.35	0.30/0.46	1.46/0.44	1.49/0.43	1.08/0.54	0.90/0.44
Uniform	2048	0.15/0.22	0.26/0.30	1.44/0.26	1.49/0.26	1.08/0.35	0.88/0.28
Random		0.14/0.17	0.23/0.27	1.42/0.25	1.48/0.27	1.07/0.37	0.87/**0.27**
FP		0.15/0.30	0.27/0.42	1.45/0.40	1.49/0.36	1.09/0.50	0.89/0.40
Uniform	4096	1.88/0.29	1.63/0.38	1.33/0.32	1.33/0.30	1.06/0.35	1.45/0.33
Random		1.89/0.29	1.53/0.39	1.49/0.42	1.17/0.47	0.93/0.63	1.40/0.44
FP		1.90/0.29	1.62/0.34	1.30/0.31	1.32/0.30	1.05/0.38	1.44/0.32

3.4 Symmetry Parameter Prediction Results

To explore the effectiveness of the proposed symmetry detection method, this section compares several existing methods: PCA, Oriented Bounding Box (OBB) [7], and PRS [3] with the proposed method in terms of mErr and CD as the evaluation indicators. The qualitative performance is shown in Fig. 3, and the quantitative results are compared in Table 2.

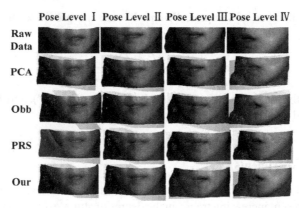

Fig. 3. Prediction of symmetry plane by different methods at different levels of poses. Note that the point cloud visualization is enhanced by mapping pixel-wise registered intensity data, while in the algorithms, only point cloud modality is used.

Table 2. Comparison of symmetry correction methods ($mErr/CD$ ($\times 10^{-3}$ m)).

Method	Model size	Pose level				
		I	II	III	IV	V
PCA	–	1.31/1.97	1.30/2.02	1.45/2.08	1.41/2.58	1.32/2.37
OBB [7]	–	1.30/1.77	1.37/1.83	1.30/1.30	1.34/1.11	1.35/0.98
PRS [3]	79k	1.07/1.04	0.99/1.01	1.38/1.11	1.31/0.60	1.37/0.48
Ours	23k	**0.13/0.60**	**0.25/0.61**	**1.22/0.58**	**1.11/0.57**	**1.19/0.19**

3.5 Lip Behaviometrics Results

Stand-Alone Lip Behaviometrics Network. In this section, we used the point cloud of the lip without symmetry correction for the experiment. PointLSTM-PSS is embedded into different feature extraction stages to determine the best network architecture. We compare the performance of baseline (without PointLSTM-PSS), PointLSTM-raw, PointLSTM-early, PointLSTM-middle and PointLSTM-late networks. The results are shown in Table 3. From the results, we can see that the model can be effectively improved by embedding the PointLSTM-PSS module, indicating that the PointLSTM-PSS module can improve the lip behaviometrics by using inter-frame information. PointLSTM-late architecture considers both inter-frame and intra-frame information better.

Table 3. Comparison of different stages of PointLSTM-PSS module embedding.

Models	Number of parameters	Acc (%) $\pm$ Std (%)
baseline	0.9M	74.23 $\pm$ 4.66
PointLSTM-raw	1.2M	77.00 $\pm$ 3.90
PointLSTM-early	1.3M	91.62 $\pm$ 3.94
PointLSTM-middle	1.2M	86.85 $\pm$ 2.58
PointLSTM-late	**0.9M**	**92.81** $\pm$ 2.62

Performance of Different Correction Levels. To explore how much self-occlusion needs to be corrected, this section investigates the effect of different levels of correction on the performance of lip behaviometrics. The correction levels are defined based on CD. When the CD of two symmetrical parts is over a CD threshold, the point cloud is corrected. The CD threshold were set at seven percentage levels, and the performance was evaluated with 10-fold cross-validation. The results are listed in Table 4. Note that all data are corrected when the threshold is 0, and no data are corrected when the threshold is 100%. According to the results, when the CD threshold is set to 58.97%, the framework achieves the highest accuracy. The correction of data in which self-occlusion is not severe may introduce some information loss.

Table 4. Comparison of lip behaviometrics performance with different correction levels

CD Threshold (%)	Acc (%) ± Std (%)
0	92.69 ± 2.26
14.74	93.92 ± 4.15
29.48	94.86 ± 4.89
44.22	94.43 ± 5.67
58.97	**95.46 ± 3.37**
73.71	94.54 ± 3.25
100	92.81 ± 2.62

Effectiveness of Symmetry Correction. This section compares the performance of symmetry correction on several off-the-shelf point cloud recognition networks, including PointLSTM [5], P4Transformer[8], SequentialPointNet [9], and PSTNet [10]. It can be seen from the result in Table 5 that these recognition methods have the accuracy improvement of 2.65%, 26.92%, 50%, and 26.93% respectively with the symmetry correction. Thus, the experimental results demonstrate that the proposed symmetry correction can be incorporated into different lip behaviometrics methods.

Table 5. Lip symmetry correction applied to different lip behaviometrics methods

Method	Acc before correction (%)	Acc after correction (%)
PointLSTM [5]	92.81	**95.46**
P4Transformer[8]	41.03	67.95
SequentialPointNet [9]	30.77	80.77
PSTNet [10]	65.38	92.31

4   Conclusions

In this paper, we propose a pose-unconstrainted 3D lip behaviometrics pipeline based on symmetry correction of lip point clouds, which is an effective solution to the problem of self-occlusion. The proposed method detects the latent symmetry plane more accurately and robustly even in the face data with a large degree of self-occlusion. The symmetry correction module is unsupervised, which does not require manual labeling the symmetry planes for training.

Acknowledgments. The work is supported by Natural Science Foundation of China (NSFC) under Grant No.61906004.

References

1. Wang, S.L., Liew, A.W.C.: Physiological and behavioral lip biometrics: a comprehensive study of their discriminative power. Pattern Recogn. **45**(9), 3328–3335 (2012)
2. Zhang, J., Fisher, R.B.: 3d visual passcode: speech-driven 3d facial dynamics for behaviometrics. Signal Process. **160**, 164–177 (2019)
3. Gao, L., Zhang, L.X., Meng, H.Y., Ren, Y.H., Lai, Y.K., Kobbelt, L.: Prs-Net: planar reflective symmetry detection net for 3d models. IEEE Trans. Visual Comput. Graphics **27**(6), 3007–3018 (2020)
4. Qi C.R., Yi L., Su H., Guibas L.J.: Pointnet++: deep hierarchical feature learning on point sets in a metric space. Adv. Neural Inform. Process. Syst. **30**, 5099–5108 (2017)
5. Min, Y., Zhang, Y., Chai, X., Chen, X.: An efficient pointlstm for point clouds based gesture recognition. In: Proceedings of the IEEE/CVF Conference on Computer Vision and Pattern Recognition, pp. 5761–5770 (2020)
6. Fan, H., Su, H., Guibas, L.J.: A point set generation network for 3d object reconstruction from a single image. In: Proceedings of the IEEE conference on computer vision and pattern recognition, pp. 605–613 (2017)
7. Chang, C.T., Gorissen, B., Melchior, S.: Fast oriented bounding box optimization on the rotation group so (3, $\mathbb{R}$). ACM Trans. Graph. **30**(5), 1–16 (2011)
8. Fan, H., Yang, Y., Kankanhalli, M.: Point 4d transformer networks for Spatio-temporal modeling in point cloud videos. In: Proceedings of the IEEE/CVF Conference on Computer Vision and Pattern Recognition, pp. 14204–14213 (2021)
9. Li, X., Huang, Q., Wang, Z., Hou, Z., Yang, T.: Sequentialpointnet: a strong parallelized point cloud sequence network for 3d action recognition. arXiv preprint arXiv:211108492 (2021)
10. Fan, H., Yu, X., Ding, Y., Yang, Y., Kankanhalli, M.: Pstnet: Point spatio-temporal convolution on point cloud sequences. arXiv preprint arXiv:220513713 (2022)

Virtual Fully-Connected Layer for a Large-Scale Speaker Verification Dataset

Zhida Song[1], Liang He[1,2(✉)], Zhihua Fang[1], Ying Hu[1], and Hao Huang[1]

[1] School of Information Science and Engineering, Xinjiang University, Urumqi, China
[2] Department of Electronic Engineering, Tsinghua University, Beijing, China
heliang@mail.tsinghua.edu.cn

Abstract. Recently, convolutional neural networks (CNNs) have been widely used in speaker verification tasks and achieved the state-of-the-art performance in most dominant datasets, such as NIST SREs, VoxCeleb, CNCeleb and *etc*. However, suppose the speaker classification is performed by one-hot coding, the weight shape of the last fully-connected layer is $B \times N$, B is the min-batch size, and N is the number of speakers, which will require large GPU memory as the number of speakers increases. To address this problem, we introduce a virtual fully-connected (Virtual FC) layer in the field of face recognition to the large-scale speaker verification by re-grouping strategy, mapping N to M (M is a hyperparameter less than N), so that the number of weight parameters in this layer becomes M/N times to the original.

We also explored the effect of the number of utterances per speaker in each min-batch on the performance.

Keywords: Speaker verification · Virtual fully-connected layer · Large-scale

1 Introduction

Speaker recognition is a typical biometric authentication technology. Speaker verification determines whether two voices belong to the same speaker by calculating the similarity of the words of two speakers. There are two categories of speaker verification, one is Text-Independent Speaker Verification (TI-SV) and the other is Text-Dependent Speaker Verification (TD-SV) [1]. In recent years, deep neural network-based approaches (e.g., TDNN [2], ResNet [3], Res2Net [4], ECAPA-TDNN [5]) have achieved excellent results in speaker recognition. A typical speaker recognition system usually consists of two phases, a speaker embedding extractor front-end and a similarity scoring back-end. The front-end network inputs the original speech to get a low-dimensional speaker embedding (e.g. x-vector [6]), while the back-end determines whether the embeddings of the two voices belong to the same speaker. Typical back-end scoring methods are cosine and Probabilistic Linear Discriminant Analysis (PLDA) [7]. The current

© The Author(s), under exclusive license to Springer Nature Switzerland AG 2022
W. Deng et al. (Eds.): CCBR 2022, LNCS 13628, pp. 382–390, 2022.
https://doi.org/10.1007/978-3-031-20233-9_39

speaker recognition research methods have matured and will likely be applied in various fields of real life in the future.

The performance of the deep neural network model depends on a large amount of training data, and the quality of the speaker front-end extracted embedding also depends on the size and diversity of the training data. Specifically, the more the number of speakers in the training set and the more the number of utterances per speaker, the better the speaker discrimination learned by the front-end neural network. As speaker recognition technology becomes more prevalent in real-life applications, the number of speakers to be discriminated by the speaker recognition system becomes more extensive. In this case, there are stringent requirements for the performance of the speaker recognition system. The speaker recognition system must also have a solid and robust discriminatory ability for large-scale speakers.

Usually, the last layer of the front-end network of a speaker recognition system is the fully-connected layer, and the output size of this fully-connected layer is the number of speakers in the training set. Therefore, the more the number of speakers in training, the larger the output size of the fully-connected layer. The neural network will generally compute a whole min-batch at once when training, so the output size of the fully-connected layer will be $B \times N$, where B is the size of the min-batch and N is the number of speakers in the training set. As the number of speakers increases, more GPU memory is required. The training process may lead to memory overflow at a specific speaker size, which makes the network model unsuccessful in training. For this potential risk, there is a need to build a network architecture that can accommodate large-scale speakers for training.

In this paper, we draw on Virtual FC layer [8] in face recognition to address the resource-constrained problem of large-scale speaker verification. The main contributions are as follows:

1) Introducing the Virtual FC layer into speaker recognition, the weight parameters of this layer are reduced to the original M/N compared to the replacement fully connected layer used for classification, and the system performance does not degrade too much.
2) Set each speaker's number of utterances K in a min-batch and map N to different M values to improve the system performance.

The subsequent contents of this paper are organized as follows: Sect. 2 describes the network structure used in our experiments; Sect. 3 illustrates our settings; Sect. 4 gives experimental results and analysis. The conclusions are drawn in Sect. 5.

2   Related Work

This section introduces the pooling method Attentive Statistics Pooling, the AAM-Softmax loss function, and the Virtual FC Layer we borrowed from face recognition and applied to large-scale speaker verification in our experiments.

2.1 Attentive Statistics Pooling

Attentive statistics pooling(ASP) [9] is the pooling method with an attention mechanism. The ASP considers each frame's contribution and calculates the weighted mean and standard deviation vectors. Next, the computed vectors were stitched together as the segment-level features. ASP makes the network more capable of speaker differentiation. It has the following equations.

$$\alpha_t = \frac{\exp\left(v^T F\left(W f_t + b\right) + k\right)}{\sum_t^T \exp\left(v^T F\left(W f_t + b\right) + k\right)} \tag{1}$$

$$\tilde{\mu} = \sum_t^T \alpha_t f_t \tag{2}$$

$$\tilde{\sigma} = \sqrt{\sum_t^T \alpha_t f_t \odot f - \tilde{\mu} \odot \tilde{\mu}} \tag{3}$$

2.2 AAM-Softmax

The Softmax function can optimize the inter-class spacing. Still, it isn't easy to reduce the intra-class spacing. It allocates all the space in the discriminative decision to the samples in the training set, resulting in insufficient generalization ability of the model. Huang et al. [10] applied the Angular Softmax (A-Softmax) [11] loss function to the speaker recognition domain to solve this problem. The A-Softmax loss function lets the network learn discriminative features by imposing an angular margin between classes. Additive Margin Softmax (AM-Softmax) [12] converts the integration of angular margins from multiplicative to additive, reducing the computational cost of the network and adjusting the cosine margin value with a hyperparameter. Based on AM-Softmax, Jiankang et al. [13] proposed Additive Angular Margin loss(AAM-Softmax), which normalizes the feature vector and weights, adding the angular interval m to θ. The angular interval has a more direct effect on the angle than the cosine interval.It has the following equation.

$$\mathcal{L}_{\text{AAM}} = -\frac{1}{n} \sum_{i=1}^{n} \log \frac{e^{s\left(\cos\left(\theta_{y_i}+m\right)\right)}}{e^{s\left(\cos\left(\theta_{y_i}+m\right)\right)} + \sum_{j=1,j\neq y_i}^{C} e^{s\cos\theta_j}} \tag{4}$$

2.3 Virtual Fully-Connected Layer

Speaker verification is a significant research direction in speech tasks. Mainstream end-to-end frameworks generally extract speech features from raw utterances, then go through convolutional neural networks and pooling layers to obtain global and local vocal pattern information, and finally, go through two fully-connected layers and softmax layers for classification and optimize the model by computing the loss function. The vector of the first fully-connected layer is often used as embedding, and we extract the embeddings of different speakers and calculate their cosine similarity to determine whether the speech belongs to the same speaker.

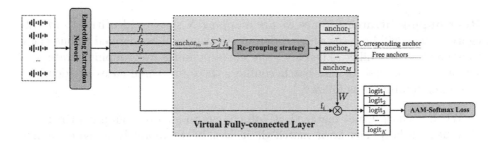

Fig. 1. Training system with Virtual FC layer. K is the number of utterances per speaker in each min-batch, and it is the hyperparameter that we need to set.

Usually, the classification is performed using one-hot coding so that the second fully connected layer often needs to be trained with weight size $B \times N$, where B is the batch size, and N is the number of speakers. In large-scale speaker verification, N is often huge, which will take up a lot of computational resources. So we borrowed Virtual FC in face recognition to replace the fully-connected layer for classification, which can effectively solve the problem of large-scale speaker recognition with limited GPU resources.The training pipeline is shown in the Fig. 1. The training weights of the second fully connected layer are reduced to $B \times M$, where M is a hyperparameter no more remarkable than N. The mapping rule of N identities to M identities can take the remainder of the original identity number to M. The following equation can express the Virtual FC.

$$y = W^T f + b \tag{5}$$

$y \in \mathbb{R}^M$ is the output of the Virtual FC Layer, $W \in \mathbb{R}^{D \times M}$ is the coefficient matrix, D is the embedding dimension, $f \in \mathbb{R}^D$ is a embedding, and b is the bias, which is often set to zero.

Corresponding Anchor and Free Anchor. When using Virtual FC Layer, we need to have more than one speaker utterance in each batch in training. First, after the previous network gets the embedding of each utterance, the embedding corresponds to the identity mapping to M groups. These identity mapping groups l share the l-th column parameter of the weight W. We call the l-th column parameter of W anchor$_l$, there are two types of weight coefficients in the W anchors, one is the corresponding anchor, denoted by anchor$_{\text{corr}}$, and one is the free anchor, denoted by anchor$_{\text{free}}$ .If there exists identity in min-batch belongs to l, then anchor$_l$ belongs to anchor$_{\text{corr}}$. Otherwise, it belongs to anchor $_{free}$, the type of anchor is dynamically changed during training. The anchor$_{corr}$ is occupied by the identity mapped to group l first in the min-batch, and its generation becomes the sum of the weights of all embeddings with the same identity. Subsequent identities mapped to group l will have conflicts, and we use the Re-grouping Strategy, which will reflect the value of anchor$_{free}$.

Re-grouping Strategy. Since we are mapping N speaker identities to M categories, there will be cases where different speakers will be mapped to one class, thus creating a conflict. Therefore, the corresponding Re-grouping strategy is set, and in the case of min-batch conflict, there are three cases of identities belonging to group l as follows.

1) When anchor$_l$ is not matched, it will change to a corresponding anchor.
2) When anchor$_l$ has been matched, it will be temporarily assigned a free anchor, making it a corresponding anchor.
3) The anchor is discarded if there is a conflict and no free anchor exists.

3   Experimental Setup

The CNN-based speaker verification models are mainly x-vector structures. It learns speaker embeddings using speaker features extracted from a speaker-discriminative network. The frequently used models include TDNN, ResNet, and ECAPA-TDNN. Usually, we extract features from raw utterances and then get embeddings with fixed dimensions by convolutional neural networks such as TDNN and pooling layers. We optimize the model according to different losses after extracting embeddings in the training phase. In the validation phase, we extract the embeddings from two speech segments and then calculate a score.

3.1   Dataset

For the large-scale speaker verification task, we use the VoxCeleb dataset, extracted from videos uploaded to YouTube. It consists of two subclasses Vox-Celeb1 dataset [14] and the VoxCeleb2 dataset [15].VoxCeleb1 is an audio dataset containing over 100,000 utterances from 1,251 celebrities. VoxCeleb2 consists of over a million utterances from 6,112 speakers. Since the dataset is collected 'in the wild', the speech segments are corrupted with real-world noise, including laughter, cross-talk, channel effects, music, and other sounds. The dataset is also multilingual, with a speech from speakers of 145 different nationalities, covering a wide range of accents, ages, ethnicities, and languages. In our work, we use the dev data containing 5994 speakers in VoxCeleb2 for training and the test dataset containing 40 speakers in VoxCeleb1 for testing. We use the list of trial pairs from the official VoxCeleb1.

3.2 Implementation Details

For convolutional neural networks, we use Fast ResNet-34 [16], which has a smaller number of filters than other ResNets, allowing us to conduct experiments in a shorter time and thus pay more attention to the impact of the Virtual FC layer on experimental performance and resource consumption. We used Sunine https://gitlab.com/csltstu/sunine/-/tree/master, an open-source speaker recognition tool from THU-CSLT, to conduct our experiments. The official Sunine open source code does not contain the structure of the Virtual FC layer, so we migrated it to speaker verification by combining the original author's article and the open source code. In the mapping from N to M of the Virtual FC layer, we set the value of M to 600, 1000, 3000 or 5994, respectively, to realize the dimensionality reduction of the FC layer.

80-dimensional Fbank features are used for model training. The pooling layer is used ASP, which can fully extract global and local utterance information. Loss is used AAM-Softmax, generally set scale equal to 30, and margin is set to one of 0.2, 0.3, 0.4, or 0.5, depending on the experiment. Adaptive Moment Estimation (Adam) [17] with learning rate 0.0002, gamma 0.4, and step size 5 is used to optimize the model. Embeddings' cosine similarity to get the scores of the two utterances, and based on the list of scores, the Equal Error Rate (EER) and Minimum Detection Cost Function (minDCF) of the system are calculated.

4 Experimental Results and Analysis

We compared the performance of the standard FC layer and Virtual FC layer in the Fast ResNet-34 network structure by setting the number of utterances per speaker K to 3 or 5 in the min-batch, respectively, and developing different N to M mappings for the network with the Virtual FC layer added, with M taking values of 600, 1000, 3000, and 5994, respectively. We find a loss in system performance EER and minDCF when replacing the FC layer with the Virtual FC layer, but the results are still within an acceptable range. But our original intention of introducing the Virtual FC layer was not to optimize system performance but to focus on dealing with the resource occupation problem of large-scale speaker verification. The number of parameters in the last FC layer of the network is reduced very effectively, and the number of parameters at M equal to 600 is about $1/10$ of that at M equal to 5994, effectively solving the problem of insufficient resources. This is necessary for systems with tens of thousands or even more speakers.

From Table 1, it can be seen that for the network structure with FC as the last layer, $K = 3$ or $K = 5$ in each min-batch has little impact on the performance. Still, for the network with Virtual FC as the last layer, $K = 3$ has better performance than $K = 5$. Especially when $M = 1000$, the performance improvement of $K = 3$ is about 13.3% compared to $K = 5$. The performance of the FC layer is better than the Virtual FC layer because the FC layer has one weight for each speaker, while the Virtual FC layer has multiple speakers sharing the weights. We are surprised that the smaller the value of M in the

Table 1. Comparison of different approaches of FC layer and Virtual FC layer. The systems are both based on the Fast ResNet-34 network, M is the dimensionality of N mapping, and K is the number of utterances per speaker in each min-batch.

Layer	Methods		EER(%)	minDCF(0.01)
FC	–	$K = 3$	2.154	0.22714
		$K = 5$	2.170	0.22783
Virtual FC	$M = 600$	$K = 3$	3.590	0.36950
		$K = 5$	3.893	0.39078
	$M = 1000$	$K = 3$	3.702	0.34840
		$K = 5$	4.271	0.40291
	$M = 3000$	$K = 3$	5.101	0.49746
		$K = 5$	5.531	0.49757
	$M = 5994$	$K = 3$	6.586	0.57170
		$K = 5$	7.180	0.62155

range, the better the system verification, which is very beneficial for large-scale speaker recognition with limited GPU resources.

Table 2. The number of model parameters.

Layer	Trainable params	Non-trainable params	Total params
FC	4.2M	–	4.2M
Virtual FC, $M = 600$	2.8M	153K	3.0M
Virtual FC, $M = 1000$	2.9M	256K	3.2M
Virtual FC, $M = 3000$	3.4M	768K	4.2M
Virtual FC, $M = 5994$	4.2M	1.5M	5.7M

Table 2 shows that the Virtual FC layer model parameters are M/N times the FC layer, effectively reducing the demand for GPU resources in large-scale speaker verification. The Non-trainable params are the tensor to temporarily save the weights for backtracking when the second method of Re-grouping strategy is applied in the Virtual FC layer implementation when conflicts are encountered, and it has the same number of parameters as the Virtual FC layer weights.

5   Conclusions

The Virtual FC layer is introduced to speaker verification to effectively solve the problem of insufficient GPU memory for large-scale speakers with limited resources. At present, we do not pursue the best performance of the system after adding the Virtual FC layer but focus more on the problem of the last layer occupying the GPU memory resources during the training process and the number of parameters of the Virtual FC layer we apply is M/N of the FC layer. M can be set to a number much smaller than N. In the following work, we will pursue the performance improvement of the system with the addition of the Virtual FC layer, using methods including but not limited to noise addition to the data, multi-task shared convolutional neural networks [18], combination of different pooling layers with different loss functions for various convolutional neural networks, expansion of data to simulate large-scale speaker datasets using speech enhancement techniques.

References

1. Hansen, J.H.L., Hasan, T.: Speaker recognition by machines and humans: a tutorial review. IEEE Signal Process. Mag. **32**(6), 74–99 (2015)
2. Snyder, D., Garcia-Romero, D., Sell, G., Povey, D., Khudanpur, S.: X-vectors: robust DNN embeddings for speaker recognition. In 2018 IEEE International Conference on Acoustics, Speech and Signal Processing (ICASSP), pp. 5329–5333 (2018)
3. He, K., Zhang, X., Ren, S., Sun, J: Deep residual learning for image recognition. In: 2016 IEEE Conference on Computer Vision and Pattern Recognition (CVPR), pp. 770–778 (2016)
4. Gao, S.-H., Cheng, M.-M., Zhao, K., Zhang, X.-Y., Yang, M.-H., Torr, P.: Res2Net: a new multi-scale backbone architecture. IEEE Trans. Pattern Anal. Mach. Intell. **43**(2), 652–662 (2021)
5. Desplanques, B., Thienpondt, J., Demuynck, K.: ECAPA-TDNN: emphasized channel attention, propagation and aggregation in TDNN based speaker verification. In: Proceedings of the Interspeech 2020, pp. 3830–3834 (2020)
6. Snyder, D., Garcia-Romero, D., Povey, D., Khudanpur, S.: Deep neural network embeddings for text-independent speaker verification. In: Interspeech 2017, pp. 999–1003 (2017)
7. Garcia-Romero, D., Espy-Wilson, C.Y.: Analysis of I-vector length normalization in speaker recognition systems. In: Twelfth Annual Conference of the International Speech Communication Association (2011)
8. Li, P., Wang, B., Zhang, L.: Virtual fully-connected layer: training a large-scale face recognition dataset with limited computational resources. In: Proceedings of the IEEE/CVF Conference on Computer Vision and Pattern Recognition, pp. 13315–13324 (2021)
9. Okabe, K., Koshinaka, T., Shinoda, K.: Attentive statistics pooling for deep speaker embedding. In: Proceedings of the Interspeech 2018, pp. 2252–2256 (2018)
10. Huang, Z., Wang, S., Yu, K.: Angular softmax for short-duration text-independent speaker verification. In: Interspeech, pp. 3623–3627 (2018)
11. Liu, W., Wen, Y., Yu, Z., Li, M., Raj, B., Song, L.: SphereFace: deep hypersphere embedding for face recognition. In: Proceedings of the IEEE Conference on Computer Vision and Pattern Recognition, pp. 212–220 (2017)
12. Wang, F., Cheng, J., Liu, W., Liu, H.: Additive margin softmax for face verification. IEEE Signal Process. Lett. **25**(7), 926–930 (2018)
13. Deng, J., Guo, J., Xue, N., Zafeiriou, S.: ArcFace: additive angular margin loss for deep face recognition. In: 2019 IEEE/CVF Conference on Computer Vision and Pattern Recognition (CVPR), pp. 4685–4694 (2019)

14. Nagrani, A., Son Chung, J., Zisserman, A.: VoxCeleb: a large-scale speaker identi-fication dataset. In: Proceedings of the Interspeech 2017, pp. 2616–2620 (2017)
15. Son Chung, J., Nagrani, A., Zisserman, A.: VoxCeleb2: deep speaker recognition. In: Proceedings of the Interspeech 2018, pp. 1086–1090 (2018)
16. Son Chung, J., et al.: In defence of metric learning for speaker recognition. arXiv preprint arXiv:2003.11982 (2020)
17. Kingma, D.P., Ba, J.: Adam: a method for stochastic optimization. arXiv preprint arXiv:1412.6980 (2014)
18. Xu, W., et al.: Jointing multi-task learning and gradient reversal layer for far-field speaker verification. In: Chinese Conference on Biometric Recognition, pp. 449–457. Springer (2021). https://doi.org/10.1007/978-3-030-86608-2_49

Gait, Iris and Other Biometrics

A Simple Convolutional Neural Network for Small Sample Multi-lingual Offline Handwritten Signature Recognition

Wanying Li, Mahpirat, Xuebin Xu, Alimjan Aysa, and Kurban Ubul$^{(\boxtimes)}$

School of Information Science and Engineering, Xinjiang University, Urumqi, China
kurbanu@xju.edu.cn

Abstract. Based on convolutional neural network, a simpler network for offline handwritten signature recognition is proposed in this paper. A total of 7,200 handwritten signature images in Chinese, Uyghur, and Kazakh languages were collected from 300 volunteers to establish an offline multi-lingual handwritten signature database. The signature images were randomly divided into training, verification, and testing sets. The average accuracy of five experiments was taken as the recognition result. Because it is difficult to collect a large number of signatures at one time, many experiments have been carried out on a multi-lingual signature database and CEDAR database with the training samples are 6, 12, and 18 respectively. Experimental results show that this method is an effective signature recognition method, and the effect is better than the existing network when there are few training samples.

Keywords: Multi-lingual · Handwritten signature · Signature recognition · Convolutional neural network

1 Introduction

Biometrics refers to the technology of automatic identification achieved by computers through acquiring and analyzing physiological and behavioral characteristics of human body [1]. Biometrics technology can be divided into physiological traits and behavioral traits. The handwritten signature is a kind of behavior traits gradually formed in human life, which is widely used in finance, public security, judicial and administrative fields, has practical significance. Signature recognition and signature verification are two different personal identity authentication methods. Recognition is a multi-classification problem, determining to which person the signature belongs. Verification is a binary classification problem, to determine whether the signature is true or forged. The handwritten signature can also be divided into online signature [2] and offline signature [3] according to the different methods of signature data collection. Online signature is obtained by the electronic signature board, which can extract dynamic information such as stroke trajectory, stroke pressure, writing speed, and writing angle. Offline signature is a static signature image written on paper, and dynamic features cannot be obtained. Therefore, offline signatures are more difficult to recognize than online signatures. However, due to the advantages of easy collection and simple equipment, the offline signature is more widely used than the online signature in daily life. Therefore, it is of practical significance to study offline handwritten signature recognition.

Considering the outstanding achievements of convolutional neural networks in the computer vision area, this paper studies the offline handwritten signature recognition technology based on a convolutional neural network. Firstly, the handwritten signature image is pre-processed by grayscale, median filtering, binarization, thinning, crop and size normalization, and five different sets of training, validation and testing are divided. Then, the signed image is input into the proposed convolutional neural network which is called OHS-Net. The convolutional layer is used to extract the high-dimensional features of the signed image, and the max pooling is used to reduce the size and calculation amount of the feature image. Finally, Softmax is used for classification. By calculating the average value of five experiments, the recognition accuracy of multi-lingual hybrid handwritten signature is obtained. The overall process of offline handwritten signature recognition is shown in Fig. 1.

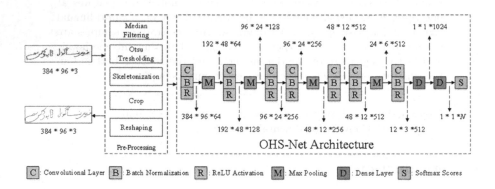

Fig. 1. Offline handwritten signature recognition system.

The main contributions of this paper are as follows:

1. Handwritten signature images of Chinese, Uyghur, and Kazakh were collected, and a multi-lingual offline handwritten signature database of 7200 images of 300 people was established through manual segmentation.
2. A convolutional neural network named OHS-Net is proposed to automatically extract high-dimensional features of signature images and classify them, which is capable of efficient recognition of multi-lingual handwritten signature database and CEDAR database.
3. A large number of experiments were carried out on the multi-lingual database and CEDAR database, with training samples of 6, 12, 18 respectively.

2   Related Works

A high-dimensional statistical feature extraction method is proposed in [4]. Local center point features and ETDT features were extracted from the mixture signatures. An offline handwritten signature recognition method based on discrete curvelet treansform is proposed in [5]. Energy features and multi-scale block local binary mode features were extracted and combined. A local central line features based offline signature recognition method is proposed for Uyghur handwritten signature in [6]. The global central line features from two horizontally centers and local central line features from two vertically centers were extracted. An offline signature identification system based on Histogram of Oriented Gradients vector features is designed in [7]. An Open Handwritten Signature Identification System is proposed by using conjointly the Curvelet Transform and the One-Class classifier based on Principal Component Analysis in [8].

A new convolutional neural network structure named LS2Net and a C3 classification algorithm based on KNN algorithm are proposed in [9]. A Fully convolutional networks is used for learning a robust feature extraction from the raw signature images in [10]. A method for signature recognition and signature forgery detection with verification using Convolutional Neural Network, Crest-Trough method, SURF algorithm and Harris corner detection algorithm is proposed in [11]. A method for learning the representations from signature images, in a writer-independent format is proposed in [12]. A framework through hybrid methods of discrete Radon transform, principal component analysis and probabilistic neural network is proposed in [13]. A Recurrent Neural Network based method to verify and recognize offline signatures of different persons is proposed in [14] which using long-short term memory and bidirectional long-short term memory for experiments.

3   Database and Pre-processing

3.1   Multi-lingual Database

The process of establishing multi-lingual offline handwritten signature database includes acquisition, scanning and segmentation. The collection of multi-language handwritten signature is the signer writes name on the collection template paper printed by A4 paper with 24 rectangular frames in the form of Chinese, Uyghur and Kazakh. A Lenovo M7400 scanner was used to scan with 300dpi accuracy and BMP image format, which was cropped with Photoshop software and stored in a numbered sequence on the computer. There are 100 people in each language, 24 signatures in each language, a total of 7200 signature samples of images, and the multi-lingual offline signature database has been established. The samples are shown in Fig. 2, the first line is Chinese, the second line is Uyghur, the third line is Kazakh.

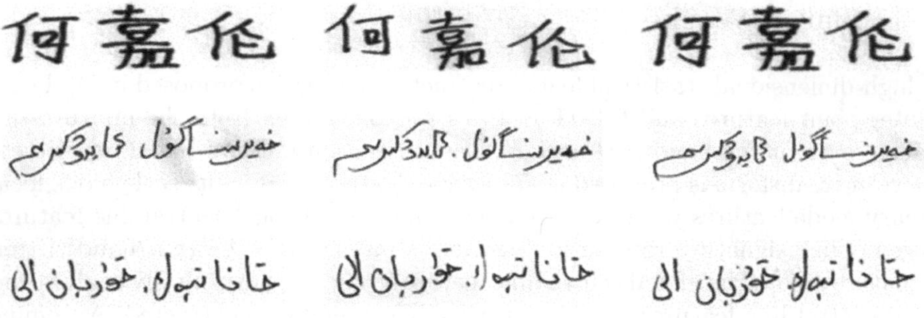

何嘉伦   何嘉伦   何嘉伦

خمىرىس ئاگۇل ئاپوكرسرمى   خمىرىس ئاگۇل. ئاپىدكرسرم   خمىرىس ئاگۇل ئاپوكرسرمى

جانا تپولو. حۆزربان ئلى   خانا تپولور. حۆزربان ئلى   خانا تپولو حۆزربان ئلى

Fig. 2. Self-built multi-lingual signature image samples.

3.2 CEDAR Database

The CEDAR [15] database contains the signature images of 55 people, with 24 true and 24 false images for each person. There are 1320 true signature samples and 1320 false signature samples in total, which are stored in grayscale image and PNG format, and the size of signed images is not uniform. The samples of CEDAR signature database are shown in Fig. 3.

Fig. 3. CEDAR database signature image samples.

3.3 Pre-processing

Both multi-lingual database and CEDAR database have problems such as discrete noise, irrelevant background, different handwriting thickness. Therefore, it is necessary to pre-process the signature image before signature recognition.

Fig. 4. Pre-processing operation step diagram.

In this paper, the weighted average method is used to gray the signed image, the median filter is used to remove the irrelevant noise, and the Otsu method is used to binarize the signed image and remove the background of the signed image. The boundary of signature handwriting is determined by scanning method, and the blank area outside the signature is clipped. Use the Skeletonize package to extract the signature handwriting skeleton and refine the handwriting. Finally, the bilinear interpolation method is used to normalize the size of all the signed images, and the image size is changed to $384 * 96$.

Through these pre-processing operations, not only the storage space and calculation amount of the signature image can be reduced, but also the influence of irrelevant factors on signature recognition can be reduced to a large extent. The pre-processing operation are shown in Fig. 4.

4 Net Architecture

Convolutional Neural Network (CNN) is a deep feed forward neural network that includes convolutional computation. As one of the representative algorithms of deep learning, it has the ability of feature learning and avoids the trouble of manual feature extraction. CNN learns the features of different levels by representing the input data in a more abstract way. Network depth is very important for solving complex learning problems, but increasing the number of layers will probably increase the complexity of computation. Therefore, it is more convenient to design a new network than to use the classic network for offline handwritten signature recognition. When CNN structures are built for a specific problem, their performance also improves [16]. Therefore, this paper proposes OHS-Net to slove the problem of offline handwritten signature recognition.

The network structures of VGG [17] and OHS-Net used in this paper are shown in Table 1. Wherein, $N * N$ represents the kernel dimension, @ represents the number of filters, and p and s represent the padding and stride parameters respectively. Experiments show that the convergence rate of the model is faster when the BN [18] layer is added between the convolution layer and the activation function. As a result, for VGG and OHS-Net, each convolution layer contains the batch normalization and ReLU activation functions. Considering the signature length of Chinese, Uyghur and Kazakh, the input size of OHS-Net and VGG

Table 1. OHS-Net and VGG architecture.

Vgg16	Vgg13	Vgg11	OHS-Net
conv3*3@64 p:1 s:1	conv3*3@64 p:1 s:1	conv3*3@64 p:1 s:1	conv5*5@64 p:2 s:1
conv3*3@64 p:1 s:1	conv3*3@64 p:1 s:1	maxpool:2*2 p:0 s:2	maxpool:2*2 p:0 s:2
maxpool:2*2 p:0 s:2	maxpool:2*2 p:0 s:2	conv3*3@128 p:1 s:1	conv5*5@128 p:2 s:1
conv3*3@128 p:1 s:1	conv3*3@128 p:1 s:1	maxpool:2*2 p:0 s:2	maxpool:2*2 p:0 s:2
conv3*3@128 p:1 s:1	conv3*3@128 p:1 s:1	conv3*3@256 p:1 s:1	conv: 3*3@256 p:1 s:1
maxpool:2*2 p:0 s:2	maxpool:2*2 p:0 s:2	conv3*3@256 p:1 s:1	conv: 3*3@256 p:1 s:1
conv3*3@256 p:1 s:1	conv3*3@256 p:1 s:1	maxpool:2*2 p:0 s:2	maxpool:2*2 p:0 s:2
conv3*3@256 p:1 s:1	conv3*3@256 p:1 s:1	conv3*3@512 p:1 s:1	conv3*3@512 p:1 s:1
conv3*3@256 p:1 s:1	maxpool:2*2 p:0 s:2	conv3*3@512 p:1 s:1	conv3*3@512 p:1 s:1
maxpool:2*2 p:0 s:2	conv3*3@512 p:1 s:1	maxpool:2*2 p:0 s:2	maxpool:3*3 p:1 s:2
conv3*3@512 p:1 s:1	conv3*3@512 p:1 s:1	conv3*3@512 p:1 s:1	conv3*3@512 p:1 s:2
conv3*3@512 p:1 s:1	maxpool:2*2 p:0 s:2	conv3*3@512 p:1 s:1	
conv3*3@512 p:1 s:1	conv3*3@512 p:1 s:1	maxpool:2*2 p:0 s:2	
maxpool:2*2 p:0 s:2	conv3*3@512 p:1 s:1		
conv3*3@512 p:1 s:1	maxpool:2*2 p:0 s:2		
conv3*3@512 p:1 s:1			
conv3*3@512 p:1 s:1			
maxpool:2*2 p:0 s:2			
dense:4096	dense:4096	dense:4096	
dense:4096	dense:4096	dense:4096	dense:1024
label:300	label:300	label:300	label:300

networks is designed as 384 * 96. Do not use a pre-training model to make a fair comparison. The networks in this paper all use cross entropy as the loss function and Softmax as the classification function.

5   Experimental Results and Analysis

The video card model of the experimental computer in this paper is NVIDIA Quadro M4000, with 8 GB of video memory, Intel(R) Xeon(R) CPU E5-1603 V4@2.80 GHz, and 16 GB of memory. Using PyCharm Community Edition 2020 to realize offline handwritten signature recognition on Windows10 64-bit system.

5.1   Hyperparameters Setting

The initial learning rate is 0.1, and it decays exponentially after each epoch. The initial weight of the network uses the method of Kaiming [19] and the NAG optimizer, with the momentum of 0.9 and the weight decay of 0.01. The batch size is 32 and the epoch is 50.

5.2   Multi-lingual Recognition Results

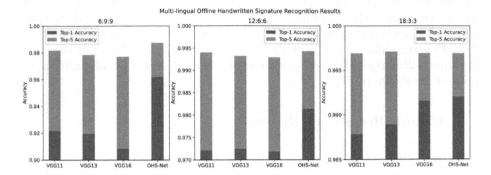

Fig. 5. Multi-lingual offline handwritten signature recognition result.

Table 2. Multi-lingual recognition results.

Ratio	Network	Evaluating Indicator		
		Training time	**Top-1 accuracy**	**Top-5 accuracy**
6:9:9	VGG11	1hours 9min	92.16%	98.17%
	VGG13	1hours 50min	91.94%	97.83%
	VGG16	2hours 43min	90.83%	97.69%
	OHS-Net	**1hours 6min**	**96.17%**	**98.73%**
12:6:6	VGG11	1hours 41min	97.21%	99.40%
	VGG13	2hours 49min	97.24%	99.32%
	VGG16	3hours 22min	97.18%	99.29%
	OHS-Net	**1hours 40min**	**98.13%**	**99.43%**
18:3:3	VGG11	2hours 54min	98.78%	99.69%
	VGG13	4hours 35min	98.89%	**99.71%**
	VGG16	6hours	99.15%	99.69%
	OHS-Net	**2hours 29min**	**99.20%**	99.69%

In Table 2, VGG11, VGG13, VGG16 and OHS-Net proposed in this paper are used respectively, and 6, 12 and 18 signature images are used as training sets for experiments. When 6 signature images are used as the training set, the highest average top-1 recognition accuracy of OHS-Net network is 96.17%, and the highest average top-5 recognition accuracy is 98.73%, which is much higher than other VGG networks. When 12 signature images are used as the training set, OHS-Net obtains the highest average top-1 recognition accuracy of 98.13% and the highest average top-5 recognition accuracy of 99.43%. When 18 signature images are used as the training set, OHS-Net achieves the highest average top-1 recognition accuracy of 99.20%. The average top five recognition accuracy of VGG13 is the highest, 99.71%, only 0.02% higher than OHS-Net, but the training time is 2 h longer. The recognition results of top-1 and top-5 of multi-lingual dataset are shown in Fig. 5.

5.3 CEDAR Recognition Results

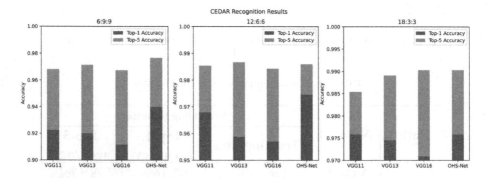

Fig. 6. Public signature dataset CEDAR recognition result.

Table 3 show the results of the CEDAR database. The radio of training set, verification set and test set are 18:3:3, 12:6:6 or 6:9:9 respectively. The database is the same as the self-built database, which is divided into five subsets, and the average accuracy of five experiments is taken as the recognition result. The recognition results of top-1 and top-5 of CEDAR dataset are shown in Fig. 6.

When 6 signature images are used as the training set, the highest average top-1 recognition accuracy of OHS-Net is 93.98%, and the highest average top-5 recognition accuracy is 97.66%, which is much higher than other VGG networks. When 12 signature images are used as the training set, OHS-Net obtains the highest average top-1 recognition accuracy of 97.46% and Vgg13 achieves the highest average recognition accuracy of 98.67% for top-5, which only 0.07% higher than OHS-Net, but the top-1 recognition accuracy is 1.58% lower than OHS-Net. When 18 signature images are used as the training set, OHS-Net achieves the highest average top-1 recognition accuracy of 97.58% and the highest average top-5 recognition accuracy of 99.03%. Although VGG11 and VGG16 also reach one of the highest values, the recognition effect of OHS-Network is more stable and less time-consuming.

Table 3. CEDAR recognition results.

Ratio	Network	Evaluating Indicator		
		Training time	**Top-1 accuracy**	**Top-5 accuracy**
6:9:9	VGG11	1hours 9min	92.16%	98.17%
	VGG13	1hours 50min	91.94%	97.83%
	VGG16	2hours 43min	90.83%	97.69%
	OHS-Net	**1hours 6min**	**96.17%**	**98.73%**
12:6:6	VGG11	1hours 41min	97.21%	99.40%
	VGG13	2hours 49min	97.24%	99.32%
	VGG16	3hours 22min	97.18%	99.29%
	OHS-Net	**1hours 40min**	**98.13%**	**99.43%**
18:3:3	VGG11	2hours 54min	98.78%	99.69%
	VGG13	4hours 35min	98.89%	**99.71%**
	VGG16	6hours	99.15%	99.69%
	OHS-Net	**2hours 29min**	**99.20%**	99.69%

6 Conclusion

In this paper, OHS-Net based on convolutional neural network is proposed to recognize offline handwritten signatures. The results show that compared with the classical VGG network, OHS-Net has the advantages of fewer parameters, smaller model, better generalization performance and higher accuracy, and can efficiently recognize the handwritten signatures of multi-lingual and CEDAR database. At the same time, considering that it is difficult to collect a large number of signature data at one time, this paper conducts comparative experiments on database with different number of training samples, which is closer to the actual needs. Experiments show that the OHS-Net proposed in this paper can achieve better performance than the classical network when the number of samples is less.

In future work, we will focus on using fewer signature image samples to realize large offline handwritten signature recognition and verification technology. At the same time, considering the difficulty of obtaining handwritten signature samples, we will conduct in-depth research on image generation technologies such as Generative Adversarial Networks (GAN) and Variational Auto-Encoder (VAE), and try to generate handwritten signature images for experimental research on signature recognition and verification.

References

1. Sun, Z., Li, Q., Liu, Y., Zhu, Y.: Opportunities and Challenges for Biometrics (2021)
2. Tanwar, S., Obaidat, M.S., Tyagi, S., Kumar, N.: Online Signature-Based Biometric Recognition (2019)
3. Das, S.D., Ladia, H., Kumar, V., Mishra, S.: Writer Independent Offline Signature Recognition Using Ensemble Learning (2019)
4. Ubul, K., Wang, X., Yimin, A., Zhang, S., Yibulayin, T.: Multilingual offline handwritten signature recognition based on statistical features. In: Zhou, J., et al. (eds.) CCBR 2018. LNCS, vol. 10996, pp. 727–735. Springer, Cham (2018). https://doi.org/10.1007/978-3-319-97909-0_77
5. Mahpirat, L.M., Zhu, Y., Mamat, H., Ubul, K.: Off-Line Handwritten Signature Recognition Based on Discrete Curvelet Transform (2019)
6. Ubul, K., Zhu, Y., Mamut, M., Yadikar, N., Yibulayin, T.: Uyghur Off-Line Signature Recognition Based on Local Central Line Features (2017)
7. Taskiran, M., Cam, Z.G.: Offline signature identification via HOG features and artificial neural networks. In: 2017 IEEE 15th International Symposium on Applied Machine Intelligence and Informatics (SAMI). IEEE (2017)
8. Hadjadji, B., Chibani, Y., Nemmour, H.: An efficient open system for offline handwritten signature identification based on curvelet transform and one-class principal component analysis. Neurocomputing **265**, 66–77 (2017)
9. Calik, N., Kurban, O.C., Yilmaz, A.R., Yildirim, T., Ata, L.D.: Large-scale offline signature recognition via deep neural networks and feature embedding. Neurocomputing **359**, 1–14 (2019)
10. Rezaei, M., Naderi, N.: Persian Signature Verification using Fully Convolutional Networks (2019)
11. Poddar, J., Parikh, V., Bharti, S.K.: Offline signature recognition and forgery detection using deep learning - ScienceDirect. Procedia Comput. Sci. **170**, 610–617 (2020)
12. Hafemann, L.G., Sabourin, R., Oliveira, L.S.: Learning features for offline handwritten signature verification using deep convolutional neural networks. Patt. Recogn. **70**, 163–176 (2017)
13. Ooi, S.Y., Teoh, A.B.J., Pang, Y.H., Hiew, B.Y.: Image-based handwritten signature verification using hybrid methods of discrete Radon transform, principal component analysis and probabilistic neural network. Appl. Soft Comput. **40C**, 274–282 (2016)
14. Ghosh, R.: A Recurrent Neural Network based deep learning model for offline signature verification and recognition system. Expert Syst. Appl. **168**(5) (2020)
15. Srihari, S.N., Xu, A., Kalera, M.K.: Learning strategies and classification methods for off-line signature verification. In: Ninth International Workshop on Frontiers in Handwriting Recognition IEEE (2004)
16. Tajbakhsh, N., Suzuki, K.: Comparing two classes of end-to-end machine-learning models in lung nodule detection and classification: MTANNs vs. CNNs. Patt. Recogn. **63**, 476–486 (2017)
17. Simonyan, K., Zisserman, A.: Very deep convolutional networks for large-scale image recognition. Comput. Sci. (2014)
18. Loffe, S., Szegedy, C.: Batch normalization: accelerating deep network training by reducing internal covariate shift. In: Proceedings of the 32nd International Conference on Machine Learning, PMLR, vol. 37, pp. 448–456 (2015)

19. He, K., Zhang, X., Ren, S., Sun, J.: Delving Deep into Rectifiers: Surpassing Human-Level Performance on ImageNet Classification. CVPR IEEE Computer Society (2015)

Attention Skip Connection Dense Network for Accurate Iris Segmentation

Shubin Guo, Ying Chen$^{(\boxtimes)}$, Yugang Zeng, and Liang Xu

Nanchang Hangkong University, Nanchang, China
c_y2008@163.com

Abstract. As a key step in the iris recognition process, iris segmentation directly affects the accuracy of iris recognition. How to achieve accurate iris segmentation under various environmental conditions is a big challenge. This paper proposes attention skip connection dense network (ASCDNet), which adopts an codec structure, and uses dense blocks as a component of encoder to obtain richer iris features and alleviate the problem of gradient disappearance. In the improved skip connection, channel attention and spatial attention mechanisms are introduced to achieve effective information fusion through the connection of high and low layers. The experimental results on two iris datasets IITD, CASIA-Interval-V4 collected under near-infrared light and one iris dataset UBIRIS.V2 collected under visible light show that the proposed improved skip connection can effectively improve the performance of iris segmentation, the accuracy rates of segmentation are as high as 0.9882, 0.9904, 0.9941, respectively, outperforming most state-of-the-art iris segmentation networks.

Keywords: Iris segmentation · ASCDNet · Attention mechanisms

1 Introduction

Nowadays, intelligent biometric technologies such as fingerprint, voice, face and iris have gradually replaced the traditional identity authentication technologies, among which iris has great advantages because of its uniqueness, durability, anti-counterfeiting, collectability and other characteristics. Due to the existence of various problems such as different acquisition devices, light reflection, pupil constriction, etc., the quality of the collected iris images is also different. The accuracy of iris segmentation results directly determines the accuracy of iris recognition. Therefore, iris segmentation is a key step in iris image preprocessing.

The early traditional iris segmentation methods are mostly based on the difference of boundary pixel values to perform iris segmentation, which is fast in segmentation, but requires high image quality and has certain shortcomings. In recent years, deep learning has developed rapidly and shown good performance in various fields. Therefore, researchers have applied deep learning to iris segmentation and achieved good results. Bazrafkan et al. [1] proposed an end-to-end full convolutional deep neural network

W. Deng et al. (Eds.): CCBR 2022, LNCS 13628, pp. 404–413, 2022.
https://doi.org/10.1007/978-3-031-20233-9_41

(FCDNN) to realize iris segmentation of low-quality iris images. Arsalan et al. [2] proposed robust iris segmentation using densely connected fully convolutional networks (IrisDenseNet) in the images by visible light and near-infrared light camera sensors. Zhang et al. [3] proposed fully dilated convolution combining U-Net (FD-Unet) for iris segmentation. Chen et al. [4] proposed a robust structure combining CNN and dense blocks, called dense-fully convolutional network (DFCN), for adaptively segmenting iris regions of iris images. Arsalan et al. [5] proposed the full residual encoder-decoder network (FRED-Net), which focuses on accurately reducing the number of parameters and layers through the unique residual connections inside the encoder and decoder. Hao et al. [6] proposed an iris segmentation method based on feature channel optimization based on U-Net, which makes the information gradient flow obtained by different layers be reused, and alleviates the problems of feature loss and gradient disappearance. You et al. [7] proposed multiscale feature fusion iris segmentation U-Net (MFFIris-UNet) based on U-Net, which is improved on the codec structure of u-net and has good segmentation performance.

Based on the method of deep learning, this paper proposes the attention skip connection dense network (ASCDNet), which not only introduces dense blocks and attention mechanisms to obtain multi-level information, but also designs an improved skip connection to integrate high-level and low-level semantic information, and improve the accuracy of iris segmentation.

2 Method of this Paper

2.1 Network Architecture

The network architecture of ASCDNet proposed in this paper is shown in Fig. 1, and the number in the figure is the number of channels corresponding to the feature map.

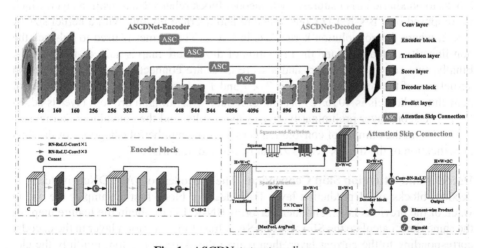

Fig. 1. ASCDNet structure diagram

ASCDNet is composed of encoder and decoder. The input image of encoder is an unprocessed iris image. Iris features are extracted by continuous convolution and down sampling. At the same time, dense block is introduced to alleviate the phenomenon of gradient disappearance. The decoder upsamples the feature map through deconvolution, and calculates the attention value of the corresponding feature map in the encoder, which are the channel attention Squeeze-and-Excitation (SE) in SENet [8] and the spatial attention (SA) in convolutional block attention module [9], respectively, to obtain rich information. At the same time, through improved skip connection, the corresponding feature map in the encoder and decoder are effectively fused. In the process of upsampling, increase the effective attention value, reduce the loss of information in the convolution, pooling and upsampling of the feature map, and finally get the prediction results.

The learning ability of deep convolutional neural network will be relatively stronger, but with the increase of network depth, the gradient may disappear, and if the number of training pictures is not large enough, overfitting may occur. Therefore, dense blocks are used as the main component of encoder in this paper, the structure is shown in the Encoder block in Fig. 1. Each dense block includes two batch normalization (BN), rectified linear units (ReLU) and convolution (Conv) modules, forming a BN-ReLU-Conv structure, in which the convolution core size of the two convolution layers is 1×1 and 3×3, respectively, and the number of convolution kernels is 48. The role of BN is to speed up the training speed and increase the learning rate, and at the same time disrupt the training set to avoid the deviation of training. The role of ReLU is to prevent overfitting. Conv is used to obtain local features. At the same time, the dense connection method is used to connect the output results with the input, and reuse the features, effectively solve the problem of gradient disappearance.

Encoder: In the encoder of ASCDNet, the input image is first subjected to a convolution operation, the size of the convolution kernel is 5×5, and the number of convolution kernels is 64, and then BN and ReLU operations are performed. Then connect 5 encoder blocks to obtain rich iris features. Each encoder block relates to a transition layer, which is composed of a BN-ReLU-Conv structure and average pooling with a kernel size of 2×2, where the convolution kernel size is 1×1. The former is used to enhance the non-linearity of features, and the resolution of the feature map is halved after pooling. Finally, two convolution layers and a score layer are connected, and the convolution kernel size of the convolution layer is 7×7 and 1×1, respectively, and the number of convolution kernels is 4096. To prevent or reduce overfitting, a dropout layer is added later. The score layer preliminarily divides the results, and the convolution kernel size is 1×1, and the number of convolution kernels is the number of categories of the final classification of the image, here is 2, that is, iris and non-iris.

Decoder and Attention Skip Connection: The decoder of ASCDNet includes 4 decoder blocks and 1 prediction layer. Each decoder block first upsamples the output value of the previous layer, and then performs BN-ReLU to obtain the feature map. At the same time, calculate the SE value and SA value of the transition layer in the encoder corresponding to the current layer, then realize the skip connection, multiply the elements with the feature map obtained by the decoder block respectively, concatenate the two feature maps of high-level and low-level information fusion, and finally perform the

Conv-BN-ReLU operation, in which the convolution kernel size of the convolution layer is 1×1, and the number of convolution kernels is the number of channels in the current layer, the role is the same as that in encoder. The final prediction layer is a upsampling. The output result is consistent with the resolution of the input image. The number of channels is 2, that is, iris and non-iris.

SA module first performs global max pooling (MaxPool) and global average pooling (AvgPool) based on the channels, and performs channel concatenation. Then perform a 7×7 convolution operation, and finally generate the final feature map through the sigmoid function.

SE module mainly includes two stages: squeeze and excitation. The squeeze stage is implemented using global average pooling to obtain global features on the channel. In the excitation stage, two full connections are mainly used to learn the relationship between each channel and obtain the corresponding weight. Finally, the excitation value of each channel is multiplied by the original feature map.

Ablation Experiments: To verify the effectiveness of the skip connection of attention mechanism in ASCDNet, this paper designs ablation experiments for SE module and SA module, replacing the Sequence-and-Exception and Spatial Attention structures of the Attention Skip Connection in Fig. 1 with ordinary connections, and designing an ordinary skip connection.

2.2 Evaluation Indexes

In this paper, accuracy (Acc), precision (P), recall (R), F1 score (F1), and mean intersection over union (MIoU) are used as the evaluation indexes of iris segmentation results. All values are within the range of [0,1]. The closer the calculation result is to 1, the better the iris segmentation result is.

3 Experiments and Results

3.1 Description of Databases and Relevant Parameters

To verify the robustness of ASCDNet, this paper intends to use three public iris datasets for experiments, namely IITD [10], CASIA-Interval-V4 (CASIA) [11] and UBIRIS.V2 (UBIRIS) [12]. IITD was collected under near-infrared light. The subjects were Indians, and the most obvious feature was thick eyelashes, which was a major challenge for this paper. CASIA was taken with a close-up iris camera, which has a circular near-infrared LED. UBIRIS was taken at a distance and in motion. There are various types of non-ideal factors, such as imaging distance, lighting conditions, etc., which have certain practical significance for ASCDNet in improving the segmentation effect of visible light and poor-quality iris images.

In this paper, all images in IITD and CASIA and 2250 images in UBIRIS are selected as experimental data. All iris datasets are randomly divided into training set and test set according to the ratio of 8:2. For the ground truth (GT) corresponding to these three iris datasets, this paper uses the public GT image used in most papers, that is, the GT image published on irisseg-ep [13]. Figure 2 shows the sample images of iris images in these three datasets and their corresponding GT images. The two lines are sample images with good and poor quality respectively.

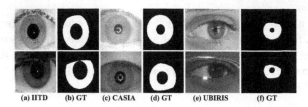

(a) IITD   (b) GT   (c) CASIA   (d) GT   (e) UBIRIS   (f) GT

Fig. 2. Sample images of the iris datasets and corresponding GT images

In this experiment, the median frequency balancing method proposed by Eigen et al. [14] is used to balance the difference between the number of iris and non-iris. The calculation of weight is shown in Formula 1, where freq represents the total number of iris and non-iris pixels in all images. Assign the calculated weight value to the opposite category to achieve the balance effect.

$$\text{weight}_i = \frac{1}{2} \sum_{j=0}^{1} \text{freq}_j / \text{freq}_i \qquad (1)$$

Due to the limited memory of the experimental equipment, the batch size is always set to 4, and the initial learning rate is set to 0.001. For every 20 epochs trained, the learning rate drops to one tenth of the current learning rate. The training model obtained with epoch of 40 is used as the completed segmentation model.

The hardware environment used in this experiment are as follows:

CPU: Inter(R) Xeon(R) Silver 4208 CPU @ 2.10 GHz (2.10 GHz).
GPU: NVIDIA Quadro RTX 5000.
Memory: 64.0 GB.

3.2 Experimental Results and Analysis

The segmentation result examples of ASCDNet on the three datasets are shown in Fig. 3, 4 and 5. Each group of images are the original image, GT image, predicted image, segmented iris image, and the effect of superimposing the difference between the predicted image and GT image in the original image. The red part in the last row of images is false negative, that is, the region is predicted to be non-iris region after segmentation, while the corresponding GT image marks it as iris region; The green part is false positive, which means the opposite.

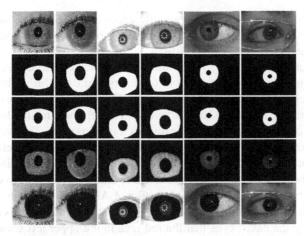

Fig. 3. Sample images with better segmentation results

Figure 3 is sample images of ASCDNet's better segmentation results in the three datasets. Every two columns are from the same dataset, from left to right are IITD, CASIA, UBIRIS. The results show that the ASCDNet segmented images are almost consistent with the corresponding GT images, whether it is the iris image collected under near-infrared light or visible light. Unfavorable factors such as eyelids occlusion, eyelashes occlusion, glasses light transmission, and angle of view deviation do not affect the segmentation of iris by ASCDNet. For the blue eye images, ASCDNet can still accurately segment the iris regions even if the pixels are different from other mostly brown iris images. In short, ASCDNet can segment iris images with different interference information accurately and has strong robustness.

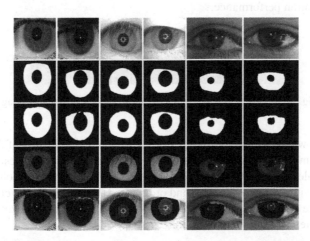

Fig. 4. Sample images with large differences in segmentation results

Figure 4 is Sample images with large differences in ASCDNet's a small amount of segmentation results in the three datasets. Every two columns are from the same dataset, from left to right are IITD, CASIA, UBIRIS.

It can be seen that it is basically iris images with thick eyelashes, serious occlusion and dim light. For example, the iris regions of the first, third and fifth columns of images are severely blocked by eyelashes. Although ASCDNet cannot recognize each eyelash, it can recognize the heavily blocked iris part with thick eyelashes and divide it into non-iris parts, while the corresponding GT image divides it into iris parts. This part is difficult to obtain iris features, which will affect the extraction of iris features. Therefore, ASCDNet is relatively rigorous. The image in the second column is dull. For the eyelashes occlusion part, the eyelashes and iris regions are interlaced, making it difficult to distinguish the iris regions. Therefore, the segmentation results of ASCDNet are quite different from GT images. The fourth column is the iris image occluded by the eyelids and eyelashes. It can be seen by the naked eyes that the red area in the upper left corner is the inner eyelid part, and the corresponding GT image mistakenly divides it into the iris area, while ASCDNet can accurately judge it as a non-iris part. It can be proved that the GT images are not necessarily completely accurate. The last column is the iris image with poor light and low contrast. The pixels in the iris, eyelashes occlusion and pupil area are extremely similar. The segmentation results of ASCDNet are quite different from the corresponding GT image. In fact, it is difficult to distinguish whether the areas with differences are iris areas with the naked eyes, and it is impossible to explain which segmentation results are more accurate, Therefore, the segmentation performance of ASCDNet cannot be directly denied.

ASCDNet can also detect the closed eye image, as shown in Fig. 5. However, this paper does not approve the annotation of the iris area of the corresponding GT image, which also proves that the GT image is not completely accurate. The ASCDNet proposed in this paper has fully obtained the features of the iris in the learning process and has better segmentation performance.

Fig. 5. Sample images of segmentation results of closed eye image

Table 1 shows the evaluation indexes of the segmentation results of ASCDNet and ablation experiments on three iris datasets. The ablation experimental results of channel attention module SE, spatial attention module SA and ordinary skip connection mode correspond to without_se, without_sa and ordinary in the table respectively. All ablation experiments are consistent with ASCDNet in terms of experimental environment and related parameters, except for the structure.

Table 1. Segmentation results of ablation experiments

Dataset	Algorithms	Acc	P	R	F1	MIoU
IITD	without_se	0.9880	0.9793	0.9815	0.9804	0.9616
	without_sa	0.9878	0.9788	0.9816	0.9802	0.9612
	ordinary	0.9880	0.9820	0.9789	0.9805	0.9617
	ASCDNet	**0.9882**	**0.9821**	**0.9834**	**0.9827**	**0.9623**
CASIA	without_se	0.9901	0.9829	0.9826	0.9828	0.9662
	without_sa	0.9903	0.9818	0.9844	0.9831	0.9669
	ordinary	0.9903	0.9830	0.9831	0.9831	0.9668
	ASCDNet	**0.9904**	**0.9877**	**0.9852**	**0.9864**	**0.9672**
UBIRIS	without_se	0.9938	0.9455	0.9630	0.9542	0.9125
	without_sa	**0.9943**	0.9545	0.9601	0.9573	0.9182
	ordinary	0.9919	0.9231	0.9583	0.9404	0.8876
	ASCDNet	0.9941	**0.9548**	**0.9696**	**0.9621**	**0.9289**

It can be seen from the results that all the experimental results are above 0.9, and the segmentation effect of ASCDNet for iris images collected under near-infrared light is slightly better than that iris images collected under visible light. Although the gap between the evaluation index results of all ablation experiments and ASCDNet is not large, the results of ASCDNet are almost the best, which proves the effectiveness of the skip connection structure designed in this paper, which combines channel attention and spatial attention.

Table 2 shows the comparison results between ASCDNet and iris segmentation algorithms based on convolutional neural network in recent years.

According to the data in the table, ASCDNet obtained the highest precision and F1 score in the IITD dataset, which were 0.9821 and 0.9827 respectively. In CASIA dataset, ASCDNet obtained the highest precision, F1 score and MIoU, which were 0.9877, 0.9864 and 0.9672 respectively. Although the accuracy of ASCDNet is lower than that of DFCN and the recall is lower than that of FRED-Net in these two datasets, the results are very close. In the UBIRIS dataset, ASCDNet has slightly lower accuracy and precision than DFCN, but higher recall and F1 score; compared with FRED-Net, the recall and F1 score are slightly lower, but the precision is higher; compared with MFFIris-UNet, F1 score and MIoU are slightly lower, but the precision and recall are higher; compared with other methods, all indexes are better. Most methods in the table improve the training effect through data enhancement, but this paper does not carry out data enhancement. Considering comprehensively, the ASCDNet proposed in this paper still has certain advantages.

Table 2. Comparison of ASCDNet and other methods based on convolutional neural network

Dataset	Algorithms	Acc	P	R	F1	MIoU
IITD	IrisDensenet [2]	—	0.9716	0.9800	0.9756	—
	DFCN [4]	**0.9884**	0.9818	0.9806	0.9812	—
	FRED-Net [5]	—	0.9682	**0.9841**	0.9761	—
	Hao et al. [6]	—	0.9801	0.9782	0.9790	—
	Proposed ASCDNet	0.9882	**0.9821**	0.9834	**0.9827**	**0.9623**
CASIA	IrisDenseNet [2]	—	0.9810	0.9710	0.9758	—
	FD-UNet [3]	—	—	—	0.9736	—
	DFCN [4]	**0.9905**	0.9827	0.9829	0.9828	—
	FRED-Net [5]	—	0.9659	**0.9910**	0.9783	—
	Hao et al. [6]	—	0.9848	0.9808	0.9827	—
	MFFIris-UNet [7]	—	0.9656	0.9262	0.9714	0.9461
	Proposed ASCDNet	0.9904	**0.9877**	0.9852	**0.9864**	**0.9672**
UBIRIS	FCDNN [1]	0.9930	0.9488	0.9398	0.9390	—
	FD-UNet [3]	—	—	—	0.9481	—
	DFCN [4]	**0.9947**	**0.9592**	0.9620	0.9606	—
	FRED-Net [5]	—	0.9431	**0.9852**	0.9630	—
	MFFIris-UNet [7]	—	0.9296	0.9287	**0.9659**	**0.9428**
	Proposed ASCDNet	0.9941	0.9548	0.9696	0.9621	0.9289

4   Conclusions and Future Work

The attention skip connection dense network (ASCDNet) proposed in this paper adopts an codec structure, uses the structure of dense blocks as a component of encoder, introduces the mechanism of channel attention and spatial attention to obtain different features, and obtains the effectively fused high-level and low-level semantic information through the improved attention skip connection. Experimental results on iris datasets collected under two near-infrared and one visible demonstrate the segmentation performance of ASCDNet, and the effectiveness of the improved attention mechanism skip connection is verified by ablation experiments. Compared with most of the most advanced iris segmentation networks in recent years, ASCDNet has a certain breakthrough, but this method also has some shortcomings. How to obtain more accurate GT images, design a lighter and more robust segmentation algorithm, and improve the segmentation accuracy of iris images collected in a variety of environments are the focus of future work.

References

1. Shabab, B., Shejin, T., Peter, C.: An end to end deep neural network for iris segmentation in unconstraint scenarios. Neural Netw. Official J. Int. Neural Netw. Soc. **106**, 79–95 (2017)
2. Arsalan, M., Naqvi, R., Kim, D., Nguyen, P., Owais, M., Park, K.: IrisDenseNet: robust iris segmentation using densely connected fully convolutional networks in the images by visible light and near-infrared light camera sensors. Sensors **18**(5), 1501–1531 (2018)
3. Zhang, W., Xiaoqi, L., Yu, G., Liu, Y., Meng, X., Li, J.: A robust iris segmentation scheme based on improved U-Net. IEEE Access **7**, 85082–85089 (2019). https://doi.org/10.1109/ACCESS.2019.2924464
4. Chen, Y., Wang, W., Zeng, Z., Wang, Y.: An adaptive CNNs technology for robust iris segmentation. IEEE Access **7**, 64517–64532 (2019). https://doi.org/10.1109/ACCESS.2019.2917153
5. Arsalan, M., Kim, D.S., Lee, M.B., Owais, M., Park, K.R.: FRED-Net: fully residual encoder–decoder network for accurate iris segmentation. Expert Syst. Appl. **122**, 217–241 (2019)
6. Hao, K., Feng, G., Ren, Y., Zhang, X.: Iris segmentation using feature channel optimization for noisy environments. Cogn. Comput. **12**(9), 1205–1216 (2020)
7. You, X., Zhao, P., Mu, X., Bai, K., Lian, S.: Heterogeneous noise Iris segmentation based on attention mechanism and dense multiscale feaures. Laser Optoelectron. Prog. **59**(04), 109–120 (2022)
8. Hu J, Shen L, Sun G.: Squeeze-and-excitation networks. In: Proceedings of the IEEE Conference on Computer Vision and Pattern Recognition, pp. 7132–7141 (2018)
9. Woo, S., Park, J., Lee, J.-Y., Kweon, I.S.: CBAM: convolutional block attention module. In: Ferrari, V., Hebert, M., Sminchisescu, C., Weiss, Y. (eds.) ECCV 2018. LNCS, vol. 11211, pp. 3–19. Springer, Cham (2018). https://doi.org/10.1007/978-3-030-01234-2_1
10. Kumar, A., Passi, A.: Comparison and combination of iris matchers for reliable personal authentication. Pattern Recogn. **43**(3), 1016–1026 (2010)
11. Chinese Academy of Sciences Institute of Automation. Casia iris image databases. http://www.cbsr.ia.ac.cn/china/Iris%20Databases%20CH.asp. Accessed 21 May 2020
12. Proenca, H., Filipe, S., Santos, R., Oliveira, J., Alexandre, L.A.: The UBIRIS.v2: a database of visible wavelength iris images captured on-the-move and at-a-distance. IEEE Trans. Pattern Anal. Mach. Intell. **32**(8), 1529–1535 (2010)
13. Hofbauer, H., Alonso-Fernandez, F., Wild, P., Bigun, J., Uhl, A.: A ground truth for iris segmentation. In: 2014 22nd International Conference on Pattern Recognition, pp. 527–532 (2014)
14. Eigen, D., Fergus, R.: Predicting depth, surface normals and semantic labels with a common multi-scale convolutional architecture. In: Proceedings of the IEEE International Conference on Computer Vision, pp. 2650–2658 (2015)

Gait Recognition with Various Data Modalities: A Review

Wei Li, Jiwei Song[✉], Yao Liu, Chen Zhong, Li Geng, and Wenfeng Wang

IoT Research Center, China Electronics Standardization Institute,
NO.1 Andingmen East Street, Beijing, China
{liwei1,songjw}@cesi.cn

Abstract. Gait recognition aims to recognize one subject by the way she/he walks without alerting the subject, which has drawn increasing attention. Recently, gait recognition can be represented using various data modalities, such as RGB, skeleton, depth, infrared data, acceleration, gyroscope, .etc., which have various advantages depending on the application scenarios. In this paper, we present a comprehensive survey of recent progress in gait recognition methods based on the type of input data modality. Specifically, we review commonly-used gait datasets with different gait data modalities, following with effective gait recognition methods both for single data modality and multiple data modalities. We also present comparative results of effective gait recognition approaches, together with insightful observations and discussions.

Keywords: Gait recognition · Sensor · Deep learning · Data modality

1 Introduction

There is a growing demand for human identification in many applications (e.g., secure access control and criminal identification). Biometrics such as face, fingerprint, iris, palmprint, .etc., have been used for human identification for years. Gait recognition aims to discriminate a subject by the way she/he walks. Compared with other biometrics, the key advantage of gait recognition is its unobtrusiveness, i.e., the gait video can be captured from a distance without disturbing the subject. Many gait recognition methods are proposed, and deep learning based gait recognition methods achieve great progresses in recent years. The general gait recognition framework can be found in Fig. 1. Most of the existing gait recognition methods utilize RGB videos as input as reviewed in [23,27,37], due to their easy access. Besides, we also have witnessed the emergence of works [5,22,29,44,47] with other data modalities for gait recognition, such as skeletons, depth images, infrared data, acceleration and gyroscope. Figure 2 demonstrates different modalities for gait recognition. This is mainly due to the development of various affordable sensors as well as the advantages of different modalities for gait recognition depending on various application scenarios.

W. Deng et al. (Eds.): CCBR 2022, LNCS 13628, pp. 414–423, 2022.
https://doi.org/10.1007/978-3-031-20233-9_42

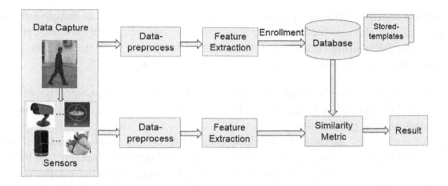

Fig. 1. Framework of gait recognition.

Generally, gait data can be roughly divided into two categories: vision-based gait data and non-vision gait data. The former are visually "intuitive" for representing gait, such as RGB images, silhouettes, 2D/3D skeletons [5], 3D Meshes [44]. Recently, vision-based gait data play important and effective roles for gait recognition. Among them, RGB video based gait data is the most common-used data modalities for gait recognition, which has been widely-used in surveillance and monitoring systems. Meanwhile, inertial-based gait data modalities, such as acceleration, gyroscope, are non-vision gait data as they are visually non-intuitive for representing human gaits. The non-vision gait data modalities can also be used in the scenarios that require to protect the privacy of subjects. Figure 2 shows several gait data modalities and more details of different modalities are discussed in Sect. 2.

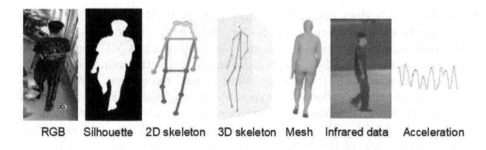

RGB   Silhouette   2D skeleton   3D skeleton   Mesh   Infrared data   Acceleration

Fig. 2. Some examples for various gait data modalities.

Compared with other biometrics, gait recognition face many challenges due to the long distance and uncooperative means. Many methods are proposed to deal with these challenges for robust gait recognition. So far, many gait recognition survey have been published, such as [23,25,27,37]. However, most of the recent surveys mainly focus on vision based deep learning, and the non-vision gait recognition draws little attentions. This paper aims to conduct a comprehensive analyze about the development of gait recognition, including gait datasets, recent gait recognition approaches, as well as the performance and trend. The main contributions of this work can be summarized as follows.

(1) We comprehensively review the gait recognition from the perspective of various data modalities, including RGB, depth, skeleton, infrared sequence, acceleration, gyroscope.
(2) We review the advanced gait databases with various data modalities, and provide comparisions and analysises of the existing gait datasets, including the scale of database, viewing angle, walking speed and other challenges.
(3) We provide comparisons of the advanced deep learning based methods and their performance with brief summaries.

The rest of this paper is organized as follows. Section 2 reviews gait recognition databases with different data modalities. Section 3 introduces related gait recognition methods and performance. Finally, conclusions of gait recognition is discussed in Sect. 4.

2   Datasets for Gait Recognition

In this section, we first introduce commonly-used gait datasets with different data modalities: vision-based and non-vision based gait data. Then, we analyze the differences among those gait databases, including the number of subjects, viewing angles, sequences, and the challenges.

2.1   Vision-Based Gait Datasets

Vision-based gait data modalities mainly include RGB image/video, infared image, depth image, skeleton data. So far, RGB image/video based gait data is the most popular gait modality for gait recognition. The CMU MoBo [8] gait database is a early gait database, which mainly study the influences of walking speed, carrying objects, viewing angles in gait recognition. CASIA series gait databases provide various data types. Specifically, the CASIA A [36] is first released with 20 subjects from 3 different viewing angles, while the CASIA B [39] contains 124 subjects with different clothes, carrying conditions and 11 viewing angles, which is one of the most commonly-used gait database. CASIA C [31] database contains infared image sequences. Besides, the OU-ISIR Speed [34], OU-ISIR Cloth [11], OU-ISIR MV [21] gait databases provide gait silhouettes with different walking speed, clothes and viewing angles.

Different with early gait database, the OU-LP [13], OU-LP Age [38], OU-MVLP [30], OU-LP Bag [35], OU-MVLP Pose [2] focus on large scale gait samples from 4007, 63846, 10307, 62528 and 10307 subjects respectively. The scale of gait database increases with the development of deep learning technologies. The GREW dataset [45] consists of 26000 identities and 128000 sequences with rich attributes for unconstrained gait recognition. The Gait3D database [44] contains 4000 subjects and over 25000 sequences extracted from 39 cameras in an unconstrained indoor scene. It provides 3D Skinned Multi-Person Linear (SMPL) models recovered from video frames which can provide dense 3D information of body shape, viewpoint, and dynamics. Figure 3 demonstrates several examples of different gait benchmark databases.

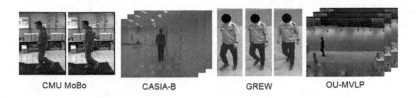

CMU MoBo   CASIA-B   GREW   OU-MVLP

Fig. 3. Examples of gait benchmark databases.

2.2 Non-vision Gait Databases

Non-vision gait recognition can be performed by sensors in the floor, in the shoes or on the body. Generally, the non-vision gait datasets are mainly focus on inertial data. Inertial sensors, such as accelerometers and gyroscopes, are used to record the inertial data generated by the movement of a walking subject. Accelerometers and gyroscopes measure inertial dynamic information from three directions, namely, along the X, Y and Z axes. The accelerations in the three directions reflect the changes in the smartphone's linear velocity in 3D space and also reflect the movement of smartphone users. The whuGAIT Datasets [47] provide the inertial gait data in the wild without the limitations of walking on specific roads or speeds. [1] provide a real-world gait database with 44 subjects over 7–10 days, including normal walking, fast walking, down and upstairs for each subject.

Table 1 show some benchmark datasets with various data modalities for gait recognition. (R: RGB, S: Skeleton, D: Depth, IR: Infrared, Ac: Acceleration, Gyr: Gyroscope, 3DS: 3D SMPL). It can be observed that with the development of deep learning technology, the scale and data modality of gait database increase rapidly. The real-world large-scale gait recognition databases draw lots of attentions.

3 Approaches for Gait Recognition

Many hand-crafted feature based gait recognition approaches, such as GEI based subspace projection method [16] and trajectory-based method [3], were well designed for video-based gait recognition. Recently, with the great progress of

Table 1. Comparisons of the gait recognition datasets regarding statistics, data type, captured environment, view variations and challenging factors. #Sub., #View. and #Sample. refer to numbers of identities, viewing point and sequences. Sil., Ske. Inf., Dep., Aud. and In. denote silhouette, skeleton, infrared, depth, audio and inertial data,respectively. VI, DIS, BA, CA, CL, OCC, ILL, SUR, SP, SH and WD are abbreviations of view, distractor, background, carrying, clothes, occlusion, illumination, surface, speed, shoes, and walking directions, respectively.

Datasets	Year	#Sub.	#View	#Sample	#Data types	#Challenges
CMU MoBo [8]	2001	25	6	600	RGB, Sil	CA, VI, SP, SUR
CASIA A [36]	2003	20	3	240	RGB	VI
SOTON [26]	2004	115	2	2128	RGB, Sil	VI
USF [24]	2005	122	2	1870	RGB	VI, CA, SU, SH
CASIA B [39]	2006	124	11	13640	RGB, Sil	VI, CL, CA
CASIA C [31]	2006	153	1	1530	Inf., Sil	CA, SP
OU-ISIR Speed [34]	2010	34	1	612	Sil	SP
OU-ISIR Cloth [11]	2010	68	1	2,764	Sil	DR
OU-ISIR MV [21]	2010	168	25	4200	Sil	VI
OU-LP [13]	2012	4007	2	7842	Sil	VI
ADSC-AWD [20]	2014	20	1	80	Sil	WD
TUM GAID [10]	2014	305	1	3370	RGB, Dep., Aud	CA, SH
OU-LP Age [38]	2017	63846	1	63846	Sil	Age
OU-MVLP [30]	2018	10307	14	288596	Sil	VI
OU-LP Bag [35]	2018	62528	1	187584	Sil	CA
OU-MVLP Pose [2]	2020	10307	14	288596	2D Pose	VI
whuGAIT Dataset1 [47]	2020	118	–	36844	In	–
GREW [45]	2021	26345	Diverse	128671	RGB, Sil., Flow,2/3D Ske	VI, DIS, BA, CA,CL, OCC, ILL, SUR
Gait3D [44]	2021	4000	39	25309	RGB, Silh., 2D/3D Ske., 3D Mesh	DIS, SP, VI, OCC, CA, BA

deep learning techniques, various deep learning architectures have been proposed for gait recognition with strong representation capability and superior performance.

Vision-based gait recognition approaches can be roughly classified into two categories: model-based approaches and appearance-based approaches. Model-based approaches model the human body structure and extract gait features by fitting the model to the observed body data for recognition. Appearance-based approaches extract effective features directly from dynamic gait images. Most current appearance-based approaches use silhouettes extracted from a video sequence to represent gait. Non-vision based gait recognition approaches mainly use inertia-based gait data as input.

3.1 Appearance-Based Approaches

RGB data contains rich appearance information of the captured scene context and can be captured easily. Gait recognition from RGB data has been studies for years but still face many challenges, owing to the variations of backgrounds, viewpoints, scales of subjects and illumination conditions. Besides, RGB videos have generally large data sizes, leading to high computational costs when modeling the spatio-temporal context for gait recognition. The temporal modeling can be divided into single-image, sequence-based, and set-based approaches. Early approaches proposed to encode a gait cycle into a single image, i.e., Gait Energy

Image (GEI) [9]. These representations are easy to compute but lose lots of temporal information. Sequence-based approaches focus on each input separately. For modeling the temporal information 3D CNN [12,17] or LSTM [18] are utilized. Sequence-based approaches can comprehend more spatial information and gather more temporal information with higher computational costs. The set-based approach [4] with shuffled inputs and require less computational complexity. GaitPart [6] uses a temporal module to focus on capturing short-range temporal features. [19] conduct effective gait recognition via effective global-local feature representation and local temporal aggregation.

For the similarity comparision, current deep learning gait recognition methods often rely on effective loss functions such as contrastive loss, triplet loss [4] and angle center loss [41].

3.2   Model-Based Approaches

In recent years, model-based gait recognition using a 2D/3D skeleton has been widely studied through view-invariant modeling and analysis. 2D poses can be obtained by human pose estimation, while 3D dynamic gait features can be extracted from the depth data for gait recognition [14]. [18] represents pose-based approach for gait recognition with handcrafted pose features. [32] utilize human pose estimation method to obtain skeleton poses directly from RGB images, and then GaitGraph network is proposed to combine skeleton poses with Graph Convolutional Network for gait recognition.

Table 2. Averaged Rank-1 accuracies in percent on CASIA-B of the recent appearance-based and model-based methods.

Type	Methods	NM	BG	CL	Mean
appearance-based	GaitNet [43]	91.6	85.7	58.9	78.7
	GaitSet [4]	95.0	87.2	70.4	84.2
	GaitPart [6]	96.2	91.5	78.7	88.8
	GaitGL [19]	97.4	94.5	83.6	91.8
model-based	PoseGait [18]	68.7	44.5	36.0	49.7
	GaitGraph [32]	87.7	74.8	66.3	76.3

In Table 2, we just compare several current the appearance-based and model-based methods due to the space limitations. We can observe that appearance-based gait recognition achieves better performance than model-based approaches. Model-based gait recognition approaches such as [32] achieve great progress compared with early model-based gait recognition method.

3.3   Inertia-Based Approaches

In the past decade, many inertia-based gait recognition methods have been developed [7,15,28,33,42]. Most of them require inertia sensors to be fastened to specific joints of the human body to obtain gait information, which is inconvenient for the gait data collection. Recently, many advanced inertial sensors, including accelerometers and gyroscopes, are integrated into smartphones nowadays [47] to collect the interial gait data. Compared with traditional methods, which often require a person to walk along a specified road and/or at a normal walking speed, [47] collects inertial gait data in unconstrained conditions. To obtain good performance, deeply convolutional neural network and recurrent neural network are utilized for robust inertial gait feature representation. So far, non-vision based recognition becomes more and more important due to its safety to protect people's privacy.

3.4   Multi-modalities Gait Recognition

Traditionally, gait data are collected by either color sensors, such as a CCD camera, depth sensors, Microsoft Kinect devices, or inertial sensors, or an accelerometer. Generally, a single type of gait sensor may only capture part of the dynamic gait features which makes the gait recognition sensitive to complex covariate conditions. To solve these problems, approaches based on multi-modalities are proposed. For examples, [46] proposes EigenGait and TrajGait methods to extract gait features from the inertial data and the RGBD (color and depth) data for effective gait recognition. [40] proposes sensor fusion of data for gait recognition which is obtained by ambulatory inertial sensors and plastic optical fiber-based floor sensors. The multi-modalities gait recognition approaches can achieves better performance but require more sensors to obtain different gait modalities.

3.5   Challenges and Future Work

Although significant progress has been achieved in gait recognition, there are still many challenges for robust gait recognition. Generally, gait recognition can be improved from the aspects of database, recognition accuracy, computational cost and privicay. For the gait database, it is significant to develop more gait databases in real scenarios. More effective gait recognition methods should be developed to deal with challenges such as different viewing angles and object carrying. Besides, the computational cost and privicy projection are also important for gait recognition.

4   Conclusions

In this paper, we provide a comprehensive study of gait recognition with various data modalities, including RGB, depth, skeleton, infrared sequences and inertial data. We provide an up-to-date review of existing studies on both vision-based and non-vision based gait recognition approaches. Moreover, we also provide an extensive survey of available gait databases with multi-modalities by comparing and analyzing gait databases from aspects of subjects, viewing angle, carrying, speed and other challenges.

References

1. Alobaidi, H., Clarke, N., Li, F., Alruban, A.: Real-world smartphone-based gait recognition. Comput. Secur. **113**, 102557 (2022)
2. An, W., et al.: Performance evaluation of model-based gait on multi-view very large population database with pose sequences. IEEE Trans. Biometrics Behav. Ident. Sci. **2**(4), 421–430 (2020)
3. Castro, F.M., Marín-Jiménez, M., Mata, N.G., Muñoz-Salinas, R.: Fisher motion descriptor for multiview gait recognition. Int. J. Pattern Recogn. Artif. Intell. **31**(01), 1756002 (2017)
4. Chao, H., He, Y., Zhang, J., Feng, J.: Gaitset: regarding gait as a set for cross-view gait recognition. In: Proceedings of the AAAI Conference on Artificial Intelligence, vol. 33, pp. 8126–8133 (2019)
5. Choi, S., Kim, J., Kim, W., Kim, C.: Skeleton-based gait recognition via robust frame-level matching. IEEE Trans. Inf. Forensics Secur. **14**(10), 2577–2592 (2019)
6. Fan, C., et al.: Gaitpart: temporal part-based model for gait recognition. In: Proceedings of the IEEE/CVF Conference on Computer Vision and Pattern Recognition, pp. 14225–14233 (2020)
7. Gafurov, D., Snekkenes, E.: Gait recognition using wearable motion recording sensors. EURASIP J. Adv. Signal Process. **2009**, 1–16 (2009)
8. Gross, R., Shi, J.: The CMU motion of body (MOBO) database (2001)
9. Han, J., Bhanu, B.: Individual recognition using gait energy image. IEEE Trans. Pattern Anal. Mach. Intell. **28**(2), 316–322 (2005)
10. Hofmann, M., Geiger, J., Bachmann, S., Schuller, B., Rigoll, G.: The tum gait from audio, image and depth (gaid) database: Multimodal recognition of subjects and traits. J. Vis. Commun. Image Represent. **25**(1), 195–206 (2014)
11. Hossain, M.A., Makihara, Y., Wang, J., Yagi, Y.: Clothing-invariant gait identification using part-based clothing categorization and adaptive weight control. Pattern Recogn. **43**(6), 2281–2291 (2010)
12. Huang, Z., et al.: 3D local convolutional neural networks for gait recognition. In: Proceedings of the IEEE/CVF International Conference on Computer Vision, pp. 14920–14929 (2021)
13. Iwama, H., Okumura, M., Makihara, Y., Yagi, Y.: The OU-ISIR gait database comprising the large population dataset and performance evaluation of gait recognition. IEEE Trans. Inf. Forensics Secur. **7**(5), 1511–1521 (2012)
14. John, V., Englebienne, G., Krose, B.: Person re-identification using height-based gait in colour depth camera. In: 2013 IEEE International Conference on Image Processing, pp. 3345–3349. IEEE (2013)
15. Juefei-Xu, F., Bhagavatula, C., Jaech, A., Prasad, U., Savvides, M.: Gait-id on the move: pace independent human identification using cell phone accelerometer dynamics. In: 2012 IEEE Fifth International Conference on Biometrics: Theory, Applications and Systems (BTAS), pp. 8–15. IEEE (2012)
16. Li, W., Kuo, C.-C.J., Peng, J.: Gait recognition via GEI subspace projections and collaborative representation classification. Neurocomputing **275**, 1932–1945 (2018)
17. Liao, R., Cao, C., Garcia, E.B., Yu, S., Huang, Y.: Pose-based temporal-spatial network (ptsn) for gait recognition with carrying and clothing variations. In: Zhou, J., et al. (eds.) CCBR 2017. LNCS, vol. 10568, pp. 474–483. Springer, Cham (2017). https://doi.org/10.1007/978-3-319-69923-3_51
18. Liao, R., Shiqi, Yu., An, W., Huang, Y.: A model-based gait recognition method with body pose and human prior knowledge. Pattern Recogn. **98**, 107069 (2020)

19. Lin, B., Zhang, S., Yu, X.: Gait recognition via effective global-local feature representation and local temporal aggregation. In: Proceedings of the IEEE/CVF International Conference on Computer Vision, pp. 14648–14656 (2021)
20. Jiwen, L., Wang, G., Moulin, P.: Human identity and gender recognition from gait sequences with arbitrary walking directions. IEEE Trans. Inf. Forensics Secur. **9**(1), 51–61 (2013)
21. Makihara, Y., Mannami, H., Yagi, Y.: Gait analysis of gender and age using a large-scale multi-view gait database. In: Kimmel, R., Klette, R., Sugimoto, A. (eds.) ACCV 2010. LNCS, vol. 6493, pp. 440–451. Springer, Heidelberg (2011). https://doi.org/10.1007/978-3-642-19309-5_34
22. Middleton, L., Buss, A.A., Bazin, A., Nixon, M.S.: A floor sensor system for gait recognition. In: Fourth IEEE Workshop on Automatic Identification Advanced Technologies (AutoID 2005), pp. 171–176. IEEE (2005)
23. Rida, I., Almaadeed, N., Almaadeed, S.: Robust gait recognition: a comprehensive survey. IET Biometrics **8**(1), 14–28 (2019)
24. Sarkar, S., Phillips, P.J., Liu, Z., Vega, I.R., Grother, P., Bowyer, K.W.: The humanid gait challenge problem: data sets, performance, and analysis. IEEE Trans. Pattern Anal. Mach. Intell. **27**(2), 162–177 (2005)
25. Shen, C., Yu, S., Wang, J., Huang, G.Q., Wang, L.: A comprehensive survey on deep gait recognition: algorithms, datasets and challenges. arXiv preprint arXiv:2206.13732 (2022)
26. Shutler, J.D., Grant, M.G., Nixon, M.S., Carter, J.N.: On a large sequence-based human gait database. In: Lotfi, A., Garibaldi, J.M. (eds.) Applications and Science in Soft Computing, pp. 339–346. Springer, Heidelberg (2004). https://doi.org/10.1007/978-3-540-45240-9_46
27. Singh, J.P., Jain, S., Arora, S., Singh, U.P.: Vision-based gait recognition: a survey. IEEE Access **6**, 70497–70527 (2018)
28. Sprager, S., Juric, M.B.: An efficient hos-based gait authentication of accelerometer data. IEEE Trans. Inf. Forensics Secur. **10**(7), 1486–1498 (2015)
29. Sun, J., Wang, Y., Li, J., Wan, W., Cheng, D., Zhang, H.: View-invariant gait recognition based on kinect skeleton feature. Multimedia Tools Appl. **77**(19), 24909–24935 (2018). https://doi.org/10.1007/s11042-018-5722-1
30. Takemura, N., Makihara, Y., Muramatsu, D., Echigo, T., Yagi, Y.: Multi-view large population gait dataset and its performance evaluation for cross-view gait recognition. IPSJ Trans. Comput. Vis. Appl. **10**(1), 1–14 (2018). https://doi.org/10.1186/s41074-018-0039-6
31. Tan, D., Huang, K., Yu, S., Tan, T.: Efficient night gait recognition based on template matching. In 18th International Conference on Pattern Recognition (ICPR 2006), vol. 3, pages 1000–1003. IEEE (2006)
32. Teepe, T., Khan, A., Gilg, J., Herzog, F., Hörmann, S., Rigoll, G.: Gaitgraph: graph convolutional network for skeleton-based gait recognition. In: 2021 IEEE International Conference on Image Processing (ICIP), pp. 2314–2318. IEEE (2021)
33. Trung, N.T., Makihara, Y., Nagahara, H., Mukaigawa, Y., Yagi, Y.: Performance evaluation of gait recognition using the largest inertial sensor-based gait database. In 2012 5th IAPR International Conference on Biometrics (ICB), pp. 360–366. IEEE (2012)
34. Tsuji, A., Makihara, Y., Yagi, Y.: Silhouette transformation based on walking speed for gait identification. In: 2010 IEEE Computer Society Conference on Computer Vision and Pattern Recognition, pages 717–722. IEEE (2010)

35. Uddin, M.Z., et al.: The OU-ISIR large population gait database with real-life carried object and its performance evaluation. IPSJ Trans. Comput. Vis. Appl. **10**(1), 1–11 (2018)
36. Wang, L., Tan, T., Ning, H., Weiming, H.: Silhouette analysis-based gait recognition for human identification. IEEE Trans. Pattern Anal. Mach. Intell. **25**(12), 1505–1518 (2003)
37. Zifeng, W., Huang, Y., Wang, L., Wang, X., Tan, T.: A comprehensive study on cross-view gait based human identification with deep CNNs. IEEE Trans. Pattern Anal. Mach. Intell. **39**(2), 209–226 (2016)
38. Chi, X., Makihara, Y., Ogi, G., Li, X., Yagi, Y., Jianfeng, L.: The OU-ISIR gait database comprising the large population dataset with age and performance evaluation of age estimation. IPSJ Trans. Comput. Vis. Appl. **9**(1), 1–14 (2017)
39. Yu, S., Tan, D., Tan, T.: A framework for evaluating the effect of view angle, clothing and carrying condition on gait recognition. In: 18th International Conference on Pattern Recognition (ICPR 2006), vol. 4, pp. 441–444. IEEE (2006)
40. Yunas, S.U., Alharthi, A.,Ozanyan, K.B .: Multi-modality sensor fusion for gait classification using deep learning. In: 2020 IEEE Sensors Applications Symposium (SAS), pp. 1–6. IEEE (2020)
41. Zhang, Y., Huang, Y., Shiqi, Yu., Wang, L.: Cross-view gait recognition by discriminative feature learning. IEEE Trans. Image Process. **29**, 1001–1015 (2019)
42. Zhang, Y., Pan, G., Jia, K., Minlong, L., Wang, Y., Zhaohui, W.: Accelerometer-based gait recognition by sparse representation of signature points with clusters. IEEE Trans. Cybern. **45**(9), 1864–1875 (2014)
43. Zhang, Z., et al.: Gait recognition via disentangled representation learning. In: Proceedings of the IEEE/CVF Conference on Computer Vision and Pattern Recognition, pp. 4710–4719 (2019)
44. Zheng, J., Liu, X., Liu, W., He, L., Yan, C., Mei,T.: Gait recognition in the wild with dense 3D representations and a benchmark. arXiv preprint arXiv:2204.02569, 2022
45. Zhu, Z.., et al.. Gait recognition in the wild: a benchmark. In: Proceedings of the IEEE/CVF International Conference on Computer Vision, pp. 14789–14799 (2021)
46. Zou, Q., Ni, L., Wang, Q., Li, Q., Wang, S.: Robust gait recognition by integrating inertial and RGBD sensors. IEEE Trans. Cybernet. **48**(4), 1136–1150 (2017)
47. Zou, Q., Wang, Y., Wang, Q., Zhao, Y., Li, Q.: Deep learning-based gait recognition using smartphones in the wild. IEEE Trans. Inf. Forensics Secur. **15**, 3197–3212 (2020)

Incremental EEG Biometric Recognition Based on EEG Relation Network

Jianghong Kang, Na Lu$^{(\boxtimes)}$, and Xu Niu

Xi'an Jiaotong University, Xi'an 710049, Shaanxi, People's Republic of China
lvna2009@xjtu.edu.cn

Abstract. Electroencephalogram (EEG) has drawn increasing attention in biometric recognition field as an emerging high-security biometric. However, personal EEG varies significantly with time and subjects' mental state, which needs to adjust or add new data and subjects to the original EEG identity database. In such cases, retraining of model leads to high computational cost and transfer learning sometimes does not work well. To address the incremental EEG biometric recognition problem, we proposed a novel method to implement incremental verification and identification using short-time EEG signals of resting state based on a specially designed EEG Relation Network (EEG-RN). The template comparison mechanism in EEG-RN has enabled incremental identification of unseen subjects. In the proposed network, an embedding module is designed to extract discriminant features of inter-subject samples. A relation module computes the similarities between the template samples and the test samples to determine the identification label. Template matching and fine-tuning were employed in the experiments to verify and classify unseen subjects with the model trained on the original dataset. We evaluated EEG-RN on public dataset and the results show that the proposed method can effectively learn efficient features from multiple-subject recognition and improve the practicability of EEG biometric recognition system.

Keywords: EEG biometric · Relation network · Incremental learning · Identity recognition

1 Introduction

Biometric recognition system is of essential importance for security application which uses various biometrics such as fingerprint, palmprint, iris to verify and identify personal identification. In recent years, besides traditional biometrics, electroencephalogram (EEG) has been an emerging and attractive biometric for personal identity recognition system due to its high complexity. EEG signal is electrical voltage fluctuation sequence recorded from the scalp reflecting subject's mental state and neural activity, which is very difficult to forge.

In this paper, an incremental EEG identity recognition method based on relation network (RN) is developed which computes the similarity between different EEG data from multiple subjects and determines the corresponding identity. A template extractor (encoder) can be learned by the metric learning of relation work, and EEG data from unseen subjects can be added and verified by incremental binary classification based on comparison which determines whether the samples from the test set belongs to the subjects in the original training set or some unseen subjects. The incremental biometric recognition is implemented by fine-tuned encoder with very few trials from the unseen target domain. The incremental verification and identification satisfy more requirements in practical application when the EEG signal of users varies with time. In addition, only few samples are necessary for training which makes potential contribution to the practicability of EEG based biometric recognition.

2 Related Work

In 1999, Poulos et al. [1] extracted autoregressive coefficient (AR) from alpha rhythm activity of EEG data as features to learn a vector quantizer network for identity recognition. This study shows the potential of EEG for person identification. Since then, various feature extraction methods were designed such as statistical feature, event-related desynchronization and synchronization (ERDS) phenomenon [2], temporal features, spatial features and power spectrum. Gelareh et al. [3] extracted spatial features and AR coefficients from resting state EEG with 100 channels and trials of 3 s long were used in their experiments. Mel-Frequency Cepstral Coefficients, Zero Crossing Point and spectrum energy were extracted as features by Phuoc Nguyen et al. in [4]. In 2012, Milan et al. [5] used Mahalanobis distance-based classifier and achieved 98% accuracy. However, the 60 s long trials with 53 electrodes were impractical to collect in practical application. Recently, more end-to-end networks have been proposed. Researchers in [6] used different kinds of convolutional neural networks to extract features of time, spatial and frequency domain. Despite the excellent performance obtained, retraining network to adapt to other datasets is time-consuming.

Besides resting state EEG, other task-related paradigms have also been used, such as emotional data, motor imagery, steady state visual evoked potential etc. In 2019 Sun et al. [7] proposed a network combining one-dimensional convolutional layers and LSTM layers which achieved high accuracy of 99.58% on Physionet EEG Dataset with 109 subjects. Trials of 1 s long were used in the experiments. However, the last convolutional layer of the model has 1024 kernels which is too expensive to compute. In order to extract discriminant information among various EEG datasets and reduce the cost of model retraining, transfer learning which aims to reduce difference of data distribution between source domain and target domain is employed in [8]. The authors employed fine-tuning in open-set verification scenarios and EEG dataset over a period of more than one year were used in the experiments.

3 Method

3.1 Dataset and Signal Processing

The EEG signal used in our experiments is Physionet EEG Motor Movement/Imagery Dataset. The dataset consists of 109 subjects performing four motor imaginary tasks (open and close left or right fist, imagine opening and closing left or right fist, open and close both fists or both feet). EEG data are recorded with BCI2000 system with sampling frequency of 160 Hz. 64 electrodes were placed on the scalp of the subjects. In this dataset, the first two runs were resting state with eye closing and opening respectively, and the rest 12 runs were recorded with specific imagery tasks. In our experiments, we only used the first two runs (resting state) to construct a model irrelevant with tasks, which has no special requirement for subjects.

The raw EEG signals can be represented as two-dimensional matrix $R[C,T]$ [10], where C refers to the number of channels (electrodes), T is the number of sampling points. Some preprocessing procedures have been employed. First, 1–48 Hz bandpass-filtering was applied on the raw EEG signals to remove the power line interference and biological artifacts (such as Electro-oculogram and electrocardiogram). Then a large factor 10^6 is multiplied to enlarge to magnitude of the input data to avoid gradient diffusion. 4 fold cross validation was used on two runs of all the EEG data. The 1 min long resting state EEG signals with eye opening and closing were segmented into 2 s trials without overlap and each subject has 60 trials.

3.2 Architecture of Relation Network

Relation network [9] is a classic backbone structure for fewer shot learning and the basic structures within it can be flexibly designed by users with respect to specific tasks. The architecture of the proposed EEG relation network is shown in Fig. 1 which includes two modules i.e. the embedding module for feature learning and the relation module for similarity computation.

The embedding module extracts discriminant features among various subjects which consists of three convolutional layers and one pooling layer. First, a convolution is performed along time dimension with large kernel size allowing a larger receptive field. A sigmoid activation function is then imposed for non-linear transformation. The output of each convolutional layer is restricted to normal distribution across samples by batch normalization. Then spatial filtering is implemented over the C channels to extract spatial patterns and components while reducing signal noise simultaneously. Approximate power of each time window of the signal is calculated subsequently by square activation function and average pooling. Based on sliding-window and splitting step of average pooling layer, spectrum energy can be calculated by

$$E = \frac{1}{2\Pi} \int_{-\Pi}^{\Pi} \left| F\left(e^{j\omega}\right) \right|^2 d\omega. \tag{1}$$

where E is the spectrum energy which is the sum of square of the signal magnitude over a frequency band, and $F(\cdot)$ means Fourier transform, which is based on Parseval theorem formulated as

$$\int_{-\infty}^{+\infty} f^2(t)dt = \frac{1}{2\Pi} \int_{-\infty}^{+\infty} |F(\omega)|^2 d\omega \tag{2}$$

where $f(t)$ is the temporal signal.

The last layer of the embedding module is a separable convolutional layer, where the convolution kernels are segmented into several parts across channels to perform on feature maps respectively. The convolutional layer split reduces computational complexity and dimension of feature map. A group of weights are assigned to all channels of feature maps simultaneously. Finally, each sample can be represented as a low-dimensional feature vector after the embedding module.

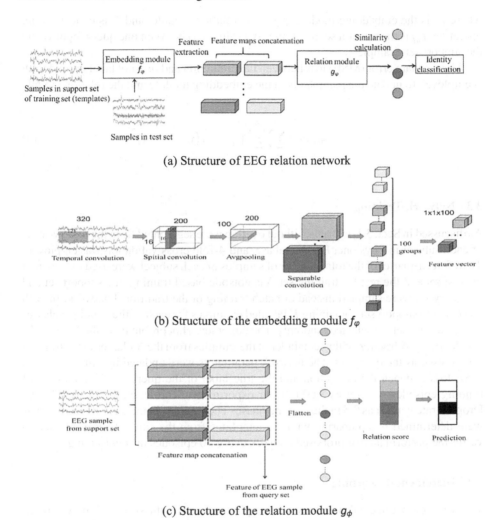

(a) Structure of EEG relation network

(b) Structure of the embedding module f_φ

(c) Structure of the relation module g_ϕ

Fig. 1. Architecture of the proposed EEG relation network.

The relation module consists of two fully connected layers. The feature maps of the test sample were concatenated with features of the support set samples (template samples). Each pair of feature vector mentioned above is fed into the relation module to determine the similarity score of the output. The dimension of the output of the last fully connected layer is the same as the number of categories.

Similarity is computed as

$$r_{i,j} = g_\Phi\big(C\big(f_\varphi(x_i), f_\varphi(x_j)\big)\big) \ i = 1, \ldots, N \tag{3}$$

where $f\varphi$ is the embedding module, $g\phi$ is the relation module, and C is concatenating operation. $r_{i,j}$ is the relation score (similarity evaluation) between one query input x_j and the support set example x_i.

Mean square error (MSE) loss between the prediction and one-hot label ground truth is employed to update the parameters in the embedding module and the relation module as

$$\varphi, \Phi \leftarrow \underset{\varphi,\Phi}{argmin} \sum_{i=1}^{m} \sum_{j=1}^{n} \big(r_{i,j} - 1\big(y_i == y_j\big)\big)^2 \tag{4}$$

3.3   Network Training

As discussed in Sect. 3.1, 60 trials without overlap were segmented from the first two runs of each subject in Physionet EEG database, and 4-fold cross validation was employed. Therefore, a quarter of the total number of samples of each subject were used to construct the test set and the rest for training set. Via episode based training, the support set and the query set were sampled instead of batch training of the traditional network. In each episode, the support set containing K labelled examples for each of the N unique classes in the training set are selected randomly. The target few-shot problem is called N-way K-shot learning. A fraction of the remainder of the samples from the N classes in the training set are used as the query set. The network parameters were updated by minimizing the MSE loss between the prediction and the true label of the query set. The number of training episodes was set as 3,000 in our experiments. The learning rate was 0.005. Dropout rate was set as 0.5 in the training phase. The samples in the test set whose labels were determined by comparing with the templates from the support set were used to verify the performance of proposed network every 50 episodes during training.

3.4   Incremental Learning

Two kinds of incremental strategies were employed to verify the subject (binary classification) and classify the identity of new subjects (multi-classification) with EEG-RN. The incremental verification determines whether the test samples belong to existed subjects in original dataset or unseen subjects. When the sample is identified as a new subject, the subject pool is increased and a new identity label is given for the test sample. Details about the incremental learning procedures were illustrated in Fig. 2.

The incremental verification was implemented by template matching without fine-tuning with any sample from the unseen subjects. When the similarity between the test sample and all the template samples is not higher than a predefined threshold, a new subject is spotted. On the contrary, it belongs to one existing subject. The similarity threshold is set as 75%, which is an empirical value.

Incremental multi-classification was conducted by fine-tuning with a few samples from the unseen target subjects. In such cases, a quarter of samples of each new subject were used to fine-tune the model which was trained on the original dataset and the remaining samples were used for test. In the fine-tuning stage, 300 episodes of training were performed to improve the generalization performance of the trained model. Feature maps of the unseen subjects became closer to the centers of all subjects by fine-tuning which means the feature representation space is more similar. Meanwhile, there is no overlap among the feature maps of unseen subjects and the subjects in original dataset, which makes it easier to recognize unseen subjects after fine-tune in EEG-RN.

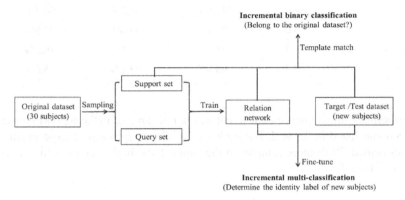

Fig. 2. Incremental learning of unseen subjects.

4   Experiment and Discussion

Three experiment settings were used in this paper. We first compared our network with three baseline models on original dataset with the number of subject fixed. Then incremental binary classification experiments were conducted which verifies whether the EEG data from the test set belongs to the existed subjects in the training set without using any sample from the target domain. In addition, incremental multiple class classification experiments were performed using a few samples in target domain to fine-tune the network to identify new subjects. The experiment scheme is shown in Fig. 2.

In first experiment setting, three networks were compared as baseline models with fixed number of subjects to verify the performance of proposed network. The first two baseline networks were CNN based model [6] and combination of CNN and LSTM [11]. Another baseline is CNN based Siamese network in [12]. Both of them were compared with the proposed model EEG relation network (EEG-RN) with 2 s long trials by 4-fold cross validation on Physionet dataset.

Different number of subjects have been selected for experiments, including 5 subjects form subject 105 to subject 109, 10 subjects form subject 100 to subject 109, 20 subjects from subject 90 to subject 109, and 30 subjects from subject 80 to subject 109 respectively. The average accuracy of 4-fold cross validation was shown in Table 1, where the best performance has been highlighted in bold. With the increasing of subject number, performance of all the models decreased by different degree. Among the four different settings in Table 1, the proposed EEG relation network has obtained the best performance on three settings, which has verified the efficiency of the proposed method.

Table 1. Comparison with baseline models on different number of subjects

Literature	Average accuracy on different numbers of subjects			
	5 subjects	10 subjects	20 subjects	30 subjects
CNN [6]	84.6%	71.8%	63.7%	60.3%
CNN+LSTM [11]	95.0%	96.1%	93.4%	94.8%
CNN+Siamese [12]	98.3%	97.2%	95.6%	**96.2%**
EEG-RN	**99.4%**	**98.8%**	**97.2%**	95.6%

Furthermore, the influence of different number of samples in the support set was also evaluated and listed in Table 2. For each setting, 3,000 episodes of experiments have been performed. With more samples in the support set, higher classification accuracy has been obtained.

Table 2. Results of different number of samples in the support set.

Model	1-shot	5-shot	10-shot
EEG-RN	84.7%	94.3%	95.6%

Results for incremental verification are shown in Table 3. In Table 3, False Accept Rate (FAR) and False Reject Rate (FRR) were also listed which were computed by taking the samples of existed subjects as positive samples. It could be seen that EEG-RN can efficiently discover unseen subjects and has excellent generalization capability.

Figure 3 shows the low-dimensional feature maps obtained by t-SNE which proves the effectiveness of fine-tuning. Before fine-tuning, the distribution of new subjects is far from that of the existing subjects in the original dataset which indicates quite different feature representation. Fine-tuning pulled feature maps of new subjects closer to the existing centers without overlapping with the old subjects.

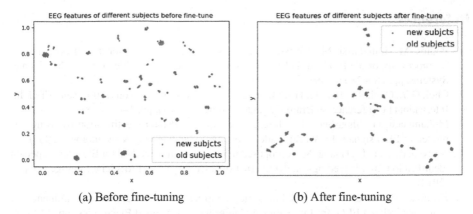

(a) Before fine-tuning   (b) After fine-tuning

Fig. 3. Visualization of the low-dimensional features of different subjects

Table 3. Result of incremental binary classification and multi-class classification

Experiment	Accuracy of unseen subjects	Accuracy of existing subjects	FAR	FRR
Incremental binary classification	86.7%	88.6%	14.0%	13.2%
Incremental multi-classification	93.3%	82.7%	18.8%	6.1%

5 Conclusion and Future Work

In this paper, discriminative representation of EEG signals was learned by relation network. Based on which, personal identity recognition based on EEG data is implemented with high identification accuracy. Incremental learning with unseen subject has been enabled. Three settings of experiments were conducted and three baseline methods were compared on Physionet EEG Dataset. The proposed EEG-RN has obtained excellent performance for identity recognition with ever seen samples in the training set. High identification accuracies for unseen subject recognition have also been obtained. These results have demonstrated the effectiveness the proposed method. In the future work, we intend to use smaller amount of data to enhance the practicality of EEG biometric recognition system and design more effective backbone model to implement recognition on more unseen subjects.

Acknowledgments. This work is supported by National Natural Science Foundation of China under Grant No. 61876147.

References

1. Poulos, M., Rangoussi, M., Chrissikopoulos, V.: Person identification based on parametric processing of the EEG. In: IEEE International Conference on Electronics, Circuits and Systems, pp. 283–286 (1999)
2. Choi, G.Y., Choi, S.I., Hwang, H J..: Individual identification based on resting-state EEG. In: International Conference on Brain-Computer Interface (BCI), pp. 1–4 (2018)
3. Mohammadi, G., Shoushtari, P., Molaee-Ardekani, B.: Person identification by using AR model for EEG signals. In: World academy of science engineering & technology (2006)
4. Nguyen, P., Tran, D., Huang, X.: A proposed feature extraction method for EEG-based person identification. In: Proceedings on the International Conference on Artificial Intelligence, p. 1 (2012)
5. Kostílek, M., Šťastný, J.: EEG biometric identification: repeatability and influence of movement-related EEG. In: International Conference on Applied Electronics, pp. 147–150 (2012)
6. Mao, Z., Yao, W.X., Huang, Y.: EEG-based biometric identification with deep learning. In: International IEEE/EMBS Conference on Neural Engineering. pp. 609–612 (2017)
7. Sun, Y., Lo, F.P.W., Lo, B.: EEG-based user identification system using 1D-convolutional long short-term memory neural networks. Expert Syst. Appl. **125**, 259–267 (2019)
8. Maiorana, E.: Transfer learning for EEG-based biometric verification. In: IEEE International Conference on Bioinformatics and Biomedicine, pp. 3656–3661. IEEE (2021)
9. Sung, F., Yang, Y., Zhang, L.: Learning to compare: relation network for few-shot learning. In : Proceedings of the IEEE conference on computer vision and pattern recognition, pp. 1199–1208 (2018)
10. Schirrmeister, R.T., Springenberg, J.T., Fiederer, L.D.J.: Deep learning with convolutional neural networks for EEG decoding and visualization. Hum. Brain Mapp. **38**, 5391–5420 (2017)
11. Das, B.B., Kumar, P., Kar, D.: A spatio-temporal model for EEG-based person identification. Multimedia Tools and Applications **78**, 28157–28177 (2019)
12. Maiorana, E.: Learning deep features for task-independent EEG-based biometric verification. Pattern Recogn. Lett. **143**, 122–129 (2021)

Salient Foreground-Aware Network for Person Search

Hongxu Chen[1,2], Quan Zhang[1,2], and Jianhuang Lai[1,2,3](✉)

[1] The School of Computer Science and Engineering, Sun Yat-Sen University,
Guangzhou 510006, China
{chenhx87,zhangq48}@mail2.sysu.edu.cn,stsljh@mail.sysu.edu.cn
[2] The Guangdong Key Laboratory of Information Security Technology,
Guangzhou 510006, China
[3] The Key Laboratory of Machine Intelligence and Advanced Computing,
Ministry of Education China, Guangzhou 510006, China

Abstract. Person search aims to simultaneously localize and identify a query person from realistic and uncropped images, which consists of person detection and re-identification. In existing methods, the extracted features come from the low-quality proposals generated by the structure like Region Proposal Network (RPN), and convolution is used to learn local features in the process of extracting features while the receptive field cannot grasp the global structural information. We propose an end-to-end network embedded with our Salient Foreground-Aware Module (SFAM). Self-attention mechanism in SFAM allows for better capture of global information. Our network incorporates our embedding method for person detection and person re-identification, which can effectively optimize the process of extracting features and improve feature expression capabilities. We merge the above modules into our Salient Foreground-Aware Network (SFAN). Extensive experiments have shown that our SFAN significantly improves the performance of end-to-end models with acceptable time-consuming and achieves state-of-the-art results.

Keywords: Person search · End-to-end · Salient Foreground-Aware Network · Embedding method

1 Introduction

Person search [1,2] is an algorithm to find specific pedestrians in scene images or video frames obtained under different cameras, which is an important task in different fields such as intelligent security, unmanned supermarket, human-computer interaction, and photo album clustering. Person search consists of two tasks: person detection, and person re-ID, (see Fig. 1(a)). The task of person detection is to find out all pedestrians in the image or video frame, including position and size, which are generally represented by bounding boxes. Person re-ID uses computer vision technology to judge whether there are specific pedestrians in images or videos of all people who have been framed [3]. It is a process

W. Deng et al. (Eds.): CCBR 2022, LNCS 13628, pp. 433–443, 2022.
https://doi.org/10.1007/978-3-031-20233-9_44

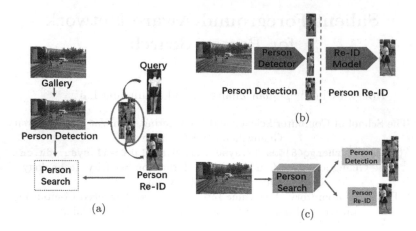

Fig. 1. Tasks and methods: (a) Person search, including person detection and person re-identification. (b) Two-stage methods. (c) One-stage methods.

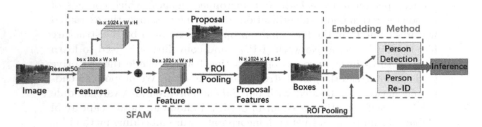

Fig. 2. Illustration of our SFAN. SFAN mainly consists of two parts: SFAM and the embedding method.

to establish a corresponding relationship between pedestrian images taken by different cameras without overlapping fields of view. Traditional person re-ID task focuses on cropped photos or video clips under different cameras [4]. Methods to solve these tasks use metric learning based on individual features. Our work is more challenging because it brings together domain-specific difficulties of the two subtasks, such as human-pose changes, occlusion, and complex backgrounds [5].

Existing works divide person search into generating boundary boxes of all people in the image and person re-ID. They tackle the problem separately either with two independent models (two-stage methods) or jointly with a multi-task model (one-stage methods, i.e., end-to-end methods). Challenges exist in feature extraction in both one-stage and two-stage methods, especially in the attention mechanism [6]. If the proposals provided for person search only adopt Faster R-CNN or other traditional structures, the obtained result and the corresponding proposal feature maps are of poor quality, and it may not be possible to accurately distinguish between people and backgrounds. To deal with the aforementioned challenges, as shown in Fig. 2, we propose a new Salient Foreground-Aware Network (SFAN) for end-to-end person search. Inspired by end-to-end method Seqnet [3], we refine the person detection and re-ID quality by a coarse-to-fine strategy. Inspired by the fact that Non-Local Network [7] can better focus on the foreground and get better results, our proposed SFAM focuses on discriminating people from background and getting proposals. Our embedding method is used to process the proposals for fine-grained classification, and get accurate person search results. The contributions can be summarized as follows:

1. We propose a Salient Foreground-Aware Module (SFAM) to further process the feature map and capture the global structure information for better attention learning. By increasing the similarities between person pixels in the same image and decreasing the similarities between the backgrounds, we get accurate proposals for person search.

2. After using our SFAM, we solve the two subtasks of person search in our embedding method. In the inference, we use the context bipartite graph matching algorithm (CBGM [3]) method. We merge the above modules into our Salient Foreground-Aware Network (SFAN).

3. The mAP (mean Average Precision) and top-1 (probability that the image with the highest search score is true) on CUHK-SYSU dataset achieve 96.1% and 96.7% respectively by our SFAN, while 48.2% and 87.6% on PRW dataset. Our SFAN has achieved state-of-the-art results on CUHK-SYSU and PRW datasets.

2   Related Work

Two/One-Stage Methods on Person Search

As illustrated in Fig. 1(b), the two-stage methods conduct person search in two steps. Researchers train the person detection model first, then they train the person re-identification model, and use two separate modules to solve the task of person search (e.g., Zheng et al. 2017 [1]; Chen et al. 2018 [8]; Chen et al. 2020 [9]; Lan et al. 2018 [10]; Han et al. 2019 [11]).

For one-stage methods (i.e., end-to-end methods), researchers use a model of multitasking federation to solve the tasks of person detection and person re-identification, as shown in Fig. 1(c). The classic framework is the OIM (Xiao et al. 2017 [2]). For end-to-end methods, Liu et al. 2017 [12] propose an end-to-end network based on a comparative attention mechanism. Yan et al. 2019 [4] propose a contextual instance expansion module. Lan et al. 2018 [10] point out that the performance of person search is limited by multi-scale matching. However, in end-to-end methods, the classification loss of person re-ID will interfere with the training of person detector while the classification loss of the person detector will interfere with the classification loss of person re-ID. Features extracted by the whole network come from the proposal obtained by Regional Proposal Network (RPN) in end-to-end methods, which are of poor quality compared with the boundary boxes obtained by the detector. Although the proposal obtained by RPN has little impact on coarse-grained classification tasks, it will greatly reduce the performance of fine-grained classification tasks such as person re-ID. This problem is caused by the parallel structure of Faster R-CNN, as the detection and re-ID are carried out at the same time, and the accurate boundary boxes cannot be obtained before person re-ID features are extracted.

Fig. 3. A progressive process using our SFAM. (a) The original input image. (b) Person attention map extracted by resnet50 and mapped to the original image. (c) Person attention map obtained through our SFAM. (d) An ideal person attention heat map.

3   The Proposed Method

We follow Seqnet, using resnet50 [13] as a backbone network for feature extraction. SFAM is used for extracting better features and provides fewer but more accurate proposals for our embedding to better complete the task of person detection and person re-ID. In the inference phase, we use a context bipartite graph matching algorithm to perform more robust matching to improve the performance of person search. The overall framework is shown in Fig. 2.

3.1   Salient Foreground-Aware Module

For an image, the pixels between each point of the person's corresponding area will have more similarities, while the pixels between the person and the background will have fewer, as illustrated in Fig. 3. So we introduce attention similarities into our feature map:

$$sim\left(x_i, x_j\right) = e^{(W_q x_i)^T (W_k x_j)}, \tag{1}$$

where the subscript i of the above formula is the index to calculate the output location of the global response, and subscript j is the index that lists all possible locations. x is the input feature map. W_q and W_k are the weight matrix to be learned in q and k dimensions, which can be obtained by 1×1 space convolution.

We calculate the similarities between each point of the feature map in the global scope and get the global feature map. The feature map we obtain can make the feature values of the area belonging to the same person more concentrated, and the feature values of the background area are more disorganized, as illustrated in Fig. 3, so as to better distinguish between people and backgrounds:

$$\mathbf{y}_i = \frac{1}{\sum_{\forall j} sim\left(x_i, x_j\right)} sim\left(x_i, x_j\right) W_v x_j, \tag{2}$$

where W_v is the weight matrix to be learned in the v dimension. Our method is mainly aimed at making the receptive field larger, rather than limited to a local field. We use the residual structure to add the result to the input feature map to

Algorithm 1: Self-attention embedded in feature map processing

---

Input:
x: [bs, c, h, w] feature map
q, k, v: 3 dimensions of x, each dimension is [bs, c, h, w]
Output:
[bs, c, h, w] output-tensor
foreach *dimension* **do**
  | 1×1conv → [bs, c/2, h, w] tensor
end
for q *and* v **do**
  | reshape → [bs, h*w, c/2] tensor
end
for k **do**
  | reshape → [bs, c/2, h*w] tensor
  | $q \cdot k \rightarrow sim$
end
for *sim* **do**
  | use Softmax normalization
  | $sim \cdot v \rightarrow SIM$
end
for SIM **do**
  | reshape → [bs, c/2, h, w] tensor
  | 1×1 conv channel expand → [bs, c, h, w] tensor
  | add original input $x \rightarrow output$
end

---

get the final attention feature map. The specific method is in Algorithm 1. After getting proposals from our optimized feature map, we use the proposal feature map obtained by ROI pooling to obtain 2048-dimensional embeddings to fix the proposal position and obtain person/background classification confidence.

3.2   Embedding Method

In order to use a combined model to solve the tasks of person detection and re-ID, we propose a new embedding method, which can obtain both person detection and re-ID results from our SFAM. On the base of OIM [2], in order to suppress the false person detection proposals, we delete the region classification branch of the original OIM model, and use the embedding norm as the classification confidence of person or background. We apply global average pooling (GAP) and a fully connected layer (FC) to get the 256-dimensional feature vector x, which consists of vector norm p and angle θ. We use a monotonic map to compress the norm p to the range of [0,1], and the original feature embedded x is replaced by the following formula:

$$\tilde{x} = \tilde{p} \cdot \theta = \sigma \left(\frac{p - E[p]}{\sqrt{Var[p] + \epsilon}} \cdot \gamma + \beta \right) \cdot \theta, \tag{3}$$

where $\tilde{p}$ is the person after norm-mapping, θ is the 256-dimensional feature of the original person vector, ϵ is used to prevent the denominator from being zero, σ is the sigmoid activation function, p is the norm of the original person, β is an offset. In this way, we get the embedding for searching.

In our re-ID method, in order to suppress false positive detections, the training process is supervised by person re-ID and person detection signals at the same time. Specifically, the detection signal is cast in the scaled norm $\tilde{p}$, and transformed into a binary classification. At the same time, we use multi-class cross-entropy loss [2] while normalizing the angle vector θ. In the inference, we use CBGM [3] to boost performance. The optimization algorithm in inference CBGM, our SFAM, and the embedding method form our Salient Foreground-Aware Network.

3.3   Optimization

Our SFAN losses mainly consist of SFAM and our embedding method:

$$L_{SFAM} = \frac{1}{N_p} \sum_{i=1}^{N_p} L_{reg}\left(t_i, t_i^*\right) - \frac{1}{N} \sum_{i=1}^{N} c_i \log\left(p_i\right), \tag{4}$$

where N_p is the number of positive samples, t_i is the calculated regressor of i-th positive sample, t_i^* is the corresponding ground truth regressor, and L_{reg} is the Smooth-L1-Loss. N is the number of all samples, p_i is the predicted classification probability of i-th sample, and c_i is the ground truth label.

We use parameters λ_1 and λ_2 to tune our end-to-end network for person detection losses and person re-ID losses.

$$L_{embedding} = \lambda_1 L_{det} + \lambda_2 L_{reID}, \tag{5}$$

The losses of person detection L_{det} are as follows:

$$L_{det} = -y \log(\tilde{r}) - (1 - y) \log(1 - \tilde{r}), \tag{6}$$

where y is a $\{0, 1\}$ label indicating if this proposal is considered as background or person and $\tilde{r}$ is the embedding norm obtained using our method.

The losses of person re-ID L_{reID} are as follows:

$$L_{reID} = \mathrm{E}_{\tilde{x}}\left[- \log \frac{\exp\left(v_i^T \tilde{x}/\tau\right)}{\sum_{j=1}^{L} \exp\left(v_j^T \tilde{x}/\tau\right) + \sum_{k=1}^{Q} \exp\left(u_k^T \tilde{x}/\tau\right)}\right], \tag{7}$$

where $\tilde{x}$ is the person vector we need to identify, $\mathrm{E}_{\tilde{x}}$ is used to maximize the expected log-likelihood, v is the person vector that has been labeled, u is the person vector that has not been labeled, i is the real label of this person x, and higher temperature τ leads to a softer probability distribution. L is the total number of people with labels and Q is the total number of people without labels. L_{SFAM} and $L_{embedding}$ are combined and optimized by Stochastic Gradient Descent (SGD).

4   Experiment

4.1   Datasets and Implementation

Datasets. Different from person re-ID, the dataset of person search contains the ground truth of person detection. CUHK-SYSU [2] dataset contains video frames sampled from movies and city scene images captured by a moving camera. This dataset provides 18,184 scene images, 96,143 person bounding boxes, and 8,432 identity labels. The dataset is divided into the training set of 11,206 images with 5,532 identities and the test set of 6,978 images with 2,900 query people. PRW [1] dataset is another widely used dataset, including 11,816 video frames captured by 6 cameras of Tsinghua University and 34,304 manually labeled bounding boxes. Similar to the CUHK-SYSU dataset, all people are divided into labeled and unlabeled identities. The training set contains 5,704 images and 482 different people, while the test set contains 6,112 images and 2,057 query people.

Implementation. We use PyTorch [14] to implement our model and conduct all experiments on one NVIDIA Quadro RTX 8000 GPU. In our experiment, we follow Seqnet [3], using resnet50 [15] pretrained on ImageNet [16] as the backbone. We set the batch size to 5 and resize each image to 900×1500 resolution in the training process. We set the ratio of λ_1 and λ_2 to 1 in Eq. (5).

4.2   Comparison with SOTA

We compare our method (SFAN) with the state-of-the-art models (SOTA) in recent years on CUHK-SYSU and PRW datasets. At present, researchers are more concerned about the results on the CUHK-SYSU dataset. Table 1 shows our comparative data. On the CUHK-SYSU dataset, compared with the most advanced end-to-end model Seqnet [3], our mAP and top-1 are 1.3% and 1.0% respectively higher. Compared with the two-stage SOTA method TCTS [17], our mAP and top-1 are 2.2% and 1.6% higher respectively. This shows that our method has powerful mAP compared with the end-to-end methods or the two-stage methods. We also introduce the use of ground truth, that is, manually marking all people for all gallery, so that the person search task becomes a person re-ID task. The PRW dataset is smaller and more difficult to train. Compared with the most advanced end-to-end model Seqnet [3], our mAP is 0.6% higher. Compared with the two-stage SOTA method TCTS (Task-Consistent Two-Stage framework) [17], our mAP is 1.4% higher. This shows that our method has excellent performance on different datasets.

We compared the speed of different methods. Our method takes 69 ms to process per frame on RTX-8000 GPU, which is close to Seqnet, the fastest work at present. NAE [18] (Norm-Aware Embedding) takes 78 ms and NAE+ [18] takes 90 ms in the same case. The speed of our method shows its great potential in real-life applications.

Table 1. Comparison with state-of-the-art

Method		Publication	CUHK-SYSU		PRW	
			mAP	top-1	mAP	top-1
End-to-end	OIM [2]	CVPR 2017	75.5	78.7	21.3	49.9
	NPSM [19]	ICCV 2017	77.9	81.2	24.2	53.1
	DisGCN [20]	MICCAI 2017	81.3	83.4	29.5	69.8
	RCAA [21]	ECCV 2018	79.3	81.3	–	–
	QEEPS [22]	CVPR 2019	88.9	89.1	37.1	76.7
	HOIM [23]	AAAI 2020	89.7	90.8	39.8	80.4
	NAE [18]	CVPR 2020	91.5	92.4	43.3	80.9
	Seqnet [3]	AAAI 2021	94.8	95.7	47.6	87.6
	CANR+ [24]	TCSVT 2022	93.9	94.5	44.8	83.9
	SFAN		**96.1**	**96.7**	**48.2**	**87.6**
	SFAN(useGT)		96.4	97.0	49.0	88.5
Two-stage	DPM+IDE [1]	CVPR 2017	–	–	20.5	48.3
	CNN+IDNet [8]	CVPR 2018	68.6	74.8	–	–
	CNN+MGTS [8]	ECCV 2018	83.0	83.7	32.6	72.1
	CNN+CLSA [10]	ECCV 2018	87.2	88.5	38.7	65.0
	FPN+RDLR [11]	CVPR 2019	93.0	94.2	42.9	70.2
	NAE+ [18]	CVPR 2020	92.1	92.9	44.0	81.1
	TCTS [17]	CVPR 2020	**93.9**	**95.1**	**46.8**	**87.5**

4.3 Ablation Study

In the ablation study, the baseline is NAE [18]. Our ablation study mainly focuses on context bipartite graph matching algorithm (CBGM), SFAM, and ground truth, as illustrated in Table 2. Using our SFAM and CBGM can effectively improve the performance of our model. The mAP and top-1 on CUHK-SYSU

Table 2. Ablation experiment on CUHK-SYSU and PRW datasets

Baseline	SFAM	CBGM	Sample	GT	CUHK-SYSU				PRW			
					Detection		Re-ID		Detection		Re-ID	
					Recall	AP	mAP	top-1	Recall	AP	mAP	top-1
✓					92.6	86.8	91.5	92.4	95.9	93.6	43.3	80.9
✓	✓		✓		92.6	89.7	95.6	96.2	96.1	93.9	47.0	84.5
✓	✓	✓	✓		92.6	89.7	96.1	96.7	96.1	93.9	47.8	87.5
✓	✓	✓	✓	✓	100.0	100.0	96.4	97.0	100.0	100.0	48.3	85.7
✓	✓				92.2	89.6	95.6	96.2	97.3	94.8	47.5	83.9
✓	✓	✓			92.2	89.6	**96.1**	**96.7**	97.3	94.8	**48.2**	**87.6**
✓	✓	✓		✓	100.0	100.0	96.2	96.8	100.0	100.0	49.0	85.5

and PRW datasets are improved. Using the ground truth can also effectively improve mAP and top-1, but the task of person search has changed into person re-ID task. After we use sampling optimization (under-sampling is introduced in h and w of k and v dimensions in Algorithm 1 to reduce computational complexity), we can see a slight improvement in the performance on the PRW dataset, while not much difference between mAP and top-1 on the CUHK-SYSU dataset.

5   Conclusion

In this paper, we propose a new end-to-end method, which can effectively optimize the process of feature extraction, improve the ability of feature expression, and finally have better effects on two datasets. We introduce our SFAM, which optimizes RPN, further processes the extracted features, and captures the global structure information for better attention learning. Moreover, our subsequent embedding method maximizes the use of the accurate proposals and feature map obtained by our SFAN. The CBGM we use during the inference improves our precision and this method does not require training. We combine the above methods into our SFAN. Finally, the results of our method on CUHK-SYSU and PRW datasets achieved SOTA, and the mAP and top-1 on the CUHK-SYSU dataset achieved 96.1% and 96.7% respectively. Extensive experiments have shown that our SFAN significantly improves the performance of end-to-end models with acceptable time-consuming and achieves state-of-the-art results.

Acknowledgment. This project was supported by the NSFC 62076258.

References

1. Zheng, L., Zhang, H., Sun, S., Chandraker, M., Yang, Y., Tian, Q.: Person re-identification in the wild. In: 2017 IEEE Conference on Computer Vision and Pattern Recognition (CVPR), pp. 3346–3355 (2017)
2. Xiao, T., Li, S., Wang, B., Lin, L., Wang, X.: Joint detection and identification feature learning for person search. In: 2017 IEEE Conference on Computer Vision and Pattern Recognition (CVPR), pp. 3376–3385 (2017)
3. Li, Z., Miao, D.: Sequential end-to-end network for efficient person search. In: Proceedings of the AAAI Conference on Artificial Intelligence, vol. 35, pp. 2011–2019 (2021)
4. Yan, Y., Zhang, Q., Ni, B., Zhang, W., Xu, M., Yang, X.: Learning context graph for person search. In: Proceedings of the IEEE/CVF Conference on Computer Vision and Pattern Recognition (CVPR), pp. 2158–2167 (2019)
5. Zhong, Z., Zheng, L., Cao, D., Li, S.: Re-ranking person re-identification with k-reciprocal encoding. In: Proceedings of the IEEE Conference on Computer Vision and Pattern Recognition (CVPR), pp. 1318–1327 (2017)
6. Zhang, Z., Lan, C., Zeng, W., Jin, X., Chen, Z.: Relation-aware global attention for person re-identification. In: Proceedings of the IEEE/CVF Conference on Computer Vision and Pattern Recognition (CVPR), pp. 3186–3195 (2020)

7. Wang, X., Girshick, R., Gupta, A., He, K.: Non-local neural networks. In: Proceedings of the IEEE Conference on Computer Vision and Pattern Recognition (CVPR), pp. 7794–7803 (2018)
8. Chen, D., Zhang, S., Ouyang, W., Yang, J., Tai, Y.: Person search via a mask-guided two-stream CNN model. In: Ferrari, V., Hebert, M., Sminchisescu, C., Weiss, Y. (eds.) ECCV 2018. LNCS, vol. 11211, pp. 764–781. Springer, Cham (2018). https://doi.org/10.1007/978-3-030-01234-2_45
9. Chen, D., Zhang, S., Ouyang, W., Yang, J., Tai, Y.: Person search by separated modeling and a mask-guided two-stream CNN model. IEEE Trans. Image Process. **29**, 4669–4682 (2020)
10. Liao, S., Zhu, X., Lei, Z., Zhang, L., Li, S.Z.: Learning multi-scale block local binary patterns for face recognition. In: Lee, S.-W., Li, S.Z. (eds.) ICB 2007. LNCS, vol. 4642, pp. 828–837. Springer, Heidelberg (2007). https://doi.org/10.1007/978-3-540-74549-5_87
11. Han, C., et al.: RE-ID driven localization refinement for person search. In: Proceedings of the IEEE/CVF International Conference on Computer Vision (ICCV), pp. 9814–9823 (2019)
12. Liu, H., Feng, J., Qi, M., Jiang, J., Yan, S.: End-to-end comparative attention networks for person re-identification. IEEE Trans. Image Process. **26**(7), 3492–3506 (2017)
13. He, K., Zhang, X., Ren, S., Sun, J.: Deep residual learning for image recognition. In: Proceedings of the IEEE Conference on Computer Vision and Pattern Recognition (CVPR), pp. 770–778 (2016)
14. Paszke, A., et al.: Automatic differentiation in pytorch. In: 31st Conference on Neural Information Processing Systems (NIPS 2017), Long Beach, CA, USA (2017)
15. Wang, F., et al.: Residual attention network for image classification. In: Proceedings of the IEEE Conference on Computer Vision and Pattern Recognition (CVPR), pp. 3156–3164 (2017)
16. Deng, J., Dong, W., Socher, R., Li, L.J., Li, K., Fei-Fei, L.: ImageNet: a large-scale hierarchical image database. In: 2009 IEEE Conference on Computer Vision and Pattern Recognition (CVPR), pp. 248–255. IEEE (2009)
17. Wang, C., Ma, B., Chang, H., Shan, S., Chen, X.: TCTS: a task-consistent two-stage framework for person search. In: Proceedings of the IEEE/CVF Conference on Computer Vision and Pattern Recognition (CVPR), pp. 11952–11961 (2020)
18. Chen, D., Zhang, S., Yang, J., Schiele, B.: Norm-aware embedding for efficient person search. In: 2020 IEEE/CVF Conference on Computer Vision and Pattern Recognition (CVPR), pp. 12612–12621 (2020)
19. Liu, H., et al.: Neural person search machines. In: Proceedings of the IEEE International Conference on Computer Vision (CVPR), pp. 493–501 (2017)
20. Ktena, S.I., et al.: Distance metric learning using graph convolutional networks: application to-functional brain networks. In: Descoteaux, M., et al. (eds.) MICCAI 2017. LNCS, vol. 10433, pp. 469–477. Springer, Cham (2017). https://doi.org/10.1007/978-3-319-66182-7_54
21. Chang, X., et al.: RCAA: relational context-aware agents for person search. In: Ferrari, V., Hebert, M., Sminchisescu, C., Weiss, Y. (eds.) ECCV 2018. LNCS, vol. 11213, pp. 86–102. Springer, Cham (2018). https://doi.org/10.1007/978-3-030-01240-3_6
22. Munjal, B., Amin, S., Tombari, F., Galasso, F.: Query-guided end-to-end person search. In: Proceedings of the IEEE/CVF Conference on Computer Vision and Pattern Recognition (CVPR), pp. 811–820 (2019)

23. Chen, D., Zhang, S., Ouyang, W., Yang, J., Schiele, B.: Hierarchical online instance matching for person search. In: Proceedings of the AAAI Conference on Artificial Intelligence, vol. 34, pp. 10518–10525, April 2020
24. Zhao, C., et al.: Context-aware feature learning for noise robust person search. IEEE Trans. Circ. Syst. Video Technol. **32**, 7047–7060 (2022)

Shoe Print Retrieval Algorithm Based on Improved EfficientnetV2

Yiran Xin, Yunqi Tang$^{(\boxtimes)}$, and Zuhe Yang

School of Investigation, People's Public Security University of China, Beijing 100038, China
tangyunqi@ppsuc.edu.cn

Abstract. The retrieval of incomplete and fuzzy shoe prints is a difficult problem in shoe print retrieval algorithm. In order to solve this problem. We improve the feature extraction network by using a new module called Dilated-MBConv on efficientV2. The new module is constructed by introducing multi-scale dilated convolution, and the original MBConv is replaced by Dilated-MBConv in stage 5–7 of the network; At the same time, in order to make the feature extraction network pay attention to the location information of shoe prints, this paper uses coordinate attention to replace the original squeeze and excitation module of the network. The improved network has achieved a better retrieve results in CSS-200 and CS-Database.

Keywords: EfficientnetV2 · Multi-scale dilated convolution · Coordinated attension

1 Introduction

In the field of criminal investigation, shoe prints are the most common trace evidence, which can provide the public security department with information about the perpetrator's crime process, personal characteristics and so on. As an important research direction of forensic science, shoe print retrieval not only provides a basis for the serial and parallel of cases, but also becomes an important part of locking suspects in the "monitoring + shoe print" technology.In recent years, that is, obtaining the shoe type information corresponding to the on-site shoe print through shoe print retrieval, and then further screening suspects through monitoring and screening. However, the on-site shoe prints not only have clear and complete high-quality shoe prints, but also incomplete and fuzzy low-quality shoe prints. With the rapid development of the information construction of the public security system, the types of shoe prints contained in the shoe print sample database of the public security organ are also increasing. Therefore, how to rank the positive samples corresponding to the on-site shoe prints in the front of the database with a large number of confused samples is very important. A good shoe print retrieval algorithm can not only greatly increase the probability of finding the corresponding shoe type information through shoe prints, but also save the time spent in screening shoe prints.

In traditional shoe print retrieval algorithms, traditional features such as sift and hog are often used for feature extraction, or features are manually labeled. This method is cumbersome and generally has low accuracy. With the rise of deep learning in recent years, more and more scholars apply deep learning to shoe print retrieval to extract the depth features of shoe print images for retrieval. This method is not only more efficient than traditional algorithms, but also has better generalization. However, the existing feature extraction networks mainly have the following two problems: first, the retrieval effect of incomplete and fuzzy low-quality shoe prints is poor; Second, the cost of network training is high due to the large number of model parameters and slow reasoning speed.

In view of the above problems, this paper improves efficientnetV2 network, replacing the shallow MBConv with Fused-MBConv, and replacing the MBConv with Dilated-MBConv; At the same time, by introducing CA attention mechanism and expansion convolution, the feature extraction network can extract more abundant semantic information of shoe print patterns, which has strong applicability to incomplete and fuzzy low-quality shoe print retrieval.

2 Related Works

The feature extraction of the traditional shoe print retrieval algorithm mainly relies on people to manually label or extract its traditional features. For example, in 2014, Wang Xinnian et al. [1] proposed to divide the shoe print into two semantic regions, and calculate its confidence according to the priority in judicial practice and the amount of reliable information. For regions with high confidence, the global invariant descriptor based on wavelet Fourier transform is used to calculate the similarity; In 2017, Nicole richetellia [2] compared three methods: phase only correlation (POC), local point interest with RANSAC and Fourier Merlin transform, and found that the performance of phase correlation method was better; In 2019, Peng Fei and others [3] called the highly recognizable areas in the shoe print image as local semantic information blocks, selected the clear and highly repetitive information blocks, matched the areas with high similarity in the sample shoe print through the normalized cross-correlation method, calculated the similarity, and fused them with the global features to achieve good results; In 2020, Zhou Siyue and others [4] used the iconic semantic information block and periodic semantic information block in the shoe prints to be retrieved to train the local semantic filter bank, and calculated the similarity between the local semantic filter model and the sample shoe prints, which has been further improved. Most of these methods start with extracting the traditional features of shoe prints, but the areas of feature extraction are mostly subject to people's cognition of shoe prints. The extraction process is cumbersome, and it is difficult to extract the rich semantic features of shoe prints.

In recent years, the development of deep learning is in full swing, and many scholars began to explore the application of deep learning methods to the process of shoe print retrieval: in 2018, Kong et al. [5] used the fine tuned resnet50 to extract shoe print features, and proposed a multi-channel normalized cross-correlation similarity measurement method, which was applied to the twin neural network and achieved good results, However, the normalized cross-correlation feature matching method used in multi-channel needs too much computation to be applied in practice; In 2021, Shi Wentao et al. [6] used the fine-tuning vgg16 network to extract the characteristics of shoe prints, expanded the tensor of conv5–1 layer directly after output as the descriptor of shoe prints, and introduced the SCDA method [7] to screen the characteristic map of incomplete shoe prints. Although this method weakened the interference of background noise to a certain extent, it needed to retrieve the complete and incomplete shoe prints separately, and the direct expansion dimension after the convolution layer output was too high, requiring a large amount of calculation.

3 Retrieval Algorithm Based on Improved EfficientnetV2

3.1 Shoe Print Retrieval Algorithm

The purpose of the shoe print retrieval algorithm is to query the shoe print images with the same pattern characteristics in the sample database according to the given on-site shoe prints.

Mark q as the on-site shoe print to be retrieved, Mark $\{g_1, g_2 \cdots g_n\}$ as the Shoe prints of sample library. By calculating the similarity score $\{d_1, d_2 \cdots d_n\}$ between the on-site shoe print q and the sample library shoe print $g_i (i \in [1, n])$, record d_i as the ranking score of g_i, and output the search results according to the ranking score.

In this paper, the shoe print retrieval algorithm uses the self-built shoe print training set to train the shoe print feature extraction network, and then put the suspected shoe prints, sample shoe prints and horizontal flip photos of sample shoe prints into feature extraction network to obtain the corresponding descriptors of three kinds of shoe print pictures, which are respectively recorded as $Descriptor$、 $Descriptor1$, $Descriptor1'$. Then calculate the cosine distance between the shoe print descriptor to be retrieved, the sample shoe print descriptor and the sample shoe print horizontal flip chart descriptor, and record it as $(cdist, cdist')$, The calculation process is shown in formula (1), (2), and $\min(cdist, cdist')$ will be recorded as the similarity score d_i between the shoe prints to be retrieved and the sample shoe prints, then sort and output the sample shoe prints according to the similarity score.

$$cdist = \frac{\|Descriptor\|^2 \cdot \|Descriptor1\|^2 - Descriptor \cdot Descriptor1}{\|Descriptor\|^2 \cdot \|Descriptor1\|^2} \tag{1}$$

$$cdist' = \frac{\|Descriptor\|^2 \cdot \|Descriptor1'\|^2 - Descriptor \cdot Descriptor1'}{\|Descriptor\|^2 \cdot \|Descriptor1'\|^2} \tag{2}$$

3.2 EfficienetV2 with Fused-MBConv

Efficientnet is the work published by Mingxing Tan et al. [8] in ICML2019. Google has proposed a concise and efficient composite scaling method, which uniformly adjusts the width, depth and image resolution of the network through composite coefficients.

Compared with the existing classification network, a series of efficientnet not only has smaller parameters, but also has higher accuracy. However, there are still some problems in efficientnet network. By using deep separable convolution, the network greatly reduces the parameters and flops of the model, and theoretically reduces a lot of computing costs. However, in fact, because deep separable convolution usually cannot make full use of some existing accelerators, this leads to the actual training of the network is not so fast. Therefore, someone proposed to use Fused-MBConv [9] to replace the original MBConv in the network to make better use of the accelerator (Fig. 1). Its structure is shown in Fig. 2, using a 3 × 3 convolution instead the depthwise separable convolution.

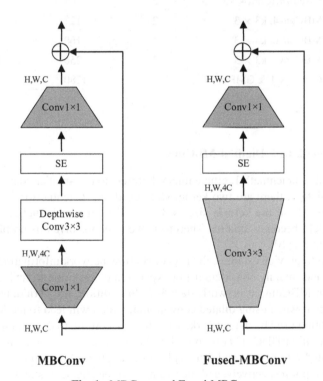

Fig. 1. MBConv and Fused-MBConv

Compared with MBConv, Fused-MBConv has more parameters, but it has stronger feature extraction ability and faster graphic reasoning speed. Tan et al. Found through NAS search method that using fused MBConv only in the shallow layer of the network (stage2–4) can give full play to the advantages of the two modules to achieve the balance of accuracy, model parameters and reasoning speed. Its architecture is shown in Table 1.

Table 1. .

Stage	Operator	Stride	Channels	Layers
1	Conv3 × 3	2	24	1
2	Fused-MBConv1, k3 × 3	1	24	2
3	Fused-MBConv4, k3 × 3	2	48	4
4	Fused-MBConv4, k3 × 3	2	64	4
5	MBConv4, k3 × 3	2	128	6
6	MBConv6, k3 × 3	1	160	9
7	MBConv6, k3 × 3	2	256	15
8	Conv1 × 1 & GMP & FC	-	1280	1

3.3   EfficienetV2 with Dialited-MBConv

Compared with efficientnetV1, efficientnetV2 prefers to use smaller convolution kernel size for calculation, there are two kernel sizes used in efficientnetv1: 3 × 3 and 5 × 5, but in effnetv2, all the kernels size is 3 × 3. The smaller kernel size means that its receptive field becomes smaller. Therefore, we hope to solve this problem by using dilated convolution[10].

According to previous studies, the loss of shallow network information is not obvious, so this paper mainly considers using expansion convolution to replace depthwise convolution in MBConv in network stage5–7. In addition, the "gridding effect" will inevitably appear when using dilated convolution, which will lead to the loss of details of the information used by the network. Therefore, according to the principle of Hybrid Dilated Convolution(HDC) [11] proposed by Wang et al., we use the dilated convolution with dilated rate of 1, 2 and 5 to replace the depthwise convolution in MBConv, convolute the input respectively, and then sum the three characteristic graphs obtained. The Dilated-MBConv module is shown in Fig. 2.

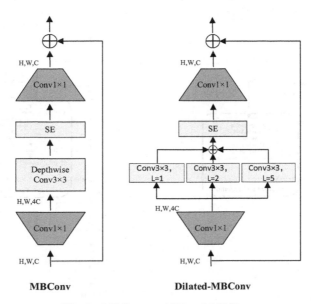

Fig. 2. MBConv and Dilated-MBConv

3.4 Coordinate Attension

In the Inverted residual module of efficientnet, a large number of Squeeze and excitation(SE) modules are used to increase the network's attention to the channel. With the help of 2D global pooling, it calculates the channel attention and provides significant performance improvement at a relatively low computing cost. However, SE attention only considers the information between coding channels and ignores the importance of location information, which is very important for capturing object structure in visual tasks. The computational overhead brought by common attention mechanisms that focus on location information, such as CBAM [12], does not meet the purpose of our requirements to reduce the computational cost. In this paper, in order to avoid a lot of computing overhead and make the network pay more attention to the location information of shoe print features, the se attention mechanism in efficientnet is replaced by coordattention attention mechanism [13] to optimize the network structure. This attention mechanism uses two one-dimensional global pooling operations to aggregate the input features in the vertical and horizontal directions into two independent direction aware feature maps, respectively, Multiply the attention map of two independent directions by the input feature map to enhance the representation ability of the feature map, as shown in Fig. 3.

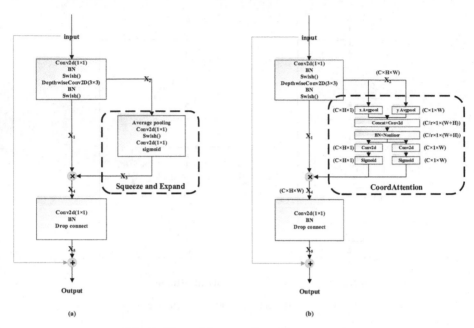

Fig. 3. The architecture of coordinate attension

4 Experimental Setup and Dataset

4.1 Dataset

In order to test the retrieval effect of this algorithm in public security practice, two shoe print data sets, **CS-database(Dust)** [2] and **CSS-200** [6], are used to test the effectiveness of the retrieval algorithm. The two shoe print data sets are collected from the real crime scene, of which CS database and css-200 data sets are obtained through the standard collection process of Chinese public security organs, The shoe prints of the three data sets were cut and removed from the scale after binarization processing by the public security organ on-site investigation system, and a few shoe prints with obvious noise impact were manually processed, as shown in Fig. 4 (Table 2).

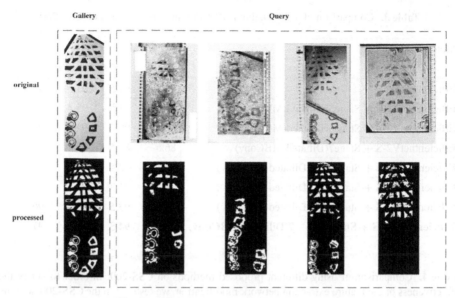

Fig. 4. The pretreatment of shoe print datasets

Table 2. The composition of different datasets

Dataset	Query	Gallery	Negative
CS-Database(Dust)	66	9	91
CSS-200	200	200	4800

5   Result

5.1   Ablation Experiment

5.2   Comparative Experiments

In order to verify the effectiveness of this feature extraction network (Table 4), this paper selects CS-database, fid-300 and css-200 as the test set, and selects the current advanced shoe print retrieval algorithms and common network models for comparison, such as local semantic filter banks, mixed features and neighborhood images [14], multi-channel normalized cross-correlation (MCNCC) Selective convolution feature descriptor fusion (SCDA) and a series of neural network models [15], the specific results are shown in Fig. 5. Considering the experimental results and the characteristics of each dataset, the feature extraction network designed in this paper extracts richer semantic information to a certain extent, which not only achieves better results in the retrieval of high-quality shoe prints, but also applies to the retrieval of incomplete and fuzzy low-quality shoe prints.

Table 3. Comparison of using Dialited-MBConv in different stage on CSS-200

Methods	Accuracy /%			
	Top1%	top2%	top5%	top10%
EfficientnetV2-S	86.5	91.5	91.5	93.5
EfficientnetV2-S + Stage5(Diliated-MBConv)	87.5	91.5	93.5	94.5
EfficientnetV2-S + Stage6(Diliated-MBConv)	88	90	91.5	92.5
EfficientnetV2-S + Stage7(Diliated-MBConv)	86.5	88.5	89	91.5
EfficientnetV2-S + Stage5、6(Diliated-MBConv)	91	92.5	94.5	95.5
EfficientnetV2-S + Stage5、7(Diliated-MBConv)	89.5	91	94	96.5
EfficientnetV2-S + Stage6、7(Diliated-MBConv)	92	93.5	95	96
EfficientnetV2-S + Stage5、6、7(Diliated-MBConv)	**92.5**	**94.5**	**96**	**97**

Table 4. Comparison of using different proposed methods on CSS-200: In order to verify the effectiveness of the feature extraction network modification, we tested it in the CSS-200, and the experimental results are shown in Table 3. It can be seen from the table that the coordinated attention (CA) used in this paper improves the accuracy with almost no increase in computing overhead. Similarly, the Dilated-MBConv used in this paper also significantly improves the accuracy with little cost.

Methods	Accuracy /%				Params	FLOPs
	top1%	top2%	top5%	top10%		
EfficientnetV2-S	86.5	91.5	91.5	93.5	24M	8.8×10^9
EfficientnetV2-S(CA)	87.5	91.5	93.5	94.5	27M	9.2×10^9
EfficientnetV2-S + Multi-scal dialited convolution	91.5	92.5	94.5	97.5	37M	5.6×1010
EfficientnetV2-S(CA) + Multi-scal dialited convolution	**93**	**94.5**	**96**	**98**	43M	6.2×10^{10}

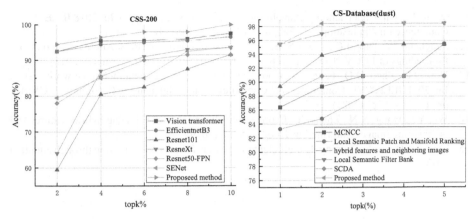

Fig. 5. The cumulative match characteristic (CMC) curve of different method on CSS-200 and CS-Database

6 Conclusion

The algorithm in this paper has achieved the best retrieval results on both the CS-Database and CSS-200 datasets. The query bases of the CS-Database(Dust) and CSS-200 datasets are composed of fuzzy and incomplete on-site shoe print images. This shows that the algorithm in this paper has good generalization in the feature extraction of low-quality shoe prints.

References

1. Wang, X., et al.: Automatic shoeprint retrieval algorithm for real crime scenes. Springer International Publishing. Springer International Publishing (2014)
2. Richetelli, N., Lee, M.C., Lasky, C.A., et al.: Classification of footwear outsole patterns using Fourier transform and local interest points. Forensic Sci. Int. **275**, 102–109 (2017)
3. Peng, F.: Local Semantic Patch and Manifold Ranking Based Shoeprint Retrieval, pp. 11–18. Dalian Maritime University, Dalian (2019)
4. Zhou, S.Y.: Local Semantic Filter Bank Based Low Quality Shoeprint Image Retrieval, pp. 15–39. Dalian Maritime University, Dalian (2020)
5. Kong, B., et al.: Cross-domain image matching with deep feature maps. Int. J. Comput. Vision **127**(3), 1738–1750 (2018)
6. Shi, W.T., Tang, Y.Q.: Research on forensic shoeprint retrieval algorithm by fine-tuning VGG-16. Journal of People's Public Security University of China (Science and Technology) **26**(03), 22–29 (2020)
7. Shi, W.T., Tang, Y.Q.: Shoeprints retrieval algorithm based on selective convolutional descriptor aggregation. Science Technology and Engineering **21**(16), 6772–6779 (2021)
8. Tan, M.X., Quoc, V.L.: EfficientNet: Rethinking Model Scaling for Convolutional Neural Networks. (28 May 2019). [2021.11.25]. https://arxiv.org/abs/1905.11946
9. Tan, M.X., Quoc, V.L.: EfficientNetV2: Smaller Models and Faster Training (1 April 2021). [2021.6.23]. https://doi.org/10.48550/arXiv.2104.00298
10. Yu, F., Koltun, V., Funkhouser, T.: Dilated residual networks. In: Proceedings of the IEEE Conference on Computer Vision and Pattern Recognition, pp. 472–480 (2017)

11. Wang, P., et al. Understanding convolution for semantic segmentation. In: 2018 IEEE Winter Conference on Applications of Computer Vision, pp. 1451–1460 (2018)
12. Sanghyun, W., Park, J.C., Lee, J.Y., Kweon, I.S.: Convolutional Block Attention Module. In: Proceedings of ECCV 2018, September 8–14, pp. 36–39. Munich, Germany (2018)
13. Hou, Q.B., Zhou, D.Q., Feng, J.S.: Coordinate attention for efficient mobile network design. In: 2021 IEEE/CVF Conference on Computer Vision and Pattern Recognition (CVPR), pp. 13708–13717 (2021)
14. Wu, Y.J., Wang, X.N., Zhang, T.: Crime scene shoeprint retrieval using hybrid features and neighboring images. Information **10**(02), 45–60 (2019)
15. Touvron, H., et al.: Training data-efficient image transformers & distillation through attention (2020)

Multi-modal Biometric Recognition and Fusion

A Novel Dual-Modal Biometric Recognition Method Based on Weighted Joint Group Sparse Representation Classification

Chunxin Fang, Hui Ma[(✉)], and Yu Li

College of Electronic Engineering, Heilongjiang University, Harbin, China
2011043@hlju.edu.cn

Abstract. Multi-modal biometric recognition technology is an effective method to improve the accuracy and reliability of identity recognition. However, there are some problems (such as feature space incompatibility) with the fusion between different modal biometric traits. To address the above problem, we propose a dual-modal biometric recognition method based on weighted joint group sparse representation classification (WJGSRC). The proposed method fuses the Pyramid Histogram of Oriented Gradients (PHOG) feature and Local Phase Quantization (LPQ) feature for each modality by the Canonical Correlation Analysis (CCA) at first. Then, the dictionary matrix is optimized by the sum of weighted scores between different modalities. Finally, the group sparse and weight constraints are constructed respectively to further improve the final recognition accuracy. The experimental results on two dual-modal databases show that the proposed method can effectively improve the performance of identity recognition.

Keywords: Dual-modal biometric recognition · Finger-vein · Fingerprint · Weighted joint group sparse representation · Joint sparse representation

1 Introduction

Biometric recognition technology mainly uses the inherent physiological and behavioral characteristics of human beings to complete the task of identity recognition [1]. Compared with traditional identification methods, biometric traits are not easily forgotten or lost, which makes biometric recognition have good security and convenience. However, more and more work shows that the unimodal biometric recognition system has some problems, such as intra-class variation, lack of identifiability, and deceptive attacks [2,3]. To overcome the above problems, multi-modal biometric recognition technology, which combines various biometric traits, is a good choice to improve the accuracy and security of identity recognition.

Compared with other biometric traits (such as iris, auricle, and so on), finger-vein and fingerprint are not only more easily accepted by the public but also

W. Deng et al. (Eds.): CCBR 2022, LNCS 13628, pp. 457–465, 2022.
https://doi.org/10.1007/978-3-031-20233-9_46

have been widely concerned by many researchers [4,5]. Fingerprint, as one of the earliest used biometric traits, has satisfactory versatility but also is easy to be copied or stolen. As an internal trait of the human body, the finger-vein has high security, but it is easily affected by the external environment (such as temperature) as well as the user's own factors in the process of acquisition, which leads to low quality images and affect the final recognition effect.

The dual-modal biometric recognition system based on finger-vein and fingerprint can not only achieve the feature complementarity between finger-vein and fingerprint but also provide more discriminant information for identity recognition, which can overcome the problems of unimodal biometric system to some extent. However, it is regrettable that the research on dual-modal biometric recognition based on finger-vein and fingerprint is still insufficient.

To solve the above problem, we propose a dual-modal biometric recognition method based on WJGSRC to improve the performance of identity recognition, as shown in Fig. 1. The proposed method first fuses the PHOG and LPQ features for each modality by CCA. Then, the dictionary matrix is optimized by the fusion of score levels. Finally, the training sample label information and weighted scores are used to further improve the final recognition performance.

Therefore, the main contributions of this paper are as follows:

(1) The CCA is introduced to combine the PHOG and LPQ features for each modality, achieving the combination of spatial and frequency features. On this basis, the score level fusion is used to optimized the dictionary matrix, providing more recognition information and improving recognition efficiency.

(2) Two weight functions constructed using similarity between the test sample and each class of training samples are proposed and acted on joint group sparse constraint to reduce the influence of heterogeneous training samples with low similarity to the test sample on the recognition results.

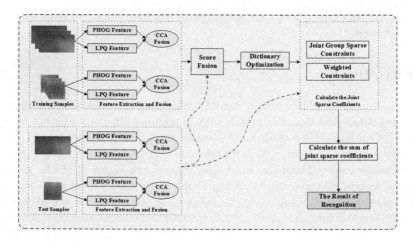

Fig. 1. The flowchart of the proposed method.

The rest of the paper is organized as follows: In Sect. 2, we introduce the WJGSRC method in detail. And the adequate experiments and analyses are carried out in Sect. 3. Finally, we summarize the paper in Sect. 4.

2   Proposed Method

Inspired by Shekhar et al. [6], we propose a dual-modal biometric recognition method based on WJGSRC to improve the effectiveness of identity recognition. The method not only makes full use of the discriminative information of training samples but also fully considers the integral similarity between the test sample and each class of training samples. Specifically, the proposed method utilizes the CCA to fuse the PHOG and LPQ features for each modality to make better characterize finger-vein and fingerprint traits. On this basis, the proposed method optimizes the dictionary matrix using the weighted scores between the test sample and each class of training samples, improving the recognition efficiency and reducing the influence of training samples that are far away from the test sample on the recognition results. Meanwhile, two weight functions are constructed and acted to the joint sparse coefficient vector, which further reduces the influence of small inter-class differences within each modality on recognition results.

The joint sparse coefficient of the proposed WJGSRC can be expressed mathematically as follows:

$$\hat{\boldsymbol{\beta}} = arg \min_{\boldsymbol{\beta}} \frac{1}{2} \sum_{i=1}^{2} \|\boldsymbol{Y}_i - \boldsymbol{D}_i\boldsymbol{\beta}_i\|_2^2 + \lambda \sum_{j=1}^{C} \omega_j \|\boldsymbol{\Gamma}_j\|_F \tag{1}$$

where $\sum_{i=1}^{2} \|\boldsymbol{Y}_i - \boldsymbol{D}_i\boldsymbol{\beta}_i\|_2^2$ represents the sum of the reconstruction errors of various modalities, $\boldsymbol{Y}_i \in \mathbb{R}^{m \times 1}$ is the fused feature of the ith modality. $\boldsymbol{D}_i \in \mathbb{R}^{m \times n}$ and $\boldsymbol{\beta}_i \in \mathbb{R}^{n \times 1}$ denote the optimized ith modality sub-dictionary matrix and the corresponding sparse coefficient vector, respectively. $\boldsymbol{\beta} = [\boldsymbol{\beta}_1, \boldsymbol{\beta}_2]$ is the joint sparse coefficient matrix, and ω_j is the weight coefficients of various classes of the training sample group. λ is the balance parameter, which is set to 10^{-3} in this paper. $\sum_{j=1}^{C} \omega_j \|\boldsymbol{\Gamma}_j\|_F$ is the $L_{1,F}$ mixed norm weighted against the coefficient matrix $\boldsymbol{\beta}$, where $\boldsymbol{\Gamma}_j = \left[\delta_{1j}\boldsymbol{\beta}_{1j}, \delta_{2j}\boldsymbol{\beta}_{2j}\right]$ is the sparse coefficient matrix after adding the weight coefficients.

2.1   Fusion of PHOG and LPQ Features

PHOG feature [7] counts the gradient information of the local region under multi-resolution conditions and has good robustness for illumination, geometric deformation, and so on. LPQ feature [8] describes the texture information of the image in the frequency domain with fuzzy invariance. Taking the fusion of PHOG and LPQ features of fingerprint image as an example, it is assumed that the PHOG feature of fingerprint image training sample is $\boldsymbol{A}$ and LPQ feature is $\boldsymbol{B}$. The fused feature can be expressed as follow:

$$X = \begin{bmatrix} W_a^T A \\ W_b^T B \end{bmatrix} = \begin{bmatrix} W_a \\ W_b \end{bmatrix}^T \begin{bmatrix} A \\ B \end{bmatrix} \tag{2}$$

where W_a and W_b denote the transformation matrix.

2.2 Dictionary Matrix Optimization

Assume training sample $t = \{X_1, X_2\}$ and test sample $z = \{Y_1, Y_2\}$, where X_i and Y_i are the training sample and test sample fused with PHOG and LPQ features, respectively ($i = 1$ is finger-vein, $i = 2$ is fingerprint). $T_i = \left[X_i^{11}, X_i^{12}, \cdots, X_i^{1n_1}, X_i^{21}, \cdots, X_i^{Cn_C} \right]$ denotes the set of all training samples for each modality, and $\bar{T}_i = \left[\bar{X}_i^1, \bar{X}_i^2, \cdots, \bar{X}_i^C \right]$ represents the mean vector, where $\bar{X}_i^j$ is calculated as follows:

$$\bar{X}_i^j = \frac{\sum_{k=1}^{n_k} X_i^{jk}}{n_k} \tag{3}$$

The dictionary matrix optimization process proposed in the paper is as follows:

(1) Determine the number of categories k in the sub-dictionary.

(2) For each modality, the Manhattan distance between test sample Y_i and the mean vector of training samples in each class is calculated and normalized by Min-Max respectively. After the normalized scores are obtained, the corresponding finger-vein and fingerprint scores are weighted and summed to get the final score $S = [s_1, s_2, \cdots, s_j, \cdots, s_C]$ in which s_j is calculated as follows:

$$s_j = w_1 \times e_{1j}^n + w_2 \times e_{2j}^n \tag{4}$$

where w_1 and w_2 are the weight coefficients ($w_1 + w_2 = 1$), e_{1j}^n and e_{2j}^n is the normalized scores of finger-vein and fingerprint.

(3) The fusion score S is arranged in ascending order to obtain S_{ascend}, and the training sample categories corresponding to the first k items of S_{ascend} are calculated. The finger-vein and fingerprint features of these categories are formed into the corresponding finger vein sub-dictionary $D_1 = [d_{11}, d_{12}, \cdots, d_{1n}]$ and fingerprint sub-dictionary $D_2 = [d_{21}, d_{22}, \cdots, d_{2n}]$, respectively.

2.3 Weighted Constraints

The weight coefficient ω_j between the test sample and each class of training samples is defined as follows:

$$\omega_j = \exp\left(\frac{s_j}{\varrho}\right) \tag{5}$$

where s_j is the fusion score corresponding to each class of training samples in the sub-dictionary and ϱ is the bandwidth parameter.

At the same time, considering the differences between various modalities, we also construct the weight coefficient δ_{ij} using the Manhattan distance between the test sample and the mean vector of various class training samples in the sub-dictionary, which is calculated as follows:

$$\delta_{ij} = \exp\left(\frac{e_{ij}}{\sigma_i}\right) \tag{6}$$

where e_{ij} denotes the Manhattan distance between the ith modal test sample and the mean vector of jth class training samples in sub-dictionary, and σ_i is the bandwidth parameter corresponding to each modality.

After obtaining the joint sparse coefficient matrix $\boldsymbol{\beta}$, the test sample can be identified using the principle of the maximum sum of joint sparse coefficients.

3   Experiments

To better evaluate the performance of score level fusion for dictionary optimization, we define the inclusion accuracy $ACC_{contain}$, that is:

$$ACC_{contain} = \frac{\sum_{i=1}^{N} s_i}{N} \tag{7}$$

where N is the total number of test samples and s_i is the inclusion score of the ith test sample, which can be calculated as follows:

$$s_i = \begin{cases} 1, c_i \in \boldsymbol{\mu}_k \\ 0, else \end{cases} \tag{8}$$

where $\boldsymbol{u}_k$ is the set of k categories corresponding to the test sample $\boldsymbol{z}_i$, and c_i is the true category of the test sample $\boldsymbol{z}_i$.

3.1   Datasets

In this paper, we mainly use HLJU310 and PolyU-FVC2006 datasets.

The HLJU310 dual-modal dataset was established by the Pattern Recognition Laboratory of Heilongjiang University. The dataset contains 256 fingers, and 5 finger-vein and fingerprint images are both captured for each finger respectively.

The PolyU-FVC2006 dual-modal dataset consists of a combination of finger-vein images of 140 fingers in the PolyU dataset and 6 fingerprint images of 140 fingers in FVC2006.

3.2   The Parameter Analysis Experiment

In these experiments, 3 images of each modality of each finger are used as training samples, and 2 images are used as test samples.

(1) k, w_1 and w_2

Figure 2 shows the inclusion accuracy $ACC_{contain}$ of each dual-modal dataset. As we can see that the inclusion accuracy of the two dual-modal datasets converges the fastest When $w_1 = 0.6$. Considering that the recognition time of the test sample is positively correlated with the number of training samples in the sub-dictionary. Therefore, in this paper, the number of categories in the sub-dictionary is set to the minimum value when each dataset tends to be stationary, that is, 35 and 30 in HLJU310 and PolyU-FVC2006 respectively.

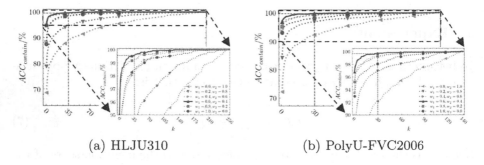

(a) HLJU310   (b) PolyU-FVC2006

Fig. 2. The inclusion accuracy $ACC_{contain}$ on each dual-modal dataset

(2) ϱ, σ_1 and σ_2

In the bandwidth parameter analysis experiment, when ϱ is set to $\{0.005, 0.1, 1, 10\}$ in turn, the values of σ_1 and σ_2 are changed in the range of $\sigma_1 = \{0.01, 0.05, 0.1, 1, 10\}$ and $\sigma_2 = \{0.01, 0.05, 0.1, 1, 10\}$, and the recognition accuracy is calculated. The average recognition accuracy for each dual-modal dataset after experiments was repeated independently is shown in Fig. 3 and Fig. 4.

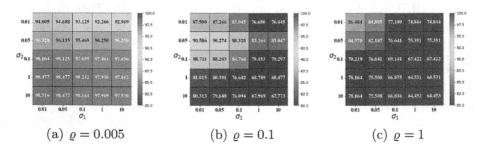

(a) $\varrho = 0.005$ (b) $\varrho = 0.1$ (c) $\varrho = 1$

Fig. 3. The average recognition accuracy of HLJU310 under different bandwidth parameter values

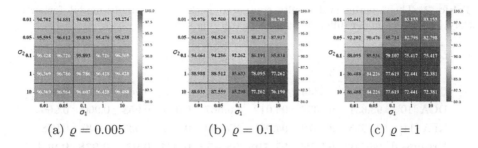

(a) $\varrho = 0.005$ (b) $\varrho = 0.1$ (c) $\varrho = 1$

Fig. 4. The average recognition accuracy of PolyU-FVC2006 under different bandwidth parameter values

From Fig. 3 and Fig. 4, it can be seen that the overall average recognition accuracy in each dataset is significantly higher than the average recognition accuracy under other values when $\varrho = 0.005$. Meanwhile, when $\sigma_1 = 0.01, \sigma_2 = 10$ and $\sigma_1 = 0.05, \sigma_2 = 10$, HLJU310 and PolyU-FVC2006 can achieve the highest accuracy, respectively.

For a fair comparison with other methods in subsequent experiments, the parameter values corresponding to the highest average recognition accuracy were used in the WJGSRC for HLJU310 and PolyU-FVC2006.

3.3 Comparison Experiments with Other Multi-modal Biometric Recognition Methods

To clarify the performance of the proposed method for finger-vein and finger-print fusion recognition, we compare WJGSRC with some existing multi-modal biometric recognition methods under different training samples. The average experimental results are shown in Table 1 and Table 2.

From Tables, it can be seen that the average recognition accuracy ACC and the average Kappa coefficient of the proposed method on two dual-modal datasets are greater than those of other multi-modal fusion recognition methods mentioned above, indicating that the recognition performance of the proposed method is better than that of existing multi-modal fusion recognition methods.

Table 1. The experimental results compared with existing multi-modal fusion on HLJU310 under different number of training samples

Method	ACC/%			Kappa		
	2	3	4	2	3	4
CCA [9]	86.693	93.672	96.797	0.866	0.936	0.968
DCA [10]	85.938	93.945	95.078	0.859	0.939	0.951
KFA [11]	96.458	97.695	98.359	0.964	0.977	0.984
Proposed	**96.875**	**98.516**	**98.750**	**0.969**	**0.985**	**0.987**

Table 2. The experimental results compared with existing multi-modal fusion on PolyU-FVC2006 under different number of training samples

Method	ACC/%				Kappa			
	2	3	4	5	2	3	4	5
CCA [9]	92.292	95.833	97.381	98.333	0.922	0.958	0.974	0.983
DCA [10]	93.631	95.357	96.012	96.667	0.936	0.953	0.960	0.966
KFA [11]	90.595	93.572	94.941	95.833	0.905	0.935	0.949	0.958
Proposed	**94.703**	**97.262**	**97.798**	**98.452**	**0.947**	**0.972**	**0.978**	**0.984**

4   Conclusion

In this paper, a dual-modal biometric recognition method based on weighted joint group sparse representation classification is proposed. The proposed method not only uses the CCA algorithm to fuse the PHOG and LPQ features for each modality to provide more discriminative information but also makes full use of the label information of training samples and the overall similarity between the test sample and various class training samples to construct group sparsity constraint and weight constraints. These constraints are used to reduce the impact of small inter-class differences within each modality on the final recognition results. Experimental results on two dual-modal datasets show that the proposed method can effectively improve the performance of identity recognition.

References

1. Adiraju, R.V., Masanipalli, K.K., Reddy, T.D., Pedapalli, R., Chundru, S., Panigrahy, A.K.: An extensive survey on finger and palm vein recognition system. Mater. Today: Proc. **45**, 1804–1808 (2021)
2. Yang, W., Wang, S., Hu, J., Zheng, G., Valli, C.: A fingerprint and finger-vein based cancelable multi-biometric system. Pattern Recognit. **78**, 242–251 (2018)
3. Khodadoust, J., Medina-Pérez, M.A., Monroy, R., Khodadoust, A.M., Mirkamali, S.S.: A multibiometric system based on the fusion of fingerprint, finger-vein, and finger-knuckle-print. Expert Syst. Appl. **176**, 114687 (2021)
4. Liu, F., Liu, G., Zhao, Q., Shen, L.: Robust and high-security fingerprint recognition system using optical coherence tomography. Neurocomputing **402**, 14–28 (2020)
5. Zhao, D., Ma, H., Yang, Z., Li, J., Tian, W.: Finger vein recognition based on lightweight CNN combining center loss and dynamic regularization. Infrared Phys. Technol. **105**, 103221 (2020)
6. Shekhar, S., Patel, V.M., Nasrabadi, N.M., Chellappa, R.: Joint sparse representation for robust multimodal biometrics recognition. IEEE Trans. Pattern Anal. Mach. Intell. **36**, 113–126 (2014)

7. Bosch, A., Zisserman, A., Munoz, X., Zisserman, P.: Representing shape with a spatial pyramid kernel, In: ACM International Conference on Image and Video Retrieval (2007)
8. Ahonen, T., Rahtu, E., Ojansivu, V., Heikkila, J.: Recognition of blurred faces using Local Phase Quantization. In: 2008 19th International Conference on Pattern Recognition, pp. 1–4 (2008)
9. Kamlaskar, C., Abhyankar, A.: Iris-Fingerprint multimodal biometric system based on optimal feature level fusion model. AIMS Electr. Electr. Eng. **5**, 229–250 (2021)
10. Al-Quraishi, M.S., Elamvazuthi, I., Tang, T.B., Al-Qurishi, M., Parasuraman, S., Borboni, A.: Multimodal fusion approach based on EEG and EMG signals for lower limb movement recognition. IEEE Sens. J. **21**, 27640–27650 (2021)
11. Khellat-Kihel, S., Abrishambaf, R., Monteiro, J.L., Benyettou, M.: Multimodal fusion of the finger vein, fingerprint and the finger-knuckle-print using Kernel Fisher analysis. Appl. Soft Comput. **42**, 439–447 (2016)

Finger Trimodal Features Coding Fusion Method

Mengna Wen, Ziyun Ye, and Jinfeng Yang[✉]

Institute of Applied Artificial Intelligence of the Guangdong-HongKong-Macao Greater Bay Area, Shenzhen Polytechnic, Shenzhen 518000, Guangdong, China
jfyang@szpt.edu.cn

Abstract. Finger carrying finger-vein (FV), fingerprint (FP), and finger-knuckle-print (FKP) simultaneously has become a research focus in the field of multimodal biometric. In this paper, a finger trimodal features coding fusion method based on vector of locally aggregated descriptors (VLAD) is proposed. First, three feature extraction models based on convolutional neural network (CNN) are designed to extract finger trimodal features individually. Then, under the direct of VLAD, feature maps of finger trimodal from feature extraction models based on CNN are encoded respectively. Finally, finger trimodal coded features are fused in series to obtain fusion features. The recognition accuracy of fusion features obtained by the proposed method can reach 99.76%, and experimental results demonstrate that the fusion features possess excellent individual characteristic expression ability, which is favourable to improve recognition accuracy and robustness.

Keywords: Multimodal biometric · Features fusion · CNN · VLAD

1 Introduction

At present, information is highly digitalized and hidden and how to identify individual by rule and line is a difficult problem that must be faced. Compared with single-mode biometric recognition technology, multimodal biometric technology is more accurate and reliable [1]. Now, research on multimodal biometric fusion is mainly divided into two fields: fusion of biometrics which is on head and fusion of biometrics which is of hand [2]. In application, hand is better than head in terms of cooperation and friendliness; for instance, generalization factors such as stature, apparel, makeup, ambient lighting and view angle make significant impact on imaging of head biometrics, yet the acquisition of hand biometrics is barely influenced [3, 4]. In addition, biometric information carried on hand is more abundant than head. There are fingerprint, finger-vein and finger-knuckle-print in one finger which integrates physiological characteristics of inner and outer layer of biological tissue, and features from FP, FV and FKP are sufficiently complementary [5–7]. Moreover, compact arrangement of finger trimodal biometrics is profitable for capturing images by one integrated device [3].

W. Deng et al. (Eds.): CCBR 2022, LNCS 13628, pp. 466–474, 2022.
https://doi.org/10.1007/978-3-031-20233-9_47

Feature level fusion can maximize the discrimination ability of features, and preferably dispose the balance between cost of processing data and amount of information contained in the data [8]. Due to the fact that attributes of finger trimodal biometrics are different, the features obtained based on artificial filters cannot be fused reasonably and effectively. Although the feature level fusion of finger trimodal biometrics can be carried out by "forcing fusion", the recognition results with the fusion features are not satisfactory [9, 10]. In recent years, neural network technology has developed rapidly and CNN is most widely used in the field of computer vision and pattern recognition [11]. CNN possesses strong ability for extracting features from image, which are more in line with characteristics of image itself [12, 13]. By changing representation of features, coding can effectively eliminate the influence caused by feature extractors, which makes multimodal features fusion more scientific and reasonable and is helpful to improve the discrimination of fused features. The coding-based feature has great advantages in illumination variance, description ability and matching efficiency, and has achieved ideal matching results.

As a result of diversity of biometrics and limitation of acquiring image, imaging principles of finger trimodal biometrics are diverse from each other, and the quality of obtained images is poor. In algorithms for extracting finger trimodal features using artificial feature extractors, it is necessary to preprocess original images, which is arduous and time-consuming [15, 16]. Besides, although the existing coding methods have solved problems of large memory space and bad real-time performance, there also exist a lot of challenges, such as, change of finger posture will affect the stability of coding; the primary and secondary relationship of features will adversely influence the discrimination of coding fusion features [17].

To attack these problems, a finger trimodal features coding fusion method based on VLAD is proposed in this paper. Firstly, three lightweight CNN models are constructed for individually extracting features from FV, FP and FKP respectively. Then, the finger trimodal features are encoded based on VLAD [18], and coded features of finger-vein, fingerprint and finger-knuckle-print are obtained respectively. Finally, the finger trimodal coded features are fused in series to obtain fusion feature.

2 Vector of Locally Aggregated Descriptors

Vector of locally aggregated descriptors (VALD) is a kind of coding method whose main idea is to aggregate feature descriptors based on local criteria in the feature space. Describing features in the form of vector is a condensed expression, which characterizes the distribution of feature vectors relative to cluster centers. The process of coding based on vector of locally aggregated descriptors is as follows: extracting features; training a codebook with extracted features. In principle, recognition accuracy will be improved with enlargement of codebook. However, the balance between computational cost and recognition accuracy should be considered comprehensively; quantifying features: assigning all descriptors to k cluster centers, calculating the residual sum of descriptor to each cluster center, normalizing the residual sum by L2-norm, concatenating the results into a $k \times d$ vector (d is dimension of feature.). The above process is shown in formula (1).

$$v_{i,j} = \sum x_j - c_{i,j} \tag{1}$$

where, x_j is the jth feature descriptor, $c_{i,j}$ is the nearest cluster center, $v_{i,j}$ means the sum of differences between the values in each dimension of x in the cluster with c_i as cluster center and the values in each dimension of cluster center.

3 Proposed Method

The key issue of biometric technology is how to convert biometrics into representations that can be measured for similarity. The effective method is to extract multiple local features, then aggregate the features into a compact vector, and finally measure the similarity of the vectors, so as to realize the identification of individual identity.

3.1 Features Extraction Models for Finger Trimodal Biometrics

Traditional feature extraction algorithms such as SIFT, SURF, etc. are based on empirical knowledge. The filters do not adapt well to images at times, and features extracted with artificial filters are inevitably influenced by anthropic factor. CNN has formidable capability for extracting features, and numerous experiments have proved that the features extracted by CNN models can preferably represent characteristics of image. And CNNs possess the ability to obtain features which cannot be gained through artificial filters.

In order to extract expressive features from raw images of FP, FV and FKP, three feature extraction models based on CNN are constructed. As we all know, under the premise of enough training samples, the performance of CNN model gradually improves with increase of model complexity. However, when the quantity of training samples is finite, complex network structure will bring disastrous problems. Consequently, we design three lightweight feature extraction models based on CNN by studying the maturely applied network structures to acquire features of FP, FV and FKP. The feature extraction models constructed in this paper mainly consist of convolution operation (Formula (2)) and mean-pooling operation (Formula (3)). Meanwhile, in order to improve the generalization ability and convergence speed of the networks, each pooling layer is followed by a batch normalization layer (formula (4)), and a full connection layer is built behind the normalization layer. Softmax function (formula (5)) is selected to realize classification at the end of structed models.

$$Z(W, X) = f\left(\sum_{i=1}^{n} w_i x_i + b\right) \tag{2}$$

where, W is weights of convolution kernels, X is pixels in receptive field, and n is the number of pixels in receptive field.

$$p = \frac{1}{M_1 \times M_2} \sum_{i=1}^{M_1 \times M_2} x_i \tag{3}$$

where p is the value in feature maps, size of down-sampling kernel is $M_1 \times M_2$, x_i is the ith element in down-sampling area.

$$\hat{Z}_j = \frac{Z_j - u_j}{\sqrt{\sigma_j^2 + \varepsilon}} \tag{4}$$

where, u_j 和 σ_j represent average value and variance of batch data respectively, ε is introduced to avoid invalid calculation with zero as denominator.

$$s_i = \frac{e^{x_i}}{\sum_j e^{x_j}} \tag{5}$$

where, $\{x_1, x_2, \cdots, x_n\}$ is output of front layer, s_i is output of the ith neuron in Softmax layer.

3.2 Feature Coding Based on VLAD

Assume that the features obtained by feature extraction model based on CNN are N feature maps whose size is $s_1 \times s_2$. First, converting feature maps above-mentioned into a one-dimensional vector with length $D = s_1 \times s_2$. Now, the features can be represented as $X_{N \times D} = [x_1, x_2, \cdots, x_n]^T$, where x_i is a one-dimensional vector. Then, building a codebook $\{c_1, c_2, \cdots c_k\}$ containing K elements, where c_k is a one-dimensional vector including D values. The above process can be expressed by formulas (6)~(7).

$$x_i = Connect(p_1, \cdots, p_{s_1 \times s_2}) \tag{6}$$

where p_i represents the element in the ith feature map, $Connect()$ can concatenate inputs into a one-dimensional vector.

$$V(j, k) = \sum_{i=1}^{N} x_i(j) - c_k(j) \tag{7}$$

where, the coding result is represented by vector V whose size is $K \times D$, $x_i(j)$ is the jth value of the ith feature descriptor, $c_k(j)$ is the jth dimension of the kth cluster center.

3.3 Finger Trimodal Features Coding Fusion Method

The framework of finger trimodal features coding fusion method based on VLAD is shown in Fig. 1. Extracting features from finger trimodal raw images using features extraction models respectively, converting feature maps into one-dimensional feature vector, encoding the feature vectors based on VLAD. Due to the coded feature descriptors represent the distance from feature to cluster centroid, the differences of finger trimodal features are eliminated, and in features fusion, the finger trimodal coded feature descriptors are connected in series directly, without considering alignment of features.

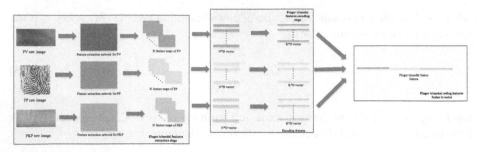

Fig. 1. Framework of Finger trimodal features coding fusion

4   Experiments and Analysis

4.1   Experimental Dataset

The dataset used in experiments in this paper comprises finger-vein images, fingerprint images and finger-knuckle-print images which are obtained by integrated finger three-modal images acquisition device. All images are from 585 fingers, and each finger is placed in acquisition device ten times at different times in various angles, that is, ten images are collected for each mode of each finger, a total of $3 \times (585 \times 10) = 17550$ images (Fig. 2).

(a) finger-vein image   (b) fingerprint image   (c) finger-knuckle-print image

Fig. 2. Raw images of finger

4.2   Experimental Results and Analysis

In order to extract finger trimodal features, three features extraction models are built for finger trimodal images respectively, as shown in Fig. 3. Among them, the model for extracting finger-vein features is composed of six convolution layers, the model for extracting fingerprint features is composed of four convolution layers, and the model for extracting finger-knuckle-print features is composed of six convolution layers. The convolution layers here include convolution operation and mean pooling operation. Each pooling layer is followed by a batch normalization (BN) layer to improve the generalization ability and convergence speed of network. When training network, a fully connected

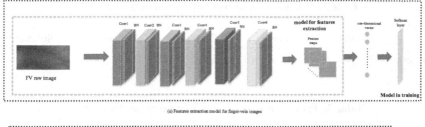

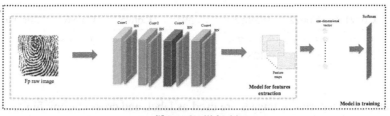

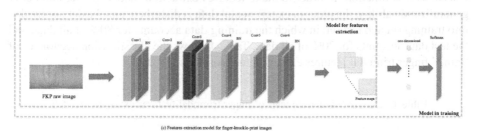

Fig. 3. Finger trimodal features extraction models

layer is embedded in the last part of single-modal features extraction network, and Softmax function is used to complete the classification, and the parameters of trained models are saved.

The specific parameters of the proposed models are shown in Tables 1, 2 and 3. When extracting features, fully connected layer and Softmax layer in single-modal features extraction network should be discarded. Finger trimodal raw images are fed into models, and outputs are feature maps.

Table 1. Parameters of features extraction model for FV

Layer	Conv1	Conv2	Conv3	Conv4	Conv5	Conv6	Softmax
Parameters	$3 \times 5 \times 32$	$3 \times 5 \times 64$	$5 \times 7 \times 128$	$5 \times 7 \times 10$	$5 \times 7 \times 10$	$4 \times 8 \times 10$	585

In order to verify whether the three-modal features extraction models we constructed can obtain highly distinguishable features, we conducted the following experiments. In training process, the raw images of finger-vein, fingerprint and finger-knuckle-print are

Table 2. Parameters of features extraction model for FP

Layer	Conv1	Conv2	Conv3	Conv4	Softmax
Parameters	$3 \times 3 \times 32$	$3 \times 3 \times 64$	$5 \times 5 \times 128$	$5 \times 5 \times 10$	585

Table 3. Parameters of features extraction model for FKP

Layer	Conv1	Conv2	Conv3	Conv4	Conv5	Conv6	Softmax
Parameters	$3 \times 5 \times 32$	$3 \times 5 \times 64$	$5 \times 7 \times 128$	$5 \times 7 \times 10$	$5 \times 7 \times 10$	$3 \times 8 \times 10$	585

used as inputs, the categories of images are used as label, and cross entropy function is chosen as loss function. In order to make features extraction models possessing better generalization ability, the order of experimental data is disturbed, and the data is divided into training set and test set, in which the training data accounts for 80% of all data, and the test data accounts for 20% of all data. Table 4 shows the classification accuracies of trained finger trimodal features extraction networks on test data.

Table 4. Classification accuracies of finger trimodal features extraction models.

Modal	FV	FP	FKP
Classification accuracy (%)	99.57	93.24	99.32

It can be seen from Table 1 that high classification accuracy can be obtained, and finger trimodal features which extracted by trained features extraction modals have strong ability of expression. The finger trimodal features extraction models constructed in this paper is effective.

In order to verify the effectiveness of vector of locally aggregated descriptors on features extracted with CNN models. Firstly, encoding extracted features according to VLAD. Then, measuring the similarity of coding features by cosine distance, and the images to be classified are classified into the category with greatest similarity. Table 5 shows the recognition accuracies based on coding features.

Table 5. Recognition accuracies of coding features.

Coding features	Fusion feature	FV	FP	FKP
Recognition accuracy (%)	99.76	99.79	96.28	99.64

As can be seen from Table 5, promising recognition accuracy can be obtained based on coded features, indicating that the coding algorithm based on VLAD is very effective for features extracted by CNN models.

For testifying the effectiveness of proposed method, we compared the method proposed in this paper with other algorithms, and the ROC curve (Receiver Operating Characteristic) is shown in Fig. 4.

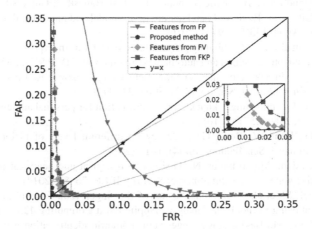

Fig. 4. Compared results of ROC for different features

It can be clearly seen from Fig. 4 that the Equal Error Rate (EER) of recognition result achieved with fusion feature can reach 0.003 or less. And the performance of fusion features obtained by proposed method is outstanding compared with other features.

Analyzing the results in Table 2 and Fig. 4 comprehensively, it can be concluded that the fusion features obtained by the proposed method is with good identification ability and strong robustness which are helpful to improve recognition accuracy.

5 Conclusion

In this paper, a finger trimodal features coding fusion method based on VLAD is proposed, firstly, three trained convolutional neural networks are used to extract finger trimodal features respectively; then, the features are encoded based on VLAD; finally, the encoded features are fused in series. A variety of experimental results prove that the proposed finger trimodal features coding fusion method can effectively improve the accuracy and reliability of individual identification by comprehensively using finger trimodal biometrics information to express individual identity attributes.

Acknowledgment. This work was supported in part by the National Natural Science Foundation of China under Grant 62076166 and 61806208.

References

1. Nguyen, K., et al.: Super-resolution for biometrics: a comprehensive survey. Pattern Recogn. **78**, 23–42 (2018)
2. Asaari, M.S.M., Suandi, S.A., Rosdi, B.A.: Fusion of band limited phase only correlation and width centroid contour distance for finger based biometrics. Expert Systems with Application **41**(7), 3367–3382 (2014)
3. Mittal, N.: Hand Based Biometric Authentication (D). Banasthali University (2014)
4. Shaikh, J., Uttam, D.: Review of hand feature of unimodal and multimodal biometric system. Int. J. Comp. Appli. **133**(5), 19–24 (2016)
5. Zahedi, M., Ghadi, O.R.: Combining gabor filter and FFT for fingerprint enhancement based on a regional adaption method and automatic segmentation. SIViP **9**(2), 267–275 (2015)
6. Shin, K., et al.: Finger-vein image enhancement using a fuzzy-based fusion method with gabor and retinex filtering. Sensors **14**(2), 3095–3129 (2014)
7. Zhang, L., et al.: Online finger-knuckle-print verification for personal authentication. Pattern Recogn. **43**(7), 2560–2571 (2010)
8. Suneet, N.G., Renu, V., Renu, G.: A survey on different levels of fusion in multimodal biometrics. Indian J. Sci. Technol. **10**(44), 1–11 (2017)
9. Alajlan, N., Islam, M., Ammour, N.: Fusion of fingerprint and heartbeat biometrics using fuzzy adaptive genetic algorithm. Internet Security IEEE, 76–81 (2014)
10. Khellat-Kihel, S., et al.: Multimodal fusion of the finger vein, fingerprint and the finger-knuckle-print using Kernel Fisher analysis. Applied Soft Computing **42**(C), 439–447 (2016)
11. Radzi, S., Hani, M., Bakhteri, R.: Finger-vein biometric identification using convolutional neural network. Turk. J. Electr. Eng. Comput. Sci. **24**(3), 1863–1878 (2016)
12. Qin, H., El-Yacoubi, M.: Deep representation-based feature extraction and recovering for finger-vein verification. IEEE Trans. Inf. Forensics Secur. **12**(8), 1816–1829 (2017)
13. Fang, Y., Wu, Q., Kang, W.: A novel finger vein verification system based on two-stream convolutional network learning. Neurocomputing **290**, 100–107 (2018)
14. Tang, S., et al.: Finger vein verification using a Siamese CNN. IET Biometrics **8**(5), 306 (2019)
15. Yang, J., Shi, Y.: Towards finger-vein image restoration and enhancement for finger-vein recognition. Inf. Sci. **268**(6), 33–52 (2014)
16. Morales, A., et al.: Improved finger-knuckle-print authentication based on orientation enhancement. Electron. Lett. **47**(6), 380–381 (2011)
17. Li, S., Zhang, H., Jia, G., Yang, J.: Finger Vein Recognition Based on Weighted Graph Structural Feature Encoding. In: Zhou, J., et al. (eds.) CCBR 2018. LNCS, vol. 10996, pp. 29–37. Springer, Cham (2018). https://doi.org/10.1007/978-3-319-97909-0_4
18. Herve, J., et al.: Aggregating local descriptors into a compact image representation. CVPR, 3304–331 (2010)

Fusion of Gait and Face for Human Identification at the Feature Level

Hui Fu[1,2], Wenxiong Kang[1,2,3(✉)], Yuxuan Zhang[1], and M. Saad Shakeel[1,4]

[1] School of Automation Science and Engineering,
South China University of Technology, Guangzhou 510641, China
auwxkang@scut.edu.cn
[2] Pazhou Lab, Guangzhou 510335, China
[3] Guangdong Enterprise Key Laboratory of Intelligent Finance,
Guangzhou 510705, China
[4] School of Automation, Guangdong University of Petrochemical Technology,
Maoming 525000, China

Abstract. Combining gait and face to identify humans can incorporate the advantages of both and improve the final recognition accuracy. Most of the previous work focuses on score-level fusion strategies. In this paper, we propose a multimodal fusion method to integrate information about gait and face at the feature level. Our approach separately concatenates the gait feature extracted by the GaitSet with the face feature extracted by ResNet50 (supervised by ArcFace loss), where the GaitSet and ResNet50 are trained in advance. The min-max normalization technique is utilized to transform the two biometric features to the common distribution space before concatenating, while a fully connected layer is used to further fuse the features after concatenating. To evaluate our approach, we built a multimodal gait-face database named CASIA-B-Gait-Face, which is based on the CASIA-B gait dataset. Extensive experiments show that our method achieves better performance than any individual biometric or other commonly used fusion methods.

Keywords: Multi-biometric fusion · Human identification · Face recognition · Gait recognition

1 Introduction

Multimodal biometric identification technology has drawn much attention in recent years. Face recognition is recently one of the most broadly used biometric technology, which performs well when people face the camera directly at a short distance. However, it has been found to be very challenging in some unconstrained scenes, such as typical surveillance scenes, where on the one hand, the long distance between people and the camera makes it difficult to capture high-resolution face images, and on the other hand, it is hard to obtain frontal face images in the case of non-cooperation of people. Gait recognition aims to identify people according to the way they walk, which can be applied at a distance without the cooperation of subjects [1,2]. But it sometimes does not work well when people are too close to the camera or walk facing the camera for a long time. It also suffers from a lot of variations such as clothing, carrying conditions, and variations in the camera viewpoint [1]. It is necessary to fuse the two biometric modalities to incorporate the advantages of face and gait recognition.

The multi-biometric fusion can be performed at various levels. Most previous work has focused on fusing at the matching score level [3–7] due to its ease of access. However, matching scores output by different classifiers contain less information about the input modality, so score-level fusion is still shallow fusion and lacks robustness in some scenarios. For example, it is hard to take advantage of multimodal fusion when one of the modalities does not work well.

In this work, we propose a feature-level fusion method to integrate gait and face biometric modalities, which is illustrated in Fig. 1. The trained GaitSet [8] and ResNet50 [9] supervised by ArcFace loss [10] are used to extract the gait and face embeddings, respectively. In the fusion part, the features of gait and face are normalized by the min-max normalization to eliminate heterogeneousness in distribution. Then, the normalized face features are copied as $2 \times \sum_{s=1}^{S} 2^{s-1}$ copies and concatenated along this dimension, where S is the output scale of GaitSet. The copied face features are concatenated with gait features along the channel dimension. Next, the concatenated features are further fused through a fully connected layer. The critical design of our fusion method is separating the gait features and concatenating them with face features, so we call that Separate Concatenate. We combine the Batch All (BA_+) triplet loss [11] and cross-entropy loss to train the network. Since GaitSet and ResNet are trained in advance, only the parameters of the feature fusion part need to be updated in the training phase. We built a gait-face dataset named CASIA-B-Gait-Face based on the CASIA-B dataset [12] and evaluated our method on it. According to the experimental results, we obtain two conclusions: On the one hand, fusing gait and face by our method performs better than any single modality, which means the fused gait and face features are more discriminative compared to any individual biometric. On the other hand, our fusion method achieves better performance than some commonly used score-level fusion methods or other feature-level fusion ways, such as fusing by self-attention structure.

In summary, our contributions lie in two folds: (1) We propose a Separate Concatenate way to fuse gait and face biometric modalities at the feature level. The extracted gait features are separated in the scale dimension and concatenated with face features separately. (2) The proposed method can integrate the gait and face features to learn more discriminative features and achieve better performance than any unimodality. (3) Based on the CASIA-B gait dataset, we built a multimodal gait-face database named CASIA-B-Gait-Face. The proposed method and other commonly used fusion methods are evaluated on it. Extensive experiments show that our method is more effective.

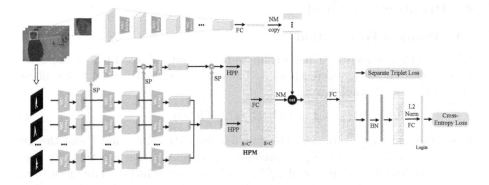

Fig. 1. Illustration of our feature-level fusion, *SP* for *Set Pooling*, *HPP* for *Horizontal Pyramid Pooling*, *HPM* for *Horizontal Pyramid Mapping*, *NM* for *Normalization*, *BN* for *Batch Normalization*, and *FC* for *Fully Connected Layer*.

2   Related Work

Most previous studies performed fusion at the score level. In [13], Kale et al. consider two fusion scenarios of score: The first involves using the gait recognition algorithm as a filter to pass on a smaller set of candidates to the face recognition algorithm. The second involves combining the similarity scores obtained individually from the face and gait recognition algorithms. Geng et al. [3] proposed an adaptive multi-biometric fusion strategy to combine the gait score and face score through the operators such as sum, product, min, and max. The group also proposed context-aware multi-biometric fusion to dynamically adapt the fusion rules to the real-time context, which considered two significant context factors, view angle and subject-to-camera distance, affecting the relationship between gait and face in the fusion [14]. In [4], alpha-matting is designed to obtain alpha gait energy images and low-resolution facial profile images, which are used to perform feature extraction, respectively. Before decision making, score-level fusion is used to combine the distance scores of face and gait. These score-level fusion methods fuse the matching score of each modality without directly exploiting the extracted discriminative features, which makes it less effective in the case of the poor effect of a certain modality. On the other hand, the range of scores for each modality may be different, so score normalization before fusion is required. But it is challenging to design a robust normalization scheme for various classifiers. Few studies focus on fusing at the feature level. In [15], the face and gait features are extracted separately, and then they are normalized and concatenated to form a single feature vector for feature level fusion. However, the features in this work are low-dimensional. With the development of deep learning, direct concatenating the features may generate a vector with a very large dimension and result in the 'curse of dimensionality' problem [16].

3   Proposed Method

3.1   Problem Formulation

Given a video sequence of pedestrian walking, gait silhouette sequence s and face image x can be extracted from it. The question of multimodal fusion of gait and face can be formulated as:

$$f = F(N(G(s)), N(R(x))) \tag{1}$$

where $G(\cdot)$ and $R(\cdot)$ represent the gait feature extraction model and the face feature extraction model, $N(\cdot)$ represents the normalization function, $F(\cdot)$ represents the feature fusion module, f is the feature after fusing. The input of the gait feature extraction model can be the silhouette sequence or gait templates generated by silhouettes, such as Gait Energy Image (GEI) [17]. In our work, GaitSet [8] is used to extract gait features, whose input data is a set of silhouettes. The face feature extraction model takes a single face image as input and outputs the feature of the face. Since the distributions of the features extracted from the two modalities are inconsistent, it is necessary to perform normalization on the features to eliminate the distributional variability of the features. The feature fusion module takes the normalized features as input and outputs the final fused feature.

3.2   Fusion

We design a multimodal fusion method of gait and face, which fuses information of the two modalities at the feature level. The overall framework is shown in Fig. 1. Given a video sequence, and we can obtain the gait silhouette sequence using background subtraction or some segmentation methods. Meanwhile, we use face detection methods like RetinaFace [18] to detect the faces and align them. Then we choose one of the detected faces. The silhouettes and the selected face are sent to the GaitSet [8] and ResNet50 (supervised by ArcFace loss [10]) to extract features, respectively. Considering that the features of various modalities have different distributions or scales, the features of the gait and face modalities are normalized and mapped to the same distribution space [16]. We have tried two techniques, min-max and Z-score normalization. The min-max normalization aims to shift the minimum and maximum feature values to 0 and 1, respectively. The Z-score normalization is to transform the given feature into Gaussian distribution space using the arithmetic mean and standard deviation of the feature. The experiments (see Sect. 4.3) show that min-max normalization achieves better performance.

The frame-level gait features are extracted frame by frame, and then they are aggregated into a set-level feature. The Horizontal Pyramid Mapping (HPM) neck of GaitSet [8] with S scales splits the set-level feature map into 2^{s-1} strips on height dimension, where $s \in 1, 2, ..., S$. As shown in Fig. 1, the output gait feature has two dimensions, scale dimension S and channel dimension C. However, the face feature has only the channel dimension, so how to fuse features with different dimensions is an important issue. We have studied several ways:

- Concatenate: Flatten the 2D gait feature to 1D, and concatenate it with the face feature along the channel dimension after normalization. A fully connected layer is used to do further fusion.
- Separate Concatenate: Separately concatenate the normalized 2D gait feature with the normalized 1D face feature along the channel dimension. Specifically, as shown in Fig. 1, the 1D face feature is copied as $2 \times \sum_{s=1}^{S} 2^{s-1}$ copies, and they are concatenated along this dimension to 2D, where S is the scale of HPM. The 2D face feature is concatenated with the gait feature along the channel dimension. The concatenated feature is further fused through a fully connected layer.
- Separate Sum: Sum the aligned face feature and gait feature. The 1D face feature is copied as $2 \times \sum_{s=1}^{S} 2^{s-1}$ copies, and they are concatenated along this dimension to 2D. Align the face feature with the gait feature in the channel dimension and sum the two features element by element.
- Separate Product: Replace the sum operation in Separate Sum with the product.

The experiments (see Sect. 4.3) show that the Separate Concatenate achieves the best performance. We choose it as our final version of fusion strategy.

3.3   Training Strategy

The GaitSet [8] and ResNet50 supervised by ArcFace loss [10] have been trained on the corresponding gait and face dataset. In our work, we freeze the gradients of parameters in two networks in the training phase and update only the parameters of the fusion part.

   We use both Batch All (BA_+) triplet loss [11] and cross-entropy loss with a label smooth to train the network. The BA_+ triplet loss is the objective of optimization on metric learning, while the cross-entropy loss is the classification optimization objective. The cross-entropy loss is followed by a design in [19] that adds a batch normalization layer before the classifier fully connected layer to make the cross-entropy loss easier to converge in the embedding space. The final loss is computed as:

$$L = L_{tri} + \lambda L_{ce} \qquad (2)$$

where λ is the weight parameter to balance the triplet loss L_{tri} and cross-entropy loss L_{ce}.

4   Experiments

4.1   Setting

Datasets. We built a multimodal dataset of gait and face named CASIA-B-Gait-Face. Since lacking of a dedicated multi-modality database of gait and face, we consider using the gait database providing RGB frames, which can help us to extract faces. We choose the CASIA-B dataset [12] to conduct experiments, which is commonly used in gait research. It contains 124 subjects with 3 different walking conditions and 11 views($0°,18°,...,180°$). The walking condition contains normal (NM) (6 sequences per subject), walking with bag (BG) (2 sequences per subject) and wearing coat or jacket (CL) (2 sequences per subject). It provides not only gait silhouettes, but also RGB video sequences. To extract face from videos, we discard the back-to-camera views and preserve the views of the face that can be detected ($0°$, $18°$, $36°$, $54°$, $72°$, $90°$). Following the general evaluation settings [8], the first 74 subjects are used for training while the rest 50 subjects are left for the test. In the test set, the first 4 sequences of the NM condition (NM #1–4) are kept in the gallery, and the rest 6 sequences are divided into 3 probe subsets according to walking conditions.

Implementation Details. The GaitSet is trained on the first 74 subjects of the CASIA-B gait dataset [12] following the setting of [8], while the ResNet50 (supervised by ArcFace loss) is trained on the MS-Celeb-1M [20] dataset following the setting of [10]. We use the RetinaFace [18] trained on the WIDER FACE dataset [21] to detect faces and align the faces to 112×112. Since multiple faces can be detected in one video, we randomly select a face during training and fix a face during testing, such as the penultimate one. For gait silhouettes, we randomly select 30 frames as an unordered set in the training phase and take all frames as an ordered set during testing. All silhouettes are aligned in size of 64×44. The number of scales S in HPM is set as 5 according to [8]. Adam is chosen as an optimizer, and the learning rate is set to be 1e–5. The margin of BA_+ triplet loss is set as 0.2. The weight parameter λ in Eq. 2 is set as 1.0. We train the network for 80K iterations and test every 1K iterations. Considering the overfitting, we take the best test results as the final results for all methods.

Baselines. We first compare our approach to the single modality, e.g., only gait or only face. Then we include some other commonly used fusion methods for comparison. Considering most previous studies focus on the score-level fusion [3–7], we evaluate three commonly used score-level fusion strategies, e.g., sum, product, and min. Since the scores of various modalities may be on different scales, score normalization is needed to transform the scores into a common scale. In our experiments, we try three normalization techniques, e.g., min-max, Z-score, and L2 normalization. Since some recent works have performed the self-attention mechanism that is also known as Transformer to handle multimodal tasks [22], we utilize the general Transformer encoder block to fuse the features of gait and face. Specifically, we flatten the 2D gait feature to 1D and use a fully connected layer to reduce the dimension to be consistent with the face feature. Then the two features are input to a Transformer block with two heads.

4.2   Results

The experimental results are shown in Table 1. We summarize the results by averaging accuracies of all walking types and views. First, the performances of unimodality and multimodality fusion are compared. For the gait modality, the mean accuracy on the NM subset is much higher than BG and CL subsets, which demonstrates gait modality is easily influenced by carrying and clothing. When fusing gait with face, the mean accuracies of BG and CL subsets boost more than the NM subset, which indicates that the incorporation of the face modality effectively mitigates the effects of gait modality on carrying and clothing. For the three score-level fusion methods, the mean accuracies are noncompetitive, which proves that the score-level fusion ways do not work when the contribution of one modality is not significant. The feature-level methods achieve higher mean accuracies and exceed the score-level methods by over 10%. Compared to the score-level fusion strategies and the feature-level fusion method using the Transformer encoder, our method obtains nice results on most of the views, which shows the effectiveness of our method.

Table 1. Averaged rank-1 accuracies on CASIA-B-Gait-Face of various methods, excluding identical-view cases.

Methods	NM#5–6	BG#1–2	CL#1–2
Unimodality-Face	9.900	9.041	7.600
Unimodality-Gait	95.567	88.867	74.767
Fuse_Score_Minmax_Sum	65.067	59.367	47.900
Fuse_Score_Z-score_Sum	65.667	58.800	46.633
Fuse_Score_L2_Sum	70.267	61.800	49.600
Fuse_Score_Minmax_Product	50.167	45.933	39.567
Fuse_Score_Z-score_Product	24.167	19.233	14.567
Fuse_Score_L2_Product	72.233	62.567	49.333
Fuse_Score_Minmax_Min	50.167	45.933	39.567
Fuse_Score_Z-score_Min	71.133	62.467	48.933
Fuse_Score_L2_Min	69.400	58.133	43.833
Fuse_Minmax_Transformer	94.033	87.567	73.467
Fuse_Minmax_Sparateconcat	**95.867**	**90.233**	**76.700**

4.3   Ablation Study

In this section, we provide the ablation experiments to analyze our design. All experiments are also conducted on CASIA-B-Gait-Face. We have tried various fusion strategies, normalization technologies, and losses. The results are listed in Table 2. Comparing the first three rows with the last row, we can see that the Separate Concatenate fusion method holds the best performance when using the same normalization and losses. We note that the Concatenate way is the least effective, which may be due to the 'curse of dimensionality' problem. Comparing the fourth and fifth rows with the last row, we can see that the min-max normalization performs better than Z-score normalization when fusing in the Separate Concatenate way. The Z-score normalization does not even help with fusion. The reason may be that the Z-score normalization requires the arithmetic mean and standard deviation of the features, which are easily affected by some outliers in the features. The results of the last two rows show that the joint training with triplet loss and cross-entropy loss is more effective.

Table 2. The ablation study for fusion strategies, normalization techniques, and losses. The Concat represents the concatenating operation.

Fusion strategy				Normalization		Loss		Acc
Concat	Sparate_Sum	Sparate_Product	Separate_Concat	Min-max	Z-score	Triplet	Cross-Entropy	
✓				✓		✓	✓	78.56
	✓			✓		✓	✓	85.83
		✓		✓		✓	✓	83.19
			✓			✓	✓	87.14
			✓		✓	✓	✓	85.81
			✓	✓		✓		87.42
			✓	✓		✓	✓	**87.60**

5   Conclusion

In this work, we propose a novel method to fuse the information of gait and face at the feature level. Based on the trained GaitSet and ArcFace, we design a fusion strategy named Separate Concatenating which separately concatenates the gait feature with the corresponding face feature. Before the concatenation, min-max normalization is utilized to transform the two features into a common feature space. The concatenated feature is further fused by a fully connected layer. The proposed method can effectively integrate gait and face features into a more discriminative feature. To evaluate the performance, we built a multimodal gait-face database named CASIA-B-Gait-Face based on the CASIA-B gait dataset. Experiments indicate that compared with the single modality and other commonly used fusion methods, our method achieves the highest recognition accuracy, which demonstrates the feasibility of our method.

Acknowledgments. This work was supported by the National Natural Science Foundation of China (No. 61976095) and the Natural Science Foundation of Guangdong Province, China (No. 2022A1515010114)

References

1. Sepas-Moghaddam, A., Etemad, A.: Deep gait recognition: a survey (2021). arXiv:2102.09546
2. Shen, C., Yu, S., Wang, J., Huang, G.Q., Wang, L.: A comprehensive survey on deep gait recognition: algorithms, datasets and challenges (2022). arXiv:2206.13732
3. Xin, G., Liang, W., Ming, L., Qiang, W., Smith-Miles, K.: Adaptive fusion of gait and face for human identification in video. In: 2008 IEEE Workshop on Applications of Computer Vision (2008)
4. Hofmann, H., Schmidt, S.M., Rajagopalan, A.N., Rigoll, G.: Combined face and gait recognition using alpha matte preprocessing. In: 2012 5th IAPR International Conference on Biometrics (ICB) (2012)

5. Geng, X., Smith-Miles, K., Wang, L., Li, M., Qiang, W.: Context-aware fusion: a case study on fusion of gait and face for human identification in video. Pattern Recogn. **43**(10), 3660–3673 (2010)
6. Kale, A., RoyChowdhury, A.K., Chellappa, R.: Fusion of gait and face for human identification. In: 2004 IEEE International Conference on Acoustics, Speech, and Signal Processing, vol. 5, p. 901 (2004)
7. Maity, S., Abdel-Mottaleb, M., Asfour, S.S.: Multimodal low resolution face and frontal gait recognition from surveillance video. Electronics **10**(9), 1013 (2021)
8. Chao, H., He, Y., Zhang, J., Feng, J.: GaitSet: regarding gait as a set for cross-view gait recognition. Proc. AAAI Conf. Artif.. Intell. **33**(01), 8126–8133 (2019)
9. He, K., Zhang, X., Ren, S., Sun, J.: Deep residual learning for image recognition. In: Proceedings of the IEEE Conference on Computer Vision and Pattern Recognition, pp. 770–778 (2016)
10. Deng, J., Guo, J., Xue, N., Zafeiriou, S.: ArcFace: additive angular margin loss for deep face recognition. In: Proceedings of the IEEE/CVF Conference on Computer Vision and Pattern Recognition, pp. 4690–4699 (2019)
11. Hermans, A., Beyer, L., Leibe, B.: In defense of the triplet loss for person re-identification (2017). arXiv:1703.07737
12. Yu, S., Tan, D., Tan, T.: A framework for evaluating the effect of view angle, clothing and carrying condition on gait recognition. In: International Conference on Pattern Recognition (2006)
13. Kale, A., Roychowdhury, A.K., Chellappa, R.: Fusion of gait and face for human identification. In: 2004 IEEE International Conference on Acoustics, Speech, and Signal Processing (2004)
14. Xin, G., Smith-Miles, K., Liang, W., Ming, L., Qiang, W.: Context-aware fusion: a case study on fusion of gait and face for human identification in video. Pattern Recogn. **43**(10), 3660–3673 (2010)
15. Zhou, X., Bhanu, B.: Feature fusion of face and gait for human recognition at a distance in video. In: 18th International Conference on Pattern Recognition (ICPR 2006) (2006)
16. Jain, A., Nandakumar, K., Ross, A.: Score normalization in multimodal biometric systems. Pattern Recogn. **38**(12), 2270–2285 (2013)
17. Ju, H., Bhanu, B.: Individual recognition using gait energy image. IEEE Trans. Pattern Anal. Mach. Intell. **28**(2), 316–322 (2005)
18. Deng, J., Guo, J., Ververas, E., Kotsia, I., Zafeiriou, S.: RetinaFace: single-shot multi-level face localisation in the wild. In: Proceedings of the IEEE/CVF Conference on Computer Vision and Pattern Recognition, pp. 5203–5212 (2020)
19. Luo, H., Gu, Y., Liao, X., Lai, S., Jiang, W.: Bag of tricks and a strong baseline for deep person re-identification. In: Proceedings of the IEEE/CVF Conference on Computer Vision and Pattern Recognition Workshops (2019)
20. Guo, Y., Zhang, L., Hu, Y., He, X., Gao, J.: Ms-celeb-1m: a dataset and benchmark for large-scale face recognition. In: European Conference on Computer Vision, pp. 87–102 (2016)
21. Yang, S., Luo, P., Loy, C.-C., Tang, X.: Wider face: a face detection benchmark. In: Proceedings of the IEEE Conference on Computer Vision and Pattern Recognition, pp. 5525–5533 (2016)
22. Huang, J., Tao, J., Liu, B., Lian, Z., Niu, M.: Multimodal transformer fusion for continuous emotion recognition. In: ICASSP 2020–2020 IEEE International Conference on Acoustics, Speech and Signal Processing (ICASSP), pp. 3507–3511 (2020)

Gait Recognition by Sensing Insole Using a Hybrid CNN-Attention-LSTM Network

Jing Yue[1], Zhanyong Mei[1,2(✉)], Kamen Ivanov[3,4,5], Yingyi Li[1], Tong He[1], and Hui Zeng[1]

[1] College of Computer Science and Cyber Security, Chengdu University of Technology (Oxford Brookes College), Chengdu, China
meizhanyong2014@cdut.edu.cn
[2] Norwegian Biometrics Laboratory, Norwegian University of Science and Technology (NTNU), Gjøvik, Norway
[3] Institute of Biophysics and Biomedical Engineering, Bulgarian Academy of Sciences, Acad. G, Bonchev Str. Bl 105, 1113 Sofia, Bulgaria
[4] Institute of Electronics, Bulgarian Academy of Sciences, 72 Tsarigradsko Chaussee Blvd., 1784 Sofia, Bulgaria
[5] Shenzhen Institute of Advanced Technology, Chinese Academy of Sciences, 1068 Xueyuan Avenue, Shenzhen University Town, Shenzhen 518055, China

Abstract. Gait recognition has become a necessary integral part of emerging smart wearables. However, considering the limitations of wearable sensing, improving the recognition performance remains an open question. In this work, we tackle the problem of gait recognition by using a large set of multimodal sensing insole data from sixty-two participants reflecting kinetic and kinematic variables of natural gait outdoors. We used this dataset to leverage a novel recognition method involving a deep architecture combining a convolutional neural network, a long short-term memory network, and attention embedding. It allows grasping the temporal-spatial gait features completely. An essential part of this work is the comparative performance exploration of fixed-length and gait-cycle segmentation. The proposed framework allows accuracy of 99.73% when using gait-cycle segmentation. The results confirm that the hybrid deep learning model using multisensory, multimodal data can be effectively applied for identity recognition in an unconstrained environment.

Keywords: Gait recognition · Deep learning · Feature extraction · Gait cycle · Sensing insole · Biometrics

1 Introduction

Biometric technologies based on intrinsic characteristics of the human body, i.e., "something you are", allow distinguishing a person from others. Already established physiological biometrics, such as fingerprint, face, and iris, have exhibited excellent performance in identity recognition [1]. However, the explicit interaction between the user and the scanning device is not practical for application in wearables.

W. Deng et al. (Eds.): CCBR 2022, LNCS 13628, pp. 484–492, 2022.
https://doi.org/10.1007/978-3-031-20233-9_49

Gait has the potential to address emerging needs for security in wearable devices. It is a behavioral biometric referring to the walking manner and unique to individuals [2]. The gait pattern is currently considered difficult to mimic or copy [3]. The implicit manner of gait data collection contributes to higher security [4], among other benefits. Motion sensors are easily integrated into most wearable devices, making gait readily available as a system modality.

Recently, electronization has reached footwear paving its path to becoming one of the compelling members of the body sensor network [5]. It possesses intrinsic benefits by allowing for fixed position and orientation of the sensors towards the foot, multi-modal sensing, and unobtrusive, continuous data collection. Despite the wide application horizons sensing footwear promises, many related aspects, including security, remain underexplored. We attribute this fact to the lack of, up until recently, powerful signal processing methods and the difficulties in constructing practical prototypes. In our systematic effort to fill this gap, we constructed a multimodal sensing insole [6] and performed an initial exploration of the possibilities it offers for person recognition [7].

In the present study, we expand the knowledge by exploring an advanced hybrid processing method involving a convolutional neural network (CNN), long short-term memory (LSTM), and an attention mechanism that brings certain improvements in recognition performance. As in our previous work, the implementation was leveraged by a multimodal insole dataset collected outdoors from multiple participants through a rich set of sensors. The particular contributions of this work are:

(1) We proposed a person recognition method based on gait that involves a deep hybrid CNN-LSTM network with attention embedding. Detailed evaluation of the complete algorithm, as well as of each of its components, was performed. The advantage of using feature-level fusion to process the data from each modality was also demonstrated.

(2) We evaluated the performance of the proposed algorithm for fixed-length and gait-cycle segmentation.

The presentation hereafter is organized as follows. Section 2 introduces the data acquisition and preprocessing; Sect. 3 explains the deep network design for gait recognition; Sect. 4 presents the experiments and performance evaluations; and, finally, Sect. 5 provides concluding remarks.

2 Dataset Preparation

2.1 Gait Data Acquisition

We used data collected during experimental sessions of our previous work [7]. We applied more liberal inclusion criteria and used all good trials, thus having data of sixty-two participants, three more than the reported in [7]. At the time of data collection, volunteers were in normal general health without known foot problems. They were from the Chengdu University of Technology and Shenzhen Institute of Advanced Technologies. Each participant performed a trial of unrestricted walking outdoors for at least ten minutes while wearing a pair of sensing insoles containing an inertial sensor and nine force sensors. Sensor data were recorded on an SD card of a data logger. A representative set of signals is shown in Fig. 1.

As this study was intended to provide an initial proof-of-concept, the signals were fed to the neural network without normalization. Thus, all captured personal characteristics, including body weight, were reflected during the classification. In doing so, however, we did not account for the imperfections of the force sensors [6] nor the differences in signal ranges between modalities and subjects.

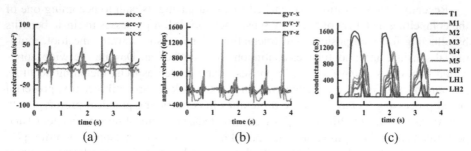

Fig. 1. Representative set of signals: (a) acceleration, (b) angular velocity, and (c) plantar force.

2.2 Signal Denoising

If trained appropriately, neural networks can extract features from noisy signals directly. However, in this study, we employ a gait-cycle segmentation method, which is sensitive to noise. We thus used denoised signals for all subsequent processing.

We adopted a wavelet threshold denoising method from [8]. The wavelet type of *symlet-8* for the three-level decomposition and the value in the threshold selection rule were determined empirically, considering preserving the useful signal components to the greatest extent. The original and denoised signals are illustrated in Fig. 2.

2.3 Segmentation by Gait Cycles

In this work, we compare the recognition performance for fixed-length segmentation and segmentation by gait cycles. Due to characteristic differences between gait and inertial sensing data, we employed different segmentation strategies for each. Segmentation points were detected in the acceleration signal over the sensor's x-axis, which reflects the vertical acceleration, and the signal from the force sensor under the medial heel. Since the channels of each modality were captured synchronously, the detected points were applied to the remaining channels of the respective modalities.

Segmentation of Inertial Data. It is based on detecting the flat regions in the signals. A window of length $a = 4$, , defined as $[\omega_i, \omega_{i+a}]$ starts moving with a stride of $s = 2$ samples from the beginning of the trial. At each position, the window is analyzed to determine whether: (1) the variance of the signal contained in the window is lower than a threshold $t_1 = 0.5$; (2) the absolute value of the difference between values of the first and last sample of the window is lower than a threshold $t_2 = 1$. Upon satisfying the two criteria, the first point of the window at the current position is considered the beginning

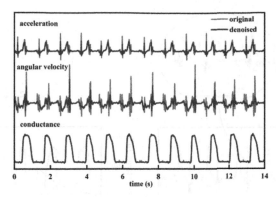

Fig. 2. Illustration of the applied denoising.

of the flat region. Then, the right side of the window expands forward, and at each step of expansion, the window is also analyzed. Failure to meet the criteria denotes the end of the flat region. The midpoint P_i of the flat region is obtained as the first point of the gait-cycle segment. The analysis continues from the point E_i before the next flat region, located at a distance $\gamma = 70$ samples from the previous segmentation point. The value of γ was determined empirically to be lower than the average duration of the gait cycle in the given dataset. Then, the procedure repeats until the end of the trial.

Segmentation of Force Data. It is based on detecting the points of rapid increase from zero. The analysis starts from the beginning of the trial with a stride $s = 1$. Each point Q_i is analyzed to determine whether: (1) the conductance at the point Q_i is zero; (2) the conductance at the point Q_{i+1} is larger than zero; (3) the values in the interval $[Q_i, Q_{i+4}]$ increase monotonically. Upon satisfying the three criteria, the point Q_i is considered the first point of the gait cycle segment.

The segmentation procedure is illustrated in Fig. 3.

Zero Padding. CNNs operate with fixed-length segments. To unify the segment lengths, we used zero padding. To avoid having segments with a padded length prevailing over the useful signal length, we empirically determined padded segment lengths of 150 and 130 samples for the force data and inertial data, respectively.

2.4 Fixed-Length Segmentation

The length of the gait cycle is in the range of 0.8–1.5 s in our dataset. For a fair performance comparison with the gait-cycle segmentation, the segment length was also chosen to be 1.3 s and 1.5 s (130 and 150 samples at a sampling rate of 100 Hz) for inertial and force data, respectively. The segmentation was performed without overlap.

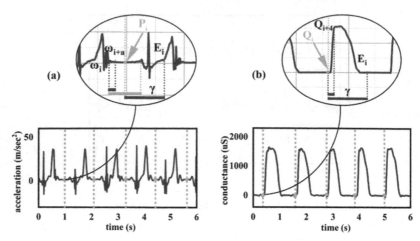

Fig. 3. Segmentation point detection: (a) in the *acc-x* signal; (b) in the medial heel force signal.

3 Proposed Neural Network Architecture

The inertial data sampling is based on an oscillator with a frequency tolerance of $\pm 1.5\%$, leading to inconsistency in the sampling frequency of inertial data between devices. To mitigate this problem, we applied feature-level fusion to process the inertial and force sensor data separately, making the classifier insensitive to the lack of precise synchronization between the two modalities. Thus, separate feature extraction pipelines were employed for the inertial and force data.

The architecture of the proposed gait recognition network is shown in Fig. 4. The dataset contained the data of left- and right-side sensors, respectively. Thus, there were six accelerometer channels, six gyroscopic channels, and eighteen force sensor channels. The input segments for model training had a shape of $130 \times 12 \times 1$ for the inertial data pipeline and $150 \times 18 \times 1$ for the force sensor pipeline. For each pipeline, a CNN extracted gait features. The structure and the parameters of the CNN are described in Table 1. Extracted features were fed into an LSTM layer. LSTMs can model temporal dependencies in time series. The combination of CNNs and LSTMs allows for capturing time dependencies from features extracted by convolutional operations. Inspired by SENet [9], we embedded an attention layer between the output of the CNN and the input of LSTM in each pipeline to improve the recognition performance further. The fused features were integrated into a one-dimensional vector and used as input to a fully connected layer for classification.

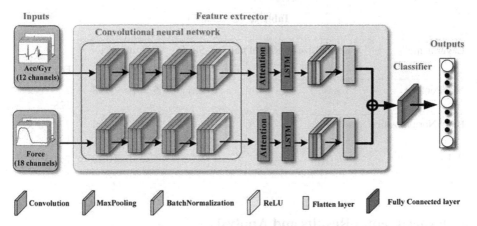

Fig. 4. Architecture of the gait recognition network.

Table 1. Structure and parameters of the CNN.

Layer name	Kernel size	Kernel num.	Stride	Feature vector	
				Acc/Gyr	Force
Conv1	3 × 1	16	(1,1)	128 × 12 × 16	148 × 18 × 16
MaxPooling	2 × 1	–	(2,1)	64 × 12 × 16	74 × 18 × 16
BatchNormalization	–	–	–	64 × 12 × 16	74 × 18 × 16
Conv2	3 × 1	32	(1,1)	62 × 12 × 32	72 × 18 × 32
MaxPooling	2 × 1	–	(2,1)	31 × 12 × 32	36 × 18 × 32
BatchNormalization	–	–	–	31 × 12 × 32	36 × 18 × 32
Conv3	3 × 1	64	(1,1)	29 × 12 × 64	34 × 18 × 64
MaxPooling	2 × 1	–	(2,1)	14 × 12 × 64	17 × 18 × 64
BatchNormalization	–	–	–	14 × 12 × 64	17 × 18 × 64
Conv4	3 × 1	128	(1,1)	12 × 12 × 128	15 × 18 × 128

(continued)

Table 1. (*continued*)

Layer name	Kernel size	Kernel num.	Stride	Feature vector	
				Acc/Gyr	Force
MaxPooling	3 × 3	–	(2,1)	5 × 10 × 128	7 × 16 × 128
BatchNormalization	–	–	–	5 × 10 × 128	7 × 16 × 128
ReLU	–	–	–	5 × 10 × 128	7 × 16 × 128

4   Experimental Results and Analysis

4.1   Experimental Method and Evaluation Metrics

In the model training, the batch size was set to 64. We split the data into a training, validation, and test set in a 6:2:2 ratio. For the evaluation, we used four metrics: accuracy, recall, F1-score, and precision. Higher scores of these metrics correspond to better performance. We trained each of the models for 50 epochs, and each model training was executed three times, then the average value of each metric was calculated. In most cases, accuracy and validation losses stabilized before reaching the 20th epoch. Categorical cross-entropy was used for the loss function, and RMSProp optimizer was applied to update the model parameters. The accuracy and loss of training and testing were saved for each epoch, and the model of the last epoch was saved for the prediction.

4.2   Experimental Results

To verify the effectiveness of the complete hybrid network, we compared the performance of different combinations of subnetworks. The results are shown in Table 2. The CNN + Attention + LSTM achieved the best accuracy of 99.73% and recall with a small number of parameters. Thus, as expected, more sophisticated feature extractors may extract better gait representations. All models based on the gait-cycle segmentation demonstrated better accuracy than models based on fixed-length segmentation. The possible reason is that the gait-cycle segmentation allows better reflection of individual gait patterns.

The proposed method was compared with similar works [7] and [10], and the results are shown in Table 3. We reached a higher recognition accuracy than [7], which could mostly be attributed to the more sophisticated neural network architecture. In [10], the classification accuracy reached 99% in the case of a study category with only 35 individuals, indicating that the recognition performance, in general, decreases as the number of categories increases.

Table 2. Results of different modules under different segmentation methods.

Architecture	Gait–cycle segm.	Accu.	Recall	Prec.	F1-score	Param. number
CNN	yes	99.64%	94.37%	96.34%	94.88%	1,428224
	no	98.98%	98.69%	98.88%	98.78%	
LSTM	yes	99.70%	98.93%	99.72%	99.26%	2,351936
	no	98.35%	98.14%	98.38%	98.25%	
CNN+LSTM	yes	99.71%	95.86%	97.92%	96.47%	1,067776
	no	99.02%	98.87%	99.02%	98.97%	
CNN+Attention	yes	99.65%	95.27%	97.52%	95.35%	1,444928
	no	99.01%	98.90%	99.00%	98.95%	
CNN+Attention+LSTM	yes	99.73%	96.32%	97.49%	96.64%	1,084480
	no	99.10%	98.94%	99.03%	98.98%	

Table 3. Performance comparison with recent studies.

Study	Modalities	Subjects	Sessions	Accuracy
Ivanov K et al. [7]	9 force sensors, accelerometer, gyroscope	59	10 min	93.3%
Wang et al. [10]	Accelerometer, gyroscope	35	5 min	99%
This study	9 force sensors, accelerometer, gyroscope	62	10 min	99.73%

5 Conclusions and Future Work

We used a large multimodal insole dataset to supply a novel gait recognition engine utilizing a CNN-LSTM network with attention embedding. The recognition accuracy reached 99.73% when using gait-cycle segmentation. A comparative evaluation of several variants of the complete hybrid architecture was performed. Even the basic feature extractor achieved accuracy comparable to more advanced architectures, suggesting that the size of the training dataset may be the determinant of the recognition performance over neural network complexity.

In future work, we will address the synchronization between the sensors of different modalities and both sides to improve the recognition performance. Also, we will explore how the variation of the gait patterns over time influences recognition accuracy. Model complexity, hardware resources, inference time, and energy consumption shall also be considered for deployment in practice.

Acknowledgments. This work was partially supported by Key R&D support projects of the Chengdu Science and Technology Bureau (No. 2021-YF05-02175-SN) and by the funding of the China Scholarship Council.

References

1. Shaheed, K., et al.: A systematic review on physiological-based biometric recognition systems: current and future trends. Archives of Computational Methods in Engineering **28**(7), 4917–4960 (2021). https://doi.org/10.1007/s11831-021-09560-3
2. Wan, C., Wang, L., Phoha, V.V. (eds.).: A Survey on Gait Recognition. ACM Computing Surveys (CSUR) **51**(5), 1–35 (2018)
3. Wang, C., Li, Z., Sarpong, B.: Multimodal adaptive identity-recognition algorithm fused with gait perception. Big Data Mining and Analytics. **4**(4), 223–232 (2021)
4. Zeng, X., Zhang, X., Yang, S., Shi, Z., Chi, C.: Gait-based implicit authentication using edge computing and deep learning for mobile devices. Sensors. **21**(13), 4592 (2021)
5. Zou, Y., Libanori, A., Xu, J., Nashalian, A., Chen, J.: Triboelectric Nanogenerator Enabled Smart Shoes for Wearable Electricity Generation. Research. 2020 (2020)
6. Ivanov, K., et al.: Design of a Sensor Insole for Gait Analysis. In: Yu, H., Liu, J., Liu, L., Ju, Z., Liu, Y., Zhou, D. (eds.) ICIRA 2019. LNCS (LNAI), vol. 11743, pp. 433–444. Springer, Cham (2019). https://doi.org/10.1007/978-3-030-27538-9_37
7. Ivanov, K., et al.: Identity recognition by walking outdoors using multimodal sensor insoles. IEEE Access. **8**, 150797–150807 (2020)
8. Guo, X.X., Yang, H.Z.: An improved compromise for soft/hard thresholds in wavelet denoising. CAAI Transactions on Intelligent Systems. 222–225 (2008)
9. Hu, J., Shen, L., Sun, G.: Squeeze-and-excitation networks. In: 2018 IEEE/CVF Conference on Computer Vision and Pattern Recognition, pp. 7132–7141 (2018)
10. Wang, T., Xia, Y., Zhang, D.: Human gait recognition based on convolutional neural network and attention model. Chinese Journal of Sensors and Actuators. **32**(07), 1027–1033 (2019)

Identity Authentication Using a Multimodal Sensing Insole—A Feasibility Study

Hui Zeng[1], Sijia Yi[1], Zijie Mei[1], Tong He[1], Jing Yue[1], Kamen Ivanov[3,4,5],
and Zhanyong Mei[1,2(✉)]

[1] College of Computer Science and Cyber Security, Chengdu University of Technology (Oxford Brookes College), Chengdu, China
`meizhanyong2014@cdut.edu.cn`
[2] Norwegian Biometrics Laboratory, Norwegian University of Science and Technology (NTNU), Gjøvik, Norway
[3] Institute of Biophysics and Biomedical Engineering, Bulgarian Academy of Sciences, Acad. G. Bonchev Str. Bl 105, 1113 Sofia, Bulgaria
[4] Institute of Electronics, Bulgarian Academy of Sciences, 72 Tsarigradsko Chaussee Blvd., 1784 Sofia, Bulgaria
[5] Shenzhen Institute of Advanced Technology, Chinese Academy of Sciences, 1068 Xueyuan Avenue, Shenzhen University Town, Shenzhen 518055, China

Abstract. With the development of intelligent electronic devices, users pay more attention to personal information privacy. Among human biometrics, gait does not require user cooperation and is difficult to imitate, making it suitable for implementing highly secure identity authentication. In this work, we demonstrate the application of a multimodal sensing insole for person authentication. For dataset preparation, fixed-length and gait-cycle segmentation were applied. We used a deep learning method to classify the legal user and imposters. The data from twenty subjects were used to train and test models. An average accuracy of more than 99% was achieved. Results confirm the feasibility and effectiveness of using the sensing insole for gait identity authentication.

Keywords: Gait authentication · Sensing insole · Gait cycle · Deep learning · Biometrics

1 Introduction

With the widespread use of portable electronic devices, there is a need to improve the existing technologies for security and unauthorized access prevention and build new, application-specific ones. Simple passwords are relatively easy to disclose, and complex ones are impractical and difficult to memorize [1]. With the aid of biometrics, it is possible to ensure continuous secure access to assets and systems. However, established biometrics such as fingerprints and facial prints are usually scanned once for authentication, and if an attacker is successfully granted access, their further actions remain unrestricted.

© The Author(s), under exclusive license to Springer Nature Switzerland AG 2022
W. Deng et al. (Eds.): CCBR 2022, LNCS 13628, pp. 493–500, 2022.
https://doi.org/10.1007/978-3-031-20233-9_50

Many studies have confirmed the feasibility of using gait as a biometric trait for identity authentication [2–4]. Ahmad et al. used the smartphone's built-in accelerometer to capture acceleration data for gait authentication, allowing subjects to carry the smartphone freely in their pockets. They trained an artificial neural network and achieved an average accuracy of 95% [2]. Papavasileiou et al. proposed a method to improve the robustness of gait-based biometric authentication by introducing multimodal learning involving inertial and pressure sensors. They used early data fusion and achieved equal error rates of 0.01% and 0.16% with smart socks and shoes, respectively [3]. He et al. designed the feature extractor of *Gait2Vec* for the gait identification task. Then they used transfer learning to apply the pre-trained feature extractor to the gait authentication task and achieved an accuracy of 97% [4].

Currently, most gait authentication methods only use an accelerometer to collect gait information and rely on devices attached to the waist or wrist or smartphones carried in clothing pockets [5]. However, in contrast with sensing insoles, devices worn on the upper body may not have a pre-determined position towards the human body, such as mobile phones, or may collect components unrelated to gait, such as wristbands. In this work, we propose the application of a multimodal sensing insole for identity authentication. It integrates a tri-axial accelerometer, a tri-axial gyroscope, and nine force sensors. They complement each other in reflecting kinematic and kinetic characteristics to provide rich information for identity authentication. For the proof of concept, we designed a deep neural network. We supplied it with training data from twenty subjects who performed free walking for about ten minutes in an unconstrained environment while wearing a pair of instrumented insoles. Also, the performance was evaluated for fixed-length and gait-cycle segmentation.

The rest of this paper is organized as follows. The proposed approach is described in detail in Sect. 2. Section 3 describes the experimental process and evaluation metrics. Section 4 provides the results and discussion. Section 5 summarizes this work.

2 Method

The proposed gait authentication method is illustrated in Fig. 1.

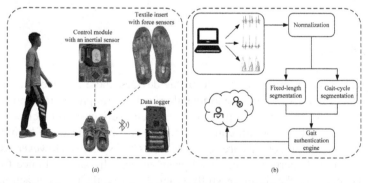

Fig. 1. Methodology of this study: (a) acquisition setup; (b) data processing sequence.

2.1 Signal Acquisition

We adopted data collected in our previous work [6], randomly selecting twenty subjects. For complete detail of the hardware setup and data collection procedure, please, refer to [6]. The sensing insole consists of a textile insert with integrated nine force sensors and an acquisition module attached to the frontal part of the shoe that contains an inertial sensor with a tri-axial accelerometer and gyroscope. The locations of the force sensors are the big toe, five metatarsal heads, midfoot, and heel. The sampling rate of all sensors was 100 Hz. Data were transferred to a portable datalogger through a Bluetooth low-energy channel and recorded on an SD card. The data from each foot involves fifteen channels, namely nine force sensor ones, and the acceleration and angular velocity signals along the x, y, and z axes. Subsequently, the total number of channels for the left and the right insole was thirty.

2.2 Normalization

To be able to process the signals on a common scale, normalization was required. As to the force signals, in principle, it would be desirable to apply the normalization over all the signals into an insole to preserve the unique amplitude relationships between the dynamic pressures under the different foot regions. Unfortunately, the thin-film force sensors reflect force imperfectly [7], and thus amplitude relationships between force sensor signals may be heavily affected by system bias. Hence, we did not aim to preserve the amplitude relationships between force channels. Subsequently, before the segmentation, we scaled each signal record between 0 and 1. In this way, body weight was not a factor, and the recognition method mainly relied on individual signals' temporal and morphological features.

2.3 Gait-Cycle Segmentation

2.3.1 Segmentation Point Detection for Inertial Sensor Data

For the detection of the gait cycles, the vertical acceleration signal could be utilized [8]. Our dataset has shown that both the vertical and forward-backward accelerations reflect the gait cycles sufficiently. We have chosen the forward-backward signal, corresponding to the inertial sensor z-axis. Liu et al. [8] used the local minimums and their subsequent transitions from positive to negative values in the vertical acceleration signal to detect segmentation points. Derawi et al. [9] determined an initial minimum point representing the beginning of the gait cycle and used average gait cycle distance and a search interval to detect the rest of the respective minimum points fast.

In our case, we preferred obtaining the midpoint P_j of the flat region at the beginning of each gait cycle as the segmentation point representing the beginning of the gait cycle, which is simpler than the methods suggested in [8] and [9]. For determining the beginning of the first recorded flat region, the variance of a window with a length of fifteen samples and a step of two samples was analyzed. When the variance was less than or equal to one, and the absolute value of the difference between the first and last sample of the window was less than two, the first window sample at the current position was considered to be the beginning of the flat region. The current window continued to expand to the right in a step of three samples, and failure of either condition denoted the end of the flat region. Then, a fast transition of seventy samples was performed, ensuring positioning before the next flat region for the given dataset. The next flat region was detected the same way as the initial one, and the procedure was repeated for all regions. The process is illustrated in Fig. 2(a). As the inertial sensor signals are mutually-synchronous, the detected segmentation points were applied to the rest of the inertial signals.

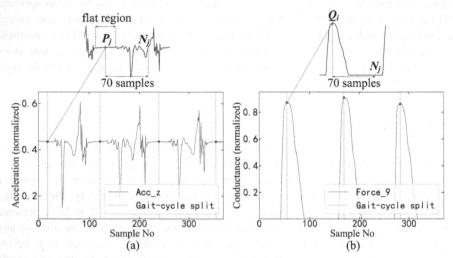

Fig. 2. Segmentation point detection: (a) in the selected inertial sensor channel; (b) in the selected force sensor channel.

2.3.2   Segmentation Point Detection for Force Sensor Data

For force data, peak points were used as the gait-cycle segmentation points. Peak point detection is simple, reliable, and avoids occasional fluctuations typical for the flat regions in the force sensor signals. In a normal gait cycle, heel sensors are activated first upon heel contact. We subsequently determined the segmentation points in the signal of sensor nine, one of the two sensors beneath the heel. Although the detected peaks have a small delay after the initial heel contact, it was deemed negligible. Peak points were detected within a sliding window with a width of five samples. A threshold value was used to ensure that the small fluctuations in the signal unrelated to plantar force would be disregarded. The detection of segmentation points in the force signal is illustrated in Fig. 2(b). As the data of force sensor channels are mutually-synchronous, the determined segmentation points were applied to the rest of the force channel signals.

2.3.3   Data Padding

Neural networks require supplying segments with a fixed length. Subsequently, zero padding was used, where the segment length was decided to be 130 samples for the two modalities, slightly larger than the longest gait cycle in the dataset.

2.4 Fixed-Length Segmentation

For a fair comparison of performance when using fixed-length and gait-cycle segmentation, we adopted the lengths of the fixed segments to be identical to the lengths of the zero-padded segments of gait-cycle segmentation. Consequently, for the fixed-length segmentation, we did not consider the positions of gait cycles in the signals and whether a full gait cycle was contained in each segment.

2.5 Neural Network Architecture

The proposed neural network structure is shown in Fig. 3. To emphasize the individual user channel importance set, we introduced a channel attention layer after the input layer. In this layer, weight values for the channels were calculated and applied to the original data as follows [10]:

$$Y = Softmax\left(ReLU\left(W_2 * ReLU\left(W_1 * X\right)\right)\right) * X \tag{1}$$

where X represents the input, W_1 is the weight value of the first linear layer, W_2 is the weight value of the second linear layer, and Y represents the weighted data of X and is used as the input of the next layer.

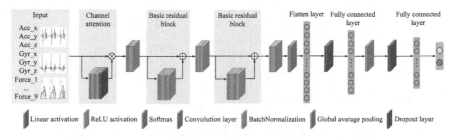

Fig. 3. Architecture of the proposed neural network for gait authentication.

Then, weighted data were supplied to a convolutional neural network (CNN) for feature extraction. The CNN feature extractor is based on the *ResNet* image classifier proposed by He et al. [11]. It uses the idea of residual connection in *ResNet* to build a feature extractor suitable for time series data. The main structure of the feature extractor we proposed is a one-dimensional basic residual block, and the residual connection of the basic residual block is an identity map. To maintain the characteristics of each channel, we kept the original number of data channels unchanged throughout the feature extraction process and performed feature fusion through the global average pooling layer in the final stage of the feature extraction. After the feature extraction, two fully connected layers were used for identity authentication.

3 Experiments

Left- and right-side accelerometric, angular velocity, and force data were taken individually and subjected to fixed-length and gait-cycle segmentation. Thus, diverse training datasets were obtained to facilitate the detailed comparative analysis of the contribution of each modality and each foot side to the recognition performance. The total number of segments for each training dataset is given in Table 1 and Table 2. For each modality combination, training was performed as described next.

For each subject, a model was trained where that subject was the intended, authorized person, i.e., the positive sample. The remaining subjects were considered negative samples or intruders. For the training set of each model, the positive data were oversampled accordingly to balance the positive and negative samples in the dataset. The training, validation, and test sets ratio was chosen as 8:1:1. We used a cross-entropy loss function and stochastic gradient descent, with a learning rate of 0.003 and a momentum magnitude of 0.9.

To evaluate the performance of each model, we used four performance metrics: accuracy, recall, precision, and F1-score. To better evaluate the robustness of the proposed architecture, the reported metrics for each modality combination were calculated as the average of the respective individual results for the corresponding set of twenty models.

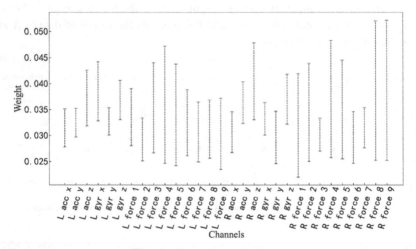

Fig. 4. Channel weight ranges.

4   Results

Individual gait characteristics determine a set of channel importance values for each subject. Figure 4 shows the weight ranges of all thirty sensor channels for all users. The distribution of weights varies between subjects, which confirms that the channel attention mechanism allows adapting a model to a particular subject.

The results are shown in Table 1 and Table 2. Overall, using gait-cycle segmentation outperforms fixed-length segmentation. For fixed-length segmentation, channel fusion allowed for better recognition performance than single-channel data. This observation is consistent with the assumption that multiple modalities complement each other in providing richer gait pattern information, thus allowing for better recognition performance.

However, we observed some deviation for multimodal fusion of gait-cycle-segmented data, where the accuracy was slightly lower than that of solely using acceleration data. This result might be attributed to the fact that a different number of unqualified cycles were discarded from the data of each side during the gait-cycle segmentation, resulting in a slight imbalance in the training dataset. Lack of precise multimodal synchronization is another likely factor that can negatively affect multimodal accuracy. Regarding the left and right sides, the results are consistent with the expectation that data from both sides allow richer discriminative information and better results than data from one side. In all cases, the accuracy of gait authentication was as high as 99%, regardless of whether data from one or two sides were used, demonstrating the feasibility of using the sensing insole for identity authentication.

Table 1. Results of fixed-length segmentation.

Modality	ANSU	Accuracy	Precision	Recall	F1-score
Acc (L&R)	4266	99.96%	99.10%	99.78%	99.43%
Gyr (L&R)	4266	99.96%	99.13%	99.89%	99.50%
Force (L&R)	12798	99.86%	98.12%	98.35%	98.22%
Acc+Gyr+Force (L&R)	21130	99.97%	99.34%	99.85%	99.59%
Acc+Gyr+Force (L)	10665	99.93%	98.65%	99.55%	99.09%
Acc+Gyr+Force (R)	10665	99.95%	99.02%	99.70%	99.35%

ANSU: average number of segments per user;
L: left-side data; R: right-side data; L&R: left-side and right-side data;

Table 2. Results of gait-cycle segmentation.

Modality	ANSU	Accuracy	Precision	Recall	F1-score
Acc (L&R)	4410	99.99%	99.94%	99.87%	99.91%
Gyr (L&R)	4410	99.98%	99.73%	99.78%	99.75%
Force (L&R)	13230	99.93%	99.28%	99.23%	99.25%
Acc+Gyr+Force (L&R)	22050	99.98%	99.72%	99.87%	99.79%
Acc+Gyr+Force (L)	11265	99.94%	99.16%	99.67%	99.39%
Acc+Gyr+Force (R)	11130	99.81%	98.43%	99.60%	98.90%

ANSU: average number of segments per user;
L: left-side data; R: right-side data; L&R: left-side and right-side data;

5 Conclusions

This work presents a gait authentication method based on a sensing insole and deep learning. We explored the recognition performance for gait-cycle segmentation and fixed-length segmentation. The method based on gait-cycle segmentation outperformed the one using fixed-length segmentation. Still, the accuracy of both methods reached 99%. The results confirm the feasibility of gait identity authentication based on a sensing insole.

Acknowledgments. This work was partially supported by Key R&D support projects of the Chengdu Science and Technology Bureau (No.2021-YF05-02175-SN) and by the funding of the China Scholarship Council.

References

1. Liu, J., Sun, W.: Smart attacks against intelligent wearables in people-centric internet of things. IEEE Commun. Mag. **54**, 44–49 (2016)
2. Ahmad, M., Khan, A.M., Brown, J.A., Protasov, S., Khattak, A.M.: Gait fingerprinting-based user identification on smartphones. In: 2016 International Joint Conference on Neural Networks (IJCNN), pp. 3060–3067 (2016)
3. Papavasileiou, I., Qiao, Z., Zhang, C., Zhang, W., Bi, J., Han, S.: GaitCode: gait-based continuous authentication using multimodal learning and wearable sensors. Smart Health. **19**, 100162 (2021)
4. He, L., Ma, C., Tu, C., Zhang, Y.: Gait2Vec: continuous authentication of smartphone users based on gait behavior. In: 2022 IEEE 25th International Conference on Computer Supported Cooperative Work in Design (CSCWD), pp. 280–285 (2022)
5. Cola, G., Vecchio, A., Avvenuti, M.: Continuous authentication through gait analysis on a wrist-worn device. Pervasive Mobile Comput. **78**, 101483 (2021)
6. Ivanov, K., et al.: Identity recognition by walking outdoors using multimodal sensor insoles. IEEE Access **8**, 150797–150807 (2020)
7. Ivanov, K., et al.: Design of a sensor insole for gait analysis. In: Yu, H., Liu, J., Liu, L., Ju, Z., Liu, Y., Zhou, D. (eds.) ICIRA 2019. LNCS (LNAI), vol. 11743, pp. 433–444. Springer, Cham (2019). https://doi.org/10.1007/978-3-030-27538-9_37
8. Liu, R., Duan, Z., Zhou, J., Liu, M.: Identification of individual walking patterns using gait acceleration. In: 2007 1st International Conference on Bioinformatics and Biomedical Engineering, pp. 543–546 (2007)
9. Derawi, M.O., Bours, P., Holien, K.: Improved cycle detection for accelerometer based gait authentication. In: 2010 Sixth International Conference on Intelligent Information Hiding and Multimedia Signal Processing, pp. 312–317 (2010)
10. Hu, J., Shen, L., Sun, G.: Squeeze-and-excitation networks. In: 2018 IEEE/CVF Conference on Computer Vision and Pattern Recognition, pp. 7132–7141 (2018)
11. He, K., Zhang, X., Ren, S., Sun, J.: Deep residual learning for image recognition. In: 2016 IEEE Conference on Computer Vision and Pattern Recognition (CVPR), pp. 770–778 (2016)

MDF-Net: Multimodal Deep Fusion for Large-Scale Product Recognition

Yanling Pan[1], Ruizhi Zhou[1], Gang Zhao[2], Weijuan Zhang[1], Delong Chen[1], and Fan Liu[1(✉)]

[1] Hohai University, Nanjing, China
fanliu@hhu.edu.cn
[2] Jiangsu Institute of Water Resources and Hydropower Research, Nanjing, China

Abstract. Large-scale production recognition systems are crucial for building efficient E-commerce platforms. However, various traditional product recognition approaches are based on single-modal data input (e.g., image or text), which limits recognition performance. To tackle this issue, in this paper, we propose a Multimodal Deep Fusion Network (MDF-Net) for accurate large-scale product recognition. The MDF-Net has a two-stream late fusion architecture, with a CNN model and a bi-directional language model that respectively extract semantic latent features from multimodal inputs. Image and text features are fused via Hadamard product, then jointly generate results. Further, we investigated the integration of attention mechanism and residual connection to respectively improve the text and image representations. We conduct experiments on a large-scale multimodal E-commerce product dataset MEP-3M, which consists of three million image-text product data. MDF-Net achieves a 93.72% classification accuracy over 599 fine-grained classes. Empirical results demonstrated that the MDF-Net yields better performance than traditional approaches.

Keywords: Multimodal fusion · Product recognition · Attention mechanism · Deep learning

1 Introduction

With the rapid development and popularization of the e-commerce, the commodity management has become one of the main tasks of e-commerce platforms, deeply influencing their economic benefits. Only reasonably classifying commodities can improve the accuracy of shopping guides and the efficiency of searching for products on e-commerce platforms. Traditional Product Recognition methods [1–3] are mainly based on single-modal data. However, on existing e-commerce platforms, the information of commodities exists in multiple modalities, such as commodity texts, images, and videos. The traditional Product Recognition methods do not make full use of this information, which extremely limit its classification performance.

Multimodal Machine Learning [4] aims to integrate two or more modal information to make classification. It merges information from different modalities to obtain comprehensive features and improve classification accuracy. Ngiam et al. [5] first introduced deep learning to multimodal learning, using deep AutoEncoders to learn the shared representation features, and the experiment verified the effectiveness of the multimodal shared representation. Multimodal Machine Learning can make full use of each modal data and establish the association between different modal data.

In this paper, we propose MDF-Net: Multimodal Deep Fusion for Large-scale Product Recognition. We first introduce an Attention Mechanism in the text feature extraction model - Bi-LSTM to improve the ability of discriminating text features. We also use the deep neural network VGG-19 [6] to extract commodity image features. Then, the extracted text and image features are fused by Hadamard product to explore the internal relationship between text and image features. And a residual struction is added to enhance the image features. Subsequently, the enhanced image features are used as the initial weights of the original text features extraction model to enhance the text features. Ultimately, the enhanced text features and image features are enforced to the matrix Hadamard product to obtain the multimodal features of product. Compared with the single-modal Product Recognition method and the Multimodal Product Recognition model based on Concatenate Fusion, the proposed method has better classification effectiveness and accuracy. The main contribution of the paper can be summarized as below.

- We proposed MDF-Net, which is able to explore complementary information from multiple modalities. Experimental results show that it achieves better classification performance than traditional single-modal counterparts.
- We integrates attention mechanism to improve text representations, and used residual connection to improve image representations. Ablation experiments demonstrated the effectiveness of these modifications.

The rest of the paper is organized as follow. Section 2 reviews the related work. Section 3 elaborates on the implementation of the MDF-Net model. Section 4 presents the data collection, model evaluation, and experimental results. Section 5 finally concludes this paper.

2   Related Work

In this section, we briefly review the existing researches via Machine Learning in the field of product recognition. The approaches can be classified into two categories, Single-modal Machine Learning based Methods and Multi-modal Machine Learning based Methods, which are respectively shown below.

2.1   Single-modal Product Recognition

Traditional product classification methods are mainly based on single modal data. Common single modal data includes text data and image data of products.

The following shows a brief introduction to the Single-modal Machine Learning based Methods using text data or image data.

Text-Based Approaches. Using the titles or descriptions data to classify product is an important task in the e-commerce industry. Zhong et al. [1] proposed a Temporal Multiple-Convolutional Network (TMN), using the text titles of product for classification. They integrated Temporal Convolutional Network (TCN) model and Multiple-Convolutional Neural Network (MCNN) model to extract features from text, which achieved higher classification accuracy than that of the state-of-the-art models at that time. The Bert model [7] has further promoted the development of text classification. Zahera et al. [2] used the fine-tuned Bert model (ProBERT) to classify product into hierarchical taxonomy with product titles and descriptions. Their work achieved great prediction performance in MWPD2020 [8]. However, with the explosive growth of product images emerging in ECommerce platforms, this kind of approach shows poor performance for lacking enough visual features. The text-based product classification uses informative and intuitive data and is widely applied because of its simplicity and efficiency.

Image-Based Approaches. Product images are essential for consumers to select product. However, product images often contain noisy information, such as promotional text and product packaging information, which make image-based product classification more difficult. And how to fuse low-level features and high-level features from the product images better still remains a key task. Wazarkar et al. [9] used linear convolution to obtain core features of product images. They then combined them with the local features of product images to improve the classification effect. Considering that Attention Mechanism can capture local information, Yang et al. [3] constructed a two-level convolutional Attention network and a cluster-based grouped Attention network to fuse low-level visual features and high-level semantic features of product images. This model performs well in fine-grained product classification. Overall, compared with text-based product classification, image-based product classification often achieves poorer accuracy, since the information implied in images is more complex and difficult to extract. Nonetheless, the images sometimes involve the information that texts lacks. Hence, it is important to integrate text data and image data to extract complementary features.

2.2 Multi-modal Product Recognition

Multimodal learning aims to obtain comprehensive information from multimodal data, generally using text data and image data. However, it is challenging task to fuse multimodal data together to obtain higher accuracy. The fusing structure of the model may deeply influence the classification performance. Additionally, the traits of deep learning models can also affect the classification accuracy. Zhang et al. [10] believed that it was necessary to infer the complex relationship between visual objects for visual question-and-answer. They used a bilinear attention module as the attention for problem guidance of visual objects to complement the fine-grained fusion of visual and textual features. Misikir et al. [11] adopted multiple neural networks, including CamemBERT, FlauBERT and SE-ResNeXt-50, to learn the features from textual data and visual data. With respect to the fusing techniques, they experimented on addition fusion, concatenation fusion and average fusion. However, these adopted fusion methods are too simple and could not solve the problem of losing low-level information when extracting visual features. Although these methods obtain better experimental results than Single-modal Machine Learning based Methods, they still achieved relatively moderate accuracy and there is still much room for improvement.

In summary, the Multimodal ML based Method can make full use of each modal data of the product, which leads to higher classification accuracy. However, there still exist two problems to solve, how to extract multimodal data better and how to fuse the extracted multimodal features to obtain higher product classification accuracy. In this paper, we propose two methods to solve these problems respectively.

3   Multimodal Deep Fusion Network

The structure of the Multimodal Deep Fusion Model for Large-scale Product Recognition (MDF-Net) is shown in Fig. 1. The model includes four parts: attention-based text feature extraction network, residual image feature extraction network, multimodal fusion, and multimodal classifier. Each part is described in detail below.

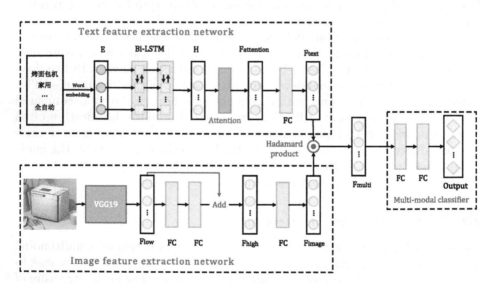

Fig. 1. The structure of the multimodal deep fusion product recognition model.

3.1 Attention-Based Bi-directional Language Model for Text Representation

We use Bi-LSTM as the backbone network for extracting features in the commodity title. Then the attention mechanism is introduced to capture semantic information in the text. The network structure is shown in Fig. 2. Our attention-based Bi-LSTM [12] model includes the input layer, embedding layer, Bi-LSTM layer, attention layer, and output layer.

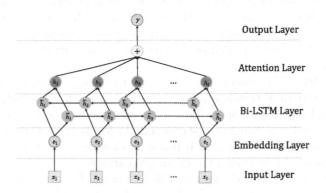

Fig. 2. The structure of Bi-LSTM model based on attention.

Firstly, word token sequences in the input layer denoted by $\{x_1, x_2, ..., x_t\}$ (t is the number of words in the text) are fed into an embedding layer that maps each word in the text to a low-dimensional space through the embedding matrix $W_{embedding}$, which is obtained by unsupervised pre-training. The output of the embedding layer is the word vector $E = \{e_1, e_2, ..., e_t\}$, where each element corresponds to a word. Then, Bi-LSTM layers perform feature extraction on the word embedding and derive $H = \{h_1, h_2, ..., h_t\}$, where h_i is represented as:

$$h_i = [\overrightarrow{h} \oplus \overleftarrow{h}]. \tag{1}$$

The $\overrightarrow{h}$ represents the historical context representation, while the $\overleftarrow{h}$ represents the future context representation, and $\oplus$ represents the concatenate operation. That is, the high-level feature H is composed of historical and future context information by concatenation. In the subsequent attention layer, we re-weight the features via attention mechanism as follows:

$$\alpha = \text{softmax}(w^T \tanh(H)) \tag{2}$$

$$F_{\text{attention}} = \tanh(H\alpha^T), \tag{3}$$

where $H \in \mathbb{R}^{d \times t}$ is the embedding extracted by the Bi-LSTM model; w represents a learnable linear projection, whose shape is $d \times 1$; the dimension of the attention map α is $1 \times t$, and $F_{\text{attention}}$ is the vector representation for classification. Finally, the output layer maps $F_{\text{attention}}$ to $F_{\text{text}} = \{f_1, f_2, ..., f_k\}$ through a fully connected layer, where k denotes the number of categories.

3.2   Residual Convolutional Neural Network for Image Representation

In this paper, we adopt VGG-19 [6] model to extract features from images. The deep network structure of VGG-19 can make the feature map broader and more suitable for large data sets. The applied VGG-19 has 19 layers, which can be divided into five groups of convolutional layers and three fully connected layers. VGG-19 also uses a 3 × 3 small convolution kernel, which can reduce the number of parameters and improve calculation efficiency. In spite of these advantages, there is a problem with this network. That is, the deep VGG-19 model is easy to lose low-level feature information when extracting image features in the transmission of information between the convolution layer and the full connection layer.

To deal with this problem and to further strengthen the complementarity of the two modal data of text and image, we introduce residual blocks to improve performance. Concatenate operation cannot complement the high-level and low-level features well. Nevertheless, the residual blocks can be used to directly transfer low-level features to high-level features so that they can reduce information loss and improve the identification of image features.

The network mainly includes the VGG-19 image feature extraction module and image feature reconstruction module based on the residual blocks. The image feature reconstruction module includes two layers of fully connected layer and addition of the skip connection.

Lastly, changing the dimension of F_{high} through a linear layer, We then obtain the final image features F_{image}.

3.3   Multimodal Fusion and Classification

In this paper, Hadamard product is applied to multimodal feature fusion. Hadamard product is a type of matrix operation between matrixes with same dimension. Suppose $A = (a_{ij})$ and $B = (b_{ij})$ are two matrixes in the same order, and the matrix $C = (c_{ij})$ is the Hadamard product of A and B, where $c_{ij} = a_{ij} \times b_{ij}$. For example, suppose $A, B \in R^{m \times n}$, then the $m \times n$ matrix shown in Eq. 4 is called the Hadamard product of matrices A and B, denoted by $A \odot B$.

$$A \odot B = \begin{bmatrix} a_{11} \cdot b_{11}, & a_{12} \cdot b_{12}, & \cdots & a_{1n} \cdot b_{1n} \\ a_{21} \cdot b_{21}, & a_{22} \cdot b_{22}, & \cdots & a_{2n} \cdot b_{2n} \\ \vdots & \vdots & \ddots & \vdots \\ a_{m1} \cdot b_{m1}, & a_{m2} \cdot b_{m2}, & \cdots & a_{mn} \cdot b_{mn} \end{bmatrix} \tag{4}$$

Compared with other traditional fusion methods, like concatenation and average fusion, the Hadamard product can mine the internal relationship between text and image. Beside, it has a smaller multimodal feature dimension than the concatenate fusion method. The parameter scale is also smaller when it is transferred to the fully connected layer.

The calculation formula of the multimodal fusion feature is shown in Eq. 5. In this case, the dimension of F_{multi} is unchanged.

$$F_{\text{multi}} = F_{\text{text}} \odot F_{\text{image}} \tag{5}$$

The multimodal classifier is composed of multiple fully connected layers and softmax activation functions. To evaluate the performance of the classification model, the cross-entropy loss function is used to optimize the model. In addition, the cross-entropy loss can also reduce the risk of gradient vanishing during stochastic gradient descent. Suppose the sample set is $\{x_1, x_2, ..., x_N\}$, the label set is $\{y_1, y_2, ..., y_K\}$, N is the total number of samples and K is the total number of labels. The cross-entropy loss function is defined as:

$$L = \frac{1}{N} \sum_{n=1}^{N} \sum_{i=1}^{K} y_i \log\left(\frac{\exp(w_i^T \phi(x_i))}{\sum_{k=1}^{K} \exp(w_k^T \phi(x_i))}\right), \tag{6}$$

where x_i is the i-th sample and w is the final linear classification layer. The y_i represents the ground-truth class lable.

4 Experiment

4.1 Experimental Setting

The MDF-Net proposed in this paper is implemented using Python, TensorFlow, and Keras. All experiments were performed using Intel Core i5-9400F CPU with 2.90 GHz, TITAN GPU. During the experiment, the batch size of each iteration is 64 and the number of epochs is 200.

In our experiments, we use MEP-3M [13] dataset, which is large-scale, hierarchical categorized, multi-modal, fine-grained, and longtailed. This dataset includes 3 million product image-text pairs of 599 categories. Each product has both image and its description text. Some image samples and the text cloud of the titles are respectively given in Fig. 3(a) and (b). The training set and the test set are divided at a ratio of 8:2. The accuracy and the precision-recall (PR) curve were used to evaluate the classification performance of each model:

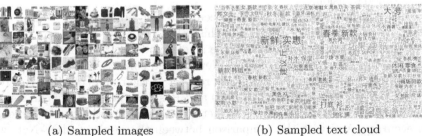

(a) Sampled images   (b) Sampled text cloud

Fig. 3. Some image examples and the text cloud of the titles in the MEP-3M dataset.

$$\text{Accuracy} = \frac{\sum_{i=1}^{N} TP_i + \sum_{i=1}^{N} TN_i}{\sum_{i=1}^{N} TP_i + \sum_{i=1}^{N} FN_i + \sum_{i=1}^{N} FP_i + \sum_{i=1}^{N} TN_i} \tag{7}$$

$$\text{Precision} = \frac{\sum_{i=1}^{N} TP_i}{\sum_{i=1}^{N} TP_i + \sum_{i=1}^{N} FP_i} \tag{8}$$

$$\text{Recall} = \frac{\sum_{i=1}^{N} TP_i}{\sum_{i=1}^{N} TP_i + \sum_{i=1}^{N} FN_i}, \tag{9}$$

where TP, FP, FN, and TN are the number of true positive, false positive, false negative, and true negative samples, respectively. The abscissa of the PR curve is Recall, and the ordinate is Precision.

4.2   Main Results

Table 1. Performance comparison between different product recognition methods

Classification type	Model	Accuracy
Text-only approaches	Attention-based Bi-LSTM	86.12%
Image-only approaches	VGG-19	74.82%
	Residual VGG-19	75.37%
Multimodal approaches	LMF [14]	89.22%
	TFN [15]	90.70%
	MDF-Net (concat)	90.69%
	MDF-Net (w/o-residual)	92.03%
	MDF-Net	**93.72%**

To verify the effectiveness of the proposed MDF-Net, we first compare the accuracy of the single-modal product recognition model and some multimodal product recognition models, such as LMF [14], TFN [15]. We further implement "MDF-Net (w/o-residual)" and "MDF-Net (concat)" to demonstrate the effectiveness of residual connection for image representation and Hadamard product for multimodal fusion.

The performance comparison between different product recognition methods are listed in Table 1. As shown in this table, the MDF-Net model proposed in this paper is more accurate than the single-mode methods and other multimodal models. The accuracy of MDF-Net reached 93.72%, achieving prominent experimental performance. Beside, with respect to the results of MDF-Net (concat), MDF-Net (w/o-residual), VGG-19 and Residual VGG-19, we can see that the residual module can make a distinct contribution to the product recognition accuracy. And with the comparison between the result of MDF-Net (w/o-residual) and MDF-Net, the Hadamard product shows great improvement of experimental performance with 1.69% increasement, which proves the effectiveness of the introduced Hadamard product.

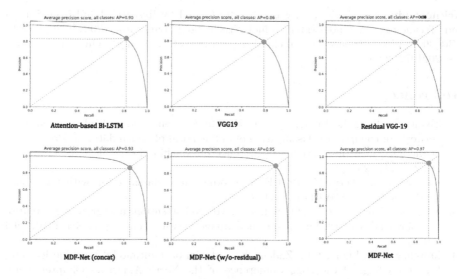

Fig. 4. PR curves. (Color figure online)

The PR curve is also used to evaluate the performance. It evaluates the model performance by comparing the value of the balance point (the red dot in the figure, where Precision = Recall) or the average precision (AP) value of different models. As shown in Fig. 4, the balance point and AP value of multi-modal model is significantly larger than that of single-modal model, and both the direct and residual MDF-Net are larger than that of MDF-Net (concat) model. In addition, compared with MDF-Net (w/o-residual), the residual MDF-Net has higher AP value and further improves the performance of Product Recognition.

The accuracy and PR curves show that the MDF-Net proposed in this paper significantly improve the accuracy and performance of product recognition. Moreover, the residual one has better classification accuracy and performance.

5   Conclusion

This paper introduces a multimodal deep fusion method for large-scale product recognition (MDF-Net). The MDF-Net uses the attention mechanism to improve text feature discrimination and introduces residual blocks to enhance image features. In addition, our multimodal model uses the Hadamard Product to explore the internal connection between the text and image features, so as to obtain better multimodal features and improve the accuracy of Product Recognition. As a result, the MDF-Net model achieves 93.72% classification accuracy, significantly improving classification performance. And the comparisons of experimental results prove the effectiveness of the introduced residula blocks and Hadamard Product.

Acknowledgment. This work was partially funded by Research Fund from Science and Technology on Underwater Vehicle Technology Laboratory(2021JCJQ-SYSJJ-LB06905), Water Science and Technology Project of Jiangsu Province under grant No. 2021072, 2021063.

References

1. Zhong, C., Jiang, L., Liang, Y., Sun, H., Ma, C.: Temporal multiple-convolutional network for commodity classification of online retail platform data. In: Proceedings of the 2020 12th International Conference on Machine Learning and Computing, pp. 236–241 (2020)
2. Zahera, H.M., Sherif, M.: ProBERT: product data classification with fine-tuning BERT model. In: MWPD@ ISWC (2020)
3. Yang, Y., Wang, X., Zhao, Q., Sui, T.: Two-level attentions and grouping attention convolutional network for fine-grained image classification. Appl. Sci. **9**(9), 1939 (2019)
4. Morency, L.P., Liang, P.P., Zadeh, A.: Tutorial on multimodal machine learning. In: Proceedings of the 2022 Conference of the North American Chapter of the Association for Computational Linguistics: Human Language Technologies: Tutorial Abstracts, Seattle, United States, pp. 33–38. Association for Computational Linguistics, July 2022
5. Ngiam, J., Khosla, A., Kim, M., Nam, J., Lee, H., Ng, A.Y.: Multimodal deep learning. In: ICML (2011)
6. Conneau, A., Schwenk, H., Barrault, L., Lecun, Y.: Very deep convolutional networks for text classification. arXiv preprint arXiv:1606.01781 (2016)
7. Devlin, J., Chang, M.W., Lee, K., Toutanova, K.: BERT: pre-training of deep bidirectional transformers for language understanding. arXiv preprint arXiv:1810.04805 (2018)
8. Zhang, Z., Bizer, C., Peeters, R., Primpeli, A.: MWPD 2020: semantic web challenge on mining the web of html-embedded product data. In: MWPD@ ISWC (2020)
9. Wazarkar, S., Keshavamurthy, B.N.: Fashion image classification using matching points with linear convolution. Multimedia Tools Appl. **77**(19), 25941–25958 (2018). https://doi.org/10.1007/s11042-018-5829-4
10. Zhang, W., Yu, J., Hu, H., Hu, H., Qin, Z.: Multimodal feature fusion by relational reasoning and attention for visual question answering. Inf. Fusion **55**, 116–126 (2020)
11. Misikir Tashu, T., Fattouh, S., Kiss, P., Horvath, T.: Multimodal e-commerce product classification using hierarchical fusion. arXiv e-prints (2022) arXiv-2207
12. Li, L., Nie, Y., Han, W., Huang, J.: A multi-attention-based bidirectional long short-term memory network for relation extraction. In: Liu, D., Xie, S., Li, Y., Zhao, D., El-Alfy, E.-S.M. (eds.) ICONIP 2017. LNCS, vol. 10638, pp. 216–227. Springer, Cham (2017). https://doi.org/10.1007/978-3-319-70139-4_22
13. Chen, D., Liu, F., Du, X., Gao, R., Xu, F.: MEP-3M: a large-scale multi-modal e-commerce products dataset
14. Liu, Z., Shen, Y., Lakshminarasimhan, V.B., Liang, P.P., Zadeh, A., Morency, L.P.: Efficient low-rank multimodal fusion with modality-specific factors. arXiv preprint arXiv:1806.00064 (2018)
15. Zadeh, A., Chen, M., Poria, S., Cambria, E., Morency, L.P.: Tensor fusion network for multimodal sentiment analysis. arXiv preprint arXiv:1707.07250 (2017)

Survey on Deep Learning Based Fusion Recognition of Multimodal Biometrics

Qiuling Yang[1](✉), Xiaoliang Chen[1], Zhaofeng He[2], and Le Chang[1]

[1] Beijing SoundAI Co., Ltd., Beijing 100084, China
[2] Beijing University of Posts and Telecommunications, Beijing 100084, China
zhaofenghe@bupt.edu.cn

Abstract. We take multimodal as a new research paradigm. This research paradigm is based on the premise that all human interactions with the outside world required the support of multimodal sensory systems. Deep learning (DL) has shown outstanding performance in detection of of iris, face, and finger vein traits from raw data and overcome many of the limitations of traditional algorithms. There is few established papers that involves multimodal biological fusion around deep learning, how to design the DL based fusion strategies, how deep learning help to relieve the problems faced by biometric systems and achieved better performance than traditional methods. This article focused on the applications of deep learning based biometric multimodal fusion. We explores recent deep learning based multimodal biometric data fusion, providing efficient fusion of multimodal biometrics to improve identification and recognition tasks. At last, we gave the potential usage and challenge.

Keyword: Deep learning · Multi-modal fusion · Biometric system · Heterogeneous data · Intermediate fusion

1 Introduction

Biometric data creates unique identifiers of individuals from the observed biological or behavioral traits for the purpose of biometric recognition of some distinguishing and reusable biometric features [1]. There are a lot of biometric systems in use today, including face recognition, fingerprint recognition, DNA recognition, gait recognition, palm print recognition, iris recognition, voice signature, shape of the periocular region, vascular or vein patterns, cardiac rhythm, and skin texture [2]. A usable biometric trait for identification or recognition in a biometric system needs the following fundamental qualities allow it to yield high accuracy and performance rates: universality (qualities per user); uniqueness (a subject's distinguishing features); permanence (its inability or unlikelihood to change over time); measurability (ease of acquisition of the biometric data sample); performance (functional and robust properties of the trait); acceptability (acceptability by the system user); and circumvention (the ability to spoof or deceive the recognition system) [3].

W. Deng et al. (Eds.): CCBR 2022, LNCS 13628, pp. 511–518, 2022.
https://doi.org/10.1007/978-3-031-20233-9_52

Systems that obtain distinctive biometric characteristic sequences from individuals are called unimodal biometric systems. While unimodality has shown powerful in biometric system, it is trained on massive, web-based datasets, in which there are many biometric applications lacking big datasets. Unimodal biometric systems are also suffered for the problems like non-universality, Lack of sensor data, etc., which pertain to its data quality, information resilience, identity overlap, and limited discriminability. There is an intuitive solving method that integrates more than two multiple biometric indicators into a concurrent system to increase accuracy in recognition, known as multimodal biometrics. Multimodal biometric systems have the advantages of minimizing the system error rate. Multimodal biometric data, depicting objects from different multiple levels with complementary or supplementary in contents, carries more information than unimodal data. By combining the evidences obtained from different levels using an effective fusion scheme, multimodal systems can improve the overall system accuracy of the biometric system. By the way, from the perspective of interaction between the human sensory system (such as vision, hearing, touch, etc.) and the external environment (such as people, machines, objects, animals, etc.), biometric multimodal paradigms are more close to the nature human interactions with the outside world. So biometric data fusion become an attractive way for related researchers (Fig. 1) [4–6].

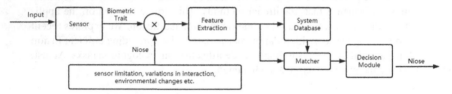

Fig. 1. Biometric System Operation. Unimodal biometric systems are suffered for the problems noise, such as sensor limitation, variations in interaction, environmental changes etc.

There is few established papers that involves multi-modal biological fusion around deep learning, how to design the DL based fusion strategies, how deep learning help to relieve the problems faced by biometric systems and achieved better performance than traditional methods. This article focused on the applications of deep learning based biometric multi-modal fusion. We explores recent deep learning based multimodal biometric data fusion, providing efficient fusion of multi-modal biometrics to improve identification and recognition tasks. At last, we gave the potential usage and challenge.

The paper is organized as follows: Sect. 2 presents neural networks which used in biometric systems; Sect. 3 surveyed existing significant deep learning based methods by using the above networks, Sect. 4 gave the challenges and future of DL multi-modal fusion. Please note that this paper is not exhaustive of all relevant articles, only some representative articles are listed.

2 Deep Learning (DL) in Biometric Systems

Most biometric systems consist of two parts: registration and identification. The registration part is responsible for capturing individual biometrics and extracting key characteristics of biometric samples, which are stored in a reference database. The recognition part is responsible for comparing the biometric samples to previously stored templates to return any matches. Traditional recognition usually require some preprocessing steps to transform the raw data into an appropriate format that fits for the later classification. Some times these steps are complex or do not work successfully with different types of biometrics. In addition, traditional methods meet many problems when come to multimodal fusion. Deep learning (DL) has shown outstanding performance in detection of of iris, face, and finger vein traits from raw data and overcome many of the limitations of traditional algorithms. It is suitable for DL to uncover underlying patterns within the data to learn multiple levels of representations via multilayer neural networks, from low level to high level. DL-based biometric models can jointly learns the feature representation process with performing classification/regression. There is a significant advantage of using DL-based biometric applications is that it also works in faces that are disguised, occluded, at turned-pose, or captured in low-illumination environments. DL played an important role in improving the ability of biometric systems. DL-based approaches achieved a milestone in face recognition tasks in 2014 and soon to other modalities as well.Development of hardware promoted the success of DL and stimulate researchers to design very deep neural networks with low cost.

There are several deep learning based models that may be implemented to fused biometric data, including convolutional neural networks (CNNs); recurrent neural networks (RNNs); autoencoders; and generative adversarial networks (GANs).

2.1 Convolution Neural Network (CNN)

The structure of CNN is comparable to the principle of the visual cortex, in which image feature representations can be learned layer by layer. An obvious benefit of CNN is that it needs less preprocessing load than other classifiers because it shares weights locally. There already have many papers that applied CNN in biometric systems. Minaee et al. proposed a iris recognition system by using a pertained VGG-Net (Visual Geometry Group, VGG) and achieved an accurate rate of 99.4% [7]. Radzi et al. used a 4-layer CNN for face recognition and got an accurate rate of 99.5% [8]. Oyedotun et al. applied a deep belief network with LeNet-5 in the diagnosis of iris nevus and got accuracy rate as high as 93.67% [9].

2.2 Recurrent Neural Network (RNN)

In recent years, many researchers start to pay attention to RNN for biometric applications. RNN is similar to a directed graph along a temporal sequence, which could exhibit both temporal and dynamic behavior. RNN has the advantages over CNN in acquiring the context of the target. RNN is spatio-temporal and is extremely complex when it is together with spatially separated measurements. Bell et al. proposed an Inside-Outside Net (ION) with RNN in detection and improved the accuracy rate from 73.9% to 77.9% [10]. Tolosana et al. designed a system based on Long Short-Term Memory (LSTM) for on-line signature verification and achieved the equal error rate (EER) of 23.75% for the best case [11].

2.3 Self-auto-encoders (Self-organizing Maps)

An autoencoder is a type of unsupervised learning and is able to learn efficient codings of unlabeled data. Autoencoder is typically used in dimensionality reduction.The applications of Self-Auto-encoders based biometrics have developed very fast and will approach the state of the art. Siddhad et al. proposed a convolutional auto-encoders based neural network architecture for palm print, palm vein, and wrist vein evaluation [12]. Sun et al. designed a Auto-encoder-based system for Electro-CardioGram (ECG)-based Identity Recognition (EIR) and improved the time efficiency that took five minutes to collect ECG data withing the identification accuracy rate of 90% [13].

2.4 Generative Adversarial Networks (GAN)

GAN has a pair of a generator (produce the target output) and a discriminator (distinguish true data from the output of the generator). GAN can create new data instances for training, providing an expanded data set for training.CAN can be used to distinguish whether two images of a face belong to the same individual. It is suitable to use GAN in in constrained or degraded sample capture conditions because GANs can resolve issues like pose or illumination. Tarek et al. proposed a biometric salting technique based on standard generative adversarial network and presented a better performance than other methods [14]. Ugot et al. designed a Convolutional Generative Adversarial Network based neural network for generating fake biometric fingerprint images [15].

3 DL Based Multi-modal Biometric Data Fusion

Deep learning based multi modal biometric fusion is a promising way to overcome the limitations of traditional, unimodal methods. Ding et al. built a deep learning framework for face recognition by using a three-layer stacked auto-encoder (SAE) for feature level fusion, which achieved accuracy rates of 99% [16]. Al-Waisy et al. designed IrisConvNet to fuse the right and left irises in the ranking-level fusion for the applicaton of user identification, which achieved recognition rate of 100% [17]. Al-Waisy et al. combined IrisConvNet and a deep belief network (DBN) for detection of the face, and left and right irises and used matching score for fusion, which achieved accuracy rates of 100% [18]. Tiong et al. proposed dual-stream convolutional neural networks based ultimodal facial biometrics and achieved a better performance than other competing networks for both recognition and verification tasks [19]. The same author designed a Multi-feature Deep Learning Network (MDLN) architecture by using facial and periocular regions and achieved better performance in the situations of variations in illumination, appearances, and pose misalignments than unimodal [20]. Gunasekaran et al. designed a local derivative ternary algorithm for feature abstracting and a weighted rank level method for fusion [21]. Gupta et al. combined three modalities viz. Face, finger, and iris by using adaptive classifier scores fusion in which conflicting belief among classifiers is resolved by adding catering dynamic environment and distinguishing between spoofing attacks and noisy inputs, and achieved the accuracy rate of 99.5% [22]. Kim et al. used several fusion methods at the score level to fuse finger vein and finger shape, such as weighted sum, weighted product, Bayesian rule, and perceptron rule [23]. Ordóñez et al. used convolutional and LSTM to create a generic deep framework for activity recognition, which achieved better performance than competing networks on the challenge dataset by 4% on average [24]. Liu et al. fused multiple finger vein images and achieved the accuracy rate of 99.53% [25]. Boucherit al. used a combination CNN to build an identification model by using finger vein traits with different qualities, which achieved the accuracy rate as high as 96.75% [26]. Jyothi et al. solved the problems of face recognition in the presence of sunglasses and scarf occlusion by using block-based mean weighted local binary patterns (MWLBP) and outperformed over other conventional techniques [27].

From the aboving examples, we can see that multimodal fusion is an effective way to exploit complementary, redundant cooperative features of different modalities with different statistical properties, sources of non-biological variation, high-dimensionality and different patterns of missing values. Multimodal deep learning can not only learn high level representations of data through simple dependencies but also be able to model nonlinear withinand cross-modality relationships. In addition, a large multi-modal biometric data are available to provide the opportunity to take advantage of this richer information. All of those made DL to be an increasing significant role in multi-modal fusion. What we concern is to reveal the key aspects in multi-modal learning with DL. We will discuss in the next section.

4 Discussion

Fusion can be divided into early, intermediate and late fusion according to when it happens in data flow. Early fusion and late fusion are usually modules integrated into deep learning modals, without effects on feature level. Heterogeneous data in intermediate fusion will transform into abstract joint feature vectors that represent higher level features and can easily be learned through DL neural networks by connecting different multi-modal features to a high level shared layer before classification. Intermediate fusion has the advantages to reduce the semantic gap and capture the correlation between heterogeneous modalities by solving the problems of feature complementarity, redundancy and cooperation between different modalities. By the way, intermediate fusion make it possible to design a gradual fusion or phased fusion in which modalities that are highly correlated fuse earlier while others fused later.

Generally, there are two main kind fusion strategies of intermediate fusion: one kind is that uni-modal input data will transform separately and joint together at the end; the other kind is that features representing latent factors will code together and follow the remain process to the end. The latter needs that uni-modals has some similarities in presentation and can simply be concatenated to a classifier or a full connecting layer. We named it as nonencoded DL multi-modal fusion.The former one is often supposed that different modalities that do not independently affect the result and there is information within modalities. We named it as encoded DL multi-modal fusion. It aggregate the elements of feature vectors from each branch and reveal more inter-modal characteristics. These two kind fusion strategies can be used separately or together.

DL multi-modal fusion can relieve some difficult situations in biometric fusion systems, such as whole modality missing, imbalance in dimensionality and limitation of small sample size.

In practice, we usually face data missing for analysis. It may become impossible in uni-modal system if the whole modality is lost. DL based multi-modal fusion method created an effective multi network to learn one modality from missing modalities by using other uni-modal input branches and task-specific output branches.

Traditional machine learning fusion approaches often require that the modalities have the same size when they are fusing. That kind problems belong to imbalance in dimensionality between modalities. Methods we often used is cutting down the dimensionality of the larger modality, which would result a significant information losing. Some researchers used nonencoded DL multi-modal fusion that integrated a smaller dimensionality of modality to the larger one. It showed that. DL based fusion can relieve the demensionality balance by adding architectural improvements.

Limitation of small sample size is more obvious for biometric systems than others. Some researchers used specific joint loss function in unsupervised learning based multi-modal fusion, which shortens the similarity of different uni-modalities within the same subjects while enlarges the distance of different modlities between different subjects.

5   Conclusion

Deep Learning shows an more significant improvement in application of multi-modal fusion than other machine learning methods. As concern from the present algorithms used today, it is easy to find out that CNN becomes more and more popular in multi-modal fusion than other methods, which we will focus on later. Attention-based fusion methods is also a promising way that gives different weights to features according to their importance. It is useful to investigate and compare performance of different fusing strategies by designing specific experiments because strategies designing might be a field- or modality- driven problem. We need to research on them in the future.

References

1. ISO/IEC: International Organization for Standardization (ISO) Information Technology, Vocabulary-Part37: Biometrics ISO/IEC 2382–37. https://www.iso.org/obp/ui/#iso:std:iso-iec:2382:-37:ed-2:v1:en:term:3.3.21 (2017)
2. Jain, A., Nandakumar, K., Ross, A.: 50 years of biometric research: accomplishments, challenges, and opportunities. Pattern Recogn. Lett. **79**, 80–105 (2016)
3. Jain, A., Flynn, P., Ross, A.: Handbook of Biometrics, 1st edn. Springer Publishing Company, Incorporated (2010)
4. Ross, A., Jain, A.: Multimodal biometrics: an overview. In: 2004 12th European Signal Processing Conference, pp. 1221–1224 (2004)
5. Zadeh, A., Chen, M., Poria, S., Cambria, E., Morency, L.-P.: Tensorfusion network for multimodal sentiment analysis. In: Proceedings of the Conference Empirical Methods Natural Language Processing, pp. 1103–1114 (2017)
6. Oloyede, M., Hancke, G.: Unimodal and multimodal biometric sensing systems: a review. IEEE Access **4**, 7532–7555 (2016)
7. Minaee, S., Abdolrashidiy, A., Wang, Y.: An experimental study of deep convolutional features for iris recognition. In: Signal Processing in Medicine and Biology Symposium (SPMB), pp. 1–6. IEEE (2016)

8. Syafeeza, A.R., Khalil-Hani, M., Imran, H., Ibrahim, M.M., Wong, Y.C.: Generalizing convolutional neural networks for pattern recognition tasks. ARPN J. Eng. Appl. Sci. **10**, 5298–5308 (2015)

9. Oyedotun, O., Khashman, A.: Iris nevus diagnosis: convolutional neural network and deep belief network. Turk. J. Electr. Eng. Comput. Sci. **25**, 1106–1115 (2017)

10. Bell, S., Zitnick, C.L., Bala, K., Girshick, R.: Inside-outside net: detecting objects in context with skip pooling and recurrent neural networks. In: 2016 IEEE Conference on Computer Vision and Pattern Recognition (CVPR), pp. 2874–2883 (2016)

11. Tolosana, R., Vera-Rodriguez, R., Fierrez, J., Ortega-Garcia, J.: DeepSign: deep on-line signature verification. IEEE Trans. Biometrics Behav. Identity Sci. **3**, 229–239 (2021)

12. Siddhad, G., Khanna, P., Ojha, A.: Cancelable biometric template generation using convolutional autoencoder. In: Singh, S.K., Roy, P., Raman, B., Nagabhushan, P. (eds.) CVIP 2020. CCIS, vol. 1376, pp. 303–314. Springer, Singapore (2021). https://doi.org/10.1007/978-981-16-1086-8_27

13. Sun, L., Zhong, Z., Qu, Z., Xiong, N.: PerAE: an effective personalized AutoEncoder for ECG-based biometric in augmented reality system. IEEE J. Biomed. Health Inform. **26**(6), 2435–2446 (2022). https://doi.org/10.1109/JBHI.2022.3145999.(2022)

14. Tarek, M., Hamouda, E., El-Metwally, S.: Unimodal-Bio-GAN: keyless biometric salting scheme based on generative adversarial network. IET Biometrics. **10**, 654–663 (2021). https://doi.org/10.1049/bme2.12034.(2021)

15. Ugot, O.-A., Yinka-Banjo, C., Misra, S.: Biometric fingerprint generation using generative adversarial networks. In: Misra, S., Kumar Tyagi, A. (eds.) Artificial Intelligence for Cyber Security: Methods, Issues and Possible Horizons or Opportunities. SCI, vol. 972, pp. 51–83. Springer, Cham (2021). https://doi.org/10.1007/978-3-030-72236-4_3

16. Ding, C., Member, S., Tao, D.: Robust face recognition via multimodal deep face representation. IEEE Trans. Multimed. **2015**(17), 2049–2058 (2015)

17. Al-Waisy, A.S., Qahwaji, R., Ipson, S., Al-Fahdawi, S., Nagem, T.A.M.: A multi-biometric iris recognition system based on a deep learning approach. Pattern Anal. Appl. **21**(3), 783–802 (2017). https://doi.org/10.1007/s10044-017-0656-1

18. Al-Waisy, A.S., Qahwaji, R., Ipson, S., Al-Fahdawi, S.: A multimodal biometrie system for personal identification based on deep learning approaches. In: Proceedings of the 2017 Seventh International Conference on Emerging Security Technologies, pp. 163–168. Canterbury, UK. 6–8 Sep 2017

19. Tiong, L., Kim, S., Ro, Y.: Multimodal facial biometrics recognition: Dual-stream convolutional neural networks with multi-feature fusion layers. Image Vis. Comput. **102**, 103977 (2020). https://doi.org/10.1016/j.imavis.2020.103977.(2020)

20. Tiong, L., Kim, S.T., Ro, Y.: Implementation of multimodal biometric recognition via multi-feature deep learning networks and feature fusion. Multimedia Tools Appl. **78**, 22743–22772 (2019). https://doi.org/10.1007/s11042-019-7618-0

21. Gunasekaran, K., Raja, J., Pitchai, R.: Deep multimodal biometric recognition using contourlet derivative weighted rank fusion with human face, fingerprint and iris images. Automatika **60**, 253–265 (2019)

22. Gupta, K., Walia, G.S., Sharma, K.: Quality based adaptive score fusion approach for multimodal biometric system. Appl. Intell. **50**(4), 1086–1099 (2019). https://doi.org/10.1007/s10489-019-01579-1

23. Kim, W., Song, J.M., Park, K.R.: Multimodal biometric recognition based on convolutional neural network by the fusion of finger-vein and finger shape using near-infrared (NIR) camera sensor. Sensors **18**, 2296 (2018)

24. Ordóñez, F.J., Roggen, D.: Deep convolutional and LSTM recurrent neural networks for multimodal wearable activity recognition. Sensors **16**(1), 115 (2016)

25. Liu, W., Li, W., Sun, L., Zhang, L., Chen, P.: Finger vein recognition based on deep learning. In: Proceedings of the 2017 12th IEEE Conference on Industrial Electronics and Applications, pp. 205–210. Siem Reap, Cambodia, 18–20 June 2017
26. Boucherit, I., Zmirli, M.O., Hentabli, H., Rosdi, B.A.: Finger vein identification using deeply-fused convolutional neural network. J. King Saud Univ. Comput. Inf. Sci. **34**, 646–656 (2020)
27. Jyothi, Ch., Ramanjaneyulu, K.: IOT-Based occlusion invariant face recognition system. In: Computer Communication, Networking and IoT. Springer, Singapore (2021). https://doi.org/10.1007/978-981-16-0980-0_39

Synthesizing Talking Face Videos with a Spatial Attention Mechanism

Ting Wang[1,2], Chaoyong Zhou[2], and Shiqi Yu[1(✉)]

[1] Department of Computer Science and Engineering, Southern University of Science and Technology, Shenzhen 518055, China
yusq@sustech.edu.cn
[2] Ping An Technology, Shenzhen, China

Abstract. Recently, talking face generation has drawn considerable attention of researchers due to its wide applications. The lip synchronization accuracy and visual quality of the generated target speaker are very crucial for synthesizing photo-realistic talking face videos. Prior methods usually obtained unnatural and incongruous results. Or the generated ones comparatively has high fidelity, but only for a specific target speaker. In this paper, we propose a novel adversarial learning framework for talking face generation of arbitrary target speakers. To sufficiently provide visual information about the lip region in the video synthesis process, we introduce a spatial attention mechanism enabling our model to pay more attention to the lip region construction. In addition, we employ a content loss and a total variation regularization for our objective function in order to reduce lip shaking and artifacts in the deformed regions. Extensive experiments demonstrate that our method outperforms other representative approaches.

Keywords: Talking face generation · Spatial attention mechanism · Lip synchronization

1 Introduction

Talking face generation, i.e., synthesizing an audio-synchronized video of a target speaker driven by arbitrary audio inputs, is of great value to various visual-audio applications, such as digital human animation and visual dubbing. Accurate lip synchronization and high visual quality (vivid and shaking-free) are two main challenges because humans are susceptible to any audio-video synchronization and facial artifacts.

To generate coherent lip motions with the input audio, previous works aimed at improving auditory and visual representations by a simple encoder-decoder structure. Jamaludin *et al.* [7] mapped a fusion of audio input and inference video frames to target frames by disentangling audio and identity features with two encoders. Some works adopted the implicit 3D scene representation of Neural Radiance Fields (NeRF) [9] to generate high-quality talking faces. However, those approaches are highly dependent on the language type of the training set or need to train different specific models for different target identities. In addition, some speaker-arbitrary methods [16,17] led to dynamic and unconstrained talking face videos without any additional speaker-specific training data, while their results suffered terrible lip synchronization. Because they ignored the spatial information extraction of the lip region during the lip reconstruction.

For those reasons, we propose an adversarial learning framework of spatial lip synchronization with an attention mechanism. The framework is divided into two parts: Attention Based Generator Network and Discriminator Network. In the Attention Based Generator Network, to cope with the problem that the spatial position information is easily ignored in the lip reconstruction process, we introduce a spatial attention module into each block of the face encoder and face decoder. By adopting average-pooling and max-pooling descriptors, information space regions are effectively highlighted so that the generator can achieve more efficient space feature selection. Furthermore, these spatial attention modules force the network to pay more attention to the lip region in the spatial dimension for fine-grained lip shape correction. Besides, we observe that there are some lip-shaking phenomena in prior works. Therefore we subtly employ a content loss and a total variation regularization in our objective function to enhance the visual quality of generated videos.

The main contribution points are summarized as follows:

(1) The proposed method results in lip synchronization for arbitrary target speakers with arbitrary driving speeches.

(2) We introduce a spatial attention module and a meticulous objective function into our framework, which can achieve higher lip synchronization accuracy and better visual quality than typical speaker-arbitrary methods.

(3) Extensive experiments and ablation studies on LRW [3], LRS2 [1] and LRS3 [2] datasets are conducted to illustrate the effectiveness and superiority of our method.

2   Related Works

2.1   Talking Face Generation

Talking face generation methods can mainly be grouped into two categories: speaker-dependent methods and speaker-arbitrary methods. For a given new speaker, speaker-dependent methods always need to retrain part or full of their models to fit each speaker's specific attributes, such as personalized lip movements and micro-expressions when speaking. Most speaker-dependent methods [5,11,14] synthesized high fidelity talking face videos by 3D face models. Suwajanakorn et al. [11] adopted a pre-built 3D face model and then drove the model by learning a sequence to sequence mapping. The weakness of this method is the cost of 3D model construction. Guo et al. [5] and Yao et al. [14] conducted conditional Neural Radiance Fields to render high-fidelity audio-driven facial videos, while still needing to train different models for different target speakers.

To generate natural talking faces of arbitrary person identities, many researchers tried to build a generic model for different target subjects. By utilizing intermediate representation, Zhou *et al.* [17] separately predicted speech content landmarks and speaker identity landmarks and further applied a speaker-aware animation model to predict spontaneous head poses alongside the audio. In [10], the ideology of introducing a pre-trained lip synchronization discriminator brought a new inspiration to further improve lip synchronization accuracy. Nevertheless, those methods yet do not pay enough attention to the extraction of spatial information in the lip region, so that the performance of their generated lip synchronization is not good enough.

2.2   Attention Mechanism

Some researchers have found that attention plays a significant role in the human visual system. When glancing at an unfamiliar visual target, humans used to pay more attention to the details of the target and ignore irrelevant information, which can greatly improve the efficiency and accuracy of capturing visual structure and useful information. Woo *et al.* [12] proposed the convolutional block attention module (CBAM), a plug-and-play module that can seamlessly embed into CNNs. In CBAM, the spatial attention mechanism generates a spatial attention map using the inter-spatial relationship of features to improve the representative ability of the whole network.

3   Lip-Synced Talking Face Generation with Spatial Attention

The outline of the proposed method is shown in Fig. 1. Our model includes two branches: (1) **Attention Based Generator Network**, which consists of two encoders (Face Encoder and Speech Encoder) and one decoder (Face Decoder), where the Face Encoder and Face Decoder are embedded with a spatial attention module respectively; (2) **Discriminator Network**, which is designed for checking audio-lip synchronization and enhancing visual quality.

3.1   Attention Based Generator Network

As described in [10], the face reconstruction loss is usually computed for the whole image while the reconstruction lecture belonging to the lip region is less than 4% of the entire reconstruction process. Therefore, we design a generator network G_{Attn} with embedded spatial attention modules for lip reconstruction. Specifically, G_{Attn} contains three parts, namely Speech Encoder, Face Encoder and Face Decoder, where the Face Encoder and Face Decoder are embedded with an attention module respectively.

Speech Encoder. The Speech Encoder is composed of a stack of convolution layers. For a source speech segment, the Speech Encoder takes an MFCC heatmap and outputs the corresponding audio feature f_a.

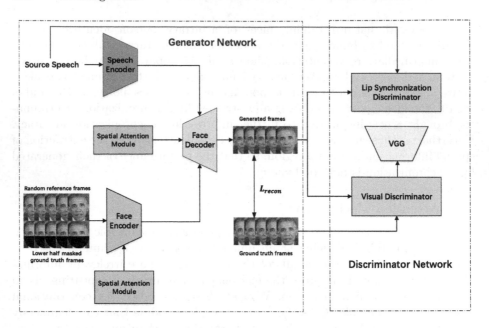

Fig. 1. The architecture of our proposed method.

Face Encoder. We send five random sequential reference frames that are con-catenated with corresponding pose-priors (target ground truth faces with lower-half masked) along the channel axis to the Face Encoder as input. Then the Face Encoder which is composed of a series of residual convolutional layers extracts the face identity feature f_i. These pose-priors are significant because they can provide the network with the target pose information of the ground-truth but nothing about the ground truth lip shape and guide the network to generate a suitable lower half mouth region that fits the upper half pose, reducing artifacts when pasting to the real videos during the inference. It should be noted that in G_{Attn}, the lower half of the face region rather than the lower half of the ground truth frame is masked, which can generate the lip region with higher fidelity.

We consider employing the attention mechanism in our generator network, to improve the feature expression of lip regions on the feature map, which emphasizes the interest area and suppresses the irrelevant area in a dynami-cally weighted way. By the attention mechanism, a set of weight coefficients that are learned autonomously by our generator network. In the first, we utilize the spatial attention module from CBAM [12] in each block of the Face Encoder to enable the generator network to focus more on extracting the effective features that correspond to lip regions while filtering redundant feature information in other regions during the training process.

The architecture of our introduced spatial attention module is shown in Fig. 2. For the given feature map F, firstly we adopt the operations of average-pooling and max-pooling along the channel axis on the feature map F. The employ of

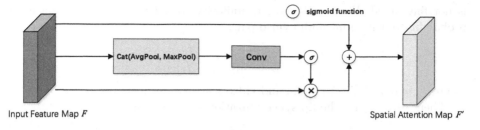

Fig. 2. The architecture of spatial attention module.

pooling descriptors aims at making informative regions stand out. And then the two feature maps with different information are concatenated. After concatenation, a 7×7 (or 3×3) convolution with a larger receptive field and a sigmoid layer are applied for feature fusion to generate a spatial attention map M_s. Finally, we can get an attention map F'. The following formula can express the calculation process:

$$M_s = \sigma(f^{7*7}(concat(AvgPool(F), MaxPool(F))))$$ (1)

$$F' = M_s \bigotimes F + F$$ (2)

where $concat$ denotes a concatenation operation, σ denotes the sigmoid function, f^{7*7} represents a convolution operation with the filter size of 7×7 and $\bigotimes$ means the element-wise multiplication.

Face Decoder. The Face Decoder consists of a stack of residual blocks with deconvolutional layers for upsampling. Similarly, we embed the spatial attention module into each block of the Face Decoder.

For G_{Attn}, we use L_1 reconstruction loss:

$$L_{recon} = \frac{1}{N} \sum_{i=1}^{N} ||L_g - L_{gt}||_1$$ (3)

where L_g and L_{gt} represent generated frames and ground-truth frames, respectively. N denotes the number of generated frames.

3.2 Discriminator Network

Lip Synchronization Discriminator. We adopt a modified SyncNet [4] as a pre-trained lip synchronization discriminator D_{sync} to discriminate the synchronization between audio and video by randomly sampling an audio sequence that is either synchronous or asynchronous. We input five contiguous video frames at a time and an audio segment corresponding to the frame sequence to D_{sync}. It should be particularly emphasized that the lip synchronization discriminator's parameters are frozen during the training process of G_{Attn}, that is D_{sync}

is not fine-tuned. We use the cosine-similarity to indicate the synchronization probability of the input audio-video pair:

$$P_{sync} = max(\frac{f_a \cdot f_v}{||f_a||_2 \cdot ||f_v||_2, \epsilon}) \tag{4}$$

where f_a and f_v indicate audio and video features, respectively.

Then we compute the lip synchronization loss L_{sync} as:

$$L_{sync} = \frac{1}{N} \sum_{i=1}^{N} -log P_{sync}^i \tag{5}$$

Visual Discriminator. As a pixel-level loss, single L_1 reconstruction loss can result in blurry images and slight artifacts in the deformed regions, so we additionally train a visual quality discriminator D_{visual} to maximize the objective function L_{disc} as follows:

$$L_{visual} = \mathbb{E}_{X \sim L_g}[log(1 - D(x))] \tag{6}$$

$$L_{disc} = \mathbb{E}_{X \sim L_{gt}}[log(1 - D(x))] + \mathbb{E}_{X \sim L_g}[log(D(x))] \tag{7}$$

D_{visual} only penalizes unrealistic face generations without any judgement of lip synchronization. Similarly, D_{visual} also consists of a stack of convolutional blocks.

3.3 Total Loss

Besides above losses, we also adopt two loss functions: the content loss L_C and the total variation regularization l_{TV} [8]. L_C is similar to the perceptual loss [13] that depends on a pre-trained VGG network. It is calculated as:

$$L_C = \min_{G_{Attn}} \mathbb{E}_X(\sum_{i=0}^{T} ||D_{visual}^i(X) - D_{visual}^i(G_{Attn}(\widetilde{X}))||_2) \tag{8}$$

where T is the total number of intermediate layers used for feature extraction and $D^i(X)$ is the extracted feature at the i-th layer of D_{visual}. In order to reduce the phenomena of shaking in the lip region of the generated video, we use l_{TV} which relies only on low-level pixel information to encourage spatial smoothness in the output frames. In the pixel discrete domain, l_{TV} is calculated as:

$$l_{TV} = \sum_{i,j}((x_{i,j+1} - x_{i,j})^2 + (x_{i+1,j} - x_{i,j})^2) \tag{9}$$

where x means each pixel value in the generated image and i and j correspond to the serial number of row and column. We combine the above terms, so the final objective function is as follows:

$$L = L_{sync} + L_{visual} + \lambda_1 L_{recon} + \lambda_2 L_C + \lambda_3 l_{TV} \tag{10}$$

In our experiments, we empirically set λ_1, λ_2 and λ_3 to 100, 0.05 and 50.

4   Experiment

In this section, we conduct a number of experiments based on the proposed method on two general metrics, *i.e.* lip synchronization accuracy and visual quality for the task of talking face generation. Considering the generalizability of the model, we compare our method with some state-of-the-art speaker-arbitrary methods that have published their training codes on several datasets: LRS2 [1], LRW [3] and LRS3 [2]. Referring to the experimental setup in Wav2lip [10], we also train the proposed model on the LRS2 dataset and evaluate it on the LRS2, LRW and LRS3 datasets. Then we discuss the advantages of our approach through some ablation studies.

4.1   Experimental Settings

Evaluate Metrics. We conduct quantitative evaluations on several metrics that have been wildly used in the field of talking face generation. For measuring the quality of the generated faces rather than the visual quality of the whole images, we employ the FID (Fréchet Inception Distance) [6]. FID is defined as:

$$F(gt, g) = ||\mu_{gt} - \mu_g||^2 + trace(\sigma_{gt} + \sigma_g - 2(\sigma_{gt}\sigma_g)^{\frac{1}{2}})) \tag{11}$$

where gt is the ground-truth data, g is the generated data, and μ_{gt}, μ_g, σ_{gt}, σ_g are the means and covariance matrices of ground-truth data distribution and generated data distribution, respectively. Lower FID means the quality of the generated image is better.

Additionally, we utilize the LSE-D (Lip Sync Error-Distance) and LSE-C (Lip Sync Error-Confidence) to evaluate the accuracy of lip synchronization. LSE-D and LSE-C proposed by [10] are a distance between the lip and audio representations (lower the better) and an average confidence score in terms of audio-video correlation (higher the better).

Implementation Details. We crop original video frames to size 96×96 at 25 FPS and process audio to mel-spectrogram of size 16×80, where the initial face detection model is S3FD [15]. With the same experimental setup as Wav2lip, we firstly pre-train SyncNet with a batch size of 64 and a learning rate of 1×10^{-4} with the Adam optimizer. Then we train G_{Attn} and D_{visual} with the batch size of 80, and the initial learning rate is set to 1×10^{-4} and 2×10^{-5}, respectively. The maximum training epochs is 500 in all experiments. And all training processes are implemented by PyTorch on a single NVIDIA Tesla V100 GPU with 16 GB memory.

4.2   Results

Quantitative Results. We compare our approach with three typical speaker-arbitrary methods, *i.e.*, MakeItTalk [17] and Wav2lip [10]. The samples of each method are generated using their released codes with the same reference audio and video. Table 1 shows the quantitative results on LRW, LRS2 and LRS3 test sets. It can be seen that our method achieves the best performance under LSE-C and LSE-D on LRW, LRS2 and LRS3. In terms of FID, we also clearly outperform other methods on LRW, LRS2 and LRS3. The above quantitative results directly demonstrate the effectiveness of our method in improving both lip synchronization performance and visual quality.

Table 1. The quantitative results on LRW, LRS2 and LRS3. The best results are in **bold**.

Method	LRW			LRS2			LRS3		
	LSE-D ↓	LSE-C ↑	FID ↓	LSE-D ↓	LSE-C ↑	FID ↓	LSE-D ↓	LSE-C ↑	FID ↓
MakeItTalk	9.642	3.754	4.135	9.771	4.220	5.976	10.194	3.548	6.010
Wav2lip	8.673	5.657	3.455	7.698	6.142	5.126	8.848	5.423	5.093
Ours	**8.331**	**5.732**	**2.740**	**7.094**	**6.663**	**4.580**	**8.712**	**5.660**	**4.745**
Real videos	6.736	7.838	–	7.012	6.931	–	6.956	7.592	–

Qualitative Results. We select a short video from the training set of [11] as the reference source video and specify another different piece of audio as the driving audio. The results are in Fig. 3. The top rows are the reference source video frames from [11]. MakeItTalk [17] can generate eye blinks while the mouth shapes are not accurate, which are marked with boxes. Wav2lip [10] achieves suitable lip motion, but some conspicuous artifacts exist between the speaker's neck edge and collar. The comparisons show that our method can synthesize more photo-realistic results. For example, the motion of our generated lips can match the driving audio better. The lip shapes are more natural and the details in the tooth regions are more realistic and delicate than other methods.

4.3 Ablation Study

To evaluate the effectiveness of the spatial attention module, the content loss L_C and the total variation regularization l_{TV} in our framework, we present an ablation study on LRS2 test set. We set up four ablated models: (1) remove spatial attention module from the generator (w/o spatial attention), (2) remove the content loss L_C (w/o L_C), (3) remove the total variation regularization l_{TV} and (4) our full model (full). The results are shown in Table 2. We can see that the effects of these components on synthesizing talking faces have been validated, and our full model obtain the best results in all three metrics.

5   Conclusion and Future Work

In this paper, we propose a new framework for talking face generation. Particularly, we embed a spatial attention module into the generator to focus on

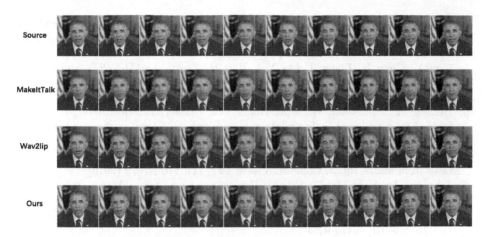

Fig. 3. The qualitative comparison results.

Table 2. The ablation study results on LRS2. The best results are in **bold**.

Method	LSE-D ↓	LSE-C ↑	FID ↓
w/o spatial attention	7.735	6.024	4.672
w/o L_C	7.151	6.563	4.897
w/o l_{TV}	7.141	6.570	4.702
Full	**7.094**	**6.663**	**4.580**

learning visual information of the emphasized lip region and introduce an objective function specifically for visual quality. A series of comparative experiments and ablation studies on multiple datasets demonstrate that our method can generate talking face videos with accurate lip synchronization and high visual quality.

With the development of digital virtual human technology, the customized requirements for talking face generation are rapidly increasing. Our method currently can not support free control of head pose. We will try to generate more personalized face attributes such as expressions and eye blinks, and explore how to further improve our introduced attention mechanism to synthesize more realistic talking face videos.

References

1. Afouras, T., Chung, J.S., Senior, A., Vinyals, O., Zisserman, A.: Deep audio-visual speech recognition. IEEE Trans. Pattern Anal. Mach. Intell. (2018)
2. Afouras, T., Chung, J.S., Zisserman, A.: LRS3-TED: a large-scale dataset for visual speech recognition. arXiv preprint arXiv:1809.00496 (2018)
3. Chung, J.S., Zisserman, A.: Lip reading in the wild. In: Lai, S.-H., Lepetit, V., Nishino, K., Sato, Y. (eds.) ACCV 2016. LNCS, vol. 10112, pp. 87–103. Springer, Cham (2017). https://doi.org/10.1007/978-3-319-54184-6_6

4. Chung, J.S., Zisserman, A.: Out of time: automated lip sync in the wild. In: Chen, C.-S., Lu, J., Ma, K.-K. (eds.) ACCV 2016. LNCS, vol. 10117, pp. 251–263. Springer, Cham (2017). https://doi.org/10.1007/978-3-319-54427-4_19

5. Guo, Y., Chen, K., Liang, S., Liu, Y.J., Bao, H., Zhang, J.: AD-NeRF: Audio driven neural radiance fields for talking head synthesis. In: Proceedings of the IEEE/CVF International Conference on Computer Vision, pp. 5784–5794 (2021)

6. Heusel, M., Ramsauer, H., Unterthiner, T., Nessler, B., Hochreiter, S.: GANs trained by a two time-scale update rule converge to a local nash equilibrium. In: Advances in Neural Information Processing Systems 30 (2017)

7. Jamaludin, A., Chung, J.S., Zisserman, A.: You said that?: Synthesising talking faces from audio. Int. J. Comput. Vision **127**(11), 1767–1779 (2019)

8. Johnson, J., Alahi, A., Fei-Fei, L.: Perceptual losses for real-time style transfer and super-resolution. In: Leibe, B., Matas, J., Sebe, N., Welling, M. (eds.) ECCV 2016. LNCS, vol. 9906, pp. 694–711. Springer, Cham (2016). https://doi.org/10.1007/978-3-319-46475-6_43

9. Mildenhall, B., Srinivasan, P.P., Tancik, M., Barron, J.T., Ramamoorthi, R., Ng, R.: NeRF: representing scenes as neural radiance fields for view synthesis. In: Vedaldi, A., Bischof, H., Brox, T., Frahm, J.-M. (eds.) ECCV 2020. LNCS, vol. 12346, pp. 405–421. Springer, Cham (2020). https://doi.org/10.1007/978-3-030-58452-8_24

10. Prajwal, K., Mukhopadhyay, R., Namboodiri, V.P., Jawahar, C.: A lip sync expert is all you need for speech to lip generation in the wild. In: Proceedings of the 28th ACM International Conference on Multimedia, pp. 484–492 (2020)

11. Suwajanakorn, S., Seitz, S.M., Kemelmacher-Shlizerman, I.: Synthesizing Obama: learning lip sync from audio. ACM Trans. Graph. (ToG) **36**(4), 1–13 (2017)

12. Woo, S., Park, J., Lee, J.-Y., Kweon, I.S.: CBAM: convolutional block attention module. In: Ferrari, V., Hebert, M., Sminchisescu, C., Weiss, Y. (eds.) ECCV 2018. LNCS, vol. 11211, pp. 3–19. Springer, Cham (2018). https://doi.org/10.1007/978-3-030-01234-2_1

13. Yang, T., Ren, P., Xie, X., Zhang, L.: GAN prior embedded network for blind face restoration in the wild. In: Proceedings of the IEEE/CVF Conference on Computer Vision and Pattern Recognition, pp. 672–681 (2021)

14. Yao, S., Zhong, R., Yan, Y., Zhai, G., Yang, X.: DFA-NERF: personalized talking head generation via disentangled face attributes neural rendering. arXiv preprint arXiv:2201.00791 (2022)

15. Zhang, S., Zhu, X., Lei, Z., Shi, H., Wang, X., Li, S.Z.: S3FD: single shot scale-invariant face detector. In: Proceedings of the IEEE International Conference on Computer Vision, pp. 192–201 (2017)

16. Zhou, H., Sun, Y., Wu, W., Loy, C.C., Wang, X., Liu, Z.: Pose-controllable talking face generation by implicitly modularized audio-visual representation. In: Proceedings of the IEEE/CVF Conference on Computer Vision and Pattern Recognition, pp. 4176–4186 (2021)

17. Zhou, Y., Han, X., Shechtman, E., Echevarria, J., Kalogerakis, E., Li, D.: MakeltTalk: speaker-aware talking-head animation. ACM Trans. Graph. (TOG) **39**(6), 1–15 (2020)

Quality Evaluation and Enhancement
of Biometric Signals

Blind Perceptual Quality Assessment for Single Image Motion Deblurring

CongLi Li, Chao Xu, ChaoYi Chen, ChengJun Xu, and Zhe Wei[✉]

PLA Army Academy of Artillery and Air Defense, 451, HuangShan Road, Hefei, AnHui, China
mrweichengjin@163.com

Abstract. Single image deblurring is a typical ill-posed problem. Although a lot of effective algorithms have been proposed, there is a lack of blind evaluation metrics for the perceptual quality of deblurred images. In this paper, we introduce a new, low-cost and lightweight dataset, called Deblurred image Quality Assessment (DeblurQA). Next, we design an extendable model named DeBlurred Quality Assessment NETwork (DBQA-NET) based on multi-resolution deep feature aggregation, and train it by a two-stage training method of classification combined with quality prediction, along with a joint loss function of ranking and regression. Finally, we demonstrate the superiority of the method and show that it can assist the existing deblurring algorithms: in the hyperparameter selection experiment, it can find the best and worst results that match human perception; when applied to the training of deep-learning-based methods, it can significantly improve the abnormal results. The model, code and the dataset are available at https://github.com/weidelongdongqiang/deblurQA/tree/IQA.

Keywords: Blind image quality assessment · Image deblurring · Deblurred dataset · Multi-resolution feature · Joint loss function · Two-stage training

1 Introduction

Image deblurring, which estimates the pristine sharp image from a single blur image, has become an active topic in low-level computer vision [1–3]. Most literatures like to use the full reference assessment methods (FRIQA), such as PSNR and SSIM, to illustrate their superiority. However, since reference images are not available in practice, it is impractical to automatically adjust algorithm parameters online. Therefore, it is necessary to design an objective and accurate blind image quality assessment (BIQA) metric for deblurring.

Although BIQAs [4–8] have made a lot of progress, the existing methods cannot be applied directly to deblurred images due to following limitations: 1) The commonly considered distortion types are far from enough; 2) The distortions in many classic IQA datasets are artificially simulated and independent, which are

© The Author(s), under exclusive license to Springer Nature Switzerland AG 2022
W. Deng et al. (Eds.): CCBR 2022, LNCS 13628, pp. 531–540, 2022.
https://doi.org/10.1007/978-3-031-20233-9_54

somewhat different from the actual distortions; 3) Although recently proposed new datasets possess more actual distortions, they do not contain enough data for image post-processing, especially deblurred images.

To this end, we propose a dataset DeblurQA using the results of multiple image deblurring methods, and introduce a novel BIQA model with multi-resolution deep feature aggregation for the post-processing perceptual quality evaluation (Fig. 1). We introduce two-stage training and a joint loss function to realize the effective measurement of deblurring quality without MOS. Our contributions include:

- A lightweight, low-cost, open image dataset, DeblurQA, consisting of 1418 deblurred images processed by different methods and parameters. To replace heavy manual scoring, pseudo-MOS values are used for supervised learning. As a result, our model successfully learns distortion features with the limited samples.
- A trainable, differentiable and extendable blind deblurring assessment model. After constructing a multi-resolution CNN model DBQA-NET, we train it with two-stage training techniques and a novel joint loss function, and finally get a new evaluator which is more in line with human perception.
- A series of important experiments including quality ranking, hyperparameter selection and optimization experiments. From these, we show the good stability and monotonicity of the proposed method, as well as the potential for the hyperparameter selection and the optimization of deblurring methods.

Fig. 1. 6 deblurred images with low quality to high. The scores predicted by DBQA-NET are 54.8598, 57.4768, 60.9279, 63.5087, 76.8988 and 81.8026 respectively, while by ILNIQE [4] are 40.5506, 57.0895, 33.9321, 41.3864, 36.5058 and 26.9327; and by SPAQ (MTA) [5] are 42.7712, 40.6773, 40.4530, 43.6014, 47.2847 and 51.5291.

2   Method

Inspired by previous work, we first establish a special dataset DeblurQA, then construct the DBQA-NET, and train it with novel loss function and learning strategies.

2.1   Dataset

The distortion caused by blurring is diverse and compound. It is difficult to define the type and measure the degree like classical datasets. Instead, we obtain diversified distortion samples by different deblurring methods and parameters.

Because the presupposition of each deblurring method is different, the results will deviate from the real world to different degrees, showing different distortion types. In order to reflect these distortions more comprehensively, we first screen pristine images from GoPro, TID2013 and Waterloo and get 142 in total, including people, animals, plants, vehicles, buildings, instructions, etc. (Fig. 2).

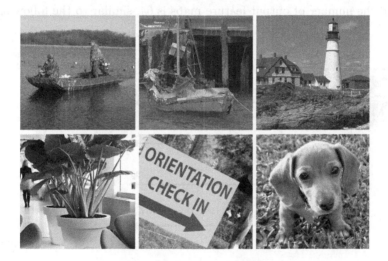

Fig. 2. Examples of the scenarios included in the proposed DeblurQA.

The motion blur generating algorithm [2] can produce a mixture of random motion blur and Gaussian blur, thus we also use it to generate blurred samples. 6 representative methods [1–3,9–11] are selected to do deblurring, including optimization-based methods, end-to-end methods, and CNN-based methods that require kernel estimation. In addition, we fine-tune the kernel size for the optimization-based methods, and obtain a group of 10 blurred images for each blurred sample. There are 2 abnormal cases, so a total of 1418 distorted images are obtained.

Manual scoring of images is time-consuming and expensive. [12] introduces a method of using the output of a supervised learning model as pseudo-labels.

Due to the constraints of conditions, given the good approximation of human perception by FR metrics, we use DISTS [13] to evaluate each distorted image, then map the score by Eq. 1 as the pseudo-MOS (pMOS) value, following [14].

$$pMOS = 100 \times \frac{maxD - DISTS(x_{ref}, x)}{maxD - minD}. \tag{1}$$

Where x, x_{ref}, $minD$ and $maxD$ denote the distorted image, the corresponding reference image, and the minimum and maximum of the $DISTS$ values in the imageset. We name the newly created dataset DeblurQA. Although no subjective scoring is used, the experimental results presented later indirectly demonstrate that this is an inexpensive and efficient alternative.

2.2 Model

Considering that image distortions may bring different changes at different CNN levels, the DBQA-NET with multi-resolution deep feature aggregation is constructed as shown in Fig. 3. Conv3-64 indicates that the convolution kernel size is 3 and the number of output feature maps is 64, similar to the following.

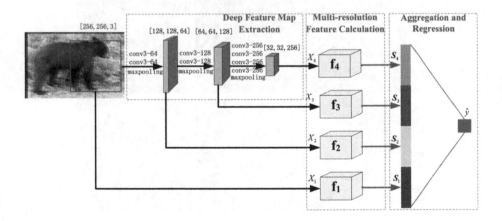

Fig. 3. The structure of DBQA-NET

The model consists of 3 parts. In Deep Feature Map Extraction, when a fixed-size image block X enters into the module, through continuous convolution-pooling resolution reduction operation, the expression of feature map $X_1 \sim X_4$ from shallow to deep is obtained. In order to reduce the number of trainable parameters, we use the first 3 layers of VGG19 pretrained on ImageNet (until conv8).

Although we have obtained spatially related feature maps, they are different in scale and quantity. Therefore, each group of feature maps needs to go through a Multi-resolution Feature Calculation to obtain their own feature vectors $S_1 \sim S_4$. We name these network branches f_k, whose function is to output vectors with the same dimension for each X_k. It is worth pointing out that the above two modules can be replaced and extended.

Finally, these feature vectors are mapped to the score or category in Aggregation and Regression. Due to space, more details are given in the supplementary material, which has been uploaded to the link mentioned in the abstract.

2.3   Loss Functions and Training

During training, the Deep Feature Map Extraction module remains unchanged. In order to better drive the model to learn distortion features, and to avoiding overfitting, we divide the training process into two stages. In stage 1, we regard the pristine images as positive examples and the deblurred images as negative examples for classification training. To avoid sample imbalance, we oversample the pristine images by 10 times. Let the label be y and the training batch size be m, the loss function in stage 1 is expressed as

$$l_1 = -\frac{1}{m} \sum_m [y \log \hat{y} + (1 - y) \log(1 - \hat{y})]. \tag{2}$$

After stage 1, we keep the convolutional layers unchanged and reset the parameters of the fully connected layer. BIQAs usually adopt L1 or Huber loss function for regression training, while ranking learning can better assist training and make the model more sensitive to image quality differences. Suppose 2 deblurred images and their pMOS values (x_1, y_1) and (x_2, y_2), assume $y_1 > y_2$, when the order predicted by the model $\hat{y}_1 < \hat{y}_2$, then penalty is given. Ranking loss can be divided into hard margin [15] and soft margin [16].

Here we choose the former, which makes the image quality sequence pairs uniformly distributed at a certain interval

$$l_H = \max(0, \hat{y}_2 - \hat{y}_1 + \delta). \tag{3}$$

Where positive δ is the hard margin. Together with the regression loss, our joint loss function can be expressed as

$$l_2 = [\frac{L_{smooth}(y_1, \hat{y}_1) + L_{smooth}(y_2, \hat{y}_2)}{2}] + \lambda_1 l_H + \lambda_2 \sum |w|. \tag{4}$$

Where $L_{smooth}(\bullet)$ represents Huber loss

$$L_{smooth}(y, \hat{y}) = \begin{cases} 0.5(y - \hat{y})^2. & \text{if } |y - f(x)| < 1 \\ |y - \hat{y}| - 0.5. & \text{otherwise} \end{cases} \tag{5}$$

The third term of Eq. 4 represents the regularization term, which is the sum of weights of all trainable layers. λ_1 and λ_2 are the weighting coefficients of the ranking and the regularization term, respectively.

3 Experiment

We randomly select 85% scenes as the training set and the rest as the validation set. In stage 1, we set the batch size to 32, verify once each round, and stop when the accuracy rate does not change significantly.

In stage 2, due to the ranking loss, we use the model as a siamese network, randomly select 2 samples each time, and then calculate the loss function. During training, we perform random cropping and flipping on the training data. For each set of hyperparameters, we train the model with 20,000 steps, and compute SRCC on the validation set. Through grid search, we obtain the optimal $\lambda_1 = 0.7$, $\lambda_2 = 5 \times 10^{-6}$ and $\delta = 0.06$.

It is noted that the optimal margin is approximately the ratio of the dynamic range of pMOS to the number of training samples, indicating that to force the uniform partition of the model response to samples is helpful for learning the pMOS values.

3.1 Quality Ranking

Due to the lack of relevant annotated datasets at present, we cannot use SRCC, PLCC and other indicators to illustrate DBQA-NET performance.

Considering that a good assessment metric should have monotonic response to continuous quality changes, we use another way to prove it. Therefore, we randomly select 42 pristine images from COCO, and process them as Sect. 3.1 using method [17–20] with different parameters. For every blur image, we get 6 deblurred results. Then, 3 human observers rank the image quality of each scene. We discard the results that are inconsistent with each other and end up with a quality order for 35 scenarios. Table 1 shows the proportion of all sorted pairs that DBQA-NET agrees with observers. For comparison, we also show the results of ILNIQE [4], BIBLE [6], SPAQ (MT-A and MT-S) [5], DBCNN [21], CaHDC [14], and 2 FRIQAs UNIQUE [22] and SSIM [23]. To be fair, SPAQ, DBCNN and CaHDC are retrained on DeblurQA. For lack of space, more results can be found in the supplementary material.

Table 1. Comparison of ranking accuracy for different methods

ILNIQE	BIBLE	MT-A	MT-S	DBCNN	CaHDC	UNIQUE	SSIM	DBQA-NET
0.869	0.771	0.867	0.830	0.808	0.859	0.631	0.586	0.956

We observe that the proposed DBQA-NET significantly outperforms other general-purpose models and specialized model (BIBLE) in accuracy, without pretraining on large-scale dataset. This indicates that the model has a strong pertinence to deblurred images and better consistency with human perception. In the following experiments, we will apply the trained DBQA-NET to achieve more functions.

3.2   Automatic Hyperparameter Selection

The optimization methods based on blur kernel estimation usually contain several hyperparameters, which are not trainable. In practice, we have to manually traverse and evaluate the result, which is very time-consuming and laborious. Here we try to embed our model into the post-evaluation of the results of Pan [1]. We get some blur images from simulation and real world and process them with Pan [1]. We traverse through the main hyperparameters, recording the best and worst results by DBQA-NET, as shown in Fig. 4.

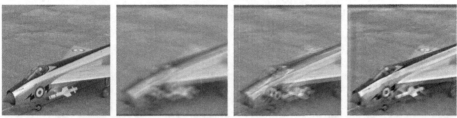

(a) Pristine image, blur image, the worst and best deblurred images of Pan [1]. The worst scores 45.5553 ($smooth = 1 \times 10^{-4}, Ksize = 20$), and the best 65.8424 ($smooth = 1 \times 10^{-4}, Ksize = 33$).

(b) Actually shot blur image, the worst and best deblurred images of Pan [1]. The worst scores 50.6876 ($smooth = 1 \times 10^{-5}, Ksize = 20$), and the best 68.3942 ($smooth = 1 \times 10^{-5}, Ksize = 36$).

Fig. 4. Automatic hyperparameters selection using DBQA-NET

It can be seen that the proposed method has the potential to replace manual traversal of hyperparameters on real blur images, which also indicates that it has the application prospect of assisting deblurring algorithms.

3.3   Optimization Experiment

Since the proposed model is differentiable, we then embed the trained model into the CNN-based deblurring method as a regularization term, and observe the changes before and after. Since the numerical range of our model is 0–100, the larger the value, the higher the quality. We add the following on the basis of the original loss function

$$l_q = 100 - f(x). \tag{6}$$

We randomly select 2000 images in VOC, follow the aforementioned steps, and respectively run the optimization method of [10] before and after adding Eq. 6. We find that the DISTS [13] values of the images decrease (quality improve) by an average of 0.003 with the regularization term. In addition, we find that on some samples with abnormalities before, our regularization terms lead to a significant improvement (Fig. 5), which shows that the proposed DBQA-NET can effectively enhance the stability of training.

Fig. 5. The result of loss function containing Eq. 6 (left side) and not (right side)

4   Conclusion

In order to solve the problem of online evaluation for deblurred images, we establish a dataset for perceptual quality assessment, and propose a novel opinion-unaware BIQA method based on multi-resolution feature aggregation. Through the proposed 2-stage training and joint loss function, we achieve better performance than other generic and specific metrics on external datasets and real blur images. Moreover, our method shows the potential of applying to other deblurring methods.

References

1. Pan, J., Liu, R., Su, Z., Gu, X.: Kernel estimation from salient structure for robust motion deblurring. Signal Process. Image Commun. **28**(9), 1156–1170 (2013)
2. Kupyn, O., Budzan, V., Mykhailych, M., Mishkin, D., Matas, J.: DeblurGAN: blind motion deblurring using conditional adversarial networks. In: Proceedings of the IEEE Conference on Computer Vision and Pattern Recognition (CVPR), pp. 8183–8192 (2018)
3. Pan, J., Sun, D., Pfister, H., Yang, M.H.: Blind image deblurring using dark channel prior. In: Proceedings of the IEEE Conference on Computer Vision and Pattern Recognition (CVPR), pp. 1628–1636 (2016)
4. Zhang, L., Zhang, L., Bovik, A.C.: A feature-enriched completely blind image quality evaluator. IEEE Trans. Image Process. (TIP) **24**(8), 2579–2591 (2015)
5. Fang, Y., Zhu, H., Zeng, Y., Ma, K., Wang, Z.: Perceptual quality assessment of smartphone photography. In: Proceedings of the IEEE/CVF Conference on Computer Vision and Pattern Recognition (CVPR), pp. 3677–3686 (2020)
6. Li, L., Lin, W., Wang, X., Yang, G., Bahrami, K., Kot, A.C.: No-reference image blur assessment based on discrete orthogonal moments. IEEE Trans. Cybernet. **46**(1), 39–50 (2015)
7. Zhu, H., Li, L., Wu, J., Dong, W., Shi, G.: MetaIQA: deep meta-learning for no-reference image quality assessment. In: Proceedings of the IEEE/CVF Conference on Computer Vision and Pattern Recognition (CVPR), pp. 14143–14152 (2020)
8. Su, S., et al.: Blindly assess image quality in the wild guided by a self-adaptive hyper network. In: Proceedings of the IEEE/CVF Conference on Computer Vision and Pattern Recognition (CVPR), pp. 3667–3676 (2020)
9. Michaeli, T., Irani, M.: Blind deblurring using internal patch recurrence. In: Fleet, D., Pajdla, T., Schiele, B., Tuytelaars, T. (eds.) ECCV 2014. LNCS, vol. 8691, pp. 783–798. Springer, Cham (2014). https://doi.org/10.1007/978-3-319-10578-9_51
10. Ren, D., Zhang, K., Wang, Q., Hu, Q., Zuo, W.: Neural blind deconvolution using deep priors. In: Proceedings of the IEEE/CVF Conference on Computer Vision and Pattern Recognition (CVPR), pp. 3341–3350 (2020)
11. Zhang, X., Dong, H., Hu, Z., Lai, W.S., Wang, F., Yang, M.H.: Gated fusion network for joint image deblurring and super-resolution. In: 29th British Machine Vision Conference (BMVC) (2019)
12. Lee, D.H.: Pseudo-label: the simple and efficient semi-supervised learning method for deep neural networks. In: Workshop on Challenges in Representation Learning (ICML), vol. 3, no. 2 (2013)
13. Ding, K., Ma, K., Wang, S., Simoncelli, E.P.: Image quality assessment: unifying structure and texture similarity. IEEE Trans. Pattern Anal. Mach. Intell. (TPAMT) **44**, 2567–2581 (2020)
14. Wu, J., Ma, J., Liang, F., Dong, W., Shi, G., Lin, W.: End-to-end blind image quality prediction with cascaded deep neural network. IEEE Trans. Image Process. (TIP) **29**, 7414–7426 (2020)
15. Liu, X., van de Weijer, J., Bagdanov, A.D.: RankIQA: learning from rankings for no-reference image quality assessment. In: Proceedings of the IEEE International Conference on Computer Vision (ICCV), pp. 1040–1049 (2017)
16. Ma, K., Liu, W., Liu, T., Wang, Z., Tao, D.: dipIQ: blind image quality assessment by learning-to-rank discriminable image pairs. IEEE Trans. Image Process. (TIP) **26**(8), 3951–3964 (2017)

17. Levin, A., Weiss, Y., Durand, F., Freeman, W.T.: Efficient marginal likelihood optimization in blind deconvolution. In: Proceedings of the IEEE Conference on Computer Vision and Pattern Recognition (CVPR), pp. 2657–2664 (2011)
18. Krishnan, D., Tay, T., Fergus, R.: Blind deconvolution using a normalized sparsity measure. In: Proceedings of the IEEE Conference on Computer Vision and Pattern Recognition (CVPR), pp. 233–240 (2011)
19. Xu, L., Zheng, S., Jia, J.: Unnatural l0 sparse representation for natural image deblurring. In: Proceedings of the IEEE Conference on Computer Vision and Pattern Recognition (CVPR), pp. 1107–1114 (2013)
20. Kupyn, O., Martyniuk, T., Wu, J., Wang, Z.: DeblurGAN-V2: deblurring (orders-of-magnitude) faster and better. In: Proceedings of the IEEE International Conference on Computer Vision (ICCV), pp. 8878–8887 (2019)
21. Zhang, W., Ma, K., Yan, J., Deng, D., Wang, Z.: Blind image quality assessment using a deep bilinear convolutional neural network. IEEE Trans. Circ. Syst. Video Technol. (TCSVT) **30**(1), 36–47 (2020)
22. Temel, D., Prabhushankar, M., AlRegib, G.: UNIQUE: unsupervised image quality estimation. IEEE Signal Process. Lett. **23**(10), 1414–1418 (2016)
23. Wang, Z., Bovik, A.C., Sheikh, H.R., et al.: Image quality assessment: from error visibility to structural similarity. IEEE Trans. Image Process. **13**(4), 600–612 (2004)

Low-illumination Palmprint Image Enhancement Based on U-Net Neural Network

Kaijun Zhou, Duojie Lu$^{(\boxtimes)}$, Xiancheng Zhou, and Guangnan Liu

Hunan University of Technology and Business, Changsha, China
ldj171428@163.com

Abstract. Palmprint has a high application prospect due to the stability, uniqueness, difficulty of reproduction, easy acquisition and high user acceptance of its own texture characteristics. However, palmprint images acquired in low-illumination conditions can lose a large amount of palmprint texture features, resulting in distortion of the palmprint image. In this paper, an improved U-Net neural network palmprint image enhancement algorithm is designed(SCAU-Net), that is, the depth and structure adjustment is made on the traditional U-Net neural network and the output feature of a hybrid attention mechanism adjustment is added to the jump connection to solve the problem that the palmprint image quality is easily affected by light intensity. The proposed method in this paper is experimented on the palmprint databases such as Idiap, CASIA, IITD and the laboratory self-acquisition, and the PSNR, SSIM, VIF indicators have been improved, which verifies that the algorithm can achieve low-illumination palmprint image enhancement well.

Keywords: Low-illumination palmprint image enhancement ·
Attention mechanism · U-Net neural network

1 Introduction

Biometrics is a modern science and technology that realizes automatic recognition of state analysis by identifying and analyzing the physiological and behavioral characteristics of the human body. In recent years, palmprint recognition technology has gradually entered people's field of vision, and has received widespread attention from researchers and the public in the field. Although the advantages of palmprint recognition technology are obvious and great progress has been made, there are still problems such as optimization and recognition of low-quality palmprint images, mobile terminals palmprint recognition, etc., which require us to further explore and optimize to improve the recognition rate of palmprint recognition to ensure the safety of palmprint recognition. Aiming at the problem that the quality of palmprint images is easily affected by light intensity, this paper designs a low-illumination palmprint image enhancement

W. Deng et al. (Eds.): CCBR 2022, LNCS 13628, pp. 541–549, 2022.
https://doi.org/10.1007/978-3-031-20233-9_55

algorithm (SCAU-Net) based on an improved U-Net neural network. The contributions can be summarized as follows:

•The depth and structure are adjusted on the traditional U-Net neural network, and a hybrid attention mechanism is added to the skip connection to readjust the output features to achieve palmprint image enhancement in low-illumination images.

•We conduct extensive experiments on four databases to demonstrate that the proposed method is well suited to achieve low-illumination palmprint image enhancement.

The rest of this paper is organized as follows: Sect. 2 describes some related works. Section 3 describes our approach in detail. Section 4 presents our experiments and results. Section 5 concludes the paper.

2   Relatex Work

Palmprint images are prone to problems such as overexposure, blur, distortion noise, etc. during acquisition, which brings challenges to palmprint image pre-processing. Jian et al. [1] present three useful approaches to correctnon-uniform illumination and eliminate the distortions for the reconstruction of 3D surface heightmaps. The algorithm proposed by BHUTADA GG [2] both preserves edge information and removes noise. Zotin et al. [3] proposed a fast image enhancement algorithm for HSV color based on multi-scale Retinex. Sun et al. [4] proposed an adaptive image enhancement algorithm based on Retinex.

In recent years, many people have adopted deep learning methods to achieve palmprint image enhancement. Lore [5] et al.experimentally verified the feasibility of deep learning in the field of image enhancement, using LLNet to improve the brightness and contrast of images. Wang et al. [6] obtained high-quality palmprint images by generating adversarial learning and achieved higher recognition accuracy. In 2020, Li et al. [7] proposed ANU-Net based on U-net++, which introduced a attention mechanism between nested convolutional blocks so that features extracted at different levels could be merged with task-related features. In 2022, Han et al. [8] proposed ConvUNeXt for medical image segmentation, which can achieve promising results with a low number of parameters. In this paper, a low-illumination palmprint image enhancement method based on mixed attention mechanism and improved U-Net neural network is proposed, and experimental verification is carried out to prove the effectiveness of the network model.

3   Method

3.1   Hybrid Attention Mechanism

The spatial attention mechanism focus on the most informative parts of the image area, and while it allows the neural network to focus on a specific area in the image based on the needs of a given task, it ignores important information in the feature channel. The focus of the channel attention mechanism is on the global information of the single channel, so the local information in the channel is ignored. According to the advantages and disadvantages of the above two kinds of attention, this section proposes a hybrid attention mechanism, which is embedded in the decoding and encoding jump connection of the U-Net, which can realize the attention complementarity of the spatial domain and the channel domain and obtain better image enhancement effects. The structure of the hybrid attention mechanism is shown in Fig 1:

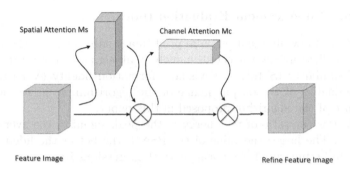

Fig. 1. Hybrid attention mechanism

3.2 SCAU-Net Network Structure

This paper follows the U-shaped structure of the original U-Net neural network and designs a 3-layer U-shaped network, which incorporates a mixed attention mechanism into the jump connection during decoding and encoding, so that the neural network learns the mapping relationship between the low-illumination palmprint image and the normal illuminance palmprint image, and pays more attention to the more important palmprint texture information in the global image.The SCAU-Net network structure is shown in Fig 2:

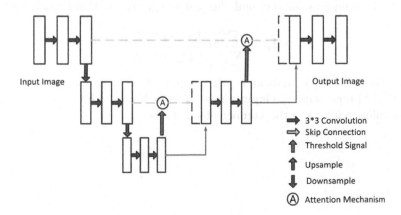

Fig. 2. SCAU-Net

In the encoding and decoding stages of the network structure, the hybrid attention mechanism can be combined to pay more attention to the image enhancement task and palmprint texture information, and suppress the feature responses of irrelevant regions. The correlation between low-level features and high-level features can be obtained, and then the weight distribution of palmprint texture features under low illumination is distributed through the weight coefficient output by the attention mechanism to achieve low-illumination palmprint image enhancement.

3.3   Image Enhancement Evaluation Index

For the effect of low illumination palm print image enhancement, three objective evaluation indicators were selected, namely peak signal-to-noise ratio (PSNR), structural similarity (SSIM), and visual information fidelity (VIF) to evaluate the image quality of the output image of the algorithm, so as to measure the performance of the algorithm proposed in this paper.

PSNR [9] is the ratio of the energy of the peak signal to the average energy of the noise. The larger the value of the PSNR, the better the fidelity effect of the image to be measured. Its mathematical expressions is:

$$PSNR = 10 log_{10}(\frac{(2^n - 1)^2}{MSE}) \tag{1}$$

SSIM [10] evaluates the similarity of the image under review and the original image from the three dimensions of brightness, contrast and structure, and its mathematical expression is:

$$SSIM(x,y) = \frac{(2\mu_x\mu_y + C_1)(2\sigma_{xy} + C_2)}{(\mu_x^2 + \mu_y^2 + C_1)(\sigma_x^2 + \sigma_y^2 + C_2)} \tag{2}$$

where, μ_x,μ_y represent the mean of x and y respectively, σ_x^2,σ_y^2 represent the variance of x and y respectively,and $\sigma_x\sigma_y$ is the covariance of x and y.

VIF [10] is a measure of image quality by calculating the mutual information between the image under test and the real image. Its mathematical expression is:

$$VIF = \frac{\sum_{k=1}^{K}[I(C_r^k; F^k|Z_r^k)]}{\sum_{k=1}^{K}[I(C_r^k; E^K|Z_r^k)]} \tag{3}$$

where $I(C_r^k; E^K|Z_r^k)$ indicates the input image information content, $I(C_r^k; F^k|Z_r^k)$ represents the input image and the distorted image's mutual information value, where k is the number of substrips.

4   Experiments

4.1   Experimental Environment

The method proposed in this paper is verified on four datasets of Idiap , CASIA , IITD and the laboratory self-collection, and the output results of the four databases were objectively evaluated, and the recognition rates before and after the enhancement were compared. The learning efficiency of the algorithm is 0.01, the momentum is set to 0.9, and the weight decay is 1e–6. The specific experimental configurations are shown in the Table 1.

Table 1. Experimental environment

Experimental environment indicators	Specific experimental environment
Operating system	Ubuntu 16.04
Programming framework	Tensorflow 1.4.0
GPU	Nvidia Geforce GTX 2080Ti
Memory	16 G

4.2   Datasets

Idiap [11] used a palm vein sensor to collect palmprint images of 110 individuals with left and right hands, for a total of 2200 palmprint images.

CASIA [12]used a digital camera to collect palmprint images of 312 individuals with left and right hands, for a total of 5502 images.

IITD [13] used a non-contact palmprint acquisition device to collect palmprint images of 230 individuals with left and right hands, for a total of 2601 images.

The laboratory self-collection database used Luxonis' acquisition equipment and OpenCV AI Kit to acquire palm positions in real time and collect palmprint images in real time, and palmprint images are collected on 9 individuals with left and right hands, for a total of 1800 images.

4.3   Ablation Experiments

In this section, ablation experiments were performed on layers 3 and 4 of U-shaped networks with spatial attention,channel attention and hybrid attention to demonstrate the advantages of layer 3 U-shaped networks in adding hybrid attention over other network models. Three metrics are used to measure the advantages of the output image of the network structure I chose and the output image of the other network structure. Perform a comparative analysis on our database, and the results are shown in Table 2:

Table 2. Attention mechanism ablation experiment of U-shaped network

	Attention mechanism	PSNR	SSIM	VIF
3-Layer U-shaped network	Channel Attention	19.6351	0.8026	0.8337
	Spatial Attention	20.8792	0.7613	0.8431
	SC Attention	**21.0431**	**0.8379**	**0.8619**
4-Layer U-shaped network	Channel Attention	20.1928	0.8094	0.7982
	Spatial Attention	19.6351	0.7982	0.8126
	SC Attention	21.7113	0.8161	0.8359

As we can see from the Table 2, the 3-layer U-Net jump connection joins the network of hybrid attention mechanisms, and the indicators are superior to other network structures. It shows that compared with other attention mechanisms, the proposed mixed attention mechanism performs best in multi-scale U-shaped networks, and can well complete the task of low-illumination palmprint image enhancement.

Table 3. Performance of multiple methods on four databases

	Ours			CASIA			IITD			Idiap		
	PSNR	SSIM	VIF	PSNR	SSIM	VIF	PSNR	SSIM	VIF	PSNR	SSIM	VIF
HE [14]	13.6451	0.5912	0.6175	11.8766	0.5912	0.6175	12.1089	0.7165	0.6874	11.3306	0.6368	0.7037
Gamma [15]	28.0662	0.8627	0.8121	18.6681	0.7139	0.7621	20.7164	0.7088	0.7392	18.6382	0.6901	0.7232
Retinex [16]	21.4382	0.7319	0.7133	20.9901	0.7218	0.7349	21.9613	0.8168	0.7893	21.6061	0.8273	0.8039
LLCNN [17]	27.8371	0.8763	0.8349	21.8671	0.7647	0.8133	22.8793	0.7891	0.7116	19.7618	0.7134	0.7116
U-Net [18]	28.6438	0.8917	0.8663	23.7343	0.8236	0.8663	22.1693	0.7963	0.8264	22.8071	0.8163	0.8486
SCAU-Net	**29.1736**	**0.9066**	**0.8901**	**24.8907**	**0.8271**	**0.8701**	**23.6814**	**0.8369**	**0.8991**	**24.0116**	**0.8387**	**0.8713**

4.4 Experimental Evaluation

The optimal network structure of the 3-layer U-Net jump connection added to the mixed attention mechanism was explored through previous ablation experiments, which are used in this section to process CASIA, IITD, Idiap and Ours, and compare the effects of the palmprint image enhancement methods of HE [14], Gamma [15], Retinex [16], LLCNN [17] and U-Net [18].

For the analysis of the three indicators in Table 3, it is not difficult to see that the SCAU-Net algorithm proposed has advantages in Ours, CASIA, Idiap and IITD databases. It is proved that the image enhancement method proposed has obvious enhancement on four databases, and is better than HE, Gamma, Retinex, LLCNN, U-Net. Among them, the worst performing palmprint image enhancement method is HE, indicating that the traditional image enhancement method is slightly less effective than the neural network enhancement method.

4.5   Comparative Experiment

In this section, CASIA and IITD are selected for comparison of recognition rate and equal error rate, and palmprint recognition experiments are performed on four recognition algorithms: AlexNet [19], VGG [20], ResNet-50 [21] and Comp code [22].

Table 4. Recognition rate and EER before and after image enhancement

Recognition rate/EER	Methods	IITD		CASIA	
		SCAU-Net	Original image	SCAU-Net	Original image
Recognition rate	Al exNet [19]	97.79%	97.27%	92.16%	92.74%
	VGG [20]	93.87%	92.12%	94.67%	94.12%
	ResNet-50 [21]	94.32%	95.57%	93.14%	95.20%
	Comp code [22]	93.83%	92.14%	93.03%	91.96%
EER	AlexNet [23]	0.37%	0.92%	1.33%	1.73%
	VGG [24]	1.47%	1.96%	0.73%	1.63%
	ResNet-50 [25]	2.30%	3.64%	2.49%	4.24%
	Comp code [26]	1.25%	1.39%	1.27%	1.38%

As can be seen from the above table, in the CASIA, the recognition rate of all three algorithms except ResNet-50 has been significantly improved. However, the recognition Rate of ResNet-50 is only 94.32%, a decrease of 1.25% compared to before the enhancement. And all four recognition algorithms achieved a lower error rate than the original image, with errors that were reduced by 0.55%, 0.49%, 1.34%, and 0.14%, respectively, relative to the original image. In the IITD, the recognition rate of both VGG and Comp code algorithms has increased, but the recognition rate of AlexNet and ResNet-50 algorithms has decreased. And all four recognition algorithms achieved lower equal error rates than the original image, which was reduced by 0.4%, 0.9%, 1.75%, and 0.11% respectively relative to the original image.

5   Conclusion

Aiming at the problem that the low brightness of palmprint images collected under low-illumination conditions affects recognition, this paper combines the hybrid attention mechanism and the improved U-Net to propose a low-illumination palmprint image enhancement model SCAU-Net. The algorithm is superior to HE, Gamma, Retinex, LLCNN, and U-Net. Compared with AlexNet, VGG, ResNet-50, Comp code and other algorithms, SCAU-Net has a better effect on image enhancement, enhances the contrast of palmprint images, and realizes palmprint image enhancement under low-light images.

Ackowledgements. We would like to thank some institutions including Chinese Academy of Sciences, Indian Institute of Technology and Idiap Research Institute for providing the palmprint dataset.

References

1. Jian, M., Yin, Y., Dong, J., Zhang, W.: Comprehensive assessment of non-uniform illumination for 3D heightmap reconstruction in outdoor environments. Comput. Ind. **99**, 110–118 (2018)
2. Bhutada, G.G., Anand, R.S., Saxena, S.C.: Edge preserved image enhancement using adaptive fusion of miages denoised by wavelet and cruvelet transform. Dig. Sig. Process. **21**(1), 118–130 (2011)
3. Zotin, A.: Fast algorithm of image enhancement based onmulti-scale retinex. Procedia Comput. Sci. **131**, 6–14 (2018). https://doi.org/10.1016/j.procs.2018.04.179
4. Sun, S.S., et al.: An adaptive segmentationmethod combining MSRCR and mean shift algorithm with K-means correction of green apples in natural environment. Inform. Process. Agric. **6**(2), 200–215 (2019). https://doi.org/10.1016/j.inpa.2018.08.011
5. Lorek, G., Akintayo, A., Sarkar, S.: LLNet:a deep autoencoder approach to natural low-Light image enhancement. Pattern Recogn. **61**, 650–662 (2017)
6. Wang G, Kang W, Wu Q, et al. Generative Adversarial Network (GAN) Based Data Augmentation for Palmprint Recognition[C]//2018 Digital Image Computing: Techniques and Applications (DICTA).2018
7. Li, C., et al.: ANU-Net: attention-based Nested U-Net to exploit full resolution features for medical image segmentation. Comput. Graph. **90**, 11–20 (2020)
8. Zhimeng, H., Muwei, J., Gai-Ge, W.: ConvUNeXt: an efficient convolution neural network for medical image segmentation. Knowl.-Based Syst. **253**, 109512 (2022)
9. Keles, O., et al.: On the computation of PSNR for a set of images or video (2021)
10. Tong, Y.B., Zhang, Q.S., Qi, Y.P.: Image quality assessing by combining PSNR with SSIM. J. Image Graph. **2006**(12), 1758–1763 (2006)
11. Tome, P., Marcel, S.: On the vulnerability of palm vein recognition to spoofing attacks. In: IAPR International Conference on Biometrics (ICB) (2015). https://doi.org/10.1109/ICB.2015.7139056. https://publications.idiap.ch/index.php/publications/show/3096
12. CASIA Palmprint Database. https://biometrics.idealtest.org
13. IITDelhiTouchlessPalmprintDatabase.   https://www4.comp.polyu.edu.hk/csajaykr/IITD/Database_Palm.htmlcsajaykr/IITD/Database_Palm.html
14. Zuiderveld, K.: Contrast limited adaptive histogram equalization. Graph. Gems, 474–485 (1994)
15. Grossmann, J.A., et al.: Decomposition of hardy functions into square integrable wavelets of constant shape. SIAM J. Math. Anal. **15**(4), 0515056 (1984)
16. Daniel J,J.: Retinex processing for automatic image enhancement. J. Electron. Imag. **13**(1), 100–110 (2004)
17. Rue, H., Martino, S., Chopin, N.: Approximate Bayesian inference for latent Gaussian models by using integrated nested Laplace approximations. J. Roy. Stat. Soc.: Ser. B (Stat. Methodol.) **71**(2), 319–392 (2009)
18. Ronneberger, O., Fischer, P., Brox, T.: U-Net: convolutional networks for biomedical image segmentation. In: Navab, N., Hornegger, J., Wells, W.M., Frangi, A.F. (eds.) MICCAI 2015. LNCS, vol. 9351, pp. 234–241. Springer, Cham (2015). https://doi.org/10.1007/978-3-319-24574-4_28
19. Alom, M.Z., et al.: The history began from alexnet: a comprehensive survey on deep learning approaches (2018)
20. Simonyan, K, Zisserman, A.: Very deep convolutional networks for large-scale image recognition. arXiv preprint arXiv:1409.1556 (2014)

21. Kong, W.K., Zhang, D.: Competitive coding scheme for palmprint verification. In: International Conference on Pattern Recognition. IEEE (2004)
22. Hinton, G.E., et al. Reducing the Dimensionality of Data with Neural Networks. Science **313**(5786), 504–507 (2006)

Texture-Guided Multiscale Feature Learning Network for Palmprint Image Quality Assessment

Xiao Sun[1], Lunke Fei[1(✉)], Shuping Zhao[1], Shuyi Li[2], Jie Wen[3], and Wei Jia[4]

[1] School of Computer Science and Technology, Guangdong University of Technology, Guangzhou, China
flksxm@126.com
[2] Department of Computer and Information Science, University of Macau, Macau, China
[3] School of Computer Science and Technology, Harbin institute of Technology, Shenzhen, China
[4] School of Computer and Information, Hefei University of Technology, Hefei, China

Abstract. Palmprint recognition has attracted widespread attention because of its advantages such as easy acquisition, rich texture, and security. However, most existing palmprint recognition methods focus most on feature extraction and matching without evaluating the quality of palmprint images, possibly leading to low recognition efficiency. In this paper, we propose a texture-guided multiscale feature learning network for palmprint image quality assessment. Specifically, we first employ a multiscale feature learning network to learn multiscale features. Then, we simultaneously use the multiscale features to learn image quality features by a QualityNet and texture features by a texture guided network. Texture features are then further used to learn texture quality features via TextureNet. Finally, we fuse the image quality features and texture quality features as palmprint quality features to predict the quality score via a regressor. Experimental results on the widely used palmprint database demonstrate that the proposed method consistently outperforms the state-of-the-art methods on palmprint image quality assessment.

Keywords: Biometric · Palmprint image quality assessment · Multiscale feature leaning · Texture guided

1 Introduction

Biometrics refers to automatically recognizing inherent physiological characteristics (such as iris, and face) of the human body [1], which has received tremendous attention in private security and crime prevention and brought great convenience to our daily life. In recent years, palmprint-based biometrics has received a great

W. Deng et al. (Eds.): CCBR 2022, LNCS 13628, pp. 550–558, 2022.
https://doi.org/10.1007/978-3-031-20233-9_56

deal of attention, not only because of its rich and reliable features but also the advantages of contactless acquisition and being less invasive.

There have been several methods proposed for palmprint recognition [3,4], which can be roughly grouped into two categories: contact-based methods [2] and contactless methods [5]. In general, contact-based methods captured palmprint images by pressing palms on the imaging devices with the help of user-pegs and under unchanged illumination, such that contact-based palmprint images usually have high quality with clear textures and fewer scale variants. This is why most existing contact-based palmprint methods can achieve very high recognition accuracies such as more than 99%. Due to its less user-friendliness, people focus most on contactless palmprint recognition methods, which are more convenient, secure, and hygienic. However, some of the contactless palmprint recognition systems work in an unconstrained environment and thus, have to deal with variabilities, such as illumination variations and hand postures, which lead to considerable degradation of recognition accuracy due to lack of palmprint image quality assessment. Therefore, image quality assessment (IQA) plays a crucial role in the preprocessing stage of palmprint recognition. Unlike other images, palmprint images are composed of rich texture lines, and the sharpness and discrimination of textures reflect the quality information of texture features. To obtain the image quality of palmprints, we need to pay attention to the texture quality of palmprints. Although existing biometric quality assessment methods (such as face IQA [7]) have achieved good performance, there is no study focusing on quality assessment of palmprint images, while existing IQA methods do not work well on palmprint images, because of the significant difference between the palmprint images and other kinds of images.

In this paper, we propose a texture-guided multiscale feature learning network for palmprint image quality assessment (PIQA). We first resize the images into three scales and feed them to three weight-shared CNN networks to extract the multiscale feature. The multiscale features are used to predict texture features by the guidance of the texture-guided network, while the image quality features are extracted from multiscale features by QualityNet. Then texture quality features are further extracted from the texture features by TextureNet and fused with the image quality features to get palmprint image quality features. Finally, the full-connected layers are used to learn the quality score of the palmprint images.

The main contributions of this paper can be summarized as follows:

- We propose a CNN-based multiscale feature learning network to learn multiscale features for palmprint image quality assessment by learning and combing different scale palmprint image features.
- To improve the efficiency and effectiveness of palmprint quality assessment, a texture-guided network has been proposed to predict texture guided features for leading the direct generation of texture features.
- We conducted extensive experiments on the Tongji synthetic distortion palmprint database based on Tongji contactless palmprint database [8]. The

experimental results clearly show that our method can perform better than advanced network models.

The rest of this paper is organized as follows. Section 2 illustrates the proposed texture guided multiscale feature learning network. Section 3 analyzes the experimental results, and Sect. 4 summarizes this paper.

2   The Texture-Guided Multiscale Feature Learning Network

In this study, we aim to develop a palmprint quality assessment network that predicts image quality features and texture quality features based on multiscale palmprint images for quality score learning. The framework of our network is shown in Fig. 1. There are three main components: image quality feature prediction, texture quality feature prediction, and palmprint image quality score prediction.

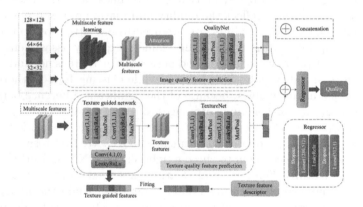

Fig. 1. Shows the basic framework of our proposed method, which mainly contains three sub-networks: image quality feature prediction (IQFP), texture quality feature prediction (TQFP), and palmprint quality score prediction (PQSP).

2.1   The Architecture of the Proposed Model

In the TQFP subnetwork, the original palmprint images are resized to three scales of 128×128, 64×64, and 32×32, and extensively exploiting different scales of palmprint features via a CNN-based network with an attention mechanism, which is converted into the quality-based features via a QualityNet. Moreover, the TQFP subnetwork takes the multiscale features from the IQFP as input to further learn the texture-guided features, which are lead to the generation of texture features that further converted into texture quality features via a TextureNet. Finally, both the image-based and texture-based quality features are fused to learn the final quality features for PIQA via a regressor. In the following, we detail the three prediction sub-networks of our proposed method.

2.2 Image Quality Feature Prediction

Many existing IQA methods feed images of different scale to the IQA model for image quality assessment. Due to palmprint images containing different scales of texture patterns, inspired by the multiscale IQA methods, we design a multiscale feature learning network to learn palmprint image quality. The network consists of three CNN-based networks. Specifically, we first resize the 128×128 palmprint image into two scales of 64×64 and 32×32, respectively, fed to three CNN networks with shared weights to learn different scale palmprint image features. Each CNN network consists of four convolutional layers, and each layer contains a LeakyReLu activation function and a maximum pooling layer with a kernel size of 2 and the step size of 2.

Secondly, we use a bilinear upsampling method to resize all scale feature maps to 16×16 and join them on the channels to get multiscale features. Let $G \in \mathbb{R}^{C \times H \times W}$ be the multiscale features, where C is 192, H and W are 16. Then the CBAM [10] is employed to weight the multiscale features so that the effective features in the multiscale features can be highlighted for more effective image quality feature extraction. Finally, after weighting the multiscale features, a QualityNet is designed to extract the image quality features from the weighted multiscale features. The QualityNet consists of two convolutional layers. Each layer contains a LeakyReLu activation function and a maximum pooling layer with the size of 2×2. Therefore, the QualityNet maps the channels of weighted multiscale features from 192 to 64, and finally outputs the image quality feature map with the size of $[64, 4, 4]$ (referred to G_I).

2.3 Texture Quality Feature Prediction

Palmprint recognition methods generally propose texture descriptors to extract texture features of palmprints and match them with other palmprints for identification and verification [11]. Moreover, the clarity of the palmprint pattern may affect the effectiveness of palmprint recognition. Therefore, in this paper, we extract the texture quality features for palmprint image quality learning. To obtain texture quality features effectively, we first introduce a texture-guided network to learn texture guided features to aid in learning texture quality features. The texture-guided network consists of eight layers, three convolution layers, three LeakyReLu layers and two max pooling layers. Specifically, we feed the multiscale features G to the texture-guided network, and the first six layers of the network map the features to a feature map with shape $[64, 4, 4]$ as texture features and denoted as G_T'. And then, the next two layers with G_T' continue to be used to predict a 32-dimensional feature vector as texture guided features, denoted as V_G. Its corresponding ground truth, marked as V_H, is extracted by a texture descriptor. Since the histogram of oriented lines (HOL) [6] feature is insensitive to illumination and robust to small transformations, we take the HOL descriptor to extract the texture feature. In order to make the network training more efficient, we downsample the HOL features by PCA algorithm from 972-dimensional to 32-dimensional feature vector as the ground truth V_H. The loss between V_G and V_H is represented by $Loss_T$, which will be summed with the loss of palmprint image quality score learning to train the network.

Subsequently, by the training of the texture-guided network, $G_T{}'$ is guided to learn more abstract palmprint texture knowledge, which contains a lot of unexplored texture information. Therefore we use $G_T{}'$ to further exploit the texture quality in it. We design a six layers CNN network named TextureNet to extract texture quality features. The TextureNet contains two convolution layers, two LeakyReLu layers and two max pooling layers that project the channel of the $G_T{}'$ from 64 to 256 and output texture quality features of shape [256, 1, 1], denoted as G_T.

2.4 Palmprint Image Quality Score Learning

After learning the image quality features G_I and texture quality features G_T, we flatten the two features and concatenate them together to obtain a 1280-dimensional feature vector as the palmprint quality features. Then two full-connected layers as a regressor is used to learn the palmprint quality features and output a quality score. A dropout layer follows each full-connected layer to reduce the parameters of the regressor to avoid overfitting, and LeakyReLu is chosen as the activation function. An L1 loss function is employed to calculate the texture feature prediction loss and palmprint quality prediction loss. And the total loss of the network is as follows:

$$LOSS = Loss_Q + Loss_T, \tag{1}$$

where $Loss_Q$ is the loss of palmprint image quality score learning and $Loss_T$ is the loss in texture feature prediction, and then the total loss of the network can be obtained.

3 Experiments

In this section, we perform comparative experiments on the Tongji palmprint database to evaluate the effectiveness of our proposed method. Our proposed approach is implemented based on the Windows 11 platform with an AMD 3700x CPU, 32 GB RAM, and a GTX1660s GPU.

3.1 Database

To the best of our knowledge, there is still no quality-labeled palmprint image database. To address the issue, we build a synthetic distortion palmprint dataset based on the widely used Tongji contactless palmprint database (TJU) [8], called

Tongji synthetic distortion palmprint (TJSDP) database for PIQA experiments. The TJU database consists of 12,000 palmprint images of 600 different palms collected in two sessions. We select 500 (50 palms × 10 samples for each palm) images from the first session baseline images. Then, we add four distortion operations with five levels on these baseline images, including the Gaussian blur, motion blur, Jpeg compression, and Jpeg 2000 compression, such that a baseline image generates 20 different distorted samples. As a result, our newly established TJSDP dataset contains 10,500 samples, including 500 undistorted and 10,000 distorted images.

To generate palmprint quality labels of TJSDP samples, we further select 500 samples from the second session of the TJU database corresponding to the same palms of the baseline images as the gallery sample set. First, we divide the images from the TJSDP into 21 groups based on the type and level of distortion. Then, for each group, we match each sample with each of the gallery samples based on the HOL feature extractor and calculate the genuine and imposter scores of the sample. According to the genuine and imposter scores, the corresponding thresholds of palms on the group can be calculated. And then false accept rate (FAR) and false reject rate (FRR) can be obtained by the threshold. Finally, the accuracy of the group can be computed as follows:

$$acc = 1 - \frac{FAR + FRR}{2}, \tag{2}$$

and then to obtain quality labels ranging from 0 to 100, we take the accuracy multiplied by 100, so that the label score can be calculated.

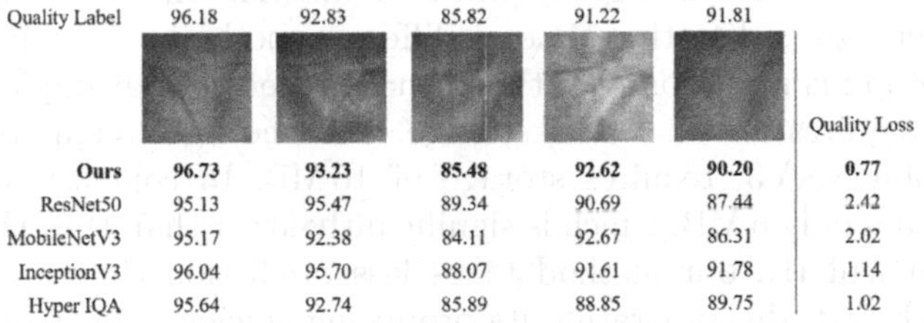

Quality Label	96.18	92.83	85.82	91.22	91.81	Quality Loss
Ours	**96.73**	**93.23**	**85.48**	**92.62**	**90.20**	**0.77**
ResNet50	95.13	95.47	89.34	90.69	87.44	2.42
MobileNetV3	95.17	92.38	84.11	92.67	86.31	2.02
InceptionV3	96.04	95.70	88.07	91.61	91.78	1.14
Hyper IQA	95.64	92.74	85.89	88.85	89.75	1.02

Fig. 2. Quality scores and quality losses of different methods on five randomly selected palmprint images.

3.2   Results of Palmprint Image Estimation

To better evaluate our proposed model, we conduct comparative experiments to compare the proposed method with the state-of-the-art approaches, including the MobileNetV3-Large, ResNet50, InceptionV3, and Hyper IQA [9], in terms of SRCC and PLCC [9]. Table 1 tabulates the SRCC and PLCC results of different approaches. It can be seen from Table 1 that our method outperforms the five compared methods by achieving higher SRCC and PLCC than them. In addition, Fig. 2 shows the quality estimation results of five typical palmprint images based on different methods. It can be seen that our proposed method obtains more accurate quality labels on the five levels of distorted palmprint images with significantly lower quality loss than other comparative methods. The experimental results prove that our proposed method can obtain more accurate quality estimation performance than others. The reason for this is that our method learns palmprint features at different scales and further learns the texture quality features of the palmprints guided by the texture guided features, which can effectively represent the quality of palmprint images.

Table 1. The palmprint quality assessment results from different methods on the TJSDP database.

Methods	SRCC	PLCC
ResNet50	0.8733	0.8626
InceptionV3	0.9533	0.9477
MobileNetV3-Large	0.9462	0.9400
Hyper IQA	0.9505	0.9503
Ours	**0.9616**	**0.9568**

3.3 Efficiency Analysis

To verify the efficiency of our method, we compare the parameter size and the computational time in the testing phase of different methods. Table 2 shows the parameter size and testing time of different methods. As can be seen, our proposed method is more compact than other models. For example, the popular Hyper IQA requires about 27 MB storage, and the lightweight representative network, MobileNetV3, requires storage of 16 MB. In contrast, our proposed model consumes only 6 MB, which is significantly lower than the other compared methods. Particularly, our method takes less prediction time on testing than the state-of-the-art, demonstrating its promising efficiency for palmprint image quality estimation.

Table 2. The parameters size and time consumed during the testing phase of different methods.

Methods	Parameter size (MB)	Testing time (second)
ResNet50	89	55
InceptionV3	83	90
MobileNetV3-Large	16	57
Hyper IQA	27	40
Ours	**6**	**34**

4   Conclusion

In this paper, we have proposed a compact convolution neural network for palmprint image quality assessment by simultaneously learning image quality features and texture quality features. We first learned the multiscale image features from three scales of palmprint images, and then projected them onto image quality features. Further, we specially learned the multiscale texture quality features of palmprints via a texture-guided CNN. Lastly, we combine the texture-specific features with image quality features as the final palmprint quality feature descriptor for palmprint image quality assessment. Extensive experimental results have demonstrated that our proposed method achieves better PIQA performance than the previous advanced models. In future work, it seems to be an interesting direction to exploit and fuse more palmprint-specific features for palmprint quality assessment.

Acknowledgments. This work was supported in part by the Guangzhou Science and technology plan project under Grant 202002030110, and in part by the National Natural Science Foundation of China under Grant 62176066 and Grant 62106052.

References

1. Jain, A.K., Ross, A., Pankanti, S.: Biometrics: a tool for information security. IEEE Trans. Inf. Forensics Secur. **1**(2), 125–143 (2006)
2. Kong, W.K., Zhang, D., Li, W.: Palmprint feature extraction using 2-D Gabor filters. Pattern Recogn. **36**(10), 2339–2347 (2003)
3. Fei, L., Zhang, B., Xu, Y., Tian, C., Imad, R., Zhang, D.: Jointly heterogeneous palmprint discriminant feature learning. IEEE Trans. Neural Netw. Learn. Syst. (2021). https://doi.org/10.1109/TNNLS.2021.3066381:1-12
4. Fei, L., Zhang, B., Jia, W., Wen, J., Zhang, D.: Feature extraction for 3-D palmprint recognition: a survey. IEEE Trans. Instrum. Meas. **69**(3), 645–656 (2020)
5. Fei, L., Zhang, B., Zhang, L., Jia, W., Wen, J., Jigang, W.: Learning compact multifeature codes for palmprint recognition from a single training image per palm. IEEE Trans. Multimedia **23**, 2930–2942 (2020)
6. Jia, W., Rongxiang, H., Lei, Y., Zhao, Y., Gui, J.: Histogram of oriented lines for palmprint recognition. IEEE Trans. Syst. Man Cybernet. Syst. **44**(3), 385–395 (2013)
7. Ou, F., et al.: SDD-FIQA: unsupervised face image quality assessment with similarity distribution distance. In: Proceedings of the IEEE/CVF Conference on Computer Vision and Pattern Recognition (CVPR), pp. 7670–7679 (2021)
8. Zhang, L., Li, L., Yang, A., Shen, Y., Yang, M.: Towards contactless palmprint recognition: a novel device, a new benchmark, and a collaborative representation based identification approach. Pattern Recognition **69**, 199–212 (2017)
9. Su, S., et al.: Blindly assess image quality in the wild guided by a self-adaptive hyper network. In: Proceedings of the IEEE/CVF Conference on Computer Vision and Pattern Recognition, pp. 3667–3676 (2020)

10. Woo, S., Park, J., Lee, J.-Y., Kweon, I.S.: CBAM: convolutional block attention module. In: Ferrari, V., Hebert, M., Sminchisescu, C., Weiss, Y. (eds.) ECCV 2018. LNCS, vol. 11211, pp. 3–19. Springer, Cham (2018). https://doi.org/10.1007/978-3-030-01234-2_1
11. Fei, L., et al.: Jointly learning multiple curvature descriptor for 3D palmprint recognition. In: 2020 25th International Conference on Pattern Recognition (ICPR), pp. 302–308. IEEE (2021)

Animal Biometrics

An Adaptive Weight Joint Loss Optimization for Dog Face Recognition

Qiwang Wang[1], Jiwei Song[2], Le Chang[3], Qing Tian[4], and Zhaofeng He[1(✉)]

[1] Beijing University of Posts and Telecommunications, Beijing, China
zhaofenghe@bupt.edu.cn
[2] China Electronics Standardization Institute, Beijing, China
[3] SoundAI Technology Co., Ltd, Beijing, China
[4] North China University of Technology, Beijing, China

Abstract. In recent years, the field of human face recognition has developed rapidly, and a large number of deep learning methods have proven their efficiency in human face recognition. However, these methods do not work well in the field of animal face recognition. There are two reasons. One is that the face recognition framework cannot fully extract the features of animal faces, and the other is that there are not enough animal datasets to fully train the model. In this paper, we collect a total of 11889 high-definition pictures containing 174 dog individuals, with an average of more than 60 samples per dog. On this dataset, we trained Swin Transformer as the backbone, and coupled with the triplet loss and cross-entropy loss function, it reaches an accuracy of 88.94%. Compared with the accuracy rate of 86.21% for using the TripletLoss alone and the accuracy rate of 86.60% for using the cross-entropy loss alone, this paper has a big improvement.

Keywords: Dog face recognition · Deep learning · Triplet-Loss · Joint loss function

1 Introduction

Now more and more people have pets and regard pets as their important friends. The increase in the number of pets has brought about a huge demand for pet personal identification technology in the pet insurance and pet medical industries. In animal husbandry, obtaining long-term health data of individual livestock is one of the important measures to know its health status and thus ensure animal health. Today, the main technologies for dog identification are tattoos, collars, and microchip implants. [1] But these methods can cause irreversible damage to animals and are often not reliable. Therefore, it is very important to develop a reliable and convenient method to identify individual animals. There are already many good algorithms in the field of face recognition, such as Facenet [2], DeepFace [3], DeepID [4], DeepID2 [5], and so on. However, there is no very effective method for animal individual recognition. The main reasons include two aspects:

W. Deng et al. (Eds.): CCBR 2022, LNCS 13628, pp. 561–568, 2022.
https://doi.org/10.1007/978-3-031-20233-9_57

one is the lack of sufficient high-quality datasets, and the other is that the framework that works well in face recognition may not be suitable for animal feature extraction. There are two contributions in this paper.

(1) Due to the lack of a high-quality dog identity dataset, we cooperated with the SAICHONGHUI Company to make a high-quality dog individual dataset. After a period of collection, the current dataset includes 174 dogs, with a total of 11,889 high-definition images. It can be used for dog recognition, dog detection etc.
(2) We proposed a method that selected Swin Transformer [6] as the backbone and coupled with the Triplet Loss [2] and Cross-Entropy loss function, it reaches an accuracy of 88.94% on this dataset.

2 Related Work

Face recognition based on deep learning is an emerging artificial intelligence technology. Compared with traditional recognition methods, it has the characteristics of safety, ease of use, and no implantation. The recognition process is mainly divided into the following steps: firstly, the face of the target individual is photographed and videoed to obtain the facial image through the acquisition equipment such as the camera; then the facial feature vector is extracted from the relevant image by using the deep learning model; The extracted facial feature vector is compared with the feature vectors of other pictures or existing categories to determine the identity.

Face recognition technology has been successfully applied in many industries, and many basic theories and practical techniques have been perfected in the process of continuous development. And its related field: animal individual recognition has gradually become a new hotspot and a new direction of research in recent years. At present, there are relatively few research works in the field of animal individual recognition, and most of them focus on cattle recognition [7]. Recently, an article designed a recognition network based on joint loss for goats with high similarity [8], which achieved an accuracy rate of 93.0007% on a closed high-similarity goat dataset. But their work can not transfer well to dog data, because the differences between individual dogs are much greater than the differences between goats. Some small-scale features are very important in the goat dataset, but some small-scale features are relatively less important in the dog data. Mougeot et al. [9] proposed a dataset containing 48 different dog faces, and obtained 88% recognition accuracy on this dataset. But this dataset is too small for recent very deep networks and pre-training weights that are getting better and better as computing power increases. In addition, the resolution of the image is also very low, which is not conducive to the extraction of high semantic features such as nose lines. For animal recognition, a large and good quality dataset is very much needed.

The use of facial recognition technology to determine and identify individual animal identities can not only help breeding enterprises to achieve intelligent management and control of individual livestock but also help the government to better manage the intelligent annual inspection of the pet industry. Therefore, the research on animal individual identification has very important practical significance and value.

3 Dataset Creation

All the face images of stray dogs used in this paper are from Beijing Pet Association and SAICHOGNHUI Company, which are taken by the staff, and the corresponding dog face images are obtained after sorting and preprocessing (Fig. 1).

Fig. 1. The left picture is the original picture, the right picture is the cropped picture.

The core difficulty of the individual identification task lies in the scarcity of datasets. Usually, animal datasets are composed of multiple species, and the sources of the same species are scattered and disordered. Many individuals usually have only one sample, and most images are of low resolution, which makes the task of individual identification difficult. For the animal individual recognition task, to make the trained model have better generalization ability, it is necessary to simultaneously train the metric method to increase the distance between different classes and reduce the distance within the same class. At the same time, achieving good recognition results requires very high-quality datasets, which have a large number of different individuals of the same species, and each animal individual needs to have a sufficient number of clear frontal pictures.

In the process of collecting images, we found that it is difficult to obtain high-quality frontal images because it is very hard for animals to obediently look at the camera. For this reason, this paper proposes a shooting method of angle rotation through the field practice of taking pictures. After fixing the animal's head, rotate the angle to the right from the left 45-degree angle to the right 45-degree angle, and take at least 25 high-definition pictures continuously during this period. In the process of cooperating with SAICHONGHUI, a new batch of data is collected every half month. So far, the dataset has included 11,889 photos of more than 174 individual dogs (Fig. 2).

Fig. 2. Examples of our dataset.

4 Proposed Method

Most of the well-known feature vector extraction networks require massive training data to have better feature extraction results. In most cases, our realistic target tasks lack a sufficient number of high-quality datasets for training. Training pre-trained models with large datasets and then fine-tuning model parameters on small scale datasets has become a mainstream approach in both academia and industry. This transfer learning method can alleviate the consequences of insufficient data in the target task domain to a certain extent, that is, the minimum in the global mode cannot be found in the gradient forest, and only the local minimum can be found.

In the selection of the pre-training model, in addition to the size of the dataset, the distance between the source data domain and the target data domain is also an important factor to be considered. For example, if you need to train a model that recognizes dogs, training a pretrained model on a human dataset will generally outperform pre-training on a car dataset with similar dataset sizes. This shows that in the case of transfer learning tasks, it is better to use pre-training datasets with closer domain distances.

So we tried several backbones that perform well on Image-Net recognition tasks, such as ResNet50 [10] EfficientNet [11] Swin [6], etc. Compared with the face dataset, both the intra-class distance and the inter-class distance are larger, especially the intra-class distance will have a greater impact on the recognition results. This is because it is difficult to obtain frontal face images in the process of animal data collection, and there will be various angles or even occlusions, while this situation will be much less in the human face dataset. Therefore, we need to reduce the intra-class distance as much as possible, so we choose Triplet-loss as the loss function, but it will be difficult for the network to fitting, so we use the combination of the cross-entropy loss function and Triplet-loss as our loss function, and add an adaptive weight to make the network fitting faster and have a higher accuracy.

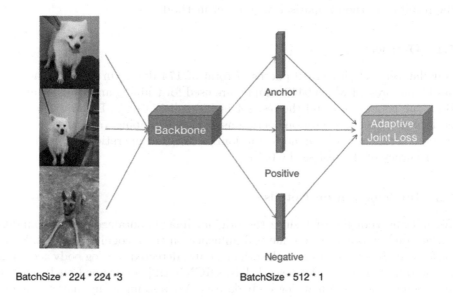

Fig. 3. The pipeline of our network

The overview of the proposed method is shown in Fig. 3. We first randomly select an anchor sample in a batch of data, then find the positive sample with the largest L2 distance of the same class as this anchor, then set a threshold T = 0.5, in this batch of data all normalized L2 distances are less than T is used as a set of negative samples. Then an adaptive loss is applied to the obtained features, because the initial Triplet-Loss is difficult to fit, so we will give Triplet-Loss a small value of weight α in the initial stage of the network, and cross-entropy loss a larger weight of $1 - \alpha$. At this stage, the cross-entropy loss dominates the descending direction of the network. Until the network has some recognition ability, the weights of these two losses are adaptively updated. In each batch, which loss drops faster will gain greater weight in the next batch. Weight update policy is shown in formula 1, $step_{value}$ is the step size for each update of the weight value, $judge_{bool}$ shows which loss from the last batch had a greater impact on the results, that is, loss dropped more.

$$\alpha = \alpha + step_{value} * judge_{bool} \tag{1}$$

$$loss = \alpha * TripletLoss + (1 - \alpha) * CEloss \tag{2}$$

5   Experiments and Results

Here are several experiments to prove the effectiveness of our method. The dataset and some experimental details are introduced first. Then we analyze the results and the comparison with other methods.

5.1   Dataset

Our dataset includes 11819 photos, a total of 174 dogs. On average, each dog has 67 pictures, of which 9447 samples are used for training and 2442 for testing. Both the training set and the test set include all 174 dogs. Before training, we performed data augmentation operations including clipping, random translation, random rotation, Gaussian noise, MotionBlur, Cutout operations. This improves the accuracy of the test set by 0.2%.

5.2   Implementation Details

We initially thought that since the original image contained the surrounding background, it would have some bad influence on the recognition results. So we performed object detection on the original data, detected the dog body according to the object detection framework FasterRCNN [12] pre-trained on ImageNet, and then segmented a new dog body dataset. We also manually marked the dog face data, then train a dog face detector, and performed dog face detection on the dataset, segmented a new dog face dataset and train it. The results show that the effects of these three datasets are similar. It may be because the network has been trained to have the ability to filter the ambient background noise.

So we use the original data to feed the backbone after data augmentation. Due to the use of Triplet-Loss, each batch of BatchSize is one third of the original size. This is because each time an anchor image is randomly selected, the corresponding positive image and negative image must be selected according

Table 1. Recognition performance of different method

Ablation study		
Model	Loss function	Recognition acc (%)
Resnet18 [10]	CE	85.94
Resnet50 [10]	CE	86.04
Swin Transformer [6]	CE	86.60
EfficientNet [11]	CE	86.72
Resnet18 [10]	CE+TripletLoss	86.51
Resnet50 [10]	CE+TripletLoss	86.49
Swin transformer [6]	CE+TripletLoss	**88.94**
EfficientNet [11]	CE+TripletLoss	87.88

to the anchor image. We take a uniform batch size of $64 * 3$ with a learning rate of $3e-4$. The initial joint loss weight parameter α is 0.01. When cross-entropy loss <9, the initial weight parameter α is 0.5, and the subsequent α is updated by Formula 1.

5.3 Ablation Study

We selected four models that performed well on the ImageNet recognition task as backbones and initialized them with pre-trained weights. We tested cross-entropy loss alone and the combination of cross-entropy loss and TripletLoss, because the network using TripletLoss alone will be difficult to fitting, so it is not listed in the Table 1.

The experimental results show that using the joint loss is about 1% higher than using CE as the loss, especially when the Swin Transformer is selected as the backbone, the improvement is most obvious, with an increase of 2.34%. This may be from the global attention mechanism of the Swin Transformer. Compared to other networks based on convolutional structures, Triplet Loss helps the network learn more inter-class differences in global features.

5.4 Comparison with Other Methods

We use the Swin Transformer as the backbone, with the adaptive joint loss function and get a pretty good results, getting accuracy of 88.94% on our dataset, which is a big advantage over other networks. Other ResNet18, Swin Transformer, and EfficientNet that only use CE as loss have slightly lower accuracy. For the two methods using Swin Transformer as the feature extraction framework, using the adaptive joint loss function can improve the accuracy by about 2%, which indicates that the joint loss function can indeed help the network learn richer features. Also, from the results, it can also help the network adapt to fewer training epochs. As shown in Fig. 4, in the case of the same epochs, our results are better than others.

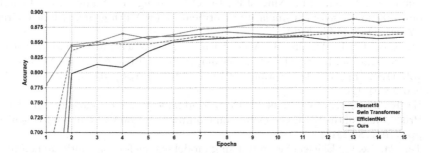

Fig. 4. Comparison with other methods

6 Conclusion

After recent development, face recognition technology has achieved very high accuracy and stability thanks to the rich face datasets and the work input of a large number of researchers. But in terms of animal identification, there has not been much breakthrough progress. Dog face recognition is much more complicated than human face recognition due to the lack of available data and the wide range of texture variations in dog face images. In this paper, we design a new method to solve the dog recognition problem by establishing a new dog dataset containing multiple dogs, each with a large number of high-definition samples, and achieve satisfactory accuracy. However, there is still room for further improvement in the recognition accuracy. In the future, it may be possible to study the fusion of dog nose texture information to further improve the recognition accuracy.

References

1. Blancou, J.: A history of the traceability of animals and animal products. Revue scientifique et technique (International Office of Epizootics) (2001)
2. Schroff, F., Kalenichenko, D., Philbin, J.: FaceNet: a unified embedding for face recognition and clustering. CoRR abs/1503.03832 (2015)
3. Taigman, Y., Yang, M., Ranzato, M., Wolf, L.: DeepFace: closing the gap to human-level performance in face verification (2014)
4. Sun, Y., Wang, X., Tang, X.: Deep learning face representation from predicting 10,000 classes. In: Proceedings of the IEEE Conference on Computer Vision and Pattern Recognition, pp. 1891–1898 (2014)
5. Sun, Y., Chen, Y., Wang, X., et al.: Deep learning face representation by joint identification-verification. Adv. Neural Inf. Process. Syst. **27** (2014)
6. Liu, Z., Lin, Y., Cao, Y., et al.: Swin transformer: hierarchical vision transformer using shifted windows. In: Proceedings of the IEEE/CVF International Conference on Computer Vision, pp. 10012–10022 (2021)
7. Yao, L., Hu, Z., Liu, C., et al.: Cow face detection and recognition based on automatic feature extraction algorithm. In: Proceedings of the ACM Turing Celebration Conference-China, pp. 1–5 (2019)
8. Shang, C., Wang, M.L., Ning, J.F., Li, Q.H., Jiang, Y., Wang, X.L.: Joint loss optimization based high similarity identification for Milch goats. J. Image Graph. **27**(04), 1137–1147 (2022)
9. Mougeot, G., Li, D., Jia, S.: A deep learning approach for dog face verification and recognition. In: Nayak, A.C., Sharma, A. (eds.) PRICAI 2019. LNCS (LNAI), vol. 11672, pp. 418–430. Springer, Cham (2019). https://doi.org/10.1007/978-3-030-29894-4_34
10. He, K., Zhang, X., Ren, S., et al.: Deep residual learning for image recognition. In: Proceedings of the IEEE Conference on Computer Vision and Pattern Recognition, pp. 770–778 (2016)
11. Tan, M., Le, Q.: EfficientNet: rethinking model scaling for convolutional neural networks. In: International Conference on Machine Learning, pp. 6105–6114. PMLR (2019)
12. Ren, S., He, K., Girshick, R., et al.: Faster R-CNN: towards real-time object detection with region proposal networks. Adv. Neural Inf. Process. Syst. **28** (2015)

Improved YOLOv5 for Dense Wildlife Object Detection

Yuhang Pei, Liming Xu, and Bochuan Zheng$^{(\boxtimes)}$

School of Computer Science, China West Normal University,
Nanchong, Sichuan, China
zhengbc@vip.163.com

Abstract. Wildlife plays a very important role in the ecological balance of the earth. With the rapid development of computer vision, we can use object detection techniques to count the number of wildlife for their better conservation; however, some wildlife live mainly in groups, so the datasets are often distributed in a dense state. It is difficult in dense environments since boxes for different objects should be preserved and duplicate detections should be suppressed at the same time. It is challenging to detect dense wildlife. To solve the problem, we propose an improved model based on YOLOv5. Firstly, we add a Convolutional Block Attention Model(CBAM) to enable the network to extract the richer wildlife features. Secondly, Distance Intersection over Union-Non Maximum Suppression(DIoU-NMS) is used to solve the problem of multiple-objects overlap in wildlife detection to reduce the redundancy of the wildlife. Finally, Efficient Intersection over Union Loss(EIoU Loss) is used to speed up the convergence of the loss function. The experimental results show that our model achieved good performance on the public dataset Wildlife. Compared with the basic YOLOv5s, it reaches 94.2% in mAP@0.5 and achieves average increments by 2.1% . It improves the application and practicability of object detection technology in dense wildlife detection, which is encouraging and meaningful.

Keywords: Wildlife detection · YOLOv5 · CBAM · DIoU-NMS · EIoU-Loss

1 Introduction

With the degradation of the environment and human intervention, natural resources are gradually being destroyed more and more wildlife are on the verge of extinction. Obtaining the number and species of wildlife in a set of photos or videos can provide valuable information for wildlife experts and scholars in related fields. Therefore, it is necessary to monitor and protect them. Most of the wildlife is collected using camera traps [1], these camera traps can take millions of images, however, extracting information from these camera-trap images is traditionally done by humans and is so time-consuming and costly that much of the valuable information in these big data repositories remains untapped. With the continuous development of deep learning and the maturity of the technology in object detection, we can solve the above problems based on deep learning. When the image of wildlife is captured, we can transmit it to the terminal and analyze the wildlife information in it with object detection techniques, object detection methods based on deep learning have evolved significantly in recent years, and have achieved solid improvements in speed and accuracy in many real-world scenes. Despite this remarkable progress, the common use case of detection in dense images remains challenging even for leading object detectors. In this paper, we focus on dense wildlife detection. Some wildlife, such as elephants, rhinos, and zebras, tend to move in clusters, so most of the datasets are densely distributed with the following three problems: Firstly, there are species in the dense wildlife population that are very similar in color to the natural background and high similarity between the same species, which makes it difficult to judge them effectively. Secondly, dense wildlife has a lot of occlusion and overlap problems with each other, which makes it difficult to precisely locate individual objects. Thirdly, dense wildlife has the problem of small objects at long distances and multi-scale variation, which increases the difficulty of feature extraction. The above three problems pose a huge challenge to the detection of dense wildlife. In the object detection task, the YOLO series is a milestone in one-stage detectors, in this paper, we propose an improved model, our model based on YOLOv5 [2] to solve the above-mentioned three problems making it more suitable for dense wildlife detection. Our contribution can be listed as follows:

1. We integrate the Convolutional Block Attention Module (CBAM) [3] in YOLOv5 to help the network find regions of interest in images to optimize the detection of multi-scale and protected-color wildlife with improved detection accuracy compared to the conventional YOLOv5.
2. For the detection of overlapping wildlife objects, we use the Distance Intersection over Union Non-Maximum Suppression(DIoU-NMS) [4] method, which improves the post-processing of overlapping boxes with full consideration of neighborhood information and shows robustness to different NMS [5] methods.
3. Considering the imbalance between high and low-quality anchor boxes in Bounding Box Regression(BBX), we use Efficient Intersection over Union Loss(EIoU Loss) [6] to replace the Generalized Intersection over Union Loss(GIoU Loss) [7] to obtain a faster convergence speed and superior regression results and enhance contributions of the most promising anchor boxes in our model optimization.

2 Related Work

2.1 Object Detection

Object detection can be divided into two types: 1. One-stage detector 2. Two-stage detector. In addition, object detectors developed in recent years often have some layer inserted between the backbone and the head, which is often referred to as the neck of the detector. In the following, we will describe each of these three structures in detail.

Backbone. The backbone often use include EfficientNet [8], CSPDarkNet [9], DenseNet [10], ResNet [11],VGG [12], Because these networks have demonstrated that they have strong feature extraction capabilities in classification and other problems. But researchers also fine-tune the backbone to make it more suitable for specific tasks.

Neck. The neck is designed to make better use of the features extracted by the Backbone. It reprocesses and rationalizes the use of the feature maps extracted by Backbone at different stages. Typically, a neck consists of several bottom-up paths and several top-down paths. The neck is a key link in the object detection framework. Commonly used path-aggregation blocks in neck are:FPN [13], PANet [14], BiFPN [15], ASFF [16]. These approaches have in common with the design of aggregated structures by iteratively using various methods of up- and down-sampling, and splicing.

Head. As a classification network, the backbone cannot complete the positioning task, and the head is designed to be responsible for detecting the location and category of the object by the features maps extracted from the backbone. Heads are generally divided into two kinds:one-stage detector and two-stage detector. Two-stage detectors are a series of candidate frames that are first generated by the algorithm as samples, and then the samples are classified by a convolutional neural network, the most representative method including R-CNN [17], Fast R-CNN [18]. Compare with the two-stage detector, the one-stage detector is also called the regression-based object detection method, which simplifies the whole detection process into an end-to-end regression problem. The bounding boxes and classification results are directly mapped by the whole image, which reduces the complexity of the operation and enables the algorithm to meet real-time requirements. The most representative including SSD [19], YOLO series [20–23].

2.2 Wildlife and Dense Object Detection Method

The study conducted by Lahiri et al. [24]. Extract simple image features and compare them based on wildlife coat markings, e.g., striped coats, and dynamic programming algorithms for individual identification of zebra. Deep neural networks (DNNs) were applied by Norouzzadeh et al. [25] to automatically extract information for wildlife identification thereby saving a tremendous amount of time by 99.3% compared to manual labor. A study by Kellenberger et al. [26] conducted wildlife recognition based on pre-trained AlexNet from CNN architecture which was optimized for fast detection based on large wildlife. Another study by Zeppelzauer [27] used a color model with different backgrounds and lighting conditions to automatically detect and track elephants in wildlife videos. Feng et al. [28] designed a novel wildlife monitoring system based on wireless image sensor networks (WISNs) and used an optimized Faster R-CNN to detect wildlife from the captured wild scene images. A pyramidal approach was proposed for dense detecting faces [29] where the gradients of all objects were back-propagated after max-pooling the responses from each scale. Different filters were used in the classification layers for faces at different scales for better detection of dense faces. Recently, a new non-max-suppression was proposed for small and crowded face detection [30]. However, The above approaches either only consider the construction of the entire wildlife detection system comprehensively, while the design of the core vision detection module is relatively simple. Either they are not targeted to apply dense object detection to wildlife, and thus this leads to their limitations. Which limits their practical applications.

3 Proposed Method

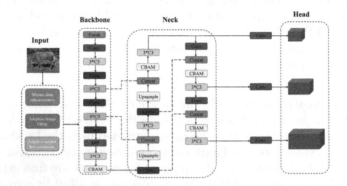

Fig. 1. The architecture of our model. a) CSPDarknet53 as the backbone. b) The neck uses a structure like PANet. c) Three heads use the feature maps from Conv.

YOLOv5 has four different models including YOLOv5s, YOLOv5m, YOLOv5l, and YOLOv5x. Because it is the most notable and convenient one-stage detector, we select it as our baseline. Considering that our wildlife dataset is at a Medium level, YOLOv5s meets real-time requirements better than YOLOv5m, YOLOv5l, and YOLOv5x and consumes less computation, making it easier to deploy on the move, at the edge. Therefore, we use YOLOv5s to pursue the best detection performance and improve based on it, the overview of the detection structure of our model is shown in Fig. 1, the improvement of our model includes the following three aspects: For the network to increase the attention to conservation-color, high similarity, and multi-scale problems in wildlife we adopt CBAM to sequentially generate the attention map along channel-wise and spatial-wise dimensions. Then, we replaced the original NMS with DIoU-NMS to avoid the redundancy of the model, which aims to eliminate redundant candidate boxes to the precise positioning of each object. Finally, we replaced the original bounding box loss function GIoU Loss with EIoU Loss to ensure faster convergence of the bounding box while maintaining precision.

3.1 CBAM

In CNN networks, the attention mechanism acts on the feature graph to obtain the available attention information in the feature graph, CBAM is a simple but

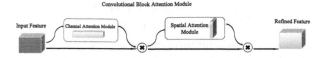

Fig. 2. Structure of CBAM

effective attention module. It is a lightweight module that can be integrated into most notable CNN architectures, and it can be trained in an end-to-end manner. Given a feature map, CBAM sequentially infers the attention map along two separate dimensions of the channel and spatial and then multiplies the attention map with the input feature map to perform adaptive feature refinement. The Structure of the CBAM module is shown in the Fig. 2. Given an intermediate feature map $\mathbf{F} \in \mathbb{R}^{C \times H \times W}$ as input, CBAM sequentially infers a 1D channel attention map $\mathbf{M_c} \in \mathbb{R}^{C \times 1 \times 1}$ and a 2D spatial attention map $\mathbf{M_s} \in \mathbb{R}^{1 \times H \times W}$. The overall attention process can be summarized as:

$$\mathbf{F'} = \mathbf{M_c}(\mathbf{F}) \otimes \mathbf{F} \tag{1}$$

$$\mathbf{F''} = \mathbf{M_s}(\mathbf{F'}) \otimes \mathbf{F'} \tag{2}$$

where $\otimes$ denotes element-wise multiplication. During multiplication, the attention values are broadcasted (copied) accordingly: channel attention values are broadcasted along the spatial dimension, and vice versa. F'' is the final refined output. The experimental results show that focusing both spatial and channel-wise is more advantageous than only using the channel-wise -attention.

In dense wildlife images, there are largely overlapping, occluded objects, and using CBAM can extract attention regions to help our model resist confusing information and focus on useful objects.

3.2 DIoU-NMS

In the actual wild environment, wildlife is often dense in groups, resulting in the problem of occlusion. In this case, the IoU-based NMS algorithm could eliminate the predicted boxes of adjacent objects or retain the low-quality detections for the current object, resulting in the problem of missing and error detection. Therefore, the confidence of predicted boxes should be considered. Zheng et al. [4]. Have verified that DIoU-NMS can obtain a better processing effect than IoU when calculating the overlaps of boxes in NMS.

The DIoU-NMS compared to NMS does not only consider the IOU value, but also the distance between the centroids of two bounding boxes. If the IOU of two bounding boxes is larger, and the distance between the two bounding boxes is also larger, it will be considered as two different bounding boxes produced by two different objects. Therefore will not be filtered out, the formula is as follows:

$$DIoU = IoU - \frac{\rho^2 \left(\boldsymbol{b}, \boldsymbol{b}^{gt} \right)}{c^2} \tag{3}$$

$$s_i = \begin{cases} s_i, IoU - \mathcal{R}_{DIoU}\left(\mathcal{M}, B_i\right) < \varepsilon \\ 0, IoU - \mathcal{R}_{DIoU}\left(\mathcal{M}, B_i\right) \geq \varepsilon \end{cases} \tag{4}$$

where box B_i is removed by simultaneously considering the IoU and the distance between central points of two boxes, s_i is the classification score and ε is the NMS threshold. We suggest that two boxes with distant central points probably locate different objects, and should not be removed.

Therefore, for the detection of overlapping wildlife objects, we use the DIoU-NMS to improve the post-processing effect of overlapping boxes and the experimental results show great robustness to the original NMS thresholds.

3.3   EIoU Loss

The bounding box in YOLOv5s is calculated using GIoU Loss, which is used to judge the difference between the predicted box (PB) and the ground truth (GT), calculated as follows:

$$GIoU = IoU - \frac{A^c - \mathcal{U}}{A^c} \tag{5}$$

$$\mathcal{L}_{GIoU} = 1 - GIoU \tag{6}$$

In the formula, IoU represents the intersection and union ratio of PB and GT, A^c represents the area of the smallest rectangular box containing PB and GT at the same time, and $\mathcal{U}$ represents the union of PB and GT. The problem with GIoU is that when PB and GT are more and more similar, the loss is directly transformed into IoU loss, resulting in its instability and slow convergence. Hence, in this paper, we selected EIoU as the loss function of bounding box regression. EIoU Loss formula is as follows:

$$\begin{aligned} \mathcal{L}_{EIoU} &= \mathcal{L}_{IoU} + \mathcal{L}_{dis} + \mathcal{L}_{asp} \\ &= 1 - IoU + \frac{\rho^2\left(\mathbf{b}, \mathbf{b}^{gt}\right)}{c^2} + \frac{\rho^2\left(w, w^{gt}\right)}{C_w^2} + \frac{\rho^2\left(h, h^{gt}\right)}{C_h^2} \end{aligned} \tag{7}$$

EIoU divides the loss function into three parts: IoU loss, dis loss, and asp loss. C_w and C_H are the width and height of two rectangles, respectively, $\rho(.)$ Represents the Euclidean distance, $\mathbf{b}$ and $\mathbf{b}^{gt}$ represent the center points of PB and GT, and c represents the length of the shortest diagonal of the minimum bounding box of PB and GT.

The EIoU loss function can optimize the convergence speed and positioning accuracy and reduce the likelihood of inaccurate regression results. Therefore, We use EIoU Loss to achieve better convergence of the bounding box.

4   Experiments

4.1   Implementation Details

We use the public wildlife dataset to evaluate our model, this experimental dataset comes from African Wildlife provided by Kaggle [31], the data was divided into a training set and a test set in the ratio of 8:2, with 1204 images in the training set and 300 images in the test set. We implement our model on Pytorch 1.10.1 All of our models use an NVIDIA Ampere 100 GPU for training and testing.

4.2 Ablation Experiments

Table 1. Ablation experiments

Model	CBAM	DIoU-NMS	EIoU-Loss	mAP@0.5%	inference time/ms
YOLOv5s	x	x	x	92.1	23
YOLOv5s+CBAM	✓	x	x	94.0	25
YOLOv5s+DIoU-NMS	x	✓	x	92.8	24
YOLOv5s+EIoU-loss	x	x	✓	93.4	22
our model	✓	✓	✓	**94.2**	**27**

This ablation comparison experiment is designed to verify the optimization of the individual improvement modules. The results show that after adding CBAM, the mAP achieved a boost of 1.9 based on an increase in inference time of only 2 ms. After the adoption of DIoU-NMS, 0.7 improvements in mAP were achieved with an increase in inference time of only 1ms. After the adoption of EIoU Loss, the inference time is reduced by 1ms while the mAP value is improved by 1.3. By adding all three to the model at the same time, the model inference time increased by only 4 ms, while mAP improved by 2.1 % compared to the original YOLOv5s, which is a great improvement for dense object detection. (Table 1)

4.3 Comparative Experiments

Table 2. Comparative experiments

Model	Weight/Mb	Precision/%	Recall/%	mAP@0.5%	Inference time/ms
Fast-RCNN	108	73.3	93.0	93.1	210
SSD	100	90.6	88.5	93.2	95
YOLOv3	233	93.4	88.7	90.2	61
YOLOv4	244	**95.8**	85.8	91.7	42
YOLOv5s	**13.9**	93.8	88.9	92.1	**23**
our model	30.8	95.3	**93.8**	**94.2**	27

To better prove the experimental results of our model in this paper, the training and testing analyses were conducted on the same data using Fast-RCNN, SSD, YOLOv3, YOLOv4, and YOLOv5s deep learning models respectively. As we can see from Table 2, our model achieves a good improvement over Fast-RCNN, SSD, and YOLOv3. Our precision is slightly lower than YOLOv4, but weight, recall, mAP, and inference time are all better than it. Compared to YOLOv5s, we have only added some weight, and inference time, precision, recall, and mAP have all been improved. In summary, our model achieves better results overall compared to other models.

a   b

Fig. 3. Comparison of the results. a) The column on the left shows the results of original YOLOv5s model. b) The column on the right shows the results of our model.

4.4 Visualisation of Results

To better validate the feasibility of our model, select some pictures in the test set test. The results are visualized in Fig. 3. As we can see from the left image of the first row, the baby zebra was not detected because it was obscured by two larger zebras, the image on the right of the first row successfully detects it. The elephant on the left of the second row was not detected because most of its body was obscured by the surrounding elephants, the image on the right in the second row successfully detects it. The buffalo on the left of the third row was not detected because it was unclear from a distance, the image on the right in the third row successfully detects it. In conclusion, our model shows better performance compared to the YOLOv5s model. It can show greater robustness in complex dense wildlife, thus exhibiting superior performance as well as more accurate localization accuracy.

5   Conclusion

For the current problems of dense wildlife detection, this paper proposes an improvement based on the YOLOv5 model. The CBAM module is used to improve the problem of protecting coloration, the similarity between each other, and multi-scale features present in dense wildlife. DIoU-NMS is used to filter redundant candidate frames in dense wildlife and to pinpoint individual objects. EIoU-Loss ensures accuracy while accelerating the convergence of the loss function. The experimental results show that our model has better superiority and applicability compared with YOLOv5s, and meets the accuracy and real-time requirements for dense wildlife under complex field conditions. The next work is to track dense wildlife with high similarity. We hope that this paper can help developers and researchers get a better experience in the analysis and processing of dense wildlife scenarios.

Acknowledgments. This study was supported by the National Natural Science Foundation of China under Grant 62176217, the Innovation Team Funds of China West Normal University under Grant KCXTD2022-3, and the Fundamental Research Funds of China West Normal University under Grant 19B045.

References

1. Kays, R., Tilak, S., Kranstauber, B., Jansen, P.A., Carbone, C., Rowcliffe, M.J., Fountain, T., Eggert, J., He, Z.: Monitoring wild animal communities with arrays of motion sensitive camera traps. arXiv preprint arXiv:1009.5718 (2010)
2. Jocher, G., Stoken, A., Borovec, J., NanoCode, Chaurasia, A., TaoXie, Changyu, L., Abhiram, Laughing, tkianai, yxNONG, Hogan, A., lorenzomammana, AlexWang, Hajek, J., Diaconu, L., Marc, Kwon, Y., oleg, wanghaoyang, Defretin, Y., Lohia, A., ml ah, Milanko, B., Fineran, B., Khromov, D., Yiwei, D., Doug, Durgesh, Ingham, F.: ultralytics/yolov5: v5.0 - yolov5-p6 1280 models, aws, supervise.ly and youtube integrations (2021)
3. Woo, S., Park, J., Lee, J.Y., Kweon, I.S.: Cbam: Convolutional block attention module. In: Proceedings of the European conference on computer vision (ECCV). pp. 3–19 (2018)
4. Zheng, Z., Wang, P., Liu, W., Li, J., Ye, R., Ren, D.: Distance-iou loss: Faster and better learning for bounding box regression. In: Proceedings of the AAAI conference on artificial intelligence. vol. 34, pp. 12993–13000 (2020)
5. Neubeck, A., Van Gool, L.: Efficient non-maximum suppression. In: 18th International Conference on Pattern Recognition (ICPR'06). vol. 3, pp. 850–855. IEEE (2006)
6. Zhang, Y.F., Ren, W., Zhang, Z., Jia, Z., Wang, L., Tan, T.: Focal and efficient iou loss for accurate bounding box regression. Neurocomputing (2022)
7. Rezatofighi, H., Tsoi, N., Gwak, J., Sadeghian, A., Reid, I., Savarese, S.: Generalized intersection over union: A metric and a loss for bounding box regression. In: Proceedings of the IEEE/CVF conference on computer vision and pattern recognition. pp. 658–666 (2019)
8. Tan, M., Le, Q.: Efficientnet: Rethinking model scaling for convolutional neural networks. In: International conference on machine learning. pp. 6105–6114. PMLR (2019)
9. Wang, C.Y., Liao, H.Y.M., Wu, Y.H., Chen, P.Y., Hsieh, J.W., Yeh, I.H.: Cspnet: A new backbone that can enhance learning capability of cnn. In: Proceedings of the IEEE/CVF conference on computer vision and pattern recognition workshops. pp. 390–391 (2020)
10. Huang, G., Liu, Z., Van Der Maaten, L., Weinberger, K.Q.: Densely connected convolutional networks. In: Proceedings of the IEEE conference on computer vision and pattern recognition. pp. 4700–4708 (2017)
11. He, K., Zhang, X., Ren, S., Sun, J.: Deep residual learning for image recognition. In: Proceedings of the IEEE conference on computer vision and pattern recognition. pp. 770–778 (2016)
12. Simonyan, K., Zisserman, A.: Very deep convolutional networks for large-scale image recognition. arXiv preprint arXiv:1409.1556 (2014)
13. Lin, T.Y., Dollár, P., Girshick, R., He, K., Hariharan, B., Belongie, S.: Feature pyramid networks for object detection. In: Proceedings of the IEEE conference on computer vision and pattern recognition. pp. 2117–2125 (2017)

14. Liu, S., Qi, L., Qin, H., Shi, J., Jia, J.: Path aggregation network for instance segmentation. In: Proceedings of the IEEE conference on computer vision and pattern recognition. pp. 8759–8768 (2018)
15. Tan, M., Pang, R., Le, Q.V.: Efficientdet: Scalable and efficient object detection. In: Proceedings of the IEEE/CVF conference on computer vision and pattern recognition. pp. 10781–10790 (2020)
16. Liu, S., Huang, D., Wang, Y.: Learning spatial fusion for single-shot object detection. arXiv preprint arXiv:1911.09516 (2019)
17. He, K., Gkioxari, G., Dollár, P., Girshick, R.: Mask r-cnn. In: Proceedings of the IEEE international conference on computer vision. pp. 2961–2969 (2017)
18. Girshick, R.: Fast r-cnn. In: Proceedings of the IEEE international conference on computer vision. pp. 1440–1448 (2015)
19. Liu, W., Anguelov, D., Erhan, D., Szegedy, C., Reed, S., Fu, C.Y., Berg, A.C.: Ssd: Single shot multibox detector. In: European conference on computer vision. pp. 21–37. Springer (2016)
20. Redmon, J., Divvala, S., Girshick, R., Farhadi, A.: You only look once: Unified, real-time object detection. In: Proceedings of the IEEE conference on computer vision and pattern recognition. pp. 779–788 (2016)
21. Redmon, J., Farhadi, A.: Yolo9000: better, faster, stronger. In: Proceedings of the IEEE conference on computer vision and pattern recognition. pp. 7263–7271 (2017)
22. Redmon, J., Farhadi, A.: Yolov3: An incremental improvement. arXiv preprint arXiv:1804.02767 (2018)
23. Bochkovskiy, A., Wang, C.Y., Liao, H.Y.M.: Yolov4: Optimal speed and accuracy of object detection. arXiv preprint arXiv:2004.10934 (2020)
24. Lahiri, M., Tantipathananandh, C., Warungu, R., Rubenstein, D.I., Berger-Wolf, T.Y.: Biometric animal databases from field photographs: identification of individual zebra in the wild. In: Proceedings of the 1st ACM international conference on multimedia retrieval. pp. 1–8 (2011)
25. Norouzzadeh, M.S., Nguyen, A., Kosmala, M., Swanson, A., Palmer, M.S., Packer, C., Clune, J.: Automatically identifying, counting, and describing wild animals in camera-trap images with deep learning. Proceedings of the National Academy of Sciences 115(25), E5716–E5725 (2018)
26. Kellenberger, B., Volpi, M., Tuia, D.: Fast animal detection in uav images using convolutional neural networks. In: 2017 IEEE international geoscience and remote sensing symposium (IGARSS). pp. 866–869. IEEE (2017)
27. Zeppelzauer, M.: Automated detection of elephants in wildlife video. EURASIP journal on image and video processing 2013(1), 1–23 (2013) pp. 40–49. IEEE (2017)
28. Feng, W., Ju, W., Li, A., Bao, W., Zhang, J.: High-efficiency progressive transmission and automatic recognition of wildlife monitoring images with wisns. IEEE Access 7, 161412–161423 (2019)
29. Hu, P., Ramanan, D.: Finding tiny faces. In: Proceedings of the IEEE conference on computer vision and pattern recognition. pp. 951–959 (2017)
30. Liang, D., Geng, Q., Sun, H., Zhou, H., Kaneko, S.: Inferred box harmonization and aggregation for degraded face detection in crowds. Multimedia Tools and Applications pp. 1–20 (2022)
31. Pei, Y.: Improved YOLOv5 for Dense Wildlife Object Detection. https://www.kaggle.com/datasets/biancaferreira/african-wildlife

Self-attention Based Cross-Level Fusion Network for Camouflaged Object Detection

Chunlan Zhan[1], Linyan He[1], Yun Liu[2], Baolei Xu[3], and Anzhi Wang[1(✉)]

[1] School of Big Data and Computer Science, Guizhou Normal University,
Guiyang 550025, Guizhou, China
andyscu@163.com
[2] College of Artificial Intelligence, Southwest University, Chongqing 400715, China
[3] Sichuan University of Arts and Sciences, Dazhou, Sichuan, China
http://gznucvmll.cn/

Abstract. Although CNN-based camouflaged object detection(COD) has made great progress in recent years, their prediction maps usually contain incomplete detail information due to the similarity between the camouflaged object and the background. To alleviate this, a CNN-based framework named SACF-Net is designed for COD via cross-level fusion that facilitates the detection of camouflaged object detail. On the one hand, the low-level features contain abundant edge detail information to distinguish the camouflaged object from the background. On the other hand, the Polarized Self-Attention(PSA) mechanism is introduced to refine high-level features that contain extensive semantic information to enhance inner details and performance. Finally, cross-level complementarity fusion is performed progressively to generate prediction maps in a top-down manner. Extensive experiments on four COD datasets exhibit that the proposed method is better than the state-of-the-art methods.

Keywords: Camouflaged object detection · Self-attention · Cross-Level fusion

1 Introduction

Camouflaged object detection(COD) is the identification of object which appearance is similar to their background that they are difficult to be distinguished. Many creatures in nature own the ability to "camouflage", for example, chameleons change their color according to the environment to hide and protect themselves at any time. Therefore, detecting camouflaged targets with a

A. Wang—This work is supported by the National Natural Science Foundation of China under Grant(62162013), the National Undergraduate on Innovation and Entrepreneurship Training Program of Guizhou Province(S202110663028, S202110663029), and the Key Laboratory of Exploitation and Study of Distinctive Plants in Education Department of Sichuan Province(TSZW2109).

high degree of similarity between the object and the background is a challenging task.

Meanwhile, camouflaged object detection has a wide range of applications, including medical diagnosis, industrial production, agriculture, security surveillance, scientific research, etc. For example, in medical image segmentation, COD task is helpful to assist physician in detecting polyp, lung infection, tumor lesion, and other condition, etc.

Most camouflaged object detection methods ignored low-level features. Sun et al. [1]. only integrated the high-level features by fusion module which considered abundant global context information. Although Mei et al. [2]. focused on the low-level features and mined richer guidance information, they only processed the information from the last four layers, and the edge details were not perfectly distinguished from the background. Instead, we advocate combining five layers of the low-level and high-level features to capture more discriminative feature information to improve performance. To this end, we perform cross-level complementarity fusion gradually in a top-down manner.

In summary, our main contributions are as follows:

- A new COD Network is proposed, denoted as SACF-Net, which is based on Self-Attention and Cross-level Fusion, and utilizes cross-level complementarity fusion gradually in a top-down manner.
- The Selective Edge Aggregation with Depthwise over-parameterized convolution, Switchable whitening and Smooth maximum unit(DSS-SEA), is designed to which mine more detail information from low-level features.
- Experiments demonstrate that the proposed model performs better than state-of-the-art on four standard metrics on four COD benchmark datasets.

2   Related Work

Edge Information Extracting Module. The edge information can assist the object detection task to locate the target precisely, and detect the foreground object entirely. In recent years, the additional edge feature has shown better performance for detection and segmentation tasks. Some salient object detection (SOD) [3–5] methods improve performance with the help of edge information. Wang et al. [7] proposed an edge detection module in edge enhancement information to improve accuracy. Wu et al. [3] utilized an edge detection module to assist in supervising the foreground object detection and solve the problem of blurred boundaries in salient prediction maps. All of the above works illustrate the effectiveness of edge information for SOD. For COD, the selective edge aggregation (SEA) [8] module is proposed to obtain better edge priors and alleviate the problem of getting unclear boundaries. This also indicates that edge features contribute to the COD. To better utilize the edge information, we design a novel module, the DSS-SEA, to fuse the rich edge information in the low-level features.

Feature Fusion Module. The fusion of multi-level features from different convolution layers is an important manner to improve performance. Low-level features own more boundary information, but have less semantics. High-level features have abundant semantic information, and low resolution. Liu et al. [6] used a bottom-up global guidance module (GGM) to provide location information of potential salient objects for different feature layers and used a feature aggregation module (FAM) to fuse the refinement information of GGM with coarse-level feature information. C2FNet [1] proposed an attention-induced cross-level fusion module(ACFM) to fuse different feature information of level layers and used the dual-branch global context module(DGCM) to fuse the rich global context information in cross-layer features. Above methods show that feature fusion module is beneficial for both SOD and COD task.

Self-attention Module. Attention mechanism is used to simulate human visual attention, which assist visual tasks in assigning different weights to a different part of the features and can obtain critical information without incurring greater computation and storage overhead. Meanwhile, self-attention mechanism [9] is able to reserve the correlation between each pixel and other pixels compared to the ordinary convolutional neural networks that only extract the correlation in local information. Hui et al. [10] calculated the correlation between pixels at a distance by introducing a self-attentive mechanism. In this paper, the polarized self-attention(PSA) [11] was introduced to reduce attention to irrelevant background, so as to obtain rich internal information of camouflaged objects in high-level features.

3 The Proposed Framework

This section describes specifically the proposed method. Section 3.1 introduces the overview of SA-CFNet and shows the architecture in Fig. 1. Meanwhile, this section also describes the role of the DSS-SEA and the PSA modules in the proposed method. Among them, Sect. 3.2 is the description of the PSA module, Sect. 3.3 is the description of the DSS-SEA module.

3.1 Overview of Network Architecture

Res2Net is usually used to extract multi-level features, it has better feature extraction ability than ResNet, which allows more detailed features to be extracted. Therefore, SACF-Net is designed based on the Res2Net pretrain model. As Fig. 1 shows that an inputting image with H × W is fed to the Res2Net backbone network, and five level-features are extracted, denoted as $\{f_i, i = 1, 2, 3, 4, 5\}$ with size $\{H/2^i, W/2^i\}$.

In previous works, most of them ignored the low-level features from Conv-1 and Conv-2, considering that the low-level features have greater spatial resolution while requiring more computational resources, as well as contributing less to performance. In contrast, we consider the low-level features, because

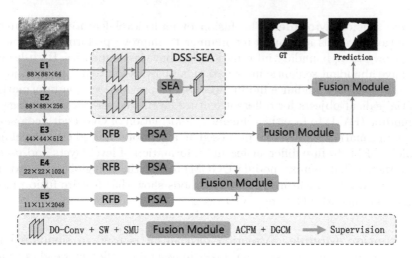

Fig. 1. An overview of the proposed SACF-Net. Res2Net is used as the backbone network. The DSS-SEA consists of three sets of DO-Conv+SW+SMU and the introduced Selective Edge Aggregation(SEA). the PSA is Polarized Self-Attention.

we argue that border information is necessary for camouflaged object detection task. Immediately afterward, considering that the high-level features contain rich semantic information, we deem that combining the high-level and the low-level features contribute to improving performance, and the PSA module is introduced to improve fusion effect and performance while maintaining the size of the feature channels and dimensions. Indeed, we find that although using the PSA module can obtain superior feature representation, the edge detail is lacking. As everyone knows, low-level features include a large number of edge features, such as colors and textures, etc. Therefore, the DSS-SEA module is designed to purify the low-level features to compensate for the deficiencies of the PSA module. The detailed structure of the PSA and the DSS-SEA modules are shown in Sects. 3.2 and 3.3.

3.2   Polarized Self-attention

In deep convolutional neural networks, extracting abundant semantic information from high-level features is momentous to enhance performance. In addition, the attention mechanism is similar to human visual attention, which is able to focus on information that is more critical to the visual task and reduce the attention to other unimportant information, which is advantageous for camouflaged object detection. Considering that PSA module can reduce the attention to irrelevant background and give greater weight to camouflage objects, the PSA module is introduced to obtain rich internal information of camouflage objects in high-level features and improve the efficiency and accurac.

In this paper, we introduce the PSA module to capture more inner features in the high-level features that namely $\{f_i,\ i=3,4,5\}$. First, we obtain a larger receptive field by the Receptive Field Block(RFB) to enhance the feature extraction capability, so that we can gain a cleaner feature map. Secondly, we utilize the output of RFB as the input image of the PSA to roughly locate and ignore the irrelevant background to extract more abundant internal features. In the PSA module, we maintain the previous channel $\{C_i, i=3,4,5\}$ of the feature map as well as the resolution $\{(H_i, W_i), i=3,4,5\}$ without compressing the input map, reducing the additional loss due to dimensionality reduction.

3.3 Selective Edge Aggregation with DO-Conv, SW and SMU

As shown in Fig. 1, the appearance of the camouflaged object has a similar texture to its surroundings which is difficult to be detected. However, there are subtle texture differences between the camouflaged objects and the background that can contribute to the acquisition of edge features. Yet since low-level features contain a lot of interference information, which has a negative impact on the subsequent result. Hence, the DSS-SEA module is designed to refine low-level features, which remove more redundant and noisy features, to improve the performance.

Firstly, the feature maps of f_1 with the resolution $(C_1 \times H_1 \times W_1)$ and f_2 with the resolution $(C_2 \times H_2 \times W_2)$ from the encoder as the input, which delivering to the DSS module to capture more edge features hidden in low-level features. The DSS module is designed as a new combination module, a combination to obtain higher accuracy while maintaining the same amount of calculation, which is composed of three sets of Depthwise Over-parameterized convolutional layer(DO-Conv) [12] with 3 × 3 kernels, Switchable Whitening(SW) [13] and Smoothing Maximum activation function(SMU) [14] to obtain feature maps as f_1' and f_2', each of them is kept to the original channel size, and the size of f_1' is $(H_2 \times W_2)$. The function of f_1' and f_2' is defined as:

$$f_i' = SMU(SW(DOConv(f_i))), \{i = 1,2\} \tag{1}$$

After performing the same operation on each pixel of f_1 and f_2, the f_1' and f_2' are fed to the SEA module for fusion, which to suppress the noise from the background and retain more edge information in low-level feature. The fusion manner is as follows f_{e_g} by:

$$f_{e\_g} = Cat(F(f_1', f_2')) \tag{2}$$

where $F(\cdot)$ and $Cat(\cdot)$ denote the SEA operation and cascaded operation, respectively.

3.4 Loss Function

We use the weighted binary cross-entropy loss($\mathcal{L}_{BCE}^{\omega}$) and the weighted IoU loss($\mathcal{L}_{IoU}^{\omega}$) for supervision. Since the low-level features include more interference information, we hope to focus on more interference information through $\mathcal{L}_{BCE}^{\omega}$

and $\mathcal{L}_{IoU}^{\omega}$, which predict the degree of disparity and the actual data. Total losses are as follows:

$$\mathcal{L}_{total} = \mathcal{L}_{BCE}^{\omega}(P, G) + \mathcal{L}_{IoU}^{\omega}(P, G) \tag{3}$$

where P, G are the prediction and ground truth, respectively.

4   Experimental Results

4.1   Experimental Setup

Implementation Details. We implement the proposed model with PyTorch on a GTX 3090 GPU. The training images are resized to 256 × 256. For optimization, we utilize AdaX optimization with a learning rate of 1e-4. We set up the batch size to 16 and the number of epochs to 40.

Datasets and Evaluation Metrics. We conduct experiments on four COD datasets including: CAMO [15], CHAMELEON, COD10K [16], and NC4K [17]. The training dataset consists of 3,040 COD10K images and 1,000 CAMO images. Among them, COD10K is the most enormous COD dataset which contains 2026 images for testing and 3040 images for training. In addition, the CAMO dataset includes 1,250 images, and the remaining(250 images) are used for testing. CHAMELEON and NC4K respectively include 76 images and 4,121 images to be used for testing. We adopt four common and authoritative evaluation metrics for comparing performance, namely S_{α}, F_{β}^{mean}, E_{ξ}^{mean}, and MAE.

4.2   Comparison with the State-of-the-Arts

We compare the proposed method with 12 state-of-the-art COD methods. For a fair comparison, we compare data and maps, which are public test results or public source code with the same parameters.

Quantitative Comparison. In Table 1, we report the quantitative results against the other 12 state-of-the-art methods on four benchmark datasets. The result shows that ours rank in the top three for almost all four standard metrics. For example, compared with the state-of-the-art SINet, we have improved the S_a by 2.9% and 2.4% on the CAMO and COD10K datasets, respectively. Note that the proposed method outperforms better than other methods on the challenging COD10K dataset.

Visual Comparison. As Fig. 2 shows the visual comparison between the proposed method among other methods. The proposed method gets a pretty result in large camouflaged objects, small camouflaged objects, multiple camouflaged objects and camouflaged objects with details. The proposed method is more accurate for detecting large and small camouflaged objects(Fig. 2 the 1st, 2nd

Table 1. Performance comparison with 12 COD models on benchmark testing datasets. The first, second and third places are marked in red, green and blue respectively.

Method	Pub' Year	CAMO				CHAMELEON				COD10K				NC4K			
		$S_\alpha\uparrow$	$F_\beta^w\uparrow$	$E_\xi^m\uparrow$	MAE↓	$S_\alpha\uparrow$	$F_\beta^w\uparrow$	$E_\xi^m\uparrow$	MAE↓	$S_\alpha\uparrow$	$F_\beta^w\uparrow$	$E_\xi^m\uparrow$	MAE↓	$S_\alpha\uparrow$	$F_\beta^w\uparrow$	$E_\xi^m\uparrow$	MAE↓
NLDF[5]	CVPR17	0.665	0.564	0.664	0.123	0.798	0.714	0.809	0.063	0.701	0.539	0.709	0.059	0.738	0.657	0.748	0.083
PiCANet[18]	CVPR18	0.701	0.573	0.716	0.125	0.765	0.618	0.779	0.085	0.696	0.489	0.712	0.081	0.758	0.639	0.773	0.088
EGNet[19]	ICCV19	0.737	0.655	0.758	0.102	0.856	0.766	0.883	0.049	0.751	0.595	0.793	0.053	0.796	0.718	0.830	0.067
CPD[4]	CVPR19	0.716	0.618	0.723	0.113	0.857	0.771	0.857	0.048	0.750	0.595	0.776	0.053	0.790	0.780	0.810	0.071
SCRN[20]	ICCV19	0.779	0.705	0.796	0.090	0.876	0.787	0.889	0.042	0.789	0.651	0.817	0.047	0.832	0.759	0.855	0.059
F3Net[21]	AAAI20	0.711	0.616	0.741	0.109	0.848	0.770	0.894	0.047	0.739	0.593	0.795	0.051	0.782	0.706	0.825	0.069
ITSD[22]	CVPR20	0.750	0.663	0.779	0.102	0.814	0.705	0.844	0.057	0.767	0.615	0.808	0.051	0.811	0.729	0.845	0.064
SINet[16]	CVPR20	0.745	0.702	0.804	0.092	0.872	0.827	0.936	0.034	0.776	0.679	0.864	0.043	0.810	0.772	0.873	0.057
LSR[23]	CVPR21	0.767	0.704	0.826	0.091	0.877	0.825	0.930	0.035	0.757	0.626	0.835	0.052	0.806	0.745	0.835	0.062
PFNet[2]	CVPR21	0.741	0.681	0.800	0.097	0.852	0.821	0.926	0.037	0.752	0.621	0.838	0.051	0.802	0.743	0.865	0.062
TINet[24]	AAAI21	0.781	0.678	0.847	0.087	0.874	0.783	0.916	0.038	0.793	0.635	0.848	0.043	–	–	–	–
C2FNet[1]	IJCAI21	0.767	0.712	0.814	0.095	0.854	0.785	0.906	0.045	0.788	0.680	0.862	0.045	0.818	0.762	0.872	0.060
Ours	–	0.774	0.715	0.828	0.093	0.881	0.828	0.932	0.033	0.800	0.702	0.864	0.041	0.829	0.782	0.876	0.056

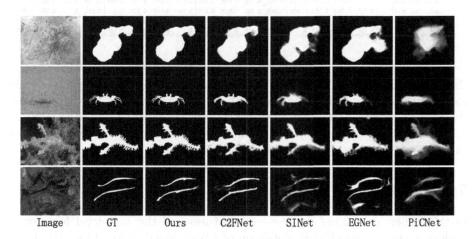

Image	GT	Ours	C2FNet	SINet	EGNet	PiCNet

Fig. 2. Visual comparison of the proposed model.

rows). Besides, other methods fail to get more details of crab and seahorse(Fig. 2 the 2rd, 3th rows). By comparison, we remove more interference information and obtain the edge details of the crab and seahorse more successfully. Not only that, but in terms of multiple object detection, we detect targets hidden in the background accurately(Fig. 2 the 4th row).

4.3 Ablation Analysis

In order to verify the effectiveness of the components in the proposed method, we conduct ablation study experiments in Table 2.

Table 2 reports that the PSA is effective in the proposed method. In addition, the DSS-SEA module obtain more detailed features in low-level features. To better verify the effect of the combination of different numbers of the DSS and the SEA modules, we compared five groups of experiments in Table 3. The experiment clearly shows that the combined effect of three groups of the DSS and

Table 2. Ablation study on the effectiveness of the PSA module, the DSS-SEA module.

	Method	CAMO				CHAMELEON				COD10K				NC4K			
		$S_\alpha\uparrow$	$F_\beta^w\uparrow$	$E_\phi^m\uparrow$	MAE↓	$S_\alpha\uparrow$	$F_\beta^w\uparrow$	$E_\phi^m\uparrow$	MAE↓	$S_\alpha\uparrow$	$F_\beta^w\uparrow$	$E_\phi^m\uparrow$	MAE↓	$S_\alpha\uparrow$	$F_\beta^w\uparrow$	$E_\phi^m\uparrow$	MAE↓
M1	basic	0.754	0.688	0.794	0.103	0.857	0.785	0.908	0.046	0.774	0.664	0.852	0.048	0.804	0.760	0.862	0.069
M2	basic+PSA	0.766	0.700	0.810	0.094	0.866	0.791	0.916	0.041	0.778	0.658	0.850	0.047	0.820	0.761	0.871	0.060
M3	basic+DSS-SEA	0.768	0.702	0.800	0.095	0.875	0.799	0.921	0.040	0.792	0.687	0.861	0.045	0.816	0.771	0.868	0.064
Ours	Ours	0.774	0.715	0.828	0.093	0.881	0.828	0.932	0.033	0.800	0.702	0.864	0.041	0.829	0.782	0.876	0.056

Table 3. Ablation study on the effectiveness of different number of DSS modules. "M2-M4" refers to adding 1, 2, 3 and 4 groups of DSS modules respectively.

Method	CAMO				CHAMELEON				COD10K				NC4K			
	$S_\alpha\uparrow$	$F_\beta^w\uparrow$	$E_\phi^m\uparrow$	MAE↓	$S_\alpha\uparrow$	$F_\beta^w\uparrow$	$E_\phi^m\uparrow$	MAE↓	$S_\alpha\uparrow$	$F_\beta^w\uparrow$	$E_\phi^m\uparrow$	MAE↓	$S_\alpha\uparrow$	$F_\beta^w\uparrow$	$E_\phi^m\uparrow$	MAE↓
Basic+SEA	0.757	0.695	0.791	0.102	0.862	0.779	0.900	0.046	0.778	0.661	0.857	0.047	0.810	0.768	0.864	0.068
Basic+SEA+DSS*1	0.747	0.685	0.774	0.101	0.862	0.785	0.908	0.046	0.774	0.664	0.852	0.048	0.808	0.762	0.862	0.069
Basic+SEA+DSS*2	0.760	0.698	0.789	0.099	0.865	0.795	0.918	0.040	0.788	0.680	0.854	0.047	0.812	0.766	0.868	0.066
Basic+SEA+DSS*3	0.768	0.702	0.800	0.095	0.875	0.799	0.921	0.040	0.792	0.687	0.861	0.045	0.816	0.771	0.868	0.064
Basic+SEA+DSS*4	0.758	0.698	0.795	0.099	0.865	0.796	0.918	0.040	0.789	0.683	0.861	0.046	0.811	0.765	0.864	0.065

the SEA("basic+SEA+DSS*3") is the best among them, and four groups begin to decline. Therefore, the proposed method uses three groups of the DSS and the SEA to remove redundant interference information from low-level features. Finally, Table 2 illustrates that the "basic+DSS-SEA" is significantly higher than the baseline. It shows the effectiveness of the DSS-SEA module.

5   Conclusion

In this paper, combining the low-level features and the high-level features to achieve accurate and efficient detection of camouflaged object in similar backgrounds, which capture more edge and inner information. Considering the characteristics of a large amount of edge information in the low-level and internal information in the high-level features, the PSA and DSS-SEA modules are utilized to reserve more feature information. Subsequently, the ACFM and DGCM modules are introduced to aggregate cross-level complementarity features in a top-down manner progressively. Experimental results demonstrate that the proposed method is better than state-of-the-art performance on four COD datasets.

References

1. Sun, Y., Chen, G., Zhou, T., Zhang, Y., Liu, N.: Context-aware cross-level fusion network for camouflaged object detection. arXiv:2105.12555 (2021)
2. Mei, H., Ji, G.P., Wei, Z., Yang, X., Wei, X., Fan, D.P.: Camouflaged object segmentation with distraction mining. In: Proceedings of the IEEE/CVF Conference on Computer Vision and Pattern Recognition, pp. 8772–8781 (2021)
3. Wu, R., Feng, M., Guan, W., Wang, D., Lu, H., Ding, E.: A mutual learning method for salient object detection with intertwined multi-supervision. Proceedings of the IEEE conference on computer vision and pattern recognition, pp. 8150–8159 (2019)

4. Wu, Z., Su, L., Huang, Q.: Cascaded partial decoder for fast and accurate salient object detection. Proceedings of the IEEE/CVF conference on computer vision and pattern recognition pp, 3907–3916 (2019)
5. Luo, Z., Mishra, A., Achkar, A., Eichel, J., Li, S., Jodoin, P. M.: Non-local deep features for salient object detection. Proceedings of the IEEE Conference on computer vision and pattern recognition, pp. 6609–6617 (2017)
6. Liu, J.J., Hou, Q., Cheng, M.M., Feng, J., Jiang, J.: A simple pooling-based design for real-time salient object detection. In Proceedings of the IEEE/CVF conference on computer vision and pattern recognition, pp. 3917–3926 (2019)
7. Wang, W., Zhao, S., Shen, J., Hoi, S. C., Borji, A.: Salient object detection with pyramid attention and salient edges. In: Proceedings of the IEEE/CVF Conference on Computer Vision and Pattern Recognition, pp. 1448–1457 (2019)
8. Ji, G.P., Zhu, L., Zhuge, M., Fu, K.: Fast camouflaged object detection via edge-based reversible re-calibration network. Pattern Recogn. **123**, 108414 (2022)
9. Vaswani, A., et al.: Attention is all you need. In: Advances in neural information processing systems 30 (2017)
10. Hui, B., Zhu, P., Hu, Q., Wang, Q.: Self-attention relation network for few-shot learning. In 2019 IEEE international conference on Multimedia and Expo Workshops, pp. 198–203. IEEE (2019)
11. Liu, H., Liu, F., Fan, X., Huang, D.: Polarized self-attention: towards high-quality pixel-wise regression. arXiv:2107.00782 (2021)
12. Cao, J., et al.: DO-Conv: depthwise over-parameterized convolutional layer. arXiv:2006.12030 (2020)
13. Pan, X., Zhan, X., Shi, J., Tang, X., Luo, P.: Switchable whitening for deep representation learning. In: Proceedings of the IEEE/CVF International Conference on Computer Vision, pp. 1863–1871 (2019)
14. Biswas, K., Kumar, S., Banerjee, S., Pandey, A. K.: SMU: smooth activation function for deep networks using smoothing maximum technique. arXiv:2111.04682 (2021)
15. Le, T.N., Nguyen, T.V., Nie, Z., Tran, M.T., Sugimoto, A.: Anabranch network for camouflaged object segmentation. Comput. Vis. Image Underst. **184**, 45–56 (2019)
16. Fan, D.P., Ji, G.P., Sun, G., Cheng, M. M., Shen, J., Shao, L.: Camouflaged object detection. In: Proceedings of the IEEE/CVF conference on computer vision and pattern recognition, pp. 2777–2787 (2020)
17. Lv, Y., et al.: Simultaneously localize, segment and rank the camouflaged objects. Proceedings of the IEEE/CVF Conference on Computer Vision and Pattern Recognition, pp. 11591–11601 (2021)
18. Liu, N., Han, J., Yang, M. H.: PiCANet: learning pixel-wise contextual attention for saliency detection. In: Proceedings of the IEEE conference on computer vision and pattern recognition, pp. 3089–3098 (2018)
19. Zhao, J.X., Liu, J.J., Fan, D.P., Cao, Y., Yang, J., Cheng, M.M.: EGNet: edge guidance network for salient object detection. In: Proceedings of the IEEE/CVF international conference on computer vision, pp. 8779–8788 (2019)
20. Wu, Z., Su, L., Huang, Q.: Stacked cross refinement network for edge-aware salient object detection. In: Proceedings of the IEEE/CVF international conference on computer vision, pp. 7264–7273 (2019)
21. Wei, J., Wang, S., Huang, Q.: FNet: fusion, feedback and focus for salient object detection. In: Proceedings of the AAAI Conference on Artificial Intelligence, pp. 12321–12328 (2020)

22. Zhou, H., Xie, X., Lai, J. H., Chen, Z., Yang, L.: Interactive two-stream decoder for accurate and fast saliency detection. In: Proceedings of the IEEE/CVF conference on computer vision and pattern recognition, pp. 9141–9150 (2020)
23. Lv, Y., et al.: Simultaneously localize, segment and rank the camouflaged objects. In: Proceedings of the IEEE/CVF Conference on Computer Vision and Pattern Recognition, pp. 11591–11601 (2021)
24. Zhu, J., Zhang, X., Zhang, S., Liu, J.: Inferring camouflaged objects by texture-aware interactive guidance network. In: Proceedings of the AAAI Conference on Artificial Intelligence, pp. 3599–3607 (2021)

Trustyworth, Privacy and Persondal Data Security

Face Forgery Detection by Multi-dimensional Image Decomposition

Tianshuo Zhang[1,2], Xiangyu Zhu[1,2](✉), Feng Pan[3], Ke Xiang[3], and Zhen Lei[1,2]

[1] School of Artificial Intelligence, University of Chinese Academy of Sciences, Beijing, China
[2] CBSR & NLPR, Institute of Automation, Chinese Academy of Sciences, Beijing, China
{tianshuo.zhang,xiangyu.zhu,zlei}@nlpr.ia.ac.cn
[3] Zhejiang Sunny Optical Intelligence Technology Co., Ltd., Ningbo, China
{fpan,xiangke}@sunnyoptical.com

Abstract. With the development of face manipulation techniques and the potential harms of fake videos and images to public safety, the field of face forgery detection has received a lot of attention. However, existing face forgery detection methods mostly rely on specific datasets, and the generalization performance appears to be degraded when testing across datasets. In this paper, we use multi-dimensional image decomposition, i.e., spatial-frequency decomposition and computer graphics decomposition, to provide additional forgery clues. On the one hand, we decompose the face image into three components: high-frequency component, medium frequency component, and low-frequency component using spatial-frequency decomposition; on the other hand, we use computer graphics algorithms to simulate the face generation process, separate the 3D model and decompose the face image into five components. For the decomposed components, we introduce a three-stream neural network to fuse multi-modality information. Extensive experiments have shown that our method achieves state-of-the-art performance.

Keywords: Face forgery detection · Face forgery · Space-frequency decomposition · Computer graphics decomposition

1 Introduction

With the rapid development of deep generative models, a series of deep face manipulation techniques have emerged in recent years. These techniques use deep learning methods such as Generative Adversarial Networks (GAN), which generate fake face images that are almost impossible to determine from RGB images. Face manipulation has attracted extensive research and is distinctly divided into two periods. The period of traditional methods relies on domain expertise and falsification experience to manipulate faces through computer graphics methods

© The Author(s), under exclusive license to Springer Nature Switzerland AG 2022
W. Deng et al. (Eds.): CCBR 2022, LNCS 13628, pp. 591–601, 2022.
https://doi.org/10.1007/978-3-031-20233-9_60

[1]. In recent years, deep learning methods have rapidly emerged to achieve their accurate manipulation of faces.

Rapid iterations of face manipulation methods and public concerns about security have contributed to the development of deep forgery detection techniques. In the beginning, researchers manually designed features [2]. With the rise of deep learning, many deep learning and multi-modal approaches have brought huge performance gains to the field, such as frequency domain features [3], ambient and direct illumination [4], optical flow, etc.

On the one hand, Extensive methods have shown that forgery traces not visible in RGB images can be found in the frequency domain [3], such as unusual upsampling patterns. On the other hand, methods that use computer graphics rendering to simulate the generation of a face image and thus reverse the decomposition of the face can provide a priori information for discriminating forged images and highlighting forgery cues in specific components [4]. In this paper, we consider combining frequency domain decomposition and graphical decomposition and designing a multimodal task to fuse the information from both. To fuse information effectively, we introduce a three-stream neural network for feature extraction and classification. The schematic diagram of our method is shown in Fig. 1.

In summary, our contributions are: 1) We fuse two image decomposition methods, computer graphics face decomposition and spatial-frequency domain face decomposition, and their positive contributions are demonstrated by ablation experiments. 2) We design a three-stream neural network for feature extraction and deep fusion of multi-modal forgery clues. 3) Experiments show that our method has performance advantages compared to other methods.

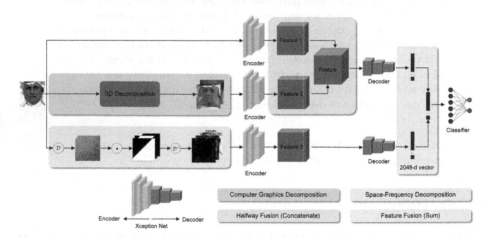

Fig. 1. Three-stream network architecture. The preprocessing process divides a face image into three information streams: face stream, frequency domain decomposition stream, and computer graphics stream. After the Encoder, we use Halfway Fusion to fuse the face and the computer graphics decomposition stream. After the Decoder, the two remaining information streams are fused to obtain the feature vector, which is followed by a Classifier.

2 Face Forgery Detection with Multi-dimensional Image Decomposition

2.1 Spatial-Frequency Decomposition

Many previous studies have shown that the forgery traces can be captured in the frequency domain. In this subsection, it is proposed to provide additional clues for forgery detection by extracting features from the frequency domain of the image through the spatial-frequency domain transform algorithm.

In this paper we use discrete cosine transform (DCT) as the spatial-frequency domain transform, considering that DCT has better energy aggregation in the frequency domain than FFT; JPEG and other algorithms widely use DCT. Using DCT to transform the image to the frequency domain, An image does not satisfy translation invariance and local consistency. In contrast, CNNs require images to satisfy local consistency and translation invariance. To solve this problem, we adopted an indirect approach to introduce frequency information into the convolutional neural network and designed the algorithm as follows.

First convert the image to the frequency domain using DCT:

$$X_{\mathrm{f}} = \mathcal{D}(X) \tag{1}$$

where X is the original spatial domain image, X_{f} is the image in the frequency domain image, and $\mathcal{D}$ is DCT. For the discrete cosine transformed frequency domain picture, the low, middle and high frequency components are extracted by designing three filters.

$$X_{\mathrm{fh, fm, fl}} = f_{\mathrm{h, m, l}}(X_{\mathrm{f}}) \tag{2}$$

where f_{h}, f_{m}, f_{l}, are high-frequency, medium-frequency, low-frequency filters, respectively, to extract the high-frequency, medium-frequency, low-frequency components of X_{fh}, X_{fm}, X_{fl}. Due to the properties of the discrete cosine transform, the three filters are three masks. The three masks are shown in Fig. 2.

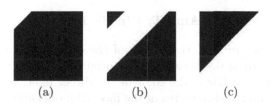

(a)   (b)   (c)

Fig. 2. Filters for extracting frequency components (a) low-frequency filter (b) medium-frequency filter (c) high-frequency filter

Then convert the three frequency domain components to the spatial domain using the discrete cosine inverse transform:

$$X_{\mathrm{h,m,l}} = \mathcal{D}^{-1}(X_{\mathrm{fh,fm,fl}}) \tag{3}$$

where X_{h}, X_{m}, X_{l} =, are high-frequency, medium-frequency, low-frequency components in spatial domain, and X_{fh}, X_{fm}, X_{fl} are high-frequency, medium-frequency, low-frequency components in frequency domain. $\mathcal{D}^{-1}$ is the discrete cosine inverse transform.

The spatial domain reconstructed components satisfy translation invariance and local consistency, and also contain part of the frequency domain information. Its pipeline has shown in Fig. 3.

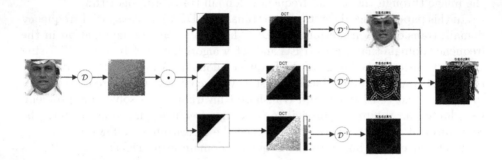

Fig. 3. Spatial-frequency decomposition pipeline

2.2 Computer Graphics Decomposition

In this section, it is proposed to use computer graphics methods to model the face generation process and to implement the graphical decomposition of faces reversibly. In computer graphics, faces can be generated by the Z-Buffer algorithm:

$$\mathbf{I}_{syn} = Z\_\,\mathrm{Buffer}(\mathbf{S}, \mathbf{C}) \tag{4}$$

where $\mathbf{S}$ is the 3D face mesh, and $\mathbf{C}$ is the RGB of each vertex in $\mathbf{S}$. Under the Lambertian assumption, the RGB value $\mathbf{C}$ of each vertex on the 3D geometry can be further decomposed:

$$\mathbf{C}_i = \mathbf{Amb}^*\mathbf{T}_i + \langle \mathbf{n}_i, \mathbf{l} \rangle \cdot \mathbf{Dir}^*\mathbf{T}_i \tag{5}$$

where the facial texture $\mathbf{T}_i$ is the albedo of the each vertex, $\mathbf{C}_i$ is the color of the ambient light, $\mathbf{n}_i$ is the vertex normal originating from the 3D mesh, $\mathbf{l}$ is the light direction, and $\mathbf{Dir}$ is the color of the direct light. $\langle \mathbf{n}_i, \mathbf{l} \rangle \cdot$ is the inner product of the normal to each vertex of the face 3D model and the light direction vector, and the value of this inner product determines color of the face 3D model rendered by direct light. They are expressed in the following form:

$$\begin{cases} \mathbf{T}_i = [R_i, G_i, B_i]^T \\ \mathbf{Amb} = \mathrm{diag}\,(R_{amb}, G_{amb}, B_{amb}) \\ \mathbf{Dir} = \mathrm{diag}\,(R_{\mathrm{dir}}, G_{\mathrm{dir}}, B_{\mathrm{dir}}) \end{cases} \tag{6}$$

For the texture $\mathbf{T}$, we can assumed that it is composed of a common texture $\mathbf{T}_{\mathrm{com}}$ and a identity texture $\mathbf{T}_{\mathrm{id}}$. The common texture is a texture pattern common to each person, and the identity texture is a texture structure unique to each person based on the common texture, which is an identifiable fine-grained texture pattern containing identity information. To obtain the common texture $\mathbf{T}_{\mathrm{com}}$, a certain number of face models are needed to solve the average texture. In this paper, we use the Basel Face Model (BFM) database and model the common texture using PCA method:

$$\mathbf{T}_{\mathrm{com}} = \overline{\mathbf{T}} + \mathbf{B}\beta \tag{7}$$

where $\overline{\mathbf{T}}$ is the average texture, $\mathbf{B}$ is the main axis of the PCA face model, β is the common texture parameter.

Finally, the difference between the texture component and the common texture is used as the individual texture.

$$\mathbf{T}_{id} = \mathbf{T} - \mathbf{T}_{com} = \mathbf{T} - \overline{\mathbf{T}} - \mathbf{B}\beta \tag{8}$$

In summary, the decomposition of the texture component is given by:

$$\mathbf{T} = \overline{\mathbf{T}} + \mathbf{B}\beta + \mathbf{T}_{id} \tag{9}$$

So far, any face image can be represented as a combination of five components: $[\mathbf{S}, \mathbf{Amb}, \mathbf{Dir}, \beta, \mathbf{T}_{id}]$, indicates 3D shape, common texture, identity texture, ambient light, and direct light, respectively. The five components are represented in Fig. 4.

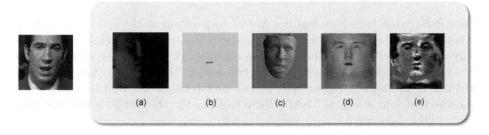

(a)   (b)   (c)   (d)   (e)

Fig. 4. The 5 components decomposed by computer graphics. (a) direct light, (b) ambient light, (c) 3D geometry, (d) common texture and (e) identity texture

To implement this graphical decomposition algorithm, it can be abstracted as an optimization problem to obtain five components by optimizing the difference between the original face image and the generated image with the following optimization objectives:

$$\arg \min_{\mathbf{S},\mathbf{Amb},\mathbf{Dir},\beta,\mathbf{T}_{id}} \|\mathbf{I} - \mathbf{I}_{syn}(\mathbf{S},\mathbf{Amb},\mathbf{Dir},\beta,\mathbf{T}_{id})\| \tag{10}$$

However, optimizing this loss function takes up a large number of computational resources. So we use an approximation method to speed up the component generation process. Specifically, we use 3DDFA [5] for face alignment and cut the face, then fit a 3DMM face model to separate the face 3D structure from the texture. For the separated face textures, they are illuminated based on the spherical harmonic function [6].

The existing method proves [6] that based on nine orthogonal spherical harmonic functions, the appearance of a face under arbitrary illumination can be expressed as:

$$(\mathbf{H}\gamma) \cdot \mathbf{T} \tag{11}$$

where $\mathbf{H} = [\mathbf{h}_1, \mathbf{h}_2, \ldots, \mathbf{h}_9]$ is nine basis functions of the spherical harmonic function, $\gamma = [\gamma_1, \gamma_2, \ldots, \gamma_9]$ is e 9-dimensional reflectance parameters of the spherical harmonic function. We consider $\gamma_1 \cdot \mathbf{h}_1$ as the ambient light and $[\gamma_2 \cdot \mathbf{h}_2, \ldots, \gamma_9 \cdot \mathbf{h}_9]$ as the direct light.

After this, the common texture and identity texture are separated according to the principal component analysis. Finally, we map these components to UV space.

3   Three-Stream Neural Networks

Xception Net [7] is based on the depth-separable convolution module, designed by the residual connection stacking of this module. In this paper, we use Xception Net as the backbone for feature extraction of the three-channel input.

3.1   Encoder and Decoder

Considering that high-level features are vectors output at the end of the feature extractor with highly abstracted information, the fusion of high-level features only may not fully utilize the input information. We divide Xception Net into two parts, Encoder, and Decoder. The two output the mid-level and high-level features of the input, respectively. In our architecture, we use the Entry Flow and the first four stacks of Middle Flow as Encoder; the last four and the Exit Flow as the Decoder.

3.2   Multi-modality Feature Fusion

For the mid-level features output by Encoder, We use Concatenate to retain all information. For the high-level feature after Decoder, the output is a 2048-dimensional feature vector, which is already very abstract and has no underlying information, so the feature fusion of this high-level feature can be performed by direct summing (Sum). The final feature fusion is shown in Fig. 5.

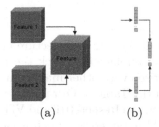

(a)   (b)

Fig. 5. Multi-modality feature fusion (a) Concatenating mid-level features, (b) Summing high-level features

3.3 Three-Stream Networks Architecture

Combining the above methods, we designed an end-to-end neural network, divided into two major parts: pre-processing and neural network classification. The schematic diagram is shown in Fig. 1. The preprocessing process divides a face image into three information streams: face stream, frequency domain decomposition stream, and computer graphics stream. After preprocessing, the Encoder extracts a mid-level feature map with shape [H, W, C] of [$19 \times 19 \times 728$]. For the mid-level feature, we use Halfway Fusion to fuse the face and the computer graphics decomposition stream. After the decoder, the two remaining information streams are fused to obtain the feature vector with the shape of [$1 \times 1 \times 2048$], which is followed by a Classifier. To address the problem of a large number of model parameters, we propose a lightweight implementation method with a small number of parameters for the above architecture. The schematic diagram is shown in Fig. 6.

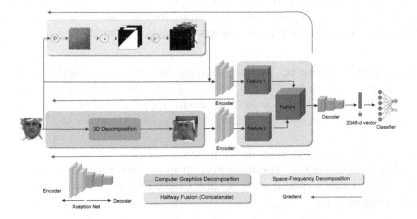

Fig. 6. Light networks architecture. We share the weights between the face information stream and the frequency domain decomposition stream. The two streams share one Feature map, which is extracted by Encoder and then Halfway Fusion with the computer graphics decomposition stream, after which only one Decoder is needed to complete the classification.

4   Experiments

Parameters. For the overall network architecture and the light network architecture, we used Pytorch to implement, check the number of parameters and make a quantitative comparison with other mainstream architecture. The results are shown in Table 1. From the Table 1, Our Three-stream network has 50.8 M parameters, which is between the Resnet-101 and ViT-Base. Our simplified light architecture has only 29.9 M parameters, which is close to 22.9 M of Xception. Both architectures achieve a usable number of parameters.

Datasets. The Face Forensics++ [11] including four state-of-the-art face manipulation methods is used as the training set, validation set and test set with a

Table 1. Comparison of parameters of multiple models

Architecture	Parameters
Xception [7]	22.9M
Resnet-50 [8]	23.5M
Ours(light)	**29.9M**
Resnet-101 [8]	42.6M
Ours	**50.8M**
ViT-Base [9]	86.6M
VGG-16 [10]	138.4M

split ratio of 0.72:0.14:0.14. We chose the c23 data. DFDC [12] and Celeb-DF [13] are used as the cross-dataset test set to simulate the test of the generalization ability of the model in the face of unknown forgery methods.

Implementation Details. We use Adam optimizer for training the model with weight decay equals to $3 \times 10^{-4}, \beta_1 = 0.9, \beta_2 = 0.999$ and batch size set to 32. The initial learning rate is 5×10^{-6} to warm up, then changed to 3×10^{-5} at epoch 2, to 2×10^{-5} at epoch 8, to 1×10^{-5} at epoch 15, to 5×10^{-6} or the rest from epoch 32.

For the frequency domain decomposition stream, we use decomposition thresholds of 0.1 and 0.2. For computer graphics decomposition, we use the settings of [4], using a combination of direct light **Dir** and identity textures $\mathbf{T}_{id}$ as input components.

4.1   Results

The converged network is tested in the FaceForensics++ test dataset and the metrics are shown in the following Table 2. It can be seen that the overall

Table 2. Test results (%) of the three-stream network in FaceForensics++

Architecture	AP (%)	AUC (%)	EER (%)
Ours	99.17	**98.57**	**5.83**
Ours (light)	**99.36**	97.35	8.51

architecture outperforms the light architecture in all metrics except for the average accuracy rate. Both designed architectures reach the mainstream of current deep forgery detection methods in terms of performance metrics. We performed cross-dataset tests on the converged network using the DFDC and Celeb-DF datasets and use the popular AUC metric to evaluate the generalization performance. The metrics are shown in the following Table 3: For the listed mainstream methods, the overall architecture designed in this paper achieves the state-of-the-art results and the light architecture has advantages over most of the results.

4.2   Ablation Study

In this paper, we design three information streams, i.e., face stream, frequency domain decomposition stream, and computer graphics decomposition streams. In this subsection, we studied the contribution of each stream. The results of the ablation studies are shown in Table 4.

Table 3. AUC (%) of the three-stream network and other SOTA methods in DFDC and Celeb-DF

Methods	DFDC AUC (%)	Celeb-DF AUC (%)
Xception [7]	62.17	63.82
EfficientNetB4 [14]	63.03	64.29
LTW [15]	69.00	64.10
F3-Net [3]	63.52	67.00
FD2-Net [4]	67.70	70.10
Ours (light)	67.71	68.66
Ours	**69.73**	**70.67**

Table 4. AUC (%) of the ablation study

Face	Frequency	Graphics	FFpp	DFDC	Celeb-DF
√			96.29	64.25	63.82
√	√		97.10(+0.81)	66.09(+1.84)	66.13(+2.31)
√	√	√	**98.57**(+1.47)	**69.73**(+3.64)	**70.67**(+4.54)

The results of the ablation studies demonstrate that both the frequency domain decomposition stream and the computer graphics decomposition stream provides a positive contribution to the overall model, and the computer graphics decomposition stream provides a greater contribution to the improvement of the overall model performance. It can also be speculated that the use of a computer graphics algorithm can better separate and highlight forgery clues.

5   Conclusion

In this paper, we propose a multi-dimensional image decomposition face depth forgery detection method combining face image spatial-frequency domain decomposition and face computer graphics decomposition by studying the field of face depth forgery detection. A detailed experimental study is conducted to show that the proposed method can perform the face depth forgery detection task with high efficiency and accuracy, and has better performance with unknown forgery methods than other state-of-the-art methods.

Acknowledgement. This work was supported in part by the National Key Research & Development Program (No. 2020YFC2003901), Chinese National Natural Science Foundation Projects (No. 62276254, 62176256, 61876178, 61976229 and 62106264), and the Youth Innovation Promotion Association CAS (No. Y2021131).

References

1. Tolosana, R., Vera-Rodriguez, R., Fierrez, J., Morales, A., Ortega-Garcia, J.: Deep-Fakes and beyond: a survey of face manipulation and fake detection. Inf. Fusion **64**, 131–148 (2020)
2. Popescu, A.C., Farid, H.: Exposing digital forgeries by detecting traces of resampling. IEEE Trans. Signal Process. **53**(2), 758–767 (2005)
3. Qian, Y., Yin, G., Sheng, L., Chen, Z., Shao, J.: Thinking in frequency: face forgery detection by mining frequency-aware clues. In: Vedaldi, A., Bischof, H., Brox, T., Frahm, J.-M. (eds.) ECCV 2020. LNCS, vol. 12357, pp. 86–103. Springer, Cham (2020). https://doi.org/10.1007/978-3-030-58610-2_6
4. Zhu, X., Wang, H., Fei, H., Lei, Z., Li, S.Z.: Face forgery detection by 3d decomposition. In: Proceedings of the IEEE/CVF Conference on Computer Vision and Pattern Recognition, pp. 2929–2939 (2021)
5. Zhu, X., Lei, Z., Liu, X., Shi, H., Li, S.Z.: Face alignment across large poses: a 3d solution. In: Proceedings of the IEEE Conference on Computer Vision and Pattern Recognition, pp. 146–155 (2016)
6. Zhang, L., Samaras, D.: Face recognition from a single training image under arbitrary unknown lighting using spherical harmonics. IEEE Trans. Pattern Anal. Mach. Intell. **28**(3), 351–363 (2006)
7. Chollet, F.: Xception: deep learning with depthwise separable convolutions. In: Proceedings of the IEEE Conference on Computer Vision and Pattern Recognition, pp. 1251–1258 (2017)
8. He, K., Zhang, X., Ren, S., Sun, J.: Deep residual learning for image recognition. In: Proceedings of the IEEE Conference on Computer Vision and Pattern Recognition, pp. 770–778 (2016)

9. Caron, M., et al.: Emerging properties in self-supervised vision transformers. In: Proceedings of the IEEE/CVF International Conference on Computer Vision, pp. 9650–9660 (2021)
10. Simonyan, K., Zisserman, A.: Very deep convolutional networks for large-scale image recognition. arXiv preprint arXiv:1409.1556 (2014)
11. Rossler, A., Cozzolino, D., Verdoliva, L., Riess, C., Thies, J., Nießner, M.: FaceForensics++: learning to detect manipulated facial images. In: Proceedings of the IEEE/CVF International Conference on Computer Vision, pp. 1–11 (2019)
12. Dolhansky, B., et al.: The deepfake detection challenge (DFDC) dataset. arXiv preprint arXiv:2006.07397 (2020)
13. Li, Y., Yang, X., Sun, P., Qi, H., Lyu, S.: Celeb-DF: a large-scale challenging dataset for deepfake forensics. In: Proceedings of the IEEE/CVF Conference on Computer Vision and Pattern Recognition, pp. 3207–3216 (2020)
14. Bonettini, N., Cannas, E.D., Mandelli, S., Bondi, L., Bestagini, P., Tubaro, S.: Video face manipulation detection through ensemble of CNNs. In: 25th International Conference on Pattern Recognition (ICPR), pp. 5012–5019. IEEE (2020)
15. Sun, K., et al.: Domain general face forgery detection by learning to weight. In: Proceedings of the AAAI Conference on Artificial Intelligence, vol. 35, pp. 2638–2646 (2021)

IrisGuard: Image Forgery Detection for Iris Anti-spoofing

Wenqi Zhuo[1,2], Wei Wang[2(✉)], Hui Zhang[3], and Jing Dong[2]

[1] School of Artificial Intelligence, University of Chinese Academy of Sciences, Beijing, China
zhuowenqi2020@ia.ac.cn

[2] CRIPAC & NLPR, Institute of Automation, Chinese Academy of Sciences, Beijing, China
{wwang,jdong}@nlpr.ia.ac.cn

[3] Beijing IrisKing Co., Ltd., Beijing, China
zhanghui@irisking.com

Abstract. With the development of generative models, new types of fake iris have emerged. Distinguished from traditional spoofing means caused by cosmetic contact lenses, such iris images are realistic and easily accessible, which poses a threat to privacy protection and information security. In this paper, we are the first to study iris forgery detection method that can simultaneously defend against contact lenses based or GAN-generated spoofing attacks. Through multi-model ensemble, we design a simple but effective detection framework. The backbone part of our method consists of three CNN networks, including ResNet-18, EfficientNet-B0 and ConvNeXt-tiny. We conduct experiments on three public iris datasets and a great deal of StyleGAN-generated iris images which are collected by ourselves. The proposed method has been proved to be effective on the detection of various iris forgeries, and it has the state-of-the-art performances.

Keywords: Iris anti-spoofing · Image forgery detection · Privacy protection

1 Introduction

Nowadays, iris recognition plays a more and more significant role in current society. It has been widely applied in diverse industries which require high-precision identity authentication, for instance, online payment and security systems. However, with the popularity of cosmetic contact lenses (also denoted as CCL) and the advances in deep generative algorithms, the biometric modality that iris recognition mainly relies on can be destroyed or falsified.

In Fig. 1, we provide several examples of real and forged iris images. Here, pictures (a)–(d) represent pristine iris, synthetic iris, pristine contact lenses and synthetic contact lenses in sequence. For simplicity, we abbreviate them as PI,

SI, PCL and SCL respectively. As one can see, for a PCL image, the CCL covers the iris region and then mixes with the original textures, which may lead to a mistake of identification. Therefore, it is regarded as one of the fake iris. SCL images have the same negative impact, but are more convenient to be obtained. To explain, with the assistant of generative models, we have no need to take pictures of genuine eyes wearing CCLs. Instead, we can directly produce such iris images by computers. Moreover, it is easy to observe that the fake iris "SI" is perfectly natural and can hardly be distinguished from the real iris "PI" just by human eyes. Because of these characteristics above, malicious users may utilize iris forgery for identity theft and financial fraud, which does a great harm to our country, society and citizens. To eliminate this risk and effectively cope with different attack means of iris spoofing, there is an urgent need to develop accurate detection methods.

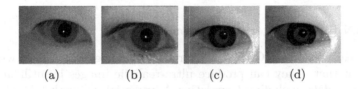

(a)   (b)   (c)   (d)

Fig. 1. Examples of real and forged iris images

Researchers have proposed lots of approaches to detect fake iris images, including algorithms depend on hand-craft features (e.g. texture analysis [1], Local Binary Patterns (LBP) [2] and hierarchical visual codebook [3]) and convolutional neural networks (CNNs) (e.g. ContlensNet [4] and GHCLNet [5]). However, existing detection approaches do not take computer-generated iris forgery into consideration. They can only deal with PCL images. In other words, they may encounter a failure when attacked by SI and SCL images. Motivated by better protection of identity information and privacy security, we design a detection framework for iris image anti-spoofing. Our main contributions are as follows:

- For the first time, we pay attention to the detection of iris forgery images produced not only by cosmetic contact lenses but also by generative models.
- We propose a simple but effective detection method for iris anti-spoofing.
- Extensive experiments are conduct on three public iris datasets and multitudes of self-collected synthetic iris images. The results show that the proposed approach outperforms state-of-the-art CCL detectors, and can accurately detect fake iris images generated by StyleGAN [6].

2   Related Work

2.1   Iris Image Anti-spoofing

There exist lots of researches on iris image anti-spoofing, and we provide a brief review of them in this section.

Early works differentiate fake iris images from the real ones through constructing hand-craft features. Daugman [7] designed a iris forgery detector by using the amplitude spectrum of Fourier transforms. [8] take full use of LBP and its variations to detect contact lenses. Based on local phase quantization and a thorough analysis of binary gabor patterns, Nigam et al. [9] developed a robust detection model for iris anti-spoofing. Benefited from the great advances in deep learning theories, CNN-based methods gradually become the mainstream. Ragvendra et al. [4] proposed ContlensNet, an detection model with 15-layers CNN. Similarly, a hierarchical network on the basis of ResNet-50 [10] was invented in [5]. Hoffman et al. [11] used a shallow version of VGG net [12] to design an iris anti-spoofing model which took a patch of the iris image and the associated segmentation mask together as the 2-channels input. Although the above methods have good performances on public iris datesets, they may lose generalization ability when facing GAN-generated fake iris images.

2.2 GAN Image Forgery Detection

In recent years, a series of GAN image forgery technologies have been widespread over the Internet. They can produce ultra-realistic images by utilizing diverse generative models, including Generative Adversarial Network (GAN) [13] and its multiple variants. To mitigate the risks introduced by GAN fake images, researchers spare no effort to develop a great deal of precise detection methods and promising results have been reported in the literature. Existing detectors can roughly be divided into two categories: spatial domain based detection and frequency domain based detection. Here, we mainly focus on the former ones.

As we all know, there exist some digital imprints in images that are acquired by the real-world cameras. Enlightened by this theory, GAN-generated fake images are also expected to present spatial domain imprints, which may be invisible and imperceptible, especially for high-quality forged images. Marra et al. [14] proposed a steganalysis model and distinguished GAN-generated imagery from camera imagery by analyzing photo response non-uniformity (PRNU) patterns. [15] points out that saturation cues can be used for GAN-generated fake image detection. Due to the remarkable performances of CNNs on image classification and other visual tasks, researchers have gradually applied in various CNN structures in fake image detection. Marra et al. [16] designed a CNN-based detectors and proved that it can perform better than conventional methods under a compression environment. In [17], Cozzolino et al. noted that the forensic models perform poorly on testing data because forged images generated by GMs are different from those used for training. To address this dilemma, they proposed a detection approach by utilizing few-shot learning and knowledge transfer. Similarly, Wang et al. [18] developed a CNN-based detector which is train only on ProGAN-generated pictures and can offer strong generalization capability when facing different GAN-generated fake images.

3   Method

Problem Definition. Inspired by traditional iris anti-spoofing and GAN image forgery detection, we model iris forgery detection as a binary classification problem. The main task is to figure out whether the suspicious image is forged. In this paper, we only define PI as real iris, while the other types are all classified as fake iris. For example, PCL belongs to mask-based iris spoofing means which changes original textures of iris region by adding a contact lens mask. Although the mask of a PCL image is usually an authentic contact lens and such images are indeed captured by camera. Recently, there emerges a novel iris spoofing attack, called GAN-generated iris forgery. It utilizes various GAN algorithms to synthesize images of pure iris or iris wearing CCL, that is SI or SCL.

Forgery Detection. To improve the accuracy and generalization ability, we use ensemble model as the backbone of our detection framework rather than a single CNN model. In effect, there are various kinds of excellent CNN structures, such as VggNet [12], ResNet [10], Xception [19], etc. According to the ranking of top-1 accuracy on ImageNet-1k dataset and the convenience of implementation, we select three SOTA CNNs and use their shallow versions, namely ResNet-18 [10], EfficientNet-B0 [20] and ConvNeXt-tiny [21] to conduct model ensemble.

For the training stage, we feed a series of iris images with their corresponding labels to the multi-model detector, denoted as the input pairs $(X, Y) = \{(x_i, y_i) | i \in 0, 1, \ldots, N\}$. Our goal is to minimize total loss of the whole detection process. Therefore, the object function can be written as:

$$\min_{\theta} \mathcal{L}(\theta) = \sum_{j=1}^{K} \lambda_j \mathcal{L}_j(\mathcal{D}_j(\theta; X), Y) \tag{1}$$

where $\theta \in \mathbb{R}^n$ is a learnable parameter, λ_j and K represent the weight coefficient and the number of sub-models $\mathcal{D}_j$ in the backbone network respectively. Besides, we adopt the cross-entropy $f_{CE}(\cdot, \cdot)$ to measure the binary classification loss $\mathcal{L}_j$ of each sub-model, i.e.

$$\mathcal{L}_j = f_{CE}(p_i, y_i) = -\frac{1}{N} \sum_{i=0}^{N-1} [y_i log(p_i) + (1 - y_i) log(1 - p_i)] \tag{2}$$

where p_i denotes the probability that an iris image x_i is classified as the label y_i, and N is the amount of input pairs.

For the testing stage, every sub-detector calculates a classification score s_j, and the final detection result is a weighted mean of these scores, i.e.

$$S_{cls} = \sum_{j=1}^{K} \beta_j s_j \tag{3}$$

4   Experiments

4.1   Setting

Data Collection. As mentioned before, there are four types of iris images in our detection settings, including the real iris "PI" and three fake iris: PCL, SI and SCL. Both PI and PCL are collected from three public iris image datasets, called CASIA-IF, ND-CL and IF-VE. Below is a brief introduction of these datasets.

CASIA-Iris-Fake (CASIA-IF) dataset [3] contains three data types, including printed iris images, plastic eyes and cosmetic contacts. Notre Dame Cosmetic Contact Lenses 2013 (ND-CL) dataset [22] consists of two sets, called ND-CL-I and ND-CL-II, which are respectively captured by LG4000 and IrisGuard AD100 sensors. Only the former part is used for our test. Iris-Fake under Various Environment (IF-VE) dataset, a large scale cross-sensor fake iris dataset, contains multiple iris images which are obtained under various environment.

While SI and SCL originate from synthetic iris images provided by our cooperators. Such data are all generated by StyleGAN [6] based on the above iris datasets. More details about the experimental data are summarized in Table 1.

Table 1. Datasets used in the experiments

Dataset	Real	Fake		
	PI	PCL	SI	SCL
CASIA-IF [3]	6000	740	18406	13610
ND-CL [22]	2800	1400	10001	40000
IF-VE [23]	40000	10000	10001	40000

Implementation Details. We train our model through using the Adam [24] optimizer with an initial learning rate of 1e−4 and a weight decay of 1e−3. A step learning rate scheduler is used for learning rate adjustment. K in Eq. 1 and Eq. 3, λ_j in Eq. 1 and β_j in Eq. 3 are set to be 3, (0.4, 0.3, 0.4) and (0.4, 0.3, 0.4) respectively. Besides, all the input images are resized to 224×224.

Evaluation Metrics. To evaluate the proposed framework, we adopt several most commonly used metrics in related arts [4,5,8,9,11,23], including the Correct Classification Rate (CCR) and Area Under the Receiver Operating Characteristic Curve (AUC). We also report the True Detection Rate (TDR) and True Negative Rate (TNR) when considering the real irises as negative samples.

4.2   Results Analysis

For a comprehensive evaluation, we conduct a series of quantitative and qualitative experiments, including intra-testing, cross-testing and ablation study. Model name with prefix "FT" means the model has been pre-trained on the ImageNet-1k classification set and then fine-tuned on specific iris forgery datasets. For example, FT VGG-16 and FT Resnet-18.

Intra-testing. This section is started by the discussion of intra-evaluation. Results are shown in Table 2. Obviously, the proposed approach has an excellent performance. For CASIA-IF and ND-CL dataset, its AUC, CCR, TDR and TNR are even all up to 100%. As the first work to study fake iris detection which contains forgery images produced by generative algorithms, we also compare our framework with current state-of-the-art PCL detection models. It has been proved in [25] that a CNN network can capture some essential location information even though it is trained only in classification scenario. Besides, the traces of forgery introduced by StyleGAN [6] generator may distribute out of the iris region. Thus, we choose the whole iris image as Region of Interest (ROI) without any extra localization and segmentation preprocessing. According to Table 3, one can see that the proposed detector outperforms traditional PCL detectors. For the fake type "PCL" on IF-VE dataset, compared with WRN [23], the CCR score of our model is increased by 0.66%.

Table 2. Intra-dataset evaluation

Dataset	AUC (%)	CCR (%)	TDR (%)	TNR (%)
CASIA-IF	100	100	100	100
ND-CL	100	100	100	100
IF-VE	99.67	99.64	99.61	99.74

Table 3. CCR (%) of different detection methods on PCL images

Model	CASIA-IF	ND-CL	IF-VE
HVC [3]	99.32	**100**	–
FT VGG-16 [12]	99.63	99.92	98.22
WRN [23]	99.70	**100**	98.58
Ours	**100**	**100**	**99.24**

Cross-testing. To evaluate the generalization ability of our approach when facing unseen forgeries, we train all models on one of the forgery datasets mentioned before and then test them on the other two datasets. As depicted in Table 4, the datasets above and below the "↓" represent the training and the tested sets separately. From this table, we observe that the proposed detection framework performs better than most of single CNN-based detectors. For instance, when trained on CASIA-IF and tested on ND-CL, our method reaches a CCR of

81.41%, which exceeds FT ConNeXt-tiny by 1.6%. In fact, utilizing ensemble trick can assist detector in learning more abundant forgery clues so that the generalization performance is boosted.

Table 4. Cross-dataset evaluation based on CCR (%)

Model	Dataset					
	CASIA-IF ↓ ND-CL	CASIA-IF ↓ IF-VE	ND-CL ↓ CASIA-IF	ND-CL ↓ IF-VE	IF-VE ↓ CASIA-IF	IF-VE ↓ ND-CL
FT ResNet-18	72.25	83.44	96.81	**82.42**	99.63	71.78
FT EfficientNet-B0	78.66	86.10	96.75	73.62	98.48	71.97
FT ConvNeXt-tiny	79.81	**92.33**	93.75	72.13	98.86	**78.06**
Ours	**81.41**	88.43	**96.90**	73.99	**99.69**	75.28

At the same time, We further calculate the correlation coefficient matrix according to the AUC scores, and then use heat maps to visually show the relationship among the forgery types that are synthesized from different sources. Figure 2 describes the cross-forgery evaluation. According to Fig. 2(a), it can be seen that intra-forgery testing naturally performances the best. For the same dataset, detectors trained on PCL images generalizes very well on SCL images. And the training on SCL images gives the best generalization performance when tested on SI images, vice verse. We also find that SI images originated from ND-CL dataset is the most generalizable forgery type. In addition, as shown in Fig. 2(b), forgery types belonging to the same meta-category usually have higher correlations mutually. For instance, for the meta-category SI, if a forgery detection method can obtain good performance on CASIA-IF dataset, it may also work for ND-CL and IF-VE dataset.

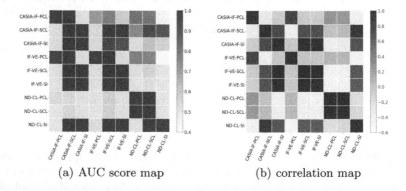

(a) AUC score map   (b) correlation map

Fig. 2. Cross-forgery evaluation. For (a) and (b), X-axis denotes the tested forgery type originated from three datasets and Y-axis denotes the forgery type for training.

4.3   Ablation Study

In this part, we conduct the ablation study on different factors to figure out how they influence our approach.

Table 5. CCR (%) of different backbones. K is the number of CNNs in Eq. 1, and in the second column, "res", "eff" and "conxt" represent ResNet-18 [10], EfficientNet-B0 [20] and ConvNeXT-tiny [21] respectively.

K	Backbone	CASIA-IF	ND-CL	IF-VE
1	1.0∗res	100	100	99.82
	1.0∗eff	100	100	99.54
	1.0∗conxt	99.89	99.97	98.89
2	0.5res+0.5eff	100	100	99.74
	0.5res+0.5conxt	100	100	99.49
	0.5eff+0.5conxt	99.98	100	99.39
3	0.4res+0.3eff+0.4conxt	100	100	99.64

Effect of Backbone Structure. In Table 5, we list the CCR (%) of using different backbones for detection. Compared with a single ConvNeXt-tiny network, we find that ensemble model indeed boosts the precision of iris forgery detection. It brings at least 0.5% CCR gains on IF-VE dataset and a slight improvement on CASIA-IF dataset. Due to high accuracy of ResNet-18 and EfficientNet-B0, reducing their proportions naturally leads to performance degradation. In practice, to reach a trade-off between detection accuracy and generalization ability, this phenomenon is acceptable. To better understand the decision-making mechanism lying behind different CNN structures, we provide the Grad-CAM [26] visualization of ResNet-18, EfficientNet-B0 and ConvNeXt-tiny in Fig. 3. For CASIA-IF dataset, the three CNN networks all focus on the central region of SI, SCL and PCL images, which indicates that the forgery is more likely to appear in iris part. On the contrary, for ND-CL and IF-VE dataset, more attention is paid to suspicious traces like unnatural eyelash and abnormal illumination, and different models may concentrate on the different parts of fake images which is beneficial to forgery detection.

Effect of Data Volume for Training. Due to the great performance of our method, we further investigate whether the detector can still work well when the data volume for training has largely shrunk. The results are presented in Fig. 4. We observe that for CASIA-IF and ND-CL dataset, just a small number of input samples contributes a high classification accuracy. For example, totally 50 real and fake iris images are enough. That is because these iris images, no matter the real ones and the forged ones, are mostly frontal and in high resolution which leads to an easy learning of forgery features. But when it comes to the detection of forgery type "PCL" in IF-VE dataset, we often need more training

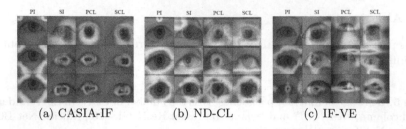

(a) CASIA-IF   (b) ND-CL   (c) IF-VE

Fig. 3. Visualization of Grad-CAM [26]. For (a)–(c), from top to bottom, each row of the heat maps are computed based on ResNet-18, EfficientNet-B0 and ConvNeXt-tiny respectively.

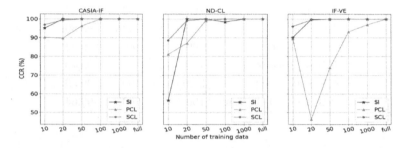

Fig. 4. The trend of CCR varying with the data volume for training

data. To explain, such fake iris images are collected in various environment which makes the detection scenario become more realistic and complicate. However, the proposed model can still achieve over 90% CCR with only 100 training samples.

5   Conclusion

In this paper, we propose a image forgery detection method for iris anti-spoofing. It can defend against various attacks on iris image, including physical attack caused by cosmetic contact lenses and synthetic attack caused by deep generative algorithms. In order to achieve a balance between accuracy and generalization performance, we consider using the ensemble model for detection, which is constructed on the basis of ResNet-18, EfficientNet-B0 and ConvNeXt-tiny. Extensive experiments are conducted on three public iris datasets and abundant StyleGAN-generated iris images. As the results prove, our framework can precisely distinguish all kinds of forged iris from the real one, and it has a state-of-the-art performance than previous work.

Acknowledgments. This work is supported by the National Key Research and Development Program of China under Grant No. 2020AAA0140003 and the National Natural Science Foundation of China under Grant 61972395.

References

1. Wei, Z., Qiu, X., Sun, Z., Tan, T.: Counterfeit iris detection based on texture analysis. In: 2008 19th International Conference on Pattern Recognition, pp. 1–4. IEEE (2008)
2. Zhang, H., Sun, Z., Tan, T.: Contact lens detection based on weighted LBP. In: 2010 20th International Conference on Pattern Recognition, pp. 4279–4282. IEEE (2010)
3. Sun, Z., Zhang, H., Tan, T., Wang, J.: Iris image classification based on hierarchical visual codebook. IEEE Trans. Pattern Anal. Mach. Intell. **36**(6), 1120–1133 (2013)
4. Raghavendra, R., Raja, K.B., Busch, C.: ContlensNet: robust iris contact lens detection using deep convolutional neural networks. In: 2017 IEEE Winter Conference on Applications of Computer Vision (WACV), pp. 1160–1167. IEEE (2017)
5. Singh, A., Mistry, V., Yadav, D., Nigam, A.: GHCLNet: a generalized hierarchically tuned contact lens detection network. In: 2018 IEEE 4th International Conference on Identity, Security, and Behavior Analysis (ISBA), pp. 1–8. IEEE (2018)
6. Karras, T., Laine, S., Aila, T.: A style-based generator architecture for generative adversarial networks. In: Proceedings of the IEEE/CVF Conference on Computer Vision and Pattern Recognition, pp. 4401–4410 (2019)
7. Daugman, J.: Demodulation by complex-valued wavelets for stochastic pattern recognition. Int. J. Wavelets Multiresolut. Inf. Process. **1**(01), 1–17 (2003)
8. Yadav, D., Kohli, N., Doyle, J.S., Singh, R., Vatsa, M., Bowyer, K.W.: Unraveling the effect of textured contact lenses on iris recognition. IEEE Trans. Inf. Forensics Secur. **9**(5), 851–862 (2014)
9. Nigam, A., Kumar, B., Gupta, P., et al.: Robust contact lens detection using local phase quantization and binary gabor pattern. In: Azzopardi, G., Petkov, N. (eds.) CAIP 2015. LNCS, vol. 9256, pp. 702–714. Springer, Cham (2015). https://doi.org/10.1007/978-3-319-23192-1_59
10. He, K., Zhang, X., Ren, S., Sun, J.: Deep residual learning for image recognition. In: Proceedings of the IEEE Conference on Computer Vision and Pattern Recognition, pp. 770–778 (2016)
11. Hoffman, S., Sharma, R., Ross, A.: Convolutional neural networks for iris presentation attack detection: toward cross-dataset and cross-sensor generalization. In: Proceedings of the IEEE Conference on Computer Vision and Pattern Recognition Workshops, pp. 1620–1628 (2018)
12. Simonyan, K., Zisserman, A.: Very deep convolutional networks for large-scale image recognition, arXiv preprint arXiv:1409.1556 (2014)
13. Goodfellow, I., et al.: Generative adversarial nets. In: Advances in Neural Information Processing Systems, vol. 27 (2014)
14. Marra, F., Gragnaniello, D., Verdoliva, L., Poggi, G.: Do GANs leave artificial fingerprints? In: 2019 IEEE Conference on Multimedia Information Processing and Retrieval (MIPR), pp. 506–511. IEEE (2019)
15. McCloskey, S., Albright, M.: Detecting GAN-generated imagery using saturation cues. In: 2019 IEEE International Conference on Image Processing (ICIP), pp. 4584–4588. IEEE (2019)
16. Marra, F., Gragnaniello, D., Cozzolino, D., Verdoliva, L.: Detection of GAN-generated fake images over social networks. In: 2018 IEEE Conference on Multimedia Information Processing and Retrieval (MIPR), pp. 384–389. IEEE (2018)
17. Cozzolino, D., Thies, J., Rössler, A., Riess, C., Nießner, M., Verdoliva, L.: ForensicTransfer: weakly-supervised domain adaptation for forgery detection, arXiv preprint arXiv:1812.02510 (2018)

18. Wang, S.-Y., Wang, O., Zhang, R., Owens, A., Efros, A.A.: CNN-generated images are surprisingly easy to spot... for now. In: Proceedings of the IEEE/CVF Conference on Computer Vision and Pattern Recognition, pp. 8695–8704 (2020)
19. Chollet, F., Xception: deep learning with depthwise separable convolutions. In: Proceedings of the IEEE Conference on Computer Vision and Pattern Recognition, pp. 1251–1258 (2017)
20. Tan, M., Le, Q.: EfficientNet: rethinking model scaling for convolutional neural networks. In: International Conference on Machine Learning, pp. 6105–6114. PMLR (2019)
21. Liu, Z., Mao, H., Wu, C.-Y., Feichtenhofer, C., Darrell, T., Xie, S.: A convnet for the 2020s. In: Proceedings of the IEEE/CVF Conference on Computer Vision and Pattern Recognition, pp. 11976–11986 (2022)
22. Doyle, J.S., Bowyer, K.W., Flynn, P.J.: Variation in accuracy of textured contact lens detection based on sensor and lens pattern. In: 2013 IEEE Sixth International Conference on Biometrics: Theory, Applications and Systems (BTAS), pp. 1–7. IEEE (2013)
23. Zhang, H., Bai, Y., Zhang, H., Liu, J., Li, X., He, Z.: Local attention and global representation collaborating for fine-grained classification. In: 2020 25th International Conference on Pattern Recognition (ICPR), pp. 10658–10665. IEEE (2021)
24. Kingma, D.P., Ba, J.: Adam: a method for stochastic optimization, arXiv preprint arXiv:1412.6980 (2014)
25. Zhou, B., Khosla, A., Lapedriza, A., Oliva, A., Torralba, A.: Learning deep features for discriminative localization. In: Proceedings of the IEEE Conference on Computer Vision and Pattern Recognition, pp. 2921–2929 (2016)
26. Selvaraju, R.R., Cogswell, M., Das, A., Vedantam, R., Parikh, D., Batra, D.: Grad-CAM: visual explanations from deep networks via gradient-based localization. In: Proceedings of the Ieee International Conference on Computer Vision, pp. 618–626 (2017)

Multi-branch Network with Circle Loss Using Voice Conversion and Channel Robust Data Augmentation for Synthetic Speech Detection

Ruoyu Wang, Jun Du$^{(\boxtimes)}$, and Chang Wang

University of Science and Technology of China, Hefei, China
{wangruoyu,changwang}@mail.ustc.edu.cn,jundu@ustc.edu.cn

Abstract. Synthesized speech in internet and telephone communications is often difficult to detect by traditional systems due to channel coding. Moreover, traditional systems limited by training data tend to perform poorly on specific synthetic attacks. Accordingly, we propose a new data augmentation strategy that training the voice conversion system without out-of-set data to synthesize specific attack data and performing single-channel data augmentation for both training and evaluation data. Further, we use multi-branching networks and introduce circle loss to improve system performance. The effectiveness of our approach is validated on the ASVspoof 2019 and 2021 LA database.

Keywords: Anti-spoofing · Synthetic speech detection · ASVspoof · Data augmentation · Channel robustness

1 Introduction

Synthetic speech detection is a task proposed against synthetic speech attacks that appear in automatic speaker verification systems and telephone scams. There have been many studies [1–4] in terms of features, network structures, and loss functions based on the ASVspoof 2019 LA track database [5] whose aim is evaluating the system's detection performance on known and unknown synthetic speech attacks. Besides unknown attacks, synthesized speech in real world internet and telephone communication is also difficult to be detected due to channel coding. To address this issue, the recent ASVspoof 2021 LA track [6] was held to evaluate the robustness of the system on different channel codings, using training set of ASVspoof 2019 as the training set and evaluation data from ASVspoof 2019 coded on various channels as the evaluation set.

Following the system with advanced performance on ASVspoof 2019, the common method is to perform channel coding data augmentation in order to improve the channel robustness. There are two main types of methods: multi-channel coding augmentation and channel coding simulation augmentation. The former is the mainstream idea of data augmentation, using various channel codes that may occur during communication to augment the data. The majority of studies in ASVspoof 2021 are using this approach [7–12]. However, a large amount of redundant data is generated due to the large number of channel formats in the communication, resulting in worse results when the evaluated data does not pass the channel coding. The latter uses the finite impulse response (FIR) filter to simulate the characteristics of the speech signal after channel coding to perform augmentation and avoid augmenting too much channel coding. STC used this method [13] to achieve excellent results in the challenge. But it is difficult to adjust the filter hyper parameters. In addition, due to the shortcomings of the training data, it is often difficult for the spectral feature-based system to discriminate the attack generated by the direct waveform modification vocoder [1].

The main contributions of this work include: 1) Improving the system performance on the hard attack by training a voice conversion model using direct waveform modification vocoder without introducing out-of-set data to generate the specific attack. 2) Achieving channel coding robustness of the system by doing single-channel data augmentation for training and evaluation data only. 3) Multi-branch network is designed to capture the synthesis information for different segments of the input speech features and circle loss is added to further distinguish between true and spoof speech.

2   Proposed Methods

2.1   Voice Conversion and Channel Robust Data Augmentation

The vast majority of networks currently constructed based on spectral features show acceptable performance on most synthetic attacks in the ASVspoof evaluation data, except for attacks generated using the direct waveform modification vocoder, such as attack type A17, which pulls down the overall evaluation results [1]. We note that A17 is a voice conversion method that mostly comes from traditional speech signal processing based algorithms [5] and does not require textual information about the data, which means that we only need a small amount of data to train an acceptable system to augment our training data. Moreover, we find that single-channel coding augmentation and multi-channel coding augmentation for the training data have similar performance on the ASVspoof 2021 evaluation set without losing system performance on the uncoded evaluation data due to the lower channel noise in the training data. We further convert all the evaluation data to the single channel consistent with the training data augmentation to reduce the channel mismatch between the training and test data.

Figure 1 shows the specific process. First, we use 2.5k utterances of real speech from the original training data to train the DIFFVC [14] voice conversion system and convert the real speech in the development set to speakers in the training set to improve the performance of the system on the attack category similar to A17 (using the development set of ASVspoof 2019 to train the system in the ASVspoof 2021 challenge is allowed). Next, we merge the original training data and voice conversion data and augment dataset by single channel coding, such as G711 alaw coding. Then, we perform triple speed perturbation on them according to perturbation factors 0.9, 1.0 and 1.1. Finally, in the test phase, we convert all evaluation data to the single-channel coding format same as the augmented training data for evaluation.

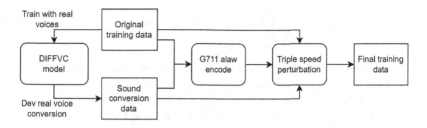

Fig. 1. The proposed data augmentation process.

2.2   Multi-branch Network with Circle Loss

By adjusting the input segment positions of the training speech, we found that the audio at different positions did not help the synthesized speech detection consistently, which inspired us to use a multi-branch network structure.

We will use a sliding window to slice the fixed-length spectral features into k parts of equal length, each part retaining an overlap of half the sliding window length to preserve contextual information, e.g., for a 750-frame input feature, taking $k = 4$, the features will be sliced into 0–300, 150–450, 300–600 and 450–750 frames and then fed to ResNet branches of the same structure without shared parameters. We then stack d-dimension embeddings of the k branches outputs into $k \times d$-dimension vectors and pass them through the BatchNorm (BN) layer as our final embeddings x_i for loss function layer.

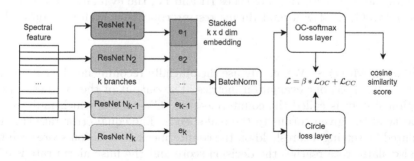

Fig. 2. The proposed multi-branch network structure with circle loss.

In terms of loss, we added a circle loss [15] term to penalize the scores of the synthesized speech to further distinguish between real and synthesized speech, based on the OC-softmax loss [3]. In the OC-softmax loss layer, the learnable w_0 refers to the optimization direction of the target class embeddings, α is the scale factor and two margins ($m_0, m_1 \in [-1, 1], m_0 > m_1$) are introduced here for real speech and spoofing attacks to bound the angle between w_0 and x_i:

$$\mathcal{L}_{OC} = \frac{1}{N} \sum_{i=1}^{N} \log \left[1 + e^{\alpha(m_{y_i} - w_0 x_i)(-1)^{y_i}} \right] \tag{1}$$

In the circle loss layer, we first calculate the circle loss similarity matrix s_p, s_n for positive and negative cases respectively by embedding vectors x_i and its corresponding labels, and then calculate the circle loss by the following equation, where $\alpha_n^j = Relu \left(s_n^j + m \right)$ and $\alpha_p^i = Relu \left(1 + m - s_p^i \right)$:

$$\mathcal{L}_{CC} = \frac{1}{N} \log \left[1 + \sum_{j=1}^{L} \exp \left(\gamma \alpha_n^j (s_n^j - m) \right) * \sum_{i=1}^{K} \exp \left(\gamma \alpha_p^i (s_p^i - 1 + m) \right) \right] \tag{2}$$

Our final loss function is the combination of OC-softmax loss and circle loss, where β is the weight factor:

$$\mathcal{L} = \beta * \mathcal{L}_{OC} + \mathcal{L}_{CC} \tag{3}$$

3   Experiments

3.1   Experimental Setup

Dataset. We designed four types of training data in Table 1 to illustrate our approach, with Type I obtaining a baseline system without any augmentation, Type II and Type III results comparing the usual multi-channel augmentation with our single-channel augmentation, and Type III and Type IV results demonstrating the change in performance before and after the addition of voice conversion data. Note that for training types III and IV, the evaluation data are fully converted to G711 alaw format during testing consistent with the approach we propose.

Evaluation Metrics. We mainly use the officially recommended EER and min t-DCF [1,16,17] as our evaluation metrics. The output of the synthetic speech detection system is called the countermeasure (CM) score, which indicates the similarity of the given corpus to the real speech. The equal error rate (EER) is calculated by setting a threshold on the countermeasure decision score such that the false alarm rate reaches the decision score and the false alarm rate is equal to the miss rate. The lower the EER, the better the synthetic speech detection system is at detecting spoofing attacks. The minimum tandem detection cost function (min t-DCF) is the metric used to rank the ASVspoof 2021 LA track.

Table 1. The four training data types based on ASVspoof 2019 LA track training set used for the experiments, where VC refers to whether we add voice conversion data, channel effect indicates which channels we use to augment, SP refers to whether we use triple speed perturbation, and size is the specific utterances number.

Type	VC	Channel effect	SP	Size
I	✘	No	✘	25380
II	✘	G711 alaw, G711 μ law, G722 and G729	✘	126900
III	✘	G711 alaw	✔	152280
IV	✔	G711 alaw	✔	194640

The EER only evaluates the performance of the spoofing system, while the t-DCF evaluates the impact of the synthetic speech detection system on the reliability of the ASV system, where the ASV system is fixed and the score results are officially provided. The lower the t-DCF, the more important the synthetic voice detection system is for improving the reliability of the ASV.

Training Details. We extract 60-dimension LFCCs through an official implementation [18]. To form batches, we set 750 time frames to a fixed length and use repetition padding for short trials, and for long trials, we randomly select a consecutive piece of the frame and discard the rest. Moreover, we calculate the mean and variance of each position of the training set spectral features and regularize the mean and variance for the training and evaluation set.

The structure of the ResNet part of our multi-branch network uses the architecture adapted from [3]. We set branch number $k = 4$ and use the 32-dimension vectors before the last fully connected layer of ResNet as the branch embedding, and the 4 partial embedding vectors are stacked together into a 128-dimensional final embedding before passing into the loss function layer. For the hyper parameters in the loss function layers, we set $\alpha = 20$, $m_0 = 0.9$, $m_1 = 0.35$ for OC-Softmax loss, $\gamma = 1$, $m = 0.25$ for circle loss, and weight factor $\beta = 3$ of the total loss.

We implement our model using PyTorch. We use the Adam optimizer with the β_1 equal to 0.9 and the β_2 equal to 0.999 to update the weights in the main model. We use the stochastic gradient descent (SGD) optimizer for the learnable parameters in the loss function. The batch size was set to 64. The learning rate was initially set to 0.0006, with a 50% decay every 5 epochs. All our experiments were performed on a Tesla-V100-PICE 12 GB GPU. We then used the ASVspoof19 eval set as our development set to select the model on which we had the lowest EER for evaluation. The output CM score of our system is the cosine similarity between the speech embedding and the weight vector w_0 in OC-Softmax loss.

3.2 Results and Analysis

Evaluation of Data Augmentation. In Table 2, when comparing the results for Type I and II, we can see that while the direct addition of multi-channel coding to the data improves the performance on the ASVspoof 2021 evaluation set, it also degrades the performance on the ASVspoof 2019 evaluation set without channel effects. Comparing the results for Types II and III, we can observe that the use of single-channel coding augmentation not only improves performance on the ASVspoof 2021 evaluation set, but also alleviates the degradation of performance on the channel-unaffected evaluation due to the effect of channel noise in the training data. Comparing Type III and IV, it is found that the addition of sound conversion data further improves the system performance.

Table 2. EER (%)/min t-DCF metrics are represented on data types I–IV, and the model uses ResNet-18 with OC-softmax loss.

Type	ASVspoof 2019	ASVspoof 2021
I	2.24/0.1237	30.17/0.8981
II	6.41/0.1790	7.96/0.3220
III	3.78/0.1403	5.39/0.2998
IV	2.31/0.1195	**4.71/0.2925**

We further compare the detection performance on each attack category in Table 3, as we expected, adding speech generated by the direct waveform modification vocoder substantially improves the performance on attack categories A17 and A18, thus improving the overall evaluation.

Table 3. EER (%) before and after adding sound conversion data to various synthesis attacks on the ASVspoof 2019 evaluation set

Type	A07	A08	A09	A10	A11	A12	A13	A14	A15	A16	A17	A18	A19	ALL
III	0.12	0.06	0.02	0.34	0.20	0.11	0.18	0.23	0.23	0.26	7.87	12.43	0.79	3.78
TV	0.14	0.04	0.04	0.41	0.15	0.10	0.06	0.15	0.14	0.23	**2.08**	**8.81**	0.35	2.31

Evaluation of Network and Loss Function. Table 4 shows the results of different network and loss function. From this table we can see that adding circle loss improves performance on the evaluation set by a small margin compared with the ResNet-18 with OC-softmax loss, and the use of a multi-branch network structure did not lead to an improvement in the results. However, the use of multi-branch network and the addition of circle loss together improved the system performance more substantially.

Table 4. EER (%)/min t-DCF metric results in network and loss function ablation experiments performed on data type IV.

NetWork	Circle loss	ASVspoof 2019	ASVspoof 2021
ResNet-18	✗	2.31/0.1195	4.71/0.2925
ResNet-18	✔	2.37/0.1185	4.43/0.2951
Multi-branch	✗	3.90/0.1564	5.81/0.3034
Multi-branch	✔	**2.17/0.1183**	**4.17/0.2751**

4   Conclusion

In this paper, we propose data augmentation using sound conversion and single-channel coding to improve the performance and channel robustness of synthetic speech detection. We also trained a voice transformation system using a limited corpus to generate fake speech to increase the diversity of synthetic speech attack systems in the training data. We added training data encoded with G711 alaw channels and used G711 alaw to encode test data with multi-channel encoding to improve the channel robustness of the system. We further improve the system performance by using a multi-branch network structure and circle loss. Experimental results on the ASVspoof 2021 LA track show that our data augmentation method, network structure and loss function design are effective. In future work, we will further explore the generalization performance of our scheme to make it applicable to more practical application scenarios.

Acknowledgments. This work was supported by the National Natural Science Foundation of China under Grant No. 62171427.

References

1. Todisco, M., Wang, X., et al.: ASVspoof 2019: future horizons in spoofed and fake audio detection. In: Interspeech (2019)
2. Lavrentyeva, G., Novoselov, S., Andzhukaev, T., Volkova, M., Gorlanov, A., Kozlov, A.: STC antispoofing systems for the ASVspoof 2019 challenge. In: Interspeech (2019)
3. Zhang, Y., Jiang, F., Duan, Z.: One-class learning towards synthetic voice spoofing detection. IEEE Signal Process. Lett. **28**, 937–941 (2021)
4. Wang, X., Yamagishi, J.: A comparative study on recent neural spoofing countermeasures for synthetic speech detection. In: Interspeech (2021)
5. Wang, X., Yamagishi, J., et al.: ASVspoof 2019: a large-scale public database of synthetized, converted and replayed speech. Comput. Speech Lang. **64**, 101114 (2020)
6. Yamagishi, J., Wang, X., et al.: ASVspoof 2021: accelerating progress in spoofed and deepfake speech detection. In: Proceedings of the 2021 Edition of the Automatic Speaker Verification and Spoofing Countermeasures Challenge (2021)

7. Chen, X.H., Zhang, Y., Zhu, G., Duan, Z.Y.: UR channel-robust synthetic speech detection system for ASVspoof 2021. In: Proceedings of the 2021 Edition of the Automatic Speaker Verification and Spoofing Countermeasures Challenge (2021)
8. Li, Z.W., et al.: A survey of convolutional neural networks: analysis, applications, and prospects. IEEE Trans. Neural Netw. Learn. Syst., 1–21 (2021)
9. Cohen, A., Rimon, I., Aflalo, E., Permuter, H.: A study on data augmentation in voice anti-spoofing. Speech Commun. **141**, 56–67 (2022)
10. Das, K.: Known-unknown data augmentation strategies for detection of logical access, physical access and speech deepfake attacks: ASVspoof 2021. In: Proceedings of the 2021 Edition of the Automatic Speaker Verification and Spoofing Countermeasures Challenge (2021)
11. Wang, X., Qin, X., Zhu, T., Wang, C., Zhang, S., Li, M.: The DKU-CMRI system for the ASVspoof 2021 challenge: vocoder based replay channel response estimation. In: 2021 Edition of the Automatic Speaker Verification and Spoofing Countermeasures Challenge (2021)
12. Cáceres, J., Font, R., Grau, T., Molina, J.: The biometric Vox system for the ASVspoof 2021 challenge. In: Proceedings of the 2021 Edition of the Automatic Speaker Verification and Spoofing Countermeasures Challenge (2021)
13. Tomilov, A., Svishchev, A., Volkova, M., Chirkovskiy, A., Kondratev, A., Lavrentyeva, G.: STC antispoofing systems for the ASVspoof 2021 challenge. In: Proceedings of the 2021 Edition of the Automatic Speaker Verification and Spoofing Countermeasures Challenge (2021)
14. Huang, W.W., Yi, C.K., et al.: Generalization of spectrum differential based direct waveform modification for voice conversion (2019)
15. Sun, Y.F., Cheng, C., et al.: Circle loss: a unified perspective of pair similarity optimization. In: CVPR (2021)
16. Delgado, H., Evans, N., et al.: ASVspoof 2021: automatic speaker verification spoofing and countermeasures challenge evaluation plan (2021)
17. Kinnunen, T., Lee, K.A., et al.: t-DCF: a detection cost function for the tandem assessment of spoofing countermeasures and automatic speaker verification. In: Odyssey (2018)
18. Official Baseline System. github.com/asvspoof-challenge/2021

Spoof Speech Detection Based on Raw Cross-Dimension Interaction Attention Network

Ye Zhou[1], Jianwu Zhang[1(✉)], and Pengguo Zhang[2]

[1] College of Telecommuncation Engineering, Hangzhou Dianzi University, Hangzhou, China
jwzhang@hdu.edu.cn
[2] Zhejiang Uniview Technologies Co., Ltd., Hangzhou 310051, China
zhangpengguo@uniview.com

Abstract. Benefiting from advances in speech synthesis and speech conversion technology, artificial speech is so close to natural speech that it is sensory indistinguishable. This situation brings great challenges to the security of voice-based biometric authentication systems. In this work, we propose an end-to-end spoofing detection method which first augments the raw-audio waveform with random channel masking, then feeds it into the lightweight spectral-temporal attention module for cross-dimensional interaction, and finally selects an appropriate attention fusion method to maximise the potential of capturing interactive cues in both spectral and temporal domains. The experimental results show that the proposed method can effectively improve the accuracy of spoof speech detection.

Keyword: Spoof speech detection · End-to-End · Data augmentation · Attention mechanism · Automatic speaker verification

1 Introduction

Automatic Speaker Verification (ASV) is a biometric-based identification technology that automatically verifies the speaker's identity by analyzing speech utterances [1]. Among the biometric recognition technologies, ASV systems have received extensive attention due to the convenience of speech collection, high discrimination, and the development of collection equipments. However, with the development of deep learning, various spoofing attacks generate spoof speech which is similar to legitimate user's voice to threaten the security performance of ASV systems. Therefore, researchers have been working on finding effective anti-spoofing methods to protect ASV systems.

The common anti-spoofing methods optimize the front-end feature extraction and the back-end classifier separately, then the hand-crafted features produced by the front-end are input to the back-end classifier. Their potential fundamentally depends on the information captured by the initial features, but the information lost in feature extraction cannot be recovered. The research also shows that the difference of handcrafted features has a greater impact on the detection performance [2]. On the contrary, end-to-end (E2E) approaches allow for pre-processing and post-processing components to be combined and jointly optimised within a single network [3]. Closer cooperation between front and back ends facilitates more effective detection. Therefore, E2E spoofing detection solutions that take raw-audio waveforms instead of 2D features as input have attracted increasing attention [4].

Artifacts indicative of spoofing attacks are known to exist in specific subbands and temporal intervals, but there is no method that works well for cross-dimensional interactions of time and frequency to learn cues spanning different subbands and temporal segments. To solve this problem, we explore E2E-oriented spoof speech detection and propose the Raw Cross-dimension Interaction Attention Network. The main contributions of this paper are as follows:

(1) Augment the raw-audio waveform by using random channel masking augmentation to highlight discriminative features and enhance the temporal-frequency implicit correlation.
(2) A novel lightweight spectral-temporal attention module for cross-dimensional interaction to capture multidimensional spoof cues at low computational cost.
(3) Explore different attention fusion strategies to maximize the capture of discriminative features.

2 Related Work

2.1 Data Augmentation

Data Augmentation (DA) based on traditional audio signal processing methods require prior knowledge to properly process audio data for getting more natural sound, which may even reduce the efficiency of acoustic models while increasing computational costs. As a result, some researchers propose some simpler, intuitive, and effective methods. SpecAugment [5] is one of the spectral-domain augmentation methods which directly wraps features and randomly masks the blocks of frequency and time frames on the log mel spectrogram. Although the original audio recovered after using SpecAugment does not sound as natural as traditional audio processing methods, it helps to train acoustic models more effectively in extreme cases. Subsequently, SpecAverage [6] was proposed, which replaces the random masking of the input feature map with a constant value during training to enhance the robustness of network in speaker recognition and spoof detection. So far, the end-to-end spoof detection techniques based on raw-audio waveform have shown great potential, but the methods mentioned above cannot be applied to it.

2.2 Attention Mechanism

In the process of human perception of things, attention will focus on essential information and suppress unnecessary ones. This mechanism can refine perceptual information and improve representation ability while retaining information context. In recent years, attention mechanisms have been widely used in various fields. Lai et al. [7] introduced Squeeze-and-Excitation Networks (SE-Net) in the field of spoof speech detection. SE-Net achieves performance gains by calculating channel attention and re-weighting the original input tensors, but the decomposition of spatial tensors results in a large loss of spatial information. Convolutional Block Attention Module (CBAM) [8] is introduced on the basis of SE-Net, usinging spatial attention as a supplement to channel attention. Since channel attention and spatial attention are calculated separately and independently, there is a lack of dependence and interactivity between the channel and spatial dimensions.

3 Raw Cross-Dimension Interaction Attention Network

In this section, we propose the Raw Cross-dimension Interaction Attention Network (Raw CIANet) based on raw-audio waveform, its architecture is shown in Fig. 1.

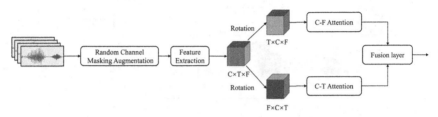

Fig. 1. Structures of the Raw CIANet

3.1 Random Channel Masking Augmentation

Frequency masking and time masking augmentation use masking to make the model focus on the most discriminative time frames and frequency patches. However, in the audio spectrogram, there is usually a implicit correlation between time frame and frequency which used alone is not conducive to discovering camouflage clues in spoof speech. Therefore, we proposes Random Channel Masking Augmentation (RCMA) to make the model jointly focus on highly discriminative time frames and frequency, and to augment the time-frequency implicit correlation, so that the model can subsequently learn high-level feature representations, thereby improving generalization.

The audio can be divided into C channels after filter processing. In each batch of training, randomly choose channels for masking. The number of masked channels F is selected from a uniform distribution between 0 and F_{mask}. F_{mask} is the maximum number of masked channels chosen based on the minimum validation loss, equation of random channel masking shows below:

$$C' = \sum_F C^i \otimes S_0 + \sum_{C-F} C^j \otimes S_1, F \in [0, F_{mask}] \tag{1}$$

where S_0 and S_1 are mask operators, representing masking and non-masking operations respectively.

In addition, due to the reduction in the number of channels, the model can significantly save computation and memory, which is more conducive to automatic learning and optimization of complex neural network structures.

3.2   Lightweight Cross-Dimensional Interaction Attention Module

The lightweight cross-dimensional interaction attention module for spectral-temporal emphasizes the importance of cross-dimensional interaction at a low computational cost to provide more reasonable feature representations, as shown in Fig. 2.

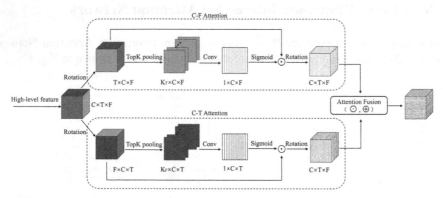

Fig. 2. Architecture of the lightweight cross-dimensional Interaction attention module

The high-level feature $X \in \mathbb{R}^{C \times F \times T}$ is used as the input of the attention module, where C, F, and T represent the channel, frequency, and time dimension. The first attention branch C-F Attention is used to construct the interaction between channel dimension and frequency dimension. Firstly, rotate the feature tensor to obtain $X_{CF} \in \mathbb{R}^{T \times C \times F}$. The value in the feature tensor represents the amount of information corresponding to each dimension. In order to realize the interaction of the channel and frequency dimensions while retaining the tensor features of the time dimension to the greatest extent, we use TopK pooling to sort the time dimension tensors according to its value, and select the top K_T tensors to generate more time-discernibility feature represents. TopK pooling can reduce the depth of temporal features while avoiding destroying their discriminability, making subsequent computations lightweight, the equation is:

$$\hat{X}_{CF} \in \mathbb{R}^{K_T \times C \times F} = TopK(X_{CF}, K_T) \tag{2}$$

The TopK-pooing output is then fed into a convolutional layer with a filter size of $f \times f$ to build a model that spans the two dimensions of channel and frequency, captures the dependencies of cross-dimensional interactions between channel and frequency, and then performs standard normalization to reshape the tensor. This tensor generates the channel-frequency interaction attention weight w_{CF} under the action of the sigmoid activation function:

$$w_{CF} = sigmoid\left(Conv\left(\hat{X}_{CF}\right)\right) \tag{3}$$

The weight indicates the importance of the feature information carried under a specific channel and frequency, and is applied to $X_{CF} \in \mathbb{R}^{T \times C \times F}$ to complete the re-weighting of the feature tensor, so as to maximize the channel and frequency to capture discriminative clues potential. Finally, the tensor is rotated to restore its original input shape:

$$Y_{CF} \in \mathbb{R}^{C \times T \times F} = Rotate(X_{CF} w_{CF}) \tag{4}$$

The second attention branch C-T Attention is used to construct the interaction between channel dimension and time dimension. The rotated tensor retains the top K_F frequency-discriminative tensor to generate features represents. Similar to C-F Attention, the output is fed into the convolutional layer to build a model that spans both channel and time dimensions can captures the dependencies of channel and time cross-dimensional interactions, as well as deforming its shape. Then the sigmoid activation function is used to obtain the channel-time interactive attention weight w_{CT}. The attention weight is subsequently applied to $X_{CT} \in \mathbb{R}^{F \times C \times T}$. And rotate the tensor to get $Y_{CT} \in \mathbb{R}^{C \times T \times F}$.

SE-Net, CBAM require many additional learnable parameters when explicitly building the dependencies among channels. The excitation operation includes two fully connected (FC) layers and a Relu. The first FC reduces the feature dimension to C/r, and then after Relu activation, the second FC restores the feature dimension to C, which increases the module computation. While the proposed attention module computes interactive attention while considering cross-dimensional dependencies, which is computationally efficient and cost effective. The required parameters for each attention module are shown in Table 1. C indicates the number of input channels, r indicates the reduction rate of the network (typically 16), f indicates the filter size, and $f \ll C$. K indicates the value set during TopK pooling.

Table 1. Comparison of attention module parameters

Attention Module	Parameters
SE-Net	$2C^2/r$
CBAM	$2C^2/r + 2f^2$
Cross-dimensional Interaction Attention Module	$2Kf^2$

3.3 Attention Fusion Strategies

Fractional fusion can achieve a certain degree of performance improvement by fusing the output scores of different detection models, but it cannot fully utilize the information complementarity among various types of features. Compared with fractional fusion, reasonable model-level fusion methods tend to obtain better complementary effects. We investigate two different model-level fusion methods to maximize the integration of discriminative features captured by the dimensionally interactive attention module. The fusion method is shown in Eq. 5.

$$Y_{fuse} = \begin{cases} Y_{CF} \oplus Y_{CT} \\ Y_{CF} \odot Y_{CT} \end{cases} \tag{5}$$

the two different operators in Eq. 5 are element-wise addition and multiplication.

Since Y_{CF} carries the interactive features of the channel and frequency dimensions, and Y_{CT} carries the interactive features of the channel and time dimensions, the two features are transformed into a shared feature subspace through model-level fusion, which can realize the complementarity of discriminative features in the time and frequency dimensions, and strengthen the correlation between the frequency dimension and the time dimension by using channel dimension.

4 Experiment

In this section, we introduce the experimental dataset, evaluation metrics and the details of experiments. We then perform ablation study and compare our model's results with existing state-of-the-art models.

4.1 Dateset and Evaluation Metrics

The ASVspoof 2019 LA dataset is used to verify the performance of the Raw CIANet. It is based on the VCTK corpus and uses a variety of advanced speech synthesis and speech conversion algorithms to generate spoof speech signals. All real speech and spoof speech signals are randomly and non-overlappingly divided into the sets of training, development, and evaluation. The evaluation set contains 11 unknown speech spoofing attack types.

In order to compare the performance of different systems, we use the official evaluation mertics of the ASVspoof2019 challenge: minimum normalized tandem detection cost function (min-tDCF) and equal error rate (EER).

$$\min -tDCF_{norm}(\tau) = \frac{C_1 P_{\text{miss}}^{cm}(\tau) + C_2 P_{fa}^{cm}(\tau)}{t - DCF_{default}} \tag{6}$$

$$EER = P_{fa}(\tau) = P_{miss}(\tau) \tag{7}$$

where C_1 and C_2 represent two kinds of error costs, which are determined by the error cost and prior probability of the two systems of ASV and speech deception detection, t-$DCF_{default}$ is the default cost for accepting or rejecting each test speech that with no information.

4.2 Setup

We apply a minimized weighted cross-entropy (WCE) loss function to address the imbalanced distribution of training data, and compare the number of real speech and fake speech, and set the weight of both to 9:1. The two K values in TopK pooling are obtained through successive iterations. After comprehensively considering the accuracy and complexity, the applied pooling number is 20 and is 15, which are used for C-F Attention and C-T Attentio attention branches respectively.

4.3 Ablation Study

Only through ablation study can we properly illustrate the advantage of the Raw CIANet. We essentially remove one of the modules or operations in the full Raw CIANet architecture demonstrated in Fig. 1. The remaining modules and operations are used as before. The default attention fusion method in the experiment is multiplication. The results are summarized in Table 2.

Table 2. Results of ablation study

System	min-tDCF	EER
Raw CIANet-mul	0.0527	1.76
Raw CIANet-add	0.0551	1.96
Raw CIANet-mul without RCME	0.0744	3.06
Raw CIANet-mul without two Attention	0.0897	3.37
Raw CIANet-mul without C-T Attention	0.0816	2.85
Raw CIANet-mul without C-F Attention	0.0566	2.04

By comparing the data of Raw CIANet-mul and Raw CIANet-mul without RCME, the min-tDCF and EER after adding the RCME module decreased by 29% and 42.5% respectively, which indicating that the masking scheme enables the model to focus not only on the most discriminative time blocks and frequency bins but also the entire time and the frequency part, the hidden relationship between time-frequency is strengthened. Generalizability and robustness are improved.

The ablation results of the attention block show that two attention branches can improve network detection performance, which proves that the dependence and interaction between the channel dimension and the spatial dimension can be used to provide potential discriminative features for the model. In addition, the performance improvement of C-T Attention is better than that of the C-F Attention module.

In order to analyze the proposed two model-level fusion methods, we train the model multiple times and summarize the detection results of the model, as shown in Fig. 3. As can be seen from the figure, Raw CIANet-mul yields lower EER than Raw CIANet-add, which indicates that fusing the features in a multiplicative manner can improve the distinction between spoofed and real inputs. Raw CIANet-mul is slightly better than Raw CIANet-add in min-tDCF performance, which verifies that Raw CIANet-mul can achieve efficient detection when used in tandem with the ASV system.

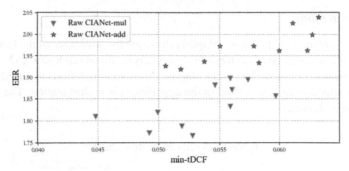

Fig. 3. Comparison of attention fusion methods

4.4 Comparison to Competing Systems

As Raw CIANet is a single-feature detection system, a comparison of performance for the Raw CIANet and competing single systems is illustrated in Table 3. The comparison shows that Raw CIANet using the attention-multiply fusion approach achieves the best detection performance, with EER and min-tDCF dropping to 1.76 and 0.0527. Furthermore, the proposed network directly takes the raw-audio waveform as input without using hand-crafted features, which saves the system computational cost and is more conducive to real-time deployment of detection compared to other acoustic feature inputs.

Table 3. Detection system performance on ASVspoof2019 LA dataset

System	Input features	min-tDCF	EER
Raw CIANet-mul	Raw-audio	0.0527	1.76
Raw CIANet-add	Raw-audio	0.0551	1.96
Capsule network [9]	LFCC	0.0538	1.97
Raw PC-DARTS Linear-L [3]	Raw-audio	0.0583	2.10
MLCG-Res2Net50+CE [10]	CQT	0.0690	2.15
Resnet18-OC-softmax [11]	LFCC	0.0590	2.19
Res2Net [12]	CQT	0.0743	2.50
Siamese CNN [13]	LFCC	0.0930	3.79
RawNet2 [4]	Raw-audio	0.1294	4.66

5   Conclusion

In this paper, we propose a spoof speech detection network based on Raw Cross-dimension Interaction Attention (Raw CIANet) and shows the architecture of the network model. The Raw CIANet operates directly upon the raw-audio waveform which reduces preparatory work by eliminating the sophisticated process of making handcrafted features. Results for an ablation study show that the effectiveness of random channel masking enhancement, lightweight dimensional interactive attention module and attention fusion strategy used in our network. According to the results in the ASVspoof2019 LA dataset, our method has a good practical effect in detecting spoof speech and advantages over other competing systems.

References

1. Wu, Z., Evans, N., Kinnunen, T., Yamagishi, J., Alegre, F., Li, H.: Spoofing and countermeasures for speaker verification: a survey. Speech Commun. **66**, 130–153 (2015)
2. Wang, X., Yamagishi, J.: A comparative study on recent neural spoofing countermeasures for synthetic speech detection. In: Annual Conference of the International Speech Communication Association, pp. 4685–4689 (2021)
3. Ge, W., Patino, J., Todisco, M., Evans, N.: ASVspoof 2021 workshop, pp. 22–28 (2021)
4. Tak, H., Patino, J., Todisco, M., Nautsch, A., Evans, N., Larcher, A.: End-to-end anti-spoofing with rawnet2. In: 2021 IEEE International Conference on Acoustics, Speech and Signal Processing, pp. 6369–6373. IEEE Press (2021)
5. Park, D. S., et al.: Specaugment: a simple data augmentation method for automatic speech recognition. In: Annual Conference of the International Speech Communication Association, pp. 2613–2617 (2019)
6. Cohen, A., Rimon, I., Aflalo, E., Permuter, H.: A study on data augmentation in voice anti-spoofing. Speech Commun. **141**, 56–67 (2022)
7. Lai, C.I., Chen, N., Villalba, J., Dehak, N.: ASSERT: Anti-spoofing with squeeze-excitation and residual networks. In: Annual Conference of the International Speech Communication Association, pp. 1013–1017 (2019)
8. Woo, S., Park, J., Lee, JY., Kweon, I.S.: CBAM: convolutional block attention module. In: Ferrari, V., Hebert, M., Sminchisescu, C., Weiss, Y. (eds.) ECCV 2018. LNCS, vol. 11211, pp. 3–19. Springer, Cham (2018). https://doi.org/10.1007/978-3-030-01234-2_1
9. Luo, A., Li, E., Liu, Y., Kang, X., Wang, Z.J.: A capsule network based approach for detection of audio spoofing attacks. In: 2021 IEEE International Conference on Acoustics, Speech and Signal Processing, pp. 6359–6363. IEEE Press (2021)
10. Li, X., Wu, X., Lu, H., Liu, X., Meng, H.: Channel-wise gated Res2Net: towards robust detection of synthetic speech attacks. In: Annual Conference of the International Speech Communication Association, pp. 4695–4699 (2021)
11. Zhang, Y., Jiang, F., Duan, Z.: One-class learning towards synthetic voice spoofing detection. IEEE Signal Proc. Let. **28**, 937–941 (2021)
12. Li, X., et al.: Replay and synthetic speech detection with res2net architecture. In: 2021 IEEE International Conference on Acoustics, Speech and Signal Processing, pp. 6354–6358. IEEE Press (2021)
13. Lei, Z., Yang, Y., Liu, C., Ye, J.: Siamese convolutional neural network using gaussian probability feature for spoofing speech detection. In: Annual Conference of the International Speech Communication Association, pp. 1116–1120 (2020)

Medical and Other Applications

A Deformable Convolution Encoder with Multi-scale Attention Fusion Mechanism for Classification of Brain Tumor MRI Images

Haipeng Zhu[1], Hong He[1(✉)], Neil Roberts[2], and Kunhao Li[1]

[1] School of Health Science and Engineering, University of Shanghai for Science and Technology, Shanghai 200093, China
hehong@usst.edu.cn
[2] Centre for Reproductive Health (CRH), School of Clinical Sciences, University of Edinburgh, Edinburgh EH16 4T, U.K.

Abstract. The diagnosis of gliomas tumors, pituitary tumors, meningiomas tumors, and normal brain (No Tumor) on MRI images is challenging and requires diligence due to the diversity of focal regions. This has motivated the development of a Deformable Convolution Encoder with a Multi-Scale Attention Fusion Mechanism (DCE-MSAF) to automatically classify brain tumors on MRI images proposed in this paper. In particular, a deformable convolution encoder is constructed to extract coarse features of interest in the region of the suspected tumor and simultaneously reduce the impact of non-tumor region features on the performance of the model, and a multi-scale attention fusion mechanism is used to extract fine tumor regional features of different scales and fuse them into more refined features. The accuracy, recall, precision, and F1 scores of the image analysis pipeline are 97.3%, 0.9713, 97.1%, and 0.9708, respectively, when it was applied to a test dataset from the Kaggle website. The new pipeline appears promising for the early diagnosis of brain tumors on MRI images.

Keywords: MRI · Brain tumor · Classification · Deformable convolution · Multi-scale Attention Fusion Mechanism

1 Introduction

Brain tumors affect the normal function of other brain cells, and seriously threaten human life and health. According to the International Agency for Research on Cancer, more than 70% of patients died each year due to malignant brain tumors all over the world [1]. Brain tumors are roughly classified as benign or malignant tumors according to their location, progression stage, nature, growth rate, and other characteristics [2, 3]. According to the development speed and obvious boundary of benign tumor cells, brain tumors can be detailedly divided into glioma, pituitary tumors, and meningiomas. Presently, Magnetic Resonance Imaging (MRI), Positron Emission Tomography (PET), and X-ray Computed Tomography (CT) are the main techniques used for the non-invasive diagnosis of brain tumors. However, the diversity and high variability of brain tumors under the MRI make

W. Deng et al. (Eds.): CCBR 2022, LNCS 13628, pp. 633–644, 2022.
https://doi.org/10.1007/978-3-031-20233-9_64

diagnosis challenging and a wide range of algorithms have been developed based on Machine Learning methods (MLs). Kumari et al. [4] used a gray level co-occurrence matrix and the support vector machine classifier to divide the images into normal and abnormal disease types with an accuracy of 98%. In a subsequent study [9], Singh et al. used principal component analysis to reduce the training feature dimension and reduce the training time. However, the accuracy of these methods mainly depends on the subjective experience of the tumor localization in brain MRI images, increasing the possibility of error.

Many researchers favor the use of Deep Learning Technologies (DLs) to diagnose brain tumors on MRI [5] because of their fast feature extraction, high accuracy, and flexibility. Tandel et al. [6] proposed an integrated algorithm based on majority voting to optimize the overall classification performance of five DLs and five MLs on four brain tumor datasets. Bodapati et al. [7] proposed a two-channel model with an attention mechanism to distinguish tumor types using MRI. A differential depth convolution neural network model to classify abnormal and normal brain tumors was proposed by Abd et al. [8]. They reported that the proposed method had good overall performance in which test accuracy reached 99.3% in a dataset comprising 25,000 MRI images. Díaz-Pernas et al. [9] designed a fully automatic brain tumor segmentation and classification model using a deep convolution neural network and obtained a classification accuracy of 0.973. Based on trained models like MobileNet V2, etc., Sadad et al. [10] used transfer learning technology to classify glioma, meningioma, and pituitary tumors with an accuracy of 91.8%. Kumar et al. [11] utilized ResNet50 and global average pooling to identify brain tumor types, achieving an average accuracy of 97.1%. Noreen et al. [12] fine-tuned the Inception-v3 and Xception and SVM to evaluate brain tumors. The test accuracy of the Inception-v3 model was 94.3%. Rasool et al. [13] introduced a new hybrid architecture based on CNN to classify three brain tumor types from MRI images. The experimental results showed that the fine-tuned GoogleNet achieved an accuracy of 93.1%.

From the above, it is apparent that both traditional MLs and DLs can play a useful role in assisting the early diagnosis of brain tumors. However, most of them focus on using transfer learning technologies or stacking basic models to improve classification accuracy, which increases model complexity and computation time. Therefore, a Deformable Convolution Encoder with a Multi-Scale Attention Fusion Mechanism (DCE-MSAF) for brain tumor MRI image classification was developed and is reported in this manuscript. The main innovations can be summarized as follows:

(1) A Deformable Convolution Encoder (DCE) was constructed to enable the extraction of coarse features of interest in the region of suspected brain tumors. The convolution function is firstly used to extract the global features and reduce the impact of non-tumor features on the classification performance of the model in the first two layers of the DCE. Afterwards, the deformable convolution is utilized to complete the location and coarse feature extraction in the region of the tumor in the last layers of the DCE.

(2) A Multi-Scale Attention Fusion (MSAF) mechanism was designed for the extraction of fine features in the region of brain tumors. The MSAF extracts the fine features by applying the attention mechanism to images that have been constructed with multiple scales. Furthermore, the features extracted by the attention mechanism are

combined into more refined features through the fusion mechanism of the MSAF, enabling the model to accurately classify various types of brain tumors on MRI images.

2 Method

Malignant brain tumors seriously pose a serious threat to human life and health because of the characteristics of high invasiveness. At present, Magnetic Resonance Imaging (MRI) technology is one of the important methods for clinicians to early diagnose and analyze brain tumors. However, manual interpretation of MRI images is a hugely time-consuming and labor-consuming project, and easy to result in misdiagnosis. Therefore, to accurately classify the types of brain tumors under the MRI, a Deformable Convolution Encoder with a Multi-Scale Attention Fusion Mechanism (DCE-MSAF) for MRI image classification of brain tumors is proposed. The overall structure is shown in Fig. 1. Firstly, we construct a deformable convolution encoder structure (DCE) to realize the coarse extraction of brain tumor region features. In the first two layers of the DCE, we use the conventional convolution function to realize the global extraction of features F^{cnn_i}, $i = 1, 2$. Reducing the impact of some non-tumor regions reducing the impact of non-tumor region features. In addition, the deformable convolution (DC) is utilized to locate the tumor regions progressively in the latter two layers of the DCE. The features of the localized tumor region are roughly extracted, i.e., F^{dce_i}, $i = 3, 4$. Secondly, considering that the features extracted by DC may still contain non-tumor region features, the MSAF composed of the attention mechanism and the fusion mechanism is designed to further extract finer features of the tumor region on the branch of the last two layers of the DCE. The attention mechanism of the MSAF is exploited to extract the fine attention features F^{am_i}, $i = 3, 4$. All the extracted fine attention features will be fused to obtain more refined features F^{msaf} through the fusion mechanism of the MSAF. Finally, three fully connected layers and Softmax functions are applied to classify the features of gliomas, meningiomas, pituitary tumors, and normal brains (No Tumor).

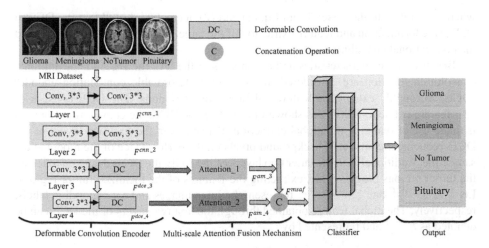

Fig. 1. Structure of the proposed model (DCE-MSAF)

2.1 Deformable Convolution Encoder for Coarse Feature Extraction of Brain Tumor Regions

It can be found that the modeling of large and unknown shape transformations by CNNs has an inherent flaw, namely that the convolutional unit only takes a fixed sampling of the input feature map. This shortcoming has implications for accurate feature extraction. To solve this problem, deformable convolution (DC) was proposed in [14] to improve the ability to model deformation. The DC is based on a parallel network learning offset vector (Offset). Firstly, the Offset is applied to generate 2N channel dimensions, corresponding to the original output features and offset features, respectively. Secondly, bilinear interpolation is developed to solve the problem of discontinuous position deformable derivation and gradients. Lastly, the convolution kernel is offset at the sampling point of the input feature map by using the back-propagation algorithm. Therefore, the shape of the feature map can be adjusted according to the actual situation by using the DC, better extracting the input features, and obtaining different scales or arbitrary sizes of the receptive field of the region.

According to the input image, a regular grid $R = \{(-1, -1), (-1, 0), \cdots, (0, 1), (1, 1)\}$ is first used for sampling and weighing operations. Finally, a convolution operation with kernel 3 is used to extract features. Each position p_0 on the output feature map y of the CNN can be calculated as follows:

$$y(p_0) = \Sigma_{p_n \in \mathcal{R}} w(p_n) \odot x(p_0 + p_n) \tag{1}$$

where the $\odot$ represents the multiplication operation, $w(\cdot)$ represents the weight, and p_n is an enumeration of the positions listed in R. The p_n defines the size and expansion of the receptive field. The feature map y obtained from Eq. (1) is used as the input, and a convolution function is applied to the feature map to obtain the deformed offset $\{\Delta p_n | n = 1, \cdots, N\}$ of the deformable convolution, increasing the regular grid R and acquiring the feature map after positioning. Formally:

$$y(p_0) = \Sigma_{p_n \in \mathcal{R}} w(p_n) \odot x(p_0 + p_n + \Delta p_n) \tag{2}$$

where Δp_n refers to the offset. From Eq. (1) and (2), it can be inferred that the DC can realize the localization and feature extraction of the target regions through the offset and the conventional convolution function.

Because of the characteristics and advantages of the DC, the DC and conventional convolution function are considered to construct a deformable convolution encoder (DCE) to roughly extract the features of brain tumor regions. The DCE consists of four feature extraction layers, as shown in Fig. 2. In the DCE, the convolution function is made use of realizing the global extraction of features in the first two layers of the DCE, reducing the impact of background pixels on the performance of the model at the same time. Additionally, in the latter two layers of the DCE, the DC is designed to locate the tumor regions progressively, extracting the features of the localized tumor regions. Let $X \in \mathbb{R}^{H,W,C}$ and $Y \in \mathbb{R}^{H,W,C}$ represent the input images and corresponding labels, respectively. The global feature obtained through the first two layers of the DCE can be denoted as F^{cnn_i} and represented by:

$$F^{cnn\_i} = f_{conv}\left(X \in \mathbb{R}^{H,W,C}; Y \in \mathbb{R}^{H,W,C}\right), i = 1, 2 \tag{3}$$

where f_{conv} represents the convolution function in the encoder pipeline. Similarly, the F^{cnn_2} is input into the third feature extraction layer. Then the DC is used for locating the tumor regions and simultaneously achieving the extraction of the features F^{dce_3} of the located regions.

$$F^{dce\_3} = f_{dc}\left(F^{cnn\_2}\right) \qquad (4)$$

where f_{dc} represents the deformable convolution function in the encoder pipeline. By analogy, it can be gradually located the tumor regions through the f_{dc} of the last two layers of the DCE, and lastly extract the coarse tumor region features F^{dce_4}. We will show the relevant ablation experimental results in Sect. 3 in detail.

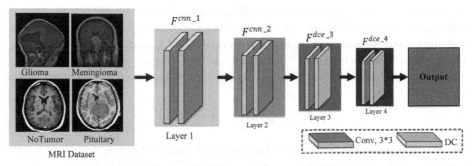

Fig. 2. Deformable convolution encoder structure. The DC indicates the deformable convolution

2.2 Multi-scale Attention Fusion Mechanism for Finer Feature Extraction of Brain Tumor Regions

It is well known that the conventional convolution function can be used in the encoder pipeline to extract the target region features layer by layer. The deeper the encoder structure, the finer the features that may be extracted. However, it will inevitably learn non-target region features and seriously affect the final performance of the model through layer-by-layer accumulation when using the convolution function to extract features in each layer. Similarly, the tumor regions may not be completely located by using the DC, resulting in the extracted lesion features being inaccurate. As the depth of the feature extraction layer deepens, the classification performance of the model will inevitably be affected. Therefore, a multi-scale attention fusion mechanism (MSAF) composed of the attention mechanism and the fusion mechanism is proposed to solve this problem. The attention mechanism of the MSAF is good for the model extracting fine attention features that are associated with the tumor regions and less for the features representing the unaffected regions. The more refined tumor region features at different scales can be fused and extracted through the fusion mechanism of the MSAF, thereby enhancing the ability of the tumor region features extraction of the proposed model. The overall model structure is shown in Fig. 3.

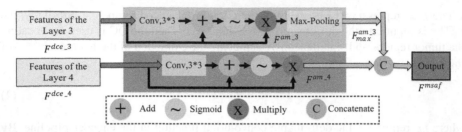

Fig. 3. Structure of multi-scale attention fusion mechanism

As shown in Fig. 3, the MSAF is built on the side branch of the DCE to extract the more refined tumor region features. Instead of treating each feature value with equal importance, paying high attention to specific tumor region features will help the classification model differentiate tumor images. Suppose F^{dce_3} and F^{dce_4} represent the corresponding features obtained by the last two layers of the DCE, and the vector W represents the attention vector, where the jth refers to the attention value given to F^{dce_i}, $i = 3, 4$. The following formula to calculate the macro representation of the attention feature vector F^{am_i}:

$$F^{am\_i} = W\left(j^{th}\right) \circ F^{dce\_i}, i = 3, 4 \tag{5}$$

where $\circ$ represents the element-wise dot product of vectors. By using different attention weights in the attention mechanism, the features F^{am_i} obtained in Eq. (5) are closer to the features of the tumor region. According to the attention mechanism structure designed in Fig. 3, the attention features can also be rewritten as:

$$F^{am\_i} = F^{dce\_i} \otimes \left(\delta\left(F^{dce\_i} \oplus f_{conv}\left(F^{dce\_i}\right)\right)\right), i = 3, 4 \tag{6}$$

where f_{conv} and δ represent regular convolution and Sigmoid functions, respectively. The $\otimes$ and $\oplus$ represent pixel-level multiplication and addition operations, respectively. Considering the problem of different scales, max-pooling is used for reducing the dimensionality, ensuring that the dimension of all attention features remains the same. Let $f_1, f_2, \cdots, f_k; k \in (W, H)$ denote the k feature maps of the attention feature F^{am_3} extracted from the $W \times H$ dimension, thus the attention feature F^{am_3} can be represented as $F^{am\_3} = \{f_1, f_2, \cdots, f_k\}, k \in (W \times H)$. The representative feature $F^{am\_3}_{max}$ obtained by the maximum pooling operation can be expressed as:

$$F^{am\_3}_{max} = f_{max}(f_1, f_2, \cdots, f_k), k \in (W \times H), \forall f_k \in F^{am\_3} \tag{7}$$

where the f_{max} represents the max-pooling function. Finally, the fusion mechanism is employed to inductively fuse all the attention features of different scales to obtain the more refined features F^{msaf}:

$$F^{msaf} = f_{fuse}\left(F^{am\_4}; F^{am\_3}_{max}\right) \tag{8}$$

where the f_{fuse} represents the fusion mechanism. Through the above theoretical analysis, it can be inferred that using the MSAF-based learning mechanism can not only extract the more refined features, but also assist the model in classifying various types of brain tumors. We will also demonstrate this inference with relevant experimental results in Sect. 3 detailedly.

3   Experiment and Comparison

3.1   Datasets and Classification Indices

Magnetic resonance (MRI) analysis is a common method for professional neurosurgeons to analyze brain tumors, but manual labeling of brain tumor MRI images is a very challenging task, resulting in a relatively small amount of brain tumor MRI data. Fortunately, some precious tumor MRI image datasets for brain tumor research are shared on the Kaggle platform in recent years [18, 19]. We collected and organized a total of 6,698 MRI images from the Kaggle website. Without using augmentation technology, there are 1,389, 1,607, 2,000, and 1,702 MRI images in the Glioma, Meningioma, Pituitary, and No Tumor datasets, respectively. The proportion of each sub-data used for training and testing is shown in Table 1 below.

Table 1. Details of the experimental dataset.

Class	Training	Testing	Total Data
Glioma	1,089	300	1,389
Meningioma	1,301	306	1,607
Pituitary	1,595	405	2,000
No Tumor	1,402	300	1,702
Total	5,387	1,311	6,698

To further verify the effectiveness of the proposed method, we adopt metrics such as accuracy (Acc), precision (P_c), Recall (recall), and F1 score (F1) to evaluate the experimental results.

3.2   Results of Ablation Experiment

(a) Ablation Experimental Results of the Deformable Convolution Encoder

To verify the effectiveness of the deformable convolution encoder (DCE) and further illustrate the contribution of the DCE to the classification performance of the overall model, the relevant ablation experiments were conducted in the laboratory. The relevant experimental results are shown in Table 2. The DCE represents the deformable convolution encoder structure constructed with 2-layer convolution layers and 2-layers deformable convolution (DC) layer. The DCE_1, DCE_3, and DCE_4 represent the DCE constructed with 1-layer DC layer and 3-layers convolution layers, 3-layers DC layers and 1-layer convolution layer, and full 4-layers DC layers, respectively. The CE denotes the encoding structure formed by the conventional convolution functions. In the

Table 2. Classification indices of the ablation experiments of the DCE.

Methods	Acc	P_c	Recall	F1
CE	0.9695	0.9682	0.9670	0.9675
DCE_1	0.9588	0.9586	0.9556	0.9567
DCE	**0.9718**	**0.9710**	**0.9697**	**0.9703**
DCE_3	0.9466	0.9459	0.9421	0.9431
DCE_4	0.8978	0.8961	0.8920	0.8936

classification structure, we adopt three fully connected layers and the Softmax function as the classifier.

On the one hand, it can be believed that the overall experimental results of the DCE are better than those of the DCE_1, DCE_3, DCE_4, and CE models from the results in Table 2. The recall scores of the DCE are 0.27%, 1.41%, 2.76%, and 7.77% higher than other models, respectively. On the other hand, it is surprising to find that the DCE_4 formed with a 4-layer DC cannot achieve optimal performance. From a theoretical analysis, the brain tumor regions can be located by using the DC in the DCE_4 layer by layer, and then continuously extracting tumor features from coarse to fine. However, when the tumor regions are initially located by using the DC, there may be problems of over-localization or incorrect localization. This problem may lead to more non-tumor region features being learned and extracted simultaneously. Different from the DCE_4 model, the MRI global features are extracted by using 4-layers conventional convolution functions in the CE model. Nevertheless, it is easy to introduce non-tumor region features, thereby affecting the classification performance of the model. The DCE combines the advantages of the convolution functions and the DC. Firstly, the convolution functions are used to learn and extract the global features in the first two layers of the DCE, reducing the impact of features of non-tumor regions. Furthermore, the DC is developed to further locate tumor regions in the last two layers of the DCE, achieving coarse tumor feature extraction.

(b) Ablation Experimental Results of Multi-scale Attention Fusion Mechanism
To verify the effectiveness of the MSAF, we performed related ablation experiments in the laboratory. The relevant experimental results are shown in Table 3. The DCE-MSAF indicates that 2-layer MSAF is constructed on the branch of the DCE. The DCE-MSAF_1, DCE-MSAF_3, and DCE-MSAF_4 indicate that 1-layer, 3-layer, and 4-layer MSAF are built on the branch of the DCE, respectively.

Since the good performances of the DCE and the MSAF, the DCE-MSAF performs well in the task of classifying different tumor types, with an accuracy of 97.25%, as shown in bold font in Table 3. Moreover, from the relevant experimental results in Table 3, it can be clearly found that the performance of the DCE-MSAF is much better than other models. The P_c indicator of the DCE-MSAF is 0.003%, 1.80%, 0.81%, and 0.84% higher than those of the DCE, DCE-MSAF_1, DCE-MSAF_3, and DCE-MSAF_4, respectively. To sum up, according to the results in Tables 2–3, it has been proved that the proposed model based on the DCE and the MSAF module can be good for assisting

Table 3. Classification indices of the ablation experiments of the MSAF.

Methods	Acc	P_c	Recall	F1
DCE	0.9718	0.9710	0.9697	0.9703
DCE-MSAF_1	0.9565	0.9550	0.9532	0.9539
DCE-MSAF	**0.9725**	**0.9713**	**0.9705**	**0.9708**
DCE-MSAF_3	0.9649	0.9632	0.9624	0.9627
DCE-MSAF_4	0.9634	0.9629	0.9613	0.9619

the model in extracting the more refined tumor regional features from the brain MRI images, thereby achieving excellent multi-type tumor classification performance.

3.3 Comparison

To fairly and justly prove that the proposed model (DCE-MSAF) has stronger classification performance than other classification models, the relevant comparative experiments were conducted in the laboratory. The relevant experimental results are shown in Figs. 4, 5 and Table 4.

The confusion matrices and ROC curves in Figs. 4, 5 show that the proposed model based on the DCE and MSAF produces good results for each tumor category (0, 1, 2, 3). Class 0 indicates the glioma tumor, class 1 is the meningioma tumor, class 2 represents the normal brain (No Tumor), and class 3 stands for the pituitary tumor. The true positive rate of class 0, class 1, class 2, and class 3 reached 0.96, 0.96, 1.00, and 99.00%, respectively. Analyzing the ROC curves, it can be inferred that the true positive rate and classification effect of the proposed model for gliomas and meningiomas tumors are inferior to No Tumors and pituitary tumors. This is mainly due to the most relevant features connected to any brain tumor are difficult to classify. Moreover, the tumor features are related to the location of the tumor regions in any MRI images, and its shape, size, and boundary vary with the tumor type. The comparison between other conventional classification methods is shown in Table 4.

With the classification indicators in Figs. 4, 5 and Table 4 for further analysis, it can be summarized that (1) the DCE-MSAF performs well in the task of identifying different types of brain MRI tumors, the accuracy, precision, recall rate, and F1 score reached 97.3%, 0.9713, 97.1%, and 0.9708, respectively. (2) Compared with the conventional classification model, the classification performance of the DCE-MSAF is also better than other models. Since the excellent performance of the proposed model constructed by the DCE and the MSAF, the F1 score of the DCE-MSAF is 2.99%, 2.11%, 1.12%, 0.33%, 0.92%, 9.55%, 1.29%, and 1.08% higher than that of the Alexnet, VGG16, ResNet, CE, CE-MSAF, and other three models respectively proposed by Sadad et al. [10], Kumar et al. [11], and Rasool et al. [13]. In the DCE-MSAF, the conventional convolution function in the first two layers of the DCE is used for extracting the global features, reducing the impact of non-tumor regional features. Additionally, the DC is developed to locate the tumor region step by step in the last two layers of the DCE, achieving the coarse feature extraction of the localized brain tumor regions. More importantly, the attention mechanism of the designed MSAF is applied to allow the model to extract fine attention features that are closer to the tumor region. Finally, the inductive fusion mechanism of the MSAF is used to further fuse all fine attention features to extract more refiner tumor region features. Although the CE, AlexNet, VGG16, and other models can achieve better overall classification performance by learning the features of brain tumor regions pixel by pixel through deep convolution layers, the above models increase the depth or width of the model, leading to unnecessary computational overhead. Literature [10, 13] and others used transfer learning technology to realize the recognition of different types of brain tumors. However, the tumor features can not be extracted accurately since the different training objects and weights are between the source domain and target domain.

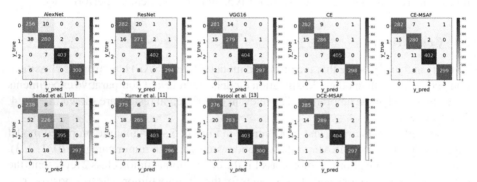

Fig. 4. Comparison of confusion matrices between DCE-MSAF and other models

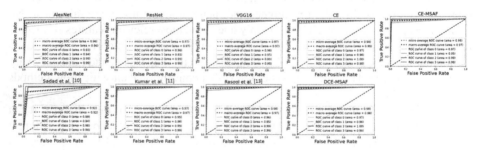

Fig. 5. Comparison of ROC curves between DCE-MSAF and other models

Table 4. Comparison of classification indicators between DCE-MSAF and other models.

Methods	Acc	P_c	Recall	F1
AlexNet [15]	0.9451	0.9432	0.9409	0.9409
ResNet [17]	0.9527	0.9503	0.9496	0.9497
VGG16 [16]	0.9619	0.9604	0.9590	0.9596
CE	0.9695	0.9682	0.9670	0.9675
CE-MSAF	0.9634	0.9624	0.9611	0.9616
Sadad et al. [10]	0.8818	0.8819	0.8743	0.8753
Kumar et al. [11]	0.9603	0.9590	0.9574	0.9579
Rasool et al. [13]	0.9626	0.9607	0.9600	0.9600
DCE-MSAF	**0.9725**	**0.9713**	**0.9705**	**0.9708**

4 Conclusions

The presence of a brain tumor seriously threatens human health and life. In medicine, clinicians often use Magnetic Resonance Imaging (MRI) for the early diagnosis of brain tumors. However, recognition of gliomas tumors, pituitary tumors, meningiomas tumors, and normal brain (No Tumor) in MRI images is time-consuming and challenging. Accurate automatic early diagnosis is highly desirable. Therefore, a Deformable Convolution Encoder with a Multi-Scale Attention Fusion Mechanism (DCE-MSAF) for brain tumor MRI image classification is proposed in this paper. Firstly, a Deformable Convolution Encoder (DCE) structure is constructed to extract coarse features of brain tumor regions. In the first two layers of the DCE, the conventional convolution function is used to extract the global features. In the latter two layers, the deformable convolution (DC) is used to locate and extract coarse features of the brain tumor region layer by layer. Secondly, a Multi-Scale Attention Fusion Mechanism (MSAF) composed of Attention and Fusion Mechanism is designed to accurately fuse and extract more refined features in the region of the tumor. The proposed DCE-MSAF shows promise for automatic identification and robust classification of various brain tumors on MRI images. The accuracy, precision, recall, and F1 scores of the DCE-MSAF for the dataset obtained from the Kaggle website are 97.3%, 0.9713, 97.1%, and 0.9708, respectively. The comparison results show that the performance of the DCE-MSAF is superior than that of the CE, VGG16, and other models in the classification of brain tumor images. The new image analysis pipeline will be potentially helpful for use by clinicians for early diagnosis and accurate management of brain tumors.

Acknowledgments. This work is supported by the National Natural Science Foundation of China (No. 61571302), Project of Ministry of Science and Technology of People's Republic of China (No. G2021013008), Key Project of Crossing Innovation of Medicine and Engineering, University of Shanghai for Science and Technology (No. 1020308405,1022308502).

References

1. Ferlay, J., Soerjomataram, I., Dikshit, R., et al.: Cancer incidence and mortality worldwide: sources, methods and major patterns in GLOBOCAN 2012. Int. J. Cancer **136**(5), E359–E386 (2015)
2. American Cancer Society. www.cancer.org/cancer.html. Accessed 9 Sept 2021
3. Brain Tumor: Diagnosis. https://www.cancer.net/cancer-types/brain-tumor/diagnosis. Accessed 9 Sept 2021
4. Kumari, R.: SVM classification an approach on detecting abnormality in brain MRI images. Int. J. Eng. Res. Appl. **3**(4), 1686–1690 (2013)
5. Nazir, M., Shakil, S., Khurshid, K.: Role of deep learning in brain tumor detection and classification (2015 to 2020): a review. Comput. Med. Imaging Graph. **91**, 101940 (2021)
6. Tandel, G.S., Tiwari, A., Kakde, O.G.: Performance optimisation of deep learning models using majority voting algorithm for brain tumour classification. Comput. Biol. Med. **135**, 104564 (2021)
7. Bodapati, J.D., Shaik, N.S., Naralasetti, V., et al.: Joint training of two-channel deep neural network for brain tumor classification. Signal Image Video Process. **15**(4), 753–760 (2021)
8. Abd El Kader, I., Xu, G., Shuai, Z., et al.: Differential deep convolutional neural network model for brain tumor classification. Brain Sci. **11**(3), 352 (2021)
9. Díaz-Pernas, F.J., Martínez-Zarzuela, M., Antón-Rodríguez, M., et al.: A deep learning approach for brain tumor classification and segmentation using a multiscale convolutional neural network. Healthc. MDPI **9**(2), 153 (2021)
10. Sadad, T., Rehman, A., Munir, A., et al.: Brain tumor detection and multi-classification using advanced deep learning techniques. Microsc. Res. Tech. **84**(6), 1296–1308 (2021)
11. Kumar, R.L., Kakarla, J., Isunuri, B.V., et al.: Multi-class brain tumor classification using residual network and global average pooling. Multimedia Tools Appl. **80**(9), 13429–13438 (2021)
12. Noreen, N., Palaniappan, S., Qayyum, A., et al.: Brain tumor classification based on fine-tuned models and the ensemble method. Comput. Mater. Continua **67**(3), 3967–3982 (2021)
13. Rasool, M., Ismail, N.A., Boulila, W., et al.: a hybrid deep learning model for brain tumour classification. Entropy **24**(6), 799 (2020)
14. Dai, J., Qi, H., Xiong, Y., et al.: Deformable convolutional networks. In: Proceedings of the IEEE International Conference on Computer Vision, pp. 764–773 (2017)
15. Krizhevsky, A., Sutskever, I., Hinton, G.E.: Imagenet classification with deep convolutional neural networks. In: Advances in Neural Information Processing Systems, 25 (2012)
16. Simonyan, K., Zisserman, A.: Very deep convolutional networks for large-scale image recognition. arXiv preprint arXiv:1409.1556 (2014)
17. He, K., Zhang, X., Ren, S., et al.: Deep residual learning for image recognition. In: Proceedings of the IEEE Conference on Computer Vision and Pattern Recognition, pp. 770–778 (2016)
18. Bhuvaji, S., Kadam, A., Bhumkar, P., Dedge, S., Kanchan, S.: Brain tumor classification (MRI): classify MRI images into four classes. Kaggle (2020)
19. Nickparvar, M.: Brain tumor MRI dataset. Kaggle (2021)

GI Tract Lesion Classification Using Multi-task Capsule Networks with Hierarchical Convolutional Layers

Mumtaz Ali, Chao Li[✉], and Kun He

School of Computer Science and Technology, Huazhong University of Science and Technology, Wuhan, China
d201880880@hust.edu.cn

Abstract. Lesions in the gastrointestinal (GI) tract of human beings are usually diagnosed with an endoscopic imaging system. Traditionally, a gastroenterologist examines the GI tract manually to diagnose the diseases. The automated systems may help to promptly diagnose the anomalous mucosal findings ranging from insignificant annoyances to extremely fatal diseases in the GI tract. Most existing techniques attempt the problem separately by dividing it into upper and lower GI lesions, and almost all the literature is concentrated on the lower GI. To this end, we propose a multi-task learning-based capsule network that incorporates shared supplementary convolutional layers along with a novel twofold margin loss to classify the lesions in upper and lower GI tracts simultaneously. The proposed work performs three tasks on endoscopic images. The first task asks the model to classify the endoscopic images into 23 classes of lesions. The second requires a classification of four groups, i.e. anatomical-landmarks, pathological-findings, quality-of-mucosal-views, and therapeutic interventions, respectively. And the third aims to classify images into two classes of upper or lower GI. Multitask capsule networks tend to be well equipped to accomplish all the three tasks concurrently by sharing the associated information. The hierarchical information of the three tasks can help the network learn the classification from the overall to the partial. Extensive experiments validate that the proposed multi-task capsule network achieves state-of-the-art performance on all the three tasks.

Keywords: GI Tract · Lesions classification · Multi-task · Capsule networks · Margin loss

1 Introduction

The recent emergence of artificial intelligence (AI)-powered support systems has shown promise in providing healthcare practitioners with the resources they need to provide high-quality treatment on a large scale [1]. The cornerstone of a successful AI-based framework is the amalgamation of valuable data and algorithms that train a deep learning model to solve practical issues such as the identification of cancers or pre-cancerous lesions in images [2], [3]. In recent years, a variety of such approaches have been used to identify abnormalities in the GI tract. The lesions in the upper and lower GI are treated independently in contemporary AI-based works [4]. For example, esophageal cancer has been diagnosed using Faster R-CNN [5] based on DenseNet [6] and Gabor features on gastroscopy [7].

Similarly, utilising Convolutional Neural Networks (CNNs) [8], an autonomous colorectal polyp identification has been developed. There are at least 23 types of lesions in the GI tract, and each of these lesions falls into one of four categories: anatomical-landmarks, pathological-findings, quality-of-mucosal-views, and therapeutic interventions. Upper and lower GI abnormalities can be identified from these lesions. As a result, AI-based systems can be trained in such a way that the lesion class and its group can be identified hierarchically.

Unfortunately, much recent research has concentrated on lower GI [9]. There is only a small amount of evidence in the literature that the systems can detect lesions from any part of the GI tract. We adopt a multi-task learning based knowledge sharing approach to determine the type of lesions, following their upper or lower GI involvement, and their respective group simultaneously, by sharing their associated information.

Capsule networks are typically better tailored for single-task problems [10]. However, such networks have also been used in special cases for multi-task learning. To classify endoscopic GI tract images for lesions, we use capsule networks in a multi-task knowledge sharing setup equipped with hierarchical supplementary convolutional layers. Mainly there are three tasks:

- Task 1 ($T1$): Classify endoscopic images into 23 classes of lesions.
- Task 2 ($T2$): Categorize the images into four groups.
- Task 3 ($T3$): Determine whether the lesions belong to the upper/lower GI.

Instead of training the model for each task separately, multi-task capsule networks are better able to do all three tasks simultaneously by exchanging the relevant information. We utilise a multi-task capsule network with hierarchical supplementary convolutional layers and a twofold margin loss to complete the tasks. To the best of our knowledge, the multi-task capsule network proposed in this research is the first of its kind for the classification of GI tract lesions. We train and evaluate the proposed approach using the prominent Hyper-Kvasir [11] dataset to validate its performance, and our model achieves state-of-the-art performance.

The major contributions of this work are as follows:

- The proposed multi-task capsule network with hierarchical supplemental convolutional layers delivers state-of-the-art performance in detecting GI tract lesions using an unique twofold margin loss.
- By correlating information from easier tasks to more hard tasks, the proposed model takes advantage of the hierarchical information of the three tasks along with the utilization of a conditional image enhancement technique.

2   Multi-task Capsule Networks and Proposed Method

Capsule networks (CapsNets) [12] have recently been found to achieve good performance. As depicted in Fig. 1, the model can perform k classification tasks concurrently, and therefore, multi-task capsule network architecture must be appropriately designed to learn as many features as possible.

In a standard approach when there is no associated information, for multiple related tasks, the common layers are designed in such a way that they extract hierarchical features. They derive n-gram features from input vectors at several points using the convolution process. The neurons in the common convolutional layers are coupled with a native region of top layers over a series of weights. Consequently, a non-linear activation gets a natively computed weighted sum to generate the final result of neurons of the convolutional layer.

Suppose that $x \in \mathbb{R}^{l \times \delta}$ symbolizes the representation of input instances when l represents the instance length and δ represents instance dimension. Similarly, assume that we have $x_i \in \mathbb{R}^{\delta}$ as the i-th instance having δ dimension and $\omega_i \in \mathbb{R}^{\Omega_1 \times \delta}$ as the filter number i to perform the convolution operation. The Ω_1 represents the size of filters and δ represents the input vector dimension. The Δ_1 are filters for the convolutional layers having a stride of 1.

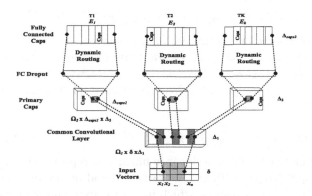

Fig. 1. Detailed diagram of a standard multi-task capsule network

Similarly, suppose the convolutional layer has θ_i as the i-th feature map. We can compute θ_i as follows:

$$\theta_i = f_{cnv}(X_{i:i+\Omega_1-1} \otimes \omega_i + \beta_i) \in \mathbb{R}^{l-\Omega_1+1}. \tag{1}$$

Here the convolutional kernel is symbolized with the sign $\otimes$ and β_i represents the vector for bias of feature map number i. We put these values then into a nonlinear function f_{cnv}, consequently, we obtain the results for the i-th feature map θ_i. We use ReLU as the activation function that can be defined as $f_{cnv} = max(0, x)$. With the help of the process described above, we can attain the output for the i-th feature map. Through this process, each filter produces one feature map, therefore, for $i \in \{1, 2, 3, ..., \Delta_1\}$, we can get Δ_1 feature maps. Finally, we can arrange such feature maps as follows:

$$\Theta = [\theta_1, \theta_2, ..., \theta_{\Delta_1}] \in \mathbb{R}^{(l-\Omega_1+1) \times \Delta_1}. \tag{2}$$

The primary capsule layers are the initial capsule layers, which substitute the features extractors of convolutional layers. In such a replacement process the initialization of parameters and the location information of features are preserved. Assume that Δ_{caps1} represents the dimension of PCps. We can get the resultant vector for each capsule with the help of convolution operation similarly as we obtained for the convolutional layer.

Primarily, the transpose of matrix Θ (the resultant vector of top layer) is performed to obtain $\Theta^T = [\theta'_1, \theta'_2, ..., \theta'_{(i-\Omega_1+1)}] \in \mathbb{R}^{\Delta_1 \times (l-\Omega_1+1)}$, such that $\theta'_i \in \mathbb{R}^{\Delta_1}$ represents the i-th column of θ^T.

Next, we describe $\zeta_i \in \mathbb{R}^{\Omega_2 \times \Delta_1}$, which is the i-th filter to perform the operation of convolution. In this expression Ω_2 denotes the filter size, and Δ_1 symbolizes the convolutional layer filters. The filters ζ_i are then multiplied with θ'_i in sequence. Here the stride is 2 and window size is Ω_2 to generate q_i. The q_i is the single feature map number i of the PCps layer. Finally, the value of q_i is obtained as follows:

$$q_i = f_{cnv}(\theta'_{i:i+\Omega_2-1} \otimes \zeta_i + p_i) \in \mathbb{R}^{(l-\Omega_1-\Omega_2+1)/2+1}. \tag{3}$$

Here q_i symbolizes the bias term. As Δ_{caps1} neurons are contained in each capsule, Eq. 3 is executed to Δ_{caps1} to obtain the resultant vector from capsule i, which is represented as $q'_i \in \mathbb{R}^{((l-\Omega_1-\Omega_2+1)/2+1) \times \Delta_{caps1}}$. Assume we have Δ_2 filters, we can get the output of PCps layer for $i \in \{1, 2, ..., \Delta_2\}$, that could be determined by:

$$Q = [q'_1, q'_2, ..., q'_{\Delta_1}] \in \mathbb{R}^{((l-\Omega_1-\Omega_2+1)/2+1) \times \Delta_{caps1} \times \Delta_2}. \tag{4}$$

A squashing function that is non-linear in nature (as reported by [12], [13]) is used to limit the input length in $[0, 1]$. The same method preserves the orientation of the input vectors of the capsules, which in turn helps to improve the probability of the presence of the features in the existing capsules. A mechanism called the nonlinear squashing function can be considered as a method for compression as well as distribution of the vector given as input. It could be determined as:

$$\nu_j = \frac{\|s_j\|^2}{1 + \|s_j\|^2} \frac{s_j}{\|s_j\|}. \tag{5}$$

Here ν_j represents the resultant vector of capsule j in the existing layer. Similarly, s_j symbolizes the total input vector.

There are two stages of vector calculation, the linear combination and the routing process can be represented as:

$$q'_{j|i} = \Psi_{ij} q'_i, s_j = \sum_i \vartheta_{ij} q'_{j|i}. \tag{6}$$

Here q_i' is the result of capsule i of the layer below, and Ψ_{ij} represents the corresponding weight matrix. Similarly, $q_{j|i}'$ denotes the prediction vectors which are obtained after the multiplication of the weight matrix and the resultant vector in the trailing layer. Term ϑ_{ij} denotes the coupling coefficients, determined by the routing-by-agreement algorithm [14], [13], [15].

Another important step is the summation of the coupling coefficients. These coupling coefficients are present between all the capsules and the i-th capsule in the preceding upper layers. The sum of the coefficients is 1. The coupling coefficients are determined with a routing procedure called leaky-softmax [16].

$$\vartheta_{ij} = leaky - softmax(\beta_{ij}). \tag{7}$$

Here term β_{ij} denotes the logits that are from the coupling coefficients, representing prior probabilities logarithmically (simply called log prior probability) expressing that capsule number i couples with the j-th capsule.

By evaluating the uniformity between the resultant vector ν_j of capsule number j of the existing layer along with the prediction vector $q_{j|i}'$ of the capsule number i in the layer underneath, the coupling coefficients β_{ij} can be updated iteratively.

$$\beta_{ij} = \beta_{ij} + q_{j|i}'.\nu_j. \tag{8}$$

A dropout mechanism [17], [13] is used before the FCCps layer for each capsule to increase the capability of the model generalization. The results of the dropout are directly transferred into a FCCs layer in such a way that the capsules are promptly multiplied with the transformation matrix $\Psi \in \mathbb{R}^{\mathbb{H} \times \Delta_2 \times E_k}$ after routing-by-agreement to generate the final capsule $\nu_j \in \mathbb{R}^{\Delta_{caps2}}$, along with the probability $\alpha_j \in \mathbb{R}$ for every single category. The predicted category in the capsule network would be the category with the greatest α_j. The symbol $\mathbb{H}$ represents the quantity of the capsules in the trailing layer underneath, and E_k is the task number k. The Δ_{caps2} is the dimension of FCCps.

2.1 Multi-task Capsule Network with Hierarchical Supplementary Layers

We propose a novel multi-task capsule network, as shown in Fig. 2, to classify the GI tract lesions. The proposed model operates conventionally other than having hierarchical convolutional layers. The convolutional layers are denoted as CL1, CL2,..., CL9, respectively. There are two types of convolutional layers. The first type contains three convolutional layers, ReLU activations operator, and an average pooling layer. The CL3 layer belongs to the first type, whereas layers CL1, CL2, CL4,..., CL9 are the second type of layers as there is no average pooling layer operation. The rest of the network is similar to a traditional multi-task capsule network. The proposed model is the result of testing several architectures of CapsNet having single-layer convolution, two-layer convolution, and three-layer convolution respectively. Finally, we obtained optimal results by using 9 convolutional layers in a shared manner as depicted in Fig. 2.

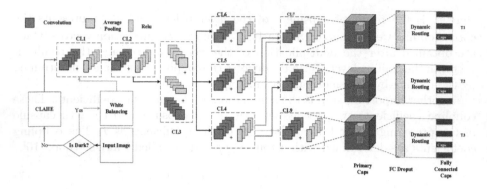

Fig. 2. The architecture of the proposed multi-task capsule network

The proposed model extracts more features than a basic approach as shown in Fig. 1. In a conventional approach, the quality of the features is considered better than the number of features. Therefore, less important features are filtered out at fully connected dropout layers. As the model extracts more features than a basic model we can afford to drop some of the features which do not contribute to the output accuracy. Such dropout of the insignificant features may reduce the computational cost as well. Each convolutional layer of the proposed model has different number of channels but the filter sizes are identical. The layers CL1, CL2 and CL3 use 64 channels, CL4, CL5 and CL6 use 128 channels, and CL7, CL8 and CL9 use 256 channels. All the layers use filter size 3×3, and 3 convolutional layers.

Similarly, we keep the number of primary capsules as 1024 for each task. As there are three tasks and the model performs each task in a parallel manner, each task has its number of higher-level capsules. Task $T1$ has 23 higher-level capsules, task $T2$ has 4 capsules and task $T3$ has 2 higher-level capsules.

2.2 Twofold Margin Loss

We use a twofold margin loss to enhance the feature learning capability of the model, written as:

$$L_1 = I_\vartheta \ max(0, \sigma_1^+ - (\|v_\vartheta\|)^2 + \lambda_1(1 - I_\vartheta) \ max(0, \|v_\vartheta - \sigma_1^-\|)^2$$
$$L_2 = I_\vartheta \ max(0, \sigma_2^+ - (\|v_\vartheta\|)^2 + \lambda_2(1 - I_\vartheta) \ max(0, \|v_\vartheta - \sigma_2^-\|)^2 \qquad (9)$$
$$L_{TF} = L_1 + L_2.$$

Here ϑ represents the class, I symbolizes indicator function. $I_\vartheta = 1$ if the existing sample is related to ϑ, else $I_\vartheta = 0$. σ_1^+ and σ_2^+ are the upper limit whereas σ_1^- and σ_2^- are the lower limit. In our method values of σ_1^+, σ_2^+, σ_1^- and σ_2^- are set to 0.90, 0.85, 0.10, 0.15, respectively. The term $\|v_\vartheta\|$ represents the Euclidean distance for the resultant vector. The symbols λ_1 and λ_2 show the lower boundary for the classes which do not exist, and these parameters assist in preventing the length of the activity vector of all fully connected capsules from being reduced during the initial learning. In the proposed method, $\lambda_1 = 0.65$ and $\lambda_2 = 0.45$. The final loss is the sum of L_1 and L_2. The final loss is symbolized as L_{TF} for FCCps.

3   Experiments

The experiments have been performed on Hyper-Kvasir dataset [11] dataset, which contains 10,662 labeled images. The proposed model has been trained and tested on a Windows 10 Personal Desktop Computer that was equipped with NVidia Gforce GTX 1060 general processing unit (GPU), having 16 GB of RAM, Intel Ci7 64 bit processor. The dataset contains 2-dimensional color images, so better color consistency and image contrast will help the model perform better. We pre-process images with Contrast Limited Adaptive Histogram Equalization(CLAHE) [18] before training the model, which is the simplification of Adaptive Histogram Equalization.

3.1   Training

We train the model up to 200 epochs where the model converges by producing encouraging training and validation accuracies. We chose a batch size of 16 images, and the model is examined for accuracy, precision, recall, and F1 score for each task on each batch. We choose a learning rate of 0.0001 and Adam [19] optimizer for all the tasks. As the dataset is imbalanced, we assign weights [20] for each class in each task. We divide the training data as 70% for training, 20% for validation, and the remaining 10% for testing.

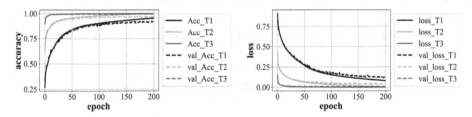

(a) Training and validation accuracy   (b) Training and validation loss

Fig. 3. The accuracy of the proposed model during training

Figure 3 depicts the precision, recall, and F1 score for each task during training. For $T1$, $T2$, and $T3$ our model has converged at the 200th epoch. Similarly, The pre-trained models ResNet50, DenseNet169 and VGG16 are also trained on same values of hyper parameters on training data upto their maximum potential.

Table 1. Macro/Micro Precision, Recall and F1 score of $T1$, $T2$ and $T3$ on test data. A: Accuracy, P: Precision, R: Recall, F1: F1 Score

Task	A	Macro_P	Micro_P	Macro_R	Micro_R	Macro_F1	Micro_F1
Bongli et al. [11]	—	0.6400	0.9100	0.6160	0.9100	0.6190	0.9100
$T1$	0.9169	0.8180	0.9169	0.7942	0.9169	0.7932	0.9169
$T2$	0.9696	0.9783	0.9696	0.9714	0.9696	0.9748	0.9696
$T3$	0.9964	0.9955	0.9964	0.9963	0.9964	0.9959	0.9964

3.2 Results and Analysis

After training, the model needs to be thoroughly analyzed on test data. Researchers [11] report the macro-precision, micro-precision, macro-recall, micro-recall, macro-F1 score, and micro-F1 score for state-of-the-art results on the dataset which we will use for comparison.

On test data that were randomly selected before training, we test the model for task 1. The results are shown in Table 1. The model, with an accuracy of 91.69%, performs fairly well for lesion classification ($T1$). As compared to the existing method(s), the model achieves 91.49% micro-precision, recall, and F1 score. Borgli et al. [11] are, to our knowledge, the only authors who report baseline results alongside the Hyper-Kvasir dataset. Our model achieves a 0.5% improvement on micro-precision, recall, and F1 score. Moreover, the model achieves at least 10% improvement on macro-precision, recall, and F1 score compared to Borgli et al. [11].

Tasks $T2$ and $T3$ are novel and to date, this paper is the only work reporting results on the two tasks. The model achieves the accuracy of 96.96% to identify the group of each lesion on task $T2$ and 99.64% for identifying whether the lesions belong to upper or lower GI on task $T3$. The model achieves very high-performance results for these tasks. Table 1 illustrates the testing results.

Table 2. Comparison of the proposed model with pre-trained models

	ResNet50	DenseNet169	VGG16	Ours
Accuracy	0.912	0.985	0.945	0.996

The performance of the proposed model in comparison with pre-trained models ResNet50, DenseNet169 and VGG16 on test data is illustrated in Table 2. It can be clearly observed the proposed model outperforms the the pre-trained models with a significant margin.

3.3 Ablation Study and Parameter Sensitivity Analysis

In this portion of the study we perform the ablation and parameter sensitivity analysis on different train and test settings.

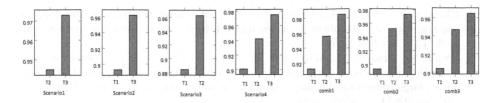

Fig. 4. Ablation study

Scenario 1: In this case, the task T1 is eliminated and the model is trained for the remaining two tasks, T2 and T3. At this point, the parameter values are left unchanged. The same test set that was employed during the entire experiment is used to test the model after training. The test results were compared based on accuracy. The accuracy for T2 and T3 was recorded as 0.945 and 0.973 respectively.

Scenario 2: Here, the task T2 is removed and the model is trained and tested on the tasks T1 and T3. In this stage results produced for both the task are 0.893 and 0.962 for T1 and T3 respectively.

Scenario 3: Here, the task T3 is removed and the model is trained and tested on the tasks T1 and T2. In this stage results produced for both the task are 0.884 and 0.963 for T1 and T2 respectively.

Scenario 4: In this stage the hierarchical convolutional layers were removed and the model is trained on direct connection of convolutional layers and primary capsule layers. In such a configuration the results for the tasks T1, T2 and T3 are noted as 0.901, 0.942 and 0.975 respectively.

4   Conclusion

To classify GI tract lesions, regardless of whether they are in the upper or lower GI, we developed a multi-task capsule network with hierarchical convolutional layers and a twofold margin loss. In addition to location, we've divided images into four categories: anatomical landmarks, pathological observations, quality-of-mucosal-views, and therapeutic interventions. The proposed model provides state-of-the-art results for lesion classification on the Hyper-Kvasir dataset by incorporating information from the three hierarchical tasks and correlating information from easier tasks to more hard tasks. In addition to lesion classification, we report benchmark results for the identification of GI tract lesions, as well as the associated group and organ information (upper or lower GI). Our research demonstrates the effectiveness of multi-task capsule networks in the classification of medical images.

References

1. Shamshirband, S., Fathi, M., Dehzangi, A., Chronopoulos, A.T., Alinejad-Rokny, H.: A review on deep learning approaches in healthcare systems: taxonomies, challenges, and open issues. J. Biomed. Inf., 103627 (2020)

2. Khan, M.A., Khan, M.A., Ahmed, F., Mittal, M.: Goyal: Gastrointestinal diseases segmentation and classification based on duo-deep architectures. Pattern Recogn. Lett. **131**, 193–204 (2020)
3. Owais, M., Arsalan, M., Mahmood, T.: Automated diagnosis of various gastrointestinal lesions using a deep learning-based classification and retrieval framework with a large endoscopic database: model development and validation. J. Med. Internet Res. **22**(11), e18563 (2020)
4. Jha, D., Ali, S., Hicks, S., Thambawita, V.: A comprehensive analysis of classification methods in gastrointestinal endoscopy imaging. Med. Image Anal., 102007 (2021)
5. Ren, S., He, K., Girshick, R., Sun, J.: Faster R-CNN: towards real-time object detection with region proposal networks. arXiv preprint arXiv:1506.01497 (2015)
6. Iandola, F., Moskewicz, M., Karayev, S., Girshick, R.: DenseNet: implementing efficient convnet descriptor pyramids. arXiv preprint arXiv:1404.1869 (2014)
7. Ghatwary, N., Ye, X.: Esophageal abnormality detection using DenseNet based faster R-CNN with Gabor features. IEEE Access **7**, 84374–84385 (2019)
8. Nadimi, E.S., Buijs, M.M., Herp, J., Kroijer, R., Kobaek-Larsen, M., Nielsen, E., Pedersen, C.D., Blanes-Vidal, V., Baatrup, G.: Application of deep learning for autonomous detection and localization of colorectal polyps in wireless colon capsule endoscopy. Comput. Electr. Eng. **81**, 106531 (2020)
9. Öztürk, Ş.: Gastrointestinal tract classification using improved LSTM based CNN
10. Mobiny, A., Lu, H., Nguyen, H.V., Roysam, B., Varadarajan, N.: Automated classification of apoptosis in phase contrast microscopy using capsule network. IEEE Trans. Med. Imaging **39**(1), 1–10 (2019)
11. Borgli, H., et al.: Hyperkvasir, a comprehensive multi-class image and video dataset for gastrointestinal endoscopy. Scientific Data **7**(1), 1–14 (2020)
12. Sabour, S., Frosst, N., Hinton, G.E.: Dynamic routing between capsules. arXiv preprint arXiv:1710.09829 (2017)
13. Lei, K., Fu, Q., Liang, Y.: Multi-task learning with capsule networks. In: 2019 International Joint Conference on Neural Networks (IJCNN), pp. 1–8, IEEE (2019)
14. Zhao, L., Wang, X., Huang, L.: An efficient agreement mechanism in CapsNets by pairwise product. arXiv preprint arXiv:2004.00272 (2020)
15. ZHang, P., Wei, P., Han, S.: CapsNets algorithm. J. Phys.: Conf. Ser. 1544, 012030, IOP Publishing (2020)
16. Yang, M., Zhao, W., Ye, J., Lei: Investigating capsule networks with dynamic routing for text classification. In: Proceedings of the 2018 Conference On Empirical Methods in Natural Language Processing, pp. 3110–3119 (2018)
17. Hinton, G.E., Srivastava, N., Krizhevsky, A., Sutskever, I., Salakhutdinov, R.R.: Improving neural networks by preventing co-adaptation of feature detectors. arXiv preprint arXiv:1207.0580 (2012)
18. Reza, A.M.: Realization of the contrast limited adaptive histogram equalization (CLAHE) for real-time image enhancement. J. VLSI Sigl. Process. Syst. Sigl. Image Video Technol. **38**(1), 35–44 (2004). https://doi.org/10.1023/B:VLSI.0000028532.53893.82
19. Kingma, J.: Adam: a method for stochastic optimization. arXiv preprint arXiv:1412.6980 (2014)
20. Johnson, J.M., Khoshgoftaar, T.M.: Survey on deep learning with class imbalance. J. Big Data **6**(1), 1–54 (2019)

Grading Diagnosis of Sacroiliitis in CT Scans Based on Radiomics and Deep Learning

Lei Liu[1], Haoyu Zhang[2], Weifeng Zhang[2], and Wei Mei[3($\boxtimes$)]

[1] Shantou University Medical College, Shantou 515041, China
[2] College of Engineering, Shantou University, Shantou 515063, China
[3] Department of Radiology, The First Affiliated Hospital of Shantou University Medical College, Shantou 515041, China
meiweist@126.com

Abstract. Ankylosing spondylitis (AS) is a disease characterized mainly by chronic inflammation of the axial joint, sacroiliitis is its early symptom and pathologic symbol. The study of the automatic grading on sacroiliac joints (SIJs) of patients in the computed tomography (CT) scans and screening the features with high correlation under different grading criterion, which can help to reduce the diagnostic differences among doctors and provide important reference for clinicians to make treatment plan. In this paper, according to 3D characteristics of CT scans, 3D features of the region of interest and 2D features of each scan are extracted respectively. After feature fusion, radiomics modeling is used for automatic classification. Experiments show that more effective features can be extracted by the multi-dimension radiomics model than the single dimension feature extraction radiomics model. In the two-category, three-category and five-category classification tasks, the accuracy is 82.02%, 79.32%, 77.91% respectively, and the recall rate is 0.8792, 0.7081, 0.5331 respectively by the multi-dimension radiomics model.

Keywords: Ankylosing spondylitis · Sacroiliitis · Computed tomography · Segmentation · Radiomics

1 Introduction

Ankylosing spondylitis (AS) is a rheumatic disease with chronic inflammation as main symptom. The incidence of this disease is 0.3% in China [1]. Sacroiliitis is the pathological and early manifestation of ankylosing spondylitis. Imaging examination is necessary for the diagnosis of sacroiliitis. The grading results of sacroiliitis can be obtained by imaging analysis. According to the New York Grading Standard of AS revised in 1984 [2], sacroiliitis can be divided into five grades from 0 to 4. Grade 0 is normal, the surface of sacroiliac joint (SIJ) is smooth and no deformation; grade 1, there are some blurring of the joint margins and suspicious changes on joint surface, but no bone destruction or hyperplasia; grade 2, there have small localized areas with erosion or sclerosis, blurred joint surface, patch-like decalcification and subchondral erosion, with no alteration in the joint width; grade 3, there are moderate or advanced sacroiliitis with erosions, evidence of sclerosis, widening or narrowing in the join width, or partial ankylosis; grade 4 is complete ankylosis in sacroiliac joint. The grading results indicate the degree of patient's disease, which are also important references to assisting clinicians in making effective treatment plans.

There are many subjective factors to the grading diagnosis results based on images made by doctors because of qualitative rather than quantitative in the grading standard of sacroiliitis [3], and different doctors may have different opinions on grading criterion. At the same time, there are lots of images need to be diagnosed for doctors every day, which will reduce the accuracy of diagnosis. Therefore, there have been preliminary studies on using radiomics [4–9] to help doctors diagnose sacroiliitis in recent years. Faleiros and his team [4] used magnetic resonance imaging (MRI) images for semi-automatic grading of sacroiliitis in 2017. They identified a dichotomous pattern of sacroiliitis using gray, texture, and spectral features on T2-weighted MRI images based on sacroiliac joints images from 51 patients. Later, they [5] used MRI images to assist classification of active inflammatory of sacroiliitis by reference to the idea of radiomics. Firstly, 24 positive patients and 32 negative patients were manually divided into regions of interest (ROI) by doctors, and 256 different features were extracted and selected by radiomics method. Finally, the multi-layer perceptron method was used for machine learning training. Using the test dataset, the sensitivity, specificity and accuracy were 100%, 66.7% and 80.0% respectively.

Compared with MRI images, CT scans have relatively higher density resolution, which are not only more sensitive to subtle bone destruction and sclerosis, but also more accurate in the classification of sacroiliitis [3]. Therefore, CT images are more favored by doctors when checking sacroiliac joins of patients and the first imaging examination of patients with back pain, low back pain, body stiffness and other symptoms [10]. Because CT scans are three-dimensional (3D) data and traditional pattern recognition algorithms only focus on single scan, which is two-dimensional (2D) features. There may have some loss of local 3D features. Based on this, in this paper, the 2D features and 3D features of the left and right unilateral SIJs are extracted respectively after using 3D-UNet network to automatically segment the ROI. Aiming at 2D and 3D features, this paper designs a multi-dimensional features automatic radiomics grading algorithm (MDARG) for sacroiliitis based on radiomics, which can balance the local and global features better and get better classification effect. Through experimental verification of CT scans of 496 patients with SIJs provided by the First Affiliated Hospital of Shantou University, the method of this paper is superior to the current advanced radiomics methods.

2 Methods

2.1 Automatic ROI Segmentation Based on Deep Learning

Initial CT scans of the patients contain a lot of information unrelated to the sacroiliac joints, which will seriously affect the accuracy of the grading. Therefore, 3D-Unet [11] is used in this paper as automatic ROI segmentation process and statistical distribution is used to clipping ROI. The overall framework is shown in Fig. 1.

The size of SIJ CT scan is $512 \times 512 \times N$, N represents the number of slices of CT images in a case, which ranged from 100 to 250. The CT scans of 31 patients are labeled with ROI by 3D Slicer [12] under the guidance of radiologists.

CT scans are not similar to gray images, the pixel value is not limited to the range of [0, 255], and the measurement index of its dicom format [13] is HU (Hounsfield scale) [14]. HU is a relatively quantitative measure of radioactivity density, which will be used by radiologists when interpreting CT scans. According to the test and experience, it is easier to highlight the target sacroiliac joint and its interspace when HU is set within the range of [150, 2000]. Finally, each slice of the overall image is standardized by z-score [15]. Its specific form is as follows:

$$Z = (x - \mu)/\sigma, \tag{1}$$

where x represents the intensity value of each pixel, μ represents the mean value of all pixels in each slice, and σ represents the standard deviation of all pixels in each slice.

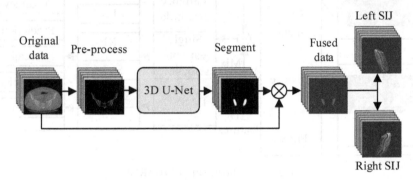

Fig. 1. Automatic segmentation and clipping algorithm based on 3D-UNET.

In order to relieve the pressure of memory and obtain faster speed, the initial input data of 3D-Unet is clipped into $160 \times 160 \times 80$ data blocks, and the overlapping parts are covered by $80 \times 80 \times 40$ data blocks.

The segmented image acquired by 3D-Unet is a binary image. It is necessary to multiply the segmented image with the original image, which is fused image. In order to adaptively segment the ROI fused images into the left and right sacroiliac joints, an automatic segmentation based on statistical distribution is proposed in this paper.

Firstly, the distribution of the binary data of the segmented image on the X, Y and Z axes will be counted respectively, and the corresponding index with more pixels is counted to determine the approximate interval distribution range of dense data on each coordinate axis. Then the appropriate coordinate range is screened through the threshold. According to the self-specified data frame range constraints (the initial coordinate range is larger than the data frame specification range), the coordinate range is gradually reduced to ensure that most pixel values can be covered. Continuously shrink the coordinate range, and then determine the specific value of the coordinates of the three axes in line with the specification of the data box. Finally, a hybrid image containing the sacroiliac joints is segmented into left and right parts.

The size of data block used in this paper is $128 \times 128 \times 96$. Under this data frame, the segmented data blocks contain all the pixels of the left and right sacroiliac joints approximately.

2.2 Multi-dimension Automatic Radiomics Grading

In order to extract more useful information about sacroiliac joints, we extract 2D features and 3D features from data blocks respectively and design a multi-dimension automatic radiomics grading (MDARG) based on sacroiliitis. The flowchart is shown in Fig. 2.

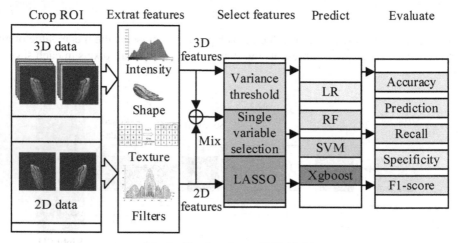

Fig. 2. The flowchart of MDARGP.

The 3D data blocks of unilateral sacroiliac joint are used to extract 3D features. Every scan of the 3D data blocks is used to extract 2D features and the final 2D features are obtained by calculating the average 2D features of all scans. Here, the pyradiomic [16] software package is used for selective extraction. The corresponding extracted features are shown in Table 1.

We extract 1169 3D features and 675 2D features from 3D data blocks. The two kinds of extracted features are combined to create a total of 1844 features, which are called "mixed dimension (MD) features". At the same time, all features were standardly processed by Z-score.

In order to select effective features, the variance threshold method will be used at first. As an unsupervised learning method based on the data, it can select out the features that are not obvious for each pathology, which is preliminary feature selecting. Then, the univariate selection method will be chosen. Similarly, it is an unsupervised learning method, which can be used to calculate the statistical metric between features. The features of 0.05 are screened out, and the features with little correlation are further screened out. Finally, LASSO regression based on supervised learning is used, which using the existing case classification as labels and combining L1 norm linear regression

Table 1. The types of features extracted from the images.

Types of features	2D features	3D features
Intensity	First Order Feature	First Order Feature
Shape	Shape Features (2D)	Shape Features (3D)
Texture	Gray Level Co-occurrence Matrix (GLCM) Features	Gray Level Co-occurrence Matrix (GLCM) Features
	Gray Level Run Length Matrix (GLRLM) Features	Gray Level Run Length Matrix (GLRLM) Features
	Gray Level Dependence Matrix (GLDM) Features	Gray Level Dependence Matrix (GLDM) Features
	Gray Level Dependence Matrix (GLDM) Features	Gray Level Dependence Matrix (GLDM) Features
Fliters	Laplacian of Gaussian filters	Laplacian of Gaussian filters
	Wavelet	Wavelet
	Local Binary Pattern 2D	Local Binary Pattern 3D
		Square
		Logarithm
		Exponential

method. As a result, we can obtain more sparse solutions and screen out the final valuable features subsequently.

The machine learning models will be established by using selected 2D features, 3D features and MD features respectively. In this paper, support vector machine (SVM) [17], logistic regression (LR) [18], random forest (RF) [19] and eXtreme Gradient Boosting (XGBoost) [20] are used for training. Consequently, we can make grading prediction of SIJ CT scans.

3 Experiments and Results

3.1 Datasets

The experimental data are obtained from the database of the Department of Radiology of the First Affiliated Hospital of Shantou University Medical College (The Ethics committee of the First Affiliated Hospital of Shantou University Medical College Approval No. B-2022-003). 496 patients CT scans are obtained with the corresponding unilateral sacroiliitis diagnostic grading labels by the radiologist. A single CT scan contains both left and right sacroiliac joints, a total of 992 data blocks are obtained after the automatic segmentation stage. The grading results are classified according to the New York standard five-category, including from zero to four.

3.2 Automatic ROI Segmentation Based on Deep Learning

The labels marked by doctors are the coarse segmentations. An accurate segmentation leads to a robust diagnosis. The 3D-UNet achieves the dice score of 90.86% on ROIs which contain almost all lesions surrounding the sacroiliac joints, thus the ROIs segmented by 3D-UNet ignore the irrelevant information and focus on the information about sacroiliitis diagnoses. Therefore, the accuracy of grading diagnoses is improved by inputting the efficient ROIs.

3.3 Multi-dimension Automatic Radiomics Grading

The two-category classification task is obtained by classifying levels 0 and 1 as healthy, levels 2, 3 and 4 as sick. In the two-category classification task, the effects of SVM under different features are shown in Table 2, the effects of different modeling methods under mixed data are shown in Table 3.

Table 2. Effect comparison of SVM under different features of binary classifications.

Types of features	Accuracy	Prediction	Recall	Specificity	F1-score
2D features	0.6214	0.6275	0.9038	0.1956	0.7407
3D features	0.7711	0.7953	0.8260	0.6884	0.8123
MD features	0.8202	0.8311	0.8792	0.7319	0.8544

Table 3. Effect comparison of MD features under different methods of binary classifications.

Methods	Accuracy	Prediction	Recall	Specificity	F1-score
LR	0.7681	0.8223	0.7826	0.7464	0.9020
RF	0.7855	0.8009	0.8550	0.6811	0.8271
XGBoost	0.7884	0.8131	0.8406	0.7101	0.8266
SVM	0.8202	0.8311	0.8792	0.7319	0.8544

The accuracy of the SVM classification algorithm based on mixed features is 82.02% which is higher than 78% of nomogram model designed by Ye [8] and 80.0% of the method proposed by Faleiros [5]. The recall rate is 0.8792. It can be seen that the algorithm based on hybrid features is better than the algorithm based on two-dimensional features alone or single three-dimensional features. Compared with the classical classifiers, the SVM model is superior to other classifiers. By comprehensive comparison, the classification algorithm of support vector machine based on mixed features proposed in this paper has higher indexes than other classical algorithms.

The three-category classification tasks are obtained by classifying level 0 as healthy, level 1 as suspicious, level 2, 3 and 4 as sick [21]. In the three-category classification task, the XGBoost effects under different features are shown in Table 4, and the effects of different modeling methods under MD features are shown in Table 5. The results of multi-category classification tasks are weighted averages of each category.

Table 4. Effect comparison of XGBoost under different features of three-category classifications.

Types of features	Accuracy	Prediction	Recall	Specificity	F1-score
2D features	0.6244	0.4576	0.5187	0.4983	0.4777
3D features	0.7601	0.6189	0.6676	0.6824	0.6313
MD features	0.7932	0.6755	0.7081	0.7095	0.6767

Table 5. Effect comparison of MD features under different methods of three-category classifications.

Methods	Accuracy	Prediction	Recall	Specificity	F1-score
LR	0.7766	0.6660	0.6908	0.6874	0.6502
RF	0.7930	0.7297	0.7225	0.6570	0.6686
SVM	0.7858	0.7380	0.7081	0.6648	0.6531
XGBoost	0.7932	0.6755	0.7081	0.7095	0.6767

According the results above we can know that XGBoost based on MD features achieves the highest accuracy of 79.32% and the recall rate reached 0.7081. Similar to two-category classification, the model based on MD features performs better than the model based on single 2D features or single 3D features. And XGBoost performances better than other methods. Unexpectedly, the SVM which could not predict suspected patients loses to achieve the high performance.

In the five-category classification task, the XGBoost effects under different features are shown in Table 6, and the effects of different modeling methods under MD features are shown in Table 7.

Table 6. Effect comparison of XGBoost under different features of five-category classifications.

Types of features	Accuracy	Prediction	Recall	Specificity	F1-score
2D features	0.6622	0.3137	0.3103	0.7605	0.3045
3D features	0.7446	0.4648	0.4726	0.8162	0.4599
MD features	0.7791	0.5208	0.5331	0.8428	0.5208

XGBoost based on MD features achieves the highest accuracy of 77.91%, which has higher than 72.25% of the method designed by Faleiros [9]. The model based on MD features still performs better than the model based on single dimension features.

Table 7. Effect comparison of MD features under different methods of five-category classifications.

Methods	Accuracy	Prediction	Recall	Specificity	F1-score
LR	0.7492	0.4768	0.4813	0.8178	0.4632
RF	0.7649	0.4782	0.5043	0.8286	0.4809
SVM	0.7760	0.6207	0.5360	0.8299	0.4916
XGBoost	0.7791	0.5208	0.5331	0.8428	0.5208

4 Conclusions

In this paper, a multi-dimensional features automatic radiomics grading algorithm has been proposed. In our method, 3D-Unet is used to segment and clip the ROI containing the unilateral sacroiliac joint. Subsequently, the features of different dimensions are extracted from the ROI containing the unilateral sacroiliac joint. Based on the selected features, an explicable classification model is obtained. It has been proved that the model based on multi-dimensional features can achieve the best effect.

For the future, it is feasible to build a more complete grading model combining with radiomics features, deep learning features and clinical features. Thus, we can not only obtain better diagnostic results, but also taking the interpretability of extracted features into account.

References

1. Zeng, Q.Y., et al.: Rheumatic diseases in China. Arthritis Res. Ther. **10**, 1–11 (2008)
2. Linden, S.V.D., Valkenburg, H.A., Cats, A.: Evaluation of diagnostic criteria for ankylosing spondylitis. Arthritis Rheum. US **27**(4), 361–368 (1984)
3. Deodhar, A., et al.: Ankylosing spondylitis diagnosis in US patients with back pain: identifying providers involved and factors associated with rheumatology referral delay. Clin. Rheumatol. **35**(7), 1769–1776 (2016). https://doi.org/10.1007/s10067-016-3231-z
4. Faleiros, M.C., Ferreira Junior, J.R., Jens, E.Z., Dalto, V.F., Nogueira-Barbosa, M.H., de Azevedo-Marques, P.M.: Pattern recognition of inflammatory sacroiliitis in magnetic resonance imaging. In: Tavares, J.M.R.S., Natal Jorge, R.M. (eds.) ECCOMAS 2017. LNCVB, vol. 27, pp. 639–644. Springer, Cham (2018). https://doi.org/10.1007/978-3-319-68195-5_69
5. Faleiros, M.C., et al.: Machine learning techniques for computer-aided classification of active inflammatory sacroiliitis in magnetic resonance imaging. Adv. Rheumatol. **60** (2020)
6. Tenório, A.P.M., et al.: A study of MRI-based radiomics biomarkers for sacroiliitis and spondyloarthritis. Int. J. Comput. Assist. Radiol. Surg. **15**(10), 1737–1748 (2020). https://doi.org/10.1007/s11548-020-02219-7
7. Tenório, A.P.M., et al.: Radiomic quantification for MRI assessment of sacroiliac joints of patients with spondyloarthritis. J. Digit. Imaging **35**(1), 29–38 (2021). https://doi.org/10.1007/s10278-021-00559-7
8. Ye, L., et al.: A predictive clinical-radiomics nomogram for diagnosing of axial spondyloarthritis using MRI and clinical risk factors. Rheumatology **61**(4), 1440–1447 (2022)
9. Faleiros, M., et al.: Computer-aided classification of inflammatory sacroiliitis in magnetic resonance imaging. Int. J. Comput. Ass. Rad. **12**, S154 (2017)

10. Feldtkeller, E., Khan, M., van der Heijde, D., van der Linden, S., Braun, J.: Age at disease onset and diagnosis delay in HLA-B27 negative vs. positive patients with ankylosing spondylitis. Rheumatol. Int. **23**(2), 61–66 (2003)
11. Çiçek, Ö., Abdulkadir, A., Lienkamp, S.S., Brox, T., Ronneberger, O.: 3D U-Net: learning dense volumetric segmentation from sparse annotation. In: Ourselin, S., Joskowicz, L., Sabuncu, M.R., Unal, G., Wells, W. (eds.) MICCAI 2016. LNCS, vol. 9901, pp. 424–432. Springer, Cham (2016). https://doi.org/10.1007/978-3-319-46723-8_49
12. Fedorov, A., et al.: 3D Slicer as an image computing platform for the Quantitative Imaging Network. Magn. Reson. Imaging **30**(9), 1323–1341 (2012)
13. Mildenberger, P., Eichelberg, M., Martin, E.: Introduction to the DICOM standard. Eur. Radiol. **12**(4), 920–927 (2001). https://doi.org/10.1007/s003300101100
14. Glide-Hurst, C., Chen, D., Zhong, H., Chetty, I.: Changes realized from extended bit-depth and metal artifact reduction in CT. Med. Phys. **40**(6Part1), 061711 (2013)
15. Kocks, J., Ward, K., Mughal, Z., Moncayo, R., Adams, J., Högler, W.: Z-score comparability of bone mineral density reference databases for children. J. Clin. Endocrinol. Metab. **95**(10), 4652–4659 (2010)
16. Van Griethuysen, J.J., et al.: Computational radiomics system to decode the radiographic phenotype. Cancer Res. **77**(21), e104–e107 (2017)
17. Cortes, C., Vapnik, V.: Support-vector networks. Mach. Learn. **20**(3), 273–297 (1995)
18. Hosmer, D.W., Jr., Lemeshow, S., Sturdivant, R.X.: Applied Logistic Regression. Wiley, New York (2013)
19. Breiman, L.: Random forests. Mach. Learn. **45**(1), 5–32 (2001)
20. Chen, T., Guestrin, C.: XGBoost: a scalable tree boosting system, In: Proceedings of the 22nd ACM SIGKDD International Conference on Knowledge Discovery and Data Mining, pp. 785–794 (2016)
21. Geijer, M., Gadeholt Göthlin, G., Göthlin, J.: The validity of the New York radiological grading criteria in diagnosing sacroiliitis by computed tomography. Acta Radiol. **50**(6), 664–673 (2009)

Noninvasive Blood Pressure Waveform Measurement Method Based on CNN-LSTM

Zheng Wang[1], Dongmei Lin[1,2,3(✉)], Aihua Zhang[1,2,3], Yurun Ma[1,2,3], and Xiaolei Chen[1,2,3]

[1] School of Electrical and Information Engineering, Lanzhou University of Technology, No. 36, Pengjiaping Road, Qilihe District, Lanzhou 730050, Gansu, China
lindm1215@lut.edu.cn
[2] Key Laboratory of Gansu Advanced Control for Industrial Processes, Lanzhou 730050, China
[3] National Demonstration Center for Experimental Electrical and Control Engineering Education, Lanzhou University of Technology, Lanzhou 730050, China

Abstract. Cardiovascular disease is a serious threat to human health. Continuous blood pressure (BP) waveform measurement is of great significance for the prevention of cardiovascular disease. Therefore, convenient and accurate BP measurement is a vital problem. This paper intends to visualize the weak pulsation of human radial artery pulse, combining the advantages of convolutional neural networks (CNN) and Long Short-Term Memory Networks (LSTM). A CNN-LSTM blood pressure measurement method based on pulse wave and blood pressure wave data is proposed. Experiments show that the six blood pressure correlation coefficients of the non-invasive blood pressure measurement method based on CNN-LSTM all exceed 0.99, and the average MSE loss is only around 0.004. This network is superior to CNN and LSTM networks and is expected to be used for blood pressure wave measurement in humans in the future.

Keywords: Blood pressure wave · Pulse wave · Convolutional neural networks · Long Short Term Memory Networks

1 Introduction

Cardiovascular disease (CVD) is a major health problem worldwide causing millions of deaths every year, according to WHO statistics report [1]. Blood Pressure (BP) is one of the four vital signs used for assessing the cardiovascular system conditions of an individual. Hypertension is known as one of the main risk factors for CVD, as well as other life-threatening diseases [2].

Nowadays, there is a high demand for continuous BP monitoring for many reasons. Firstly, hypertension is treatable, but there are few reliable high BP detection methods, particularly in low resource settings [3]. Secondly, BP can fluctuate rapidly over time and is influenced by several factors, such as stress, emotions, food, exercise and use of medication. Thirdly, chronic hypertension leads to organ damage [4]. For all these reasons, continuous BP monitoring, not just at a specific point in time, is important for the early detection and treatment of hypertension.

W. Deng et al. (Eds.): CCBR 2022, LNCS 13628, pp. 664–675, 2022.
https://doi.org/10.1007/978-3-031-20233-9_67

Common clinical BP devices often fail to capture the true BP values of patients due to the "white-coat hypertension" syndrome [5]. Moreover, oscillometry [6] and auscultation [7] methods can only provide BP measurements intermittently, with a 2 min interval between measurements, and therefore are not suitable for estimating BP continuously for long-term monitoring. Patients have reported discomfort and inconvenience when measuring BP using these devices due to the compression of the artery by the cuff attached to the arm [8]. Some of these challenges can be avoided using the invasive BP measurement method. Particularly, direct BP measurement is continuous in nature, and thus it provides instantaneous BP for every heartbeat in real time [9]. This can only be achieved using catheterization, which is considered the "gold standard" BP measurement method internationally [10]. However, it requires medical intervention since it is invasive and restricted to hospital setting.

Other BP measurement methods include volume clamping [11] and tonometry [12]. Both methods are non-invasive and provide continuous BP values, but they are predominantly utilized in research settings. Volume clamping uses a small finger cuff and a photoplethysmography (PPG) sensor. This method measures BP instantaneously for a long period of time, but it is expensive and still requires a cuff, which is cumbersome and painful. Tonometry is a cuffless approach for measuring BP continuously using a manometer-tipped probe pressed on an artery. This method is sensitive to arm and probe movement which has been proven to be difficult to maintain in practice and requires constant calibration with a cuff BP device [13, 14]. All the aforementioned methods are not suitable for cuffless and continuous BP monitoring. An ideal BP technology should be non-invasive, cuffless, preferably optical, wearable and inexpensive.

But thanks to the rapid development of artificial intelligence, machine learning methods have emerged as a potential solution to this problem. Some scholars have begun to use intelligent algorithms such as machine learning to measure continuous blood pressure. At present, the most widely studied is the blood pressure measurement method based on pulse wave. For example, Zhang et al. [15] used a genetic algorithm to estimate blood pressure after extracting 13 parameters from the PPG signal. Chen et al. [16]. Proposed a continuous blood pressure measurement method based on a KNN algorithm, and in reference [17] the authors established a support vector machine regression model for blood pressure prediction. However, the above methods all require manual feature extraction, so we consider introducing a convolutional neural network for automatic feature extraction. In addition, considering that the pulse wave is a time series, the time series is the result of a series of observations, and the human physiological state changes with time, which makes the blood pressure measurement a dynamic system, so the blood pressure can be measured through the past historical physiological state. We can introduce a long short term memory network (LSTM) with global feedback for further feature processing. In this paper we focus on the CNN-LSTM method of pulse wave for blood pressure prediction. The advantages of this study are as follows:

1. Precious human physiological signals are difficult to obtain. We collect pulse waveform and blood pressure waveform as experimental data by designing a human pulse simulation platform. This approach avoids the difficult acquisition of human data.
2. By analyzing the time series characteristics of pulse wave data, a deep learning method CNN-LSTM for predicting blood pressure waveform is proposed, which

can make full use of the time series of pulse data to obtain more reliable predictions. We compare with traditional neural network methods such as CNN and LSTM, and prove that our method has less loss, higher correlation coefficient, and is more suitable for the prediction of blood pressure waveform.

2 Acquisition of Pulse and Blood Pressure Signals

2.1 Acquisition of Pulse and Blood Pressure Signals

The data in this paper are all from the human pulse simulation platform and binocular vision acquisition system in the laboratory of the research group [18], shown as Fig. 1. The binocular vision acquisition system uses a flexible film and a steel tube wall to make a balloon probe, which simulates the action of the fingers of traditional Chinese medicine on the radial artery of the wrist of others. Under the appropriate pressure in the probe, the pulse of the radial artery will cause the membrane to move, and the two cameras fixed above the probe simultaneously capture the image of the membrane movement.

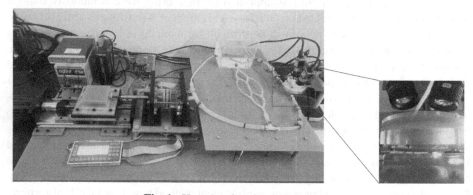

Fig. 1. Human pulse simulation system

Then, based on the binocular stereo vision measurement theory, the calibration of the dual camera system, the extraction of image feature points and the stereo matching are carried out. According to the imaging model, combined with the theory of digital image processing, multi-point spatial displacement information can be obtained, and then the extraction of multi-dimensional pulse waves can be realized. Figure 2 shows the thin film image processing flow. Figure 3 shows the extracted six 16-dimensional radial artery pulse waves, that is, each group of images can extract radial artery pulse waves with 16 dimensions and 20 cycles.

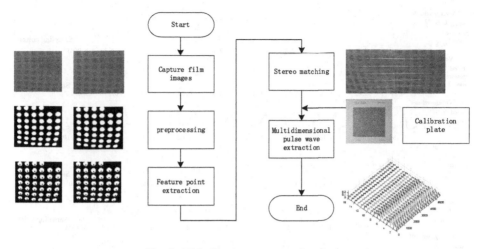

Fig. 2. Thin film image processing flow

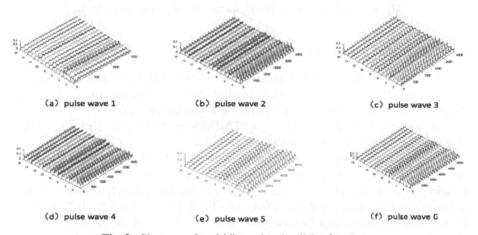

(a) pulse wave 1   (b) pulse wave 2   (c) pulse wave 3

(d) pulse wave 4   (e) pulse wave 5   (f) pulse wave 6

Fig. 3. Six types of multidimensional radial pulse waves

At the same time, the pressure waveform in the simulated blood vessel (the blood pressure waveform simulated in the experiment) displayed by the host computer of the human pulse simulation platform is collected, and the pulse and blood pressure signals collected in the experiment need to be synchronized. The collected pulse and blood pressure data are used as the input data X and label data y of the subsequent blood pressure measurement model. In the experiment, the heart module of the human pulse simulation system simulated six different types of blood pressure waveforms. At the same time, the pressure transmitter in the experimental platform collected six different types of radial artery blood pressure waves. Figure 4 shows six different types of radial artery blood pressure waveform data collected by the pressure transmitter.

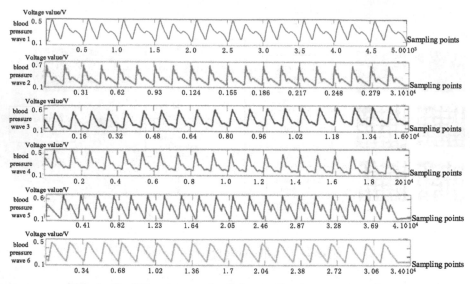

Fig. 4. Six different types of radial artery blood pressure waveforms

2.2 Pulse Signal Processing

In order to improve the accuracy of data analysis and the reliability of data, this paper will de-noise the collected pulse wave. Due to the characteristics of the experimental platform, the pulse waveform contains a lot of medium and high frequency noise. This paper adopts several denoising methods: EEMD [19], CEEMDAN and VMD [20]. Through spectrum analysis, the optimal denoising algorithm is selected.

It can be seen from the denoising analysis of the three algorithms EEMD, CEEMDAN and VMD. The energy of the signal spectrum after denoising by the three algorithms remains basically unchanged in the low frequency band and the energy before the signal denoising, and the energy in the high frequency band is reduced to 0.01–0.02, 0.05, and 0.03–0.05 respectively. It can be seen from Table 1 that the denoising effects of the VMD algorithm and the CEEMDAN algorithm are both better than the EEMD algorithm, and the denoising effect of the VMD algorithm is more significant.

Table 1. Comparison of denoising effects of three denoising methods

	High frequency band energy of the signal after denoising	Signal peak amplitude after denoising
EEMD	0.01–0.02	0.16
CEEMDAN	0.005	0.15
VMD	0.003–0.005	0.16

Figure 7 shows the pulse waves before and after denoising using EEMD, CEEM-DAN and VMD algorithms respectively. It can be seen from Fig. 5 and Table 1 that, compared with the EEMD and VMD algorithms, the blood pressure amplitude of the CEEMDAN algorithm after denoising is greatly reduced. The CEEMDAN algorithm filters out excessive blood pressure wave signals, and the VMD algorithm is selected as the final denoising algorithm.

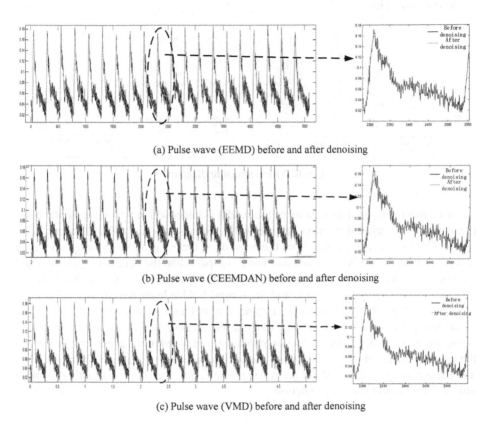

(a) Pulse wave (EEMD) before and after denoising

(b) Pulse wave (CEEMDAN) before and after denoising

(c) Pulse wave (VMD) before and after denoising

Fig. 5. Pulse wave before and after denoising by three algorithms

3 Blood Pressure Measurement Method Based on CNN-LSTM Network

This paper uses a hybrid model consisting of CNN and LSTM to predict the blood pressure waveform from the pulse waveform. After inputting the pulse waves extracted from the thin film images, the pulse waveform features are first extracted automatically by the CNN module, and then these features are input into the LSTM module for further training. The proposed model topology is shown in Fig. 6.

We choose two layers of one-dimensional convolution, and the activation function of the first layer of convolution (filter = 80, kernel = 1) is the Relu activation function. The filter of the second layer of convolution is 48, and the rest of the parameters are the same as the settings of the first layer of convolution. The unit of the first layer LSTM is 32, and the unit of the second layer LSTM is 16. There are two fully connected layers using the Relu activation function, and the last fully connected layer is used to predict blood pressure values.

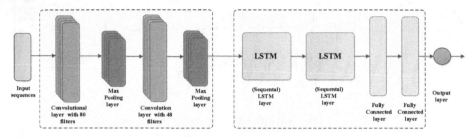

Fig. 6. Model structure diagram

Note that the input data volume of the model is huge, which will increase the complexity of the model, and the input features will become sparse and difficult to extract.So we use CNN to extract features from the pulse data, further use max pooling, so far the features are successfully extracted and more compact than the original input data, and then the extracted features are passed to two LSTM hidden layers for further training. The first hidden layer has 32 units and the second hidden layer has 16 units. Since the blood pressure prediction problem is a regression problem, we use two fully connected layers to receive the tensors from the hidden layers and output the blood pressure waveform, and the last fully connected layer outputs the predicted blood pressure wave. Since the proposed network model combines the excellent feature extraction ability of CNN and the advantages of LSTM for processing time series, the proposed method is more effective for blood pressure prediction.

3.1 Model Training

Establish an experimental simulation environment: the hardware part uses the i5-6200U processor, the mechanical hard disk is 1000GB, and the memory is 8GB; the software part uses the anaconda environment with pycharm to build the model through the tensorflow framework.

The model data in this paper are 6 different types of pulse waves and their corresponding blood pressure waveform data, and the cycles and trends of different types of pulse waves are quite different. The model can set different window lengths and training iterations for different types of pulse waves and blood pressure waves. First, each pulse wave and blood pressure wave are divided into training set and validation set according to 4:1. Due to the large amount of data, the Batch_size of the network is set to 128. The epoch starts from the fifth round and is superimposed every 5 rounds. It can be seen from the CNN-LSTM network model that the number of training rounds is 35 rounds when the validation set achieves the best training effect. The comparative models CNN, LSTM, BiLSTM, GRU, and RNN models were obtained at rounds 55, 40, 70, 500, and 200, respectively. Save the training parameters, and the model training ends when the six types of pulse waveforms and blood pressure waveforms are all trained.

4   Experimental Results and Analysis

4.1   Evaluation Standard

To demonstrate the effectiveness of the CNN-LSTM model, we compare the method with CNN, LSTM, BiLSTM, GRU, RNN network models in the same setting using the same training and test set data. In order to better compare the performance of each model, the loss function of the six types of network models tested in this paper is the Mean Square Error (MSE) loss function. And the correlation coefficient R^2 of the validation set of the six types of models is determined, and the Adam optimizer is selected as the back-propagation optimizer of the six types of models. In order to prevent overfitting, both CNN and LSTM models add a dropout layer, and the dropout layer parameter is set to 0.2.

1)   Mean Square Error (MSE), is the average formula that describes the sum of squares of the difference between the predicted value and the true value, as shown in formula (1).

$$MSE = \frac{1}{T} \sum\nolimits_{t=1}^{T} \left(Y^t - \hat{Y}^t \right)^2 \tag{1}$$

where Y^t is the true value and $\hat{Y}^t$ is the predicted value.

2)   Determine the correlation coefficient (R^2 score). The correlation coefficient is an index to measure the effect of the model in measuring unknown samples. The higher the value, the better the model, and the calculation formula is shown in formula (2).

$$R^2 = 1 - \frac{\sum_{t=1}^{T} \left(Y^t - \hat{Y}^t \right)^2}{\sum_{t=1}^{T} \left(\overline{Y}^t - \hat{Y}^t \right)^2} \tag{2}$$

4.2   Results Comparison and Analysis

After training models such as CNN-LSTM, CNN, LSTM, BiLSTM, GRU, and RNN using the denoised dataset, the trained models are used to predict the test set data, and the real values are compared with the predicted values. It can be seen from Fig. 7 that the CNN-LSTM model has the highest fitting degree, which is almost coincident, followed by the LSTM model, the CNN model, the GRU model and the BiLSTM model, and the RNN model has the worst fitting effect.

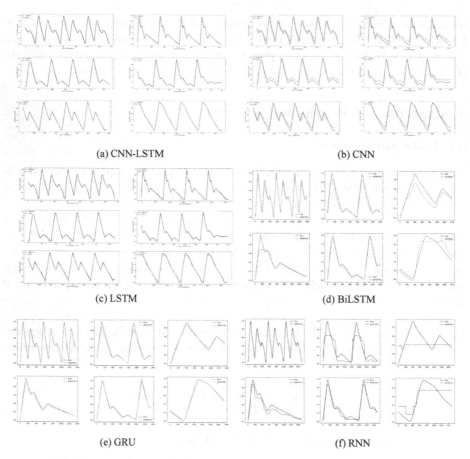

Fig. 7. Comparison of the predicted value of the model with the true value

As can be seen from the figure, the prediction result of CNN-LSTM is the best. The network model uses 1D-CNN for feature extraction, then uses LSTM for time domain modeling, and finally uses the fully connected layer to predict blood pressure, and finally measures blood pressure perfectly. Although the CNN network fits the blood pressure waveform well, it only extracts its features from the spatial domain, ignoring the time series characteristics of the pulse wave. Since CNN is more commonly used to solve problems such as image classification and feature extraction, the accuracy of blood pressure waveform prediction using CNN alone is worse than that of CNN-LSTM. Although the LSTM network has noticed the time series characteristics of the pulse wave, only the LSTM layer cannot predict the blood pressure waveform very well when there is too much sequence data of the input pulse wave. The evaluation indicators of the six types of methods are shown in Table 2.

Table 2. Six types of method evaluation indicators

(a) Evaluation metrics of CNN-LSTM method

	Test set 1	Test set 2	Test set 3	Test set 4	Test set 5	Test set 6
R	0.994	0.996	0.999	0.999	0.999	0.999
MSE	0.0007	0.0004	0.0002	0.0001	0.0001	0.0001

(b) Evaluation metrics of CNN method

	Test set 1	Test set 2	Test set 3	Test set 4	Test set 5	Test set 6
R	0.993	0.995	0.997	0.995	0.996	0.998
MSE	0.001	0.0006	0.0005	0.0007	0.0006	0.0006

(c) Evaluation metrics of LSTM method

	Test set 1	Test set 2	Test set 3	Test set 4	Test set 5	Test set 6
R	0.996	0.998	0.999	0.997	0.996	0.998
MSE	0.002	0.003	0.003	0.003	0.001	0.003

(d) Evaluation metrics of BiLSTM method

	Test set 1	Test set 2	Test set 3	Test set 4	Test set 5	Test set 6
R	0.984	0.952	0.763	0.726	0.962	0.912
MSE	0.001	0.004	0.013	0.015	0.002	0.008

(e) Evaluation metrics of GRU method

	Test set 1	Test set 2	Test set 3	Test set 4	Test set 5	Test set 6
R	0.998	0.995	0.976	0.957	0.993	0.997
MSE	0.001	0.003	0.002	0.002	0.004	0.002

(f) Evaluation metrics of RNN method

	Test set 1	Test set 2	Test set 3	Test set 4	Test set 5	Test set 6
R	0.959	0.803	0.012	0.763	0.767	0.438
MSE	0.002	0.015	0.057	0.013	0.015	0.054

5 Conclusions

In this paper we propose a CNN-LSTM blood pressure prediction model based on pulse wave and blood pressure wave data. In the CNN-LSTM model, two convolutional layers and two pooling layers are used for feature extraction of pulse waves, and two LSTM layers are used for further training. We set two sets of benchmarks to determine whether the training results are good or bad. The experimental results in this paper show that the proposed method is close to the accuracy of the existing blood pressure measurement methods or has a higher accuracy than the existing methods. Especially because of the combination of CNN and LSTM networks, the proposed method achieves a correlation coefficient of 0.99 for predicting blood pressure, and the training time is low.

However, since our datasets all simulate the pulse wave and blood pressure wave data of healthy people, they cannot be applied to a large number of patients. In the future, we will further improve the network model and improve the generalization ability of the model to be suitable for various types of patients. And introduce the current advanced deep learning method, that is, the transfer learning method, and successfully apply the network model trained from the data collected on the experimental platform to the blood pressure measurement of the human body.

Acknowledgments. This work was supported by the Science and Technology Program of Gansu Province of China (Grant No. 20JR5RA459, 20JR5RA438) and the National Natural Science Foundation of China (Grant No. 61967012).

References

1. World Health Organization: World health statistics. Monitoring health for the SDGs, Sustainable Development Goals (2016)
2. Kearney, P.M., Whelton, M., Reynolds, K., Muntner, P., Whelton, P.K., Jiang, H.: Global burden of hypertension: analysis of worldwide data. Lancet **365**, 217–223 (2005)
3. Burt, V., Whelton, P., Roccella, E.: Prevalence of hypertension in the US adult population. Results from the Third National Health and Nutrition Examination Survey, 1988–1991. Hypertension **25**, 305–313 (1995)
4. Irigoyen, M.C., De Angelis, K., Dos Santos, F., Dartora, D.R., Rodrigues, B., Consolim-Colombo, F.M.: Hypertension, blood pressure variability, and target organ lesion. Curr. Hypertens. Rep. **18**, 1–13 (2016)
5. Tientcheu, D., et al.: Target organ complications and cardiovascular events associated with masked hypertension and white-coat hypertension: analysis from the Dallas heart study. J. Am. Soc. Hypertens. **66**, 2159–2169 (2015)
6. Drzewiecki, G., Hood, R., Apple, H.: Theory of the oscillometric maximum and the systolic and diastolic detection ratios. Ann. Biomed. Eng. **22**, 88–96 (1994)
7. Perloff, D., et al.: Human blood pressure determination by sphygmomanometry. Circulation **88**, 2460–2470 (1993)
8. El-Hajj, C., Kyriacou, P.A.: A review of machine learning techniques in photoplethysmography for the non-invasive cuff-less measurement of blood pressure. Biomed. Signal Process. Control **58**, 101870 (2020)
9. McGhee, B.H., Bridges, E.J.: Monitoring arterial blood pressure: what you may not know. Crit. Care Nurse **22**, 60–79 (2002)
10. Sharma, M., et al.: Cuff-less and continuous blood pressure monitoring: a methodological review. Technologies **5**, 21 (2021)
11. Imholz, B.P., Wieling, W., van Montfrans, G.A., Wesseling, K.H.: Fifteen years experience with finger arterial pressure monitoring: assessment of the technology. Cardiovasc. Res. **38**, 605–616 (1998)
12. Drzewiecki, G., Melbin, J., Noordergraaf, A.: Deformational Forces in Arterial Tonometry (1984)
13. Hansen, S., Staber, M.: Oscillometric blood pressure measurement used for calibration of the arterial tonometry method contributes significantly to error. Eur. J. Anaesthesiol. **23**, 781–787 (2006)
14. Peter, L., Noury, N., Cerny, M.: A review of methods for non-invasive and continuous blood pressure monitoring: pulse transit time method is promising? IRBM **35**, 271–282 (2014)

15. Zhang, Y., Wang, Z.: A hybrid model for blood pressure prediction from a PPG signal based on MIV and GA-BP neural network. In: 13th IEEE International Conference on Natural Computation. Fuzzy Systems and Knowledge Discovery, Chongqing, China, pp. 1989–1993 (2017)
16. Yi, C., Jian, C., Wenqiang, J.: Continuous blood pressure measurement based on photo-plethysmography. In: 14th IEEE International Conference on Electronic Measurement and Instruments (ICEMI), Guilin, China, pp. 1656–1663 (2019)
17. Chen, X., Yu, S., Zhang, Y., Chu, F., Sun, B.: Machine learning method for continuous noninvasive blood pressure detection based on random forest. IEEE Access 9, 34112–34118 (2021)
18. Lin, D.M., Zhang, A.H., Gu, J., Chen, X.L., Wang, Q., Yang, L.M.: Detection of multipoint pulse waves and dynamic 3D pulse shape of the radial artery based on binocular vision theory. Comput. Methods Programs Biomed. 155, 61–73 (2018)
19. Zhang, Y., Lian, J., Liu, F.: An improved filtering method based on EEMD and wavelet-threshold for modal parameter identification of hydraulic structure. Mech. Syst. Signal Process. 68, 316–329 (2016)
20. Gao, Y.B., Zhang, F.: Fiber optic gyro de-noising based on VMD algorithm. IOP Conf. Ser. J. Phys. Conf. Ser. 1237, 022183 (2019)

Recurrence Quantification Analysis of Cardiovascular System During Cardiopulmonary Resuscitation

Shuxin Chen[1], Lijun Jiang[2], Chang Pan[2], Jiaojiao Pang[2], Feng Xu[2], Jiali Wang[2(✉)], Yuguo Chen[2(✉)], and Ke Li[1(✉)]

[1] The Institute of Intelligent Medical Engineering, Department of Biomedical Engineering, School of Control Science and Engineering, Shandong University, Jinan, China
kli@sdu.edu.cn

[2] Department of Emergency, Qilu Hospital, Shandong University, Jinan, China
wangjiali_2000@126.com, chen919085@126.com

Abstract. Sudden cardiac arrest (CA) is a common cause of death, and cardiopulmonary resuscitation (CPR) can improve the survival rate of CA patients. However, the in-depth study of the pathophysiological mechanism of patients during CPR is limited, and the characterization of the dynamic structure behind the electrical activities of the cardiovascular system from the perspective of nonlinear time series analysis is still lacking. This study used recurrence quantitative analysis (RQA) to quantify changes in the cardiovascular system during CPR and analyze its pathophysiological mechanisms. In artificially constructed porcine CA models, data were divided into four periods: Baseline, ventricular fibrillation (VF), CPR, and Recovery of spontaneous circulation (ROSC). RQA parameters of electrocardiogram (ECG) were analyzed to compare the changes in cardiovascular system dynamics in four periods. The RR, ENTR, and TT of ECG were significantly higher than those of VF and CPR at Baseline and ROSC, indicating that the period and stability of electrical activity of the cardiovascular system were significantly reduced under pathological conditions. The RQA is valid in cardiovascular system analysis in CA patients. This may be useful for future research on the diagnosis and prediction of CA.

Keywords: Cardiac arrest · Cardiopulmonary resuscitation · Recurrence quantitative analysis · Electrocardiogram

1 Introduction

Cardiac arrest (CA) refers to the disappearance of circulatory signs, the cessation of effective heart beating, or the sudden cessation of systemic blood flow directly caused by arrhythmia or the disappearance of the effective heart beating [1]. Ventricular fibrillation (VF) is the cause of most SCD episodes. After the onset of the VF, the survival rate of patients decreases by 10% per minute [2]. Early high-quality cardiopulmonary resuscitation (CPR) is the key to the survival of patients, which can effectively improve the survival outcome of patients.

The CA leads to systemic blood flow interruption, and all organs of the body are injured by ischemia and hypoxia. Recovery of spontaneous circulation (ROSC) after CPR leads to blood reperfusion of the whole body, resulting in a series of pathophysiological changes. Myocardial dysfunction, including mechanical and electrical damage to the heart, can occur within hours to days after ROSC, leading to hypotension and low cardiac output index [3]. Therefore, continuous assessment of cardiac function during CPR and understanding of the mechanism of cardiovascular system changes may help improve the survival rate and functional prognosis of cardiac arrest patients.

The CA and the CPR have long been research hotspots in emergency medicine, including but not limited to the prediction of CA [4, 5], the prediction of resuscitation outcome [6, 7], and the identification of defibrillation timing [8, 9]. However, due to the interference of many factors in clinical research, in-depth research on the pathophysiological mechanism of patients during CPR is limited to some extent. Moreover, the characterization of the dynamic structure behind the electrical activities of the cardiovascular system from the perspective of nonlinear time series analysis is still lacking. The nature of this problem suggests that recurrence quantitative analysis (RQA) may provide an interesting solution for the study of underlying cardiac dynamics.

In fact, the development of RQA is intrinsically related to the analysis of cardiac signals [10]. RQA has been used to specifically characterize the dynamics of intracardiac signals during heart disease [4, 11–13]. These studies suggest that RQA-based features represent a promising set of tools for identifying phase transitions and distinguishing different electrophysiological features associated with cardiac tissue [14].

In the current work, we attempted to quantify the changes in the cardiovascular system during CPR and describe its mechanisms from the perspective of nonlinear time series. Based on this, we constructed a CA model of pigs and compared the changes in cardiovascular system dynamics during four periods: Baseline, VF, CPR, and ROSC. We assume that the dynamic parameters are significantly different in these four periods.

2 Method

2.1 Experimental Design

The CA model of 5 small healthy Bama pigs was established, and fasting was required one night before the experiment. After the subjects were weighed and anesthetized, the electrocardiogram (ECG) was collected by the multichannel parameter monitor, as shown in Fig. 1. The sampling frequency of ECG was 500 Hz, and then ECG signals were resampled to 250 Hz.

The experimental flow chart is shown in Fig. 2, which is described as follows:

First, collect the baseline data of 20 min. Then make the cardiac arrest due to ventricular fibrillation (VFCA) model. After successful modeling of CA, there was no intervention for 6 min. CPR was then performed for 20 min, during which time CPR was stopped if the pig was ROSC. Otherwise, failure was declared.

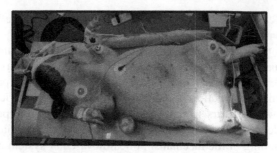

Fig. 1. Position of ECG electrode.

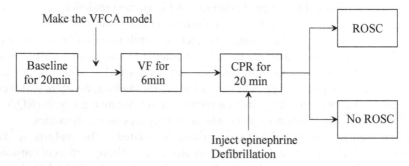

Fig. 2. Experimental flow chart.

2.2 Data Processing

MATLAB (The Mathworks, Natick, MA, USA) was used to preprocess and analyze the collected ECG signal.

The pretreatment method consists of three steps. The first step was to rule out unusable signals (shedding of electrocardiogram electrodes). The second step was to remove the baseline drift noise of all signals by median filtering. The third step was that during the pressing period, the ECG signal would be affected by the pressing artifacts and be submerged in the pressing artifacts, so the pressing artifacts in the ECG signal need to be removed. The frequency of compression is generally around 2 Hz, and the frequency of ECG signals in pigs during VF is 4–8 Hz [8]. Most of the pressing artifacts in ECG signals could be filtered by using a 3–30 Hz bandpass filter.

All data were divided into four periods, Baseline period, VF period, CPR period, and ROSC period, with the onset of VF, initiation of CPR, and initiation of ROSC as nodes. We select the stable signal stage among the four periods and use the sliding window method for signal segmentation. The window length is 5 s, and the sliding distance is 1 s.

2.3 RQA Technology

RP is a two-dimensional graphics technology proposed by Eckmann, aiming at analyzing the structure of attractors of multidimensional dynamical systems [15]. RP captures a representation of multidimensional states by a binary matrix $R_{i,j}$, where states X_i and X_j are close to each other, and the state X_i is represented by ε, otherwise 0. Binary modes with observations of potential generation dynamics can be used to assess different oscillatory properties by diagonal (capturing states coevolving in phase space) and vertical (capturing the remaining trends remaining in a given state) [15].

Here, a total of three parameters need to be set, namely, embedding dimension M, time delay T, and proximity distance E. The time delay is calculated by calculating mutual information, and the embedded dimension is calculated by the false nearest neighbor method. The proximity is an empirical parameter, and its default value is 0.1. In this case, the recurrence matrix $R_{i,j}$ can be defined according to the distance between their respective reconstructed states X_i and X_j and the selected distance threshold ε, which can be expressed as:

$$R_{i,j}(\varepsilon) = \Theta\{\varepsilon - \|X_i - X_j\|\} \tag{1}$$

where, Θ is the Heaviside function. The recurrence plot (RP) is obtained by drawing the black and white binary image of the recurrence matrix.

The following parameters are used in this work:

Recurrence rate (RR): Indicates the density of recurrence points in an RP.

$$RR = \frac{1}{N^2} \sum_{i,j=1}^{N} R_{i,j} \tag{2}$$

Determinism (DET): represents the ratio of recurrence points that form diagonal structures (of at least length l_{min}) to all recurrence points.

$$DET = \frac{\sum_{l=l_{min}}^{N} lP(l)}{\sum_{l=1}^{N} lP(l)} \tag{3}$$

Entropy (ENTR): refers to the Shannon entropy of the probability $p(l) = P(l)/N_l$ to find a diagonal line of exactly length 1 in the RP.

$$ENTR = -\sum_{l=l_{min}}^{N} P(l) \ln P(l) \tag{4}$$

Trapping time (TT), which represents the average length of vertical structures in the RP.

$$TT = \frac{\sum_{v=v_{min}}^{N} vP(v)}{\sum_{v=1}^{N} P(v)} \tag{5}$$

The embedding dimension used in this study was 1, the time delay was 1 sample, and the threshold was set to 0.1 [16]. RQA parameters are implemented by MATLAB cross recurrence plot toolbox 5.16.

3 Result

Figure 3 shows the changes in the RPs of ECG for the first subject over four periods. There were significant differences in the RPs for the four periods of ECG (Fig. 3). Diagonals associated with the deterministic structure were found in RPs during Baseline and ROSC. Moreover, in the RPs calculated by ECG, there were recurrence blocks in the RP during Baseline. In RPs during VF and CPR, only the main diagonals were significant.

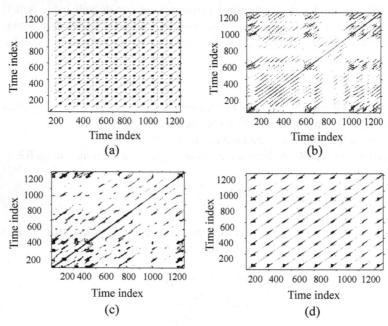

Fig. 3. RPs of ECG for the first subject. (a) is in Baseline. (b) is in VF. (c) is in CPR. (d) is in ROSC.

Figure 4 shows the changes in RQA parameters of ECG of subjects 1 and 2 in four periods. The overall changes were similar in both pigs. For RR, ENTR, and TT, the values in Baseline and ROSC are higher than those in VF and CPR. DET during Baseline and ROSC in the first subject was significantly higher than that during VF and CPR, but this relationship was not significant in the second subject. In addition, DET, ENTR, and TT of both subjects were significantly increased during CPR compared with VF.

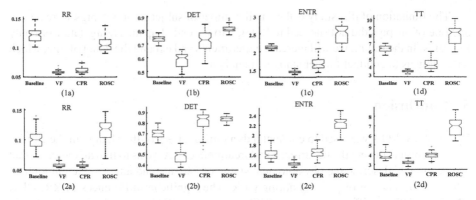

Fig. 4. RQA parameters of ECG for the first and second subjects in 4 periods. (1a) RR for the first subject. (1b) DET for the first subject. (1c) ENTR for the first subject. (1d) TT for the first subject. (2a) RR for the second subject. (2b) DET for the second subject. (2c) ENTR for the second subject. (2d) TT for the second subject.

4   Discussion

As a malignant arrhythmia, VF is the main cause of CA [3], and CPR is an effective means to treat CA. The electrical and mechanical activities of the cardiovascular system have obvious complex patterns in different periods from the onset of VF to ROSC. In addition, complex biological systems have autonomous control mechanisms that produce nonlinearity and non-stationarity in signals [14]. The complexity of the biological system and some uncontrollable clinical factors bring challenges to the in-depth study of the pathophysiological mechanism in the occurrence and treatment of CA.

In this study, we attempted to analyze the dynamics of ECG signals during the onset and treatment of CA. The RPs represent the recurrence dynamics of the cardiovascular system in different periods and can effectively capture the transient, intermittent, and steady-state behaviors of the system [14]. In the RPs of ECG, more diagonal structures associated with deterministic structures were found during both Baseline and ROSC, suggesting that the state evolution of the system is similar during these two periods [15], which may indicate the existence of stable periodic orbits. The decrease of the diagonal structure during VF and CPR suggested that the stability and periodicity of the system may be disrupted due to pathological reasons.

This study used RQA to analyze the dynamics of the electrical activity (ECG) of the cardiovascular system during the onset and treatment of cardiac arrest, as shown in Fig. 5. RR, DET, ENTR, and TT of ECG were higher than those of VF and CPR at Baseline and ROSC. A lower TT represents a reduced probability that the system will remain in one state for an extended period of time [15]. This indicated that the periodicity and stability of electrical activity of the cardiovascular system are poor in a pathological state [12]. This may be due to disturbances in the electrical activity of the heart during VF, which does not accurately control the contraction of the heart muscle [17].

The limitation of this study is the small number of subjects, only 5 pigs were tested, and one of the pigs did not succeed in ROSC. So we ended up analyzing data from only four pigs. In the future, we will increase experiments and expand the data volume, which will allow us to conduct further statistical analysis.

5 Conclusion

In this study, RQA was used to conduct a dynamic analysis of the change in the cardiovascular system during the occurrence and treatment of CA, so as to find an indicator that can accurately describe the physiological status of patients and analyze the pathophysiological mechanism of patients during CPR. The significant differences in RR, DET, ENTR, and TT at different stages of CPR suggest that RQA technology is effective in the cardiovascular system analysis of CA patients. This could lead to the development of an effective way to diagnose and predict CA in or out of the hospital.

Acknowledgments. This study was supported by National Key Research and Development Program (2020YFC1512701), Technical Innovation Guidance Plan of Shandong Province, and Youth Interdisciplinary Scientific Innovation Project of Shandong University.

References

1. Mozaffarian, D., Benjamin, E.J., Go, A.S., Arnett, D.K.: Heart disease and stroke statistics—2016 update: a report from the American Heart Association. Circ. (New York, N.Y.) 133(4), e38–e360 (2016)
2. Rea, T.D., Page, R.L.: Community approaches to improve resuscitation after out-of-hospital sudden cardiac arrest. Circ. (New York, N.Y.) 121(9), 1134–1140 (2010)
3. Perkins, G.D., Jacobs, I.G., Nadkarni, V.M., Berg, R.A.: Cardiac arrest and cardiopulmonary resuscitation outcome reports: update of the utstein resuscitation registry templates for out-of-hospital cardiac arrest a statement for healthcare professionals from a task force of the international liaison committee on resuscitation (American Heart Association, European Resuscitation Council, Australian and New Zealand Council on Resuscitation, Heart and Stroke Foundation of Canada, InterAmerican Heart Foundation, Resuscitation Council of Southern Africa, Resuscitation Council of Asia). Circ. (New York, N.Y.) 132(13), 1286–1300 (2015)
4. Acharya, U.R., Fujita, H., Sudarshan, V.K., Ghista, D.N.: Automated prediction of sudden cardiac death risk using Kolmogorov complexity and recurrence quantification analysis features extracted from HRV signals, pp. 1110–1115. IEEE (2015)
5. Chae, M., Gil, H.-W., Cho, N.-J., Lee, H.: Machine learning-based cardiac arrest prediction for early warning system. Math. (Basel) 10(12), 2049 (2022)
6. Nanayakkara, S., Fogarty, S., Tremeer, M., Ross, K.: Characterising risk of in-hospital mortality following cardiac arrest using machine learning: a retrospective international registry study. PLoS Med. 15(11), e1002709 (2018)
7. Coult, J., et al.: Continuous assessment of ventricular fibrillation prognostic status during CPR: implications for resuscitation. Resuscitation 179, 152–162 (2022)
8. Zuo, F., Ding, Y., Dai, C., Wei, L.: Estimating the amplitude spectrum area of ventricular fibrillation during cardiopulmonary resuscitation using only ECG waveform. Ann. Transl. Med. 9(8), 619 (2021)

9. Gaspari, R., et al.: Echocardiographic pre-pause imaging and identifying the acoustic window during CPR reduces CPR pause time during ACLS – a prospective Cohort Study. Resusc. Plus **6**, 100094 (2021)
10. Luongo, G., Schuler, S., Luik, A., Almeida, T.P.: Non-invasive characterization of atrial flutter mechanisms using recurrence quantification analysis on the ECG: a computational study. IEEE Trans. Biomed. Eng. **68**(3), 914–925 (2021)
11. Clayton, R.H., Murray, A.: Linear and non-linear analysis of the surface electrocardiogram during human ventricular fibrillation shows evidence of order in the underlying mechanism. Med. Biol. Eng. Comput. **37**(3), 354–358 (1999)
12. Wessel, N., Marwan, N., Meyerfeldt, U., Schirdewan, A., Kurths, J.: Recurrence quantification analysis to characterise the heart rate variability before the onset of ventricular tachycardia. In: Crespo, J., Maojo, V., Martin, F. (eds.) ISMDA 2001. LNCS, vol. 2199, pp. 295–301. Springer, Heidelberg (2001). https://doi.org/10.1007/3-540-45497-7_45
13. Desai, U., Martis, R.J., Acharya, U.R., Nayak, C.G.: Diagnosis of multiclass tachycardia beats using recurrence quantification analysis and ensemble classifiers. J. Mech. Med. Biol. **16**(1), 1640005 (2016)
14. Yang, H.: Multiscale recurrence quantification analysis of spatial cardiac vectorcardiogram signals. IEEE Trans. Biomed. Eng. **58**(2), 339–347 (2011)
15. Marwan, N., Carmen Romano, M., Thiel, M., Kurths, J.: Recurrence plots for the analysis of complex systems. Phys. Rep. **438**(5), 237–329 (2007)
16. Li, K., Li, Z.-M.: Cross recurrence quantification analysis of precision grip following peripheral median nerve block. J. Neuroeng. Rehabil. **10**(1), 28 (2013)
17. Tseng, W.C., Wu, M.H., Chen, H.C., Kao, F.Y.: Ventricular fibrillation in a general population– a national database study. Circ. J. Off. J. Jpn. Circ. Soc. **80**(11), 2310–2316 (2016)

UAV Aerial Photography Traffic Object Detection Based on Lightweight Design and Feature Fusion

Xuesen Ma[1,2](✉), Tianbao Zhou[1,2], Ji Ma[1,2], Gonghui Jiang[1,2,3], and Xuemei Xu[1,2,3]

[1] School of Computer and Information, Hefei University of Technology, Hefei, China
mxs@hfut.edu.cn
[2] Engineering Research Center of Safety-Critical Industrial Measurement and Control Technology, Ministry of Education, Hefei, China
[3] Intelligent Interconnected Systems Laboratory of Anhui Province (Hefei University of Technology), Hefei, China

Abstract. Real-time and accurate traffic object detection is one of the important technologies to support intelligent traffic management. Focusing on the problem of poor detection accuracy in aerial photography scenes of drones, the algorithm of lightweight design and multi-scale feature fusion for traffic object detection based on YOLOv5s (LMF-YOLOv5s) is proposed. First, a lightweight network is designed. Then a fast-spatial pyramid convolution module based on dilated convolution is constructed. Finally, an improved spatial pyramid pooling layer module is introduced before the detection layers of different scales, which can enhance the multi-scale feature fusion ability of the network. The experimental results in the public dataset VisDrone show that the detection accuracy of the proposed method is improved by 7.4% compared with YOLOv5s. The model's parameters are reduced by 67.3%, and the model's size is reduced by 63.2% compared with YOLOv5s.

Keywords: Drone aerial photography · Multi-scale feature fusion · Lightweight network · Small object detection

1 Introduction

The continuous advancement of the modern city process has led to an increasing urban traffic flow, urban traffic congestion has become more and more serious, and the increasing travel demand has also led to frequent traffic accidents [1].

UAVs (unmanned aerial vehicles) have high mobility, are not restricted by ground traffic, and have a wider monitoring field of view. UAV monitoring systems have the advantages of low maintenance costs and easy deployment. UAVs have been widely used, including surveillance, aerial photography, and infrastructure inspection [2–4]. By integrating the object detection algorithms into the UAVs, the position of the object can be detected more accurately from different heights and angles, which is more in line with

© The Author(s), under exclusive license to Springer Nature Switzerland AG 2022
W. Deng et al. (Eds.): CCBR 2022, LNCS 13628, pp. 684–693, 2022.
https://doi.org/10.1007/978-3-031-20233-9_69

the real-time and accurate detection requirements of the intelligent traffic supervision system [5].

Object detection algorithms can currently be divided into two categories: one is called two-stage detection algorithms, such as R-CNN [6], Fast R-CNN [7], and Faster R-CNN [8], FPN [9], etc. This kind of algorithm classifies the proposed candidate frame of the region that may contain the object and corrects the object position. Usually, the detection accuracy is high but the speed is slow. Another type is called a single-stage detection algorithm, such as SSD [10], YOLO [11], RetinaNet [12], etc. These methods do not include the region generation link, and directly classify and regress the detection object on the feature map. Compared with the two-stage method, this kind of algorithm has a faster detection speed but lower accuracy.

Zhang et al. [13] proposed to apply L1 regularization to the channel scaling factor and pruned the feature channels with less information to design a new lightweight network. The proposed algorithm could maintain the detection accuracy of the original network while reducing the weight of the network, but the detection accuracy was relatively low. Wang et al. [14] proposed an efficient end-to-end detector SPB-YOLO for UAV images, which introduced SPB into the original network. Improving the detection accuracy of objects at different scales in UAV images by using an attention mechanism. Although the detection accuracy of the model had been improved compared with YOLOv5s, some parameters had been introduced, and the detection speed of the model had also been relatively reduced. Sun et al. [15] proposed an algorithm called RSOD that can detect small objects in real-time, the algorithm predicts the location of small objects in dense areas of the image by using the details contained in the shallow features. However, compared with the previous model YOLOv3 [16], the detection accuracy of the model was improved, but the detection speed of the model was lower, and the complexity of the model was also higher.

Under the condition of ensuring real-time performance, improving the accuracy of object detection in this scene is the key to the application of UAVs to traffic object detection. The YOLOv5 algorithm is one of the better detection algorithms currently. After iteration of the previous version [17], the improved YOLOv5 algorithm has been widely used in various object detection tasks. The shape of the receptive field of its backbone network is fixed, and the PANet [18] structure in the network does not fully utilize the information of the underlying features.

2   LMF-YOLOv5s

To address these challenges, we propose an algorithm called LMF-YOLOv5s in this paper. The network structure is shown in Fig. 1.

First, a lightweight detection network (SlimYOLOv5s) is designed. To further improve the detection accuracy of the model, a fast-spatial pyramid convolution module based on dilated convolution (DSPPF) is introduced into the multi-scale feature extraction network. It integrates features of different sizes and retains the location information of the object to improve the accuracy of object location positioning and object recognition. Aiming at the problem that the spatial pyramid pooling module (SPP) [19] has insufficient ability to extract object features, the redesigned spatial features with different

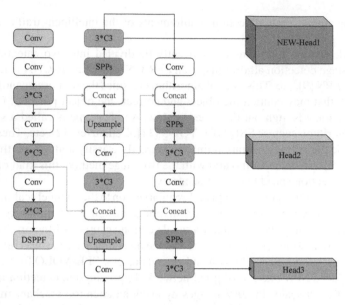

Fig. 1. Structure of LMF-YOLOv5s

pooling kernels are embedded in the multi-scale feature extraction network. The spatial pyramid pooling-small module (SPPs), uses a smaller max-pooling kernel to perform max-pooling operations, and further fuses feature of different sizes so that the network can better represent the feature map. Through experimental analysis, the improved algorithm has a better detection effect on small objects in UAV aerial photography.

2.1 Design Lightweight Network SlimYOLOv5s

The original model uses {P3, P4, P5} feature layers as detection heads respectively, while the three detection heads have low detection resolution, and are insensitive to small object detection. The model has insufficient feature extraction ability for small objects, and it is difficult to learn the features of small objects. Therefore, to improve the detection accuracy of the model, a higher resolution P2 feature layer is used based on the original three layers. A new detection head is added to detect low-level and high-resolution feature maps. The feature map of the higher resolution contains more abundant feature information of small objects. The original feature layer is expanded to {P2, P3, P4, P5}. Based on the original YOLOv5s, low-level, high-resolution shallow feature information is fused.

After the small object detection head is added, the calculation and storage costs of the model increase accordingly. Although the accuracy of the model is improved, it introduces several parameters and increases the calculation cost. To increase the performance of the model while reducing the computational and storage costs of the model, it can be more suitable for the detection requirements of the UAV aerial photography scene. Inspired by YOLO-Z [20], on the premise of not changing the size of the input image, modifying the depth and width of the model, and changing the layer connection method of neck and head to make the model focuses on detecting specific feature maps. Based on the above analysis, a suitable lightweight network SlimYOLOv5s is designed, and three detection heads are reserved for more effective detection of small objects. Lower resolution feature layers that are not friendly to small object detection are removed.

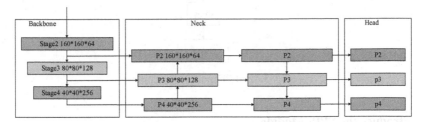

Fig. 2. The structure of SlimYOLOv5s

As shown in Fig. 2, by modifying the network structure, the model is lightweight while maintaining the performance of small object detection.

2.2 Construct DSPPF Module

The original SPPF module obtains different features through different layers of pooling. Enriching the representation ability of feature maps by fusing feature information of receptive fields at different scales. However, the maximum pooling operation will bring about the problem of loss of resolution, and the input feature map will lose the details of the object through the module. Therefore, the dilated convolution is used to replace the maximum pooling operation of the SPPF module to make up for the loss of image details due to the loss of resolution caused by the max-pooling operation. In Fig. 3, the DSPPF module replaces the maximum pooling layers in the SPPF module with a 3×3 dilated convolution with dilation rates of r1 = 2, r2 = 4, and r3 = 6. The DSPPF module fuses a part of the features obtained by dilated convolution, and another part of the features after the dilated convolution continues to be convolved. Dilated convolution obtains features of different sizes. The DSPPF module increases the receptive field without losing the detailed information of the image, and can more fully fuse the local and global features of the input feature map. To a certain extent, the loss of object details is avoided.

The improved DSPPF layer is introduced into the original feature extraction network. DSPPF fuses the object position information of different receptive fields through dilated convolution to improve the accuracy of object positioning, which is beneficial to detecting objects with large differences in size in the aerial photography scene of UAV and can improve the ability of the algorithm to detect small objects.

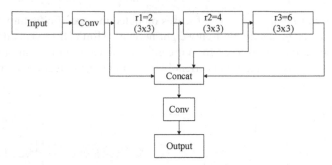

Fig. 3. DSPPF module structure

2.3 Introduce the SPPs Module

Based on the original spatial pyramid pooling layer structure, we designed a new SPPs module. As shown in Fig. 4, the pooling kernel size of the SPPs structure is adjusted to 11×11, 7×7, and 3×3. Based on the SPP module, to further improve the detection accuracy of the model with a smaller computational cost. The adjusted SPPs modules are embedded in the front of different detection heads.

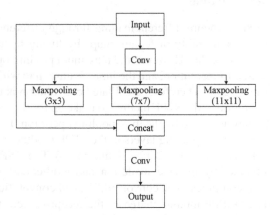

Fig. 4. SPPs module structure

The main purpose of the SPP layer is to solve the problem of non-uniform input image size. Avoid image distortion caused by operations such as image scaling by achieving size-consistent output for the input of different sizes. However, a single SPP module cannot effectively extract the feature information of objects at different scales. Introducing a new spatial pyramid pooling layer before the detection layer at different scales can make up for the defect of insufficient detection accuracy of small objects in complex backgrounds. Integrate local features and global features of different receptive fields to improve the multi-scale feature fusion ability of the model. Further fusion of local features and global features makes the model's ability to represent feature maps better.

3   Experimental Results and Analysis

The experiment uses the evaluation index of the COCO dataset and uses average precision (AP) to measure the detection performance of the model, mean average precision (mAP) is the average of multiple categories of AP. The main indicators are mAP0.5 and mAP0.5:0.95. Where mAP0.5 refers to the average accuracy of all object classes computed at an IOU threshold of 0.5. mAP0.5:0.95 refers to the average accuracy of 10 thresholds between 0.5 and 0.95. Using the frame rate per second (FPS) as the evaluation index of the model detection speed, the specific definitions of recall and precision are as follows:

$$\text{Recall} = \frac{TP}{TP + FN} \tag{1}$$

$$\text{Pr ecision} = \frac{TP}{TP + FP} \tag{2}$$

$$mAP = \int_0^1 P(R)dR \tag{3}$$

Fig. 5. Some images of the VisDrone dataset

Figure 5 shows some images of VisDrone under different scenes and perspectives. The VisDrone2019-Det dataset used in this paper is a dataset of aerial traffic images of 14 cities in China that were captured by the Tianjin University team AISKYEYE at low altitudes under different conditions [21]. The training set and validation set contain 6471 and 548 images, respectively, and the test set contains 1610 images. Most of the labels in the VisDrone dataset are people and daily vehicles, with a total of 10 categories, namely pedestrians, cars, trucks, tricycles, motorcycles, etc.

The experimental running environment of this paper is based on the 64-bit operating system Ubuntu 18.04LTS, the CPU is Intel(R) Core(TM) i9-10900K, and the GPU is NVIDIA GeForce RTX3080. The deep learning framework is Pytorch v1.8.0. SGD optimizer is used during training, the learning rate is set to 0.01, the batch size is set to 32, and the number of learning epochs is set to 300. The input of Yolov5 adopts the Mosaic data enhancement method, randomly selects four images for cropping and splicing and enhances the scene diversity to improve the detection effect. In the inference stage, the NMS algorithm is used to filter out candidate object frames generated by model inference to get the final result. To speed up the convergence speed of model training, the model trained on the COCO dataset is used as the preloaded training model to speed the training speed of the model.

3.1 VisDrone Experimental Analysis

In this paper, experiments are conducted on the public dataset VisDrone to verify the effectiveness of the proposed method. The experiment is mainly divided into two parts: (1) A comparative experiment is carried out on the VisDrone dataset to verify the effectiveness of the proposed method, and the experimental results of some other mainstream object detection methods on this dataset are compared to illustrate the advantages of LMF-YOLOv5s; (2) An ablation experiment is designed to further illustrate the effectiveness of the improved method proposed in this paper for object detection in UAV aerial images. To test the performance and speed of the improved algorithm, the method proposed in this paper is compared with other object detection algorithms on the VisDrone dataset. The experimental results are shown in Table 1:

Table 1. Comparison of algorithm performance on VisDrone dataset

Methods	mAP0.5	FPS
YOLOv5s	34.9	163
YOLOv3 [16]	39.9	32
SPB-YOLO [14]	40.1	145
NAS-FPN [22]	40.6	20
Ours	**42.3**	**162**
DMNet [23]	42.4	24
ClusDet [24]	43.2	21
RSOD [15]	43.3	28

The experimental results in Table 1 show that the mAP0.5 of LMF-YOLOv5s is 7.4% higher than YOLOv5s, which can meet the requirements of real-time detection of UAVs. Although DMNet, ClusDet, and RSOD have relatively high detection accuracy, the FPS is low and it is difficult to deploy on mobile terminals. Figure 6 shows the comparison of the detection effect on the VisDrone dataset between YOLOv5s and LMF-YOLOv5s in this paper.

Fig. 6. Comparison of experimental results between YOLOv5s and LMF-YOLOv5s

Since the small objects of pedestrians and some cars in the image are small and dense, the background is complex and the object edge is blurred. The original algorithm has missed detections during detection, and the original algorithm has certain false detections on some occluded objects. Compared with YOLOv5s, LMF-YOLOv5s can obtain more abundant small object features, the detection effect of small objects is better, and at the same time, a reasonable judgment can be made on the recognition of small objects based on context information. It can be seen that LMF-YOLOv5s can detect farther and smaller objects in aerial images.

3.2 Ablation Experiment

To further verify the effectiveness of the proposed algorithm, an ablation experiment was performed on the VisDrone dataset, and the results are shown in Table 2.

Table 2. Comparison of the results of ablation experiments

Methods	mAP0.5:0.95	mAP0.5	FPS	Model size (MB)	Parameters (M)
YOLOv5s	19.2	34.9	163	14.4	7.04
YOLOv5s+P2	22.9	40.9	138	15.1	7.18
SlimYOLOv5s	22.5	40.5	188	4.8	2.04
SlimYOLOv5s+DSPPF	22.9	41.2	182	4.8	2.07
SlimYOLOv5s+3SPPs	23.1	41.5	167	5.2	2.27
LMF-YOLOv5s	23.9	42.3	162	5.3	2.30

The parameters of LMF-YOLOv5s are reduced by 67.3% compared with YOLOv5s and the size of the model has been reduced by 63.2% compared to YOLOv5s. The detection accuracy of LMF-YOLOv5s is increased by 7.4% compared with YOLOv5s. Which meets the requirements of lightweight detection and high-precision detection.

4 Conclusion

This paper proposes an improved UAV aerial photography traffic object detection method LMF-YOLOv5s based on YOLOv5s. First, the SlimYOLOv5s model is designed based on adding a detection layer for detecting small objects. Then a new DSPPF module is constructed, and the object feature information of different receptive fields is fused by dilated convolution so that the model can better represent the feature map. Finally, the redesigned SPPs module is embedded in the object detection layer of different scales, and the local and global features of different receptive fields are fused to improve the multi-scale feature fusion of the model. The method proposed in this paper can reduce the weight of the model and improve the detection accuracy of the object compared with the original algorithm. In the next step, we can try to find a more effective use of context information and feature fusion methods, further optimize the network structure, and improve the detection accuracy of small objects. Moreover, we can try to deploy algorithms on edge devices to achieve real-time detection.

Acknowledgments. This work was supported by the National Key R&D Program Funding Project (No. 2020YFC1512601); Hefei Natural Science Foundation Project (No. 2022015).

References

1. Zhao, P., Hu, H.: Geographical patterns of traffic congestion in growing megacities: big data analytics from Beijing. Cities **92**, 164–174 (2019)
2. Bhaskaranand, M., Gibson, J.D.: Low-complexity video encoding for UAV reconnaissance and surveillance. In: 2011-MILCOM 2011 Military Communications Conference, pp. 1633–1638. IEEE Press, New York (2011)
3. Madawalagama, S., Munasinghe, N., Dampegama, S.D.P.J., Samarakoon, L.: Low cost aerial mapping with consumer-grade drones. In: 37th Asian Conference on Remote Sensing pp. 1–8 (2016)
4. Sa, I., Hrabar, S., Corke, P.: Outdoor flight testing of a pole inspection UAV incorporating high-speed vision. In: Mejias, L., Corke, P., Roberts, J. (eds.) Field and Service Robotics, pp. 107–121. Springer, Cham (2015). https://doi.org/10.1007/978-3-319-07488-7_8
5. El-Sayed, H., Chaqfa, M., Zeadally, S., Puthal, D.: A traffic-aware approach for enabling unmanned aerial vehicles (UAVs) in smart city scenarios. IEEE Access **7**, 86297–86305 (2019)
6. Girshick, R., Donahue, J., Darrell, T., Malik, J.: Rich feature hierarchies for accurate object detection and semantic segmentation. In: Proceedings of the IEEE Conference on Computer Vision and Pattern Recognition, pp. 580–587. IEEE Press, New York (2014)
7. Girshick, R.: Fast R-CNN. In: Proceedings of the IEEE International Conference on Computer Vision, pp. 1440–1448. IEEE Press, New York (2015)

8. Ren, S., He, K., Girshick, R., Sun, J.: Faster R-CNN: towards real-time object detection with region proposal networks. In: Advances in Neural Information Processing Systems, 28. (2015)

9. Lin, T.Y., Dollár, P., Girshick, R., He, K., Hariharan, B., Belongie, S.: Feature pyramid networks for object detection. In: Proceedings of the IEEE Conference on Computer Vision and Pattern Recognition, pp. 2117–2125. IEEE Press, New York (2017)

10. Liu, W., et al.: SSD: single shot Multibox detector. In: Leibe, B., Matas, J., Sebe, N., Welling, M. (eds.) ECCV 2016. LNCS, vol. 9905, pp. 21–37. Springer, Cham (2016). https://doi.org/10.1007/978-3-319-46448-0_2

11. Redmon, J., Divvala, S., Girshick, R., Farhadi, A.: You only look once: unified, real-time object detection. In: Proceedings of the IEEE Conference on Computer Vision and Pattern Recognition, pp. 779–788. IEEE Press, New York (2016)

12. Lin, T.Y., Goyal, P., Girshick, R., He, K., Dollár, P.: Focal loss for dense object detection. In: Proceedings of the IEEE International Conference on Computer Vision, pp. 2980–2988. IEEE Press, New York (2017)

13. Zhang, P., Zhong, Y., Li, X.: SlimYOLOv3: narrower, faster and better for real-time UAV applications. In: Proceedings of the IEEE/CVF International Conference on Computer Vision Workshops, pp. 37–45. IEEE Press, New York (2019)

14. Wang, X., Li, W., Guo, W., Cao, K.: SPB-YOLO: an efficient real-time detector for unmanned aerial vehicle images. In: 2021 International Conference on Artificial Intelligence in Information and Communication (ICAIIC), pp. 099–104. IEEE Press, New York (2021)

15. Sun, W., Dai, L., Zhang, X., Chang, P., He, X.: RSOD: real-time small object detection algorithm in UAV-based traffic monitoring. Appl. Intell. **52**(8), 8448–8463 (2021)

16. Redmon, J., & Farhadi, A.: YOLOv3: An Incremental Improvement. arXiv preprint arXiv:1804.02767 (2018)

17. Bochkovskiy, A., Wang, C.Y., Liao, H.Y.M.: YOLOv4: optimal speed and accuracy of object detection. arXiv preprint arXiv:2004.10934 (2020)

18. Wang, K., Liew, J.H., Zou, Y., Zhou, D., Feng, J.: PANet: few-shot image semantic segmentation with prototype alignment. In: Proceedings of the IEEE/CVF International Conference on Computer Vision, pp. 9197–9206. IEEE Press, New York (2019)

19. He, K., Zhang, X., Ren, S., Sun, J.: Spatial pyramid pooling in deep convolutional networks for visual recognition. IEEE Trans. Pattern Anal. Mach. Intell. **37**(9), 1904–1916 (2015)

20. Benjumea, A., Teeti, I., Cuzzolin, F., & Bradley, A.: YOLO-Z: improving small object detection in YOLOv5 for autonomous vehicles. arXiv preprint arXiv:2112.11798 (2021)

21. Zhu P, Du D, Wen L, et al.: VisDrone-VID2019: the vision meets drone object detection in video challenge results. In: Proceedings of the IEEE/CVF International Conference on Computer Vision Workshops, pp. 227–235. IEEE Press, New York (2019)

22. Ghiasi, G., Lin, T.Y., Le, Q.V.: NAS-FPN: learning scalable feature pyramid architecture for object detection. In: Proceedings of the IEEE/CVF Conference on Computer Vision and Pattern Recognition, pp. 7029–7038. IEEE Press, New York (2019)

23. Li, C., Yang, T., Zhu, S., Chen, C., Guan, S.: Density map guided object detection in aerial images. In: Proceedings of the IEEE/CVF Conference on Computer Vision and Pattern Recognition Workshops, pp. 737–746. IEEE Press, New York (2020)

24. Yang, F., Fan, H., Chu, P., Blasch, E., Ling, H.: Clustered object detection in aerial images. In: Proceedings of the IEEE/CVF International Conference on Computer Vision, pp. 8311–8320. IEEE Press, New York (2019)

UMixer: A Novel U-shaped Convolutional Mixer for Multi-scale Feature Fusion in Medical Image Segmentation

Yongxin Su[1], Hongbo Huang[2,4(✉)], Zun Song[1], Lei Lin[3], and Jinhan Liu[2]

[1] Mechanical Electrical Engineering School, Beijing Information Science and Technology University, Beijing, China
[2] Computer School, Beijing Information Science and Technology University, Beijing, China
[3] School of Economics and Management, Beijing Information Science and Technology University, Beijing, China
[4] Institute of Computing Intelligence, Beijing Information Science and Technology University, Beijing, China
hhb@bistu.edu.cn

Abstract. Medical image segmentation plays a critical role in assisting diagnosis and prognosis. Since the transformer was first introduced to the field, the neural network structure has experienced a transition from ConvNet into Transformer. However, some redesigned ConvNets in recent works show astonishing effects, which outperforms classic elaborate ConvNets, and even complicated transformers. Inspired by these works, we introduced large-kernel convolutions to improve the ConvNets in capturing the long-range dependency. Cooperated with a novel multi-scale feature fusion method, we proposed a U-shaped convolutional structure, dubbed UMixer, which effectively integrates shallow spatial information with deep semantic information and high-resolution detailed information with low-resolution global information. Without any attention mechanism and pre-training on large datasets, UMixer achieves more accurate segmentation results than traditional ConvNets and Transformers on the Synapse dataset. Experiments demonstrate the effectiveness of this multi-scale feature fusion structure and its capability in modeling long-range dependency.

Keywords: Medical image segmentation · Multi-scale feature fusion · Large-kernel convolution · Transformer

1 Introduction

With the increasing demands in healthcare, AI technology as an impactful auxiliary means has been becoming more and more essential in diagnosis and prognosis under various medical conditions. Improving the medical practice by the adoption of technologies such as computer vision, big data, etc. has progressively attracted the attention of researchers. Since the introduction of deep learning, many superior models have been proposed and made a breakthrough in the medical field. Medical image segmentation is one of the hottest topics in this domain. Most typically, FCN [1], which first introduced convolutional neural networks into medical segmentation, proposed a pixel-to-pixel segmentation method. It creatively employed upsampling blocks to integrate feature maps with different resolutions and thus can deal with multi-scale images effectively. The method gave rise to wide discussions and sequentially led to a series of improved variants. Among them, U-Net [2] adopted multilevel convolution blocks with symmetric U-shaped structures and fused the features via skip-connections between the same level. Furthermore, Unet++ [3] redesigned the skip-connections as a dense cascade structure for more efficient multi-scale feature fusion.

Due to the locality property of convolution operations, CNN-based models inevitably have restrictions in modeling long-range dependency. The emergence of ViT [4] inspired some researchers to introduce transformer mechanism into segmentation architecture. However, directly combining convolutional layers and fully-connected layers will destruct the consistency of semantic information [7]. To solve this problem, hierarchical transformer structures, such as Swin-Unet [8] and MISSFormer [9], were successively put forward, which reintroduced the design philosophy of convolutional network mechanism and the convolutional operation itself. It has also put the pure convolution networks back in the spotlight.

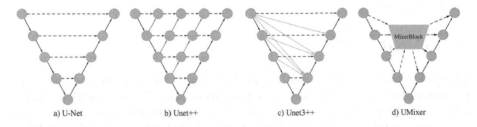

a) U-Net   b) Unet++   c) Unet3++   d) UMixer

Fig. 1. Comparison of different fusion methods. a) indicates the disadvantages of Unet which cannot integrate multi-scale feature information. b) and c) represent the upsampling and downsampling in the multi-scale fusion of Unet++ and Unet3+, respectively. d) shows the fusion structure adopt in our model.

The recent success of ConvNeXt [10] led to a discussion about whether pure convolutional architectures can achieve the equivalent or even exceed the performance of Transformer. Furthermore, whether the strong performance of vision transformers results more from its patch-based representation or the Transformer intrinsic superiority [11]. Although there is no definitive explanation for these doubts yet, to some extent, these works demonstrate that the pure convolutional architecture consisting of large-kernel depth-wise convolutions and point-wise convolution can achieve competitive performance as transformer in modeling long-range dependency. Therefore, we rethought the pure convolutional

U-shaped structure and proposed a novel model, attempting to introduce these aforementioned convolution structures into the medical image segmentation network to enhance the capability of extracting global context. The proposed model was validated on popular datasets and the results confirmed our intuition.

To make it more specific, let's review the architectures of traditional U-Net and its variants. The topology structures are shown in Fig. 1. We can learn the different feature fusion methods used in the segmentation community. To fuse features of different scales, many models adopt upsampling and downsampling blocks before concatenating the different-level feature maps, which will cause the loss of semantic information during the sampling. UCTransNet [12] presented a new approach that uses different sizes of patches from four feature maps to align different scales before stacking them up. Inspired by this idea, we introduce different sizes of feature patches into pure CNN-based networks.

RepLKNet [13] disclosed that large-kernel convolutions can achieve comparable or superior results than Transformer. We argue that large-kernel convolutions have the capability in capturing long-range dependency. Followed by this intuition, this paper designed a new CNN block (MixerBlock), which is based on large-kernel convolutions, and capable of gathering different scale features. Without an attention mechanism or dense block involved, our proposal, named UMixer, consists only of the primary U-shaped architecture and a simple multi-scale feature fusion module. UMixer can be categorized into a pure convolutional structure, thus being free of pre-training and large datasets. Despite the simplicity itself, UMixer has even surpassed some transformer-based networks on the Synapse dataset.

2   Related Works

The earlier works in the medical segmentation area focus on the two points: the extension of receptive fields and the improvement of the feature fusion method. To eliminate irrelevantly and noise response in segmentation, some architectures employed attention mechanism, like Attention U-Net [14], which achieved better accuracy with less parameter growth.

With the boom of transformers, Transunet [5] and MedT [6] are typical Transformer-based medical segmentation networks, which employed transformer layers to improve the capability of capturing long-range dependency in CNN-based models. UCTransNet [12] proposed a multi-scale Channel Cross Fusion method using Channel Wise Cross-Attention to guide the fusion of multi-scale channel-wise information and effectively eliminate ambiguity. Some recent works [15–17] pointed out the limitation of self-attention in a local context [18], Seg-Former [7] and Swin-Unet [8] tried to embed convolutional operations into feed forward layers and achieved remarkable performance.

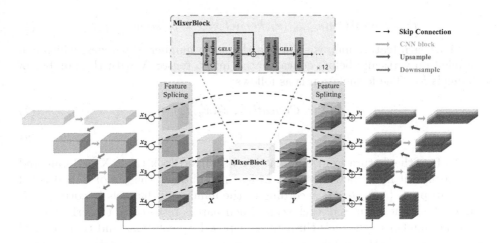

Fig. 2. The overview of proposed UMixer architecture.

3   Method

3.1   U-shaped Convolutional Structure for Feature Extraction

As a widely used architecture in medical segmentation, U-Net achieved an equilibrium between the ability of feature extraction and computational complexity. Following this structure, the proposed UMixer is also a U-shaped convolutional model, which is composed of an encoder-decoder structure and a multi-scale feature fusion block, as shown in Fig. 2. Specifically, the encoder of the U-shaped convolutional model will generate four feature maps $\{x_1, x_2, x_3, x_4\}$ in different scales. The features x_i are then input into the multi-scale fusion block, which fuses the maps and generates four stacks of mixed maps represented by $\{y_1, y_2, y_3, y_4\}$. The generated feature maps y_i contain detailed and spatial information from the lower levels, as well as semantic information from the higher levels. Then, the decoder uses these mixed maps to recover the resolutions of four scales. Therefore, this model has the advantage of a U-shaped structure in extracting multi-scale features and enhances the capability of modeling long-range dependency.

3.2   Multi-scale Feature Fusion Strategy

The multi-scale feature fusion structure contains three components: feature splicing, MixerBlock, and feature splitting.

The feature splicing block takes patches as input. The feature maps of four different scales from the encoder of a U-shaped structure are split into the same number of patches, with p_i referring to the patch size in level $i(i = 1, 2, 3, 4)$. Then, patches embedding operation with patch size p_i and embedding dimension h_i can be implemented as convolution with c_i input channels, h_i output channels, kernel size p_i, and stride p_i, which can be formulated as:

$$x'_i = BN(\sigma(Conv_{c_i \to h_i}(x_i, kernel\_size = p_i, stride = p_i))) \tag{1}$$

Since each feature map is split into the same number of patches, which can be piled up vertically before concatenated into a tensor X with the number of channels h_Σ. The formulation is as follows:

$$X = Concat(x'_1, x'_2, x'_3, x'_4) \tag{2}$$

$$h_\Sigma = \Sigma h_i \tag{3}$$

To fuse the feature from different levels, MixerBlock takes X as input and transformed it into a new tensor Y. In feature splitting, the tensor Y is divided into four parts $\{t_1, t_2, t_3, t_4\}$ according to the number of channels h_i corresponding to the input features of each scale. Each part is restored to the original size and the number of channels through transposed convolutions and then merged by skip connections to generate tensors $\{y_1, y_2, y_3, y_4\}$. The operation above can be formulated as:

$$Y = MixerBlock(X) \tag{4}$$

$$t_1, t_2, t_3, t_4 = split(Y, dim = 1) \tag{5}$$

$$y_i = BN(\sigma(TransposedConv_{h_i \to c_i}(t_i, kernel\_size = p_i, stride = p_i))) + x_i \tag{6}$$

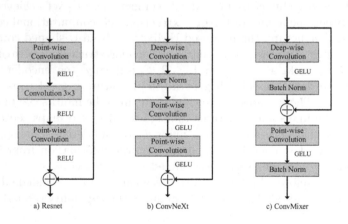

Fig. 3. The various explorations of the mixer modules, from left to right: a) Resnet in traditional modules. b) The vanilla ConvNeXt structure c) The enhanced mixer block ConvMixer

3.3   MixerBlock

To improve the capability of capturing long-range dependency for ConvNets, we follow the operations as some superior-performance algorithms. As illustrated in Fig. 3, ConvNeXt and ConvMixer both employed large-kernel convolutions and split them into two parts: depth-wise convolution and point-wise convolution. It has been demonstrated that large-kernel convolutions have a larger valid receptive field and can capture more global information than traditional Resnet modules, which can even achieve comparable performance with transformers.

We tested the performance of traditional Resnet, ConvNext, and ConvMixer with different depths. It finally turns out that ConvMixer achieved superior performance and surpassed TransUnet by 4.5%, approximately.

4   Experiments

4.1   Experiments Settings

Our model was implemented by PyTorch and trained with NVIDIA GeForce RTX 2080Ti. We did not use any pre-training models, and the model was trained from scratch on the Synapse training dataset. The images were augmented by random flips and rotation. We first split the 3D CT scans into 2D axial slices, then reduce the resolution from 512×512 to 224×224. The initial learning rate is set to 0.05 and the poly learning rate scheduler is used in the training process. The max training epoch is 150 with batch size 12. SGD optimizer with momentum 0.9 and weight decay 1e-4 is adopted for UMixer. The model was tested on Synapse multi-organ segmentation dataset and the preprocessing was similar to Transunet [5] to ensure comparability.

Table 1. Performance of different configurations h_i in feature splicing. When conducting these experiments we set the depth as 12 and use ConvMixer modules in MixerBlock.

H	Average		Aorta	Gallbladder	Kidney(L)	Kidney(R)	Liver	Pancreas	Spleen	Stomach
	DSC ↑	HD↓								
$\{32, 32, 32, 32\}$	79.46	23.85	88.6	69.5	86.1	79.5	93.8	58.8	86.2	73.2
$\{64, 64, 64, 64\}$	80.54	21.03	89.3	70.1	86.5	81.3	94.9	59.1	89.0	74.1
$\{16, 32, 64, 128\}$	78.26	24.505	86.6	65.6	84.5	79.6	93.1	55.4	87.9	73.4
$\{128, 64, 32, 16\}$	82.06	18.83	87.8	72.1	88.7	84.1	94.4	59.9	90.6	78.9

4.2   Ablation Studies

Numbers of Channels h_i in feature splicing. The number of output channels h_i affects the proportion of each scale mixed in the tensor X. Empirically, we tested four configurations to explore their effect in the multi-scale feature encoder. The results are shown in Table 1. In our experiments, the configuration of $\{128, 64, 32, 16\}$ shows the best performance, which suggests that the larger the scale, the bigger the role. We argue that segmentation tasks rely more on spatial information like shape, edge and texture etc., some of which may be lost during convolution and sampling.

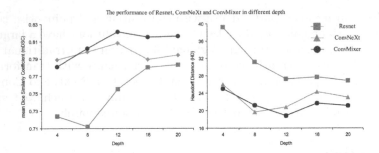

Fig. 4. The performance of Resnet, ConvNeXt, and ConvMixer modules in different depths.

Comparison of Different Feature Fusion Modules. In this section, we tested three aforementioned modules: traditional Resnet, ConvNeXt and ConvMixer in different depths. It turns out in Fig. 4 that both ConvNext and ConvMixer show higher DSC and lower HD than traditional Resnet, which demonstrate that large-kernel convolutions play a critical role in more efficient feature extraction. Furthermore, ConvMixer modules peaked at depth 12 and achieves the maximum DSC, and outperforms ConvNeXt.

Table 2. Comparison to state-of-the-art methods on Synapse dataset.

Methods	Average DSC ↑	Average HD↓	Aorta	Gallbladder	Kidney(L)	Kidney(R)	Liver	Pancreas	Spleen	Stomach
V-Net	68.81	–	75.34	51.87	77.10	80.75	87.84	40.05	80.56	56.98
DARR	69.77	–	74.74	53.77	72.31	73.24	94.08	54.18	89.90	45.96
R50 U-Net	74.68	36.87	87.74	63.66	80.60	78.19	93.74	56.90	85.87	74.16
U-Net	76.85	39.70	89.07	69.72	77.77	68.06	93.43	53.98	86.67	75.58
R50 Att-UNet	75.57	36.97	55.92	63.91	79.20	72.71	93.56	49.37	87.19	74.95
Att-UNet	77.77	36.02	89.55	68.88	77.98	71.11	93.57	58.04	87.30	75.75
R50-ViT	71.29	32.87	73.73	55.13	75.80	72.20	91.51	45.99	81.99	73.95
TransUnet	77.48	31.69	87.23	63.13	81.87	77.02	94.08	55.86	85.08	75.62
SwinUnet	79.13	21.55	85.47	66.53	83.28	79.61	94.29	56.58	90.66	76.60
MISSFormer	81.96	**18.20**	86.99	68.65	85.21	82.00	**94.41**	**65.67**	**91.92**	**80.81**
UMixer	**82.06**	18.83	87.8	**72.11**	**88.68**	**84.12**	94.40	59.87	90.62	78.91

Comparison with Other Methods. In this part, we made a comparison with the state-of-the-art segmentation models on the Synapse dataset, including TransUnet, SwinUnet and MISSFormer etc. The results are listed in (Table 2). Our proposed UMixer model surpasses U-Net by 5% approximately, which demonstrated the addition of multi-scale fusion structure that significantly enhanced the capability of capturing long-range dependency.

We also visualized the segmentation results of the comparable models in Fig. 5. It can be found that UMixer can effectively eliminate the confusing false positive lesions and performs better than other methods in some regions.

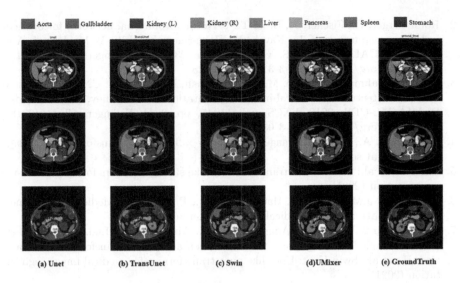

Fig. 5. The visualization of Qualitative comparison with different approaches.

5   Conclusion

In this paper, we reconsidered the pure convolution model and designed a U-shaped network, dubbed UMixer. The proposed UMixer model uses large-kernel convolutions, which can remarkably enhance the capability of capturing the long-range dependency of the pure convolution model. Meanwhile, the experiments turn out that the proposed multi-scale feature fusion method effectively improves the segmentation result and reduces the detailed and spatial information loss along with the convolution and sampling. UMixer achieves excellent performance with DSC 82.1% and HD 18.83 in the Synapse dataset, which is even better than some transformer-based models. Its success provides a new choice for the medical segmentation method, as well as a new feasible approach for multi-scale feature fusion.

Acknowledgments. This work is supported by the Beijing municipal education committee scientific and technological planning Project (KM201811232024), and Beijing Information Science and Technology University Research Fund (2021XJJ30, 2021XJJ34).

References

1. Long, J., Shelhamer, E., Darrell, T.: Fully convolutional networks for semantic segmentation. In: Proceedings of the IEEE Conference on Computer Vision and Pattern Recognition, pp. 3431–3440 (2015)

2. Ronneberger, O., Fischer, P., Brox, T.: U-Net: convolutional networks for biomedical image segmentation. In: Navab, N., Hornegger, J., Wells, W.M., Frangi, A.F. (eds.) MICCAI 2015. LNCS, vol. 9351, pp. 234–241. Springer, Cham (2015). https://doi.org/10.1007/978-3-319-24574-4_28

3. Zhou, Z., Rahman Siddiquee, M.M., Tajbakhsh, N., Liang, J.: UNet++: a nested U-Net architecture for medical image segmentation. In: Stoyanov, D., et al. (eds.) DLMIA/ML-CDS -2018. LNCS, vol. 11045, pp. 3–11. Springer, Cham (2018). https://doi.org/10.1007/978-3-030-00889-5_1

4. Dosovitskiy, A., et al.: An image is worth 16 × 16 words: transformers for image recognition at scale (2020)

5. Chen, J., et al.: TransUNet: transformers make strong encoders for medical image segmentation (2021)

6. Valanarasu, J.M.J., Oza, P., Hacihaliloglu, I., Patel, V.M.: Medical transformer: gated axial-attention for medical image segmentation (2021)

7. Xie, E., Wang, W., Yu, Z., Anandkumar, A., Alvarez, J.M., Luo, P.: SegFormer: simple and efficient design for semantic segmentation with transformers (2021a)

8. Cao, H., et al.: Swin-Unet: Unet-like pure trans-former for medical image segmentation (2021)

9. Huang, X., Deng, Z., Li, D., Yuan, X.: MISSFormer: an effective medical image segmentation transformer (2021)

10. Liu, Z., Mao, H., Wu, C.-Y., Feichtenhofer, C., Darrell, T., Xie, S.: A ConvNet for the 2020s (2022)

11. Trockman, A., Zico Kolter, J.: Patchecs Are All You Need? (2022)

12. Wang, H., Cao, P., Wang, J., Zaiane, O. R.: UCTransNet: rethinking the skip connections in U-Net from a channel-wise perspective with transformer (2021)

13. Ding, X., Zhang, X., Zhou, Y., Han, J., Ding, G., Sun, J.: Scaling up your kernels to 31 × 31: revisiting large kernel design in CNNs (2022)

14. Oktay, O.: Attention U-Net: learning where to look for the pancreas (2018)

15. Islam, M.A., Jia, S., Bruce, N.D.: How much position information do convolutional neural networks encode? (2020)

16. Chu, X., et al.: Conditional positional encodings for vision transformers (2021b)

17. Li, Y., Zhang, K., Cao, J., Timofte, R., Van Gool, L.: LocalViT: bringing locality to vision transformers (2021)

18. Wang, Z., Cun, X., Bao, J., Liu, J.: Uformer: a general U-shaped transformer for image restoration (2021d)

Author Index

Printed in the United States
by Baker & Taylor Publisher Services

Printed in the United States
by Baker & Taylor Publisher Services